Texan Jazz

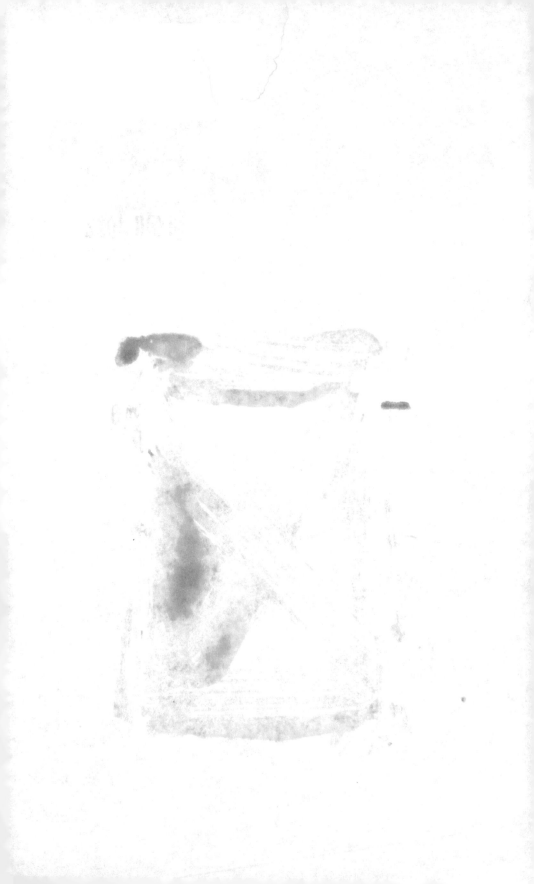

TEXAN JAZZ

By Dave Oliphant

 University of Texas Press • Austin

First edition, 1996

Requests for permission to reproduce material from this work should be sent to Permissions, University of Texas Press, Box 7819, Austin, TX 78712-7819.

∞ The paper used in this publication meets the minimum requirements of American National Standard for Information Sciences—Permanence of Paper for Printed Library Materials, ANSI Z39.48-1984.

Library of Congress Cataloging-in-Publication Data

Oliphant, Dave.

Texan jazz / by Dave Oliphant. — 1st ed.

p.   cm.

Includes bibliographical references and index.

ISBN 0-292-76044-2. — ISBN 0-292-76045-0 (pbk.)

1. Jazz—Texas—History and criticism. I. Title.

ML3508.7.T4045 1996

781.65'09764—dc20   95-4416

MN

CONTENTS

PREFACE

In *Cosmic Canticle*, Ernesto Cardenal's contemporary epic poem on the origins and meaning of the universe, this Nicaraguan poet-priest confesses that he is not a man of science and therefore has relied, for the poetic treatment of his subject, on theories and laws advanced by leading figures in the field of physics. As a teacher of literature, I likewise gratefully acknowledge my immense debt to the work of so many jazz scholars who have written of this American music. Much of my information on Texans in jazz history is owing to seminal studies by Franklin S. Driggs, Albert J. McCarthy, Gunther Schuller, and Ross Russell, all of whom have documented the role of territorial bands in Texas and the Southwest. I also wish to extend my special thanks to Thomas Hennessey, author of *From Jazz to Swing* (1981), for having read my original manuscript so closely and perceptively and for having offered valuable suggestions for its revision.

Even before encountering the indispensable writings of jazz scholars, it was fundamental to my appreciation of this music that a Beaumont orchestra teacher, Harold Meehan, found in 1954 a place for me as third-chair trumpet in the South Park High School dance band. It was this inspirational teacher from St. Louis who awakened me to musicians like Dizzy Gillespie and Charlie Parker, whose live performances "Mr. Meehan" had heard in his hometown and whose recordings he played for us during lunchtime or before or at the end of the school day. Only after such music had fired my imagination and prompted me to seek out recordings by earlier jazzmen did my own father reveal his awareness of and fondness for the music of Duke Ellington, Jimmie Lunceford, Cab Calloway, and Charlie Christian. Following my father's death, my mother recalled to me that, when they were first married, my dad had made 500 addressograph cards at a penny a piece to earn five dollars so they could hear the Ellington orchestra when it came to Fort Worth in the 1930s. She remembered how they would stand behind the Duke and watch him at the piano, and when Dad would speak to me of Ellington, it was clear that this jazzman was something of a hero, that the Duke in fact was his all-time favorite musicmaker. It always impressed me that, as a man born in the one-horse railroad town of Baird, with only an eighth-grade education and with no real talent for music (except as a dancer), he recognized, understood, and deeply appreciated Ellington's artistic achievement. Dad would attempt to describe to me, from having watched the Duke and his men, how the pianist, the bassist, and Sonny Greer on drums would all hit together on the offbeat to build up for the rest of the group a marvelous type of revolving, swinging rhythm. For Dad, Lunceford too was extraordinary, and he loved to reminisce about dancing with Mother to Jimmie's orchestra during those Depression years before World War Two. Cab's "hi-de-ho" songs he never tired of hearing, and Charlie Christian's "Blues in B" he had me play over and over.

Guided by my father's memories and by his great delight in listening to the records I would purchase at local stores, including the neighborhood supermarket that offered a series of twelve albums forming the RCA Victor Encyclopedia of Recorded Jazz, I slowly unearthed the work of many of the jazz figures who have meant so much to me, among them Ellington and Jelly Roll Morton. Although my school-mates declared these earlier musicians "old hat," I was and still am captivated by their music, having experienced "love at first sound," as Paul F. Berliner has termed it in Thinking in Jazz: The Infinite Art of Improvisation (1994). During those Beaumont days I also became aware of Benny Goodman's star soloist, Harry James, whose boyhood home had been moved to Florida Street where we lived in the 1950s and early 1960s and which I passed regularly as a high school and later a college student. In a downtown music store I once overheard the instrument repairmen speaking in hushed tones of this trumpet virtuoso who they said had dropped by just the week before. It was in high school as well that I discovered the music of Jimmy Giuffre, who recorded in the 1950s as part of the West Coast movement. In 1964, as the editor of Riata, the student literary magazine at the University of Texas at Austin, I solicited an article on Jack Teagarden from Morton Stine, a fellow student and trombonist who wrote a delightful piece on Big T. In later years I found myself drawn to writing and publishing poems on a number of jazzmen, including King Oliver, Louis Armstrong, Duke Ellington, Fats Waller, Jimmie Lunceford, Count Basie, Lester Young, Charlie Parker, and Ornette Coleman.

Although I had long been interested in Texas musicians like Teagarden, James, Christian, Giuffre, and Coleman, the idea of investigating the place of Texans in jazz history did not take hold until Bill Traylor, a longtime friend, invited me in 1989 to speak on jazz to his academic decathlon students at Conroe High School. The thought that Texans had contributed significantly to this music had first occurred to me years before when I realized the major role that Eddie Durham had played in the 1932 band of Bennie Moten. But only after the Conroe presentation did I follow through and write for the *Southwestern Historical Quarterly*, with the encouragement of its managing editor, Dr. George Ward, an article entitled "Eddie Durham and the Texas Contribution to Jazz History," a "try cake" for the present study. Decherd Turner, a distinguished bookman who furnished me with that colorful phrase, also encouraged this project by telling my wife that she had to see to it that I wrote "the jazz book." And without my beloved Maria's support when spirits flagged and without her unfailing belief that I could do it, this study would never have seen the light of day.

I also am deeply grateful to Dr. Hugh Sparks, public affairs officer in the School of Music of the University of Texas at Austin, and to his wife Kay, whose knowledge and expert performances of ragtime and boogie-woogie were crucial to the sections of this book that deal with those musical forms; to Dr. Douglass Parker, a professor in the university's Department of Classical Languages and an active jazz trombonist, who made possible the transcriptions of Louis Armstrong's trumpet phrases from his recordings with blues singers Maggie Jones and Sippie Wallace; to Dr. Karl Miller and Beth Brotherton, of the university's Fine Arts Library, who always were more than willing to assist me with questions and materials; to John Wheat, of the university's Center for American History, who provided access to hard-to-find 78 rpm recordings; to Louis Harrison, of the university's radio station, KUT-FM, who supplied tapes of several vital recordings; and to Dr. Thomas Staley, director of the Harry Ransom Humanities Research Center, who allowed the use of the Ross Russell Collection of recordings, periodicals, and photographs that proved so essential to this undertaking, as was the assistance of the Ransom Center's staff, in particular Dell Hollingsworth, George Leake, Jack Blanton, Robert N. Taylor, and Beverly Deutsch.

Parts of this study were originally based on 78 rpm recordings, which were not at the time available on compact disc. Dan Morgenstern, of the Rutgers University Institute of Jazz Studies, generously prepared tapes of 78 rpm recordings required for the sections on blues and boogie-woogie, but as these and other recordings were being reissued as compact discs, Dave Laczko of Austin's Tower Records, Hayes McCauley of Austin's Waterloo Records, and T. Sumter Bruton III of Fort Worth's Record Town enabled me to update my discographical references. To Alison Tartt I am especially beholden for the exemplary job she did in copyediting my text. Theresa May, executive editor at the University of Texas Press, promoted this project from its inception, and I heartily thank her for cheerfully seeing the manuscript through a time-consuming process. Finally, I wish to express an enduring sense of gratitude to all those Texans whose music remains for me a source of profound pleasure and native pride.

Texan Jazz

INTRODUCTION

In large part, the history of jazz in the United States has been written of the music's principal figures, bands, and styles as they developed in five cities: New Orleans, Chicago, New York, Kansas City, and Los Angeles. While these metropolitan areas have accounted for the rise of many individual performers, small and larger ensembles of short or long duration, and the jazz styles associated with each, the regional origins of the musicians and of the types of jazz they played have never been limited to these five urban centers. It is true, for now well-documented reasons, that these five cities each in turn served at particular moments in jazz history as the spawning or proving grounds for highly significant groups and featured soloists. Yet not only has jazz been a well-traveled music—in the early years developing much of its technique and its audience on the road and often through "battles" between touring and local bands—but the musicians both as individuals and as group members journeyed from all sections of the country to gather in at least four of the "birthplaces" of jazz. Although New Orleans, as the first jazz city, remained more self-contained in the sense that its musicians were generally homegrown, even here there were influences from such bordering or nearby states as Mississippi, Tennessee, Missouri, and Texas.

Making their presence known musically in all five of the jazz crucibles, a sizable and vital contingency of musicians came from almost every part of the Lone Star State to join with their fellows from communities and states around the nation. Not only were Texas jazz musicians present during the rise and development of the stylistic periods denominated by the music's five principal birthing places, but in many instances Texans were major figures in the growth and success of jazz as it evolved in those same areas, identified either by city or region: New Orleans–Gulf Coast; Chicago-Midwest; New York–East Coast; Kansas City–Southwest;

and Los Angeles–West Coast. From the beginnings of jazz up to the present time, Texans have made their mark on this native American music, and to name but a few of those active during the various movements—from ragtime, blues, boogie-woogie, and swing through bebop, Third Stream, and free jazz—is to mention seminal figures leading up to or active in all these period movements. Scott Joplin of Texarkana has long been acclaimed the greatest composer of ragtime, and in his day he influenced New Orleans and Chicago jazz and the rise of stride piano in New York. George and Hersal Thomas of Houston helped popularize blues and boogie-woogie in Chicago and to some extent in New Orleans. Blind Lemon Jefferson of Couchman was one of the first important male blues singers in Chicago, just as Sippie Wallace of Houston was a central female blues singer in 1920s Chicago and New York. Buster Smith of Ellis County, Hot Lips Page of Dallas, Eddie Durham of San Marcos, and Herschel Evans of Denton were all prominent jazzmen in Kansas City during the heyday of swing, and Charlie Christian of Dallas was at the forefront of bebop in New York. Jimmy Giuffre, also of Dallas, was one of the earliest experimenters in the Third Stream idiom, while Ornette Coleman of Fort Worth initiated almost singlehandedly the free-jazz movement in Los Angeles.

It should be evident from this abbreviated list of Texas jazzmen that a major instrumentalist like Jack Teagarden of Vernon has been left out, along with any number of other figures—from Budd Johnson and Red Garland of Dallas to Booker Ervin of Denison. These Texas musicians may not be so clearly associated with any one city or stylistic school among those listed above; however, they too had a significant impact on the larger history of jazz, both as individual instrumentalists and as participants in such movements as swing, the birth of the cool, and hard bop. Furthermore, any mere survey of cities and styles does not indicate, for example, the special brand of blues practiced by Texans from Hersal Thomas through Ornette Coleman, nor by the countless other Texans from Teagarden and Lips Page to Kenny Dorham of Fairfield. In addition, Texas musicians were either members of bands led by major stars in jazz history—from Louis Armstrong, Duke Ellington, Count Basie, Jimmie Lunceford, Cab Calloway, Earl Hines, Benny Goodman, and Charlie Parker to Woody Herman, Stan Kenton, Miles Davis, Art Blakey, and Charles Mingus—or were themselves leaders of traditional or innovative groups, particularly the avant-garde units of Jimmy Giuffre and Ornette Coleman.

Another notable fact about Texas jazzmen is that they have performed and recorded on almost every instrument associated with this democratic music. Any comprehensive list of Texans and their instruments would include the following:

piano: Scott Joplin, Hersal Thomas, Lloyd Glenn, Peck Kelley, Teddy Wilson, Red Garland, Cedar Walton, Horace Tapscott, Joe Sample, Joe Gallardo, James Polk

bass: Gene Ramey, Harry Babasin

electric bass: Wilton Felder

drums: Clifford "Boots" Douglas, Gus Johnson, Ray McKinley, Granville Theodore Hogan, Jr., Charles Moffett, Nesbert "Stix" Hooper, Ronald Shannon Jackson, Quinten "Rocky" White, Sebastian Whittaker

guitar: Eddie Durham, Charlie Christian, Oscar Moore, Herb Ellis, Larry Coryell

clarinet: Buster Smith, Albert "Budd" Johnson, Ernie Caceres, Jimmy Giuffre, William "Prince" Lasha, John Carter

flute: Leo Wright, James Clay, Prince Lasha, John Carter, Hubert Laws

piccolo: Hubert Laws

soprano saxophone: Budd Johnson, Gene Roland, Julius Hemphill

alto saxophone: Buster Smith, Budd Johnson, Ernie Caceres, Eddie "Cleanhead" Vinson, Jimmy Ford, John Handy, Leo Wright, Prince Lasha, John Carter, Julius Hemphill

tenor saxophone: Herschel Evans, Budd Johnson, Tex Beneke, Buddy Tate, Arnett Cobb, John Hardee, Illinois Jacquet, Jimmy Giuffre, Booker Ervin, Ornette Coleman, John Carter, King Curtis, James Clay, David "Fathead" Newman, Jesse Powell, Dewey Redman, Marchel Ivery, Wilton Felder, Billy Harper

baritone saxophone: Budd Johnson, Ernie Caceres, Jimmy Giuffre, Leroy "Hog" Cooper

trumpet: Harry "Big Jim" Lawson, Lammar Wright, Oran "Hot Lips" Page, Milt Larkin, Joe Keyes, Carl "Tatti" Smith, Charlie Teagarden, Harry James, Harold "Money" Johnson, Russell Jacquet, Kenny Dorham, Richard "Notes" Williams, Ornette Coleman, Bobby Bradford, Martin Banks, Dennis Dotson, Marvin "Hannibal" Peterson, Roy Hargrove

trombone: Jack Teagarden, Eddie Durham, Allen Durham, Dan Minor, Tyree Glenn, Keg Johnson, Henry Coker, Wayne Henderson, Joe Gallardo

valve trombone: Gene Roland

mellophone: Hot Lips Page

mellophonium: Gene Roland

euphonium: Wayne Henderson

tuba: Gene Ramey

vibraphone: Tyree Glenn

violin: Emilio Caceres, Ornette Coleman, Michael White

viola: Will Taylor

cello: Harry Babasin

All of these are native Texans or, like Harry James, Illinois and Russell Jacquet, Bobby Bradford, and Will Taylor, grew up in the state. Another jazzman who was born in Texas but left at a very early age is tenor saxophonist Harold Land.

While the number of Texans involved in jazz history has been extensive, no cities in the state have served as the site of major jazz movements, with the possible exception of Fort Worth, which unknowingly fostered the beginnings of free jazz. And although certain stylistic features associated with cities in other states had their roots in Texas, no Texas city brought to fruition the native ideas and techniques that assisted in achieving for cities on the east and west coasts their historic places in the story of jazz. For the most part, no city in Texas provided the benefits of nationally recognized night clubs or the availability of a viable recording industry such as those offered by Chicago, New York, and Los Angeles. Dallas, San Antonio, and Houston hosted several locally successful bands, but none of these enjoyed a national reputation, nor for the most part were they so innovative as to affect the development of jazz, except through individual musicians who only later and elsewhere had an impact on this music's history.[1]

In the early years, the largest group of Texas jazzmen were either natives of Dallas or began playing in that city's Deep Ellum section, but once again it was only in out-of-state cities that Dallas musicians made a name for themselves. Compared with the regular work, recording contracts, and national exposure offered by cities outside the state, the metropolitan areas of Texas could not promote and thereby retain within its borders its own native artists, nor did it attract jazz musicians from beyond the state's borders on a significant basis. In the mid-1920s Alphonse Trent from Arkansas brought his entirely non-Texan band to Dallas, and during the late 1920s and early 1930s, trumpeter Don Albert of New Orleans recruited much of his San Antonio band from the Crescent City.[2] Perhaps it is precisely because no single city in Texas has been identified as a center for the making of jazz that the state and its musicians have not received the level of attention accorded the five cities that have been synonymous with the evolution of this music through its predominant periods and styles. Frequently, in fact, Texas jazz musicians have not been identified as such—that is, they have been discussed by and large in terms of one of the handful of jazz cities with which their work is most closely connected rather than as Texans who left their home state to find work in Kansas City, Chicago, New York, or Los Angeles.

What is clear, nonetheless, is that wherever they have gone, Texas musicians have performed an important role in the creation of jazz and have made a distinct contribution that can be described as peculiar to those Texans who derived their musical approach from their state's cultural traditions. While jazz is recognized worldwide for its blend of African, American, and European strains and by its prominent styles from hot through swing, from bebop to cool, from hard to free, it is also possible to hear in the work of certain Texas musicians the elements of a jazz heritage that is at times as distinctive in its way as any style or period named for New Orleans or the West Coast. Indeed, jazz from the music's five recognized centers of activity often owes much of its distinction to a sound and an expressive conception that originated in the rural and urban areas of Texas.[3]

The aim of the present study, then, is primarily to identify the native jazz musicians of Texas who took from their residence in the state a regional feel or spirit that shaped their musical expression. However, because not every Texan's work lends itself to characterization in terms of a native tradition, and because at times little documentation, if any at all, is available regarding the early years of a musician's career, there is no attempt merely to define each Texan's music by means of a specific set of regional attributes. Nor is the purpose of this study to establish the existence of a so-called "Texas jazz," even though certain traits that may be associated with such a designation do emerge on occasion in the course of citation, discussion, and analysis.[4] More precisely, the object is to recognize in jazz history those Texans who made their mark on the music as major figures or who participated as sidemen in many of the important bands and movements during the principal periods of jazz's development. In this regard, the emphasis here is on the evidence provided by recordings. In particular, this study traces the contributions made by Texas musicians to the recorded history of jazz as it unfolded in the four cities of Chicago, New York, Kansas City, and Los Angeles. Finally, it is the hope of this survey of Texans in jazz to encourage a greater appreciation for the intellectual, artistic, and personal accomplishments of those musicians who, through dedication and perseverance, have added not only to Texas culture but to a music regarded universally as one of the highest artistic achievements of the twentieth century.

PART 1

BEGINNINGS IN EAST TEXAS

RAGTIME

Many types of nineteenth-century American music entered into the making of jazz, and a number of these originated in West Africa and from that region were brought by slaves to the New World. Among the African, antebellum traditions of southern blacks was the music of their everyday lives: work songs, play songs, story songs, satirical songs, field and street cries, and spirituals. All of these forms of black music contributed to the development of jazz, especially such practices as flatting the sixth and seventh tones of melodies in major scales, syncopating melodies against an established, repeated beat, establishing a call-and-response pattern between a soloist and a group, and adding improvised, spontaneous phrases to a song or instrumental part.[1] Out of these various traditions came two of the predominant elements in early jazz: ragtime, with its syncopated rhythms, and the blues, with their use of improvisation. Both of these vital elements, combined with European forms of music and instrumentation, account fundamentally for the beginnings of jazz in the American South and Southwest.

Although most histories of jazz have credited New Orleans and the Mississippi Delta region with being the source of the first stirrings of jazz-related musical practice, the Piney Woods region of East Texas has also received recognition as the origin for this twentieth-century music that began among the black minority and eventually spread to the white majority in the United States and abroad. Among the principal features associated with early jazz are its references to life in the cotton fields, along the railroad, and in lumber camps, jails, and prisons. The theme of separation from loved ones and of mistreatment by overseers and employers is allied with the joy of shared labor and the hope of better times. Such social and interpersonal motifs were characteristic of the way of life of blacks in East Texas and carried over into their music making. Crucially important to the experience of black East Texans was the fact that while their existence there was subject to the same hardships and cruelties common to their lives in the South before and after the Civil War, there was nonetheless the possibility of greater freedom and mobility. The theme of movement and its reproduction through sound is clearly present in such early jazz-related forms as the blues and boogie-woogie, and can be heard as well in the driving syncopated rhythms of ragtime.

Scott Joplin, whose ragtime tunes took the country by storm during the first two decades of the twentieth century, died a disappointed composer in 1917, the same year in which the Original Dixieland Jazz Band made the first jazz recording ever. As Gary Giddins has so aptly conceived it, Joplin's 1911 ragtime opera, *Treemonisha*, was his tar baby into which "he stuck one limb . . . and then another," but he could not escape the rejection of this work with its rag tunes and its theme of education versus superstition, which "concerned him no less than it did Booker T. Washington."[2] Nevertheless, Joplin's 1899 *Maple Leaf Rag* became "the first million-selling song . . . in the history of popular music"[3] and an unexcelled example of the ragtime form, "a hallmark, a milestone."[4] More than fifty years after Joplin's death, the composer's ragtime music helped make possible in 1973 the success of *The Sting*, a film starring Paul Newman and Robert Redford, which won seven Oscar awards, including Best Musical Adaptation for Marvin Hamlisch, and which in turn revived the popularity of Joplin's infectious tunes, in particular *The Entertainer*.[5] Although this Hollywood film employs the composer's rag tunes as theme music to a 1936 plot that is more than a decade removed from the height of the ragtime craze, the movie demonstrates an awareness of, and an appreciation for, Joplin's inspiriting music over seventy years after it was first being composed and performed by this native of northeast Texas. Significant as well is the fact that, at Scott Joplin's death on April 11, 1917, which coincided with the entrance of the United States into World War One, his compositions were still widely popular on the eve of three of this century's most influential revolutions, through two of which his music would live on and in which his rags would have a consequential role to play.

While the Russian Revolution in October 1917 seemed for over seven decades to have had the most profound and lasting effect on the modern world, the other two "revolutions"—of telecommunications and the spread of jazz—have exerted their own influences on the present age, and these may prove in the long run more enduring and more meaningful for humanity than the Marxist hegemony of the Bolsheviks. In 1918 American inventor Edwin Armstrong developed the superheterodyne circuit that made possible a fixed frequency for the transmission of radio

Scott Joplin of Texarkana,
"The King of Ragtime."

signals amplified hundreds of times before reaching a receiver. The first regular commercial radio broadcasts began in 1920 and marked the commencement of a revolution that has affected every realm of modern life, from war and medicine to business and industry. In the wake of live radio broadcasts came music beamed from coast to coast and continent to continent, either from on location in ballrooms or concert halls or from radio studios presenting live or recorded performances. In many ways, Joplin's ragtime music was part of this global revolution, which began with the widespread sale of printed editions of his compositions and was followed by recordings of his and other composers' ragtime tunes by countless bands like the Original Dixieland Jazz Band, whose repertoire "consisted of ragtime and early dance music played in the jazz idiom."[6] Through ragtime, jazz would make its way around the world, overcoming geographical, language, and political barriers to establish an international following that survives to this day and shows no signs of losing its avid enthusiasts among each new generation of listeners. The sound of Joplin's rags heard at movies and from the loudspeakers of ice cream trucks passing down the streets of our towns and cities is testimony to his ongoing place in the era of telecommunications and its debt to him as a creative artist who assisted in popularizing the radio and recording media, through which he also helped to gain an audience for serious black music.

Born in Texarkana on November 24, 1868, Scott Joplin was the first Texan whose music would influence the development of jazz.[7] Although not strictly jazz, ragtime was an important ingredient in the mix that is now identified as that revolutionary black music. Joplin's "classic" rags were in fact a type of dance suite that contained themes with a lyrical flow (as in *The Entertainer*) and a structural form based on the European march (four themes, with a reprise of the first theme after the second, and a "conscious or unconscious reference to rondo form"),[8] combined with polyrhythms and stop-time breaks and choruses (as in his *Stoptime Rag*) based on African folk music. In effect, Joplin's rags represent the two sources from which jazz would develop: the musical traditions of Europe and Africa.

In Texarkana, Joplin was exposed to both traditions through trained music teachers and through the experience of his own race's music making. At home Joplin probably heard the popular musical forms of the day—waltzes, schottisches, polkas, and quadrilles—performed by family members, with his father on fiddle, his mother on the banjo, and his siblings singing or playing various instruments. A variety of music also stimulated Joplin at the Mt. Zion Baptist Church, the only black church in Texarkana, established in 1875 on the Texas side of this town that straddles the Texas-Arkansas border. Here Scott would have been exposed to spirituals, shouts and hollers, and perhaps ring plays, as well as the syncopated patterns superimposed over the melodies of church hymns. Equally important, if not more so, was the training he received from a black piano teacher, Mag Washington, and a "professor" of music, variously identified but perhaps a German by the name of Julius Weiss, born about 1841 in Saxony.[9] From these teachers, Joplin learned to read music, which was crucial to his success as a composer, since in creating his ragtime compositions Joplin utilized black folk music collected from itinerant musicians too unskilled to write down their own syncopated tunes. Thus Joplin combined the black idiom with the formal design of European notation to produce works that could be performed from sheet music by musicians anywhere, regardless of race.

Like a number of other important Texas musicians, Joplin was able to affect the history of jazz primarily through his skills as a composer more than as an instrumentalist. While jazz is largely an improvised rather than a written music, much jazz has been dependent on notated compositions that can be performed by musicians other than the composer. In this way, those who can read the music make possible its performance on a broader basis, for those who cannot read but can learn the music by ear are able to do so whenever reading musicians happen to perform such written compositions. Therefore, the value of Joplin's skills as a reader and composer of music cannot be overemphasized in tracing the impact of his music on early jazz. Buster Smith, one of the earliest composer-arrangers among Texas jazzmen, commented that Count Basie and such fellow Texans as Hot Lips Page, Joe Keyes, and Dan Minor "all had good ideas but couldn't write them down."[10] Only those musicians like Joplin who could compose on paper— or those like Count Basie who could communicate their ideas to Texans like Buster Smith and Eddie Durham, who then would notate and arrange them—were able to transmit their music widely and to preserve it in the form they conceived for its performance. Much jazz was originally based on "heads," or arrangements invented as a group, and only when such head arrangements were recorded could musicians imitate them or use them as a basis for their own improvisatory interpretations. Joplin's music, however, depended for transmission on its being written and then published, for his rags predated both radio and the recording industry, although he did leave behind several pianola rolls of his rags recorded for the Connorized label in April 1916.[11]

Joplin's ability to compose on paper was important not only because his rags could be published, recorded, and broadcast but also because they gave a permanent form to folk elements and elevated them to the level of serious music. Even though ragtime later became adulterated through its commercial exploitation, Joplin's work was consistently rooted in a folk music that he consciously shaped into an artistic form which expressed a forward-looking vision of and for his people. As Rudi Blesh and Harriet Janis have pointed out in their classic study, *They All Played Ragtime*, Joplin's music (in particular his *Maple Leaf Rag*) is an "incomparable fusion of folk music and learned music, of prairie and town," and when his exacting scores from 1904 are performed, they "become a beautiful, light syncopation unlike any music ever heard before ragtime. All of them, too—and especially *Chrysanthemum*—are exultant with triumph."[12] Given the origin of Joplin's rags in his early experience in Texarkana, such forward-looking, triumphant music may seem inexplicable; yet Texas in the late nineteenth century offered greater freedom and hope for blacks than they had known in the South, from whence most had been forced to come as slaves. Schools were available, and Joplin probably attended Central High on the Texas side of Texarkana.[13] The town boasted an opera house, his mother was able to afford a piano for her talented son, and there were opportunities to perform at church socials and for such black organizations as fire companies, benevolent societies, fraternal orders, and clubs, as well as for school functions. Eventually Joplin would play in area dance halls. Yet despite all these outlets for Joplin's musical talents, conditions in East Texas were still extremely repressive for blacks, and Scott ultimately would use his gifts to escape the usual fate of his race by settling in Missouri, where he found a publisher for what would become his lucrative rags.

Even before the Civil War, slave owners had left the Deep South with its depleted soil and limited possibilities for the wide-open and expansive Texas frontier. Many in the westward migration made it no further than the tri-state border of Arkansas, Texas, and Louisiana where the Red River had been used as a crossing by Caddo Indians, early French and Spanish explorers, and travelers heading into the interior of what would become in 1845 the thirty-sixth state of the Union. Finding waterways available for transporting the cotton and cattle they raised or the timber they cut and milled, settlers from the South brought with them slaves who shared with their masters the hope of a new life. The blacks themselves brought along their musical traditions, which they adapted to their lives in an environment that differed little in terms of climate and geography but that promised a less rigid system of bondage and servitude.

Scott Joplin's father Jiles and his mother Florence came to East Texas from South Carolina and Kentucky, respectively, he in 1850 as a slave at the age of six and she perhaps in the late 1850s as a freeborn black.[14] Several years before the Emancipation Proclamation of 1862, when Jiles Joplin was in his late teens, he was given his freedom. Then, probably around 1859, Jiles married Florence Givens by jumping with her over a broomstick ("the only marriage-like arrangement available to blacks, slave or free, at that time").[15] The couple had their first child, Will, shortly before the outbreak of the Civil War, with Scott, their second son, arriving three years after the end of that sectional conflict. By the early 1870s, the Joplins, like many freed blacks, found in Texarkana a growing, prospering community, owing largely to the establishment in 1871 of the Texas and Pacific Railway Company, which was to construct a line from Dallas to the northeast corner of Texas. With the advent of the railway, jobs were plentiful and there was little discrimination in hiring practices. Jiles Joplin was taken on as a common laborer, while other blacks were employed as track layers, menders, brakemen, engineers, and mechanics.[16]

The railroad brought with it the rise of the lumber industry, a cotton compress, stockyards, and the production of natural gas. The grand antebellum homes of the East Texas area were constructed by slaves whose workmanship is evident through the survival today of those richly columned buildings, even though throughout the rural area blacks still occupied shotgun shacks in their own "quarters." Lured by the prosperity of Texarkana's frontier boomtown, freed blacks left the cotton fields and found work on the railroad, in the lumber camps, and at sawmills; yet most were still assigned to menial tasks and had little hope of improving their condition, lacking for the most part the advantages of education as a means of bettering their lot. As always, music remained an integral part of their lives, in church and in work gangs where they chanted in time to their manual labor; even the poorest homes in Texarkana tended to own secondhand pianos. The importance of education was stressed in the Joplin family by Scott's mother, who encouraged his interest in music. Joplin's lessons with "The Professor"—who was so impressed with the boy's talent that he taught him for little or nothing—would ground the young musician in sight-reading and harmony. The professor also talked to Scott about the great European masters and about opera. During these early years in Texarkana, Scott was already beginning to compose, and one citizen reported hearing him play what would later be published as his *Maple Leaf Rag* (1899),[17] "the first great instrumental sheet music hit in America" and the most widely influential of Joplin's more than fifty printed compositions.[18]

Unavoidably Joplin must have been aware of the sentimental ballads, minstrel tunes, and popular Sousa marches of the day and must have tried his hand at these different styles, for reportedly he "worked on his music all the time."[19] At sixteen he formed the Texas Medley Quartette with his brother Will and two neighborhood friends. For their first engagement, the group traveled to Clarksville, some eighty miles west of Texarkana, and afterward found other jobs in nearby towns. From about 1884 to 1888, Joplin performed with this quartet, which became a quintet with the addition of his brother Robert. Around the age of twenty, Scott Joplin left Texarkana and sought his fortune as an itinerant pianist, joining the ranks of musicians who were in demand in the South, Midwest, and Southwest, mainly in saloons and bawdy houses. Around 1890, after a couple of years of travel that took him possibly into the Indian Territory, through Arkansas, and eventually to Missouri, Joplin settled in St. Louis, which had become a center for the railway as well as for riverboats. The pianist-composer first found work in Chestnut Valley, the redlight district that had developed in this "Gateway to the West" and that was home to a number of early ragtime practitioners, among them John Turpin, owner of the Silver Dollar Saloon, and his son Tom Turpin, whose Rosebud saloon was commemorated by Joplin's 1905 *Rosebud Two-Step*.

From St. Louis, Joplin probably visited surrounding towns and cities, continuing to play as a traveling pianist, improving his skills, and picking up on the work of his fellow musicians in these important training grounds for ragtime. In 1893 Joplin apparently moved to Chicago at the time of the World's Columbian Exposition and formed his first band there, consisting probably of cornet, clarinet, tuba, and baritone horn.[20] As a serious and dedicated musician, composer, and bandleader, Joplin would eventually influence the rise of ragtime brass bands, which have been considered "undoubtedly the models for the earliest dance and quasi-jazz bands of Kansas City and the Southwest."[21] It was at the Columbian Exposition that the word "ragtime" was coined to describe the lively style of this music, heard in Chicago for the first time by a larger public, as performed by Joplin's band and by the many itinerant piano players who gathered for the occasion.

During his time in Chicago, Joplin made the important discovery that "black music and music by blacks might have a chance at respectability."[22] This notion may have been reinforced by Scott's possible hearing at the exposition of a minstrel show by W. C. Handy, his "revitalized" Mahara's Minstrels, and an all-black revue, the *Creole Show*. In place of the blackface tradition with its clownish "Jim Crow" depiction of blacks—a stereotypical impersonation first introduced in 1830 by Thomas D. Rice and referred to in Hawthorne's 1851 novel *The House of the Seven Gables* as a "world-renowned dance"[23]—Joplin found that black music in Handy's minstrel show and in the all-black revue emphasized his race's talents and showed the potential for expressing black experience through musical composition. As a result, Joplin began to take his writing more seriously, encouraged by a fellow pianist, Otis Saunders, whom Scott met while in Chicago.

Accompanied by Saunders, Joplin returned to St. Louis in 1894 or 1895, and soon thereafter the two men continued on to Sedalia. Like Texarkana, Sedalia was another railway center where Scott would settle for the next five or six years. In Sedalia, Joplin was joined by his older brother Will, who sang and played violin and guitar, and by his younger brother Robert, who sang, played several instruments, and had himself composed some popular songs.[24] Together the Joplin brothers revived the Texas Medley group as an octet or double quartet by adding five new members. From Sedalia, Joplin and his ensemble traveled extensively, seemingly even as far as Syracuse, New York, where in 1895 Joplin published his first songs, *A Picture of Her Face* and *Please Say You Will*, considered "typical sentimental ballads of the era."[25] In 1896, apparently during a tour of Texas that took the group to Temple, Joplin had his first piano compositions published in that city by John R. Fuller: *The Great Crush Collision March*, *Combination March*, and *Harmony Club Waltz*.

Even though *Crush Collision March* may not be a full-blown ragtime composition, it is significantly related to Joplin's musical beginnings in East Texas. According to James Haskins, this march is Joplin's first publication to contain elements of ragtime, and in his own playing of the piece the composer "would have infused it with considerable syncopation."[26] As a number of jazz historians have indicated, it was the march to which both ragtime and much early jazz were indebted for their sense of form. In general, the march involves a multithematic structure,[27] and many early ragtime compositions included "march" or "march and two step" in their titles or subtitles.[28] While the description of a train wreck in Joplin's march is brief and perhaps tacked on as a result of a collision that occurred in 1896 in or near Temple—the piece is dedicated to "the M. K. & T. Ry."—this work belongs to a jazz tradition that includes countless blues songs with their references in word and through guitar accompaniments to midnight trains: the boogie-woogie train imitations of Meade "Lux" Lewis's famed *Honky Tonk Train Blues* (1927), Duke Ellington's recordings of *Choo-Choo* (1926) and *Daybreak Express* (1937), the Ellington-Strayhorn classic *Take the "A" Train* (1941), and Jimmy Giuffre's *The Train and the River* (1957).

Not that Joplin's composition directly influenced any of the above-mentioned works constructed on a railroad analogy, but the fact that he attempted to reproduce sounds associated with trains places him at the forefront of a tradition in black music related to the development of many of the major movements in jazz: blues, boogie-woogie, hot and swing, and the post–World War Two cool, funky, and Third Stream schools. As in Ellington's orchestration for *Daybreak Express*, Joplin incorporates in his piano piece a number of noises associated with the railroad: a speeding train; "whistling at the crossing," represented by four-note treble discords, two long and two short; more frantic whistling before the crash, suggested by higher discords; and the collision recreated by a loud chord on a low diminished seventh. The effect is a type of program music or tone poem of precisely the sort that Ellington sought to create. A later composition by Joplin, *Cascades* (1904), was also programmatic in its imitation of a watercourse at the 1904 St. Louis Exposition.[29]

Joplin's writing at this early point in his career is mostly marked by its classical/ pop music qualities—based on light classics and popular marches—and shows the composer's awareness of a serious use of piano technique in terms of form, variation, theme, and modulation more than it does his use of a black folk tradition. What Joplin did early on was to employ his music for a serious mimetic purpose, and having such a serious intent would prove true of all his efforts, culminating with his 1911 folk ragtime opera, *Treemonisha*, set near Texarkana and encompassing a wide variety of music from Joplin's early life: a cornhuskers' ring dance; blue moaning choral responses; barbershop harmony; a "quittin'-time song"; and a slow drag. In a sense, Joplin looked forward to the urge of many major jazz figures to create an art form that would be recognized and appreciated as such. This vision would be carried on some sixty-five years later in the improvisations and first compositions of another Texan, Ornette Coleman, whose *Space Flight*, a work for string quartet recorded in 1968, is perhaps an extension or fulfillment of Joplin's far-reaching conception, which is echoed in Coleman's comments on this composition and its performance by the Chamber Symphony of Philadelphia Quartet: "In *Space Flight* the quartet achieved something I really thought came off as I had envisioned it—a sound being made from Speed and Destiny of notes not restricted even though they are written down. The players created from Speed what I had envisioned—they really took a trip!"[30]

Following the Medley's 1896 tour of Texas, the group disbanded and Joplin made Sedalia his home for the next four years. Here he attended Smith College of Music to study piano, theory, and composition. In Sedalia Joplin also met other young men who would become prominent ragtime composers—Joe Jordan, Arthur Marshall, and Scott Hayden—and, perhaps most important of all, Joplin found in John Stark & Son a publisher who would champion his music on the same serious level as that of European composers. John Stark even asserted in print that Joplin's "classic" rags could "possibly contain more genius and psychic advance than a Chopin nocturne or a Bach fugue" and that classic rags "lifted ragtime from its low estate and lined it up with Beethoven and Bach."[31] Even before Stark & Son issued in 1899 Joplin's most famous and influential composition, *Maple Leaf Rag*, Scott's first ragtime work, *Original Rags*, had been purchased by the firm of Carl Hoffman in St. Louis. Although *Original Rags* was not published until 1899, it is thought to be an earlier work by as much as two years.[32] In any event, it was only with the Stark & Son publication of *Maple Leaf Rag*, named for a local Sedalia saloon, that Joplin achieved fame and a steady income, making it possible for him to earn a living as a composer of ragtime music. This one piece would, in the first dozen or so years after its publication, sell hundreds of thousands of copies; of Joplin's more than fifty published ragtime works, *Maple Leaf Rag* would exert "the widest, deepest, and most lasting effect."[33] However, Joplin was not the first to publish a ragtime piece for piano; his *Original Rags* and *Maple Leaf Rag* of 1899 were both preceded by white bandleader William H. Krell's *Mississippi Rag* of January 1897 (considered the first true rag) and by black composer-pianist Tom Turpin's *Harlem Rag* of December 1897.[34] But Joplin's distinction lay in the quality of his music, which has been called "the essence of ragtime in its most perfect composed form,"[35] and in its singular impact on its listeners, especially Joplin's fellow musicians. With his *Maple Leaf Rag*, Joplin is credited with establishing "the style that was to add a new musical form to the cakewalks of Kerry Mills and the dances of Stephen Foster and Louis Gottschalk."[36]

By 1901 Joplin had left Sedalia to return to St. Louis with his first wife, Belle Hayden, sister of Scott Hayden, Joplin's co-composer on *Sunflower Slow Drag* (1901). At this time, Joplin's talent was recognized by Alfred Ernst, director of the St. Louis Choral Symphony, who declared that "the work Joplin has done in ragtime is so original, so distinctly individual, and so melodious withal, that I am led to believe he can do something fine in compositions of a higher class when he shall have been instructed in theory and harmony."[37] It was in the direction of something "of a higher class" that Joplin aspired for the rest of his career, ultimately spending the better part of his remaining sixteen years on *Treemonisha*. He began his ragtime opera while he was still in St. Louis and continued work on it in New York from about 1907 to 1917. While Joplin went on producing ragtime pieces for piano, there was no essential change in the kind of music he composed in this form, although Guy Waterman observes that "Joplin's 'last period' is a strange collection of contradictions. Some of his rags reach more toward concert music than did any jazz up to Lennie Tristano's, while others seem to revert to his 1900 style. Profoundly ambitious passages lie side by side with meaningless, mechanical ditties!"[38] Waterman outlines three main features of Joplin's style from 1909 to 1917: "increased freedom in the left hand; the attempt to keep rhythmic momentum implicit rather than explicit; and a new, or at least increased, concern with structure."[39]

Of Joplin's effort late in life to "synthesize the ragtime he helped to create with certain methods and devices of concert composition," Guy Waterman finds that this part of his work "left no mark on American music—it has been almost completely ignored." One reason Waterman offers as an explanation for such disregard is that with the advent of jazz, this music's "rougher syncopation and more flexible harmonies . . . moved in and absorbed the younger musicians." However, considering Joplin's total production, Waterman concludes that not only were all his rags "fine, but the development from *Original Rags* in 1899 to *Reflection Rag* in 1917 is clearly that of one man working out his musical ideas." Waterman goes on to compare Joplin's "dynamic quality" to that of Bach and Haydn, of Stravinsky, Schoenberg, and Hindemith, calling the fresh outlook Joplin maintained throughout his career "the true measure of his stature," and asserting that the last rags (*Euphonic Sounds, Magnetic Rag, Scott Joplin's New Rag, Solace,* and the posthumous *Reflection Rag*) represent his "real achievement," which "still stands among the finest in ragtime and jazz."[40]

Before Joplin left St. Louis and the Southwest, never to return (his last visit to Texarkana would come in 1907),[41] he was active composing his second extended work, *A Guest of Honor* (1903), a lost one-act ragtime opera. His first longer work (nine printed pages of music lasting twenty minutes) had been *The Ragtime Dance*

(1899), a dramatic folk ballet containing a vocal introduction and ten dance themes: "Ragtime Dance," "Clean Up Dance," "Jennie Cooks Dance," "Slow Drag," "World's Fair Dance," "Back Step Prance," "Dude Walk," "Sedidus Walk," "Town Talk," and "Stop Time." The term "slow drag," which also appears in the title of the 1901 Joplin-Hayden composition *Sunflower Slow Drag—A Ragtime Two-Step*, derives from "a social dance of the late 19th and early 20th centuries performed by couples to a slow blues with leisurely, sensuous rhythms . . . so called because the musical rhythms drag behind the beat, reflecting the smooth, voluptuous movements of the dance."[42] Later, in Joplin's three-act opera of 1911, *Treemonisha*, the composer would include "several set pieces drawn from the older tradition of black African music, especially 'We're Goin' Around,' a ring game, and 'A Real Slow Drag,' which closes the opera."[43]

Many of the terms and techniques found in the titles and forms of Joplin's dance music would figure meaningfully in the later history of jazz. The use of the word "drag" in the title of pianist Fats Waller's *The Minor Drag*, recorded with His Rhythm in 1929, is but one instance of a jazz version of this social dance, but even more important is the impact of the slow drag's characteristic "behind the beat" rhythm, as found in the tenor saxophone solos of Lester Young in the late 1930s. As for Joplin's dance theme entitled "Stop Time," this phrase (which he later employed for his 1910 *Stoptime Rag*) refers to a discontinuous rhythm—as in the playing of only the first beat in every two bars—and was an accompaniment typically for tap dancers. Later, the use of "stop time" would figure significantly in Louis Armstrong's 1928 *West End Blues*, which combines the trumpeter's famous opening "break" with an extended stop-time chorus.[44] With regard to the break in jazz, which is a "short rhythmic-melodic *cadenza* interpolated by an instrumentalist (or singer) between ensemble passages," this practice "existed in an embryonic form" in Joplin's 1901 *Easy Winners*.[45] It is also notable in the case of Armstrong that another performance considered the zenith of his early career, *Weather Bird*, a King Oliver composition recorded in 1928 by Armstrong and pianist Earl Hines (as was *West End Blues*), adheres to "the original three-part ragtime format."[46] Even the words "talk," "cook," "prance," and "walk" in Joplin's dance themes would become part of the jazz parlance and serve as a source for the mimetic tendencies of the music in seeking to capture the rhythms of physical movement (often with sexual connotations)[47] and the speech patterns of African Americans. These terms also served as titles for such tunes and albums as *Hear Me Talkin' to You* (recorded by Ma Rainey in 1928), *Cookin'* (a 1956 recording by the Miles Davis Quintet with John Coltrane on tenor and Texan Red Garland on piano), *Pfrancin'* (a tune recorded by another Davis quintet in 1961),[48] and *Walkin'* (performed frequently by Davis and others in the 1950s and 1960s). In this regard, Rudi Blesh has observed that ragtime is "in its broadest sense of a racial rhythm . . . in all truly Negroid music today and in a great deal of white music too. It is in Negro speech, in Negro preaching, and in the syncopated surge of the shouting spiritual. It is in Negro song and Negro jazz. It is so basically of the race, whatever its environment, that one might say that ragtime rhythm infuses Negro motor activity itself, activating both work and play."[49]

More important for the direct link between ragtime and jazz was Joplin's influence on the first great jazz composer, Ferdinand "Jelly Roll" Morton. During Joplin's St. Louis years, from 1901 to 1907, Jelly Roll Morton was reportedly working on the composition of one of his most often performed tunes, *King Porter Stomp*, which has been dated to 1902 or 1905. According to Joplin's second wife, Lottie Stokes, Morton mailed this piece to Joplin because he and fellow pianist Porter King were having trouble with it.[50] Morton asked for help and Joplin obliged by completing the piece and mailing it back, but the tune (copyrighted in 1906) was not published until almost twenty years later in 1923.[51] Joplin apparently added to and arranged what would become *King Porter Stomp*, but according to Campbell Brun, a white pianist who first heard Joplin's music in 1898 in Oklahoma City, Morton and later Joplin himself told Brun that "'Jelly Roll arranged it over again.'"[52] True or not, it is clear that Joplin had an impact on Morton, for Jelly Roll himself stated that Scott Joplin was "known throughout the world as the greatest ragtime writer that ever lived,"[53] a tribute uncharacteristically accorded by Morton to one of his contemporaries. Louis Armstrong even considered Joplin "the principal source of Jelly Roll's ideas."[54] Another view of Morton's debt to Joplin has been recorded in Jelly Roll's autobiography as reported to Texas folklorist Alan Lomax, who quotes Morton's publisher, Walter Melrose: "But, so far as Jelly Roll originating anything, he didn't do that. All Jelly did was to come along and write additional numbers in the style that goes back to Scott Joplin in the '90s. Scott Joplin was his God; and, really, things like *Maple Leaf Rag* and *Grace and Beauty* [a 1910 rag by James Scott] were his models. Jelly always worked with two twelve-bar strains, modulating into trio, just like Joplin." Lomax comments that "Jelly Roll's music, like all early jazz, reflects the influence of Scott Joplin; but it is astonishing that Melrose, after all his experience with hot music, would deny the important differences."[55] Evidence of the influence of Joplin's music on Morton and the "important differences" between Jelly Roll's jazz and Joplin's ragtime is to be found in Morton's own performances of the Texan's *Original Rags* and *Maple Leaf Rag*, the latter called by James Collier "the single most popular of all rags" and "the best loved by students of the form."[56]

While critics have said of *The Ragtime Dance* from 1899 that "some of Joplin's most beautiful work is embedded in this score,"[57] and although the later *Treemonisha* represents "one of the first—and finest—examples of opera in a truly American idiom . . . a thoroughly original, imaginative, and enjoyable work of music,"[58] it was Joplin's first two published rags of 1899, *Original Rags* and *Maple Leaf Rag*, that would exert the greatest influence on jazz. *Maple Leaf Rag* would first enter the history of this music through one of the earliest of jazz recordings, those made by the New Orleans Rhythm Kings in 1922 and 1923. In July 1923, Jelly Roll Morton was recorded by the Gennett Company of Indiana with the New Orleans Rhythm Kings, a white group that had recorded earlier in the year Morton's *Wolverine Blues*. The New Orleans Rhythm Kings had first recorded for Gennett in August 1922, and this recording is considered more significant than that of the Original Dixieland Jazz Band in 1917 as a result of its influence on the greatest of all white jazz musicians, trumpeter Bix Beiderbecke. The New Orleans Rhythm Kings has been called "the earliest and most authentic link between the Negro New Orleans ensemble tradition (as epitomized by King Oliver's Creole Jazz Band) and a host of white imitators" and is credited with reproducing the rhythmic flow of the New Orleans jazz tradition of polyphonic, group improvisation.[59] At their second recording session for Gennett in March 1923, the New Orleans Rhythm Kings performed Scott Joplin's *Maple Leaf Rag* along with Morton's *Wolverine Blues*, as well as such classic jazz tunes as *That Da Da Strain* and *Tin Roof Blues*. The group's recording of Joplin's all-time favorite composition (that is, his own as well as the music-listening public's), in addition to a popular ragtime piece from 1915 entitled *Weary Blues*, illustrates the Rhythm Kings' wider variety of accents and "more legato flow"—in contrast to the Original Dixieland Jazz Band's jerky, "abrupt articulation."[60] Through the Rhythm Kings' "greater flexibility," the band "adroitly transformed" both ragtime pieces "into jazz," years before "more celebrated groups such as Bennie Moten's" had managed "to eliminate the tenacious influence of ragtime from their music."[61]

In many ways, Joplin's *Maple Leaf Rag* is hardly itself when played by the New Orleans Rhythm Kings, partly because it is no longer simply a piano piece but a performance by five instruments: trumpet, clarinet, trombone, drums, and piano. Certainly other groups with varying instrumentation had performed Joplin's tune long before the New Orleans Rhythm Kings, among them probably the band of legendary New Orleans trumpeter Buddy Bolden. According to the recollections of one early trumpeter, Sam Rickey, ragtime was being played by bands in New Orleans in 1885,[62] for even though Joplin was among the first to write down ragtime for piano, this style of music was known decades before. Years prior to the

Rhythm Kings recording, ragtime numbers performed on the Mississippi riverboats included such tunes as *Raggin' the Scale, Tiger Rag,* and *Maple Leaf Rag.*[63] But the distinction of the New Orleans Rhythm Kings lies in its transformation of Joplin's rag into a work full of identifiable jazz elements that were already characteristic of the music of unrecorded black jazz bands and would become essential to most every subsequent jazz performance.

One of the first developments to be noticed is that the role of the piano has changed from that of a solo instrument to primarily an ensemble instrument, functioning more as part of a rhythm section with the drums. The first exception to this shift in role occurs when the pianist, Mel Stitzel, takes a break—that is, interpolates a series of phrases when the rest of the band stops playing, after the fashion of the stop-time device noted earlier, which was originally designed to allow tap dancers to fill the pause in the music with a rapid flourish of footwork. The second exception comes when Stitzel takes an extended solo or chorus, which is not in the ragtime style but a free variation on the tune's chords. Although ragtime could involve improvisation to a limited extent, more in the form of embellishment and a "careful addition of figures," this kind of embellishment differs from "the wholesale transfiguration of ragtime by jazz-oriented pianists."[64] Another notable feature of the piano's role is the speed with which its parts are played, in keeping with the upbeat tempo of the band's overall performance, which runs counter to Joplin's admonishment that his rags were not to be played too fast.[65] From the opening notes of the Rhythm Kings recording of *Maple Leaf Rag,* the tempo is so fast that Joplin's tune is barely recognizable, and the trumpet and clarinet's playing of the repeated two-bar pattern of four sixteenths and an eighth is almost a blur compared with the piano-roll version of Joplin's rag as he recorded it in 1916.[66] The clarity of Joplin's ragtime is in direct contrast to the emphasis of the New Orleans Rhythm Kings on an ensemble sound that blends piano, clarinet, trumpet, trombone, and percussion (drums, woodblock, and cymbal) into a hectic rush. The excitement generated by this jazz performance of Joplin's classic rag is owing not only to the upbeat tempo but to the constant shifts in tonal combinations, to the group's rapid starts and stops in their playing of the tune's melodic phrases, and to the variations on the rag's basic motivic and rhythmic patterns. As Schafer and Riedel point out, "Ragtime scores rarely indicate shifts in tempo or allow for a free *rubato* style,"[67] so the New Orleans Rhythm Kings performance departs dramatically from the written form of the "classic" rag.

Not only does the Rhythm Kings rendition change the tune's patterns quickly and often, but several other important elements of jazz style are introduced in this 1923 recording. First, the trombonist, George Brunis, does not function as the bass line does in the piano rag—keeping a steady eighth-note beat—but plays a type of countermelody, syncopating runs up and down the scale and at times swinging out in inventive rhythms of his own or going into double time as the other instruments continue in the established rhythmic meter. Meanwhile, the clarinetist, Leon Rappolo, weaves in and around the rag's patterns, leaping to and holding a blue note, joining the trumpet line, or generally wandering as something of a free spirit against Joplin's repeated phrases. In the singing trio section that is traditional to the march form on which the rag is modeled, trumpeter Paul Mares plays with growls and wah-wahs (characteristic of such early great brassmen as King Oliver and Duke Ellington's Bubber Miley), while drummer Frank Snyder keeps up a steady barrage of offbeats to complement and encourage the instrumentalists. With the variety of tone colors, rhythms, and variations achieved by the New Orleans Rhythm Kings, Joplin's *Maple Leaf Rag* loses its crystalline sound and its repetitive patterns and is metamorphosed into the all-out, seemingly every-man-for-himself freedom that characterizes the group improvisation of New Orleans jazz.

It was not until fifteen years later, during the last three years of his life, that Jelly Roll Morton would himself record *Maple Leaf Rag*. However, in his "Discourse on Jazz," recorded by Alan Lomax in June 1938, Morton tells Lomax that he had played Joplin's "great rag . . . one of the best writings . . . long before" going to "the state of Missouri" in 1904. Morton says that he will play Joplin's piece in the style in which it was performed in St. Louis in that year, "but maybe I say I hate to make the remark like that but maybe not as good [as his own playing] because the boys couldn't finger so good."[68] As with all of Jelly Roll's seemingly outrageous claims, he backs this one up by ripping off Joplin's rag thirty-four years later in an almost flawless performance, providing listeners with his memory of how the piece was played by ragtime pianists a few years after the turn of the century. In *Mister Jelly Roll*, Lomax comments that "for the record, Jelly Roll imitated the piano style of some of these great old-timers [Joplin, Tom Turpin, Louis Chauvin, Audie Mathews, James Scott]. These remarkable imitations . . . prove his phenomenal musical memory, for they faithfully mimic the style of these long-dead pianists, and can be checked with piano rolls of the period."[69] Listening to Joplin's own 1916 piano roll of *Maple Leaf Rag* and comparing it with Morton's performance makes it clear that in fact Jelly Roll's version differs in at least two important ways. First, Morton plays the rag at a considerably quicker pace than Joplin—against the composer's frequent injunctions not to perform ragtime fast. Second, Morton adds in the right hand upward "rips" like those of Louis Armstrong in all his jazz recordings. Both the increased speed and the heightened excitement of the rips lend to Morton's performance something of a jazz feel even in his "straight" version of Joplin's rag.

After finishing a "faithful" version of *Maple Leaf Rag*, Jelly then turns to his own rendition, which will thoroughly transform the ragtime composition into jazz and demonstrate, in his estimation, "a vast difference." Morton goes on to say that in effect this is what he did to all music: "I changed every style to mine."[70] In fact, this is true of a jazz treatment of any piece of music, with ragtime serving as simply one source of material on which jazz musicians have based their improvisations and interpretations. While not unusual as a basis for jazz, ragtime was more significant than other works of music in that it already provided many of the devices incorporated into and extended by jazz, such as those noted earlier: stop time, the break, embellishment, the three-part march form, the drag with its bluesy feel and behind-the-beat rhythm, and of course syncopation. In the case of Morton's impressive reproduction of the "straight" rag style of 1904 and his own jazz version of Joplin's piece, these particular performances are important not only because they exhibit Jelly's phenomenal memory but because they illustrate the transformation of a work of ragtime into jazz, the differences between the two but also their kinship in rhythm, form, and spirit.

Much has been written on Morton's version of Joplin's *Maple Leaf Rag*, particularly in comparison with Joplin's own 1916 piano roll of his famous rag.[71] Joplin's composition has been characterized as "keenly structured" with "fine contrasting themes and their repeats (AABBACCDD)." As for Morton's transformation of Joplin's rag, it has been called "one of the most revealing examples of [the New Orleans] contribution to jazz. It is immediately evident that the basis of the contribution was rhythmic. Morton embellishes the piece two-handedly, with a swinging introduction (borrowed from the ending of the A strain) followed by ABACCDD (with a hint of the tango in the first D and a real New Orleans stomp variation in the second). In accordance with his belief that piano styles should follow band styles, Morton is here clearly playing a trumpet-clarinet part with his right hand and a trombone-rhythm part with his left."[72] Gunther Schuller credits Texas folklorist Alan Lomax—in his "moving, sympathetic, and definitive account of Morton's life"—with first pointing out that "trombone phrasing is the Jelly Roll trademark."[73]

While Joplin created one piece with a tango rhythm (*Solace—A Mexican Serenade*, 1909), it is unlikely that this single composition would have influenced Morton's rather frequent use of what he called a "Spanish tinge" in such works as his *Mama Nita*, *Creepy Feeling*, *New Orleans Blues*, *Fickle Fay Creep*, *Spanish Swat*, and *The Crave*. Nevertheless, Joplin's tango rhythm antedates Jelly Roll's earliest recording of 1918 (according to Morton's statement in *Mister Jelly Roll*) and apparently even Jelly's first published composition from around 1915.[74] While Morton only published his *New Orleans Blues* in 1925, he claimed to have written it around 1902: "Now in one of my earliest tunes, *New Orleans Blues*, you can notice the Spanish tinge. In fact, if you can't manage to put tinges of Spanish in your tunes, you will never be able to get the right seasoning, I call it, for jazz."[75] By seasoning Joplin's *Maple Leaf Rag* with a Spanish tinge, Morton transforms the rag—by his own definition—into jazz. In this regard, Gunther Schuller comments that Morton's remarkable use of the Habanera rhythm in the left hand for "an unequal-beat pattern" in the 1923 recording of his *New Orleans Joy* is something "not again seriously explored by jazz musicians until the sixties, and then in a more arhythmic than polyrhythmic sense."[76] In general, Morton's jazz version of Joplin's rag is marked by right-hand "manipulations," as Jelly Roll called them, which give his melodic lines "a much freer, looser feeling than ragtime had ever known." Morton also avoids ragtime's strict repetitions, creates more contrasts in structure and dynamics, and adds another essential ingredient: the expressive and improvisational "melodic leavening" of the blues.[77]

As noted earlier, Joplin's brand of ragtime during the period from 1907 to 1917 featured greater attention to structure, since for the composer the form or structure of ragtime was an end in itself.[78] This concern for structure was indeed one of Joplin's major contributions to the creation of ragtime as a serious, composed music. Comparing Joplin's compositions with those of Jelly Roll Morton and Duke Ellington, jazz critic Martin Williams observes that, like Joplin's ragtime, the best jazz works of Morton and Ellington are "instrumentally conceived in comparatively simple ways."[79] Williams extends the comparison by including the work of Thelonious Monk, which the critic suggests is also based on a simple framework but is transmuted compositionally. Within the ragtime formula, Joplin would over the years develop certain structural innovations by varying the sequence of themes, adding or lengthening repeated sections, creating contrasts, and modulating through different keys before returning to a piece's home base. Form and variation were both crucial to Joplin's achievement as a composer of ragtime, and both of these features of his music appealed to a fellow composer like Jelly Roll Morton. But in transforming ragtime into jazz, Morton would seek more freedom within musical structure by moving beyond mere thematic variation to the use of an improvisational technique that allowed for wider-ranging invention in terms of harmony and melody, at the same time that it "made possible a rhythmic forward momentum, the *sine qua non* of swing" and "a whole new sense of continuity."[80] Like Morton's jazz treatment of Joplin's *Maple Leaf Rag*, his recording of Joplin's first published rag, *Original Rags*, demonstrates—perhaps even more fully—how Jelly Roll could transform Joplin's four-square pattern of repeated themes into a work of first-rate jazz.

On December 14, 1939, a year and a half after his June 1938 recording of *Maple Leaf Rag* and only a year and a half before his death on July 10, 1941, Jelly Roll Morton recorded Joplin's *Original Rags*.[81] It is especially appropriate that Morton recorded both of these two 1899 Joplin rags and transformed them into jazz, for they have been considered "the keystones of [Joplin's] priceless contribution to American music."[82] Although Joplin's first published rag is not as sophisticated as his later ragtime compositions, Morton incorporates in his version of *Original Rags* a practice in which Joplin later came to delight: a harmonic progression from tonic to submediant, "the change which all of jazz made so rich and varied."[83] Jelly Roll also syncopates Joplin's composition "more than ragtime usually allows . . . adding syncopations to Joplin's treble line" to produce "what Morton commonly called 'stomp' piano, a propulsive two-handed improvisatory style that departs from ragtime's classical restraints but retains its form."[84] Even more significantly, Morton creates a richer harmonic vocabulary by playing chromatics and accidentals not in the original, changes passages from major to minor, adds blue notes and sevenths, flats thirds and fifths, and builds augmented chords. In the area of rhythm, Morton not only syncopates by leaving one beat unsounded but also shifts accents before or after a strong point, bringing emphasis to the offbeats, which also is so characteristic of jazz. Likewise, Morton achieves a strong anticipation in both hands by tying over the last half of the last beat of a measure into the next bar. Finally, throughout his performance Morton never plays a single eighth note straight but swings them all, so Joplin's music becomes unrecognizable as such and is thus transmuted into Jelly's own jazz creation.

Most important of all in Morton's playing of Joplin's *Original Rags* is Jelly Roll's handling of the form of the piece. Joplin's composition contains five themes, the first three of which are repeated, although not immediately—the A theme returning only after the C has been stated and repeated. Whereas Joplin varies his music by moving to another theme, Jelly Roll "forces all of the first three themes to be identical in spirit, fused together to build up his new jazz-type momentum."[85] Morton also achieves this momentum by developing his improvisations out of a single phrase without repeating it exactly but varying it through his spontaneous invention. In addition, Morton revises Joplin's themes and makes of them bridges to link his various choruses. Guy Waterman has observed that "this way of tying together a piece, by having the phrasing overlap the bounds of the four-square structure" is "a splendid artistic achievement." And he adds that "this is the basic resource of Charlie Parker's musical genius" and "what elevates J. S. Bach to his high place." This same critic does confess, however, that Morton's transformation of Joplin's *Original Rags* is not "all net gain," since Jelly's "wandering left-hand sixths," though "most interesting," must serve at one point as a "substitute for some very pretty little left-hand lines in the Joplin original, especially the endings of the first and last strains."[86] But overall it is to be admitted that Jelly Roll Morton's jazz version of the Joplin rag is a more thrilling, more imaginative, more swinging piece of music, and it was this combination that spelled the end of the ragtime craze long before Morton recorded *Original Rags* in 1939 in his mid-1920s New Orleans style.

Ragtime had, in fact, concluded its reign by the date of Scott Joplin's death or shortly thereafter. But before that time, Joplin had established ragtime as a serious music that inspired countless imitators and served as the basis of jazz, the greatest achievement in American music. The lasting effect of Joplin's compositions, however, was not limited merely to their influence on this new African American musical form, even though the impact of ragtime on jazz was surely its most vital contribution to twentieth-century American music. Other musical genres, from concert music to rock and roll, have also been profoundly affected by ragtime, and in some ways this infectious music has become "part of our speech."[87] When a literary critic like Camille Paglia can hear in Emily Dickinson "the first modernist master of syncopation,"[88] such a retrospective reading of Dickinson's poetry owes much to an awareness of the rhythmic form popularized by Scott Joplin. As for Joplin's first hit, the composition that would, as he prophesied, make him the King of Ragtime, *Maple Leaf Rag* lives on as the most popular rag ever. The far-reaching effect of this one tune is perhaps best exemplified by its having been the source for the last complete dance choreographed by Martha Graham, her 181st composition, created in 1990. When this creator of modern dance suffered from "dancer's block" in her early years, she would ask her pianist, Louis Horst, to play *Maple Leaf Rag*, "the one piece of music that could cheer her."[89]

❧ ❧ ❧

While Scott Joplin is the acknowledged King of Ragtime, another Texan also created at least one piece of ragtime which, until the 1970s ragtime revival of Joplin's music, had been ranked as "the most popular rag of all time."[90] Referred to as "ubiquitous,"[91] Euday L. Bowman's *Twelfth Street Rag* was recorded by more jazz groups than any single work by Joplin or even all his compositions combined. Not only was Bowman's rag popular as a jazz vehicle but many of the performances of this work figure significantly in the development of jazz as a form of artistic improvisation. Numbered among the individual performers of Bowman's rag are

Louis Armstrong, Sidney Bechet, Bennie Moten, Duke Ellington, Fats Waller, Count Basie, and Lester Young, representing a range of styles from New Orleans hot jazz through stride piano to the swing era and the rise of the cool school of tenor saxophone playing. The variety of groups recording Bowman's rag covers the field from Armstrong's Hot Seven and smaller ensembles led by Waller and Bechet to the big bands of Bennie Moten, Duke Ellington, Count Basie, and Andy Kirk. In all, the *Twelfth Street Rag* has been recorded in more than 120 versions.

Born in Fort Worth on November 9, 1887, Euday L. Bowman played in a shoeshine parlor on Main Street between Tenth and Eleventh streets, where he would practice and work on his compositions.[92] According to one account, he recorded his *Twelfth Street Rag* on the same piano on which he originally composed it.[93] As a performer, Bowman has his problems with his own composition, missing notes and in places failing to keep steady time; and yet he definitely swings, while his recorded introduction to his theme is reminiscent of Jelly Roll Morton's style and even includes blue notes. Although some music critics have thought that the *Twelfth Street Rag*, first published in 1914, represents Bowman's only composition, he also wrote other rags between 1914 and 1917 as well as *Kansas City Blues* (1914), which, "though using a chorus and verse structure, helped popularize blues among white audiences."[94] As for the *Twelfth Street Rag*, whose title has been attributed both to a numbered street in Fort Worth and to one in Kansas City, the piece was unusual for ragtime in having a theme-and-variations structure, but what made it a major hit was its use of a "repeating three-note motif (sometimes called 'secondary rag')," a device that proved "catchy and easy to play."[95] As a type of binary-ternary mixture "using a three-note melodic cycle against the duple-metered ragtime bass," the *Twelfth Street Rag* is "perhaps the best-known example and most extensive employment of this rhythmic device," which is "frequently found in ragtime and jazz" and is "rhythmically exciting . . . though mild in comparison to melodic-rhythmic figures found in present-day jazz."[96] While Bowman's rag has often been disparaged as a piece of music "remarkable more for surface brilliance than for content," it has been noted that "this is the most familiar form of ragtime . . . and there is no denying its exuberance."[97]

The attraction of the *Twelfth Street Rag* for jazz groups may be owing merely to the tune's popularity; yet the results of a number of the recordings suggest that Bowman's piece could prove inspiring for the purposes of improvisation in spite of its repetitious three-note motif. Generally jazz critics have credited the jazz performers themselves with transforming Bowman's rag into great music. As Gunther Schuller remarks of Lester Young's extended solo in a 1939 recording with the Count Basie Orchestra, it "mercifully bears no relationship to the original tune."[98] Likewise, Eric Thacker seems grateful that Sidney Bechet, in his 1941 solo, "completely recomposed" Bowman's "puerile theme."[99] Nonetheless, Lester Young, Louis Armstrong, and other outstanding jazz figures managed to produce some of their finest musical moments in basing their improvisations on Bowman's popular rag, and in doing so they were to give new direction to jazz as an art form.

The earliest jazz recording of Bowman's rag dates from May 11, 1927, when Louis Armstrong and His Hot Seven cut their version in Chicago, although this take remained unissued until 1940.[100] Comments on this performance by critic John Chilton begin with the declaration that "making great jazz out of 'Twelfth Street Rag' . . . is a task that has defeated countless jazz musicians." Predictably, Chilton goes on to observe that it is only when Armstrong begins "presenting his version of the tune" that he is able through "his ingenious reallocation of time values" to transform "the old rag into something startlingly intricate."[101] Critic Martin Williams goes even further in his estimate of Armstrong's performance:

> As written, *Twelfth Street Rag* is a fair rag-style piece, but its manner was already dated by the 'twenties and it is still used today as a vehicle for a deliberately corny quasi-jazz. Armstrong's performance, a brilliant revelation, opens up the jazz tradition. . . . In its way, *Twelfth Street* is more interesting, or at least more indicative, than such justly celebrated Armstrong performances as the brilliant stop-time choruses of *Potato Head Blues*, the series of sublime descents on *Gully Low (S.O.L.) Blues*, the recomposition of *Hotter Than That*, or the lovely and sober form of *Big Butter and Egg Man*. With *Twelfth Street Rag*, we are prepared for the beautifully free phrasing on the 1928 recordings with Earl Hines, *West End Blues* and *Muggles*. We are prepared for the later passionate melodies that swing freely without rhythmic reminders and for the double-time episodes that unfold with poise. We are prepared for a fuller revelation of Armstrong's genius.[102]

One month later, on June 11, 1927, a second jazz-oriented version of Bowman's rag was recorded in Chicago by the Bennie Moten band, demonstrating "how tenaciously ragtime survived in Kansas City . . . even at that late date."[103] Although British critic Brian Rust claims that "once you have heard this account of the famous rag, you need bother with no other, dozens of which have been recorded by big bands, small bands, Hawaiian guitars, ukeleles, cinema organs and piano-accordions," there are certainly, aside from the Armstrong recording, at least two other versions—those by Ellington and Basie—that deserve special attention. Also contrary to Rust's assertion, the Moten rendition of Bowman's rag does not resort to "deliberate corny effects of doo-wacka-doo trumpets and gurgling clarinets," although it is marked by a dated banjo and tuba sound and a generally rick-a-tick style. After Moten's concert piano opening, the piece features a pyramid-building introduction by the brasses and saxes, and then the whole band cranks up Bowman's three-note motif. A slightly stiff sax solo is followed by a more lively trombone chorus; after this the cornets play the rag's theme straight, followed by Moten's very raggy piano treatment. A rousing ensemble section leads to the conclusion with its nifty passing of single notes around from brasses to saxes. Moten's band definitely, as we shall see, produced more important work in the early 1930s, but as Rust observes, Bowman's composition served "to establish the credentials of the great band that gives it such a very warm, even elegant reading."[104]

On January 14, 1931, Duke Ellington and his orchestra recorded *Twelfth Street Rag*, and this version is notable for its two-piano antiphonal treatment of Bowman's theme. Even as Ellington and Benny Payne play the rag in a fairly straightforward statement of its three-note motif, the Duke introduces his trademark rippling arpeggios, this time a descending run of minor thirds on the diminished seventh, the most unstable chord in Bowman's composition, which makes the Duke's resolution to the tonic all the more satisfying. Many of Ellington's most outstanding sidemen are present on this recording, among them trombonists Tricky Sam Nanton with his talking plunger and Juan Tizol with his Latin-tinged valve trombone, as well as trumpeters Cootie Williams and Freddie Jenkins.[105] Tizol plays the rag's theme with exaggerated syncopation in both a tongue-in-cheek manner and in a wildly swinging call-and-response style. Especially impressive here is the percussion work of the Duke's remarkable drummer, Sonny Greer, who keeps the band energized throughout. In arranging the rag, Ellington emphasized the high-pitched sound of the clarinet, which is even voiced for the baritone saxophonist, the inimitable Harry Carney. Like Ellington's many railroad tunes, this rendition of Bowman's rag steams along at an unrelenting clip until the last bars, when the train is abruptly stopped by the brass section's three short whistlelike blasts. This rollicking performance illustrates the Ellington orchestra's power, regardless of the genre—blues, tone poem, character sketch, solid swing-era warhorse, or a seemingly outgrown piece of ragtime.

While Stanley Dance considers the Duke's performance of the *Twelfth Street Rag* a departure from "what might be regarded as Ellington canon," as an instance of the pianist-composer's "concessions to popular taste,"[106] the orchestration is nonetheless as complex at times as in any other Ellington composition. In its sophisticated, inventive approach to jazz arranging and its exciting swing, the arrangement features contrapuntal writing for the saxes and brasses that shows off the orchestra's great section work. For each soloist, Ellington provides a slick modulation into a different key, and despite its repetitious nature, Bowman's rag in the hands of Ellington results in an exhilarating performance that compares favorably with Duke's own compositions from the 1930s, such as the highly regarded *Daybreak Express* (1933) and *Merry-Go-Round* (1935).

Quite a different interpretation of Bowman's *Twelfth Street Rag* is the one by Fats Waller and His Rhythm dating from June 24, 1935, complete with the pianist's comic outbursts in the middle of his sidemen's solos.[107] Lyrics had been added to the tune, and Fats delivers them in his spirited, infectious style of good humor, along with his impeccable stride piano. Also in evidence here is what Wilfrid Mellers calls Waller's "right-hand technique, full of twittering thirds in tremolando and dancing dotted arabesques" that "become increasingly delicate" as "the music's energy is wittily released by the repeated-note bass."[108] Al Casey on guitar is a fringe benefit of this recording, while Rudy Powell on clarinet and Herman Autry on trumpet stir things up with their own brand of jovial jazz, the latter with his conversational repartee and repeated high-note shakes as Fats shouts "Baby, get those hotdogs ready" and "Turn it loose!" This reading of Bowman's rag is sheer, unadulterated fun, and even though many jazz devotees have regretted Waller's lowering himself to the level of a clown, there is nothing in jazz history so enduringly invigorating as Fats rippling through the most innocuous tunes and transforming them into swinging or lilting renditions that are at once riotously comedic and virtuosic in their control and rhythmic drive. Opening with a melodramatic flourish at the keyboard, Waller does his own very typical stride approach to Bowman's three-note motif, altering its entire character, and then ends the piece with a classical-like arpeggiated run, which is followed by the trumpet's mocking nursery-rhyme tag. What makes Waller's version so appealing is this very combination of a virtuosic technique with a light-hearted touch. Given the basis of his treatment, it is totally appropriate and the results truly representative of Waller's unique contribution to 1930s jazz.

The Count Basie Orchestra's April 5, 1939, recording of *Twelfth Street Rag*, featuring Lester Young on tenor, finds Bowman's piece in a full-blown swing-era rendition. Even so, this version begins with a Basie piano (accompanied by some consciously dated woodblock hokum from drummer Jo Jones) that remains fairly close to the rag before the Count moves into his patented lightly swinging right hand against a left-hand stride. In addition to the crisp brass punctuations, so much a part of the period's big-band sound, this reading includes two outstanding choruses by Young and one by trumpeter Harry Edison. Although opinions differ on Young's performance here, there is no doubt that his approach is vintage swing-era tenor and looks forward to a long line of imitators. As critic Eric Thacker points out, Young's "gently honking entry . . . with a distinctly oral quality in execution represents an element in his playing that was popularly exaggerated" (in particular by Texas tenorist Illinois Jacquet).[109] Here, as elsewhere in his solo outings, Young is relaxed yet paradoxically swinging by way of a kind of intensity imparted to each vibratoless note. Whereas Stanley Dance considers Young's playing to be unstimulated by Bowman's rag and finds that in Edison's solo, which splits Young's two choruses, the trumpeter "seeks valiantly to update the material,"[110] Albert McCarthy avers that during 1939 and 1940 Young "recorded some of his greatest solos with the band, most notably being those heard on *Twelfth Street Rag, Miss Thing* (the first tenor solo), *Clap Hands Here Comes Charlie*, and *Louisana*."[111] Likewise, Benny Green considers Young's solos on *Clap Hands Here Comes Charlie* and *Twelfth Street Rag* "perhaps the very zenith of Lester's greatness," adding that "one can sense instantly the detachment of the aphorist and the presence of an original spirit. Young is the great epigrammatist of jazz, which is perhaps why he remains the most quoted man in all jazz."[112] Gunther Schuller, who is never enthusiastic about Bowman's rag, judges this Basie recording to be "another anomaly . . . a totally mechanical rendition of that old warhorse—except for Young's extended solo."[113] As Schuller's remarks reveal, Lester Young, at the date of this Basie recording, was already improvising on pop tunes, as would the beboppers within the next few years, by working from a tune's chords without stating its melody—yet another forward-looking aspect of this important version of Bowman's rag.

From a November 7, 1940, session by Andy Kirk and his Twelve Clouds of Joy comes a recording of *Twelfth Street Rag* that represents yet another interpretation of Bowman's tune.[114] Featured on piano is one of the most outstanding women in jazz history, Mary Lou Williams, who not only provides two brief stride piano solos but also arranged Bowman's rag.[115] Williams's orchestration, like Ellington's, contains some ingenious modulations, beginning with the sax section's statement of the theme, to which she adds written phrases and accents not in the original, and like Basie's arrangement, Mary Lou's transforms the tune into quintessential swing. Aside from Williams and tenorist Dick Wilson, who played with a Lester Young–like sound but with a more frantic approach, the Kirk band did not offer the same level of soloists as the Ellington or Basie orchestras, but on *Twelfth Street Rag* Harold Baker is present to take one of his "characteristic solos," exhibiting his "deliciously melodic" trumpet with a "tone full of light and shade."[116] Ben Thigpen on drums is a highly effective big-band percussionist. In addition to other solos by trombone, tenor sax, and clarinet, this version of Bowman's rag showcases the orchestra's ensemble work. Leading the trumpet section is Harry "Big Jim" Lawson, who was born in Round Rock near Austin on December 25, 1904.[117] The "arrangement" of the rag theme is made up almost entirely of swing-style written lines that reflect, as Rex Harris suggests of the reed and brass scoring for the Kirk orchestra's selections, "a touch of the Ellington brush . . . ; a hint of Glenn Miller . . . ; a finger jab of the imperious Basie brass section-work."[118] Nonetheless, Bowman's rag theme remains central to the performance and reveals how adaptable it proved as a jazz vehicle. The tune concludes with a typical swing-era, full-orchestra grand finale, with a phrase from *Sailors' Hornpipe* thrown in for good measure as a kind of witty, boplike ending.

In 1941, when the big bands were still enjoying widespread popularity and combos were already beginning to congregate in such New York nightspots as Minton's and Monroe's to play what would become known as bebop, the traditional New Orleans style was simultaneously experiencing a revival with the return to active careers of trumpeter Bunk Johnson and other jazzmen who had been prominent in the early 1910s and 1920s. Among these "moldy figs," as the traditionalists were branded by advocates of the new experimental music, was Sidney Bechet, the clarinetist and soprano saxophonist who has been considered by some critics as "one of the great creative figures in the history of jazz."[119] Bechet, noted for "his moving interpretations of blues and ragtime,"[120] had impressed classical conductor Ernest Ansermet as early as 1918 when the clarinetist performed in Europe with Will Marion Cook's Southern Syncopated Orchestra. Bechet had continued to play with various groups throughout the 1920s and 1930s, and on October 24, 1941, he and his New Orleans Feetwarmers, featuring Charlie Shaver on trumpet and Willie "The Lion" Smith on piano, recorded Bowman's *Twelfth Street Rag*. Earlier, in September 1932, another group of Feetwarmers, with Tommy Ladnier on trumpet, had recorded the *Maple Leaf Rag*, which illustrates "the important influence of the St. Louis piano ragtime style on New Orleans music. All four themes of Scott Joplin's famed *Maple Leaf Rag* are rendered at breakneck tempo."[121] Bechet himself called his version of Joplin's 1899 rag "one of his best recordings," and critics have considered his "fierce, inventive, and over-all exuberant playing" in this recording "one of his greatest performances on soprano saxophone."[122] Bowman's rag is likewise taken at an up-tempo pace, but this time Bechet "displays some of his finest clarinet work."[123] While Bechet and pianist Willie Smith stick close to the ragtime tradition, Charlie Shavers exhibits more of the swing style and even hints at the later bop showmanship of a Dizzy Gillespie. But it is Everett Barksdale with some of his fills on guitar who indicates the impact on his own playing of revolutionary Texas guitarist Charlie Christian and the new sound of augmented and diminished chords that was already beginning to mark the music of the bop movement. In a way, then, this recording of Bowman's rag stands as something of a miniature history of jazz from the pre–World War One period up to the entrance of the United States into World War Two.

Even more than Scott Joplin's admittedly superior ragtime compositions, Euday L. Bowman's *Twelfth Street Rag* offers, through some half-dozen recordings, a sampling of the various jazz styles that were dominant in each of the three decades covered by the work of Louis Armstrong, Bennie Moten, Duke Ellington, Fats Waller, Lester Young, Mary Lou Williams, and Sidney Bechet and his sidemen. Thus, the development of jazz is, perhaps surprisingly, demonstrated by means of Bowman's single rag, from the early practice of New Orleans hot jazz to the arranged big-band style, from the unique but highly influential solo conceptions of Armstrong to those of Lester Young, and from the distinctively exhilarating swing of Fats Waller to the revolutionary rhythmic, melodic, and harmonic ideas of bebop. Regardless of its outmoded sound and structure, Bowman's *Twelfth Street Rag* yet served a wide range of jazz styles and jazz soloists to develop their own peculiar approaches to the music that would supersede ragtime and spread throughout the world as America's greatest contribution to the creative arts of the twentieth century.

COUNTRY BLUES

Jelly Roll Morton's "invention of jazz" in 1902 resulted from his combination of the formal, harmonic, and rhythmic characteristics of ragtime with the "improvisational freedom and emotional expressiveness" of the blues.[1] Even though two of Morton's earliest compositions, *New Orleans Blues* (1902–1903) and *Jelly Roll Blues* (1905), bear the word "blues" in their titles, Jelly Roll did not claim to have invented this musical form. The term itself, or the phrase "blue devils," has been traced back to the sixteenth and seventeenth centuries in England and was used in America as early as 1807 by Washington Irving in his *Salmagundi*, in 1810 by Thomas Jefferson, and in 1854 by Henry David Thoreau in *Walden*,[2] meaning in all these cases a state of sadness, loneliness, or low spirits. The blues sound in music derives from a simultaneous use of major and minor tonalities— a "blue note" on the piano is a black key played together with the white key below it, producing a sound that apparently originates from an African practice of singing a leading tone flatter than in European music.[3] While the color red tended to signify a hotter type of music, fast and spirited, blues suggested a slower, more melancholy feeling, even though many blues were played up-tempo. Speed in many ways did not determine the nature of a blues, nor did its duration, since a blues could vary in the number of measures for its call-and-response-like breaks, which were played following each of the standard three-line verses of a song based on a three-chord harmonic structure. It was this flexibility of the blues that allowed for freedom and improvisation, and it was this feature of the music that appealed to Jelly Roll Morton and led, in conjunction with the more patterned form of ragtime, to the creation of jazz.

Like ragtime, blues were in existence long before Morton began to perform and compose. As one of Jelly's early associates, Louis de Lisle Nelson, would comment to Alan Lomax, "The blues always been. Blues is what cause the fellows to start jazzing."[4] Morton remembered hearing blues in New Orleans when he was quite young, and the tune was the famous *See, See Rider* as sung and played on the piano by Josky Adams.[5] In the 1920s *See, See Rider* would be recorded by the classic blues singers Ma Rainey and Bessie Smith and by Texas country blues singer Blind Lemon Jefferson. Another blues recorded by these three major figures is *Boll Weevil Blues*, a folksong traced to Texas because it was the first state in the cotton belt to be hit by the boll weevil that crossed over from Mexico in the 1860s.[6] According to Gunther Schuller, the blues in Texas is "one of the oldest indigenous traditions and probably much older than the New Orleans idiom that is generally thought to be the primary fountainhead of jazz."[7] Ma Rainey, acclaimed as the "Mother of the Blues," recalled hearing her first blues in 1902 in a small Missouri town, so she herself only incorporated this musical form into her repertoire after that date, having previously sung minstrel songs of the day.[8] As for the New Orleans bands that are credited with creating jazz, they reportedly did not become familiar with the rural blues until the mid-1890s, prior to which ragtime was the basis of the music made by the legendary Buddy Bolden and other figures working in the French Quarter.[9] Paul Oliver has even asserted that New Orleans did not have "an important part to play in the story of the blues, the transition there being from the songs of the field and the dance into jazz."[10] Bolden's significance lies in his having fused the country blues with the march form of the ragtime band at the same time that he united the popular stringed instruments with wind instruments to form a rhythm section and a front line of clarinet, cornet, and trombone. Paul Oliver speaks of Bolden "having improvised a 'blues' . . . presumably a field holler played instrumentally."[11] It was probably upon this innovative approach of Bolden's that Jelly Roll Morton built his own music, with the important difference that Morton was more improvisatory in his playing and yet more formal in his written compositions, which largely determined the solos or breaks taken by his band members.

In their creation of jazz in New Orleans, both Bolden and Morton were indebted to the rural or country blues, which originated following the Civil War and developed in the South's cotton belt, particularly from the Mississippi Delta to East Texas. Sidney Finkelstein has observed that "no other city holds a place in jazz history comparable to that of New Orleans. The reason is that New Orleans jazz itself was more than the music of a city. It was the concentrated music of the entire lower Mississippi valley, Texas, and the Gulf Coast."[12] In general, Texas blues are marked by "imaginative and witty lyrics which tell a story, and they rarely fall into the trap of putting one traditional phrase after the other, common in Delta blues."[13] The Texas country blues tradition is further distinguished from the blues of other regions by its "somewhat lighter touch; guitar playing [that] tends to be less chordal, with an emphasis on single-string melodic dexterity; more relaxed vocal qualities and an open rather than a dense accompaniment texture."[14] The rural blues, as their name implies, were born in the cotton fields, later spreading to workers in the lumbering, milling, and turpentine industries in the Piney Woods region, to the stevedores along the Gulf Coast and the Mississippi and its tributaries, to laborers building and maintaining railroads, and to the black domestic workforce. The style and textual content of the rural blues was influenced as well by work songs sung by prison inmates or those prisoners sent out on road gangs. As an offshoot of African cross-rhythms, the blues were created by pitting the melody line against the bass line and thereby emphasizing offbeats, much as in ragtime but with a difference: whereas ragtime employed a regular rhythmic line against which a melody could syncopate, the blues were unpredictable in their placement of the beat, tending not to play on either strong or weak pulses but to stretch a phrase through a normal accent or to set up irregular groupings of accents. The freedom achieved by the blues came about from within the harmonic structure of their generally three four-measure phrases of three chords (in tonic, subdominant, and dominant, usually in this order: I IV V, or I IV I V I). In creating the blues, black rural musicians expressed their emotions with falling pitches and by bending or flattening certain notes, practices also deriving from their African heritage.

The themes of country blues were largely drawn from the experiences of the singers as well as from black folklore. The various forms that the blues took were owing to their roots in spirituals and hymns, moans and hollers or cries, shouts and chants, and ballads and dance steps. In all of these roots and sources the central preoccupation was a desire for freedom—freedom from a socioeconomic condition of injustice, prejudice, and exploitation or simply from "the blues" brought on by the pangs of love. An oft-repeated motif in the rural blues is the desire to escape the cotton fields and their backbreaking labor. But what remains most moving about the blues as sung and performed by black musicians is that the music is essentially uplifting, full of racial pride, and memorable in its blend of simple form with complex rhythms and emotional expression.

❂ ❂ ❂

Henry "Ragtime Texas" Thomas, an early exponent of country blues, was born in 1874 in Big Sandy, Texas, the son of former slaves who sharecropped on a cotton plantation in the northeastern part of the state. One of nine children, Thomas learned to hate cotton farming, and he left home as soon as he could, around 1890, to pursue a career as an itinerant "songster," as he has been called by various commentators on his music. Derrick Stewart-Baxter writes that, for his money, Thomas was the best songster "that ever recorded."[15] Thomas first taught himself to play the quills, a folk instrument made from cane reeds that sounds similar to the *quena* used by musicians in Peru and Bolivia; later, he picked up the guitar. On the twenty-three recordings made by Thomas from 1927 to 1929,[16] he sings a variety of songs while he accompanies himself on guitar and at times on the quills.[17] The range of Thomas's work makes him something of a transitional figure between the tradition of early minstrel songs, spirituals, square-dance tunes, hillbilly reels, waltzes, and rags and the rise of blues and jazz. Most of his repertoire, which consists largely of dance pieces, was out of date by the turn of the century when the blues began to grow in popularity. Thomas's nickname, "Ragtime Texas," is thought to have come to him because he played in fast tempos, which were synonymous for some musicians with ragtime. Five of Thomas's pieces have been characterized as "rag ditties," among them *Red River Blues*, and such rag songs have been considered the immediate forerunners and early rivals of blues.

Out of Thomas's twenty-three recorded pieces, only four are "bona fide blues," so he has been looked upon as more of a predecessor rather than a blues singer as such. One commentator has claimed that Thomas's blues are original with him and that other musicians seem not to have performed his pieces.[18] However, Thomas's *Bull Doze Blues* ends with the four-bar *Take Me Back*, a Texas standard of the World War One era, which Blind Lemon Jefferson would record around August 1926 as *Beggin' Back*.[19] It would seem, then, that Thomas's blues represent many of the traditional themes and vocal phrases that, as Louis de Lisle Nelson suggested, have "always been."[20] For example, Thomas's *Texas Easy Street Blues* contains the verse made famous by Jimmy Rushing and Joe Williams in their 1930s to 1950s versions of the Basie-Rushing tune *Goin' to Chicago*: "When you see me comin', baby, raise your window high." Another well-known phrase found in this same Thomas piece is "blue as I can be," which is heard in W. C. Handy's *St. Louis Blues* of 1914 as recorded by Bessie Smith in 1925, accompanied on cornet by Louis Armstrong. Thomas's own vocal delivery on *Texas Easy Street Blues* can even be related at one point to the practice of ripping upward to a note the way Armstrong would on his horn or when he would scat-sing—for instance, in Satchmo's *Hotter Than That* from 1927. As for Thomas's free picking and strumming on the guitar, his accompaniment work has been ranked "with the finest dance blues ever recorded," and its "intricate simultaneous treble picking and drone bass" have been described as "a challenge to any blues guitarist of any era."[21] But perhaps most indicative of Thomas's transitional position between the early black music and jazz is his *Cottonfield Blues*, which contains several standard blues themes: field labor, the desire for escape, and the role of the railroad in providing a freer lifestyle.

Henry Thomas's *Cottonfield Blues* begins with a twelve-bar instrumental intro-duction, and along with his *Texas Worried Blues* and *Texas Easy Street Blues*, this piece has suggested to William Barlow that "here was the beginning of a distinctive regional blues style. His thumb provides the repetitive groundbeat, while he picks the melody higher up the guitar neck."[22] After his instrumental introduction on *Cottonfield Blues*, the songster says he is going to Texas and has "to ride the rods," but rather than leaving the cottonfields, he seems to be returning to his home state and remembering why he left in the first place. He makes reference to a popular black song, *Alabama Bound*, from the first decade of the twentieth century,[23] and then begins to recall his reasons for having taken up a wandering life on the rails. For one thing, he had to be up at four o'clock to "turn that land" with a mule and plow; yet no matter how early he started, the weeds kept getting ahead of him. In the end he says that—again by way of reminiscence—one morning they will call him and he'll be gone.

Thomas did in fact escape from a life of farm work by taking to the rails to make a living by singing along the Texas Pacific and Katy lines that ran from Fort Worth–Dallas to Texarkana. In *Railroadin' Some*, Thomas supplies his itinerary, which includes Texas towns like Rockwall, Greenville (with its infamous sign, "Land of the Blackest Earth and the Whitest People"), Denison, Grand Saline, Silver Lake, Mineola, Tyler (where Thomas was last heard during the 1950s), Longview, Jefferson, Marshall, Little Sandy, and his birthplace of Big Sandy. Texas communities are not the only ones cited in this song, for Thomas traveled into the Indian Territory, as he still calls it, to Muskogee, over to Missouri and Joplin's stomping grounds of Sedalia, and on up to Kansas City, then into Illinois: Springfield, Bloomington, Joliet, and Chicago, where he attended the 1893 Columbian Exposition, as did Joplin. In speaking of *Railroadin' Some*, William Barlow calls it the most "vivid and intense recollection of railroading" in all the early blues recorded in the 1920s. The cadences in this early rural blues "depict the restless lifestyle of the vagabonds who rode the rails and their boundless enthu-siasm for the mobility it gave them."[24] What is especially remarkable about this recording is Thomas's imitation of the train sounds on his quills at the same time that he keeps the rhythm moving by simultaneously puffing on the cane reeds and strumming his guitar. As he travels from point to point along the route, he yells out "Hello," naming each town as he passes, and whistles to the High Ball to come on through. Finally, on reaching Chicago, he even suggests the train's slowing down for the Fourth Street depot. Thomas ends the piece with a catchy melody on the quills, complete with ragtime syncopation.

Freedom for blacks could have its dangerous as well as its adventurous side, for they were not always welcome in the Texas towns where the trains stopped for passengers or freight. A wandering, "shiftless" black was suspicious and would find himself in jail at the slightest provocation or under the mere pretense of making trouble. Many blues originated in jails or prisons or were based on experiences shared with the singers by those who had served time. Several of Thomas's songs deal with this theme, among them *Don't Ease Me In, Run Molly Run, Shanty Blues*, and *Bull Doze Blues*, the latter alluding to the floggings received by inmates. In *Don't Ease Me In*, the singer laments that his girl brings him coffee, tea, and everything "except the jailhouse key." Escape from incarceration or the fear of flogging should the singer be caught leads him to declare that he is heading for Tennessee "where I'll never be bulldozed." Although in saying good-bye to his gal and her parents he repeats that he is not going away for long, return does not seem likely, which makes the farewell all the more poignant. The case is similar for *Run Molly Run*, in which the singer tells of having gone to Huntsville Penitentiary, where, though he says he did not go to stay, once there he had to wear the ball and chain. He now seems on the run. Likewise, the singer is at large in *Shanty Blues*, this time being tracked down by hounds and "the man on his horse." While on *Bull Doze Blues* and *Run Molly Run* Thomas performs upbeat tunes (the first on quills and the second on guitar) that tend to offset the melancholy situation described in his lyrics, on *Shanty Blues* he responds on guitar to the plaintive words with minor thirds high up on the neck of the instrument, producing a type of call-and-response crucial in the blues, a keening parallel to the crying tone of his voice as he sings of leaving home for the Indian Nation. If not a blues but rather a "truncated version of a hillbilly song,"[25] Thomas's rendition of *Shanty Blues* nevertheless creates the urgency of escape, both in its minor feel and the banjolike whining of his strumming and his upper-register picking, all of which are related to the blues form.

Other songs by Henry Thomas concern his need for someone to care for him, as in *Texas Worried Blues*, in which he says he has "got no one to tell his trouble to." Often the themes of Thomas's songs, such as *Honey, Won't You Allow Me One More Chance*, are typical of the blues in their appeal for forgiveness and their promise to treat the woman right and never "to stay out all night." And yet, as with most of the songster's work, *Honey* derives from another tradition, in this case the 1880s "coon song," a form of white syncopated ragtime with lyrics that stereotyped blacks as drifters and ne'er-do-wells. In general, Thomas's recordings represent a wide variety of sources for his Texas brand of country music, dating back to a time before the blues became popular and before in essence they subsumed many other popular song forms. This eclecticism perhaps accounts for the fact that three of Thomas's songs—*Fishing Blues, Woodhouse Blues*, and *Red River Blues*—are not in reality based on the blues but may have taken the name as a way of capitalizing on the form's growing popularity. According to Stephen Calt, both *Fishing Blues* and *Woodhouse Blues* are of vaudeville origin, while *Red River Blues* has been associated melodically with *Comin' Round the Mountain*, published in sheet music form in 1889 but deriving from an earlier spiritual.

The importance of Thomas's recordings as something of a compendium of the popular song forms of the late nineteenth and early twentieth centuries—from spiritual to "coon song," from "rag ditty" to blues—is enhanced by the similar range of instrumental techniques found in his work with guitar and quills. Sounding at times like the banjo that was, along with the fiddle, the favorite instrument for accompanying the voice, Thomas's guitar playing returns to the African roots of black music in America, both in his guitar sound that is akin to African drums when he strums and in his use of the call-and-response pattern that is the soul of the blues.[26] At other times, Thomas's guitar playing looks forward to its use by later Texas bluesmen like Blind Lemon Jefferson and Leadbelly as a versatile melodic solo instrument. On *Shanty Blues* (where Thomas employs open tuning and utilizes a knife or a bottleneck to stop the strings) and in his bona fide blues, he comes close to matching the skills of Jefferson and Leadbelly in creating complex passages of free improvisation. Samuel Charters has provided a concise description of Thomas's guitar playing as well as his vocal practice:

> Like most Texas singers he kept the guitar close to standard pitch, instead of slackened considerably below it, as in Mississippi. Also he played in the middle strings to a great extent. There were other techniques that he also shared with later Texas singers, and he could be considered one of the earliest Texas blues men as well as a songster. Three of his recorded pieces, "Texas Worried Blues," "Cotton Field Blues," and "Texas Easy Street Blues," had nearly all the elements that became part of the emerging Texas blues style. The voice was unforced, and the melody, although close to the conventional city blues melody, was faster and lighter. The accompaniment technique was one of the first to completely define the Texas guitar style. . . . The thumb played repetitive 4/4 on the tonic of the key, the sound light and insistent. Usually there was the brush back on the upper strings with the first fingers, and a melodic figure was picked against this background up the neck of the guitar. Thomas might have been the first to play in this style, although it seems unlikely that he could have created it.[27]

Perhaps most striking of all is Thomas's ability to imitate on the guitar the vocal expression of his singing, particularly, as noted above, in his *Shanty Blues*. This feature of Thomas's playing places him squarely in the jazz tradition, in which woodwind and brass instruments attempt to reproduce the highly expressive qualities of the human voice. As early as their 1917 recordings, the Original Dixieland Jazz Band musicians tried to imitate barnyard noises in their *Livery Stable Blues*, but these were mere novelty effects compared with the human sounds of crying, moaning, and laughing reproduced through the mutes and hand-in-bell techniques of King Oliver, Bubber Miley, Charlie Irvis, Tricky Sam Nanton, Dickie Wells, and Texan Tyree Glenn and later through the voicelike inflections of the tenor saxophone in the playing of Coleman Hawkins, Lester Young, John Coltrane, and Ornette Coleman. To a greater degree than the Original Dixieland Jazz Band's mimesis, Thomas's imitation of train sounds is also more in keeping with jazz and its connection with the blues-railroad tradition that would ultimately lead to Ellington's masterworks in this vein, as well as such related compositions as the Duke's *Merry-Go-Round* and Jimmie Lunceford's *The Merry-Go-Round Broke Down*. In a sense, then, Henry Thomas represents a vital link between the roots of black music in Africa—that is, nineteenth- and twentieth-century American folksong (including spiritual, hillbilly, "rag," and "coon")—and the coming of the blues. All of these forms contributed in turn to the creation of jazz in its various styles, which are reflected in the many approaches to rhythmic, tonal, and thematic expression practiced by Ragtime Texas decades before he made his series of recordings from 1927 to 1929.

If Henry Thomas was a forerunner or a transitional figure, Blind Lemon Jefferson was the undisputed "King of the Country Blues." Born around 1880 near Couchman in east-central Texas, Jefferson became the most famous male blues singer of the 1920s, and his success on records rivaled that of the "Empress of the Blues," Bessie Smith.[28] Jefferson's first recordings were released in 1926, one year before those of Henry Thomas, with whom Blind Lemon shared the same producer in J. Mayo Williams of Paramount Records.[29] Whereas Thomas rarely played the blues and is thought to have come to this form late in life, Jefferson is considered "strictly a blues man," "the kinda bluesman you didn't have every day on the street. He was the king."[30] Like Thomas, Jefferson had grown up and performed in the country towns of Texas; but because he had been born blind, he never worked in the fields as "Ragtime Texas" had. Nonetheless, Jefferson also "escaped" from the limitations placed on blacks by taking to the Central Texas trains that passed through the area of Wortham and Mexia, where he performed regularly. Beginning by entertaining for all-night parties, community picnics, and Saturday-night dances in the Wortham area sometime around 1911 or 1912, Jefferson also seems to have played in the barrelhouses of the lumber and levee camps. Around 1917 he traveled by train to Dallas, where he found it profitable to play on the streets or in the redlight district known as Deep Ellum. Galveston also attracted Jefferson, and it was there that "the loping boogie-woogie beat of Texas

Blind Lemon Jefferson of Couchman, "The King of the Country Blues."

blues evolved . . . through the fingers and voices" of Jefferson and such Houston figures as Sippie Wallace, Hersal Thomas, and Victoria Spivey, who reported that she first met and performed with Jefferson at a house party on the island city.[31] Eventually Lemon traveled as far as Mississippi, Tennessee, Alabama, Georgia, and the eastern seaboard, but it was his move to Chicago in 1925 that resulted in his recordings with the Paramount company, which issued eighty-nine Jefferson sides before his death there in 1929 or 1930.[32] In Lemon's *Long Lonesome Blues* of 1926, which immediately revolutionized the "race record" industry by becoming both the first country blues hit as well as the first successful recording by a male blues singer, Jefferson produced a work that is still "startling" today in that its "speed and sheer number of riffs come close to setting a blues record."[33]

The influence of Jefferson's singing and guitar playing has been considered at once pervasive and yet less extensive than that of "any commercially successful blues artist."[34] At the same time that Pete Welding claims that "there is scarcely a blues performer alive, major or minor, who has not acknowledged his debt to Lemon," that Jefferson "saturated . . . the blues traditions of his state," and that he "was probably the most widely influential blues artist of the 1920s," this critic also observes that Jefferson's music "is totally unlike that of any other Texas bluesman of the period."[35] Stephen Calt echoes this assertion when he notes that the average listener was doubtless "captivated" by "Jefferson's uncommonly expressive singing" and yet no other musician truly resembles him.[36]

What is unique in Jefferson's playing and singing is that he had a "highly irregular guitar style," which he used "in juxtaposition with his equally unusual voice, the two carrying on an intense and competitive dialogue." Like Henry Thomas, Jefferson would strum a "drone bass" figure against which he would pick the treble strings, simultaneously singing in an "ordinary" voice that "was comforting and easy to identify with" and "tinged with melancholy."[37] But whereas Thomas's lyrics are at times difficult to decipher because of a heavy black dialect, Jefferson's enunciation is "clear and fairly understandable."[38] The vocal range of the two singers differs in that Thomas rarely went beyond an octave plus a minor third,[39] whereas Jefferson could cover over two octaves.[40] While Thomas could at times, as on *Texas Easy Street Blues*, offer some impressive treble passages against his drone bass, Jefferson excelled in constructing "playful single-string arpeggios high up the neck of the guitar, which moved the melody of his songs forward in tandem with his voice."[41] Like Thomas, Jefferson would take periodic breaks, but these were more extensive and complex than Thomas's responses on guitar or quills. Jefferson's guitar responses, in fact, were the despair of other musicians, and it was perhaps not until Charlie Christian a decade later that a guitarist would manage such intricate breaks. In this regard, Jefferson has been cited as "one of the earliest rural blues guitarists to have regularly used improvisation in his playing."[42] In speaking of the standard role of the blues guitar as an accompaniment to the voice, Welding notes that Jefferson's instrumental passages were not just "marvels of invention, light and brilliant," nor were they merely responses to vocal phrases; rather, they served as "independent yet interactive lines with a complementary motion of their own."[43] It was this rhythmic and melodic flexibility in the call-and-response tradition that the blues introduced into jazz as part of this later music's appealing and enduring style.

Another feature of Blind Lemon Jefferson's blues performances is their creation of riffs, a fundamental development in what would become known as Kansas City jazz. Whereas Henry Thomas tended to patch together a medley of tunes and lyrics in each performance, Jefferson combined a "crazy quilt" of riffs beginning with his first blues recordings in 1926, *Long Lonesome Blues* and *Rabbit Foot Blues*, and continuing with one of his best-known songs, *Matchbox Blues* from 1927, and with *Mosquito Moan*, from his last recording session in September 1929. Gunther Schuller defines a riff as "a relatively short phrase that is repeated over a changing chord pattern, originally as a background device, although it later came to be used as foreground material in the so-called riff tunes of the Swing Era."[44] Schuller relates the riff to African music based on repetition and to "the whole concept of drum patterns," which are repeated in African ensemble playing "until the master drummer signals a change to another set of related patterns."[45] As noted earlier, Jefferson's *Long Lonesome Blues* of 1926 set something of a record for the number of riffs it stitched together. On *Matchbox Blues*, Jefferson produced a "spontaneous performance" of "crazy-quilt riffing" that is "more rhythmically intricate and precise than Texas dance music had any hope of becoming, and is astonishingly cohesive."[46] In contrasting Jefferson's recorded performances with those of other representative bluesmen of his time, Pete Welding concludes that one must "come to a speedy recognition of Blind Lemon's . . . astonishing musical sensibility. It must have all but staggered listeners accustomed to the more modest ways of local bluesmen."[47] In large part it was Jefferson's ability to invent an endless series of imaginative riffs that made him the inimitable performer he still is and "the source of much that remains valuable in American popular music."[48]

Dating probably from early 1927, *Matchbox Blues* is deservedly celebrated as among Jefferson's finest recordings. For in this one performance Lemon offers a wide variety of styles in his guitar playing, from leaps to upper-register blue notes in response to the lyrics and contrasting riff commentaries, to simultaneous drone bass and treble riffs behind the voice as well as in the breaks. In addition, this piece swings more than most of Jefferson's blues, with the guitar either playing riffs, single-note lines, or fills without letup, and even incorporating in two different breaks a type of eight-to-the-bar barrelhouse rhythm. Arpeggiated riffs add to the momentum-keeping swing, as do tremolos, which Lemon employs elsewhere in his music. Here his scalewise runs on the guitar are especially in evidence, either starting high and working downward through bluesy intervals or moving up and down in the eight-to-the-bar barrelhouse manner. Jefferson ends *Matchbox Blues* on an off note, a final unexpected touch to this unusual performance. Other songs contain some of the same techniques, such as *Black Horse Blues*, which ends on an unresolved chord. Lemon's wide range of styles is absent from this performance, although it is noteworthy for having as its symmetrical introduction "one of the most carefully knit blues breaks ever constructed, balancing not only unusual phrases and rhythms but creating an almost humorous bass/treble dialogue in the process."[49] Unlike *Matchbox Blues*, *Black Horse Blues* does not vary from the guitar's basic rhythmic and harmonic pattern established in the introduction, except in the final break with its unresolved ending.

On *Rabbit Foot Blues* the introduction is also symmetrical in construction, with the guitar echoing the vocal phrases. Here, however, the rest of the piece does not continue with the same pattern but creates countermelodies, with the vocal delivery moving at the normal speed of conversation while the guitar plays at a faster tempo. The truest blend of voice and guitar is found on *Rambler Blues*, where the vocal line is accompanied rhythmically, note for note, by the stringed instrument, although in the breaks the guitar offers contrasting but typical blues interpolations. On *Rambler Blues* the voice makes the leaps to the same upper-register blue notes that were given to the guitar on *Matchbox Blues*, and Jefferson also bends and embellishes his vocal notes in the blues tradition that distinguishes it so clearly from ragtime. In this regard, *Mosquito Moan* is notable not so much for the number of its riffs but for the variations on a basic riff pattern, which again differs from ragtime in giving rein to the greater improvisatory skills of each performer. Also present on *Mosquito Moan* are many examples of blue notes as well as a repeated two-note dissonance probably intended to suggest the mosquito's nagging off-key buzz.

Rambler Blues is also noteworthy in terms of its lyrics, for at least two verses figure significantly in jazz history. The first is the verse that asks, "Don't your house look lonesome when your baby pack up and leave?" This theme of loneliness in love, of being abandoned by the loved one, takes many forms in the blues, but this particular version was given a classic jazz treatment in 1938 by Jimmy Rushing and the Count Basie band. Entitled *Sent for You Yesterday and Here You Come Today*, the Rushing-Basie recording opens with this traditional three-line verse:

Don't the moon look lonesome shining through the tree?
Don't the moon look lonesome shining through the tree?
Don't your house look lonesome when your baby pack up to leave?

As with so many blues, the lyrics may have existed in this form long before Jefferson inserted them into his *Rambler Blues*, but it seems likely that it was from

Blind Lemon that Rushing took this verse for what Gunther Schuller considers the Basie blues shouter's "crowning achievement."[50]

As for *Sent for You Yesterday*, the possible Jefferson connections with this 1938 Basie-Rushing recording include not only the tune's lyrics but the arrangement done by Texan Eddie Durham, who at this point in his illustrious career had "hit his stride with a series of well-made arrangements," among them this blues featuring two instrumental soloists—Herschel Evans (another Texan) on tenor saxophone and Harry "Sweets" Edison on trumpet. Evans's solo showcases his full-bodied blues sound with the bent notes and soulful vibrato that would influence an entire generation of Texas tenors. Likewise, Edison's solo also incorporates "a wave-like bent-note effect" that Durham "immediately picked up and featured" in his background ensembles, as on *Now Will You Be Good* (1938).[51] Not only does this "bent-note" effect hark back to Jefferson's *Rambler Blues* but Edison's improvised responses behind Rushing's vocal are directly reminiscent of Jefferson's guitar work behind his own vocal delivery on *Matchbox Blues*. In addition, Durham's arrangement utilizes a number of ensemble riffs between solos and in backing them up, which is characteristic of Jefferson's practice from the beginning to the end of his brief four-year recording career. Finally, the Basie performance demonstrates how Durham's arrangement, with its swinging, upbeat rhythms, is "a typical example of blues music counterstating negative lyrics."[52] Stephen Calt contrasts Jefferson with other street singers by asserting that Blind Lemon "did not (if one excludes *One Dime*) proffer self-pitying panhandling lyrics, but made his songs as entertaining as blues ever became."[53] Offering a related view, William Barlow observes of Jefferson's *Mosquito Moan* that its "deadpan humor" thwarts "the insect's perseverance."[54] The blues as performed by Blind Lemon and Basie and his band counteracted persistent hardships and pain through humor and upbeat up-tempos that achieved a joyful, triumphant music, which still entertains and uplifts.

Another verse in Jefferson's *Rambler Blues* that relates to a jazz classic is the one containing the line "I got a gal in Texas, one in Tennessee." In rendering W. C. Handy's *Beale Street Blues* (1916), Jack Teagarden, a trombonist–blues singer and another native Texan, introduced into his 1931 version of the song the now famous lines "I was born down in Texas, raised in Tennessee. / No one woman is gonna make a fatmouth out of me." (Contrary to the lyrics' claim, Teagarden was actually raised in Texas and Oklahoma.) Teagarden was himself already recording while Jefferson was still alive, having cut a record of Clarence Williams's *Basin Street Blues* on June 11, 1929. However, the source for Teagarden's line in *Beale Street Blues* is probably not *Rambler Blues* but rather Blind Lemon's recording from about March 1926 entitled *Got the Blues*, which contains the following verse:

I was raised in Texas\\schooled in Tennessee
I was raised in Texas\\schooled in Tennessee
Now sugar you can't make no fatmouth out of me

As with Henry Thomas's lyrics, these lines from Jefferson's song were traditional and "found in many blues stanzas," but since Handy's original verses for *Beale Street Blues* do not include the Texas-Tennessee line, it seems likely that Teagarden heard Blind Lemon's recording and borrowed the references to Texas and Tennessee as well as to the woman not being able to make a "fatmouth" out of the singer.[55] He may have found the verse attractive not only for its rhyme but also because the Tennessee reference fits a song about Beale Street, which is in Memphis. For this same 1931 recording of *Beale Street Blues*, Benny Goodman was the leader, Glenn Miller the arranger, and Jack's younger brother, Charlie Teagarden (barely eighteen at the time), the trumpet soloist, producing what Gunther Schuller calls "an impassioned solo . . . which would stand unequalled as a fine example of white blues trumpet-playing for many years."[56] While these developments may be somewhat incidental to Jefferson's recordings of *Got the Blues* and *Rambler Blues*, they are historically significant and indicate the influence of country blues in Texas on jazz figures like the Teagarden brothers, who were well aware of early blues in their home state.

Yet another possible connection between Jefferson's lyrics—this time in his *Gone Dead on You Blues* (ca. October 1927)—and a historic jazz recording is the verse containing the line "Hello Central, won't you please ring Dr. Brown?" This variation of a similar verse—"Hello Central, give me Dr. Jazz. / He's got what I need, I know he has"—in Jelly Roll Morton's "flamboyant" recording of King Oliver's tune, *Doctor Jazz*,[57] links Blind Lemon's lyrics with those of a piece of classic New Orleans jazz. The Morton rendition, recorded in December 1926 by Jelly's Red Hot Peppers, is "notable for its breaks, some of them duet and some of them ensemble."[58] Morton's lyrics are making an appeal for the power of jazz to cure the singer's ills, which of course is the object of the blues as well. But most important in the performance of blues or jazz—and particularly when the lyrics are as "flamboyant" as Jelly Roll's—is not the words but the music. As Albert Murray points out, whether we can understand the words or not—even the best performers can garble or mumble their lines—the musical quality of blues or jazz is the primary consideration.[59] What endures most from Blind Lemon's *Gone Dead on You Blues* and Jelly Roll's *Doctor Jazz* is not so much the words as the music, especially the inventive breaks, though with Jefferson the words are treated with such expressive musicality that they can be compared favorably with the best improvised or written instrumental breaks in Morton's classic New Orleans jazz.

Blind Lemon Jefferson's range of subjects for his blues equals that of Henry Thomas, who, as we have seen, included in his repertoire songs on country life, the railroad, love, and prison, among many others. Jefferson's *Rambler Blues*, like a number of his songs, refers to the railroad, saying at one point that it is "train time" and he will be taking the "number nine." Lemon's *Bad Luck Blues* speaks of his desire to escape his ill fortune by traveling on the Santa Fe, and in *Sunshine Special* he plans to catch that Texas train that will "run me away from here." Although there is no evidence that Jefferson was ever incarcerated, he recorded several songs concerning prison life: *Blind Lemon's Penitentiary Blues*, *Prison Cell Blues*, *'Lectric Chair Blues*, and *Lock Step Blues*. A related song, *Hangman's Blues*, is about a man in the county jail awaiting a noose around his neck. The most musically interesting of these five performances is *Prison Cell Blues*, with Jefferson's voice rising to heart-rending heights of melancholy, bending notes with great power and passion. Simultaneously his guitar reiterates the same basic riff pattern of the vocal line, underscoring the singer's sense of unrelieved misery. Not only is he losing his mind from sleeping without Nell, his "rider" who he says is responsible for his being in a cell, but he seems to have no hope of having his time reduced. Even the ploy of appealing to the governor to let him loose, which worked for Leadbelly, does not appear to have been successful for Blind Lemon's inmate.[60]

Other of Jefferson's songs involve sexual themes: *That Black Snake Moan*, his own more symbolically sexual version of Victoria Spivey's *Black Snake Blues*; *That Crawling Baby Blues*, which contains a verse dating back to the days of slavery;[61] *Corinna Blues*, Blind Lemon's version of the famous *See, See Rider*; and *Easy Rider Blues*, which uses the same riff as *Prison Cell Blues* but at a faster tempo, thus producing less of a melancholy impact. Still other Jefferson songs concern poverty, the frequent Delta theme of the devastating effects of flood waters, and, as noted earlier, the boll weevil, scourge of cotton farmer and picker alike. Finally, Jefferson's moving *See That My Grave Is Kept Clean*—the "phrasing and carpentry" of which "were probably suggested by *Careless Love*," one of the best-known blues ballads—employs a riff similar to the one heard on *Prison Cell Blues* and *Easy Rider Blues*.[62] Here, however, even though the riff is played about as fast as on *Easy Rider Blues*, the effect is deeply melancholy by dint of the singer's mournful subject of death and his very somber delivery. At the end of *See That My Grave*, Jefferson twice plays two low notes on the guitar at a much slower tempo, as if to suggest an approach to death. Some listeners have heard in this song, released in early 1928, Jefferson's premonition of his own impending demise. Despite the fact that Blind Lemon would only live two more years, his musical genius, as Pete Welding declares, "has ensured that his admonition in song—'Please see that my grave is kept clean'—will continue to be respected."[63]

❀ ❀ ❀

The most famous country blues singer to be influenced by Blind Lemon Jefferson was Huddie Ledbetter, known as Leadbelly, who was born in Mooringsport, Louisiana, in 1885 but was raised in Texas in the area of Caddo Lake. As early as 1917, Leadbelly recalled hearing Blind Lemon in Dallas, and according to Leadbelly's own account, the two men traveled together, playing in the East Texas lumber camps and barrelhouses. Since Jefferson was quite independent, despite his blindness, and because his own free-form guitar playing was quite different from Leadbelly's "rhythmically redundant" repertoire, their collaboration has been doubted.[64] In any event, for many listeners Leadbelly ranks in his own right as the most representative blues man of the Southwest, partly on the basis of his versatility and his extensive discography, which numbers some 300 songs, and partly because in his lifestyle

> we find, inflated to proportions that sometimes seem larger than life, the salient characteristics of . . . vitality, a roving disposition, a fierce independence, and a kind of Western arrogance that stems from pioneer self-reliance. These same qualities appear in varying degrees in many other singers from the area— Ragtime Texas, Texas Alexander, Blind Lemon Jefferson, Ramblin' Thomas, and T-Bone Walker—and are carried forward with certain changes, in the lifestyles of the singers of the following generation, purely urban singers of the Southwest, like Big Joe Turner, Cleanhead Vinson, Lightnin' Hopkins, John Lee Hooker, Mercy Dee, Black Ace, Jimmy Witherspoon, and Wynonie Harris.[65]

Of principal interest in relation to jazz is the fact that Leadbelly's repertoire included almost every African American song form. In execution he ran the gamut of vocal techniques for blues and folksong—the "elastic and unpredictable approach to pitch . . . in the turn, *appoggiatura*, grace notes, slides, slurs, scoops, rips, and . . . leaps of a third, a fifth, or even an octave"—and such techniques of guitar accompaniment as stopping and "worrying" the strings "with a knife blade held in the fret hand to produce vibrati, pitch changes, and glissandi."[66] Leadbelly's "titanic voice" and his "slide work"[67] on the twelve-string guitar—"an instrument common among Mexican folk musicians but used by very few East Texas bluesmen"[68]—produced in combination "a miniature treasure house of southwestern blues and folksong."[69] The singer's "pitiless, iron-hard voice"[70] and his twelve-string guitar, with its "resonant, impressive accompaniments" (even though more repetitive and less inventive than those of Blind Lemon), can be heard in particular on Leadbelly's *Pig Meat Papa*, recorded on March 25, 1935.[71] Here Leadbelly generates a more solid swing than usually found in Jefferson's work, which may demonstrate that Leadbelly's music derives more out of a tradition from which jazz evolved one of its most readily recognizable and basic ingredients, or it may simply indicate the influence of jazz on the blues singer, since by the date of this recording and of much of Leadbelly's work, jazz already had taken its place as a fully identifiable musical form in its own right.

Like Ragtime Texas and Blind Lemon, Leadbelly sang of the most common experiences of blacks: country and prison life (he himself having served two terms for shootings), love and death, and the ubiquitous Texas railroad,[72] as well as more urban and social themes not so characteristic of Thomas and Jefferson. According to Ross Russell, southwestern blues had their "roots in delta style," but whereas that area's blues are "dense, tragic, hopeless, and poignant," the new locales in Texas where blacks migrated, either as "uprooted slaves" or "sometimes as mere adventurers," offered "a new hope, a new vision of emancipation, and the music began to change. The blues became less cryptic, more outspoken, more powerful and exuberant in delivery, more traveled in reference."[73] This difference is certainly seen in the music of Ragtime Texas and Blind Lemon but even more so in Leadbelly's field hollers, ballads, blues, and protest songs. While Leadbelly recorded some of the same tunes as Blind Lemon, such as *Matchbox Blues* and *See, See Rider*, he also created a hit song in his *Irene* and achieved what Ross Russell considers the singer's masterpiece with *Ella Speed*, a ballad—the form in which Leadbelly "excelled"—based on the murder of a "popular lady of the Dallas streets by her paramour, the gambler Bill Martin, and Martin's sentencing, incarceration, and bitter remorse."[74]

While apparently Leadbelly was aware of New Orleans jazz as early as 1910, only the left-hand figures of the piano player intrigued him, according to Marshall Stearns, and he reportedly copied these on his guitar. However, as Stearns goes on to say, if Leadbelly's "contact with jazz per se was early and tangential," it was "he and a host of guitar pickers like him" who "kept alive an enormous reservoir of music to which jazz and near-jazz returned again and again." Stearns identifies within Leadbelly's music "its powerful elements of the work song, the ring-shout, and the field-holler" as those that provide "a dynamic blend in which many of the qualities of West African music are fully represented." The critic-historian concludes that "without this original mixture, jazz could never have developed."[75]

CLASSIC BLUES

Even though the blues originated among the working blacks in the country—whether in the cotton fields or in lumber camps, on the levees or in the shacks of field hands or housemaids—the first recordings of the blues were made by popular female vocalists who toured the South with minstrel and variety shows. The earliest such recording, *Crazy Blues*, made by Mamie Smith in November 1920, was not, however, in the blues form and the vocalist was not actually a blues singer. Yet the success of this first "blues" recording, which sold 75,000 copies in the first month,[1] paved the way for the great female blues singers: Gertrude "Ma" Rainey and Bessie Smith. This "blues craze" also resulted in the first recordings on which black jazzmen performed. Whereas the Original Dixieland Jazz Band recordings of 1917 represented white players whose approach was basically the repetitious style of ragtime, Mamie Smith was accompanied on her first and succeeding recordings by the Jazz Hounds, a black band that included pianist Willie "The Lion" Smith and cornetist Johnny Dunn. These jazzmen brought with them to New York—where Mamie recorded for the Okeh company—such jazz instrumental traits as the break, a "lean, hard tone and clean attack," a "considerable versatility with mutes," and "great inventiveness."[2] This joining of forces by the classic vocalist singing "blues" and jazz musicians as instrumental accompanists would serve to introduce both types of music and would later encourage the recording of rural songsters and bluesmen like Henry Thomas and Blind Lemon Jefferson, as well as such jazzmen of the 1920s as King Oliver, Louis Armstrong, and Jelly Roll Morton.

❦ ❦ ❦

Even before "Ragtime Texas" and the "King of the Country Blues" made their way into the studios of Paramount Records, Texas urban female blues singers

Sippie Wallace of Houston,
"The Texas Nightingale."

produced their own recordings, with important New Orleans jazzmen in the role of instrumental accompanists. Just as Ma Rainey and Bessie Smith were active members of traveling troupes prior to recording in 1923, Beulah "Sippie" Wallace nee Thomas, born in Houston on November 1, 1898, was attracted as early as 1910 by the slow drag blues of the touring vaudeville troupes. Later, Sippie would join a touring tent show as a singer and dancer when it visited her city's Fifth Ward around 1914.[3] In the spring of 1916 Sippie joined her older brother George W. Thomas, Jr., in New Orleans, where he was a successful pianist-songwriter-publisher. There in the Crescent City, before the redlight district known as Storyville was shut down in the following year, Sippie was surrounded by many of the jazz musicians with whom she would later record, among them Louis Armstrong. In 1917 Sippie returned to the tent shows as a featured blues and ballad singer, developing with other female vocalists a style that would contribute to the "blues craze."

In 1923, the same year that Ma Rainey and Bessie Smith were first recorded, Sippie was called to Chicago by her brother George, who had moved there along with other New Orleans musicians following the closing of Storyville. Also in Chicago was Sippie's younger brother Hersal Thomas, who as a teenager (having been born in Houston around 1908) was a prodigy on piano and would accompany his sister on her finest early recordings.[4] As Ernest Borneman indicates, one of the changes that marked the difference between rural and urban blues was "the switch-over in accompaniment from banjo or guitar to piano."[5] As for Sippie's brother George, he was the composer of a number of hit songs for Okeh Records and thus was able to find work for Sippie in Chicago.[6] Within three months after the release of Sippie's first recording, pressed on October 26, 1923, she was a black recording star. The date of Sippie's first record falls between the earliest recorded performances by Bessie Smith on February 11, 1923, and by Ma Rainey in December of the same year. While Ma would become the "Mother of the Blues" and Bessie the "Empress of the Blues," Sippie would earn the epithet "The Texas Nightingale" for the "beautiful quality" of her voice and for its power "chiefly in the upper register"; her lower range was said to lack "the full richness and force which Ma and Bessie possessed."[7] Nevertheless, as we shall see, Sippie, along with brothers George and Hersal, George's daughter Hociel Thomas, and Moanin' Bernice Edwards (who was "raised up" in the household), formed a group of musicians of which it may be said that in the history of the blues none "contributed more important personalities than the Thomas family of Houston."[8]

For Sippie Wallace's first recording date she was accompanied on piano by Eddie Heywood, Sr., whose "stride piano set a loping pace to allow the vocal a full range of flexibility."[9] As Gunther Schuller points out, "The essentially musical aspects of blues singing, as opposed to its textual elements, can best be measured by the quality of the musical accompaniments."[10] The tunes recorded at this session were *Shorty George Blues* and *Up the Country*, the former based on a prison work song from "the blues tradition centered in East Texas"[11] and written jointly by Sippie and her brother Hersal. Of this performance, Daphne Duval Harrison has observed that Sippie exhibits "an unorthodox sense of timing and accentuation of words" that lends to her lyrics "punch and tension." Harrison also notes that "the plaintive swoop in the last verse is a device Wallace used to wrench tears from the most ordinary melody. Her slide down a fourth on 'Shorty' and up a fourth on 'only man' gives a twist that ends that song with a dynamic surge of melodic emotion." As for *Up the Country*, Harrison finds that it offers a "contrast in mood," demonstrating that Sippie "could convey a broad spectrum of mood and feeling." Whereas *Shorty George Blues* laments that her man has left her, *Up the Country Blues* concerns a woman who "ushers [a] mistreating two-timer out of her house and out of her life."[12] This initial recording session introduced Wallace's "Texas-style blues singing" to an expanding audience,[13] and following her success in Chicago, Sippie moved on to New York, where on November 28, 1924, she would record for the first time with the era's leading jazz figures.

Much of Sippie's repertoire during her peak years from 1923 to 1927 is close in feeling to spirituals and church music. In the case of Sippie's 1924 New York session, her *Trouble Everywhere I Roam* recalls such spirituals as *Nobody Knows the Trouble I've Seen* and *Rocks Cried Out, "There's No Hidin' Place."* Both spirituals and blues derive from the "same bedrock of experience,"[14] and even though Sippie commented that she tried to "keep her blues from sounding 'churchy,'" the link between religious and secular ideas in her blues "reaffirms the belief that the blues is a universal experience" and supports her assertion that the Bible was the source for all her songs.[15] Rudi Blesh describes Sippie's phrasing as "varied and full of the feeling of the spirituals and the church," and goes on to characterize her style as having "a shouting quality [that] abounds in the downward quavering phrases which we hear in the congregations, those numes, centering around the third and seventh intervals, which are so characteristically African. Sippie's ending of the shouted phrase with a nume recalls and symbolizes both the preacher and the responding congregation."[16] On the reverse side of the 1924 Okeh recording is "another fine blues" entitled *Baby I Can't Use You No More*, although, according to Blesh, both sides "suffer from inadequate accompaniment."[17]

For the most part, the classic blues sung by women "lived halfway between the older country blues of the male singers and the modern blues of the jazz players."[18] The influence of the women blues singers on jazz resides in their greater affinity for the "framework of strict meter and the twelve-bar form."[19] The reason for this more "classical" approach was the fact that the women vocalists were not actually blues singers but came up through the variety shows where they performed popular songs of the day. Unlike male blues singers, the women were not so bound by blue notes or minor keys but would resolve their blue thirds "upwards into an ordinary major third," whereas a Blind Lemon Jefferson probably never sang a major third.[20] Yet in working with jazz musicians who would play for them in strict time and employ formal harmonies, the women tended to sing against this "a loosely phrased, blue-note inflected melody line" so characteristic of jazz, with the result that there was a reciprocal influence between the two and the development of a certain uniformity of style.[21]

At the November 28, 1924, New York session, Sippie was accompanied by the Clarence Williams Blue Five, which included Louis Armstrong on cornet and Sidney Bechet on clarinet and soprano saxophone. For Armstrong, who also performed with Ma Rainey and Bessie Smith, the experience of playing as an accompanist with these women blues singers allowed him to "stretch out," which was not the case when he performed in New York with the Fletcher Henderson band from October 1924 to October 1925. Even though Armstrong's solos with Henderson in 1924 remain as modern today as most anything in jazz, Armstrong felt inhibited by the band's arrangements and its musicians' rather stiff style of playing. Even when Armstrong had performed with King Oliver's band in Chicago before joining Henderson in New York, Louis was not able to express himself so freely as he could on the recordings with the blues singers and as he would with his own Hot Five in November 1925 when he returned to Chicago and made with this band the first of a series of historic, groundbreaking recordings. While Rudi Blesh finds that the Blue Five ensemble with Armstrong and Bechet is "muddy" and that the singer on *Trouble* only "shines through" because of her "severe and beautiful melody,"[22] Sippie Wallace would record again with Armstrong, and the results would prove superior to this first date with the great jazz cornetist.

In February 1925, back in Chicago, Sippie Wallace and Hersal Thomas recorded for Okeh in the company of King Oliver, mentor to Armstrong and one of the finest of all blues trumpeters. Speaking of the King's work with Sara Martin, another singer of the period, Martin Williams observes that "on the blues accompaniments Oliver usually confines himself to plaintive and simple wa-wa crying, and these performances hardly compare to, say, his *Morning Dove Blues* with Sippie Wallace."[23] In accompanying Sippie, Oliver exhibits on *Morning Dove Blues* his marvelous moaning, low-down style full of passionate and penetrating blue notes. While his playing is a traditional approach to the form and offers little of the bravura style associated with Armstrong, Oliver's performances are so impassioned that they never lose their emotional appeal. Throughout the recording, Hersal's piano, which is heard behind the singer and Oliver's cornet, adds to the steady movement of the piece and to Sippie's deeply felt delivery of her mournful lyrics. On the same date, the trio recorded two other compositions, *Devil Dance Blues* and *Every Dog Has Its Day*, both of which feature Oliver's muted trumpet in its sympathetic, conversational responses to Sippie's accounts of painful dreams and of shabby treatment at the hands of her man.[24] Hersal's accompaniment on *Devil Dance Blues* provides an inventive filigree behind his sister that maintains an interest of its own, even as it backs up the vocal with well-chosen notes and phrases. At the end of this tune, Oliver and Hersal offer a final understanding response to the vocalist's melancholy tale. Oliver employs few notes—many fewer than Hersal, who is everywhere on the piano—but the King makes them count, varying his rhythms and accents in his supportive role as condoler. Hersal and Oliver—each within his own particular style—work together beautifully, the pianist as a constant and uplifting presence behind the singer and Oliver commiserating at the ends of lines, turning the blues into a means of triumph in the face of pain and misery.

On March 1 and 3, 1926, some four months prior to the sudden death of her brother Hersal Thomas, apparently by poisoning, Sippie again recorded with Louis Armstrong, along with Hersal on piano. The trio performed two of Sippie's own compositions, *Special Delivery Blues* and *Jack O' Diamonds Blues*, and a piece entitled *A Jealous Woman Like Me*, credited to Thomas—either Hersal or George.[25] Here Armstrong is truly able to stretch out, partly because, as on the Oliver sides, Louis is the only horn player and partly because Hersal's own playing on piano must have inspired the cornetist more than pianist Clarence Williams had earlier. At the March 1 session the trio recorded *A Jealous Woman Like Me*, and all three musicians were in top form. Louis opens the piece alone with a strong four-note rising motif, and as he begins to repeat it a third lower, Hersal comes in with the same figure, which Sippie too will sing following Louis's lengthy introductory passage that ends with a two-note flourish announcing the vocalist's entrance. As Sippie belts out the blues lyrics, Louis fills the breaks with "lines which will be the definitive basis all jazz musicians to come (instrumentalists, singers or arrangers) assimilate in order to create their own style."[26] After Sippie has sung the lyrics, Louis takes a solo break that is a marvelous example of his genius for extending a tune's melodic, harmonic, and rhythmic components into imaginative flights of artistic invention. At the same time, Hersal, a mere teenager, is pounding away, moving all over the piano and sounding like Jelly Roll Morton in his ability to fit perfectly with the other musicians no matter what he plays.

On *A Jealous Woman Like Me*, Hersal's handsful-chord approach looks forward to the technique of Earl "Fatha" Hines, who would later record with Armstrong's Hot Seven. And just as Louis invents his own motifs, so does the young Texan, who varies his rhythms and the range within which he plays, alternating between supporting Sippie's lines and improvising on his own. As for Sippie, she is beautifully in tune with the piano, even as she gives to her tones the slightly lowered pitch appropriate to the blues. All three performers engage in simultaneous but complementary music making, each one going his or her own way yet blending into a unified whole. To compare this performance with so many others Louis made with vocalists, such as May Alix, who sings on *Big Butter and Egg Man*, recorded on November 16, 1926, is to hear how the unity achieved with Sippie and Hersal is unique, even if Louis's individual part is not as brilliant as it is on *Big Butter and Egg Man*, which has been considered by several critics to be among Armstrong's finest solos.[27] Louis's solo work on the March 1 recording with Sippie and Hersal does contain, however, many jewels that make this another pace-setting performance. In combination with Hersal's exceptional piano and Sippie's classic blues intonation and full-bodied sound, Louis achieves one of his more satisfying overall outings.

Like several of the classic Jelly Roll Morton tunes that the pianist-composer would record the following September with his Red Hot Peppers, such as *Sidewalk Blues,* and *Dead Man Blues,* the Wallace-Armstrong-Thomas trio recording of Sippie's *Special Delivery Blues* opens with nonmusical sound effects and the kind of hoakum associated with minstrels: two blasts on a pitch pipe used to signal the arrival of the mailman, followed first by the word "special" in Louis's gruff voice, which rises on the last syllable, and then by Sippie saying, "Lord, it must be from *my* man." After this minstrel routine, Hersal begins a tremolo on the piano that will be repeated effectively throughout the piece. Daphne Duval Harrison touches on the complementary nature of the Armstrong-Thomas duo behind Wallace when the critic comments that "the mellow rolling piano [of Hersal] in the introduction is ably contrasted by Armstrong's crisp staccato notes." In describing the interaction among the three musicians, Harrison observes that "Hersal's use of tremolo chord progressions, which follow Wallace's ascending melodic line, builds each line to an intensity, which is relieved by Armstrong's brief broken phrases. She slides up a fourth on the last word of the first line in each stanza, imitating the piano roll, dragging out every ounce of melancholy from each word. The last line of each stanza releases the tension with an upbeat tempo and syncopated chord progressions."[28]

Hersal Thomas's use of tremolo for the song's melodic line does indeed have a dramatic effect that underscores Sippie's melancholy vocal, and in itself the pianist's playing is amazingly authoritative. By means of the tremolos, Hersal reflects the lyrics' allusions to the departure of the singer's man and to the passing train she hopes is bringing him back, as well as to the line where she remembers her man saying it almost broke his heart to leave his baby but that "sometimes the best of friends must part." After Sippie sings that she had the blues so bad she thought she would die, Hersal plays a tremolo sliding downward to echo this melancholy state, his diminished and dominant sevenths in F adding to the unsettling atmosphere of the lyrics. The singer and pianist also echo one another when both reach for the high note in the first stanza on the word "away" and later in the stanzas where the high notes come on the words "by" and "news," with both musicians sliding upward to suggest the emotional text and its meaning of loss and longing. Meanwhile, Armstrong's interpolations contribute to the blues feeling, but overall it is the rapport between the brother on the piano and the sister singing the lyrics that makes for a remarkable performance. The musical relationship between Hersal and Sippie had obviously developed over many years and achieves on *Special Delivery Blues* one of Sippie's most powerful recordings. It is clear from this session of March 1926 why Hersal's death the following July 3 affected Sippie so deeply. As Ronald P. Harwood has reported, "Until Hersal's untimely death . . . he was the only piano player Sippie would have at her side, both in the studio and on the vaudeville circuit," and years later she was "unable to talk of him without tears filling her eyes."[29] Certainly Sippie's subsequent recordings in 1927 without Hersal on piano were not nearly so successful. Fortunately, before Hersal died, additional sides were recorded by the trio of Thomas, Wallace, and Armstrong.

Wallace's *Jack O' Diamonds Blues*, also recorded at the March 1, 1926, session, probably derives from folk tradition and is traceable to a group of musicians in Houston around 1910 to 1915.[30] Shortly thereafter, in April 1926, Blind Lemon Jefferson would also record a tune by the same title.[31] Although the two performances have little in common, it is nevertheless revealing to compare them, for there are stylistic similarities that suggest a shared source for their approaches to lyrics and accompaniment. Blind Lemon's guitar, like Hersal's piano, follows the singer's vocal line, duplicating it note for note. Although other accompanists for blues singers like Ma Rainey and Bessie Smith also follow the melody line, they do not tend to limit their notes to those sung by the vocalist and more often are playing countermelodies of their own.[32] It would seem that the practice of Blind Lemon and Hersal has its roots in the Southwest guitar tradition, which did not embellish so much as it duplicated the melody line and thus, by creating a closer connection between song and accompaniment, could achieve a more unified impact on the listener. Hersal, through his use of the tremolo, supports Sippie's held notes and lends them greater emotive force, just as Blind Lemon's simple guitar imitation reinforces his sung notes and gives them a richer sound and poignancy.

Nonetheless, neither Blind Lemon (as we have seen) nor Hersal Thomas eschewed embellishment, and in Sippie's *Jack O' Diamond Blues* Hersal is especially impressive in his variations on the melodic vocal phrases and in his countermelodies that complement Armstrong's breaks and obbligato lines. Indeed, piano and cornet can at times weave a rich tapestry of sound in and around Sippie's largely unadorned and straightforward delivery. The vocalist on occasion approaches Blind Lemon's singing style, in particular when she suddenly leaps a minor sixth in A flat (a difficult interval to sing and therefore more vocally challenging) on the second syllable of the word "money," much as the bluesman does on *Broke and Hungry*, recorded in June 1926. The moaning tone of both Blind Lemon's and Sippie's brand of blues carries a distinctly Texas or southwestern feel, whose origins the two singers document in their respective country and classic styles.

On March 3, 1926, Sippie again recorded with Louis and Hersal, producing three more tunes: *The Mail Train Blues*, *I Feel Good*, and *A Man for Every Day in the Week* (the first by Blair-Lethwick and the last two credited to Thomas). With *The Mail Train Blues*, both Louis on cornet and Hersal on piano turn in fine performances, though quite different in their approaches, and Sippie renders this blues with intensity and conviction, bending her lines to imbue them with greater feeling and shouting out her high notes with both power and control. Together Louis and Hersal take an extended simultaneous break that is a wonderful instance of the improvisatory skills of both men, and equally fine are their responses to and support of Sippie's vocal lines. *I Feel Good*, which sounds more like a pop song in a slow four, showcases Hersal's versatility as he handles this tune with a rocking, somewhat satirical style that suggests at moments a Fats Waller spoof. While Sippie delivers the lyrics in a rather plodding but authoritative fashion, Louis for his part finishes off his introduction with an upward rip and then fills throughout with phrases recognizable as those of none other than the premier cornetist of his day. Armstrong's solo is thoroughly captivating, and his concluding break is a Satchmo trademark, predating his playing of a similar phrase to open his *Skid-Dat-De-Dat* of November 16, 1926. (His first use of this signature phrase came in a December 9, 1924, recording of *Poor House Blues*, in which he accompanied Texas singer Maggie Jones.) As for *A Man for Every Day in the Week*, this tune features a type of stop-time vocal, where the accompanists lay out while the singer takes the "breaks" with her lyrics. There is also another delightful extended simultaneous break by Louis and Hersal, the latter even sounding at one point like Bix Beiderbecke on piano.

On May 6, 1927, Sippie would once again join Armstrong, and three other accompanists, for recordings of *The Flood Blues*, *Dead Drunk Blues*, *Have You Ever Been Down?*, and *Lazy Man Blues*, but with Hersal's death, these sides lack to some extent the spirited quality of the 1926 sessions. The pianist, who is possibly Sippie herself, is competent, but there is not the same rapport with Armstrong, even though Louis manages to demonstrate his artistry as he always could under any circumstances and on whatever tune.[33] Sippie's vocal delivery seems a bit strained at times, and in spots the clarinetist has a rather irritating sound. However, *Have You Ever Been Down?* can be singled out as an excellent performance that features an interesting piece of collective improvisation that includes the instrumentalists and Sippie as vocalist. The most intriguing of these four compositions is definitely *The Flood Blues* by Porter Grainger (the other three tunes are credited to Thomas).[34] As an instance of the blues tradition of songs based on the effects of flooding in the South, this piece (inspired by the devastating Mississippi flood of 1927) is notable for its

Ellington-like opening and the guitar that sounds close to the thumping bass of Wellman Braud in the Duke's early rhythm section. Sippie's singing and Louis's obbligato playing both contribute effectively to the gloomy atmosphere.

For the next two years Sippie went unrecorded, but in 1929 she issued two sides under contract to RCA Victor. One of these, *I'm a Mighty Tight Woman*, is "one of the few erotic blues recorded by Wallace" and also reveals her abilities as a pianist.[35] With the onset of the Depression, Sippie's career suffered a decline, and she did not record again until 1945, when she was accompanied by Albert Ammons and his Rhythm Kings. Two tunes, *Buzz Me* and *Bedroom Blues*, unfortunately tend to confirm the view of Rudi Blesh that at this point Sippie "seems not to have grown in stature . . . but to have deteriorated into mere sophistication and cliché."[36] Even though *Buzz Me* shows Sippie's voice still to be expressive and *Bedroom Blues* has a certain appeal, the latter lacks the true intensity of an authentic blues performance. As a swing-era treatment of the form, *Bedroom Blues* offers a sentimental saxophone that is no substitute for the passionate responses of Oliver and Armstrong. But nonetheless, Sippie demonstrates her adaptability to the times, which has been characteristic of many Texas musicians. Sippie Wallace staged a fuller comeback in 1966 when, with the support of fellow Houstonian Victoria Spivey, the "Texas Nightingale" traveled to Europe "and captivated a new, younger generation of blues enthusiasts."[37]

❧ ❧ ❧

Sippie Wallace was not the first blues singer to record with Armstrong—both Ma Rainey and Virginia Liston were accompanied by a group of musicians that included Louis for Okeh recordings made in October 1924. (In addition to Armstrong, the Rainey recording has Buster Bailey on clarinet, Kaiser Marshall on drums, Fletcher Henderson on piano, and Charlie Dixon on banjo, while the Liston has the Clarence Williams Blue Five.) At Ma Rainey's session, the Mother of the Blues performs *See, See Rider*, on which Louis already contributes some of his recognizable phrases, as he does to a lesser extent on *Jelly Bean Blues* and *Countin' the Blues* from the same recording date. But Louis was not able to stretch out so fully or effectively as he did when it was only he and Hersal Thomas accompanying Sippie Wallace.

Following the November 1924 session with Hersal and Sippie, Armstrong would record with another Texas singer, Fae Barnes, who took the name Maggie Jones when she moved from her hometown of Hillsboro, where she was born around 1900 to a family of sharecroppers. Jones actually recorded earlier than any other Texas singer, having participated in a session on July 26, 1923, but it produced only an unissued trial recording. Two sides by Jones were issued from a session in August 1923, and two others were released from a September 4, 1923, date, the former with Don Redmond on piano and the latter with Fletcher Henderson. Like other black women who went east in the 1920s to pursue careers as professional performers, some of whom sang on Broadway and toured Europe "on the wave of popularity for all-black shows," Maggie Jones only "used hints of blues phrasing and intonation."[38] Nevertheless, on a half-dozen tunes recorded by Jones on December 10 and 17, 1924, for Columbia Records, this Texas singer's record date would allow for both Louis Armstrong and Fletcher Henderson—her accompanists in this recording session—to improvise at length and with notable results.

On *Poor House Blues*, Louis opens with a phrase that is strikingly close to the one that begins *Skid-Dat-De-Dat*, the latter described by John Chilton as "a sombre, unaccompanied phrase . . . that is breathtakingly original."[39] As noted earlier, Armstrong's phrase on *Poor House Blues* predates by more than two years the November 16, 1926, recording of *Skid-Dat-De-Dat* as well as his use of a similar phrase to conclude *I Feel Good*, cut on March 3, 1926, with Sippie Wallace.[40] In all three instances, the phrase (which Armstrong uses to open or close the tunes) contains a two-note pick-up involving the dominant note (an F), a blue-note D flat in the second bar, the tonic note on the first beat of the last bar, and a descending three-note pattern beginning on the first beat of the first bar and descending to the dominant scale degree (see Fig. 1).

According to critic William Russell, Armstrong reveals on this first session with Maggie Jones "a return to the purely melodic, hot style of Bunk [Johnson]" and the New Orleans tradition that Louis inherited and developed during his time with King Oliver in Chicago before joining the Fletcher Henderson orchestra in New York. For Russell, Armstrong's time was not wasted and his stay in New York "was made worthwhile by the memorable series of recordings in which Armstrong accompanied many blues singers, including Bessie Smith."[41]

Certainly Maggie Jones was no Bessie Smith, but the Texan was a professional in her delivery and at times rises to the occasion of having two inventive jazz accompanists for her recording date. Even though *Thunderstorm Blues* employs clichéd sound effects for the thunder and for the howling and moaning wind, Louis turns in a freewheeling commentary on Maggie's lyrics, as does Fletcher with his own tasteful runs in the background. After Maggie takes a break from the corny lyrics of *Anybody Here Want to Try My Cabbage?*, which only co-composer Fats Waller could have brought off with his customary élan and good humor, both Louis and Fletcher swing out with some fine polyphonic improvisation. *If I Lose, Let Me Lose* is pretty much a total bust, even though both men give it the old college try in this "losing" effort. With *Screamin' the Blues*, Armstrong is back on solid ground for this tune credited to Jones and Henderson. Here Louis manages to show his virtuosity

Poor House Blues

(closes)

[in B♭]

I Feel Good

(closes)

Skid-Dat-De-Dat

(opens)

[in B♭; transposed from B for purposes of comparison]

1 Dominant degree note in both examples and occurs on 3rd beat of each.
2 Blues 3rd on last beat of measure.
3 Descending 3-note pattern beginning on beat 1, descending to dominant scale degree.
4 2-note pick-up involving dominant note (F).
5 First beat last bar = tonic (B♭).

Figure 1. Louis Armstrong's three similar phrases from *Poor House Blues* with Maggie Jones (December 9, 1924), *I Feel Good* with Sippie Wallace (March 3, 1926), and *Skid-Dat-De-Dat* (November 16, 1926).

throughout, especially toward the end, and at a slower tempo Maggie is able to inject more of a blues feeling and to make better use of her rather refined vibrato to instill the song with greater affectivity.

Above all, it is on *Good Time Flat Blues* that both Louis and Fletcher really find a groove and dig into this Spencer Williams tune with a "dirty" sound that complements Maggie's slightly "low down" delivery. Armstrong's cornet lines sing with the same type of vibrato utilized by the vocalist, and at times he employs a flutter-tongue effect that adds to the low-down feeling of this more authentic blues. For Richard Hadlock, this recording "serves only as a stepping-off place for Armstrong the virtuoso cornetist" and "is of value precisely because it is a fine example of early Armstrong bravura playing, and Miss Jones indeed is playing 'second fiddle.'"[42] However, here at last the trio achieves its most unified and bluesy performance, and it was probably this side that Rudi Blesh had in mind when he wrote that "the cornet of Louis Armstrong, loftily inspired, may sing with moving, human accents, weaving with Ma Rainey's voice, or Maggie Jones's, or Bertha Hill's, an inexpressibly moving antiphony of two voices."[43]

While Maggie Jones's vocal style generally lacks the emotive power and richness of a true blues singer, her voice is not unpleasant and can at times be impressive in executing with delicacy and precision certain surprising intervals and pitches. More often than not, however, her vocal control does not save the performances from tedium, which is relieved only by the rather restrained yet imaginative playing of Fletcher Henderson, who makes the listener long for more from him and less from the singer. Armstrong definitely fails to salvage *If I Lose, Let Me Lose*, but otherwise he does stretch out and gives signs of greater things to come, with a number of breaks offering the kind of work that would startle listeners when he recorded some two years later in the company of his Hot Five.

❧ ❧ ❧

The day before the Hot Five's first recording date on November 12, 1925, three of this historic quintet's members—Armstrong, Johnny Dodds on clarinet, and Johnny St. Cyr on banjo—joined with Hersal Thomas as accompanists for singer Hociel Thomas on a series of Okeh recordings of tunes written by the vocalist.[44] The daughter of George W. Thomas and the niece of Hersal Thomas and Sippie Wallace, Hociel was born July 10, 1904, in Houston. In commenting on one of Hociel's tunes, entitled *Gambler's Dream*, which was recorded by the group on November 11, 1925, Rudi Blesh describes Louis's playing as having "a compelling, authentic New Orleans quality"; Dodds's "slow, slashing clarinet" as supplying "an ecstatically melancholy obbligato for Hociel's spoken words"; and Hersal's "solid piano chords" as alternating "with player piano tremolandi of great beauty."

Of Hociel's singing, Blesh characterizes it as "avoiding the beat" rather than following it "in the usual strong Negroid tendency," and as moving the beat "forward by very slight anticipations." On the other hand, Blesh also finds Hociel's phrasing "often solidly on the beat thus sacrificing swing and the provocative, unpredictable, imaginative quality derived from inner rhythms." Blesh concedes that *Gambler's Dream* does exemplify "the tendency of even the classic blues to develop through change." After having said of her voice that it "had a fruity richness, a little less powerful than that of Ma and Bessie," Blesh declares that Hociel is "a classic blues singer" because of her "expressive power" that transcends "any technical lack."[45] Hociel Thomas's enunciation, compared with that of her aunt Sippie Wallace, is rather sappy (in particular on *Sunshine Baby*) and her sound pinched, while her control definitely leaves something to be desired. But what makes performances by the "Hot Four with Hociel Thomas" most notable is, once again, the presence of Armstrong and Hersal Thomas, especially on *Wash Woman Blues* and *I've Stopped My Man*, although even on *Sunshine Baby* Louis and Hersal contribute some swinging moments to an otherwise plodding vocal.

On *Adam and Eve Had the Blues*, Hociel varies her delivery with better results, which in turn allows the accompanists to provide her with a more varied backing. Hersal follows Hociel's sliding and falling voice with similar effects on the piano, while Louis fills in with some choice breaks. Even though Hociel's vocal in her *Put It Where I Can Get It* is uninspiring in its repetitive dotted-eighth and sixteenth rhythm, Louis, Johnny Dodds, and Hersal all engage in a lively polyphonic exchange, including a fine double-time passage. But it is on *Wash Woman Blues* and *I've Stopped My Man* that the three soloists (St. Cyr only faintly supplying the beat) create the same kind of swinging, high-energy jazz that the Hot Five would achieve more famously on the very next day. On *Wash Woman Blues* it is a duet break by Louis and Hersal that saves the tune from a rather tired, predictable blues, although here Hociel turns in a more interesting performance by giving to her voice a greater forcefulness and by delivering her lyrics with stronger conviction. Throughout the recording, Hersal backs the singer with tasteful chords and runs, but when he joins Louis for the break, he makes one regret even more deeply his premature death. Sounding like Jelly Roll, yet with an astoundingly sophisticated and advanced note choice, Hersal plays beyond his youthfulness and looks forward to Earl Hines and Teddy Wilson. On *I've Stopped My Man*, all three soloists launch into simultaneous improvisation that again presages the exciting classic recordings by the Hot Five, except that Hersal contributes the kind of piano part that Lil Hardin—Armstrong's wife and pianist-composer for the Hot Five sessions—was never quite capable of providing. Hersal seems to supply both cornet and clarinet with just the right notes and rhythms to inspire them to a swinging, thrilling piece of jazz.

Hociel Thomas was also joined by Louis and Hersal on four of her songs recorded on February 24, 1926, and these are marked by a different style from cornet and piano and by greater warmth on the part of the vocalist. Although Hociel still lacks the accuracy in her delivery that would place her in the same class as Ma Rainey and Bessie Smith, she does manage to add a touch of vibrato, especially on *Listen to Me*, that enrichs her voice and lends it a heightened expressiveness. However, *Listen to Me* is not a blues but rather in the vaudeville mode, so *Deep Water Blues* offers a better example of her emotional depth, with the result that both Louis's and Hersal's performances also prove superior in their expressive qualities. Hersal shows a definite change in style in that he has moved away from the Morton ragtime or Dixieland-inspired accompaniment and is now backing up Hociel more in the way he would Sippie on March 1 for *A Jealous Woman*—doubling the vocalist's notes an octave lower to underscore the melancholy of *Deep Water Blues*, executing downward smears, and filling in with tremolos that are effective in enhancing the abusive nature of the lyrics, which in themselves owe much to Sippie and Hersal's earlier *Trouble Everywhere I Roam* of November 1924. On *Listen to Me*, Louis begins by muffling his horn so that it sounds trombonelike and therefore is not at first recognizable as that of the cornet great. Throughout this piece Louis demonstrates his ability to match the style of the vocalist and her song. Once he takes his extended break, backed by a comping Hersal, Louis continues in the same rather maudlin vein of this vaudeville song, yet invests it with a bit more genuine feeling than it naturally possesses. On *Lonesome Hours*, the style is closer to the blues, and again both Hersal and Louis contribute a richer accompaniment as well as a classic blues ending. Armstrong is especially strong and inventive on *G'wan I Told You*, and Hociel's delivery is quite forceful, while Hersal backs up both vocalist and cornetist with earthy rhythms and telling note choices. Hersal also takes a tasteful eight-bar solo, and then he and Louis conclude the tune in classic style.

Throughout three of these tunes both Hociel and Hersal demonstrate their authentic feeling for the blues form, which they learned early in their Houston homes and later in New Orleans among the same leading figures with whom they would record in Chicago. Like so many Texans to follow, Hersal and Hociel Thomas evince their ability to create a variety of styles both as performers and as composers.[46] As revealed in these and other recordings, the Thomases shared this capability with Louis Armstrong, and at the same time they provided the cornetist with an opportunity to develop his interpretive gifts, just as they themselves grew artistically along with this all-time jazz master. Unfortunately, the recordings in February with Hociel and those with Sippie in March 1926 would mark the end of Hersal's advancement as a promising piano star. Nonetheless, as we shall see,

Hersal's influence would survive his early death to influence later generations of blues as well as boogie-woogie pianists.

❂ ❂ ❂

Another Texas female vocalist from the 1920s who recorded with major jazz artists was Victoria Spivey, also of Houston. Born on October 15, 1906, Spivey was performing at the age of twelve at the Lincoln Theatre in Dallas and made her first recording in St. Louis on May 11, 1926, accompanying herself on piano on *Black Snake Blues*, one of her many original compositions.[47] Shortly after, in June, Blind Lemon Jefferson made Spivey's song famous by investing it with sexual connotations and retitling it *That Black Snake Moan*, which Spivey resented since apparently her own version did not intend to convey such associations.[48] Nonetheless, the two singers were friends and had sung together in Galveston for picnics and house parties.[49] For this reason, it is thought that "both artists had a rightful claim to . . . this blues, whose lyrics and melody were a part of the folk literature."[50] Even Spivey acknowledged that "everyone in the west Texas clique performed versions of the 'Ma Grinder,'" which was probably the source for her *Organ Grinder Blues*.[51] Although Spivey never recorded with Jefferson, she made a number of notable recordings with the blues-jazz guitarist Lonnie Johnson, who was a member of Louis Armstrong's Hot Five that recorded *I'm Not Rough* and *Struttin' with Some Barbecue* in 1927. In that same year, Johnson accompanied Spivey on *Arkansas Road Blues*, in which the singer exhibits the moaning that "was soon recognized as her musical signature . . . sliding easily from words into moans and back—a vocal device found in religious singing throughout the South from slavery times."[52]

After recording *Black Snake Blues* in 1926, Spivey, known as Queen Vee, became the "new blues star" of the late 1920s and "wrote and recorded no fewer than thirty-eight blues for the Okeh label in St. Louis and New York."[53] Two of her tunes written during this period were *No. 12, Let Me Roam* (another blues based on train travel and "one of Spivey's best compositions and recordings")[54] and *TB Blues*, made famous by its frequent performance by other recording artists. *TB Blues*, which describes the congested conditions of city living, represents the type of urban blues most closely associated with Spivey's recording career. As she reported in an interview, "There was a lot of T.B. goin' around then—especially among poor black folk. We had it down in Houston and that's where I got the idea for the song. Seein' those poor folks with T.B. in the streets, coughin' and sufferin' so . . . that's what I put in my blues, true things nobody wanna talk about."[55] The social realism of Spivey's work is also evident in another song of this genre, her *Blood Hound Blues*, which reports on the singer's poisoning of her man (after he has kicked her and blacked her eyes), on her being thrown in jail, and on her escape.

As the song makes clear, the singer is now on the run, as in so many of the country blues, but this time it's a woman "on the lam" because "presumably, no jury back then would have believed a woman if she claimed self-defense due to life-threatening abuse."[56]

Both Spivey's *Blood Hound Blues* and her *Dirty Tee Bee Blues* were recorded by her on October 1, 1929, with a jazz group that included Henry Allen on trumpet and J. C. Higginbotham on trombone. In characterizing Spivey's singing, Billy Altman writes that it is "bold music" that "gives a somewhat frightening, but also thrillingly provocative feel of wicked metropolitan life in the Roaring Twenties."[57] Another description of Spivey's vocal style calls it "lean and nasal,"[58] perhaps indicating why her delivery on *Blood Hound Blues* seems to lack musicality, or at least to sound harsh and almost unpleasant, in keeping with the realism of her lyrics. The jazz musicians on this recording appear to give it their best but can do little to help make the performance musically appealing. *Dirty Tee Bee Blues* is a better effort in this regard, but still Spivey's voice seems out of control, and even the story told in the song does not move one because the music remains so flat and unexpressive, though this was apparently the singer's intention. At one point, before Spivey ends her first chorus, the piece seems about to take off but then lapses back into a rather dull treatment. Other tunes from this 1929 session include *Moaning the Blues*, featuring Spivey's sliding moans, and *Telephoning the Blues*. Here again the jazzmen try their best to generate some excitement, but Victoria's unmusical voice seems to affect their fills, which are unsuccessful in offsetting her rather dull moaning. On *Telephoning the Blues*, the singer never seems to get into the tune, her notes completely unrelated to the jazzmen's work. Spivey's voice and delivery are simply painful to hear, and the only thing that saves this piece is J. C. Higginbotham's chorus—which not only saves it but gives the listener a needed moment of relief with what Billy Altman calls "a terrific solo." Spivey seems to have done better without a jazz band and to have achieved her best efforts when accompanied—as in the February 3, 1930, recording of *Showered with Blues*—by only a piano and guitar, although even here her affected pronunciation of "away" and "turned" tends to turn one off.

Unlike the singing of Sippie Wallace and Hociel Thomas with Louis Armstrong, Victoria Spivey's collaboration with Henry Allen and J. C. Higginbotham did not produce great or influential jazz, and Richard Hadlock even brands Armstrong's last Hot Five session with Spivey a "dismal . . . affair."[59] On the other hand, Stanley Dance seems more favorably impressed by Spivey's July 10, 1929, recording of *Funny Feathers*, with a six-piece group including Armstrong: "An entertaining lady from Dallas, Spivey delivered her lyrics in an offhand, almost disdainful fashion, telling both tall tales and funny stories deadpan. Armstrong could be relied upon to inject color and emotion."[60] At this same session, Spivey also recorded with Armstrong the tune entitled *How Do You Do It That Way?*, and here she "deal[s] sharply with loneliness," singing with her "aggressive sound" and "tough, hard-edged voice" that Linda Dahl finds characteristic of the "state of Texas, in earlier decades as now," in supplying "many blues and jazz artists."[61] Although Armstrong contributes some color and feeling to both of these performances, the band generally drags and seems to be going through the motions. More impressive is Spivey's recording session on October 15, 1936, with a quartet composed of Lee Collins on trumpet, Freddy Shayne on piano, John Lindsay on bass, and an unidentified clarinet. On this occasion Spivey sings *Any Kinda Man* and *I Ain't Gonna Let You See My Santa Claus.*[62] Here her voice is sweeter, and the band backs her up with a more responsive, sympathetic performance. The boogie-woogie style piano on *I Ain't Gonna Let You See My Santa Claus* is particularly good, and Lee Collins on trumpet gives spirited, driving support to the vocalist, who growls and bends her vowels to good effect. By this date, however, jazz had already moved beyond the point that Spivey's work would have exerted any effect on the music's historical development. While Spivey's voice is certainly the most distinctive of all the Texas women blues singers, her delivery does not have the low-down blues feeling of a Sippie Wallace—or a Lillian Glinn or even a Bessie Tucker, two other Texas blues singers who unfortunately never recorded with prominent jazz figures, as did Maggie Jones and the three Houston vocalists, Sippie, Hociel, and Queen Vee.

❂ ❂ ❂

Between 1910 and 1920, Lillian Glinn, who was born about 1902 near Dallas, traveled with the Rabbit Foot Minstrels, as did Ma Rainey and Bessie Smith.[63] On December 2, 1927, when Columbia Records "made its first of several annual visits to Dallas,"[64] Glinn recorded four tunes with Willie Tyson on piano and Octave Gaspard on brass bass.[65] A Columbia promotional blurb billed Glinn as "a new singer of blues, full of pep and personality. She possesses an extraordinary voice, of which every word gets over on the phonograph."[66] Later, on April 24, 1928, Glinn made her most remarkable recording in New Orleans when she performed with four unidentified musicians, cutting only one tune with this group, *Shake It Down.* Paul Oliver writes of this performance that Glinn sings "in the grand manner. She has the heavy contralto voice of the more impressive women singers of the day."[67] Although Glinn is accompanied on *Shake It Down* by unknown musicians, she is obviously inspired by the cornetist, tuba player, and pianist, who are true jazzmen, and Glinn's delivery of the lyrics definitely approaches that of a Bessie Smith. Here Glinn's voice is rich and expressive, managing many nuances and effective grace notes, and her performance with this trio achieves more swing than perhaps that of any other Texas blues singer. As the lyrics express it, this recording by Glinn is "the real thing," as she follows the injunction of the song to "just lose control." Lillian lets loose with all she has, belting out her song with power and emotive gruffness. More than Glinn's other recordings, *Shake It Down* demonstrates the positive effect of a genuine jazz band on this blues singer, which, as we have seen, was often the reciprocal effect of such instrumental accompanists and vocalists on one another. As Paul Oliver points out, "Jazz, of course, owed much—some might hold, everything—to the blues, and blues qualities are to be heard in the playing of the greatest jazzmen of any period." Oliver goes on to comment that there are a number of women blues singers who "deserve far greater recognition than they have had" and that one such was Lillian Glinn.[68]

While *Shake It Down* is clearly Glinn's most outstanding recorded performance, there are other extremely interesting pieces among her twenty-two issued sides. On *Come Home Daddy*, from the December 2, 1927, session in Dallas, Glinn exhibits her strong contralto delivery that can remind one, both here and on *Shake It Down*, of Victoria Spivey, at least in the vocal inflections and the dips on second added syllables ("me-he" for "me" and "dow-hown" for "down"). If Glinn was influenced by Spivey, it is certain that she lends greater musicality to Queen Vee's technique. Glinn not only has a much richer, more appealing voice, but she also hums effectively in a number of her recordings, in particular *Moanin' Blues* from the December 6, 1929, session in Dallas when a fine unknown banjoist strums and picks to Glinn's affective humming. (Glinn may have been influenced in her practice of humming by Texas Alexander, who also employed this approach regularly in his many blues recordings, concluding his songs "with the low humming moan which often ended his syllables.")[69] The range of Glinn's work is indicated by her performance from this same session of *I'm Through (Shedding Tears Over You)*, a pop song that Lillian manages to swing nicely, showing off her lovely voice and offering more of her humming to Willie Tyson's piano. At the first Dallas session, Tyson and an unknown guitarist had already turned in a remarkable accompaniment for the vocalist on *Brown Skin Blues*, with the guitar close to Leadbelly's ringing, percussive, twelve-string sound.

Glinn also recorded in Atlanta on April 9 and 10, 1929, in the company of what may have been a group of white jazzmen. The trumpeter, Pete Underwood, is reminiscent of Bix Beiderbecke and can on occasion prove quite ambitious, delivering on *Black Man Blues* some fine blue notes in the upper register, which are more under control than is usual with this musician's work. At times the tunes recorded at the Atlanta sessions are overly arranged and the commercial lyrics a bit on the corny side. More authentic blues marked the New Orleans session of April

24, 1928, when Glinn sang *Lost Letter Blues*, with lyrics similar to those of Sippie Wallace's *The Mail Train Blues*.[70] Both Wallace and Glinn were essentially products of the African-American church, where Dallas blues singer Hattie Burleson discovered Glinn and encouraged her to record.[71] After only two years, Glinn ended her professional career and returned to the church, but not before she had recorded one truly classic performance in the stunning 1928 *Shake It Down*.

✿ ✿ ✿

Like Glinn, Bessie Tucker also was active in Dallas, although little is known about this "powerfully-voiced singer . . . whose songs were largely about prison."[72] According to James Collier, there were few truly good women blues singers, some were even atrocious, and "out of the whole lot not more than a dozen at the very outside left a body of music sufficient in quantity and quality to interest anyone but a scholar. The list would include Bessie Tucker, a strong singer with a dark voice."[73] Collier also includes Sippie Wallace, Maggie Jones (given as Mae Barnes), and Victoria Spivey among the "better-known names," but makes no comment on their voices or recordings. Tucker can be heard on *Fort Worth Denver Blues*, from an August 29, 1928, recording made in Memphis, sounding a bit like Spivey but with a deeper pitch that gives her voice a more bluesy tone.[74] *Penitentiary*, from the same August 1928 session, is perhaps of interest only as an instance of a female version of a prison blues, for it adds nothing to our understanding of the relationship between this musical form and jazz. On *Better Boot That Thing*, from an August 10, 1929, recording date in Dallas, Tucker is accompanied by a booting, unidentified tuba player who infuses the performance with a peppy, infectious swing. The pianist, K. D. Johnson, is also inspired to "kick" the group along with an elemental rock. *Whistling Woman Blues*, recorded in Dallas on October 21, 1929, features Johnson's piano introduction as well as Jesse Thomas's guitar accompaniment. As noted earlier in the case of Blind Lemon Jefferson and Hersal Thomas, here the guitar parallels the vocal, which is notably controlled in Tucker's delivery of her lyrics. *Bogey Man Blues*, from October 17, 1929, is the most successful tune in capturing a spark of true blues, depicted in the words to the song that concern a certain nobility of spirit in the face of racial maltreatment.

All the songs recorded in 1928 and 1929 by Bessie Tucker contain fundamental blues themes and at times achieve a higher caliber of musical content than much of Victoria Spivey's work; yet Tucker had no real contact with the development of jazz, as did Queen Vee, who, like Maggie Jones, Sippie Wallace, and Hociel Thomas, took part in recording sessions that included top-flight jazz musicians in the process of exploring their art and expanding its limits for themselves and for future generations. Even though Maggie, Hociel, and Victoria may not have approached the level of a Ma Rainey or a Bessie Smith, their singing of the classic blues attracted to the form an important audience and directly or indirectly affected the growth of jazz, if in no other way than by making the blues form and the blues spirit integral parts of this twentieth-century American music. And in the case of Maggie Jones and Sippie Wallace, these Texas blues women, "in using some of the finest jazz musicians of the day as their accompanists, . . . made possible some of the earliest recorded jazz breaks by these great artists."[75]

BOOGIE-WOOGIE

Just as ragtime and blues originated to an important extent in East Texas and were developed by Texas musicians who influenced the rise of jazz, boogie-woogie can be traced to the Piney Woods area along the Texas-Louisiana border. According to several early commentators on jazz history, boogie-woogie was first played in the lumber and turpentine camps and in the sporting houses of Texas.[1] Although "Stavin' Chain" of Arkansas is noted for being boogie-woogie's "first semimythological figure . . . a metaphor for sexual prowess in [Jelly Roll] Morton's 'Winin' Boy'"[2] and was heard around Donaldsville, Texas, in 1904 "during the building of the Texas-Pacific railway," Leadbelly remembered boogie-woogie being played as early as 1899 in the Texarkana and Marshall area of Texas.[3] Eventually, the boogie-woogie conceived and performed by black musicians in Texas would find its way to New Orleans, Chicago, and New York and would be recorded by the major swing orchestras of the 1930s and 1940s; it would even influence one of the founders of modern jazz, Thelonious Monk.

Considered the most pianistic of all styles in jazz because it makes "full use of the resources" of the piano, boogie-woogie is related to ragtime in its use of a repeated and unvaried ground rhythm as well as of African cross-rhythms.[4] Boogie-woogie differs from ragtime in allowing more freedom for improvisation within its twelve-bar harmonic form, leaving room—as does the blues—for greater extemporaneous expression, which would destroy "the overall patterns and balance of a ragtime composition."[5] Deriving largely from its association with sacred music performed in the South during the period of slavery, boogie-woogie developed an ecstatic but secular style similar to that of the spiritually heightened music heard in fundamentalist black churches.[6] Unlike the blues, which "in its various moods evokes sadness," boogie-woogie at any tempo "transmits a raw, buoyant energy."[7] A related style, barrelhouse, is said to bridge the gap "between boogie-woogie and ragtime," as it "combines some of the melodic properties of ragtime with the driving bass rhythm of boogie-woogie."[8] Barrelhouse, boogie-woogie, and jazz all originate to some degree in the religio-sexual customs of primitive African societies, for as Wilfrid Mellers notes, one of the meanings of the phrase "boogie-woogie," and of the word "jazz" itself, is sexual intercourse,[9] even as the ritualistic-orgiastic nature of the music also represents an ecstatic form of a spiritual order. In a sense, boogie-woogie remained closer to the spirit of the black church, while barrelhouse "ministered" to customers in the railroad and rural bars from which it took its name—so-called from the barrels that were used to support a plank that served as a bar in the rudest joints.[10]

Although the neighboring states of Arkansas, Louisiana, and Missouri would also produce boogie-woogie players and their boogie-woogie tunes, and despite the fact that Chicago would become known as the center for this music through such pianists as Jimmy Yancey, Albert Ammons, and Meade "Lux" Lewis, Texas was home to an environment that fostered the creation of boogie-woogie style: the lumber, cattle, turpentine, and oil industries, all served by an expanding railway system from the northern corner of East Texas to the Gulf Coast and from the Louisiana border to Dallas and West Texas. Identifying boogie-woogie with this area were the various labels attached to the music: "fast western," "fast Texas," and "Galveston." A boogie pianist's playing could be so distinctive that his style would be associated with a city or district, or the tunes performed by certain pianists would have their origins in specific places, as in the case of *Hattie Green*, named for the madam of an Abilene brothel.[11] In jazz music of all periods and styles, it is true as well that a listener comes to distinguish an individual player by the contours of a single solo or even by a few notes that bear the stamp of each musician's unique sound production, regardless of the instrument. This may in fact be characteristic of all types of music worldwide. Certainly in classical music it is possible to identify a composer after hearing only a phrase or two or a characteristic combination of sound elements. But along with the irresistible rhythmic and harmonic features of jazz, the peculiar qualities—including at times regional traits—that set off one performer from another account in large part for the distinct appeal of this music.

Between 1870 and 1900 the number of miles of railroad tracks laid in Texas went from 711 to 9,886, almost doubling that of any other southern state in which a black population was concentrated.[12] By 1873, the Southern Pacific line had arrived in Abilene to furnish transportation for the cattle raised in the surrounding area, and black entertainers would travel by railway to find work in such outlying areas. But it was along the East Texas lines that boogie-woogie musicians found the most opportunities for employment. Itinerant musicians followed the railway logging camps, which were usually converted railroad cars on wheels that moved on as the forest was cleared and the tracks were laid down. Such railroad shacks functioned as a combination dance hall, crap-game dive, and brothel and were known as barrelhouses, honky tonks, or juke joints.[13] Other rail lines connected the oil fields and such oil-boom towns as Beaumont, with its Spindletop gusher that blew in on January 10, 1901. A barrelhouse circuit also connected the port cities of Galveston, Houston, and nearby Richmond, and branching off to east and west the main side lines "claimed to serve eighty-eight Texas counties."[14]

Speaking of the boogie-woogie style of "a fast, rolling bass" that gave this music its "tremendous power," E. Simms Campbell remarks that "in Houston, Dallas and Galveston—all Negro piano players played that way." Campbell goes on to observe that this Texas style, also known as "fast western" or "fast blues," could be differentiated from the "slow blues" of New Orleans and St. Louis.[15] In general, boogie-woogie is highly percussive and is marked by a repeated left-hand bass, which is usually played with eight beats to the bar and moves "to the three blues-chord positions (C, F and G in the key of C)"[16] while the right hand improvises over this continuous bass figure "in fascinating and varied polyrhythmic, polymetric patterns."[17] For Wilfrid Mellers, boogie-woogie piano represents the triumph of the percussive guitar over the lyricism of the country blues vocal.[18] On the other hand, Rudi Blesh contends that "boogie-woogie is a special phase or development of blues piano. The whole barrel-house style is often connected with singing and with the spoken monologue, like the speaking blues." Yet even Blesh affirms that this "definitive piano version of the blues . . . like that of the parent blues . . . developed from banjo and guitar playing."[19] This more primitive, unsophisticated music has been called "the bad little boy of the rag[time] family who wouldn't study."[20] Nonetheless, the freer, improvisational style of boogie-woogie gained for it greater spontaneity and, through its "powerful 'striding bass,'" added to the refined ragtime form "the rugged virility of the barrelhouse chugging triads."[21]

As noted earlier, Leadbelly reportedly heard boogie-woogie being played in 1899 in the area of Texarkana and Marshall where the Texas and Pacific Railroad was laying track, but as jazz critic Martin Williams is quick to observe, "We don't know where the blues came from, or when, [just as] we don't know where boogie woogie came from, or when," even though the critic concedes that it "seems to have been a midwestern style, heard early in urban and rural Texas, Oklahoma, and Missouri in barrooms and mining camps, honky-tonks and lumber camps."[22] According to Williams, Fletcher Henderson on his *Chimes Blues* (ca. March 1923) was one of the first to record using the "intermittent walking bass" identified with boogie-woogie. Williams adds that a Clay Custer, in his recording of *The Rocks* from the same year, also employed this technique but then "dropped into obscurity."[23] However, Peter J. Silvester reveals that in fact Clay Custer was none other than George Washington Thomas, Jr., elder brother of Sippie Wallace and Hersal Thomas, who recorded his own composition *The Rocks* in February 1923 using as a sobriquet his mother's maiden name.[24] According to Silvester, this piece "can claim the distinction of being among the earliest known recorded works with a boogie-woogie structure"—that is, "a twelve-bar blues."[25] *The Rocks* is also credited with being "the first recorded example" of a work including "a walking bass."[26]

❧ ❧ ❧

The boogie-woogie compositions of George W. Thomas and his brother Hersal were vital to the spread of this music that blended ragtime and blues. As early as 1911 George Thomas had composed his *New Orleans Hop Scop Blues* when he still lived in Houston prior to moving to New Orleans.[27] This piece, which was not published until 1916, would be recorded by Bessie Smith in 1930, continuing in "her barrelhouse mood."[28] More important historically is the fact that *New Orleans Hop Scop Blues* is thought to be "the first twelve-bar blues to be written and published with a boogie-woogie bass line."[29] Even more significant to the development of boogie-woogie in Chicago, where the Thomases moved in 1919, was George and Hersal's composition *The Fives*, copyrighted by the brothers in 1921 and published in 1922 by George's publishing company. According to Peter Silvester, the title refers to the time of arrival of a train from Chicago to San Francisco.[30] *The Fives* looks back to the origins of barrelhouse piano along the railway lines in East Texas and forward to the boogie-woogie rage in Chicago of the late 1920s and its "tidal wave" that "swept America" in the 1930s and 1940s.[31]

In common with the blues, boogie-woogie was inspired by train journeys and by the sounds associated with this form of transportation so appealing and accessible to blacks. A composition by Texas barrelhouse pianist Edwin "Buster" Pickens, born northwest of Houston in Hempstead in 1916, is entitled *Santa Fe Train* and is characteristic of boogie-woogie's imitation of railroad travel, with a bass that, although "played in an unusual 6/4 time, typifies the relentless power of the engine and is embellished by a series of chiming chords in the treble, reminiscent of a train bell." As Peter Silvester goes on to say, "The many compositions that drew their inspiration from train journeys not only illustrate the significance of this form of travel for pianists, but also helped to shape the music itself."[32] George and Hersal Thomas's *The Fives* is also representative of boogie-woogie's railway origins and would lead to the popularity of this musical form in Chicago.

The Fives consists of a number of characteristic boogie-woogie bass patterns: stride (a broken octave interposed between on- and off-beats in the left hand), walking bass (broken or spread octaves repeated through the blues progression to provide the ground for improvisation), and stepping octave chords.[33] The title of this composition became synonymous with boogie-woogie bass patterns employed by certain Chicago pianists, even though the exclusive or predominant use of the first and fifth fingers in a walking bass differed in *The Fives* in that the bass parts found in the Thomases' composition varied the left-hand fingering.[34] Nonetheless, the influence of *The Fives*, as well as *The Rocks*, was such that every boogie-woogie player would be judged by his performance of these pieces: "In those days if a pianist didn't know the *Fives* and the *Rocks* he'd better not sit down at the piano at all."[35] Little Brother Montgomery, a Louisiana pianist born in 1906 who came to Chicago in 1928, was quoted as saying that "it was impossible to get work unless a pianist could play the Chicago 'Fives'—a possible reference to the George and Hersal Thomas composition."[36] Furthermore, two Chicago pianists, Albert Ammons, who popularized the use of the "powerhouse walking bass so much a part of jazz," and Meade "Lux" Lewis, whose 1927 recording of his *Honky Tonk Train Blues* was "the most phenomenal Boogie Woogie solo ever composed,"[37] both asserted that *The Fives* "was instrumental in shaping 'modern boogie-woogie.'"[38]

Even though George Thomas was an accomplished musician who played cornet, saxophone, and piano, he preferred to compose music, which ranged in style from ragtime tunes, such as *Bull Frog Rag* and *Crawfish Rag*, to such blues numbers as *Shorty George Blues*, *Mussel Shoal Blues*, *Houston Blues*, and *New Orleans Hop Scop Blues* as well as such songs as *I'll Give You a Chance* and *Love Will Love*.[39] His brother Hersal, in addition to being the joint composer of *The Fives*, also wrote the classic piano piece *Suitcase Blues*, which he recorded in 1925 and which is considered one of the "great barrel-house records."[40] Hersal's recording of *The Fives*, made in Chicago in 1924, makes clear that this work is structured as a blues but also reveals its ragtime roots beneath the new growth of a boogie-woogie eight-to-the-bar rhythm.[41] One wonders what Joplin would have made of this upstart fifteen-year-old fellow Texan who, after this, his first commercial recording, was touted by the April 19, 1924, issue of *The Music Trade Review* as "one of the youngest songwriters in the world."[42] Had he lived longer, surely Hersal would have gone on to write more such work, alone or in collaboration with his brother George.

Certainly *The Fives* as played by Hersal has to be heard to be believed, not only for his flawless execution but for the work's structure. Incorporating allusions to Joplin's rags and to *Pop Goes the Weasel*, Hersal avoids the rather repetitive quality of much boogie-woogie by developing his performance more along the lines of Joplin's compositions that featured variations, polyrhythms, syncopation, and alternating sections, all of which are here ingeniously integrated as a whole. However, the young Thomas is not as consistent structurally as Joplin, for he varies the chord patterns, playing eight-, eleven-, and twelve-bar blues, as well as

Hersal Thomas of Houston,
the boogie-woogie prodigy.

one six-bar blues, and extending a ten-bar passage to eleven by quoting *Pop Goes the Weasel*. At times he stretches an eight-bar blues to eleven, changing the harmony to do so. Hersal will also vary his rhythms from bar to bar by moving from duplet to triplet time—the latter the swing meter of Jelly Roll Morton—and even keeping both tempos going simultaneously. One striking feature of this recorded performance is that it runs to four minutes and seventeen seconds, the longest of all the piano selections included on *Boogie Woogie Blues*, the Biograph compact disc that contains Thomas's piece among a total of sixteen numbers from the 1920s.[43] And even though there are many masterful performances on this disc—including James P. Johnson's 1922 *Birmingham Blues*, Everett Robbins's 1923 *Hardluck Blues*, Clarence Johnson's 1923 *Low Down Papa*, and Cow Cow Davenport's 1925 *Hurry and Bring It Home Blues*—Hersal's clean execution of the Thomas brothers' composition stands out and exhibits the indelible stamp of a thought and technique that recall Joplin and Morton while working toward a uniquely individual style all its own. Only toward the end of this long piece does the pianist seem to tire somewhat, falling into a repeated figure that loses the energy and variety exhibited earlier. On the other hand, the conclusion suggests the slowing of the train that must have originally inspired so much early boogie. In any event, it is easy to see from this recording why Hersal has been pronounced "king of Chicago's house-rent party pianists in the middle 1920s."[44]

As noted earlier, Hersal served as an accompanist for his sister Sippie and his niece Hociel on their 1920s blues recordings, along with Louis Armstrong and King Oliver, among other jazz greats. On these recordings, Hersal employed many of the treble figurations associated with boogie-woogie, such as "short descending scale figures, chord clusters, arpeggiated or unfolded chords, trills, tremolos or glissandi—but in all cases, the harmonic thought is derived from the twelve bar blues sequence."[45] Hersal's solo performances also exhibit characteristic features of boogie-woogie in combination with variant patterns or nonboogie elements. The fact that Hersal's *Suitcase Blues*, recorded for Okeh on February 22, 1925, is the work of an eighteen- or nineteen-year-old makes this performance an amazing feat in itself, but it is the elegant, controlled quality of Hersal's playing that would be impressive at any age, in particular among untrained musicians who mastered the piano by imitation and experiment. No other recorded boogie-woogie pianists of the period possess the full-handed technique found on Hersal's recording of his *Suitcase Blues*. Although Albert Ammons's interpretation of the tune fourteen years later "captured the spirit of the Hersal Thomas original," it "contained fewer embellishments than that pianist brought to the playing."[46] That the performance by Ammons "retains the flavor of the original" leads Max Harrison to speculate on Thomas's importance "as a formative influence in the early Chicago days."[47] Hersal's use of the sequence of tremolo chords in his accompaniment for Sippie Wallace's *Special Delivery Blues*, analyzed earlier, was recorded two years before Clarence "Pinetop" Smith's famous *Pinetop's Boogie-Woogie* (December 29, 1928), which employs "the same substantive accompaniment played by Thomas."[48] Yet another of Hersal's compositions, *Hersal's Blues*, recorded in June 1925, is an extraordinary performance and together with *Suitcase Blues* makes his "a name to remember."[49]

In a sense, Hersal Thomas's *Suitcase Blues* and *Hersal's Blues* look backward and forward in terms of the development of jazz. While *Hersal's Blues* occasionally employs the boogie-woogie bass pattern of the four-to-the-bar "crotchet accom-paniment in the left hand," as does *Suitcase Blues*, the former tune "mainly uses a vamping type ragtime bass."[50] Although the four-to-the-bar crotchet is present only in the first half of *Suitcase Blues* and the second half of the tune "is completely non boogie-woogie in all respects," this classic piece "possesses a certain amount of melodic movement" and thus "assumes something more of a boogie-woogie character."[51] It is the "melodic movement" that gives to Hersal's form of boogie-woogie a quality that perhaps overcomes the "severest handicap" of the music: the repetitions in both the left-hand figures and the corresponding chordal patterns of the right hand, which "tended toward automation."[52] Eventually this severe disadvantage would spell the end for boogie-woogie's widespread popularity, but before its decline came in the late 1940s, the music that George and Hersal Thomas brought to Chicago from an East Texas tradition had, like ragtime before it, "seeped into what is believed the younger form"—jazz.[53] Indeed, boogie-woogie would be disseminated throughout the land through the work of countless pianists as well as by a multitude of popular swing-era orchestras.

❂ ❂ ❂

By the 1940s, as Martin Williams points out, boogie-woogie was obligatory: "Every dance band (whether a real swing band or not), every small group, every solo pianist had to have at least one boogie-woogie number—or, if not, had to call something 'boogie' whether it really was or not."[54] On a more positive note, it was through the impact of ragtime and boogie-woogie (or barrelhouse) that the great New York stride pianist James P. Johnson affected the work of Duke Ellington, Fats Waller, and Count Basie. Wilfrid Mellers writes that Ellington emulated Johnson's piano playing, which "combined the improvisatory passion of jazz with the formalized art of ragtime," and that Basie was capable of "thin, wiry, boogie-rhythmed piano" as well as "the kind of honesty he achieved in his powerhouse manner." As a comic version of Johnson, whose own "habitual manner" was happy, Fats Waller could "charm with boogie rhythms" in the left hand but could also deliver with his right the kind of elegant arabesques associated with ragtime. Through these three jazz figures, Thelonious Monk in turn would perpetuate ragtime and boogie-woogie as well as the blues, developing all three into his own modern style that in synthesis blends the warmth and formality of Ellington's haunting blues-inflected compositions with what Mellers has characterized as Monk's use of "all the traditional formulae of barrelhouse piano: the boogie rhythm, the teetering blue thirds, the rocking tremolos, the sharply chittering repeated chords in the treble." As Mellers goes on to remark, regardless of where Monk begins, even "from the compulsive energy of Latin American rhythm, as in *Bye-Ya*, the texture turns into [his] nervous re-creation of barrelhouse tradition."[55]

Like these eastern jazzmen, Texas musicians other than the Thomases also picked up on the rhythms and accents of boogie-woogie. Sammy Price, born in Honey Grove in north-central Texas on October 6, 1908, knew Hersal Thomas in Houston and recalls him in his autobiography, *What Do They Want?*[56] This was long before Price took up the piano and led his own band, the Texas Blusicians, during the early 1940s, a band that at one time included Lester Young on tenor. In later years, according to Leonard Feather, Price retained in his own piano playing "the forceful authority of the early boogie-woogie catalysts."[57] Many Texans like Price would travel to Kansas City to become members of such bands as those of Bennie Moten, Count Basie, and Jay McShann, who all played ragtime- and boogie-inspired piano. As we shall see, Carl "Tatti" Smith, a trumpeter born in Marshall in 1908, recorded with Lester Young in a small Basie group that went under the name Jones-Smith, Inc. In a 1935 session, Smith takes a muted solo on *Boogie-Woogie* that James Collier calls "excellent . . . controlled, spare, and clean,"[58] while Harry James, who grew up in Beaumont, would join Kansas City pianist Pete Johnson on a recording of their own *Boo-Woo* of February 1, 1939.[59] It was in Kansas City that ragtime, blues, and boogie-woogie would all come together to produce, through the playing of an important group of Texans, some of the most exciting and enduring jazz of this music's entire history.

PART

2

GOING TO KANSAS CITY

THE BENNIE MOTEN BAND, 1921–1927

In *The Swing Era*, the second part of Gunther Schuller's projected three-volume history of jazz, this composer–music critic remarks that "it is always a source of surprise to discover in what diverse regions of the country many of the major and lesser figures of jazz were born and/or grew up."[1] Speaking of the creation of a specifically southwestern jazz, Ross Russell, in his classic study *Jazz Style in Kansas City and the Southwest*, observes that "the state of Texas, the largest and most populous in the Kansas City–Southwest area, predictably yielded the greatest number of musicians and bands."[2] Like Scott Joplin, most of the Texas jazz musicians moved on to Missouri to pursue their careers, finding in Kansas City a stable working environment for their music as well as the attraction of recording contracts. The first important jazz figure to make his way to Kansas City was Lammar Wright, a trumpet player who, like Joplin, was a native of Texarkana. Born on June 20, 1907, Wright was reportedly in Kansas City by the age of fourteen, beginning his "formidable career" in his early teens as a member of Bennie Moten's first band, formed in 1921.[3] Wright trained under Major N. Clark Smith in the music department at Kaycee's Lincoln High School, where later Charlie Parker and other distinguished jazzmen would learn or sharpen their skills.[4] Although the music being played in Kansas City in 1921 was either ragtime or blues, Lammar Wright would participate in the advent of jazz, which, according to Ross Russell, arrived "in Moten's time, or with Moten."[5]

It was Bennie Moten, a ragtime pianist born in Kansas City in 1894, who conceived the idea of "projecting ragtime style by means of other instruments, possibly taking his cue from the raggy bands, like Joplin's, which were fairly common in Missouri."[6] At the time that Lammar Wright joined Moten's band playing in Kansas City nightspots, the city already was the scene of a wide-open gambling, prostitution, and bootleg beer and liquor operation controlled by its mayor, Tom Pendergast. Entertainment was available at all hours, and the dozens of saloons and cabarets provided steady work for musicians, who developed their individual techniques and their ensemble sounds while earning more than they could on construction jobs or by menial labor. Following the success of the Original Dixieland Jazz Band's 1917 recordings and those by blues singer Mamie Smith in 1920, record companies sought out talent for their catalogs of "race records," and Okeh was among the first to concentrate on blues and jazz, beginning in 1923 with Bessie Smith, Ma Rainey, and the various Texas blues singers recorded during that historic year. The first great jazz band to be pressed in wax was King Oliver's Creole Jazz Band, also recorded in 1923 by an acoustical horn before the introduction of the electric recording process in 1925.[7] At Oliver's initial Okeh session of June 22 and 23, 1923, his Creole Jazz Band recorded *Snake Rag* and *Dippermouth Blues*, which had already been recorded by the group on April 6, 1923, for the Gennett label. The Okeh recordings are important not only because they improve on or differ from the Gennett performances but also because they continue the influence of ragtime and blues, yet demonstrate the emerging new form of jazz, marked by the excitement and swing of the two-cornet breaks by Oliver and Armstrong on *Snake Rag* and of Oliver's muted solo on *Dippermouth Blues*, which became "one of the classic trumpet riffs that was imitated by hosts of other trumpet players."[8] In September 1923, the Okeh company would also record Bennie Moten's six-piece band, with Lammar Wright, "the best player in the group," showing "a marked King Oliver influence."[9] That a Texas jazzman not only was active during this first significant year of jazz recording but that he sounded like the leading cornetist of the day indicates that participating Texans were fully aware of the early developments in this new music.

During the first two decades of the twentieth century, jazzmen from New Orleans traveled into the Southwest and even as far west as California. As early as about 1904, Bunk Johnson toured through Texas, playing his New Orleans brand of Buddy Bolden–inspired cornet in a theater band in Dallas.[10] Sidney Bechet, born in 1897, reports that at the age of fourteen he was playing his clarinet in Texas, often in dime stores in places like Plantersville, but also in jail in Galveston, where he first performed the blues with a bunch of cellmates.[11] A few years later, Jelly Roll Morton ventured into Texas—"Dallas, Denison, Cuero, Yoakum, Brownsville (where I saw a bullfight), San Antonio, and more towns I can't remember," and everywhere he went he "looked up the piano players, and they were all terrible."[12] In Houston, Morton tried to start a stock theater and bought a tailor shop, but he soon grew tired of the place because "there wasn't any decent music around there, only jews-harps, harmonicas, mandolins, guitars, and fellows singing the

Lammar Wright of Texarkana. Reprinted by permission of *Down Beat.*

spasmodic blues—sing awhile and pick awhile till they thought of another word to say."[13] According to Clarence Williams, with whom Sidney Bechet traveled about 1914, Joe Oliver also went to Texas with Williams's show.[14] But it is more likely that Lammar Wright would have heard the King along the Mississippi when Oliver played on steamboats plying the river or performed in nearby towns and cities. Ed Lewis, a trumpet player who joined Moten's band in 1926, remembered having heard King Oliver in Kansas City when his band came to town playing with a circus: "He rehearsed during the morning, and every musician in town was there listening. He was one of the greatest, and I can appreciate what Louis was trying to do then."[15] Lewis was "very young" at the time, which would seem to have been considerably before Oliver's 1923 recordings, so the fact that Wright already was imitating Oliver on a recording made the same year as the King's first recordings demonstrates again Lammar's early awareness of the major developments in jazz prior to its being captured on the phonograph record.

Like the music of Oliver's Creole Jazz Band, Bennie Moten's early recordings consist of blues and ragtime tunes, with his band's first session in 1923 producing *Crawdad Blues* and *Elephant Wobble*, the former a standard twelve-bar blues and the latter what Ross Russell calls "a kind of riffed blues and, as such, an interesting artifact."[16] On both numbers, Lammar Wright utilizes a cup mute in the manner of Oliver, who virtually invented this device and made it one of his trademarks. The moaning effect achieved through Wright's use of the mute on *Crawdad Blues* owes much to Oliver, but the same technique employed on *Elephant Wobble* creates a more original sound, as Wright plays more notes and at a faster clip than was usual with the King. Both brassmen exhibit a driving style that is direct and forceful, with Wright characterized by Russell as playing "with authority" on *Crawdad Blues*.[17] Ed Steane asserts that "it is doubtful if anything [Wright] has done since 1923 can surpass the beauty of the cornet work on this record; even the poor recording possible at this time cannot dim the immediacy of his searing, stabbing style."[18] Although Gunther Schuller considers Moten's first two recorded titles "rhythmically stiff beyond belief," he still commends the playing of Wright and finds it significant that out of twenty sides recorded by the Moten band, half were blues; he points out that "the blues had always had strong roots in the Southwest" and "the larger Southwestern orchestras quickly adopted the form and used it more consistently than bands anywhere else. Audiences throughout the region insisted on a large diet of blues, and out of this earlier, deeper feeling in the music developed a way of playing jazz which was eventually to supercede the New Orleans, Chicago, and New York styles."[19]

From the Moten recording date of May 1925, which produced eight tunes, Wright's solo on *Sister Honky Tonk* is a wonderful piece of blues—poignant, crying, and inventive, moving away from the chords unlike the other soloists, who stick close to the tune's basic notes. Schuller singles out *Eighteenth Street Blues* (or *Strut*) from this session as "a fascinating mixture of the pure New Orleans ensemble style and the more heavily accented, blues-drenched feeling typical of the Southwest."[20] In *The Making of Jazz*, James Collier observes that by this time Moten's band "was a solid, swinging, New Orleans-style group: trumpeter Lammar Wright, who in 1923 had played almost without vibrato, was using the fast terminal vibrato characteristic of the New Orleans cornetists, and on '18th Street Strut' he used whole phrases taken directly from Oliver."[21] Eventually, as both Schuller and Collier acknowledge, Moten's band would become in the late 1920s the best in the Southwest and would develop its own riff style with shouting brass figures, although by then Lammar Wright had moved on to another Missouri band.

Before the Bennie Moten unit developed out of the blues its "fundamental jazz orchestral technique" of the riff statement, thereby influencing every swing band of the 1930s, the organization tended during Lammar Wright's tenure, which ended in 1927, to play "with a plodding, on-the-beat, even-eighth-note rhythm that was not even good ragtime."[22] However, at its May 1925 recording session the band performed *Kater Street Rag*, an original rag that demonstrates "the ties between ragtime and early Kansas City style" at the same time that it is "converted to instrumental jazz treatment."[23] Again, Wright utilizes his cup mute, at first delivering a straight ragtime tune, with no real attempt at more than a slight embellishment of the syncopated melody. Following Moten's very fine ragtime piano solo, Wright returns with more of a jazz feel, although reminiscent of the New Orleans Rhythm Kings rather than anything forward-looking or original. More interesting, and more up to date, is Wright's performance at the December 13 and 14, 1926, recording sessions for RCA Victor, especially in Jelly Roll Morton's *Midnight Mama* and George W. Thomas's *Muscle Shoal Blues*.[24]

The December 1926 recording date, the last Moten session at which Wright was present, is noteworthy in that it came only three months after the first recordings made by Jelly Roll Morton and his Red Hot Peppers on September 15, 1926, also for RCA Victor. It seems apparent that Morton's recordings were heard by Moten and his men, for *Midnight Mama* is clearly rendered in the Hot Peppers style, even though this is not a tune ever recorded by Morton's Chicago-period band. The performance of Thomas's *Muscle Shoal Blues* is also close in spirit to the Hot Peppers orchestration, while Moten's piano style is similar to that of Jelly Roll. Even Wright's open and muted horn echoes the sound of Morton's trumpeter, the outstanding George Mitchell. On *Midnight Mama*, there is still the annoying "novelty" clarinet of Woodie Walder, lamented by Schuller from the time of the first Moten sides in 1923,[25] but this is definitely tempered now, and Wright's driving cornet generates more swing than most of Moten's early recordings. When Wright plays a muted obbligato behind La Forest Dent on baritone, Lammar is the one who harks back to the novelty routine. But when he solos afterward, it is one of his most impressive breaks during his time with Moten and shows what he might have achieved as a soloist rather than as the big-band lead trumpet he later became with Cab Calloway's orchestra.

It may be that Lammar Wright tired of carrying the Moten band, but it seems unfortunate that he left Moten just when this unit was moving toward its greatest period—one in which a number of other Texans would join Moten and contribute fundamentally to his success. Although it is true that at this time the Moten band's performances "still did not have the elegance and structural cohesion of Jelly Roll Morton's recordings of the period,"[26] this ensemble, and particularly Wright, had made great strides toward creating the kind of swing essential to jazz.

THE BLUE DEVILS, 1925–1934

While Texarkana was home to the King of Ragtime and the birthplace of the first important Texas musician to record as a member of a major jazz band, Dallas gave rise to more Texas jazz figures of the early period than any other town or city in the state. A center for urban blues and boogie-woogie piano as well as gospel sounds, Dallas attracted such musicians as Henry "Ragtime Texas" Thomas, Blind Lemon Jefferson, Leadbelly, Alger "Texas" Alexander, and T-Bone Walker, who came from other parts of the state to play on the streets and in the saloons and dance halls of the city's tenderloin section located along Central Avenue, which was intersected by the other major thoroughfare, Elm Street. Known locally as Deep Ellum, this redlight district operated at all hours and served as a training ground for many apprentice musicians like Henry "Buster" Smith, who was born on August 26, 1904, in Alsdorf, south of Dallas, and who moved into the city from a cotton farm. To earn his first instrument—a clarinet he had seen for sale in Celina for $3.50—Buster picked over four hundred pounds of cotton a day for five days.[1] Self-taught on both clarinet and alto saxophone, Buster began playing around 1922 a type of barrelhouse music with the Voddie White Trio in the Tip-Top Club on Central Avenue. By 1925 he had joined the Blue Devils, a band whose home base was the Ritz Ballroom in Oklahoma City but which would include, along with Buster Smith, two other Texans—Eddie Durham of San Marcos and Hot Lips Page of Dallas. This band's seven members were, in the estimation of Ross Russell, among "the finest musicians produced in two decades of jazz in the Southwest." Russell also believes that Smith approaches the stature of Leadbelly among southwestern bluesmen, representing an "archetypal jazzman of the Southwest" in his own right and a "major saxophone stylist . . . with roots in the urban blues."[2]

Although Buster Smith never played with the Alphonse Trent Orchestra, the foremost band in Dallas during the early 1920s, he was quite familiar with the Trent orchestra and with the Troy Floyd band out of San Antonio—two outfits that he considered "as good as you could find anywhere."[3] The Trent orchestra had been formed in the leader's native state of Arkansas, and its finest soloists through the years included Snub Mosley from Arkansas on trombone and Peanuts Holland from Virginia on trumpet. By 1925 Trent's orchestra played regularly at the Adolphus Hotel, with Terrence Holder on trumpet, Mosley on trombone, and A. G. Godley on drums. Budd Johnson, another native of Dallas, remembered the band as the greatest he had heard: "They were gods back in the twenties, just like Basie was later, only many years ahead of him. . . . They made $150 a week a man. Imagine! They worked nothing but the biggest and finest hotels in the South."[4] Snub Mosley himself recalled those heady days when the Trent orchestra was "the first colored band to play for a white audience in the state of Texas." Mosley was reminded how this "was a big step forward, and the Ku Klux Klan planned to tar and feather us, just because we were playing for the white people. That wasn't the feeling of the majority, especially not of the big, rich people, but only of the lower element, the crackers."[5]

Another first for the Trent orchestra was its regular radio program, aired over station WFAA in Dallas beginning around 1925. No other black band in the nation had been accorded such an honor. However, recording companies apparently remained unaware of the band, for it was not until October 28, 1928, that the Trent orchestra cut two sides with Gennett, and only six more between 1930 and 1933. Nonetheless, even these few recordings demonstrate the polish of the orchestra and the advanced conceptions and techniques of its soloists. Gunther Schuller says of Snub Mosley's "lightning-fast" trombone that it "forecasts" the work of trombonists of the bop era. On *Black and Blue Rhapsody* from the 1928 session, Mosley "saunters in blithely" on a high E flat, "toying with rapid cascading figures as if they were child's play."[6] Even so, Ross Russell finds that the Trent orchestra "was an anomaly rather than a model of Texas style." Russell characterizes the group as "an eastern dance band, masquerading in high heel boots, with a Texas flavor to its music." He goes on to declare that Trent's band "represented the top level of professional aspiration in Texas and, in attaining this goal, removed itself from the nurturing root material of the Southwest, the blues and folksong and loose ad-lib style of the early bands that worked with nothing more advanced than head arrangements and set great store on individual improvisation, thus encouraging and developing the solo talents in their ranks."[7]

At times a few Texas musicians were members of Trent's orchestra, including such important figures as Dan Minor, Charlie Christian, and Carl "Tatti" Smith, and as early as 1923 Sammy Price was a featured Charleston dancer with the band.[8] But it would seem that no Texan was among the Trent personnel when the orchestra recorded its total of eight sides.[9] In addition to the Trent orchestra, other groups made the circuit from Kansas City, Oklahoma City, Houston, Dallas, San Antonio, and the smaller towns in between; among these were the bands of Jap Allen, Terrence Holder, and George E. Lee, as well as traveling shows that included Louis Armstrong on occasion and more often King Oliver, both of whom Buster Smith heard playing at "the big places" in Dallas, the L. B. Mose theater downtown and the Hummingbird on Hall Street. According to Smith, the jazz played in Dallas started with medicine shows where four-piece groups consisted of trombone, clarinet, trumpet, and drum, with "every man blowing for himself as loud as he could blow to attract a crowd for the 'doctor.'" Smith recalled that in 1922 the medicine shows tried to get him to join, but he turned them down, and after performing around Dallas "at Saturday night suppers and that sort of thing" during 1923 and 1924, he was urged in 1925 by the touring Blue Devils to go on the road as part of their "commonwealth" band.[10]

Formed originally around 1923, the Blue Devils, at the time that Buster Smith became a member of the group in 1925, was led by Ermir Coleman, a trombonist known as "Bucket." Also in the band was Walter Page, who by the end of 1927 was the Blue Devils' leader, playing string bass, tuba, and baritone sax. Operating on the "commonwealth plan," all "hirings, firings, itineraries, fees, in fact all important decisions were left to a majority vote; earnings were pooled, the net divided equally, and, if one of the musicians had a personal problem, his needs were considered."[11] With the addition of Buster Smith, the Blue Devils became "equal in strength to any band in the Southwest, including Alphonso Trent and Bennie Moten, and were improving rapidly."[12] Although the Blue Devils did not enjoy the prestige of Moten's band or "the impressive musicianship of Trent," the group developed a style that was largely based on the blues tradition associated with the Southwest, making "generous use of riffs" and building up improvised solos of great power and imagination.[13] The music of the Blue Devils represented, in William Barlow's words, a fusion of "certain blues practices with jazz instrumentation. Most notably, blues vocal techniques were transferred to the musical instruments used in the brass and reed sections: in essence, the blues vocal became the blues instrumental."[14] As a territory band that competed with other touring groups for the best jobs, the Blue Devils gained a reputation as a successful and even feared unit that took delight in "cutting" other bands in "battles" of music. With the recruitment of Smith, the reeds became the Blue Devils' "best section" and made the band a fierce competitor, but on other recruiting drives into Texas the organization added to its brass section two more members who helped make the Blue Devils a formidable opponent and the envy even of Bennie Moten.

The first important find was Oran "Hot Lips" Page, a trumpeter and blues singer who was born in Dallas on January 27, 1908. Hot Lips joined the Blue Devils in part through Buster Smith. At the time that Page was picked up by the commonwealth band, which systematically raided other bands and auditioned, evaluated, and cajoled its recruits, the future trumpet star was working with Eddie and Sugar Lou's band in Austin.[15] Page had attended college to become a doctor but never finished because he was "much more interested in music," which he began to take seriously when he discovered he "could make more money blowing a trumpet than shining shoes."[16] According to Hot Lips, Walter Page was his older half-brother, which also may account for his being invited to join the Blue Devils. In turn, Lips was responsible, by his own report, for adding another vital member to the commonwealth, Bill (not then Count) Basie, a stride pianist from New Jersey who had not been "out West long" and was "still more or less unknown."[17] Lips, whose playing was inspired by Louis Armstrong and King Oliver, "was neither as subtle nor as inventive as the New Orleans master players, but he possessed an impressive trumpet sound, had worked up a brawling muted delivery, and sang a creditable blues vocal. . . . Lips came in and at once the trumpet section took on a new authority. Page's infectious rhythmic drive, blasting tone, and ability to pile chorus upon chorus made the Blue Devil brass section go."[18]

The third Texan to join the Blue Devils was Eddie Durham of San Marcos, born there on August 19, 1906, into a family of seven who all played instruments. The eldest of the brothers and sisters, Joe Durham, would perform for a time on bass with Nat King Cole,[19] and it was this brother who had a crucial impact on Eddie's career. Before being invited to join the Blue Devils, Durham had experienced the typical life of a Texas jazz musician, beginning in 1916 at the age of ten as a member of a group formed with another brother and a cousin named Allen Durham (place and date of birth unknown). Allen would become the best soloist, along with Mary Lou Williams, on the first recording made in 1929 by Andy Kirk's Clouds of Joy.[20] Another cousin, Herschel Evans of Denton, would later join Eddie Durham during the finest years of the Count Basie band. After playing with his siblings in the Durham Brothers Band, Eddie went on the road at the age of eighteen with the 101 Ranch Brass Band, a marching band that played circuses.[21] Having traveled as far as New York City, where he performed at Yankee Stadium, Durham left the 101 when the show went on to Europe, after which he joined Edgar

Battle's Dixie Ramblers and later Gene Coy's Happy Black Aces out of Amarillo.[22] Andy Kirk, a member of the George Morrison Orchestra in Denver when Coy's band visited there, recalled how the musical establishment in the Mile-High City was "shook up" by the "hottest and liveliest music" they had heard.[23] Such territory bands in Texas not only provided entertainment for audiences in the region but also served as "traveling 'music conservatories'"[24] or training organizations in which young players like Eddie Durham could develop their skills as players or arrangers and in general come into their own musically and professionally.

In acquiring the services of Eddie Durham, the Blue Devils gained a triple-threat musician in this Texan's skills as trombonist, guitarist, and composer-arranger. Like Buster Smith, who learned to read music while working at the Tip-Top Club in Dallas[25] and would contribute a number of important arrangements to the Count Basie book, among them *The Blues I Like to Hear* and *Smarty*,[26] Durham could read and arrange, having been exposed to music theory at an early age. Although Eddie's father, who played the fiddle and performed at square dances, had "instilled a love of music in his children," he "didn't want to even see [written or printed] music. . . . He figured that people couldn't hear you read; they hear you play."[27] But Eddie's oldest brother, Joe, "subscribed to lessons from what was called the U.S. School of Music," which, as Eddie explained, was a correspondence course whose system taught only two- and three-part harmony: "A sixth was unknown."[28] Eddie subsequently taught himself to write five- and six-part harmony and to add sixths and ninths to his and others' arrangements of many outstanding tunes of the swing era, which would have far-reaching effects on jazz history.[29]

Eddie Durham's early training in the rudiments of music theory was perhaps an even more significant factor in determining his contributions to jazz than his ties to a Texas blues tradition. While it is thought that most of the tunes played by the Blue Devils were "head arrangements"—that is, pieces "improvised or worked out collectively by an entire band or group; usually not written down, but memorized 'in the head'"[30]—Count Basie recalled that, along with playing the trombone, Durham "did a great deal of arranging" for the band.[31] Basie did not mention Durham's guitar work at the time, but it was with this instrument that Eddie would make jazz history, having taken it up after beginning on the banjo. Durham first played the four-string guitar, then added the trombone, and later learned the six-string guitar, on which he claimed that he "could have been a kind of genius," but after he "started getting up in the world," he divided his time "between arranging, composing, trombone, and guitar, not sticking to any one."[32]

Unfortunately, Durham had left the Blue Devils to join the Bennie Moten band a month before the Blue Devils held their only recording session in November

1929. However, Durham already was present on an October 1929 recording by the Moten band, featured on both trombone and guitar. Basie, too, would desert the ranks of the Blue Devils for the Moten band, but, according to Ross Russell, it was Basie who played at the Blue Devils' 1929 session, not Willie Lewis, who "appears in some discographies as the pianist of record."[33] The Blue Devils recorded two tunes, *Squabblin'* and *Blue Devil Blues*, the latter featuring a vocal by Jimmy Rushing, a native of Oklahoma City who had joined the band in 1927.[34] Although Russell concedes that the section work on *Squabblin'*—"a riff original taken at a headlong and demanding tempo"—lacks Alphonse Trent's precision, he finds that "this is a different kind of a band. The sections here are more flexible and the support for the solo passages superior." Russell goes on to make two observations about the historical significance of this recorded riff:

> The beat is headed in the direction of the supple 4/4 time that would eventually characterize Kansas City style. Buster Smith is heard twice on alto saxophone and once on clarinet. The alto work is years ahead of any saxophonist recording in the Southwest—in fact, it forecasts Charlie Parker. The tone is round and airy; the notes have a floating quality and a nostalgic blues timbre. The hard edge of phrasing heard in saxophone playing in bands all over the country is now beginning to lose its diamond-like brilliance and move toward the softer, more fluid Kansas City style.[35]

Gunther Schuller's earlier analysis of this same recording had anticipated Russell's conclusions by finding Buster Smith's solos "advanced for their time" and "especially fascinating because the tone, with its sinewy fullness and slight edginess, was clearly emulated by Parker." Yet Schuller seems to prefer the playing of Hot Lips Page, who for the critic was freer and more relaxed. On *Blue Devil Blues*, Schuller also prefers the trumpeter's work, observing that "Page's muted trumpet behind Rushing is in the classic ornamental blues style, perfectly filling in and responding to the voice."[36] Page's performance style is understandable since Page had played with the great Ma Rainey at the Lincoln Theatre in New York City during earlier years when he, like Durham, toured the country, performing at carnivals, with minstrel shows, and at theaters. During one summer in Atlanta, Lips played "a theater date with Bessie Smith."[37]

Russell and Schuller agree that *Blue Devil Blues* is a lesser performance than *Squabblin'*—the one branding the former piece "only moderately interesting"[38] and the other observing that the piece "ends inconclusively with dull, arranged riff harmonies under a meandering piano solo."[39] While Schuller points out that "in a sense the whole performance has neither a beginning nor an ending," he allows that Page's opening solo "is a workable substitute for a beginning." In this solo Schuller praises the trumpeter's "great rhythmic freedom" as seeming "to be an almost bar-less music, stemming directly from the blues." Schuller also notes that Page "produces a remarkably cohesive solo built on two ideas, both constantly varied. The quality of this achievement must be measured against the fact that for the sixteen bars of this introductory solo the harmonic background remains unwaveringly locked in C minor. Yet Page turns this harmonic construction to advantage, as he builds over it a solo that is in effect a miniature composition." As for *Squabblin'*, Schuller remarks that this tune clearly demonstrates "how concrete the Southwestern tradition had become by 1929, and how different in spirit and direction this was from a band like Ellington's, for example." Although Hot Lips Page and Buster Smith are the main soloists, Schuller also credits the "relaxed propulsion" of Walter Page's two-beat bass line and the "flowing cymbal work" of Alvin Burroughs with combining "to make a fluid, swinging beat that became the recognizable rhythmic trademark of the Kansas City style."[40] Dan Minor, who was born in Dallas on August 10, 1909, and occupied Durham's trombone chair after his fellow Texan left for the Moten band, is not featured. Minor was in fact rarely a soloist, but along with Smith and Page, he also contributed to the Blue Devils as part of what Ross Russell characterizes as "a remarkable collection of talents."[41] Gunther Schuller even includes Minor on the list of "the best players of the region," which consists of Buster Smith, Eddie Durham, Hot Lips Page, Alvin Burroughs, Jimmy Rushing, and Count Basie.[42]

One name not included on Schuller's list is that of Lester Young, who joined the Blue Devils only after most of the band's outstanding musicians had already gone with Moten. Prez, as Young would come to be known when he starred later with the Count Basie orchestra and played his "cool" tenor sax behind Billie Holiday's sensual lyrics, is certainly among the major jazz figures of the Southwest, but by the time he became a member of the vaunted Blue Devils the band was in decline, with only Buster Smith left from the early commonwealth musicians and even from the group of latterday Texans. Stranded in the East after a job in West Virginia turned sour, both Lester Young and Buster Smith made it to Cincinnati, where they were picked up by a car sent over by Bennie Moten, whose band they too joined at the end of 1933, a year after Moten's last recording session and barely two years before his sudden death in 1935.[43]

This marked the end of the Blue Devils, which Gunther Schuller calls "a spunky outfit" that "would take on all comers," one whose recordings "are of great historical importance, quite apart from their musical merits, since much of the personnel of the Blue Devils sparked the Moten band of the early thirties, which in turn became the nucleus of the Basie band. Of perhaps even greater significance is Buster Smith's presence in the Blue Devils band, he being the main musical influence on young Charlie Parker in the mid- and late thirties."[44] Likewise, Ross Russell summarizes the impact of Buster's playing by taking his cue from Kansas City bandleader Harlan Leonard, who characterized the sort of solo work done by Smith as typical of "naturals," musicians whose methods "were their own and made for a resourceful, self-reliant jazzman to whom improvisation came naturally, almost as self-defense. When they were at their best, improvisation was a constant series of discoveries. One usually has this feeling in the playing of Buster Smith, Lester Young, and Charlie Parker."[45]

From towns and cities throughout the state of Texas, and with territorial bands based in such cities as Dallas, San Antonio, Houston, Amarillo, Wichita Falls, San Angelo, Austin, and Tyler, jazz musicians toured the Southwest and as far away as Minnesota and Maine. As Frank Driggs has observed in the first major study of southwestern jazz, the musician from this region "tended to be well educated musically, which enabled him to meet the challenge of constantly developing styles."[46] The musical education obtained by the Texas musician, in particular, was due largely to his being well traveled, often changing bands and joining such outfits from Oklahoma and Arkansas as those headed up by Walter Page, Nat Towles, and Terrence T. Holder. Eventually, many of the best musicians ended up in Kansas City, where they found better-paying, more dependable jobs and were afforded opportunities to record for money *and* posterity. Others remained in Texas and were, for the most part, never recorded; as a result, they died unknown or lived on as legendary figures, compared in memory with the giants of southwestern jazz who made it to Kansas City and joined the seminal bands of Bennie Moten and later of the great Count Basie.[47]

BENNIE MOTEN, 1929–1935

After the departure of Lammar Wright in 1927, Bennie Moten's band produced some excellent sides that show the influence of other jazz orchestras both from back east and in the Southwest. The eastern styles of Fletcher Henderson and Don Redman's big-band arrangements had by now, in Gunther Schuller's account, "penetrated the Southwest," and Louis Armstrong's "individualism of lines" can be heard in the solos of players like Moten's Ed Lewis and the Blue Devils' Hot Lips Page. Jesse Stone's Blues Serenaders were traveling through Missouri and Kansas, expressing "the tragic spirit of the blues in a manner that even Moten, who reflected more a white urban culture than Stone's rural touring territory, never achieved." In Texas, Alphonse Trent, Troy Floyd, and Terrence Holder were also proving strong competition and were causing Moten to change his approach in order "to appeal to a wider (white) audience." As a result, Moten's band began to deemphasize the element that had brought him success—the riff technique of the blues. Moten did hang on to the ragtime strain, as we have seen in his 1927 recording of Euday L. Bowman's *Twelfth Street Rag*, and he also exploited on *The New Tulsa Blues* the popularity at the time of "the boogie-woogie piano style that was spreading like wildfire throughout the Southwest." However, by 1928 "the lingering ragtime influences" were gone, but an overreliance on arrangements had homogenized the band's sound, making it "nationalized as it were, and in the process causing regional characteristics to disappear." Having avoided doing "battle" with the Blue Devils, Moten finally met them in 1928 and was reportedly "wiped out" by this commonwealth band.[1] Since Moten always wanted the best musicians and needed new ideas, he began to raid the Blue Devils, and the first to go over was Eddie Durham.

In October 1929, the month of the stock market crash—commemorated in jazz by Ellington's December recording of *Wall Street Wail*—Bennie Moten's band made a trip to the RCA Victor studio in Chicago. Two of the sides cut on October 23 were *Rhumba Negro* (subtitled *Spanish Stomp*) and *Rit-Dit-Ray*. These show the marked influence of Ellington, the first in its use of clarinet and trombone in a nicely composed passage and the second both in Jack Washington's baritone solo, which owes much to the Duke's great saxophonist Harry Carney, and in the general lines of the tenor sax's solo (probably Harlan Leonard), as well as the bouncy support from the band, including tuba.[2] The saxes lack the flowing swing and originality of Buster Smith and show how far ahead he was—or how far behind they were with a sound still of the novelty type compared with Buster's more fluid and sophisticated approach. Only with the piano solo on *Rit-Dit-Ray* by Basie, who had joined Moten after working up some arrangements with Durham, is there something new and different, even though Basie rambles at times, as he does in other piano solos from this recording session.[3] Nonetheless, Basie's extended solo on *Rit-Dit-Ray* is definitely superior to his shorter efforts on *The Jones Law Blues* and *Small Black*, which, even so, reveal "the young Basie's potential talent and budding originality of style."[4] Indeed, the piano solo on *Rit-Dit-Ray* contains many ingredients in the Basie recipe for a light, swinging treatment, largely unaided by the heavy rhythm section that he must attempt to carry along with him. Likewise, *New Vine Street Blues*, another tune recorded at this Chicago session (on October 24), shows that "the band was clearly moving ahead,"[5] with Basie furnishing further evidence of his light, ringing touch that would win for him many future accolades.

Also notable on *New Vine Street Blues* is Eddie Durham's most impressive early performance on guitar, with something approaching the single-note lines made famous much later by Charlie Christian. Here Durham performs on acoustic guitar in the rather stiff style of Eddie Lang, as in the latter's 1927 solo on *For No Reason at All in C* with Bix Beiderbecke and Frankie Trumbauer. Unlike Lang, however, Durham alternates single-note lines with modulating chords, which is typical of his solos in the coming decade but not of the more relaxed, entirely single-note lines of his 1937 performance on *Time Out* with the Count Basie band. In speaking of Durham's solos on *The Jones Law Blues* and *Small Black*, Gunther Schuller finds them "somewhat unformed" but marked by "the advanced harmonic thinking of a man who was to become an important arranger in the Kansas City style"; as such, they are "beyond the stylistic frame of reference set by the Moten band at that time."[6] It is true that Durham's rather stiff guitar solo on *Small Black* is "somewhat unformed," but he does end this piece with some forward-looking chords. Durham's brief guitar solo on *Rhumba Negro* is nice enough but not up to his work on *New Vine Street Blues*, which is only approached by his single-string technique on *Band Box Shuffle*.

On *The Jones Law Blues*, Durham also takes a fine trombone solo that illustrates perfectly the Texan's remark that he always liked this instrument because "a guy could make it sound like he was crying."[7] Not only does Durham's solo belong to the Texas blues tradition of moaning and crying, but it anticipates a line of Texas sax players that includes Booker Ervin and Ornette Coleman, who made names for themselves in the late 1950s and early 1960s with their own style of moaning on tenor and alto, respectively. Although Durham, like Dan Minor, was rarely featured as a soloist on trombone, he began playing "jazz breaks" on this instrument as early as his time with the 101 Ranch Band, whose other members "stayed very close to the melody."[8] Durham remembered trying to solo a bit and found that "it wasn't hard for me to learn the value of notes, but a guy who could swing a break was something new to them. So when we played for dances at night [in addition to their circus work], I asked them if I could swing in the jazz breaks. They were all trained musicians playing solid trombone—not faking—so jazz breaks on trombone were different."[9] As late as 1981, Durham would still be recording on trombone with a technique that remained impressive,[10] amazingly so, as captured in 1973 at a reunion of Kansas City musicians for the video entitled *The Last of the Blue Devils*.[11]

In addition to soloing both on trombone and guitar, Durham would bring a further dimension to the Moten band with his arranging skills. The next recording session for RCA Victor took place in Kansas City in October 1930, and by this time two other Blue Devils had defected—Hot Lips Page and Jimmy Rushing. But as Schuller notes, it was an arranger who was beginning to reshape the Moten band's destiny: Eddie Durham.[12] Ross Russell concurs, observing that with the coming of Basie and Durham, "the band took on a surprising amount of polish, and the quality of the book improved."[13] According to Schuller, on the 1930 sides "Durham's first inclination was to emulate the Henderson-Redman-Carter style very closely," with the result that "their ideas now appear consistently," as in Durham's *Oh! Eddie*.[14] For Schuller, the beat is "beginning to flow" and is "clearly headed toward the marvelous swing" of the Moten band's classic 1932 recordings.[15] Also important on *Oh! Eddie* is the presence of Hot Lips Page, who delivers an opening solo with mute that exhibits what Russell calls "Page's explosive trumpet," which "gave the band another lift and brought the brass section up to five pieces, more than any other band in the Southwest, even [that of] Alphonso Trent."[16]

Although Martin Williams feels that Durham's *Oh! Eddie* is "over-arranged," this critic does find that "the last chorus teasingly sketches out ideas that later turned up on *Moten's Swing*," one of the all-time classics of Kansas City jazz created by Basie and Durham.[17] Another Durham arrangement, *That Too, Do*, also looks forward, not just to the historic 1932 recording session by Moten's band but to the 1937 *Good Morning Blues* and the 1938 *Sent For You Yesterday*, both arranged by Durham for the Basie band. *That Too, Do* is, as Williams indicates, Jimmy Rushing's "only recorded blues vocal with Moten" but "each of Rushing's choruses has a life of its own on a later blues with Basie." Once again, after Jack Washington's assertive baritone opens the piece, Lips contributes a strong muted solo and Basie sounds more as he would in later years, his chiming chords played with their notes widely spaced. Durham's obbligato guitar behind Rushing's vocal establishes a tradition that would be carried to its greatest heights with the work of Buck Clayton and Dickie Wells when they later played behind this blues shouter in the Basie band. Durham also contributes two of his very fine swinging blues guitar solos on *When I'm Alone*, which, as arranged by Durham, shows "the tempo at which the four-beat of the later band was worked out" and "hints of things to come in those crisp brass figures at the end."[18]

Much of the commentary on the 1930 sides—by Schuller, Russell, and Williams—emphasizes these "hints of things to come." However, only with the 1932 recordings, the last by a Moten band before his untimely death in a dentist's chair in 1935, would the music making of this group come together fully at the RCA Victor studios in Camden, New Jersey, to produce what "still stands as one of the dozen or so most thrilling single sessions in this history of jazz. Here is the epitome of the Kansas City big band sound before it became absorbed into the swing movement."[19] For this final session, Moten acquired the services of two more members of the Blue Devils, its nominal leader, Walter Page, and Dan Minor, the Texas trombonist. In addition, Moten brought in another Texan on trumpet, Joe Keyes, who was born in Houston about 1907 and who played there with Johnson's Joymakers.[20] Also added by Moten were Ben Webster, a native of Kansas City who had been playing with Coy's Black Aces out of Amarillo, and another reed player, Eddie Barefield, from Iowa. The brass section, with the possible exception of trumpeter Prince (Dee) Stewart (whose place of birth has not been identified but who also had been with the Blue Devils and later led his own band in Kansas City), was composed entirely of Texans, with Hot Lips Page and Joe Keyes on trumpet and Dan Minor and Eddie Durham on trombone. The main arrangements were by Durham and Barefield.

Although the influence of Fletcher Henderson is still evident in the Moten band's use of "brass and reed riff choruses," these "have been extended," as Schuller allows, "into a rhythmic realm that gives them another dimension, as in the way each successive riff chorus builds upon its predecessor, in *Toby* for instance."[21] Schuller comments that the "hair-raising, exciting *Toby*," a riff by

Bennie Moten Orchestra, 1931. Among those pictured in the front row are Oran "Hot Lips" Page of Dallas (third from left) and Eddie Durham of San Marcos (sixth from left). Reproduced from the Ross Russell Collection, courtesy of the Harry Ransom Humanities Research Center, University of Texas at Austin.

Durham arranged by Barefield, was "certainly known to all the black musicians of the day."[22] Every commentator on this tune would tend to agree with Ross Russell that "against the background tapestry, the solos take on new depth and definition."[23] The major soloists here are Durham on guitar; Hot Lips Page on trumpet in a classic muted, driving, and blues-inflected performance; Ben Webster on tenor sax for a version of southwestern swing; Basie in his patented stride piano style; Barefield on clarinet for a few bars; Dan Minor on open trombone, showing the impact on a black jazzman of the revolutionary technique of fellow Texan Jack Teagarden; and finally Durham, completing the string of solos with a bluesy plunger-muted trombone. As Walter Page pulses away on his walking bass, the smooth flow of the soloists emerging one after another from the ensemble riffs creates "a perfectly integrated unit and at exactly the right tempo."[24]

Hot Lips Page and Ben Webster are clearly the principal wind soloists, and in Basie and Durham's *Moten's Swing*,[25] these two horn players exchange searing choruses before the famous riffs of this "Kansas City Anthem" are shouted at the end by the brass and reeds.[26] Both Schuller and Williams remark on the personal melodiousness of Page's playing, with Schuller noting that Lips "is harmonically freed to produce pure melodic essence."[27] While Schuller finds that Webster tends to play too many notes, typical of the early tenormen, he feels that Page is more modern in limiting himself to "a minimum of activity with a maximum of expression, a lesson Lester Young was to extend several years later."[28] Durham solos effectively on guitar, but it is his arrangement of the tune that represents his most important contribution. In a discussion of *Moten's Swing*, Martin Williams summarizes the achievement of the 1932 recording session: "*Moten's Swing* succinctly reveals what this band achieved. Here, by late 1932, was a large jazz orchestra which could swing cleanly and precisely according to the manner of Louis Armstrong— a group which had grasped his innovative ideas of jazz rhythm and had realized and developed them in an ensemble style. Further, the piece features original melodies on a rather sophisticated chord structure borrowed from a standard popular song."[29]

While the members as a group, the individual soloists, and Moten as the leader all made possible the success of the band's 1932 recording date, it seems undeniable that the contribution of the Texas players and Durham as arranger and soloist was considerable. The impact of Durham's work was indeed far-reaching, as indicated by this commentary: "Despite their poor reception, Moten's band, and one of their records, 'Moten Swing' on Victor 23384, was a very popular release. The piece, and the fine arrangement by the trombone player Eddie Durham, were picked up by every swing band in the country. . . . [Moten's] trumpet soloist, 'Lips' Page, attracted as much attention as Basie did."[30] And even though this would be the last Moten recording, many of the same musicians would gather again under the leadership of Count Basie to continue and expand on the ideas and techniques introduced on this historic date in the evolution of big band jazz and of the later rise of the combo styles of the cool and bebop movements.

THE COUNT BASIE ORCHESTRA, 1935–1963

With the sudden death of Bennie Moten at the age of thirty-nine, his band struggled on under the direction of Bennie's accordion-playing brother Buster, whose "volatile and inconstant temperament" differed so greatly from Bennie's steady, easygoing ways that the sidemen soon drifted off, leaving mostly those who had come over to Moten from the Blue Devils—Basie, Walter Page, Jimmy Rushing, Lips Page, Buster Smith, and Lester Young. Eddie Durham had already left Moten in 1934, and the other Texans, Joe Keyes and Dan Minor, were still working in Kansas City but in other bands. After Bus Moten failed in the role of director, a new band was formed, originally under the co-leadership of Basie and Buster Smith. Organized around the nucleus of the old Moten band, this new group had Basie and Walter Page as the rhythm section, to which was added Jesse Price on drums and Clifford McIntyre on guitar. Once again, the brass section was dominated by Texans: Joe Keyes, Carl "Tatti" Smith, who came by way of the Terrence Holder and Gene Coy bands, and Hot Lips Page, all on trumpet, while Dan Minor led the trombone section, which consisted of himself and George Hunt. The sax section was composed of Lester Young on tenor, Jack Washington on baritone, and two Texans, Buster Smith on alto and a second tenor player, Herschel Evans. Evans, born in Denton in 1909, had arrived in Kansas City after working with the Troy Floyd band in San Antonio and with Lionel Hampton and Buck Clayton in Los Angeles. As Ross Russell sums things up, "The musicians, former Blue Devils and recruits from Texas bands, had at last found the right companions and a happy home."[1]

It would seem that Texas jazzmen felt drawn to one another, for time and again both black and white players from the state tended to congregate and to seek out groups with fellow Texans. The fact that four-fifths of the Basie-Smith brass section was made up of Texans would certainly suggest that a geographical consideration may account for the mutual attraction, but it may also be explained simply by a desire to play with other good musicians. In the case of the sax section, half of whose members were Texans, this latter explanation is the one that appeals most to Ross Russell, who states that the four reed men "represented the pick of saxophonists in the Southwest. The only comparable reed section in all of jazz was the Harry Carney–Johnny Hodges–Barney Bigard reed team with Duke Ellington from 1928 to 1932."[2] Unfortunately, this aggregation with Buster Smith on alto and Lips Page on trumpet was never to record. In the fall of 1936, just when the band had signed with Decca records—through the recommendation of promoter John Hammond, who had caught the Basie-Smith band on the radio and traveled to Kansas City to hear it at the Reno Club—both Smith and Page departed, the former "skeptical of the grandiose plans in the making" and the latter to become a leader of his own band.[3] Smith's and Page's careers faltered as a result, while the Basie orchestra went on to national recognition as one of the finest jazz units of the entire swing era, with neither Texan being heard as he would have been in the context of such a great band. Smith and Page spent their prime years with lesser groups that could never provide them with such an ideal setting or bring them the exposure their talents deserved. Nonetheless, in the case of Buster Smith, it would seem that he left his indelible stamp on the Count's unit, for as Gene Ramey told Stanley Dance, "It was Buster who really made the Basie band what it was, a riff band with very little music."[4]

With the departure of Buster Smith, not only did Basie lose an important section leader who taught the reeds "to harmonize" and "to learn to breathe at the same time,"[5] but the Count suffered throughout the 1930s from the lack of an alto star. However, in Lester Young and Herschel Evans the new leader had brought together an incomparable tenor duo that complemented one another as never before or since in the history of jazz. With regard to the view that Young and Evans did not get along, Jo Jones set the record straight in this way: "Herschel Evans was a natural. He had a sound on the tenor that perhaps you will never hear on a horn again. As for the so-called friction between him and Lester, there was no real friction. What there was was almost like an incident you would say could exist between two brothers. No matter what, there was always a mutual feeling there."[6] The contrast between Evans and Young worked so well for Basie that it established a pattern for all the rest of his bands. Stanley Dance has written that "in the beginning there was a tendency for the band's success to be credited to its two tenor stars, Lester Young and Herschel Evans. Since then, Basie has always featured a couple of tenor soloists," three of these being Herschel's fellow Texans, Buddy Tate, Illinois Jacquet, and Budd Johnson.[7]

Herschel Evans of Denton. Reprinted by permission of *Down Beat.*

Representing the older tradition of tenor saxophone playing was Evans, who modeled his approach to the instrument after Coleman Hawkins, the premier tenorman of the day who made his reputation with the Fletcher Henderson Orchestra in New York in the 1920s and early 1930s. Against the warm, full-bodied sound of Hawkins that Evans admired and emulated, Lester Young developed a vibratoless, restrained, airy style that concentrated on creating a melodic story line rather than a robust, bursting-at-the-seams tone quality that expressed power and passion through the Hawk's chromatic and arpeggiated runs and sweeping, rhapsodic phrases. Even though Evans clearly belonged to the Hawkins school of tenor playing, he was not completely beholden to the elder statesman for his conception of the horn. On *Dreamland*, Herschel's earliest recording, made on June 21, 1929, with the Troy Floyd band out of San Antonio, the Texan provided "this band's most satisfying moments . . . during a rhythmically-searching tenor solo."[8] Gunther Schuller calls attention to the fact that Evans's solo is "very much *unlike*, and in advance of, the Hawkins of 1929. It is a more fluent, more melodic, and blues-tinged approach, perhaps more elegant, too."[9] Ross Russell seconds this view, remarking that Herschel's first recorded solo "is a minor landmark in tenor saxophone style and shows that he was securely rooted in the Texas blues tradition."[10]

By the time Herschel came to record with Basie for the Count's first session, held on January 21, 1937, the Texas tenorist showed that he was in total control of his own passionate style, pouring out the emotion in a brief solo on *Swinging at the Daisy Chain*.[11] Herschel's solos are almost always brief and make the listener yearn for more, which is perhaps as it should be. Despite the richness of his breaks, they never cloy, but one wonders how Evans would have held up in later years when tenors could go on for one entire side of a long-playing record. Had there been a microphone at the legendary late-into-the-night meeting at the Cherry Blossom in Kansas City early in 1934 between Hawkins and several Kaycee sax players, among them Lester Young, Ben Webster, and Herschel Evans, when by all reports Lester "cut" the Hawk, it might have been possible to catch Herschel improvising beyond the time limit imposed by the 78 rpm record. At this famous cutting session, Evans apparently did not hold back but was intent on showing his mentor "how much he had improved since they had last met."[12] Despite the time limitations, Herschel managed on his recordings with Basie to take full advantage of the few bars allotted him, his entrances ever authoritative and imaginative, his lines telling their own story—if a different, more urgent one than Lester Young's— in what Gunther Schuller has termed Herschel's "unique sense of drama."[13] Even though Young is indisputably the supreme soloist in the Basie band—and along with Armstrong and Parker one of the greatest in jazz history—Lester rarely, as Sidney Finkelstein points out, overbalances the other players: "There seems to be a fine interchange of ideas between him and Edison, Wells, Clayton, Collins, and Evans, so that all the solos stand up as music and all sound born out of the same musical source."[14]

Speaking of an earlier performance of *Swinging at the Daisy Chain*, broadcast on January 10, 1937, from the Chatterbox at Pittsburgh's Hotel William Penn, Frank Driggs has commented that he, for one, "can't get enough of" Herschel's soulful tenor. Here Evans is "heard at length" whereas his role on the commercial recordings was often smaller.[15] While Lester Young's solo on this broadcast transcription is the kind of technical and swinging treatment that awoke listeners to his new approach, Evans in the "older" tradition is equally impressive as he swings hard in an extremely fine performance that differs considerably from his solo on the January 21 recording. In Jelly Roll's *King Porter Stomp*, also from January 10, Evans takes a hot solo, utilizing some rhythmic ideas not heard elsewhere in his recorded work. On yet another piece from this date, *You Do the Darndest Things, Baby!*,

Evans takes a terrific break, just eight bars, but soaring beautifully with the tune's chords. Transcriptions of radio shows from the Chatterbox also include a February 8 performance of *Oh! Lady Be Good*, which has Herschel soloing superbly, his rich sound a combination of feeling and rhythmic invention. Another version of *Oh! Lady Be Good* from February 12 finds Herschel crying, moaning, impassioned, soulful—so different from Lester's "cool" interpretation of this tune. Although Driggs regrets "the somewhat square trumpet riffs behind Herschel's solo," this take of *Oh! Lady Be Good* does feature the "stabbing sound" of a trumpet solo with plunger mute, which may be by Texan Carl Tatti Smith, whose solos were "hard to separate" from those by Buck Clayton.[16]

With a March 26, 1937, recording session, Evans also was given a longer chorus than usual on *The Glory of Love*, but this performance by the entire band is an example of what Schuller brands "patchwork."[17] Herschel's solo, though extended, is broken up by meaningless ensemble passages and never coheres. There is a moment when Evans soars in what would become identifiable as the soulful "Texas tenor" style, but to no avail on this occasion. On July 7, 1937, the band would make the first recording of what proved to be the Basie theme song, *One O'Clock Jump*, a number created for Moten by Buster Smith and Eddie Durham, according to the latter's account, and based on a Fats Waller motif by way of a 1929 Chocolate Dandies recording of *Six or Seven Times*.[18] Although Schuller considers the quality of this first recording of *One O'Clock Jump* "inconsistent" with other performances, he does find Herschel's solo "excellent."[19] Here, with the terminal vibrato at the end of his impassioned phrases, Evans established a tradition for almost every Texas tenor player of the 1940s, among them Illinois Jacquet and Arnett Cobb. However, far superior is Herschel's performance on *One O'Clock Jump* from the November 3, 1937, air check recorded at the Meadowbrook in Cedar Grove, New Jersey. Here Evans is again allowed more time for his solo, and the results are much improved over his extended break on *The Glory of Love*. This time there is great variety in the tenor's chorus, with each segment of the solo having its own well-conceived idea and intensity of expression. Here also Lester Young's complementary solo exhibits his lightly swinging style to better advantage than in the March 26 recording. Another air check from July 9, 1938, of *One O'Clock Jump* has Herschel in good if somewhat predictable form, although Young and especially Dickie Wells seem more enthused about what was by then a warhorse recorded by every band of the period.[20]

Herschel Evans's best-known solo came on *Blue and Sentimental*, which Eddie Durham apparently worked out with his fellow Texan after the arranger joined the Basie band in the summer of 1937.[21] Of this performance, Joachim Berendt writes that "though Lester [Young] was the greater musician, Evans played the most renowned solo in the old Basie band: 'Blue and Sentimental.'"[22] Before recording this tune on November 9, 1938, as a showcase for Evans, Basie featured the tenorman in 1937 and early 1938 in five other pieces by Durham: *John's Idea* (July 7, 1937, arranged by Jimmy Mundy); *Time Out* and *Topsy* (both on August 9, 1937, the latter one of Durham's finest and most popular originals); and *Every Tub*, a perennial favorite, and *Swingin' the Blues* (both on February 16, 1938), the latter considered by Gunther Schuller "perhaps the most appropriately named title in the entire Basie library."[23] Bending his notes, warbling, and turning some catchy phrases, Evans opens the soloing on *John's Idea* with a spirited chorus that James Collier rates as Herschel at his best, along with the tenorman's solo on his own composition, *Doggin' Around*.[24] More effective despite their brevity are Herschel's solos on *Time Out* and *Every Tub*. In the former his four-bar break is a little masterpiece of controlled emotion, with every note contributing to the total effect of his musical statement, at the same time that it leads beautifully into Lester Young's extended chorus. This brief solo by Herschel exemplifies Albert Murray's observation that "Evans usually but not always made the hot getaway or set-up tenor statement, and Young made the cool wrap-up, clean up, or knockout before the out chorus."[25]

On *Every Tub*, one of the hardest-swinging arrangements Durham ever concocted, with brass and reeds slashing and biting their sharp punctuations, Evans enters after the band and its various soloists have been driving fiercely for the better part of this three-minute, sixteen-second piece, with Lester Young having opened the soloing instead of Herschel. In spite of his late arrival, Evans maintains the tune's high energy level even when it seems at first that his held notes might slow things down. Once again, Herschel makes the listener wish for more from his distinctive voice, especially after the ensemble closes in on him just as he appears to be catching fire. On *Topsy*, Evans participates in a type of call-and-response pattern, trading off his intensely swinging phrases with riffs shouted by the trumpet section. Durham's arrangements of *Time Out*, *Every Tub*, and *Topsy* buoy up the soloists through rocking rhythms and, in the case of *Topsy*, through his syncopated theme with its testifying muted trombones descending in minor thirds. As Gunther Schuller remarks, Durham, "who had contributed so creatively to the Moten band with his stunning arrangements for the 1932 recordings," helped "to solidify the [Basie] band's performance and gave it a more cohesive style, within the basic swing concept set by Basie."[26] *Swingin' the Blues*, another masterful arrangement by Durham, features, in addition to Evans, solos by Bennie Morton on trombone, Lester on tenor, Buck Clayton on trumpet, and Harry Edison on trumpet, as well as a marvelous three-trombone break. Durham's ensemble buildup to the penultimate solo by Evans is especially fine and sparks Herschel to a thrilling few bars of his passionately quaking, erupting tenor. From Evans's performances in these Durham originals and arrangements, it would appear that Herschel must have been especially pleased by and indebted to the services of his fellow Texan.

In creating a showcase for Evans with *Blue and Sentimental*, Durham provided just enough background ensemble passages to set the bluesy mood without obliging the tenorist to overblow.[27] Herschel is relaxed but impassioned in his delivery, and his soft vibrato achieves a rhapsodic effect that never lapses into mushy sentiment. Another Durham arrangement that features the tenor's lusher side is *I Keep Remembering*, recorded October 13, 1937. Here Herschel also avoids the saccharine tendency of so many tenor players yet adds during his few bars to the romantic flavor of this Isham Jones song, whose lyrics are effectively sung by Jimmy Rushing.[28] In characterizing the playing of Texas tenor saxophonists, Ross Russell notes that they "favored a softer sonority . . . with less vibrato [than Coleman Hawkins] and more blues inflection." Russell goes on to observe of Evans that, compared with Hawkins, he is "a dreamier and more imaginative saxophonist" and "his tone is warmer and softer and his phrasing somewhat more legato."[29] This is true even of Herschel's solo on his own upbeat composition, *Doggin' Around*, recorded on June 6, 1938. Here Evans plays at a much faster tempo than is usual for him; yet he remains relaxed and legato even as he invests his chorus with great intensity of feeling and drive. It is understandable why James Collier cites this solo as one of Herschel's two best, for certainly there is, in spite of the speed with which Evans plays, none of what Collier criticizes as Herschel's occasional "effect of frenzy that a jazz musician sometimes produces when he is striving for excitement but lacks the necessary ideas."[30] For his part, Gunther Schuller aptly describes Herschel's tenor solo on *Doggin' Around* as "virile eloquence" and identifies "the strong clarinet riding atop the final ensemble" as Herschel's as well.[31]

Owing to Schuller's own work as a composer, he tends throughout his writings on jazz to emphasize compositional artistry; thus he finds in Herschel's original composition *Texas Shuffle*, recorded on August 22, 1938, "something of the simplicity of method and cumulative energy fundamental to one of the better prototypical Basie-style riff arrangements."[32] In analyzing Evans's *Texas Shuffle*, Schuller is particularly struck by the fact that "the registral distribution of choirs . . . goes right back to the early days of jazz: every instrument has its assigned range and function, staying out of each other's way." Schuller reiterates this point and elaborates on it at length: "As Evans arranged things, they not only avoid colliding but complement each other, fusing—one could hear it that way—into a combined new melodic riff. . . . It should also be noted that this layering of three competing superimposed riffs would not have been possible had not the basic riff material been so extremely simple, thus avoiding polyphonic chaos. . . . The final half-chorus, softly marching off into the distance, is a minor miracle of musical-culinary artistry."[33] Herschel's *Texas Shuffle* not only stands as a classic riff arrangement, but it furnished the framework for four superb Basie soloists to improvise brilliantly: Harry Edison on trumpet, Lester Young on clarinet, Dickie Wells on trombone, and Herschel himself on tenor.

Even though the Basie band lost Buster Smith as a leading soloist and as an original arranger—"the man upon whom others relied to organize their musical ideas into new repertory pieces by means of sketches and skeleton arrangements"[34]—the acquisition of Herschel Evans and the "return" of Eddie Durham as soloists, arrangers, and composers gained for the band the crucial work of two other Texans who were responsible in large measure for the cohesive ensemble swing achieved by the Basie organization. One Buster Smith composition that was in fact recorded by the band is *The Blues I Like to Hear*, from November 16, 1938, which Schuller considers an indication of "how much further to the southwest Buster's Texas-based style was rooted, compared even with the somewhat peppier, 'smarter' Kansas City idiom. Listening to this side . . . , one cannot fail to note its distinctive sound and voice-leading, its 'crying' blues-drenched harmonies. Clearly, it has a totally different feel: simple and uncomplicated, earthy low-down blues with a heavy rocking beat."[35]

While the compositions of Evans and Durham may not have provided so much of this "Texas-based style," certainly both musicians subscribed to the blues and riff traditions developed in their home state, and both would greatly influence later developments in jazz, Evans standing as the first in a long line of Texas tenormen "with opulent, big thrashing sound"[36] and Durham—whose *Out the Window*, *Time Out*, and *Topsy* "are almost always included in listings of the Best of Count Basie"[37]—epitomizing the effective big-band jazz arranger who left ample room for soloists and generated high-energy riffs for the wind sections, a feature that, in the case of the Basie band, drove his sidemen to their most imaginative solo flights. Durham's *Time Out* has been declared "an exemplary Basie arrangement" that "encouraged a fine effect of suspense during Lester Young's solo"; likewise, Evans's *Doggin' Around* has been credited with providing the occasion for a solo by Basie that is "probably his masterpiece."[38]

Both Evans and Durham were gone from the Basie band by 1939—Herschel dying unexpectedly of a heart attack and Eddie leaving to do freelance arranging for other big bands. Evans's penultimate recorded solo came on *Panassie Stomp*, from

November 16, 1938, which is not up to his earlier work and may be explained perhaps by his failing health.[39] Taking Herschel's place would be yet another Texan, Buddy Tate, born in Sherman on February 22, 1915. Tate and Evans had played together in Troy Floyd's San Antonio band. Buddy was another Texan associated with Kansas City, having been with the Nat Towles band and with Andy Kirk's Twelve Clouds of Joy, which had originally been Terrence Holder's band. Like Lips Page, when the Blue Devils hired him, Tate also worked with Eddie and Sugar Lou's Austin band. Ross Russell has summarized Tate's career by relating it to the life of the southwestern jazzman, who was

> conditioned to change, and this accounts for the fluid personnel of some of the bands and the appearance of the same musician in many different bands. . . . Adjustment to change and the ability to work with other jazzmen from the general area helped create a common musical language. Change, tolerance for catch-as-catch-can living and eating arrangements, adversity and, in the case of black musicians who clearly dominated jazz in the area, the usual, expected, but always unpleasant and sometimes ominous Jim Crow situation—all seem to have combined to create in the Southwestern jazzman a musician of unusual originality, endurance, and self-reliance, and this spirit, in keeping with the character of the plains country, is reflected in the musical style.[40]

Buddy Tate's first recording date with Basie came on March 19, 1939, when the Count Basie Orchestra cut what was probably a head arrangement of *Rock-a-Bye Basie*, though credited to Jimmy Mundy as arranger.[41] This first appearance in place of Evans reveals Tate's similar sound but a style all his own—a tighter vibrato and wider interval leaps than in Herschel's solos. The medium tempo suits Buddy's relaxed but solidly swinging manner, though he would also be quite at home in a tune like the October 19, 1947, *Seventh Avenue Express*, which, as its title suggests, is a spirited piece taken at nearly runaway speed.[42] On *Taxi War Dance*, from the same date as *Rock-a-Bye Basie*, Tate's brief solo breaks do not amount to much but are marked by the identifiably Texas blues tradition of smeared notes falling off in a crying moan.[43] Certainly Buddy's two short passages cannot compare with Lester Young's opening chorus, which for Martin Williams "contains a bold enough use of . . . horizontal, linear phrases to have captivated a whole generation of players, and to seem bold still."[44]

Buddy Tate's personal favorite was his May 31, 1940, recording with Basie of *Super Chief*, a busy Jimmy Mundy arrangement that has Tate running the chords smoothly and with his own brand of relaxed drive.[45] By this time, as Gunther

Schuller suggests, Tate may have picked up some of Young's traits "without relinquishing entirely his more Hawkins/Evans–oriented approach."[46] Tate may well have been intimidated more by Young than Evans was, but by 1947 Buddy played with complete self-confidence, though by then other Texas tenors in the Herschel Evans mold, such as Arnett Cobb, were performing with equal authority if with less inventiveness than Tate. For a Jimmy Rushing vocal, *Bye, Bye, Baby*, recorded on December 12, 1947,[47] Tate was in top form, squealing in the upper register as would so many other tenor saxophonists who adopted this device, among them Texan Illinois Jacquet, Sonny Rollins, and Eddie "Lockjaw" Davis. Unlike Evans and Durham, Tate did not bring with him the skills of a composer-arranger, so in this respect he did not leave behind the same kind of legacy as his fellow Texans. However, during his ten years with Basie, Tate did carry on admirably in the Texas tenor tradition obviously favored by Basie and identified with his finest years as a leader of what some have thought to be the greatest jazz band of all time.

After a decade with Basie, Tate continued to record extensively with various groups, including one formed by another ex-Basie sideman, trumpeter Buck Clayton. On an album entitled *Buck and Buddy*, recorded on December 20, 1960, Tate still sounds much as he did during his time with the Count, utilizing some of his alternate fingerings in a fine rendition of *High Life*, which also includes some solid bass work by another Texan, Gene Ramey of Austin, who even takes what was for him an infrequent extended solo. In the album's final tune, *Kansas City Nights*, both Ramey and Tate are in a typical Basie-like groove, with Clayton's riff recalling "the good old days" when Buck played in the Count's Kansas City Seven.[48] Tate also recorded with three other brass players whose styles differ from Clayton's: cornetist Ruby Braff and trumpeters Humphrey Lyttleton and Clark Terry. On sampler albums released by the Black Lion label, Tate joins Braff and the Newport All-Stars on Ellington's *Take the "A" Train* and on *Mean to Me*, from October 1967, and turns in sterling performances in both tunes. Tate is featured with Lyttleton, one of the top British jazzmen, on *The One for Me*, from July 1974; here each takes an excellent solo, with Buddy performing this ballad in a lovely style reminiscent of Ben Webster at his best.[49] On *Tate-a-Tate* from 1962, one of a number of albums under his own name, Buddy, accompanied by Clark Terry, performs "in his usual brawny, muscular fashion—the tone . . . very large and the solos . . . free-and-easy, unhurried and swinging all the time."[50] In 1975 Tate made *The Texas Twister*, and the style of this album's title tune is straight out of the Basie book. Also included are two of the Count's classics, *Boogie-Woogie* and Eddie Durham's perennially popular *Topsy*.[51]

When Buddy Tate joined Basie in 1939, only one member from the original unit was a Texan, trombonist Dan Minor, who departed in 1941 (the same year that Lester Young left, which marked the end of the classic period of the Basie band). In 1948, when Tate moved on after the Count briefly disbanded, two other Texans would come to contribute significantly to the Basie organization: Gus Johnson of Tyler and Henry Coker of Dallas. Johnson, as we shall see in Chapter 10, was an important member of the Jay McShann Orchestra before figuring as "one of the most effective drummers ever heard with the Basie band"[52] and the first of Basie's "effusive drummers."[53]

Gus Johnson replaced Jo Jones on drums in 1948 and stayed with Basie until 1954, soloing to great effect on *Tootie*, a fast boogie recorded with Basie's octet on November 3, 1950.[54] A representative album of Johnson's work with Basie is entitled *Basie Rides Again* and was recorded on July 22 and 23, 1952. On *Be My Guest*, Johnson supports the Count's piano solo with a steady beat, and Gus's drums drive the tune's closing ensemble with great percussive power. Johnson's razzle-dazzle drumming on *No Name* rocks the band along, and his sharp snare work at the beginning of the tune shows off his tight time-keeping talents. With *Blues for the Count and Oscar*, Johnson provides behind the organ and piano a chink-chink rhythm that keeps, once again, a tight control over the proceedings and yet at the same time intensifies the swing. One of the most exciting tunes from this 1952 recording is *Every Tub*, which opens with Gus's shimmering ride cymbal that symbolizes the entire album, as truly "Basie rides again," especially on this Basie-Durham classic. The other big swinger is *Blee Blop Blues*, which features some of Johnson's rapid-fire drum fills and the closest thing to a break that he takes on this album. In general, Gus Johnson was a timekeeper, a foundational rhythm man. In what was billed as Basie's "New Testament" band (to distinguish it from the "Old Testament" unit of the late 1930s), Johnson preached his belief in the solid beat rather than showmanship.[55]

Trombonist Henry Coker was born in Dallas on December 24, 1919, and attended college in Marshall.[56] He started out with John White's band at sixteen and then joined Buddy Tate in the Nat Towles band during 1937. At the time of Pearl Harbor, Coker was playing in Hawaii, but in 1943 he returned to the States and worked for some four years with the Benny Carter Orchestra, recording his first solo on April 9, 1945, on *Malibu*.[57] Later, in February 1948, Coker showed that he could do his thing on *Bop Bounce*, a tune performed by the Carter orchestra for a radio broadcast, and in fact much of Henry's solo work with the Basie band would show the influence of bebop.[58] From 1949 Coker was a member of the Illinois Jacquet band, after which he joined Basie in 1952.[59] On September 2, 1954,

Coker would be showcased as the soloist on *Yesterdays*, and both Coker and Gus Johnson add greatly to the rocking treatments given by a Basie nonet on *In Case You Didn't Know*, *Ain't It the Truth*, and the Count's driving riff *Ingin' the Ooh* from September 7, 1954 ("a more than close derivative" of Eddie Durham's *Swinging the Blues*).[60] During his tenure, Coker was present on innumerable albums, including the highly popular *"April in Paris,"* on which the trombonist takes an outstanding solo on *Did'n You*, recorded on July 26, 1955,[61] and the equally exciting *Basie in London*, recorded on September 7, 1956, when Coker turned in an explosive opening break on *Jumpin' at the Woodside* and a blaring, bluesy, double-time solo with rapid tonguing, high notes, everything, yet controlled and full of meaning.[62] Coker also participated in perhaps the most popular Basie postwar recording, *The Atomic Mr. Basie*, which was made on October 21 and 22, 1957, and which introduced something of a hit tune in the delightful *Lil' Darlin'.*[63]

Most significantly, Henry Coker is the featured soloist on the Basie band's 1960 albums, *The Count Basie Story* and *Kansas City Suite*. The former is a retrospective of classic Basie tunes primarily from the 1930s (including Eddie Durham's *Swinging the Blues*, *Topsy*, and *Time Out* and Herschel Evans's *Texas Shuffle* and *Doggin' Around*),[64] and the latter a modern version of "the elements of Kansas City stomp jazz . . . tailored [by Benny Carter] for the big brash sound of the Basie band of today."[65] Coker also solos prominently on *Kansas City Wrinkles* from the 1963 album *Li'l Ol' Groovemaker . . . Basie!*[66] In many ways these three albums from the 1960s revisit the history of Kansas City jazz as developed from Bennie Moten to Count Basie, and Henry Coker's low-down blues solo on *Kansas City Wrinkles* is part of the unforgettable Kaycee story as retold by the last in a long line of vital Texas sidemen.

JONES-SMITH, INC., AND THE
KANSAS CITY FIVE AND SIX

The jazz scene in Kansas City during the 1930s was given over as much to jam sessions among small groups at all hours as it was to big bands, many of the latter having to travel out of town to find enough work to support their larger numbers. Smaller groups could gather in almost any saloon or night club so long as there was a piano, drum set, or guitar available to lay down a riff, a steady beat, or chords for a blues ballad or pop tune.[1] Owners often welcomed the jazz musicians and even treated them to sandwiches and drinks for the entertainment value of the "cutting sessions." Out of these small after-hours gatherings, held once the big-band jobs had ended, came much of the technique and many of the ideas adapted for use in the larger units. Indeed, for some musicians the real jazz was created in the more intimate setting of a small group, while the bigger bands tended to lose the true Kansas City spirit. Two such smaller groups made up of regular members of the Basie band were given the opportunity to record, and from these sessions came music closer to the Kansas City jam tradition, which in turn influenced developments in jazz known as the cool and bop revolutions. Both of these groups—Jones-Smith, Inc., and the Kansas City Five and Six—were nominally co-directed or led by Texans: Carl Tatti Smith and Eddie Durham.

Prior to the January 1937 recordings by the full thirteen-piece Basie band, John Hammond arranged a "clandestine" small-group session on October 9, 1936,[2] which was issued by the Brunswick-Vocalion label without Basie's name (for contractual reasons) under the "deceptively faceless heading" of Jones-Smith, Inc.[3] On this occasion a quintet—composed of Basie on piano, Walter Page on bass, Jo Jones on drums, Lester Young on tenor, and Carl Tatti Smith on trumpet—produced four sides that exhibit an easygoing style so different from the killer-diller approach of most of the swing-era big bands. Originally Hot Lips Page was slated to be the trumpet player for this date, but he had split his lip during the Basie band's show at Chicago's Grand Terrace and Carl Tatti Smith was brought in at the last minute. The inclusion of Smith may have been fortuitous in that his relaxed but very precise and under-control execution was more in keeping with the manner of Lester Young, while Lips Page represented the older Armstrong tradition of the hot, virtuoso trumpet style with its bold and power-house approach.

With this session, Lester Young would make his recording debut. Historically, these first sides by Lester and the rest of the combo mark the arrival of a new kind of jazz as well: cool rather than hot, restrained instead of exhibitionistic, under-stated in place of the endless string of notes adding up to very little that was becoming the fashion among both tenor saxophone and trumpet players in the popular big bands of the swing era. Not that Young and Smith could not keep pace with those musicians who specialized in running up and down the scales or rapidly repeating single notes to different rhythms and accents. On *Shoe Shine Boy* both soloists manage many sixteenth notes at an upbeat tempo, but the ideas contained in their choruses are fresh and singular, even today, with each phrase evolving naturally out of the one before.

Even though it was the performance by Lester Young that signaled a new epoch in jazz, the value of Smith's presence on this recording date has been appreciated by several prominent commentators. While acknowledging that Lips Page was "a superior soloist" with "a much more distinguished career," Gunther Schuller offers the view that "Smith was no mere 'surrogate' second-rater." He character-izes Smith's solo work as "fluent, clear in thought and form, at times inspired, as in his exciting entrance on *Shoe Shine Boy*," and finds Smith's note choices "inter-esting" and his solos "well shaped in overall form."[4] James Lincoln Collier calls Smith's solo on *Boogie-Woogie* "excellent . . . controlled, spare, and clean."[5] Eric Thacker, who also admires the trumpeter's solo work, terms his chorus on *Shoe Shine Boy* "vigorously lyrical," and in commenting on the quintet's recording of *Boogie-Woogie*, he speaks of Lester's "subdued but purposeful accompaniment to the trumpeter's muted solo."[6] Together the two hornmen engage in a call-and-response exchange, in which Lester "shows his cooperative generosity."[7] For Schuller, the full-band version of *Shoe Shine Boy*, entitled *Roseland Shuffle* and recorded on January 21, 1937, is "much less good" than the earlier quintet performance, and he notes that on the "slightly beefed-up arranged version" of 1937, "Lester repeats some of the same licks, now quite a bit staler."[8]

Schuller judges Lester's "crowning achievement" to be his solo in the George Gershwin tune *Oh! Lady Be Good*, which he designates "quintessential Lester Young: economical and lean, no fat, nothing extraneous, and masterful in its control of form."[9] Of this one solo, Martin Williams observes that "every phrase . . . has been imitated and fed back to us a hundred times in other contexts by Lester's followers."[10] Jo Jones simply called it "the best solo Lester ever recorded."[11] According to Schuller, Young's solo on *Oh! Lady Be Good* "led directly to a harmonic freeing up of the language of jazz without which Bop, Modern Jazz . . . and eventually musicians like Ornette Coleman, John Coltrane, and Eric Dolphy could not have evolved."[12] Indeed, the effect of Lester's solo on the next generation of bop musicians can be heard in the first rendition of this same Gershwin tune by Charlie Parker, recorded with the Jay McShann Orchestra on November 30, 1940.

As for Carl Smith's solo on *Oh! Lady Be Good*, Schuller suspects that even though it is a fine effort, the trumpet player "felt somewhat strait-jacketed by Young's not very inspired riffing behind him." Nonetheless, Schuller seeks to redress "the prevailing uncritically handed-down opinions on some of the lesser lights in jazz" by documenting the fact that, as in the case of Carl Smith, there were countless musicians from the territory bands "who for one reason or another never received the recognition they deserved."[13] Schuller may be correct in saying that Smith is "somewhat strait-jacketed," but in many ways his solo on *Oh! Lady Be Good* remains on a par with Lester Young's classic chorus. For one thing, Smith follows Young in limiting the range of his solo to concentrate on working out the harmonic and rhythmic possibilities of the Gershwin melody. Smith's use of a cup mute adds to the greater introspection of his performance and to its notable restraint vis-à-vis the excesses of the more virtuosic soloists of the era. In both respects Smith leads the way for a number of better-known Basie trumpeters who developed essentially the same approach, among them Buck Clayton, who replaced Lips Page for the January 1937 full-band recordings,[14] and Harry "Sweets" Edison, who joined Basie in September of that year. Certainly Smith's chorus on *Oh! Lady Be Good* is neither so varied nor so imaginative as Young's, yet it maintains the same type of "groove" in which Young worked out his startling innovations in terms of "melodic contours," "coherence, . . . simplicity, . . . linear fluency," and "harmonic shifts or modulations."[15]

Along with the groundbreaking work of Lester Young and the Basie rhythm section, in particular Jo Jones's unobtrusive but tasteful fills that support and stimulate the soloists, Carl Tatti Smith was a pioneer of sorts who showed the way but did not gain "the promised land" of recognition and fame, largely because after his brief stint with Basie he "sank into oblivion."[16] Reportedly, Smith moved to South America after World War Two and continued to play through the 1950s in Argentina and Brazil, but nothing more is known about this important "minor" figure.[17] Nonetheless, this Texan's part in the Jones-Smith, Inc., recording session places him at the scene of a "remarkable breakthrough—one which was to have far-reaching consequences and implications for later jazz."[18]

On March 18, 1938, John Hammond produced another session for Brunswick-Vocalion, this time devoted to the Kansas City Five, with Buck Clayton on trumpet, Jo Jones on drums, Walter Page on bass, Freddie Greene on acoustic guitar, and leader-arranger Eddie Durham on electric guitar. After Brunswick showed no interest in issuing the Kansas City Five recordings, Hammond informed Milt Gabler of the Commodore Music Shop in New York that he could purchase the sides if Gabler paid Brunswick for the cost of the session. Gabler did so with the idea that he would put together a total of eight sides using the same combo plus Lester Young.[19] Even though the sides by the Kansas City Five were designed to be the first "to feature jazz electric guitar," in point of fact Eddie Durham had already recorded on this instrument when he soloed on *Time Out* with the Count Basie Orchestra on August 9, 1937.[20] Nevertheless, the Kansas City Five recording session did allow Durham to "stretch out" on electric guitar and furnishes the fullest evidence of his influence on Charlie Christian, who would become the instrument's greatest proponent.

Of the four sides recorded by the Kansas City Five, the least interesting is *Love Me or Leave Me*, which was not issued with the other three takes in 1938 but was released only after it was discovered by Milt Gabler in 1978.[21] Although both Durham and Clayton play proficiently enough on *Love Me or Leave Me*, their ideas are not inspired, and Durham's solos tend to be chord changes rather than inventive lines or rhythms, although his second chorus does give glimpses of the kind of single-line technique that Charlie Christian would develop into his own unique style. As a precursor of Christian, Durham best exhibits his skills in this direction on *Laughing at Life*, where he plays in the long-lined, single-string manner identified with Christian. One can detect something of the entire early history of the Texas guitar tradition in Durham's chorus and in his brief break following Clayton's second muted chorus. Durham's performance abounds with rifflike figures as well as sixteenth-note pickups to boppish licks. He leaps from low to high notes, plays bluesy, falling-off moans, and utters sudden whines in the upper register. Even though Durham has at his command the power of amplification, his playing remains subtle and "cool" rather than "overblown," as with so many subsequent electric guitarists. Prior to Charlie Christian's first recordings with Benny Goodman in the fall of 1939, Durham had already indicated the potential for a full range of expression on the electric guitar. His solo on *Laughing at Life* can easily be taken as a preview of Christian's coming attractions.

Durham's arranging skills, as we have seen, were important to the Moten band as well as to the Basie band of the 1937–1938 period. As Eric Thacker points out, Durham attempted "to translate orchestrally what he heard happening in Kansas

City jam sessions."[22] This skill is particularly evident in the Kansas City Five recordings, where Durham achieves a relaxed, intimate relationship with Buck Clayton, backed by Page, Greene, and Jones. Both Page and Jones are given space for extended solos, which they rarely took as members of the full Basie band. More important is the interchange between Durham and Clayton that demonstrates Eddie's skills both as arranger and as a sensitive partner in a duo that listens to and feeds off one another. Thacker remarks on this aspect of the Kansas City Five's recordings when he observes, "The success of the unusual combination of trumpet and electric guitar in the three quintet performances is substantially due to [Durham's] linear and harmonic imagination. Clayton's indefinable amalgam of delicate sounds (whether his instrument is muted or open) and interior force complements Durham's conception beautifully, as their shared passages on *Laughing at Life* well show."[23]

While *Laughing at Life* is the fullest witness to Durham's talents as soloist and arranger, *Good Mornin' Blues* represents but one version of a Durham composition that enjoyed a distinguished career—from the August 9, 1937, recording with Jimmy Rushing doing the vocal to the rendition by Joe Williams on his famous Basie album of 1958, *Everyday I Have the Blues*. In the quintet version of *Good Mornin' Blues*, the mood is quite subdued and is taken at a slower tempo than in the 1937 and 1958 vocals. Page's bass is prominently featured and adds effectively, along with Durham's electric guitar, to Clayton's closing theme statement. Thacker notes that Durham's "wittily-timed guitar chords urge on the several swinging Clayton improvisations," especially in the final tune, *I Know That You Know*.[24] In this last piece in the set, Durham again solos nicely, recalling the work of Blind Lemon Jefferson with his bluesy pings and inventive riffs. Not so wide-ranging as his solo on *Laughing at Life*, this chorus still illustrates Durham's modern conception of a Texas tradition reaching back to the 1920s and looking forward to Christian's basic down-home blues that influenced the creation of bop through melodic invention based on riffs and extended chords and intervals.

With the Kansas City Six session of September 27, 1938, we have what a number of commentators have considered one of "those exceedingly rare works of man that do not beome stale."[25] Although the principal interest in these sides has been with the tenor saxophone performances of Lester Young and with his infrequent but highly prized appearances on clarinet, Durham's role in this session is historically significant for several reasons. For one thing, this recording date showcases the multitalented Texan as trombonist (on *Paging the Devil*), electric guitarist, and arranger and represents the culmination—though by no means the end—of a career that produced some of the finest jazz ever recorded. Even though Eric

Thacker has found fault with Durham's arrangement for Young's clarinet, especially on *Way Down Yonder in New Orleans,* James Lincoln Collier considers this "the masterpiece of the session," at least after Lester "reverts to the saxophone":

> In his handling of the tune [Young] departs to a degree from his more typical style. There are fewer open spaces; the phrases are not cut so neatly into two- and four-bar segments; and he shifts away from the bar lines more than usual in his practice. . . . Another characteristic of Lester's playing apparent in this solo is the constant rising and falling of the line. He runs upwards, pauses, then runs down and pauses at the bottom; then he surges upward again, shifting the volume of sound to follow the shape of the line.[26]

Much the same thing may be said of Durham's fine solo that follows. Eddie maintains the "cool" feeling of Lester's chorus and concludes his own solo with a smooth and satisfying transition into the ensemble's group improvisation that ends the performance. Like Lester, Eddie leaves behind for the most part the Dixieland tune and creates instead his own melodic ideas. Single-string lines that rise and fall and shift in volume and accent mark Durham's chorus, which is totally in keeping with the spirit of Young's celebrated "urbanity."

For many listeners, it was Lester's use of the clarinet on the Kansas City Six sides that resulted in his fashioning on *I Want a Little Girl* and *Paging the Devil* "two of the most beautiful jazz solos ever recorded on that instrument."[27] Nat Hentoff goes so far as to say that he would trade the collected works of "yes, even Benny Goodman" for the passages in which Young plays the clarinet.[28] On *Countless Blues,* Lester delivers a lightly swinging solo, also on clarinet, following Durham's western guitar routine, and as a whole this blues riff provides "substantial hints of what inspired the more celebrated Christian," demonstrating that "the ensemble approach of these small Basie units is usefully compared with the music of the Goodman sextets which featured Christian."[29] Taken together, the recordings made by the Kansas City Five and Six and those produced by Jones-Smith, Inc., stand as pinnacles of jazz history, bringing to bear on the tried and true practices of the past a new conception that would prove prophetic of developments in the 1940s and on into succeeding decades. The importance of both recording sessions was owing in part to the presence of two Texans who remain less known in the annals of jazz than some of the other musicians performing on these occasions, yet the roles played by Carl Tatti Smith and Eddie Durham deserve not only continued recognition but closer attention for their own special contributions to these two historic dates in the story of Kansas City jazz.

THE JAY MCSHANN ORCHESTRA, 1938–1942

With the conviction in 1938 of Tom Pendergast for income-tax evasion and his incarceration in the federal penitentiary at Leavenworth, the flourishing jazz scene fostered by the Kansas City mayor and his corrupt political system began to fall on hard times. The source of employment and support for the bands still operating in the city evaporated with the closing of the night clubs and cabarets. Into this twilight of the Kansas City heyday came the city's last important band, that of Jay McShann, who had arrived from Oklahoma to make his way as a blues and boogie-woogie pianist. After working with jazzmen from the earlier generation, among them Buster Smith, McShann organized his own trio and eventually expanded it to a sextet and later to a full big band. In McShann's orchestra he featured on alto saxophone the next great jazz star after Lester Young, Charlie "Bird" Parker, as well as two Texans, Gus Johnson on drums and Gene Ramey on bass. It was with the Jay McShann Orchestra that Charlie Parker would make his first recordings, accompanied by Johnson and Ramey. According to Ramey, who had known Parker since the altoist was about fifteen, or four years before he joined McShann,[1] all Bird needed to start on his road to stardom was the 1936 Jones-Smith recordings. Following the famous humiliation of Parker during a jam session at the Reno Club, when drummer Jo Jones threw his cymbal on the floor to stop Bird's dreadful performance, Charlie took those 1936 sides up into the Ozark hills and on returning after three months "startled everybody by playing Lester Young's solo on *Lady Be Good* note for note."[2]

Gene Ramey, who was born in Austin on April 4, 1913, began his career on tuba at thirteen, playing for a time with a local group, George Corley's Royal Aces. After high school Ramey received a scholarship to Western University in Kansas City, and when he arrived there in 1932 he immediately found music jobs and even organized his own fifteen-piece band. Although Ramey intended to major in

Charlie "Bird" Parker (left) and Gene Ramey of Austin.
Reprinted courtesy of Duncan Schiedt.

electrical engineering, he ended up concentrating on his music and in 1933 switched to string bass, studying with Walter Page and listening to the Moten band and later to Basie. At one point, after Basie's band went east, Ramey joined Bus Moten's band,[3] but it was meeting Jay McShann at a jam session that led in 1938 to Gene's joining the McShann orchestra, in which he "teamed admirably with Gus Johnson, a drummer with an aggressive style and bright, almost metallic sonority."[4] Johnson, who was born in Tyler on November 15, 1913, grew up in Beaumont and Houston and attended Booker T. Washington High School in Dallas, where he was a classmate with Basie trombonist Henry Coker. After graduation, Johnson went to live with his father in Kansas City, where Gus studied at Southern Junior College. In Kaycee, Johnson heard the bands of Moten, Andy Kirk, and George E. Lee, and while sitting in with pianist Pete Johnson at the Lone Star, Gus met drummer Jo Jones, who at the time had recently joined Basie's band.[5] Jones landed Johnson a job with a six-piece band, and after leaving that group Gus played with various units, touring the Midwest. When he returned to Kansas City in 1938 and met McShann, he joined forces in Jay's orchestra with Gene Ramey.

Together, Ramey and Johnson would help swing the McShann orchestra from the rhythm section, which was characteristic of the Kansas City bands, largely under the influence of Basie, Jo Jones, and Walter Page.[6] In Ramey's own words, "No band was great unless it had a strong rhythm section. It had to have a motor."[7] As members of the McShann orchestra, Ramey and Johnson would find themselves, beginning in 1939, in the company of Gene's lifelong friend, Charlie Parker, and would serve as the "motor" for the early days of Bird's monumental career. With regard to his long-range effect on Parker's development, Ramey remarked in one interview:

> I, myself, will take credit to this extent as far as Charlie Parker's career in jazz is concerned. It was I, his close friend and associate, who made Bird jam every day as a means of helping him to "evolve."
>   We would jam together—just the two of us, working out the relationship between notes and chords.[8]

Once the jobs in Kansas City had dried up, the McShann orchestra went on the road touring the Deep South, returned to Kaycee, and then went to Wichita, Kansas, where in the summer of 1939 the orchestra performed at the Plaza and was heard by two Wichita University students, Pete Armstrong and Fred Higginson. So impressed were these students that when the McShann orchestra returned to Wichita the following summer, they arranged to capture its August 1940 performance at the Trocadero Ballroom on a portable disc recorder. On *I Got Rhythm*, one of three numbers to survive from this recording session, the alto toward the end of the tune may be Parker's, although it is not clearly in the style of his solos recorded just three months later. But Ramey's bass and Johnson's drums come through loud and clear despite the poor sound quality of the recording. In fact, Ramey's bass is about as clear as it ever was, for his tone did not always seem to carry that well—possibly because he was double-jointed[9]—although on small group recordings Gene's sound is much more audible. Ross Russell has commented that "Ramey played with a flat, broad tone . . . he was a steady, unobtrusive, behind-the-beat section man, felt more often than heard, the pivot man around whom the band pulse centered."[10] It is clear from what Ramey had to say about Duke Ellington's early bass-drums combination that he was aware of the problem, for bass players like himself, of cutting through a big band: "I remember when *Ring Dem Bells* came out [April 20, 1930]. That was a totally different kind of rhythm section. For the first time you could hear the bass player [Wellman Braud] coming through, and [drummer] Sonny Greer knew how to team with that bass fiddle because it wasn't as strong and couldn't cut through like the bass horn had been doing."[11] Of course, Jelly Roll Morton's bass player with his Red Hot Peppers, John Lindsay, was probably the first to handle this problem, thanks in part to a fine RCA Victor recording of 1926. On the McShann recording of *I Got Rhythm*, Gus Johnson solos on drums with exceptionable spirit and expertly drives the band along with rolls, rim shots, and bass drum kicks. Without one of Parker's thrilling solos, however, the recording offers just another rocking Kansas City big band. Fortunately, the two university students interested Bud Gould, a staff musician at Wichita station KFBI, in hearing the orchestra, and subsequently Gould arranged for a recording session in the radio station's studio.

On the KFBI date of November 30, 1940, Parker is first heard in a full chorus on *Body and Soul*, made famous in jazz circles just the year before by Coleman Hawkins. The next tune with a Bird solo is the Basie-Durham classic, *Moten Swing*, where Parker "enters with a lilt, his bridge a marvelous mixture of note values: a happy, sweet solo."[12] Also on this take is a tenor solo by Bob Mabane, who plays in the style of Herschel Evans. Both Ramey and Johnson fulfill their supporting roles competently, but it is on *Coquette* that Ramey is especially effective behind the Bird, though rather repetitious when he backs the trombone solo by Bud Gould, who sat in with the band during this session. Even more interesting is Ramey's bass work on *Oh! Lady Be Good*, in which he lays down an inspiring beat and a choice of notes that could explain why, thanks to a glowing article by Dave Dexter in a *Down Beat* issue of 1938, Ramey was among those voted "promising new players" in a poll by the magazine.[13] During Parker's solo on *Oh! Lady Be Good*, Bird's dancing answer to Prez with quotes from *Mean to Me* that echo Lester,[14] the bassist is right on the beam, throbbing away in the upper range to approach the altoist's higher register and to urge him on. Both Ramey and Johnson are also effective in backing up McShann's piano solo.

For the final tune of this November 1940 session, Fats Waller's *Honeysuckle Rose*, Ramey seems more agile than ever and again complements Parker's solo by working the higher range of his instrument, plucking the strings at the neck for all they're worth and at an up-tempo. Ross Russell observes that Johnson's "fast hands and feeling for accents made him an ideal companion for Gene Ramey."[15] Johnson is punctuating throughout the piece, but gives just one push at the beginning of Parker's solo; then, with the exception of a few light accents, he leaves it to the Bird to do the rest, staying out of the soloist's way in deference to this teenage master. Johnson does take a short drum solo before an ensemble riff leads to Parker's second break, but afterward Gus remains unobtrusive in his role as timekeeper. As for Parker's solo work on *Honeysuckle Rose* and *Moten Swing*, Gunther Schuller has declared,

> Nothing quite like it had ever been heard before on the saxophone, and for that matter, in jazz. . . . [T]hink across the 1940 spectrum and see if you can find anything even remotely as fresh, daring, *and* substantial as Parker's playing. It is, in fact, remarkable in retrospect that, given Parker's precocious originality [he was only nineteen], virtually nobody took notice of him until years later, say, in 1945.[16]

It is interesting to recall that *Honeysuckle Rose* and *Lazy River* were the only tunes Parker knew when he first tried to jam at the High Hat in Kansas City. When he tried to play *Body and Soul* with the rest of the group and went into a "double tempo," one of his trademarks in later years, he was laughed off the stage and reportedly "went home and cried and didn't play again for three months."[17]

Charlie Parker's 1942 recordings include what is thought to be his first recorded version of *Cherokee*, a tune that became for him the means of a breakthrough into "something else . . . the thing I'd been hearing."[18] Done with a different orchestra in New York, using what sounds to Dan Morgenstern like a "pre-arranged accompaniment," this version is "an antecedent of Parker's 1945 masterpiece *Koko*" and "reveals a harder, more lifting sound than the McShann sessions." Even though Morgenstern finds that "there is increased rhythmic freedom" in this performance, he comments that the orchestra's rhythm section "hasn't the drive of McShann's."[19] On February 13, 1942, Parker was back with the McShann orchestra for a number of sides recorded live at the Savoy Ballroom in New York.

Gus Johnson of Tyler. Reproduced from the Ross Russell Collection, courtesy of the Harry Ransom Humanities Research Center, University of Texas at Austin.

Although the McShann unit was now in New York, it remained "a genuine Kansas City riff orchestra, which, during the years of Parker's internship, served as an incubator to bop."[20] This connection is evident in the group's recording of *Swingmatism*, which illustrates "how, with a good 'swing' rhythm section, one can play bebop and still have it fit."[21] Gene Ramey is solid on the 1942 *Swingmatism*, swinging with ensembles and soloists alike, pulsating with a particularly strong beat in tandem with Bird's brilliant chorus, which, as so often, seems to come soaring in from "Out of Nowhere." An earlier version of *Swingmatism*, recorded in Dallas on April 30, 1941, found the band delivering its phrases with more bite, and this briefer rendition also has Gus Johnson kicking the band along with even more precision and punch.[22] In general, Johnson's drums are almost a melodic instrument, as he underscores the band's notes with just the right sound on his trap set.

It is understandable from his work with the McShann orchestra why Johnson was later selected in 1956 for the album *The Drum Suite*, "the first time that anyone had attempted to integrate four drummers in a jazz composition." On this composed suite of six movements featuring the different percussion instruments employed by jazz musicians (drums, sticks, brushes, cymbals, etc.), Manny Albam and Ernie Wilkins wrote out "a series of melodic, swinging, carefully constructed sketches in which the drums share with—but rarely supersede—the horns and reeds in carrying out the development of the composers' ideas." As one of the "four top stick men" at the time and a steady hand, Gus Johnson was chosen as the main drummer, "always keeping time" when he was not soloing.[23]

Another outstanding tune from the 1942 Savoy Ballroom recordings is the seemingly unlikely *I'm Forever Blowing Bubbles*. This 1919 chestnut was ordinarily "the stuff of which swing band flagwaver dreams" were made, but here it is translated "into a Kaycee style riff."[24] In this number Ramey is at his best, his tone carrying beautifully and his notes just the ones needed to send chills down one's spine. Johnson too is superb, his driving accents adding verve and punch to a ripping performance. With all the energy generated by the McShann rhythm section and the orchestra's swinging treatment of the theme, it might seem impossible to heighten the excitement any further, but just then Parker bursts out with a chorus that is breathtaking, his dips and flips in anticipation of bop simply astounding. The audience's yells in the background are obviously a spontaneous reaction to the showstopping entrance of this rising star.

It is easy to see why Bird would have grown impatient with playing in big bands, where opportunities for blowing and developing his ideas were limited to a few brief solos. This problem is best illustrated by the long wait he has for a chorus in the first tune broadcast from the Savoy, McShann's *St. Louis Mood*. But for a listener the wait is well worth it, especially since the orchestra builds nicely through a blues progression that "showcases each section," with Johnson and Ramey doing their thing ever so well. The pair of rhythm makers is particularly fine behind the trumpet solo that precedes Bird's chorus. Once Parker enters, one can only agree with Robert Bregman that "all superlatives apply to the ease in which Bird handles his solo—it's buoyant, joyful, and smooth, a pleasure to listen to."[25] Again, Parker's conception is in advance of the advent of bop and exhibits so many of his later tricks of the trade, including the bebop artist's inclination to quote from other tunes (in this case, *Isle of Capri*), fitting the pieces seamlessly into the fabric of a blues chord progression. A slow blues composed by McShann and Parker, *Hootie Blues*, reveals Bird's Kansas City pedigree and indicates the direction his playing would soon take, for the sound, swing, and blues-inspired ideas are all there, waiting for him to find a way to go beyond "the stereotyped changes."[26]

At the Dallas session of April 30, 1941, the rhythm section of McShann, Ramey, and Johnson recorded as a trio when the group cut three sides, one of which, *Hold 'Em Hootie*, anticipated the gospel and funky styles that developed in the 1950s.[27] *Hold 'Em Hootie* contains a wonderful "running commentary by Gus Johnson's sticks on the rim of his snare drum" that "sounds much like a tap-dancer," while *Vine St. Boogie* exhibits Johnson's "smooth brushwork." *So You Won't Jump* demonstrates Johnson's fine handling of a snare-drum solo, which he rarely took in his work with Basie. On *Vine St. Boogie* and *So You Won't Jump*, Ramey not only pumps along with solid swing behind McShann but the bassist also solos quite effectively. Indeed, Ramey and Johnson both contribute mightily to this trio performance. Later in Chicago, on November 18, the trio was joined by guitarist Leonard Enois to record seven tunes. On *Red River Blues* Ramey and Johnson exhibit what aptly has been called their "prescient accents." With *Baby Heart Blues*, the quartet is "loose as a goose," and on *Crying Won't Make Me Stay* Johnson's cymbal "breathes" and leaves "a lot of space for both McShann and Ramey to swing in." Johnson's snare drum is especially impressive on *Hootie's Ignorant Oil*, lending to this "double-time blues" a fresh and infectious feeling.[28]

Gus Johnson left the McShann band in 1943, and not until 1972 would he, Ramey, and McShann come together for a reunion on the album *Going to Kansas City*. On this retrospective recording Jay recalls the boogie-woogie era with his fine performance of *Hootie's Ignorant Oil*, while the trio—plus Buddy Tate on tenor—revives *Moten Swing* from the Moten-Basie-Durham days. Tate also recaps the career of Herschel Evans in his solos for *Doggin' Around* and *Blue and Sentimental*, while Ramey's tune, *Say Forward, I'll March*, which was featured in the early 1940s by McShann's orchestra, contains the seeds of bebop, another of the great Kansas City–inspired developments.[29] The rhythm section is well recorded here, with Johnson sounding as steady as ever, Ramey better than ever, and McShann his irrepressibly spirited self. In the album's liner notes, Bill Weilbacher sums things up: "The McShann-Johnson-Ramey rhythm section . . . had confounded and delighted jazz fanciers in the late 'Thirties, following the miraculous Basie rhythm section out of Kansas City, suggesting in their wonderful cohesiveness and superb drive that the Basie emergence was not a chance happening but that rather Kansas City was the seat of a very important, until just then unsuspected, tradition in the making."[30]

After 1943, Gene Ramey and Gus Johnson would continue their careers as respected timekeepers, Ramey participating, as we shall see, in a number of developments during the bop and hard bop movements, and Johnson, as already noted, joining forces with the later Basie band, appearing with his fellow Texan

Henry Coker on the early 1950s albums *The Best of Basie* and *Basie Rides Again.*[31] Like the other Texas jazzmen who made their way to Kansas City, Ramey and Johnson were an integral part of the history of jazz that was made by or with the support of Texas musicians. Although jazz has never been the exclusive property of any one time or place, it is true, as Marshall Stearns has pointed out, that toward the end of the 1920s "the real peak of jazz intensity was shifting to the Southwest," where "one of the focal points for this musical revolution was Kansas City," as it remained until the collapse of the Pendergast machine.[32] In the meantime, other areas of the country continued to produce jazz figures, many of whom tended to congregate in New York and Chicago and many of whom, once again, included Texans from every part of the state. The pull of these two northern cities was natural and for the most part inevitable, for they were the centers of the recording industry and the music business in general. Some few Texans avoided the frantic lifestyle that went along with the advantages of a metropolitan existence; others tried their luck in New York and Chicago and failed or, if they succeeded, simply preferred to return to Texas.[33] Of those who did try their luck up north, a goodly number would leave permanent marks on the jazz associated during the 1920s and 1930s with both the Big Apple and the Windy City.

PART

3

GOING TO NEW YORK AND CHICAGO

A TROMBONE TRIO

When Jack Teagarden arrived in New York City in the fall of 1927 and began playing his trombone in such established venues as the Roseland Ballroom opposite the Fletcher Henderson Orchestra that had been the featured attraction there since 1924, the Texan was taken as someone from "another world."[1] Henderson was stopped in his tracks by what he heard, and according to a member of the Scranton Sirens, the band with which Teagarden was performing in April 1928, Henderson "would take Jack all over Harlem at the end of our evening, showing him off as if he were a man from Mars."[2] Another view held that Teagarden was a "phenomenal young trombonist who had just blown into town from the wild and woolly Southwest . . . through whose completely new style the entire concept of what a jazz trombone could sound like was being changed."[3] Still another version of the Teagarden story maintains that if there are classifications by school—Dixieland, swing, bop, or modern—and "convenient subdivisions of Kansas City, Chicago, New York," none of these applies to Jack, who "not having planted his adolescent roots in the soil of the traditional jazz orchards . . . is afforded a separate slot. Woe be to the critic who dares approach the maverick with branding iron in hand."[4] The consensus was and remains that Jack Teagarden figures as "one of the sturdy oaks of jazz who bends to no one,"[5] and that "after the shock of his 1927 charge on New York wore off, most Eastern trombonists set about the task of reorganizing their concepts of what could be done with the horn."[6]

In many ways, Jack Teagarden's appearance on the New York scene in 1927 was comparable to the startling emergence of Charlie Parker in Kansas City around 1940. Just as a number of different observers and commentators have described Teagarden as seemingly dropping from the skies and as a maverick, others have remarked on the similarities between the Texan's revolutionary approach to jazz and that of Bird and the beboppers. Richard Hadlock, for example, has noted Teagarden's construction of a melodic line—on his April 18, 1929, recording of *Indiana*—using "sixths and diminished, major, and minor sevenths and ninths," which, as Hadlock sees it, suggests some of the notions propounded by Parker and others ten or fifteen years later: "Teagarden, like Charlie Parker in later years, played rhythmically propulsive, blues-touched, emotionally satisfying jazz *first*, then added the melodic and harmonic interest."[7] Max Harrison also comments on Teagarden's ear "for harmonic subtleties" that in the late 1920s was

> matched only by Coleman Hawkins, Bix Beiderbecke and a very few others, and his interpolation of ambiguous diminished chords and treating major triads as if they were minor are especially noteworthy. This last is related to his sensitive use of blue notes—flat sevenths as well as the commonplace flat thirds—and the authenticity of his feeling for this idiom is apparent in . . . , above all, *Dirty Dog* [ca. April 1929] and *St. James Infirmary*, two of the best recordings of his career.[8]

In referring to the February 8, 1929, recording of *That's a Serious Thing*, Gunther Schuller has observed that this is "vintage Teagarden . . . in already a very modern stance: concise, economical, fluent, ornamented with lots of tricky bop-ish turns."[9] Later, in 1950, Teagarden "floored the beboppers of the time" with a version of *Lover* that astounded them with "its technical and inventive prowess."[10] Finally, George Hoefer found that although Teagarden was "not a bop musician," he nevertheless "made bop possible for trombone, handling the quick changes with the ease of a skilled trumpet player."[11] How this young trombonist from Texas showed up in New York with a mature technical and stylistic command of his instrument may never be fully explained, but it is clear from all accounts that even when Teagarden "toys provocatively with minor sevenths and augmented chords," he never loses "the blues idea."[12] As a player of the blues, Teagarden was, even from the beginning of his career, fundamentally a soloist rather than an ensemble jazzman in the New Orleans tradition of group improvisation. Gunther Schuller attributes this tendency to "the influence of the Texas solo blues-singing he grew up with."[13]

Born in Vernon on August 29, 1905, Jack Teagarden remembered, from his youth in that farm community near the Oklahoma border, how he listened to spirituals at "Holy Roller" tent revivals and hummed along "with no trouble at all."[14] Like Bob Wills, inventor of Texas Swing and another Texas musician influenced by the blues, Teagarden seems to have heard his first great blues through the singing of Bessie Smith.[15] Between 1921 and 1923, in the Houston home of legendary pianist Peck Kelley, Teagarden and clarinetist Pee Wee Russell apparently studied Bessie Smith recordings,[16] but reportedly Jack also heard Bessie, as Wills did, in person: "[Teagarden's] feeling for the blues, unique among white musicians, was already stirring. It awakened fully one night in a shabby theatre on the north side of [Galveston] when, tears blurring his eyes, he heard Bessie Smith sing *Cold in Hand* and a number of other blues."[17] Around 1924, Teagarden also reportedly heard recordings of Louis Armstrong accompanying "blues singers of the coloured vaudeville circuit,"[18] which may well have included some of the Texas women discussed earlier. On Armstrong's recordings, Teagarden not only encountered blues in a jazz setting, but he picked up on Louis's trumpet technique that he would carry over into his own playing of the trombone.[19] Martin Williams emphasizes the idea that Teagarden himself was "authentically a blues man . . . he could play the twelve-bar blues with a real feel for the idiom, and not just playing in the form. . . . His blues playing was not like any other man's blues." For Williams, this "attests to the individuality Teagarden was able to find in the idiom, not to a lack of authenticity."[20]

When Teagarden arrived in New York, the leading white trombonist of the day, Miff Mole, was rhythmically still playing in the tradition of ragtime, even though harmonically he was quite progressive for the 1920s. On Teagarden's first important recording date, March 14, 1928, Jack would substitute for Miff Mole in the orchestra of Roger Wolfe Kahn: "His full-chorus solo on *She's a Great, Great Girl*, though suggestive of Mole's approach and less positive than later Teagarden solos, is unmistakably the work of a mature jazz trombonist with ideas well in advance of most of his contemporaries. Furthermore, he sets forth these ideas in the warm blues dialect of the South rather than in the more stilted rag-time based phraseology of the Northeast. The effect is stunning."[21] No one in New York would have mistaken Teagarden for Mole, not with Jack's smooth entrance that has all the "cool," casual, "lazy," and lyrical flow that remained his inimitable trademark. As for technique, Teagarden will suddenly pick off a high note in passing, just as Mole would, but Miff's method of single-note rapid tonguing and Jack's legato but deceptively quick note production were worlds apart. More unique, however, is the southwestern style that Teagarden exhibits in this early jazz solo—the paradoxical ease of his phrasing has in it a relaxed yet driving rhythm that *sounds* regional. This is the same feeling that one has from Ornette Coleman's 1959 *Ramblin'*, which has been called "an idealized Texas-style improvisation."[22] Otis Ferguson, writing in the *New Republic* in the mid-1930s, may have touched on this sound when he noted of Teagarden that "in both tonal and rhythmic attack there is that constant hint of conquest over an imposed resistance which is peculiar

Jack Teagarden of Vernon, 1920. Reproduced courtesy of Duncan Schiedt.

to jazz and therefore indefinable in other terms."[23] But even this description does not capture the peculiar "Teagarden style" that sets off his playing from that of the musicians of his day, including those in New York and elsewhere who attempted to imitate the Texan's fluid, blues-inflected manner.

In general, commentators on Teagarden's career have relied on accounts of his formative years to explain a technical proficiency that featured "a highly plastic embouchure and a fast, close-to-the-chest right arm."[24] According to the story told of his being drafted into the Vernon City Band at the age of eleven, Teagarden at that time had arms too short to reach beyond fourth position on the slide, so he learned to lip the notes he needed to play. Teagarden also had perfect pitch and "could call off the overtones of a thunder clap."[25] While technical shortcuts and natural abilities provided Teagarden with special skills, it was perhaps more than anything his being well traveled, as Frank Driggs observed about southwestern jazzmen, that holds the secret to Jack's bursting on the New York scene as a full-blown jazz artist who was, like Eddie Durham, something of a triple threat: a "perfunctory 'hot' soloist, [an] earthy blues singer-instrumentalist, and [a] creative melodist."[26] Unlike Durham and the black jazz figures from Texas who were also well traveled, Teagarden moved in another circle and did not end up, as they did, in Kansas City. He did, however, visit there with the Ben Pollack Orchestra around 1931 and met Mary Lou Williams, who heard Jack sing some blues and later recalled: "I thought he was more than wonderful."[27] Teagarden may have also worked in Kaycee as early as 1924, when he was with the Will Robison Deep River Orchestra.[28] But Teagarden's more particular circuit began in 1921 at the age of sixteen, when he left home to play with an uncle in San Angelo, moving from there to San Antonio, where he played at the Horn Palace with Cotton Bailey's band. To "the Horn Palace boys," jazz was "pure adventure": "None of them had heard any of the jazz and ragtime records just beginning to flow into the limited city markets. No publicized trends or predecessors' talents influenced them. Their origins were aural."[29]

In the summer of 1921 Teagarden worked in Shreveport, Louisiana, at the Youree Hotel; in the fall he joined Peck Kelley's Bad Boys and played the Houston area until 1923. Howard Waters reports that during this period, in 1922, Teagarden participated in the Musicians Jazz Festival in Houston, which Richard Hadlock concludes is "almost certainly the first jazz festival on the books."[30] Kelley's band departed from the usual dance hall groups in not sticking to the melody of the trite popular tunes of the day but improvising instead, and thus "their endeavours formed the mainstream of authentic jazz."[31] After working for a time in the oil fields, Teagarden toured with R. J. Marin's Southern Trumpeters as "The South's Greatest Sensational Trombone Wonder," traveling through Texas, Oklahoma, and as far as Mexico City. Marin claimed that a 1924 broadcast by the Southern Trumpeters had elicited 640 letters and telegrams, more than had "any orchestra in the entire U.S.A. since radio started."[32] That radio served to spread jazz and to influence its performers is perhaps the most significant interpretation to be placed on this particular claim.

In 1924 Teagarden left Marin's band for Doc Ross and his Jazz Bandits, which played at theaters, dance halls, open-air shows, tank towns, and saloons, making "every hamlet in Texas with a population over five hundred." After the Ross band traveled to California and foundered in Los Angeles, Teagarden and a few of the members headed for New York, where, instead of finding the sort of "barnstorming vigour" they were accustomed to in the Southwest, they encountered "a pattern of grimly sentimental melodies framed within heavy ornate arrangements."[33] This style is apparent in *She's a Great, Great Girl*, where even jazz violinist Joe Venuti sounds simply saccharine next to Teagarden's virile trombone rooted solidly in the blues tradition.

Despite the fact that professionally Teagarden worked most often with white groups, he was drawn to black jazzmen when the occasion permitted. Either musicians like Coleman Hawkins and Jimmy Harrison invited Jack to visit their homes in Harlem for jam sessions or, on those rare opportunities when studios in the 1920s and 1930s allowed mixed groups to record, he was included on historic sessions with those figures he so admired and emulated, in particular Louis Armstrong and Bessie Smith. The first such meeting of black and white jazz musicians in which Teagarden participated was a recording date on February 8, 1929, with Eddie Condon's Hot Shots. To illustrate how original an improviser Teagarden was, Gunther Schuller observes that on one of two takes of *That's a Serious Thing*—in which there are "dramatic differences" between Teagarden's solos—the trombonist plays a phrase that is "almost identical to the melody of *Stormy Weather*," a Harold Arlen song composed four years later.[34] This recording also exhibits the complementary styles of black trumpeter Leonard Davis and Big T, who is "at his most elegant and a perfect foil for the fervent playing" of Davis.[35] This meeting of black and white shows how at home Teagarden was with an authentic jazzman like Leonard Davis, whose stop-time obbligato behind Jack's vocal chorus is intensely exciting but does not detract from Teagarden's "purring lacy delivery and languid Texas drawl."[36] Even more remarkable is the fact that in the collective improvisation at the end, Teagarden is obviously inspired by Davis to contribute to the ensemble with unusual success. This is no accident, for in the second tune recorded on this date, *I'm Gonna Stomp Mr. Henry*, Teagarden again renders some fine ensemble work, returning the favor with a hot lick behind Davis's statement of the theme; he then joins the trumpeter for a collective passage that is superior to most of Jack's ensemble efforts.

I'm Gonna Stomp Mr. Henry was also recorded with another group on March 5, 1929, but this time Eddie Lang on guitar replaced Condon on banjo, Kaiser Marshall replaced George Stafford on drums, Louis Armstrong replaced Davis, and clarinetist Mezz Mezzrow dropped out, while Teagarden, Joe Sullivan on piano, and Happy Caudwell on tenor sax remained from the earlier date. Although *I'm Gonna Stomp Mr. Henry* was never issued,[37] the other tune from this session—*Knockin' a Jug*—resulted, as Ross Russell declares, in an outstanding performance that illustrates "the disservice done to musical culture in this country by the American apartheid system."[38] However, despite the many glowing accounts of *Knockin' a Jug*, this recording is not "an arresting performance,"[39] largely because Kaiser Marshall's percussion work is so intrusive and ill advised. Even though Teagarden's opening statement shows "the rapid advance then being made on jazz trombone, especially when his is compared with the trombone solos on Armstrong's previous records,"[40] the solo is almost covered up first by Marshall's sticks on the snare drum rim and then by his heavily recorded brushes on the drum head. This is so distracting that even if Teagarden can be heard, his playing seems to take a back seat to the drummer's tasteless timekeeping. The same thing happens to the other soloists, including Armstrong. The effect is to make this piece a feature for Kaiser Marshall instead of for the horn players. The louder Louis plays, the more overbearing is the drummer's insistence, except during Armstrong's cadenza. Here Marshall relents and lays his brushes aside, but unfortunately not nearly soon enough, for the damage has been done from the beginning of Teagarden's solo up to the cadenza, which is followed only by the ensemble close. Neither trombonist nor trumpeter can really show his stuff under these conditions, which are hardly optimum: not only does the drummer spoil the occasion of Teagarden and Armstrong's first meeting on records, but the early eight o'clock hour of the recording session after a night out, not to mention the gallon jug of whiskey for which the tune was named, certainly did not help matters. To hear Louis to better advantage, it is only necessary to listen to his performance later that same day when he recorded *Mahogany Hall Stomp*, on which even J. C. Higginbotham turns in a superior trombone solo in terms of its swing.[41]

While the first Armstrong-Teagarden recording is a memorable meeting and still carries with it historical significance, the performance cannot compare with the interchange between Teagarden and Leonard Davis. As corny as the vocal is in *To Be in Love*, recorded by Armstrong on June 4, 1929, even Tommy Dorsey takes a fine break that shows how much he has already learned from Teagarden. It is simply difficult to find in Teagarden's playing in *Knockin' a Jug* what Gunther Schuller calls an "expansive, explosive solo,"[42] for even without the distracting racket made by Marshall, there is little in this solo that can hold up against Teagarden's best, although it may be superior, as Schuller asserts, to Jimmy Harrison's recorded work up to this date. The one thing that is undeniable is that

Teagarden's playing on this 1929 recording is his alone, immediately identifiable as the sound and phrasing of the man who changed jazz trombone forever.

Following this historic union with Armstrong, Teagarden would perform with one of many Red Nichols groups, replacing Miff Mole on trombone and singing one of the tunes with which the Texan would be identified for the rest of his career, *Basin Street Blues*, recorded on June 11, 1929. As Stanley Dance remarks, Teagarden's vocal with its "burnished tone" gave him "a permanent lien" on this number,[43] and as Gunther Schuller observes, Teagarden's singing is mirrored by his "fine Armstrong-like trombone solo in his best 'vocal' style."[44] Whitney Balliett has described Teagarden's singing as "a distillation of his playing" that "formed a kind of aureole around it. He had a light baritone, which moved easily behind the beat. The rare consonants he used sounded like vowels, and his vowels were all puréed. His vocals were lullabies—lay-me-down-to-sleep patches of sound."[45] The other tune that became almost the sole property of Teagarden was W. C. Handy's *Beale Street Blues*, with its lyrics about being born in Texas and raised in Tennessee—which some writers took as literal truth about Teagarden and "had him learning his licks in the Great Smokies!"[46] Recorded on October 22, 1931, with the Eddie Lang–Joe Venuti All-Star Orchestra, the *Beale Street Blues* session included Benny Goodman and Jack's brother Charlie, whose "considerable talent can be sampled" in such tunes as this and the other numbers recorded on the same date, especially *After You've Gone* and *Farewell Blues*, the latter of which contains a driving solo by Charlie that even upstages Big T.[47] Jack's vocals in all three of these tunes are "explosive and exhilarating," and that goes for his trombone solos as well.[48] Teamed with his brother Charlie, Jack seems both secure and relaxed in his playing, as he would be in an October 23, 1934, session with the great bass saxophonist Adrian Rollini's orchestra, which included Bunny Berigan on trumpet and Benny Goodman on clarinet. On this occasion, both the slow version of Bix Beiderbecke's *Davenport Blues* and the medium-tempo rendition of *Riverboat Shuffle* feature Teagarden in top form, even though he was no longer free to record whenever he wished with suitable ensembles like this one, having by this time become a permanent member of the basically nonjazz Paul Whiteman Orchestra.

Two historic sessions that preceded the 1934 date with Adrian Rollini found Teagarden participating in the last recordings ever made by Bessie Smith and the first sides cut by Billie Holiday. On November 24, 1933, Bessie recorded four tunes with a mixed group that included Teagarden on all four numbers and Benny Goodman on the one entitled *Gimme a Pigfoot*. Even though it seemed that by 1931 Bessie was "washed up as a commercial recording artist," she still managed to belt out four songs "constructed in the style of 16-bar blues," which "abound in colorful slang."[49] Admittedly, Teagarden's part on this recording is minimal, but his presence at this final session by the "Queen of the Blues" must have meant much to the Texan. On *Do Your Duty* Teagarden does just that, contributing one of his patented blues choruses, fitting in beautifully with Frankie Newton's trumpet and Chu Berry's tenor sax. On *I'm Down in the Dumps*, Teagarden also has the rare privilege for a white jazzman of playing obbligato behind Bessie's vocal and does so with very convincing results, infusing the background figures with Jack's peculiar blues quality.

Through Teagarden's own blues singing he could well appreciate Bessie's great artistry, and on an early recording like his *It's So Good*, dating from June 6, 1929, he had already shown that he knew the meaning of the blues. With what was another first for Teagarden, the trombonist recorded on *It's So Good* a bluesy solo on trumpet before singing "a kind of classic" in his "slightly reedy vocal timbre, slurred-over lyrics, and casually free rhythms."[50] In Gunther Schuller's evocative description,

> Teagarden sounds like an itinerant Texas blues-shouter, suddenly transported into the New York studios. Take away Rodin's band and imagine a simple four-string guitar accompaniment instead, and the listener is transported right back to central Texas blues country. Whether by choice or by accident, Bud Freeman's harshly guttural tenor and, later, thinnish, amateurishly clarinet underline the strange primitivism of this performance. Without knowing the record, one would assume it to have been recorded on location in San Angelo, Texas, at 2:00 a.m.[51]

A later vocal by Teagarden rates in Schuller's estimation as one of the Texan's greatest accomplishments as a singer, his rendition of *Nobody Knows the Trouble I've Seen*, recorded on July 7, 1941: "In the understated intensity of its feeling, the inner radiance and genuine soulfulness, it ranks with the finest jazz-singing offered through the years—from Bessie and Billie to Calloway, Sinatra, and Rushing."[52]

In 1933, Billie Holiday was the rising new female vocalist who would, in a sense, be the first and the last great jazz singer—not a blues singer but a jazz musician whose instrument was her voice. Although some critics have felt that Holiday's debut—on two sides cut with a Benny Goodman group composed of white players and black trumpeter Shirley Clay—does not show her as the artful, personally expressive "Lady Day" that she would become, Billie is already masterful and appealing in her delivery of the lyrics on *Your Mother's Son-in-Law* and *Riffin' the Scotch*.[53] Even here, with a unique blend of girlish innocence and knowing musicality, Holiday swings subtly and enunciates with a delicious sensuality that no other female singer has ever duplicated. As for Jack Teagarden, he comes riding in with more of his smooth but fiercely driving choruses that seem to arrive in the New York studios from right off the open plains. If the two styles sound incompatible, they are not, for Teagarden's horn solo on *Your Mother's Son-in-Law* shares with Holiday's vocal some of the same exuberance in the face of the wistful (and even inappropriate) lyrics, as well as the same sort of relaxed swing that Billie would be attracted to in the playing of Lester Young.

Certainly Holiday's later performances with Young and another native Texan, Teddy Wilson, are more representative of her mature artistry.[54] However, on her recording of *Your Mother's Son-in-Law*, made on November 27, 1933, Billie is already utilizing to great effect her slight quavering drop at the end of words—a type of shake probably adopted from Armstrong's trumpet style. The articulation of syllables is as clear and expressive as it will be in her majestic years from 1935 to 1939, at the same time that she begins certain words with a gruffness that lends them emotive force and personality. Likewise, Teagarden's notes can be alternately clear and raspy, and at times they will be suspended with a bluesy falling off at the end much as Holiday's. While in her early recordings Billie sings the melodies fairly straight, she will later improvise more freely. Teagarden, however, is inventive both melodically and rhythmically, creating original phrases that are not restricted by the theme or by the bar lines. Teagarden, in fact, is the consummate swing artist, just as Goodman is with his solo on *Your Mother's Son-in-Law*. For this reason Teagarden's performance is particularly poignant when one realizes that just at this time Jack was signing a five-year binding contract with Paul Whiteman that would essentially terminate for half a decade the trombonist's work as a free-wheeling jazz improviser. Whitney Balliett has concisely summarized Teagarden's achievement by this date and its relationship to his Texas heritage: "His famous style had set, and it changed little. It was very much of the Southwest, which has produced many of the most lyrical and affecting of all jazz musicians. Their music is imbued with the blues, they wear their emotions on their sleeve, they swing effortlessly, their sounds are rich and spacious."[55]

Before going with Whiteman's commercial orchestra, Teagarden took part in one other recording session, on October 18 and 27, 1933, with the same Benny Goodman studio group (minus Shirley Clay) that would cut the two sides with Billie Holiday in November and December.[56] This earlier group includes Jack's brother Charlie (who accompanies Clay on trumpet for the Holiday date) and features the trombonist-vocalist on all of four sides, which in content are only a step above Whiteman's novelty numbers. A tune entitled *Dr. Heckle and Mr. Jibe* was composed by the guitarist, Dick McDonough, who, along with Goodman and a certain Buck, also contributed *Riffin' the Scotch* in the Holiday session of December 18. Sounding like *Your Mother's Son-in-Law* in the beginning, *Dr. Heckle and Mr. Jibe* finds Goodman falling from the same high note as that later recording, and Teagarden also solos on his first chorus in a style similar to his performance on the Holiday song but here uses a cup mute. Even though the lyrics are corny, Teagarden manages to sing them with conviction. On his trombone chorus following his vocal, Jack even incorporates the tune's pathetic theme and elevates it to the high level of jazz. But it seems that just the presence of Billie Holiday and Shirley Clay on *Your Mother's Son-in-Law* and *Riffin' the Scotch* lifted Teagarden to another plane of inspiration. Clearly Billie makes more music out of *her* insipid lyrics, but Teagarden also rises to greater heights in his ad lib solos preceding and following Holiday's vocals.

For all the praise due to Teagarden as a technician and despite the suggestion that he was highly inspired by Benny Goodman, it was the black musicians who brought out Jack's best as an artist. On the other hand, Teagarden's four-year association with Louis Armstrong's All-Stars from 1947 to 1951 did not always result in the kind of quality jazz of which both giants were capable. Circumstances may never have been ideal for Teagarden, but he seemed to make the most of whatever he was offered. Yet the realization that Teagarden spent the greater part of his career playing with white musicians lacking in his technical and intellectual gifts and that he locked himself into a deadening arrangement with Whiteman (something of an allegorical relationship) disappoints and frustrates anyone who has heard the difference between his more profound creativity in stimulating company and his noted tendency to take it easy when surrounded by members of the Whiteman organization or Jack's own big bands, led by him beginning in 1938. Nonetheless, it is true that "even when Teagarden was coasting, he tossed off casual trombone passages that could send novices running back to their wood-sheds."[57]

On another tune from the October 1933 sessions, *Texas Tea Party*, Teagarden sings a version of his famous lyrics on Texas and Tennessee and then plays one of his trombone solos full of what Gary Giddins has aptly described as "casual triplets percolating unexpectedly from his warming Texas blues riffs."[58] *Ain't Cha Glad* contains a fine solo by Charlie Teagarden and demonstrates why Gunther Schuller regards him as "unduly overshadowed not only by his brother but by the likes of Berigan, Spivak, Eldridge, James—even Wingy Manone." Schuller, who claims he never heard a bad solo by Charlie, goes on to say that the trumpeter was "a consistent contributor to quality jazz" who always played "with taste and integrity."[59] Jack's solos, however, are so full of his unique musical personality that it is understandable how he was the family star.[60] Here too his vocal chorus is a plus and is as infectious in its way as one by Billie Holiday. But it is Jack's "tossed off" trombone cadenza at the end of the piece that stamps this recording with the mark of an individual style whose place in jazz history is not to be denied. Even more impressive is the final tune of the four, *I Gotta Right to Sing the Blues*, which became Teagarden's theme song for his big band and in many ways is a comment on his life—with its multiple divorces, the unfortunate mistake of signing up with Whiteman, and the years of drinking to excess. Yet Jack's singing of the lyrics is bright and positive in tone, and his closing trombone work is as forceful and upbeat as anything he ever recorded. Of course, there are probably few listeners who have heard all of Teagarden's more than 1,000 recordings—which makes the Teagarden discography "one of the most extensive in jazz, comparable to Louis Armstrong, Fats Waller, Duke Ellington, and Coleman Hawkins"[61]—so there may be many candidates for the most vigorous and affirmative. And it may well be true of Teagarden's vast production, as Gunther Schuller has said of brother Charlie, that Jack never played a bad solo, even though during his days with Whiteman his performances could become regrettably predictable.

Jack Teagarden went on in the 1940s, 1950s, and 1960s to record works that maintained his "image of invincibility" that he first created in the twenties.[62] Among these, for Martin Williams, was a half-chorus on *Pennies from Heaven* with the Louis Armstrong All-Stars. Williams observes that "most of Teagarden's best solos are paraphrases of melodies as written, and they show his taste in knowing what to add, what to leave out, what to rephrase"; in this category Williams names as his favorite the 1957 version of *My Kinda Love*.[63] On November 30, 1947, Teagarden performed with the Armstrong All-Stars at Symphony Hall in Boston and on *Lover* exhibits once again his technical prowess, the purity of his tonal quality, and his triple-tonguing ability in a display that few could duplicate even today, maintaining a driving swing at the same time that he provides another example of his phenomenal execution of exercise-like figures.[64] Likewise, on *Stars Fell on Alabama* from the same concert, Jack rips off scale runs and triplets and delivers a lovely vocal in his inimitable lazy, relaxed style that is yet rhythmically right on the mark. Here too, just as Armstrong's singing is an extension of his trumpet work, so Teagarden's vocalizing follows from his trombone style, though the latter is more technically exhibitionistic.

With his own big bands, Teagarden could produce from time to time a blues that would be "a masterpiece of sustained upper-register virtuosity."[65] But for most students of jazz, Teagarden's playing in the twenties and early thirties remains the abiding evidence that he was, in the words of Gary Giddins, "the best trombone player in the world," whose music is characterized by "restrained virtuosity, easy ingenuity, and personal charm." At the same time that Giddins offers this assessment—or rather echoes Pee Wee Russell's rating of Teagarden—the critic also suggests that the trombonist's importance to the development of jazz may not be as "integral . . . as Armstrong or even Hawkins and Beiderbecke" and instead a consequence of the way he "haunts the music with his individuality."[66] Technically speaking, however, various critics have wondered in print whether without Teagarden the jazz trombone would have evolved on its own beyond "the inflexibility of its tone, the awkwardness of its action and its inability to do more than grunt and stutter at fast tempos."[67] Certainly Teagarden's impact on trombonists can be heard in every generation, beginning with his own and continuing to the present. For Gil Rodin, a Chicagoan who joined Ben Pollack's orchestra in 1927 and heard Teagarden when he arrived that same year in the Big Apple, it was the Texan who gave him his "first taste . . . of real, genuine hot trombone," and at least as far as Rodin was concerned, Jack's "rise in music was inevitable and the swing world should be thankful that he came to New York when he did."[68]

❂ ❂ ❂

Like Jack Teagarden, trombonist Frederic "Keg" Johnson and his better-known brother Budd, the saxophonist and arranger, were born into a musical family. Their father was a trumpet player, organist, and choir director who made his living with the Studebaker firm in Dallas. Both Keg and Budd studied music in their hometown with Portia Pittman, the daughter of Booker T. Washington. Born in Dallas on November 19, 1908, Keg worked with Budd in various bands in the area, the two brothers traveling to Oklahoma while still in their teens and playing "all over Texas as the Blue Moon Chasers" and battling "all the bands around there."[69] About 1927 the brothers even traveled as far as El Paso and Mexico while playing with Ben Smith's Music Makers. At one point Keg and Budd were with Gene Coy's Happy Aces in Amarillo and "went back and forth between many a band in those years."[70] In 1929, the brothers joined up with the Jesse Stone band and headed for Kansas City, where Keg, Budd, and Stone became members of the George E. Lee band, which at the time rivaled Bennie Moten's. In 1930 Keg left for Chicago, where he played with the Ralph Cooper band at the Regal Theatre and with the Clarence Moore band at the Grand Terrace Ballroom, along with pianist and fellow Texan Teddy Wilson. After Budd arrived in Chicago in 1932, the brothers played in a combo with Wilson, and in early 1933 they all three joined the orchestra of Louis Armstrong, directed by Zilmer T. Randolph.[71]

It was with Armstrong's orchestra in January 1933 that Keg recorded his first solo, on *Basin Street Blues*, one of Teagarden's signature pieces. In his own solo

Johnson shows the influence of Teagarden and he carries it off well, though not quite up to Jack's form, falling off a bit at the end. Gunther Schuller calls Keg one of the major soloists with Armstrong's orchestra (another being his brother Budd on tenor) and notes that he is "especially fond of . . . Johnson's soulful open-toned, unfancy solo on *Basin Street Blues*."[72] More impressive in exhibiting Keg's upper-register work is *Mahogany Hall Stomp*, in which the trombonist executes his solo with great swing, sliding down and suddenly popping high notes and also utilizing shakes to good effect. While Schuller considers Armstrong's performance on this piece "one of his crowning achievements and thus, by definition, in all of jazz,"[73] George Avakian calls Satchmo's unaccompanied solo on *Laughin' Louie* of the same date "one of Armstrong's greatest."[74] On *Laughin' Louie*, Keg Johnson also takes a nice break, but this and the other two choruses mentioned above are unfortunately all the solo space allotted to the trombonist. As James Lincoln Collier notes, Keg Johnson was "an excellent jazz player, who did not record often enough to receive the recognition he deserved."[75]

After the Armstrong orchestra disbanded in July 1933, Keg Johnson played in New York with the orchestra of Benny Carter, again along with Teddy Wilson, who, on *Blue Lou* from October 16, 1933, reels off what Johnny Simmen considers "a fantastic chorus." While playing with Carter, Johnson himself took, in Simmen's view, one of his finest solos on record,[76] a judgment perhaps based on the fact that Keg performs his break in the jumping, spirited *Devil's Holiday* at the tune's very demanding up-tempo, even though his rapid tonguing is not quite under control.

In 1934 Johnson joined the Fletcher Henderson Orchestra, and during this year Keg recorded solos on five tunes in which he demonstrates that, although he was no Jimmy Harrison, Henderson's former trombone star, the Texan was an effective soloist and fit in well with Fletcher's brand of swing. On two dates from September 1934, Johnson displays his use of trills, which can at times become something of a crutch that he depends on overmuch, as on *Rug Cutter's Swing* of September 25, when his first solo is given over to this device. But later he does more interesting work on this same tune when he trades swinging eight-bar breaks with tenor Ben Webster.[77] Another device Johnson employs is a legato sliding around that is evident on *Limehouse Blues* from September 11 as well as on *Liza* from September 25. With the latter, the tune seems too fast for this technique, so it is difficult for Keg to manage the kind of accented, legato half-time approach he often employs quite effectively. Here it sounds as though he were in slow motion against the upbeat tempo. On *Wild Party*, of the same date, he handles the up-tempo well and produces some fine swing in the process. Keg also achieves some nice syncopated work on *Limehouse Blues*, accurately hitting his high notes as well. Johnson is perhaps most swinging on *Memphis Blues* from September 12, which finds the trombonist executing Teagarden-like shakes and swoops, proving Keg to be a very solid performer, if not a spectacular one.

The next year, Keg Johnson began his fourteen-year association with the orchestra of Cab Calloway. On September 10, 1937, Johnson took part in a recording date with one of Calloway's featured soloists, tenorist Chu Berry, a rival of the great Coleman Hawkins. As one of Berry's Stomp Stevedores, Keg contributes solo work to three tunes on this occasion: a short break at the beginning of *Chuberry Jam* that gives evidence of his fine upper-register technique and an extended solo that demonstrates his facility at achieving a swingingly flowing chorus; a bit of his high-note effects and tricky slide (or lip) work on *Maelstrom*; and a Teagarden-like fluidity and swing on *Ebb Tide* as well as more examples of Johnson's high-note agility.[78] Johnson did not solo often with the Calloway orchestra, but he can be heard on the August 30, 1938, recording of *At the Clambake Carnival*, a typical swing-era riff that has Keg combining Teagarden triplets with ascending smears in the style of Trummy Young. Although this solo cannot compare with Johnson's impressive choruses on *Basin Street Blues* and *Mahogany Hall Stomp* with Armstrong, in one of Calloway's most popular songs, *The Jumpin' Jive*, recorded on July 17, 1939, Keg delivers in his best Teagarden manner a series of triplets that exhibits his technical proficiency and his talent for creating a very swinging and beautifully phrased break.[79]

Essentially, Keg Johnson was a section man in the Calloway orchestra, one of the fine hard-swinging big bands of the 1930s and 1940s. In later years, Johnson recorded with Gil Evans and toured with the Ray Charles Orchestra from 1960 to 1967.[80] A 1960 album with brother Budd, entitled *Let's Swing*, provided Keg with more room to stretch out than he normally enjoyed, and even though the results are not so interesting as his first recordings with Armstrong or his brief appearances as a soloist with Cab Calloway, his playing here has been characterized as "extremely pliant" and his blues deeply felt.[81] What Keg Johnson offered most often was a mastery of the new fluidity and easy swing introduced by Teagarden, along with a high-note execution that looked forward to the development of the bop trombone with its extension of the range of the instrument and its soloistic capabilities.

❂ ❂ ❂

Tyree Glenn, unlike Keg Johnson, was not a Teagarden protégé. More eclectic, Glenn ranged from a hot style to the romantically mellow sound of Tommy Dorsey and Glenn Miller, and in later years Glenn took up the tradition that began with Duke Ellington's first trombonist, Charlie Irvis, and was carried on by the magnificent mute-and-plunger work of Joe "Tricky Sam" Nanton. Born in Corsicana on November 23, 1912, Glenn took his first lessons from Snub Mosley[82] and played with local bands before appearing on the scene in Washington, D.C., in 1934. According to Albert McCarthy, Glenn also worked with the Los Angeles band of trumpeter Charlie Echols in 1935, along with Buck Clayton and Herschel Evans. These three musicians later recalled that the Echols band "was outstanding and should have been recorded," but, as McCarthy reports, "unfortunately it never was."[83] In D.C., Tyree worked in the Tommy Mills Orchestra from 1934 to 1936, after which he joined Bennie Moten's former reed man, Eddie Barefield, in New York, where Tyree later played with Benny Carter for two years, from 1937 to 1939. While with Carter, Glenn would record on trombone more in the Dorsey-Miller style on such tunes as *Vagabond Dreams* and *Love's Got Me Down Again* from November 1, 1939. But most impressive from this period with the Carter orchestra is Glenn's work on vibraphone. On May 20, 1939, Tyree took a truly first-rate solo on *Oh! Lady Be Good* during a live radio broadcast from the Savoy Ballroom in Harlem. This solo surely ranks not only among the finest vibraphone performances of his career but as the equal of any ever recorded.[84]

In 1940 Tyree Glenn went with the Cab Calloway Orchestra, joining Keg Johnson and Lammar Wright in the brass section and doubling on vibraphone and occasionally recording as a vocalist. At this time, Glenn and Johnson were present on *Pickin' the Cabbage*, which was Dizzy Gillespie's first recording on trumpet as well as his debut as a composer-arranger. Although *Pickin' the Cabbage*, made in Chicago on March 8, 1940, does not signal the beginnings of the bop movement that Gillespie would help to institute in the 1940s, it is "prophetic" in "using revolutionary rhythmic ideas" as reflected in his long solo "utilizing whole-tone scales."[85] Following a chorus by Gillespie on trumpet on *Calling All Bars*, recorded in New York on May 18, 1940, Glenn takes something of a hot solo, and after Dizzy's solo on *Bye Bye Blues*, recorded in Chicago on June 27, 1940, which "demonstrates the beautiful ensemble playing of the band,"[86] Glenn contributes a fine chorus on vibes. On this same date, Tyree also takes a terrific short break on *Come On with the "Come" On*, showing what he could do even in a pinch. Perhaps Glenn's best hot chorus on trombone comes in the Calloway version of Jelly Roll Morton's classic, *King Porter Stomp*, recorded in New Jersey on July 27, 1940. Here Glenn leads off what Albert McCarthy considers a group of "driving . . . solos of quality,"[87] with Tyree's own chorus in the upper register sounding at first like a trumpet, then settling down into a recognizable trombone groove that is brassy and blaring but tastefully so. For the July 24, 1941, New York recording of *Hey Doc!* Glenn served as vocalist along with Calloway in a novelty routine, but this is neither a notable moment for Glenn nor one of Cab's memorable efforts among his long line of exciting songs, such as *The Jumpin' Jive, Miss Otis Regrets, The Honeydripper, Minnie the Moocher, Hi De Ho Man, Eadie Was a Lady*, or even the 1949 *I Beeped When I Shoulda Bopped*.[88] On the other hand, Glenn's performances on trombone and vibraphone during his stay with Calloway require no apology whatsoever.

Glenn stayed with the Calloway orchestra until 1946, after which he toured Europe with Don Redman and then in 1947 joined the Ellington orchestra for a five-year stint. During his time with the Duke, Glenn developed a wah-wah mute approach that originated with King Oliver and was picked up by Ellington's early "growl" trumpeter, Bubber Miley, who in turn instructed Charlie Irvis to employ this technique on trombone. Subsequently, Tricky Sam Nanton inherited this mute sound that became indispensable to the Ellington "jungle" and impressionistic styles. The "unmistakable" influence of Irvis's blues growl trombone began in 1923 in New York's Kentucky Club at a time when Ellington "was little more than a moderate ragtime pianist revealing a most limited faculty for composition," but the Duke "instinctively sensed the importance of Irvis's grotesque style."[89] Later Ellington would create through the use of Bubber and Tricky Sam's "bizarre, menacing mute-and-plunger blues style" his sophisticated "primitive" compositions that first made him the greatest of all jazz composers during his four-year engagement at Harlem's famous Cotton Club, where the Duke opened in December 1927, shortly after the arrival in New York of Jack Teagarden. When Glenn joined the Ellington orchestra twenty years later in 1947, he took over the plunger duties from Tricky Sam Nanton.

While Glenn rarely if ever reminds one of his fellow Texan from Vernon, he was, like Teagarden, completely at home in the blues, and during his stay with Ellington, Glenn revealed this side to his varied musical talents. On *H'ya Sue*, recorded on August 14, 1947, and considered one of the Ellington orchestra's "best blues," Tyree builds a wah-wah solo on trombone through which he "conjures the image of a great blues singer; indeed, one can almost visualize Big Bill Broonzy throwing back his head as Glenn leads into each of his choruses."[90] On *Three Cent Stomp* from the same session, Glenn exhibits yet another side to his multifaceted musical personality in an open solo that reveals "a distinctive style . . . good humoured, with a freely flowing melodic line and supple swing."[91] Ellington himself had this to say about Glenn: "Tyree, to me, is a very beautiful trombone player. He plays real good, legit trombone, and when he applied the plunger to it, his tone remained very precise and clean, so that you were tempted to like it better than Tricky's, because it was so clean. . . . He still uses the plunger, and he is one of the most effective plunger trombones I have ever heard."[92]

Even though James Lincoln Collier regrets Ellington's choice of Glenn to replace Tricky Sam Nanton when he might have gotten Dickie Wells or Benny Morton, Collier does acknowledge that Glenn and Quentin Jackson were the best of several trombonists who "came the closest to Nanton," although the critic believes that "none of them were really able to get that haunting human sound that Nanton had made his own."[93] On the other hand, Vic Bellerby finds that Tyree's achievement in "adapting his phrasing to Tricky Sam's trombone style was very remarkable."[94] Nonetheless, on *Mood Indigo*, the Ellington classic dating from 1930 and the Duke's first major hit, Glenn fails to capture with his December 19, 1950, version the eerie beauty of the role played by Nanton in the famous *Mood Indigo* trio with Arthur Whetsol on trumpet and Barney Bigard on clarinet. Of course, Ellington rarely repeated a tune's instrumentation or its interpretation, so the 1950 rendition is, as would be expected, quite different from the 1930 original. But undeniably, as Bellerby points out, Glenn's mute effects tend to come across as "ludicrous."[95] In fact, the total performance pales considerably beside the 1930 version or any number of other recordings with Nanton. One problem with Glenn's approach is that the wah-wah is overdone and becomes a mere sound device rather than a means to a musical end. However, on the December 28, 1947, recording of Ellington's *Liberian Suite*, Glenn performs with distinction on both trombone and vibraphone. His vibraphone chorus, which was the first for an Ellington orchestra, demonstrates once again the Texan's very real ability on an instrument made famous in jazz by Lionel Hampton, Red Norvo, and Milt Jackson. More important, Glenn's solo fits perfectly into the context of Ellington's dance suite, adding a rhythmic and melodic quality that is quietly exotic.

In describing the live performance of *Liberian Suite*, which was premiered at Carnegie Hall on December 26, 1947, Raymond Horricks writes, "It is when Tyree Glenn lays down his normal instrument, the trombone, and takes his stance behind a vibraharp that the excitement is really turned on in full . . . selecting a series of short, neat melodic figures and hammering them out with a maximum drive. The percussive riffs he builds in his conclusion set the entire band rocking out behind him."[96] In the last section, Dance No. 5, Glenn contributes a wah-wah solo on trombone that is far superior to his effort on *Mood Indigo*. Horricks reports that in the live performance "Tyree's solo actually heralds the finale to the suite. Inserting a rubber plunger mute into his instrument, he half imitates the style of the late Joe Nanton, though he cannot retard completely the more rounded, lush sound of his own highly-individual trombone tone."[97] On the recording of the *Liberian Suite*, made two days later, Glenn's mute effects are controlled, though at times intentionally fierce to reflect "the wild, virile, majestic pulse of Africa."[98] Glenn's participation in this musical celebration of the centenary of the African republic, founded in 1847 by freed slaves, is, like Teagarden's concert at the site of Hiroshima in January 1959, one of the more meaningful connections created between the Texas jazz heritage and events in world history.[99]

Glenn would record in later years with an Ellington studio band that included Texas trumpeter Harold "Money" Johnson, who was born in Tyler on February 23, 1918. In the early 1930s, Johnson was with Eddie and Sugar Lou's Hotel Tyler Orchestra as well as with Nat Towles for a number of years, with Horace Henderson in 1940,[100] briefly with Basie in 1944, and with the Cootie Williams orchestra in 1944 (recording then with Texan Eddie "Cleanhead" Vinson) and during the late 1940s; in 1966 Johnson toured Russia with Earl Hines and again in late 1968 was with Hines in Europe. Johnson was also occasionally with Ellington in 1968 and 1969,[101] and in 1970–1971 he was a regular member of the Duke's band. From the 1969 to 1972 period, both Johnson and Glenn are present on the album entitled *Up in Duke's Workshop*.[102] Johnson solos on *Blem*, an Ellington riff from April 25, 1969,[103] playing somewhat in the Cootie Williams manner, but Money also exhibits his own driving attack that fits perfectly into the Ellington mold of penetrating trumpeters who artfully crafted their choruses within the Duke's original material. Glenn takes a very fine wah-wah break that swings forcefully and once again manipulates the mute effects in the grand tradition of Irvis and Nanton.

Just as Jack Teagarden was a member of the first Louis Armstrong All-Stars formed in 1947, Tyree Glenn joined with Satchmo in 1965 in the great trumpeter's last all-star combo.[104] Even though Armstrong was reaching the end of his highly productive career, he was still able to perform with his characteristic power and swing. As for Glenn, he has been called "one of the great and unsung heroes of jazz trombone," in reference primarily to his work with Armstrong on such an album as *What a Wonderful World*, the song that still has great popular appeal from Louis's singing of its lyrics.[105] In his final years, Louis managed with amazing and touching intensity to interject some of his inextinguishable fire into his offerings of such standards as *When the Saints Go Marchin' In* and *Tin Roof Blues*, but even more so in *Bye 'n' Bye*, *Short But Sweet*, and *Mame*.[106] With his internationally renowned gravelly voice, Armstrong delivers the lyrics to the *Saints* and then calls on Tyree Glenn by name to come on in, and the Texan responds with the only worthwhile break on this cut, sounding as fresh and vital as he did when he worked with Cab Calloway, if more relaxed and mellow.

Tyree's unison work with Satchmo on *Tin Roof Blues* compares favorably with the fine duos performed with Louis by his earlier trombonists, Teagarden and Trummy Young. On *Bye 'n' Bye*, Armstrong's vocal, the clarinet solo, and Glenn's break, as well as the trumpeter's chorus, are all excellent, but especially Satchmo's vocal, even though it does not equal his moving delivery on *Short But Sweet*. On *Mame*, Glenn has another wah-wah solo that is nicely done and maintains the solid swing created by Louis's trumpet-style vocal, while *The Circle of Your Arms* opens with Armstrong doing a kind of scat vocal backed nicely by Glenn's wah-wah trombone. *So Long Dearie*, a *Hello Dolly*–like, bouncy, banjo-strummed tune, finds Tyree leading the Dixieland improvisation with fervor. In this last piece and *Tyree's Blues*, a tune named for Glenn, Louis and Tyree do some splendid duowork, then bring back the durable blues form for "one more once." *Pretty Little Missy* has Louis finishing off the piece on trumpet with his high-note shake that will never be mistaken for that of any other player on his instrument.[107]

While this group of tunes may represent a sentimental revisiting of the jazz past, it still offers a genuine bit of Armstrong showmanship and artistry that has spread happiness throughout the world. Tyree Glenn adds to this nostalgic return to the roots of jazz with a special feeling for the traditions he knew so well, as did Jack Teagarden and Keg Johnson. From banjo to blues, from swing to bop, from hot to cool, from scat and jive singing to impressionist tone poems, these three trombonists ranged through the entire gamut of African American music, joining with such masterful figures as Bessie Smith, Duke Ellington, and Louis Armstrong to help create America's greatest native art form.

BY WAY OF KAYCEE

After Lammar Wright left the Bennie Moten band in 1928, he joined up with a group originally from St. Louis that had journeyed to New York City in 1924 and even played and recorded in 1925 as the Cotton Club Orchestra. When Duke Ellington took the place of this band at the Cotton Club in 1927, the Missouri group went on tour with Ethel Waters and picked up Wright along the way, returning to New York in 1928 as the Missourians. By this time, jazz had experienced a number of major developments through the recordings of Armstrong and Fletcher Henderson, but as Max Harrison observes, "The Missourians are the rare case of a territory band that long preserved something of its regional flavour," demonstrating that "earlier modes of expression" can survive, even though this fact "is not allowed for in strictly evolutionist views of jazz history." Harrison also points out that despite the notion that Moten's Kansas City style had influenced the Missourians, owing in part to Wright's earlier association with Bennie's various units, the impact of such orchestras as those of Henderson and Ellington was undeniably apparent in "the Missourians' treatments of their simple themes."[1] Nevertheless, while the ensemble riffs, use of banjo, and reliance on variants of the *Tiger Rag* all date the approach of this group when Wright recorded with it on August 1, 1928, June 1 and August 8, 1929, and February 17, 1930, there is still a recognizable blues spirit to much of the solo and ensemble work of this lively Missouri band that remains timelessly rooted in the Southwest.

Lammar Wright, as he had during his stay with Bennie Moten, performed with power and feeling in this orchestra that must have given the leading New York organizations "many an uneasy night."[2] In fact, in 1929 the Missourians had soundly beaten no less than Duke Ellington's band in one of the more famous "battles of jazz."[3] According to Gunther Schuller, New York had not curbed the "rough, brash style" of the Missourians, as is evident in Lammar Wright's "boisterous trumpet solos."[4] Whether muted or open, Wright's playing is outstanding, as shown respectively on *Scotty Blues* and *400 Hop*.[5] On *Ozark Mountain Blues*, the two trumpeters, Wright and Roger Q. Dickerson, one muted and one open, are "responsible for a telling antiphonal sequence towards the close," and in the briskly performed *Market Street Stomp* both are muted.[6] But it is on *Prohibition Blues* that "one of the most memorable passages in the entire series occurs," when Dickerson "masterfully declaim[s] with plunger and wah-wah"[7] and Wright contributes a "vehemently sad" open-horn solo.[8] In general, the Missourians represented a blues-oriented band that could play very danceable music and could therefore compete successfully in the New York market. With a driving, earthy energy based on its "ragtime ancestry," the Missourians could "outswing anybody within earshot."[9] The twelve sides cut by the Missourians, in Gunther Schuller's estimate, "are virtually unique in jazz-recording history and contain, in their particular idiom, at least a couple of masterpieces."[10] But the Missourians soon ended as a group under this name, for in 1930 they were taken over by Cab Calloway, who brought them back for a longstanding engagement at the Cotton Club. As we have seen, Keg Johnson and Tyree Glenn would also form part of the Calloway organization, but it was Wright who was the first Texan to contribute to the rise of this important swing-era big band.

The Cab Calloway orchestra had as its primary function to support the vocalist, who in 1931 recorded *Minnie the Moocher* and gained national recognition as a scat singer nicknamed "the hi-de-ho man," from the lyrics of the song of this title concerned with marijuana or opium smokers. Consequently, as Gunther Schuller explains, the music played by Cab's sidemen "became increasingly jazz-oriented and professional" rather than the "powerful and raucous" style of the Missourians, which could readily be found "in the riverfront joints in . . . the Midwest and Southwest, but not indigenously in New York." Among the main soloists in Calloway's band was Lammar Wright, who "was responsible for the open-horn or straighter solos. His playing was characterized by a propulsive bullet-like attack . . . and by well-designed solos which often featured rising scalar or chromatic figures." One of the earliest recordings by Calloway's combined Missourians and Alabamians (the group he had brought with him from Chicago in 1928) is of the tune *Some of These Days*, recorded on December 23, 1930, which Schuller calls "amazing to this day for its hell-bent break-away tempo, upwards of 300 to the quarter-note beat . . . a staggering technical achievement for its time and . . . the fastest tempo achieved by any orchestra up to that time." On this historic performance Lammar Wright is "prominently featured" as a soloist in a driving chorus,[11] and on other tunes recorded from 1930 to 1933 the Texarkana product is also given solo space. But after 1933 Wright worked with the Calloway orchestra primarily as a section leader, remaining with Cab until 1947.

In addition to soloing on *Some of These Days*, Wright takes choruses or breaks on *St. James Infirmary*, recorded December 23, 1930; on *Somebody Stole My Gal*, of October 12, 1931; on *Reefer Man*, of June 9, 1932; and on *Margie*, recorded on December 19, 1933.[12] On all of these performances recorded in New York, Wright plays with his intense King Oliver–inspired sound that is in full evidence on *Some of These Days* and is just barely heard in a short break at the end of *St. James Infirmary*. After Cab's straight vocal on *Somebody Stole My Gal*—he will scat later in the song—Wright bursts out with a gripping solo that employs his penetrating tone and some dandy single-note tonguing that evokes the old Kansas City barrelhouse roughness in the midst of a rather sedate ballroom rendition, complete with simpering saxes. It is revealing to compare this version with the October 31, 1930, recording of the same tune by Bennie Moten's band, which includes a scat vocal by Count Basie. Although both readings are moving toward dominance by the sax section in the Swing Era, it is already clear why the Basie reed sound would prove more virile and robust than that produced by the East Coast orchestras—that is, the saxophones in Moten's band, anchored by Jack Washington's manly baritone, swing as a unit with the aid of a well-orchestrated arrangement by Eddie Durham. Lips Page's red-hot chorus drives as only Lammar Wright's does among the Calloway soloists, although the preeminence must go to Page for inventiveness.

By mid-1932, when the Calloway orchestra recorded *Reefer Man*, it was beginning to develop into what would become one of the period's top big bands, with "direct power and unremitting swing."[13] But here Lammar Wright's solo is obviously a throwback to King Oliver in being limited to a few searing notes built up to a high-note intensity that by this time owed something as well to Armstrong's example. Even though this is another instance of Wright's clear-toned, ringing style, which, if its day was past, had served him well in what Schuller calls his "formidable career,"[14] amazingly the 1933 recording of *Margie* shows that Wright has suddenly adapted his approach to the era's new faster-paced, high-acrobatic virtuosity. Without forsaking his Oliver-inspired conception and swing, Wright fits comfortably, it would seem, into the more flowing, showmanlike style of the Swing Era. Proving himself to be as adaptable as many of his fellow Texans, Wright endured the changes of the 1930s and 1940s with Calloway, and in later life continued to perform with a wide variety of bands in the 1950s, including the Sy Oliver orchestra in 1947, when Wright was featured on *Lammar's Boogie*, and the Sauter-Finegan orchestra and George Shearing big band in the late 1950s.

Beginning with Bennie Moten's first recordings and stretching through some four decades, Lammar Wright demonstrated that the rudiments of jazz he mastered in the 1920s could stand him in good stead throughout his career and that such "prehistoric" skills could survive the times to serve him and the bands he played with despite any "evolutionist view of jazz history."

Just as a comparison of the Moten and Calloway recordings of *Somebody Stole My Gal*, made a year apart, is instructive with regard to jazz developments in Kansas City and New York, it is equally revealing to compare the Calloway recording of *Margie* with the work of Jimmie Lunceford, whose orchestra was drawn largely from his former students in Memphis and Nashville. For the most part, Lunceford's 1938 version of *Margie* is far removed from the Calloway reading of this 1920 hit. Yet both bands could rely on their sax sections to maintain a driving energy from which the often dazzling soloists are launched into orbit, as in the case of Lammar Wright, who is the most exciting soloist on the Calloway recording of 1932. In Lunceford's later arrangement of the tune, Trummy Young is featured as vocalist and as trumpet-range trombone virtuoso, with the various sections of the orchestra serving in a concerto-like supporting role. What is particularly contrastive in these two recordings is the guitar work in each—Morris White in the Calloway version and Al Norris in the Lunceford.[15]

The only glaring weakness in the Calloway performance is White's out-of-date, unswinging solo on guitar, whereas Norris's tasteful fills add to the overall swing of the Lunceford version and are quite modern-sounding compared with White's chorus. Even so, Norris's 1938 style on guitar seems somewhat anachronistic (or anti-evolutionary) when one considers that as early as October 1929, on the Moten recording of *New Vine Street Blues*, Eddie Durham had already indicated a new direction for jazz guitar. Furthermore, Durham's ideas that looked forward to Charlie Christian had not only been advanced in 1937 by his solo on a Basie recording of Eddie's arrangement entitled *Time Out* but were manifest in Lunceford's 1935 recording of Durham's arrangement of *Hittin' the Bottle*, which marked the Texan's first recorded experiment with an amplified guitar. For after leaving Bennie Moten in 1933 and working for a year with Willie Bryant's band (which included Teddy Wilson on piano), Eddie Durham joined Lunceford's orchestra in New York as trombonist, guitarist, and composer-arranger—positions he had filled in Moten's band and would likewise fill later in Count Basie's. As he had for Moten's band, Durham helped account for the success of the Lunceford organization, providing the arrangement for its hit tune entitled *Lunceford Special*, which has been called "one of the most genuine and brilliant illustrations" of the Lunceford orchestra's style[16] and "a prototype of the classic swing band."[17]

✷ ✷ ✷

In joining Jimmie Lunceford's orchestra, Eddie Durham became a vital member of one of the four greatest big bands of the Swing Era, along with those of Ellington, Basie, and Goodman. Among the big four, Lunceford's band had a "unique reputation as the best-disciplined and most showmanly Negro jazz orchestra" from 1934 to 1944.[18] Born in Fulton, Missouri, in 1902, Lunceford studied music in Denver with Paul Whiteman's father, Wilburforce Whiteman, later in Nashville at Fisk University, and also at New York City College. Gunther Schuller has called Lunceford "a black Paul Whiteman" and has compared their personal and professional habits, including their teetotaling dispositions. Schuller points out that Lunceford's aversion to drink is immortalized in the last line of the lyrics to *Hittin' the Bottle*: "Everybody—except Jimmie—hits the bottle."[19] While teaching at Manassa High School in Memphis, Lunceford organized a band to play for student dances. When his band members graduated, Jimmie followed them to Fisk University in order to keep the group together, with five of the nine original Manassa players still with the leader at his death in 1947. When his group members graduated from Fisk around 1929, Lunceford organized a tour through the Midwest, after which he and his band ended up in New York State, playing in Buffalo and Lakeside before being hired around 1933 to play the Lafayette Theatre in New York City.

The Lunceford orchestra's first big success came when it entered the Cotton Club in 1934 and played its odd assortment of arrangements that all reflected the Lunceford philosophy, exemplified in the 1934 recording of *Rhythm Is Our Business*, a kind of response to Ellington's 1932 *It Don't Mean a Thing If It Ain't Got That Swing*. Indicative of Lunceford's disciplined approach is the title of a tune recorded on January 3, 1939, *Tain't What You Do, It's the Way That You Do It*. The strange and unusual fact about Lunceford's orchestra was that it did not play the blues, as did Ellington, Moten, Basie, and most of the other big bands of the Swing Era. Largely given over to novelty numbers arranged effectively for a band that rehearsed religiously—and attended church on Sundays—the Lunceford book was created by an eclectic group of arrangers, although because of the demands made on them by their leader and by the need to produce danceable music, the styles of the various arrangers tended to merge "into more or less *one* Lunceford style." For this reason, as Gunther Schuller goes on to observe, "it became increasingly difficult to differentiate Durham from [Sy] Oliver and the latter from [Ed] Wilcox."[20] However, Eddie Durham's special contribution to the Lunceford band lay in the fact that, as even Sy Oliver acknowledged, the Texan was the best jazz arranger in the organization, which indicates a distinction between Durham's approach and

Oliver's own popular, more commercial style.[21] Nonetheless, as Durham himself told Stanley Dance, even when Eddie wrote swinging numbers, Lunceford and his men would "go back and put novelty on top of them."[22]

Gunther Schuller describes the emergence of Eddie Durham as a new arranger in the Lunceford band when he analyzes Durham's "fine composition and arrangement" of *Oh Boy!*—a tune that is "especially ingenious in its use of the versatile five-man sax section (which was sometimes enlarged to six by the addition of Lunceford himself on alto)."[23] Schuller's discussion of Durham's writing and arranging is valuable for two reasons: it recalls the importance of Eddie's early training in music theory, noted previously, and it indicates why for some time Lunceford had been seeking the services of Durham (just as Moten sought to enlist Eddie for his own band when the Texan was with the Blue Devils), that is, because the Lunceford organization was made up of highly intelligent, mostly college-educated musicians who aimed at creating a sophisticated brand of music that appealed to black and white audiences alike. Even though Durham had not studied at Fisk University, as had many of the members of Lunceford's orchestra, Eddie fit in because he was musically adept. Willie Smith, Lunceford's masterful lead alto, held a degree in chemistry from Fisk, but as Durham recalled, he taught Smith "how to voice for the instrumentation we had, and he was even willing to pay me,"[24] which is testimony to the Lunceford musicians' avid interest in self-improvement, even as proven professionals. Although the blues, which were the basis of Durham's compositions for the Moten and Basie bands, were not an essential part of the Lunceford orchestra's musical offerings—the Lunceford sound encompassing rather a wide variety of styles, featuring musicians who could play with precision and great swing—nonetheless, Durham's versatility as a composer-arranger, a soloist, and a sideman allowed him to contribute significantly to the success of the Lunceford organization and thus to important developments in the Swing Era.

Among the works Durham composed and arranged for Lunceford, Schuller has singled out both *Oh Boy!* and *Lunceford Special* as outstanding, remarking of the latter that it gives "ample solo space for four of the band's major soloists and a generally spirited performance."[25] For the most part, Durham's compositions are intended as hard-swinging instrumentals rather than as novelty numbers. In the case of Eddie's *Harlem Shout*, this piece not only provides for five soloists to take their turns but creates some intriguing passages to show off the band's well-rehearsed section work. Counterpoint-like writing for two or more sections alternates with riff-style punctuations from the trumpets and some descending figures by the trombones, with Durham among them. Recorded on October 14, 1936, the performance cannot compare, however, with the Basie band's reading of such a chart—for it

Eddie Durham of San Marcos. Reprinted by permission of the Ernest Smith Collection.

would have achieved far more swing—nor with the solos of the Count's sidemen, in particular those of Lester Young, Herschel Evans, and Buck Clayton. In the hands of Basie's players Durham's composition would surely have swung harder, but even so, the Lunceford rendition has the band's distinctive flavor that was uniquely its own and thus for many was incomparable.

An earlier purely instrumental arrangement is Durham's version of *Avalon*, recorded September 30, 1935, in which Eddie also takes some brief opening breaks on acoustic guitar. Here there are superior solos to those on *Harlem Shout*, and Durham's arrangement also contains a number of notable differences. For one thing, the arranger creates some original rifflike but nicely varied lines played by the trumpets behind the muted trombone's theme statement. Eddie also writes for the full trombone section an arranged improvisation based on the tune's melody. Throughout Durham's arrangement, the soloists are urged along by well-placed fills, and toward the end of the piece Eddie builds the kind of tiered pyramid that would become so popular with period bands. This is followed by a swinging solo by trombonist Russell Bowles, who just gets going when the dread three-minute limit forces Durham to shut things down with an unsatisfyingly abrupt ending. Nevertheless, as Charles Fox has pointed out, in the penultimate four bars of *Avalon*, Durham has managed to include the riff that also "provides a climax" for *One O'Clock Jump*,[26] which predates any Basie recording of the Count's theme song. As for Durham's guitar breaks, these are rather typical of much of his lesser work, as are those on another tune from this recording date, the novelty vocal entitled *I'll Take the South*. But in one other piece from this same session, *Hittin' the Bottle*, Durham would make jazz history when he utilized for the first time on record an amplified guitar.[27]

Along with *Runnin' a Temperature*, recorded on October 26, 1936, *Hittin' the Bottle*, from the September 30, 1935, session, is an exception among Durham's arrangements in that both tunes contain novelty vocals. But this fact does not detract from the excellence of the two numbers, especially not from Durham's performance on *Hittin' the Bottle*, where he first employs an electric guitar after having experimented with a tin resonator. Although Durham had recorded earlier on acoustic guitar with Moten, it was during his Lunceford years that the amplified guitar became a prominent part of Eddie's repertoire. As mentioned earlier, Durham divided his time among composing, arranging, trombone, and guitar, never concentrating entirely on any one, so he never achieved the expertise on guitar that he thought he could have. Nonetheless, while with Lunceford, Eddie seemed to devote more attention to the guitar, which resulted in his 1935 solo on *Hittin' the Bottle* and its introduction of an amplified sound. In discussing Durham's use of amplification, Gunther Schuller observes that because orchestras were becoming larger in size and power, the acoustic guitar lost its listeners, and since Durham wanted to exploit the melodic possibilities of the instrument, he first came up with a tin resonator that could project his solo and ensemble work.[28] Durham himself described his invention of a homemade amplified guitar in a 1985 interview: "I made a resonator with a tin pan. It was back in the early 1930s. I'd carve out the inside of an acoustic guitar and put the resonator down inside there. It was the size of a breakfast plate. I'd put something around the guitar to hold it. And when I hit the strings, the pie pan would ring and shoot out the sound. I didn't have to do that for long because I ran up on a National. It had a resonator in it."[29]

On *Hittin' the Bottle* Durham opens the tune in a type of call-and-response interchange with Willie Smith on clarinet. The delicacy of the combination of clarinet and amplified guitar demonstrates the potential for Durham's instrument. According to Alain Gerber, because of "the simplicity and effectiveness of his conceptions," this remains "one of [Durham's] most successful orchestrations."[30]

However, although Gunther Schuller finds Durham's amplified guitar "on the plus side," he places Durham's arrangement "on the minus side" for being "too fancily sectionalized, its modulations strained and pretentious."[31] Despite this difference of opinion as to Durham's arrangement, Eddie's guitar work stands as a breakthrough that would influence important new developments in jazz. In particular, Durham's blues interpolations during Sy Oliver's vocal represent an extension of the blues tradition within the practice of southwestern guitar playing. The impact of this innovation on the history of jazz guitar can best be measured by the work of those who followed Durham's lead. Durham himself claimed that he had introduced Charlie Christian to a form of the amplified guitar in 1937. At this time Durham was still with Lunceford and was playing in Oklahoma City, where Christian grew up. As Durham tells the story,

> one day Charlie showed up with an old beat-up guitar that had cost him five dollars [Christian had originally played the string bass with the Alphonse Trent orchestra]. He had big eyes to sound like a saxophone [which is possible on an amplified guitar], and I showed him how by using down strokes he could get a sharper tone, and how if you use the up stroke you get a more legato sound, which the horns couldn't get. With no legato the sound is more like a horn, but it takes an awful fast wrist to play the down strokes.[32]

As Durham acknowledges, Christian learned quickly and was soon playing single-string solos on electric guitar. Just as Durham's interpolations on *Hittin' the Bottle* with Lunceford's orchestra are blues responses, so too are Charlie Christian's contributions to modern jazz based on southwestern blues. Gunther Schuller defines the blues connection in Christian's solo work when he comments on Charlie's performance on *Breakfast Feud*, recorded with the Benny Goodman sextet on December 19, 1940: "Not only does Christian emulate the types of twangy slides, scoops, and string-crossings [of country blues guitarists], but he also uses less syncopation, staying more on the beat and relying a great deal on straight even eighth-note lines."[33] Of the latter trait, Schuller also observes that such even-note lines were common among country-style Texas guitarists like Leon McAuliffe and Zeke Campbell, who played with Bob Wills and the Light Crust Doughboys. While Schuller acknowledges that these Western Swing musicians performed in a rhythmic style that was "more 'square' and less swinging," he finds that "the similarity is undeniable."[34] Schuller's point is that Christian would have heard such bands both on radio and on recordings in the Oklahoma area where he grew up and that, although he may not have taken his style directly from Texas guitarists, such a tradition was in existence long before Christian arrived in New York in 1939. It was this tradition that Eddie Durham helped pass along to Charlie Christian and to modern jazz.

Al Avakian and Bob Prince have described Charlie Christian's work as a blues riff approach that "gave a full range of expression to the guitar, utilizing all its basic rhythmic, melodic, and sound potential."[35] Many of these possibilities are evident in Durham's performance on *Hittin' the Bottle*, though certainly on a very limited scale compared with Christian's achievement. The early Lunceford recording does not, in fact, allow Durham the kind of solo space he would later enjoy on the Basie and the Kansas City Five recordings, which show Durham moving in the direction of what later would prove Christian's improvisations that brought forth "a new, mobile, swinging jazz" and that are "familiar in their basic blues allusion."[36] Yet what makes Durham such a unique figure in the history of this period is the fact that he not only contributed to new developments in the area of jazz guitar but that he also composed or arranged such a variety of important works for the major big bands of the Swing Era.

Among the works that Durham composed and arranged for Lunceford, there is an amazing mix of styles and approaches. *Harlem Shout*, which Durham called a flagwaver, was constructed on Kansas City riffs. Durham once remarked that Lunceford's orchestra "always opened and closed the show with a number of mine,"[37] and *Harlem Shout* obviously would have served the purpose, as would Durham's *Lunceford Special*. *Avalon*, a standard, was turned by Durham into one of Lunceford's more jazz-oriented selections. As noted above, *Hittin' the Bottle* and *Runnin' a Temperature* were novelty numbers. Recorded on October 26, 1936, *Runnin' a Temperature*, in spite of its rather overly cute lyrics, is, as the song says, "infectious," and it features Lunceford's unusual two-beat rhythm and some precisely played section writing that illustrates Durham's ability to arrange perfectly in the Lunceford style. As Gunther Schuller notes about Durham's *Hittin' the Bottle* and *Runnin' a Temperature*, such novelty numbers "stimulated not only the arrangers' musical imaginations, often directly inspired by the lyrics, but also brought a welcome element of humor and wit. And this was one of the important ingredients that made the Lunceford band such an entertainment delight."[38]

Perhaps most representative of Durham's achievement is *Pigeon Walk*, an arrangement that has been considered one of Durham's best scores for the Lunceford orchestra.[39] Based on a tune by James V. Monaco, *Pigeon Walk* is essentially a novelty number that attempts to evoke in music the stiff, jerky walk peculiar to the bird of the work's title. In responding to Monaco's descriptive piece, Durham was able to transform *Pigeon Walk* into something of a jazz classic, both for Lunceford and later for Count Basie. As we have seen, Durham joined Basie's band in the summer of 1937, and as Chris Sheridan, Basie's bio-discographer, has remarked, it was Durham, "above all," who "ensured the Count's permanence, by providing the necessary formality and polish in a way that preserved the band's individuality."[40] In this regard, Sheridan makes the following comment:

> Both in its parts and as a whole, Basie's 1930s orchestra personified South Western swing, and, initially at least, one looked in vain for the grand theme statement and development that typified the work of New York bands. Instead, performances grew organically from the simplest materials, something borrowed or something Blues being built, often quite spontaneously, in riffs to climax both solos and entire performances. This is the process that gave the band its immense drive and momentum.[41]

Gunther Schuller suggests that it was with the recording of Durham's composition *John's Idea* that the Basie band first achieved "a degree of creative and performance cohesiveness that might qualify as both distinctive and truly creative." Schuller mentions three other instrumental numbers created for Basie by Durham that "had a salutary effect on the band": *Time Out*, *Topsy*, and *Out the Window*.[42] *Time Out* is in fact the same tune as *Pigeon Walk*, as Charles Fox points out.[43] On the Basie recording of *Pigeon Walk* under the title *Time Out*, the original composer, James V. Monaco, is not credited, but this was fairly common practice on jazz recordings that employed the chord changes of a popular tune and created in many ways a quite different piece of music. (During the bebop period, this was frequently done, largely as a way of avoiding the payment of royalties for famous pop songs like those of George Gershwin, whose tunes provided the basis for many if not most jazz compositions.) While *Time Out* is recognizable as the same tune as *Pigeon Walk*, the differing arrangements and performances reveal the contrasting styles of the Basie and Lunceford bands. *Pigeon Walk* and *Time Out* are highly instructive not only for an understanding of the peculiar styles of these two great swing orchestras but also for an appreciation of Durham's arranging skills and his talents as a pre-bop guitarist.

Pigeon Walk was recorded by Lunceford on November 5, 1937, after Durham had already left to join Basie.[44] Durham's departure explains the guitar interpolations by Al Norris, who delivers his basically four-square chordings on an acoustic guitar. (As a team on *The Merry-Go-Round Broke Down*, recorded on June 15, 1937, Durham and Norris perform what Gunther Schuller calls a very rare combination of Eddie's low-register electric against Norris's acoustic guitar.)[45] In many ways the Norris interpolations on *Pigeon Walk* are more in keeping with the tune's stiffness as performed by the Lunceford orchestra than Durham's electric-guitar style would have been. And the entire band's performance of *Pigeon Walk* emphasizes the precision of the various sections as they execute their passages to an almost stomping beat, with solos limited to the kind of rigid, four-square rhythm that allows for little in the way of imaginative improvisation but serves rather to replicate the stiff motion of the tune's namesake. Durham thus provided an arrangement that was made to order for Lunceford's style—precision section work and solos that are designed primarily to characterize the original tune or to relate musically to its lyrics.

Durham's *Time Out* was recorded by the Count Basie band on August 9, 1937, almost three months prior to the Lunceford version of Monaco's piece, and the Basie performance is a typical example of the Kansas City riff style with its emphasis on swinging, imaginative, blues-derived solos. Here the *Pigeon Walk* theme is only stated briefly, and then Herschel Evans on tenor bursts out passionately for four bars, followed by Lester Young. Of this recording and Young's performance, Martin Williams observes that

> Many of the best early Basie arrangements were casually worked out by the band's members in the act of playing, and many others were revised by them in the act of replaying. But when scores were written for the band, Basie himself would frequently cut and simplify them, and one can well imagine that this happened to Eddie Durham's *Time Out*. Durham seems to have profited from, and improved on, Edgar Sampson's *Blue Lou*, and his structure encouraged a fine effect of suspense during Lester Young's solo. The resultant *Time Out* is an exemplary Basie arrangement: its ideas are sturdy and it is flexible, it might be expanded almost indefinitely—by more solos, longer solos, and by repeats of its written portions—without losing its casual, high effectiveness. (And incidentally, the performance of that piece shows how much technical polish the band could achieve by 1937.)[46]

After Lester Young's solo, the theme is repeated, and then Buck Clayton takes a solo on muted trumpet that is also characteristic of the driving Kansas City style. Next comes Durham himself on electric guitar, with a solo that predates Charlie Christian's revolutionary recordings and yet sounds so close to his work that it could easily be taken for that of the guitar master. As Leonard Feather observes, "At the time this was a total revelation; [Durham's] clarity and fluency in delineating single-note passages was like nothing before in jazz."[47] Indeed, Durham's single-note lines are in dramatic contrast to the stiff, traditional solo by Al Norris on *Pigeon Walk* and again demonstrate the flowing drive of the Kansas City brand of swing. Finally, Basie takes his turn with a Fats Waller–inspired solo that is representative of the leader's stride piano, backed by the subtle but powerful rhythm section of Jo Jones on drums, Walter Page on bass, and Freddie Green on acoustic guitar.[48] As the band rides out, the Durham arrangement has the sax and brass sections punctuating in the riff mode made famous by the Bennie Moten band and perpetuated here by Basie. The excitement generated throughout this performance makes it clear why Durham's *Time Out* is "almost always included in listings of the Best of Count Basie."[49] Once again, this rendition of Monaco's *Pigeon Walk* demonstrates Durham's ability to arrange a tune in the style of the band for which it was intended.

The rise of the arranger as the principal figure in determining the style and emphasis of the big band during the Swing Era inevitably brought about a decline in the jazz quality of the music performed by the successful bands led by Lunceford, Cab Calloway, Fletcher Henderson, Chick Webb, and such white leaders as Goodman, Tommy and Jimmy Dorsey, and Artie Shaw. Smaller ensembles like Goodman's trio and sextet and John Kirby's sextet emerged in an attempt to restore the prominence of the jazz soloist and to replace the arranger, who had come to emphasize section work by adding more reed and brass instruments in order to produce louder sounds, higher notes, and a greater array of tone colors and flashy effects, with the end result that the big band became unwieldy and unprofitable.[50] (Much the same thing happened in concert music at the end of the nineteenth century and the beginning of the twentieth, when Wagner, Bruckner, Strauss, Mahler, and even the early Schoenberg in his *Gurre-Lieder* called for larger and larger orchestras, until a reaction set in from such French composers as Erik Satie and Les Six, who were opposed to the heavy German symphonic works that required for their performance prohibitive funds and instrumental forces.) While Eddie Durham was praised for providing many opportunities for soloists in his own arrangements, he too was responsible in part for the demise of the big band as an outlet for authentic jazz. On the other hand, as we have seen from his Kansas City Five recordings, Durham also made possible some of the most important small group recordings of the period.

After a year and a half with Basie, Eddie Durham made his arranging skills available to other big-band leaders, including Benny Goodman, Artie Shaw, and Glenn Miller. The story of Durham's work for Miller merits retelling because it not only involves another aspect of the Texan's career as an arranger but underscores the bigotry that all black musicians faced, regardless of their talents. At a time when whites often considered blacks shiftless and incapable of intellectual pursuits, African-American jazz musicians suffered economically in spite of their proven artistry and professional capacity. Durham's arrangement for one of Glenn

Miller's biggest hits, *In the Mood*, earned him a mere five dollars while it made the bandleader a millionaire.[51] Recounting his experiences with Miller in a 1971 interview, Durham stopped short of discussing any particular compositions or the amount of his compensation for services rendered; he merely told why he had gone to Miller with his "book." Having left Basie in 1938, Eddie organized in 1940 a mixed band, which included fellow Texans Buster Smith and Joe Keyes along with a white altoist, but he was told by the president of a local union that "it was too smooth for a colored band, and that I'd be more successful if I went with Glenn Miller."[52] Durham believed in his group and was doing so well that he was hurting the business of some of the big-name bands (in particular, that of Harry James), but in the end Eddie was talked out of keeping his unit together and offered his talents to Miller instead. Walter Gilbert Fuller's account of Durham's work for the white bandleader is more specific and even credits the Texan with giving Miller his famous sound by using a lead clarinet on top of the band, a device Durham had employed earlier in arrangements for Jimmie Lunceford.[53] Among the arrangements that Durham supplied to the Miller orchestra were those for such numbers as *Slipborn Jive, Wham, Glen Island Special, Tiger Rag, Baby Me,* and *I Want to Be Happy.* Bio-discographer John Flower attributes the original arrangement of *In the Mood* to Durham on the basis of a radio interview:

> Chummy MacGregor, reading from his forthcoming book "Moonlight Serenade Revisited" [no such published title seems to exist], stated that the band bought an arrangement of "In the Mood" from Eddie Durham for five dollars. All they used of the original arrangement were the two front saxophone strains and another part that occurred later on in the arrangement. MacGregor mentioned that additional solos were added to the original arrangement and he wrote the finishing coda. Miller probably edited some of the arrangement along with MacGregor (and others?).[54]

While *In the Mood* represents a falling away from true jazz and the growing, almost universal dependence of the big bands on written compositions that called for very little improvisation or spontaneity, Durham's work for the Miller organization illustrates once again his great versatility as an arranger. Durham did try to allow in his arrangements for the essential jazz ingredient of personal expression, but because of the greater emphasis on a prearranged performance rather than a looser, more individualistic approach, even his compositions were doctored for popular consumption. Although Durham was involved in these big-band developments, he remained close to the spirit of the blues-infused Kansas City tradition, which would be revitalized in the mid- to late 1940s and the early 1950s by Charlie

Parker, carried on through the 1950s by Count Basie and by Jimmy Giuffre in his work with Shorty Rogers, and extended by Ornette Coleman and others into the 1960s, 1970s, and 1980s.

Durham's career did not end in the early 1940s, but by that time he had accomplished his major work as a composer-arranger and a soloist. During the war years, Eddie trained the International Sweethearts of Rhythm, the all-woman jazz orchestra, and later organized his All-Star Girl Orchestra, disbanding it after V-J Day in 1945.[55] Durham also brought together a number of early Kansas City figures for small group sessions. In 1973 he joined forces with Snub Mosley for two recordings made on the English RCA Victor label,[56] and then in 1981, while on his first European tour, Durham made the album *Blue 'Bone* with a quartet of tenor, piano, bass, and drums, on which there are two originals by Eddie, *Sliding Along* and the title tune. *Blue 'Bone*, a slow, low-down blues, shows off Durham's still considerable trombone technique at the age of seventy-five, while his guitar work on *Front and Centre* and *Out of Nowhere* (a tune immortalized by Charlie Parker) finds him still improving on the amplified instrument he introduced to jazz in 1935. As a versatile and highly proficient musician who was willing to experiment with new approaches to jazz and who was capable of adjusting to changing styles, Durham was representative of many black and white musicians of his own and later generations. Like other of his fellow Texans, Eddie was an enduring figure who remained active for seven decades, changing with the times yet remaining true to the southwestern traditions from which he took his inspiration. Native Texas jazzmen like Durham have exhibited above all an openness to change and innovation, an Emersonian self-reliance, and an adventuresomeness that has led them to participate in widely divergent groups, to which they have effectively adapted themselves and to the common funds of which they have made a significant and lasting contribution.

❡ ❡ ❡

Like Eddie Durham, Albert "Budd" Johnson was a versatile figure who played vital roles in the history of jazz, both as a performer on the woodwind family of instruments and as an arranger and business manager for several top bands and for a number of historic recording sessions. Born in Dallas on December 14, 1910, Budd was active from his teenage years in local bands organized by himself and his older brother Keg. The first group started by the Johnson brothers was called the Moonlight Melody Six and shortly thereafter, about 1925, it became the Blue Moon Chasers.[57] Under this name the group traveled to Tulsa, meeting up with the Blue Devils and Jimmy Rushing, who fed them at his family's restaurant when the brothers were broke. Back in Dallas, Budd knew Buster Smith in Deep Ellum and heard the bands of Alphonse Trent and Terrence Holder, thinking at the time and recalling for years afterward that Trent's Snub Mosley "was the greatest trombone player I'd ever heard in my life."[58] In 1952 Budd would tour Europe with Mosley for the USO, and in 1967 he would perform for the first time with Jimmy Rushing, two of the many jazz stars that Budd met early in his life in the Southwest and with whom he would eventually play as a star in his own right.[59]

While still in Texas, Budd journeyed to El Paso in 1927 with Ben Smith's Music Makers, playing "for room and board and tips—no salary," after which in 1928 he and Keg joined Gene Coy's Happy Black Aces out of Amarillo, where Budd met Ben Webster and showed him how to play the saxophone.[60] From here the brothers returned to Dallas to become part of Holder's band, opening up what Budd remembered as the city's first nightclub. It was at this time that Budd was with Eddie Durham briefly in what was the Twelve Clouds of Joy *in Dallas* (before it went to Kansas City) and later with Jesse Stone's Blue Serenaders, which ended up in Kaycee as "the first black band that brought music on paper."[61]

In Kansas City, Bennie Moten's biggest rival was the George E. Lee Band, which Jesse Stone and Budd Johnson joined around 1929. Budd made his first recordings late in that year. On *Paseo Street*, Budd takes an eight-bar solo, which, according to Frank Driggs, "shows him to have been a tenor player of fluent technique and an unusually light tone for that time. His style already seemed personal and original, and he seemed to owe little to Coleman Hawkins, Prince Robinson, or other established tenor soloists of the time."[62] Reportedly Moten tried to raid Lee's band to get "the fine tenorman and arranger Budd Johnson,"[63] for by 1929 Budd was writing arrangements as well as playing sax. During his stay with Lee's band, Johnson met Coleman Hawkins for the first time in Tulsa at Dreamland Hall. At nineteen, Budd was impressed that "young as I was, [Hawkins] gave me some attention when I let him know who I was. That is one of the reasons I always respected this guy."[64] Although Budd's playing may not owe much to Hawkins, Johnson himself acknowledged that "nobody influenced me before him. It was definitely Hawk."[65] In 1932, Budd took his leave of Lee's band and headed for Chicago, where he would join his brother Keg. It was in the Windy City in 1934 that Budd met the other great tenor player in early jazz history, Lester Young, who had taken Hawkins's place with the Fletcher Henderson orchestra. As Driggs and other critics have commented, Budd and Lester sounded very much alike on tenor, even though they had developed their styles quite independently. Johnson remarked that "it's a funny thing, because before ever we heard one another we played similar styles. . . . We were eager then to show each other what we learned. . . . I really never tried to copy Pres, until maybe later, when I may have thought I wanted to do something like he was doing."[66]

In Chicago, Johnson worked with several bands—Ed Carry, Cass Simpson, Irene Eadey, Eddie Mallory, Clarence Moore, and Jimmie Noone—but it was with Earl Hines that Budd most wanted to play. He got his chance on May 10, 1935: "I'll never forget the date."[67] Before this, Budd was with his brother Keg and with Teddy Wilson in Louis Armstrong's band. Johnson often called this "one of Louis's worst bands," but it was on two tunes recorded with Armstrong in January 1933 that Budd exhibited his tenor sound with its tone that reminds one of Lester Young: *Mahogany Hall Stomp* and *Some Sweet Day*, the latter with a solo that "utilizes space in much the same manner that Lester Young was later noted for and shows [Johnson's] ability to swing using the simplest of statements."[68] As noted earlier, these solos predate Budd's meeting of Lester by at least one year and Prez's first recording by almost four years.

Following the accidental death of Cecil Irwin, the tenorman and arranger with the Earl Hines band, Budd Johnson was called in May 1935 to join Hines at the Orpheum Theatre in Minneapolis. Budd had previously sat in with Earl's band, taking Irwin's place when he was doing some writing for the group. At such times, Johnson said, he would "sight-read the book, because by this time I was quite a musician. 'Don't never come to Chicago if you can't read,' they used to say, and scare us to death in Kansas City. But I was prepared, and I had made up my mind I was going to join Earl's band when I used to hear it over the radio in K.C."[69] While with Hines, Budd began to write arrangements for such tunes as *Blue Because of You*, *Rosetta*, and *You Can Depend on Me*. Only later, in 1940, would this last arrangement be recorded, and by that time Budd had returned to the band, after having been with Gus Arnheim at the Hotel New Yorker as an arranger and at the same time doing work in New York for Mickey Alpert. Johnson recalled that in 1937 "I was really in the writing business. I was turning it out like crazy."[70] Johnson went back to Chicago and jobbed around, recording in October 1937 with the Lionel Hampton orchestra, which included on *Rock Hill Special* many of the Hines sidemen. Afterward, Budd received a call from Fletcher Henderson to play alto for a radio show broadcast from the Grand Terrace, where once again he would later join Earl Hines and reorganize "Fatha's" band. Johnson had left Hines for more money with Arnheim, who in 1937 had Stan Kenton on piano and paid three times what Budd was getting with Earl. In 1935, when Johnson first went with the Hines band, it "didn't always seem to click," so at that time Earl began to leave the hiring and firing up to Budd.[71] When Johnson returned to Hines in 1938, Earl once again left Budd in charge and the Texan ran things "just like a business. That was the beginning of his greatest band."[72]

The Hines Grand Terrace recordings of this period feature Budd Johnson both as an alto and tenor soloist as well as an arranger, especially of some of Earl's most notable tunes: *Piano Man, Father Steps In, G.T. Stomp,* and *Grand Terrace Shuffle.* As the band's "straw boss," Johnson was responsible for rehearsing the band and for writing "a large proportion of the arrangements in the book."[73] *Piano Man,* recorded on July 12, 1939, is, in Gunther Schuller's view, Budd's "exciting setting for Earl's exciting pianistics" and "a fitting introduction . . . to the 'King of Pianology.'"[74] Discussing a tune entitled *Pianology,* recorded on February 10, 1937,[75] Schuller finds Hines's piano solo "quite conservative and 'held-in,' with none of the usual surprises," but the critic nevertheless deems this recording notable "for an excellent solo by Budd Johnson, who, already an admirer of Lester Young, was bringing the first influence of that 'modern' style to the Hines band."[76] With Johnson's arrangement of *Piano Man,* Hines takes off on what Schuller terms "a brilliantly confident excursion in stride piano, the left hand leaping infallibly at the brisk tempo." Johnson solos on alto in his arrangement of *Father Steps In,* also recorded on the same date as *Piano Man,* and here Budd sounds at moments as fluid and modern as Charlie Parker. Johnson's obvious mastery of the Bird's instrument is demonstrated by his bending of notes upward, by his executing of shakes and runs with ease yet with intense swing, and in general by his creating an alto quality and technique that, as Schuller suggests of Budd's tenor break on *Pianology,* is modern in style. But to Schuller, the "real achievements" of the Hines band "were centered in a number of fine Johnson compositions and arrangements, recorded in New York in July 1939," the two most successful of which were *G.T. Stomp* and *Grand Terrace Shuffle.*[77]

While *Father Steps In* (and also Johnson's *Riff Medley*) is reminiscent of Eddie Durham's arrangements with their punctuating sax riffs—Hugues Panassié observed that even Johnson's later advanced arranging for Billy Eckstine, Woody Herman, Boyd Raeburn, and Dizzy Gillespie "particularly lend themselves to swing; they are in the great Kansas City tradition resembling those of Eddie Durham and the Count Basie style"[78]—both *G.T. Stomp* and *Grand Terrace Shuffle* offer passages in the reed section that are at times more freewheeling and generate something of a contrapuntal feeling against the solo work. Although Schuller calls Johnson's *Grand Terrace Shuffle* "an even more ambitious piece" than *G.T. Stomp,* the critic defines Johnson's major contribution on the former work as his tenor solo, which is "economically constructed" and in which "Johnson works with only two or three note motivic fragments . . . , varying them slightly and placing them, like Prez, in different contexts in the phrase structure." Schuller characterizes Budd's two solos in his arrangement of *XYZ,* recorded in Chicago on October 6, 1939, as "even more Prez-like," especially the first solo, in which the phrases and the sound are trademark Lester Young. For a quartet recording of *Honeysuckle Rose* on the February 10, 1937, date, Budd had joined Hines, Omer Simeon on clarinet, and Wallace Bishop on drums, and here again Schuller finds Johnson's playing "Lester-like,"[79] but on this occasion Budd rushes more than Young would have with his laid-back style of relaxed swing. Somehow, Johnson's faster fingering even manages a legato sound that recalls Herschel Evans more than Lester, especially in Budd's use of vibrato. Still, Johnson's rhythmic patterns are close to those of Young, although, as Frank Driggs would have it, Johnson only parallels rather than imitates Young's work.[80] The fact that Johnson could sound on tenor like Young and on alto like Parker was no mean feat, particularly when he was doing so on records before either of these giants of modern jazz.

In Gunther Schuller's view, Earl Hines did not take full advantage of Budd Johnson's talents as an arranger, and when Budd and Billy Eckstine recruited some of the "young turks"—Dizzy Gillespie and Charlie Parker among them—Hines could not hold on to these innovators.[81] In 1942 Johnson left Hines, who would give up his band in 1948 and join Armstrong's All-Stars along with Jack Teagarden, after which Hines's career in the 1950s and early 1960s was unremarkable until, once again, Budd Johnson rejoined "Fatha" and essentially rejuvenated his old boss.

An album recorded by Frank Driggs at New York's Village Vanguard on June 29 and 30, 1965, has both Johnson and his fellow Texan Gene Ramey in exceptionally fine form, as is Hines, who—along with Ramey, "one of the swingingest bassists in jazz history," and drummer Eddie Locke—is particularly impressive on an up-tempo version of *Lover Come Back to Me*.[82] "Selfless" Ramey is also superbly swinging (and very clearly recorded) on *Tea for Two, Breezin' Along with the Breeze*, and *Rosetta*, with Gene's genius for remarkable note choices especially in evidence. As for Budd Johnson, he amply demonstrates on *Sometimes I'm Happy* the truth of Stanley Dance's assertion that Budd "was one of the greatest of the many great musicians introduced during the two decades Hines led big bands." This exceptional piece of work contains all the finest qualities of tenor saxophone playing and shows that, thirty years after first joining Hines, Budd was still "an improvising soloist" who "had very few peers."[83] Indeed, Budd's extended solo, which takes up almost the entire six-minute performance, is a textbook lesson in Texas tenor that swings all the way, with everything from blues phrases and honks, touches of the funk-gospel feeling of the 1950s, and some of the most advanced musical thinking of the 1960s. This tune also exhibits the marvelous chemistry between Hines and Johnson, with both musicians inspired to some simultaneous moments of the intensest swing on record. On *Cavernism* and *Red River Remembered*, the latter credited to Hines and Johnson, Budd plays soprano sax, and each tune offers a different facet of the Texan's multitalented skills. *Out of Nowhere* reveals Johnson's warmth, feeling, and even humor, expressed so beautifully on tenor with all the control of a master musician. Finally, in Basie and Durham's *Moten Swing*, Budd shows how thoroughly he understood the Kansas City style and could swing in it with the best, from Herschel Evans and Lester Young to the Bird.

Another fine album, recorded on July 19, 1967, presents Hines, Johnson, and Jimmy Rushing in top form—the first time for both Earl and Budd to record with the blues shouter. Johnson displays all his skills as a soloist and an accompanist, performing again on both soprano and tenor. This is vintage Budd, with his tenor solo on *Louisana* warm, searching, in control, inventive, and with little surprise shifts and interpolated phrases—playing that is called "relaxed" and "attractive" in the unsigned liner notes.[84] On *Summertime* Budd plays soprano in a tribute to Sidney Bechet, which he later performed as "one of the highlights of the 1967 Newport Jazz Festival."[85] For Rushing's vocal on *Exactly Like You*, Budd provides some fine riffs and obbligato work that are identifiable with Lester Young's style but still recognizable as Johnson's own distinctive manner. On *Am I Blue?* Budd does the same thing, producing at times on tenor the light alto sound toward which Lester so often inclined. Certainly Johnson maintained throughout his career an approach closer to the "cool" school rather than to the impassioned tenor style of Coleman Hawkins or Herschel Evans. Nevertheless, Budd would also team up effectively with Hawkins when the Swing Era tenorist began to listen to and be influenced by the bop movement of the mid-1940s.

After leaving Earl Hines in 1942, Budd Johnson performed with numerous groups during the war years, among them the bands of Cab Calloway (on alto), Dizzy Gillespie, Woody Herman, and Billy Eckstine. It was on a USO tour during the war that Johnson played with Lester Young and another tenor, Al Sears, after which Budd joined Dizzy Gillespie on Fifty-second Street in New York, scene of the early developments in bop. Here Johnson renewed his association with Dizzy, who had gone with Earl Hines partly because of Budd. Before Bird arrived to take Budd's place and join Gillespie in their historic quintet of 1945, and before Don Byas was the tenor with Diz on the classic 1946 recordings, Johnson worked with Gillespie "playing those unison-line things that became so famous on records later on." As Budd tells it, he and bassist Oscar Pettiford encouraged Dizzy "to write them down, but we had to do it ourselves. They were the basis of the style then."[86] Playing at the Onyx Club on Fifty-second Street in early 1944, this group with Johnson, Gillespie, and Pettiford has been labeled "the first organized small bop combo," and Leonard Feather credits Budd with developing "the unison ensemble style that became definitive of small band bebop."[87]

Another tenorman, Kermit Scott, who according to Budd Johnson was also from Texas, worked with Gillespie even earlier,[88] in the years 1939–1942. Scott's

Onyx Club, 52nd Street, New York, 1944. Pictured are (left to right) Max Roach, Budd Johnson, Oscar Pettiford, George Wallington, and Dizzy Gillespie. Reproduced courtesy of Duncan Schiedt.

Texas connection is reinforced by Cedric Haywood, who remembered that Kermit was in Milt Larkin's Houston band during the period from 1936 to 1940 when Haywood played piano.[89] At Minton's Playhouse, Scotty, as Kermit was called, performed with Thelonious Monk on piano, Joe Guy on trumpet, Kenny Clarke on drums, and Nick Fenton on bass, and Budd recalls how Lester Young tried to "go up there and cut this guy Scotty" but Kermit knew the new music "backwards" and Lester and Ben Webster "would get a good lesson when they sat in."[90] Johnson again emphasizes the need for writing down the new music: "You gotta have some music in front of you to read or something; your ear will not carry you to where these guys were going."[91] Scott's part in the development of bop was acknowledged by Gillespie himself: "Kermit Scott had his own little style going. He lives in California now and came out on the stage with me in Monterey, in 1974, and played 'Manteca.' He went right out there and took care of business. I introduce him every time I go out to California as one of the founders of our music."[92] Jazz critic Ira Gitler, from interviews with pianist Allen Tinney and tenorman Dexter Gordon, reports that "a tenor player around Minton's named Kermit Scott" is "where Jaws [Eddie 'Lockjaw' Davis] is coming from" and that "Scotty was a heavy influence."[93]

Unfortunately, no recordings by Scott with Monk or Gillespie seem to exist, but there are several sides with Kermit playing with the Coleman Hawkins orchestra on August 9, 1940, and with Billie Holiday on various sides in the same year, although on only one of these Holiday takes does the tenorman solo, the February 29, 1940, recording of *Falling in Love Again*.[94] Sounding so much like Lester Young that it is hard to hear how Scott "had his own little style going," this solo tells us nothing about Kermit's role in the bop movement, but it certainly seems to explain why he was featured on this recording—as a stand-in for Prez, who was Billie's soul mate. Scott plays beside Lester on other Holiday sides—notably on the June 7, 1940, takes of *I'm Pulling Through, Laughing at Life,* and *Time on My Hands*—in which Prez solos and works his magic that Kermit could not quite duplicate, though almost.[95] (It may be that Scott is actually the tenor heard on *Time on My Hands.*) On these same sides with Billie, Lester, and Roy Eldridge, Scott is also in the company of another Texan, Teddy Wilson, who, along with Prez, is credited with helping Holiday create some of her very finest recordings.

As for Budd Johnson, on February 16, 1944, he would participate in—and reportedly was responsible for organizing—"the first bop record date ever cut."[96] Dan Morgenstern points out that "the main reason why this is considered the first bebop recording date" is Gillespie's composition, *Woody 'n You,* with its "effective counter melody and harmonic daring," which was "indeed a strong whiff of something new in the air."[97] It is also important for containing Gillespie's first recorded solo "that fully shows him as himself, not as the earlier Roy Eldridge disciple."[98] Dizzy's solo on *Woody 'n You* became a favorite with countless young trumpeters, including Miles Davis.[99] Significant as well is the presence of Coleman Hawkins on this date, when he not only demonstrates his ability to adapt to the new music but records a second version of his 1939 masterpiece, *Body and Soul,* this time entitled *Rainbow Mist.* As Hawkins told Budd Johnson on this occasion, *Body and Soul* "was such a big hit and it's my solo [he never plays the tune's melody], so I'm gonna do that over and call it 'Moon Mist' or something like that."[100] Although critic John Chilton suggests that *Rainbow Mist* was recorded by Hawkins to make himself some money as the "composer" and feels that this second version lacks "the creative magic of the original,"[101] Morgenstern considers both versions to be masterpieces, with the Hawk's "sound alone fuller" on the later recording and "a thing of beauty."

Johnson's tenor forms only part of the ensemble on *Rainbow Mist*, just as his baritone sax does on *Woody 'n You*. The latter tune derives from "a minor-sixth chord to the dominant seventh" and "the influence of Monk"[102] and was dedicated to Woody Herman, who recorded it under the title of *Yenta*. Budd's outstanding contribution to the session (aside from his role as its organizer) is *Bu Dee Daht*, written with pianist-arranger Clyde Hart. This "hip riff number"[103] also features Dizzy's trumpet, which is "no less startling" than on *Woody 'n You*, even though "the sequence, with its more or less conventional use of diminished chords, is not as challenging."[104] Ira Gitler credits his own introduction to the new music to ravings over the recording of this Johnson-Hart composition.[105] Other tunes recorded on this date are Hawkins's *Disorder at the Border*, a blues on which Gillespie provides "the more daring improvisations" and Hawkins branches off "into new territory," and the standard *Yesterdays*, on which Hawkins "hits a stunning high note (not so common with him) along the way." Hawk would record *Yesterdays* again magnificently in 1960 at the Essen Festival in Germany, accompanied by three of the early bop masters, Oscar Pettiford, Bud Powell, and Kenny Clarke.[106]

A little over a month later, on March 23, 1944, Budd Johnson recorded with Woody Herman. Further evidence of the Texan's amazing versatility is provided by his fine tenor solo on the novelty number entitled *It Must Be Jelly 'Cause Jam Don't Shake Like That*. Unlike Johnson's solo on *Cherry*, which is inappropriately broad for the style of the band's crisp interpretation of this Don Redman tune,[107] his chorus on *It Must Be Jelly* fits perfectly into the swing tradition of this number. On this recording date, Johnson was joined in the reed section by fellow Texan Ernie Caceres on baritone. It was at this time that Herman was just finding his "own particular groove," a type of bebop big-band style that would lead to the creation of his First Herd.[108] Even though Budd was not quite right for this band, which "zoomed to the country's number one spot" on the basis of its biting brass and swinging sax ensembles and the writing of Neal Hefti and later Shorty Rogers and Jimmy Giuffre,[109] it is a tribute to Johnson's all-around musicianship and his rapport with other jazzmen—both black and white—that he was sought out by so many prominent bandleaders in every period of jazz to fill a necessary role, whether as soloist, arranger, organizer, or section man.[110]

Other recording sessions from the 1940s that included Budd Johnson were those of April 13, 1944, with the Billy Eckstine Deluxe All-Stars; of February–March 1945 with Eckstine at the Plantation Club in Hollywood; and of December 1947 with the Coleman Hawkins orchestra in New York. On the 1944 All-Star session with Eckstine, the group performs Gillespie's *Good Jelly Blues*, which, according to Dizzy, is "one of my best and . . . the first 'double up' arrangement."

Gillespie goes on to explain this term and to comment on the musicians, many of whom would soon become members of Eckstine's regular band, including Budd Johnson: "In our style with all the riffs, we played very few riffs slowly. Very few phrases weren't 'doubled up,' double the time of the music, except for whole-note phrases. So on 'Good Jelly Blues,' when we were playing behind a vocalist, Billy Eckstine, the saxophones would hold the harmony behind him. It was nice, and we had some good players on that session."[111]

Johnson joined Eckstine in 1945 and did much of the writing for Billy's band, contributing, along with such tunes as *Rhythm in a Riff* and *I'm in the Mood for Love*, a "fantastic arrangement" of *Airmail Special*, on which the tenorist plays a Lester-like solo from a performance by the band at the Plantation Club in early 1945.[112] As Johnson's longest solo on the album issued from the February–March engagement, this extended offering, which follows a solo by Fats Navarro on trumpet, allows Budd to stretch out effectively, and even though he recalls Prez in the alternate fingerings for the same notes and in the generally similar sound and style, Johnson is convincingly his own man. On *Blowing the Blues Away* Budd takes a break that is also Lester-like but fuller toned, as is the solo by Gene Ammons, whose playing is even broader and more robust. As for Johnson's arranging skills, these are exhibited on *Together*—a "lame duck tune" that Budd "revitalised"[113]—with its fine sax work following Eckstine's trumpet solo. After the saxes and brasses swing out, Budd ends his arrangement with a boppish allusion to Glenn Miller's *Pennsylvania 6-5000*. Mark Gardner notes that "clearly none of [the band's] members suffered under the discipline of playing the same section parts nightly. All found this experience of playing *together* invaluable. The ensemble work is of a very high order."[114] The excellent section work is again in evidence on *Mr. Chips*, which may have been arranged by Johnson, who solos briefly. In what Gardner calls a "fine composition and arrangement" that "must, for the moment at least, remain uncredited," drummer Art Blakey is the featured soloist.[115] Speaking of Johnson's career as an arranger, Leonard Feather has written that the Texan "played a unique role in the development of modern jazz. The only large bands of the early 1940s involved in the transition from swing to bop were those of Earl Hines and Boyd Raeburn in '42–44, Billy Eckstine and Woody Herman in '44–45, and Gillespie in '45–46. The only common thread linking them was Johnson, who wrote music for all five bands and played tenor sax in person or on records with all but Raeburn's."[116]

By the time Johnson recorded again with Coleman Hawkins on December 17, 1947, the bop movement was in full control, as bands large and small had picked up on the innovations of Gillespie and Parker that could not be denied. Although, as we have seen, Budd could sound like Parker as early as the 1939 *Father Steps In*, previous to any known recording by the Bird, there is no doubt that the 1947 session with Hawkins, which produced *Jumping for Jane* and *Half Step Down Please*, would not have been the same without the revolutionary developments introduced by Gillespie and Parker in 1945. While Hawkins is essentially his old self playing within the bop framework, Johnson seems to have listened closely to Parker, for in Budd's solo on the upbeat *Jumping for Jane* he plays alto "of a very Parkerish hue."[117] The turns of phrase, the half quote from Parker's *Ornithology*, the long flowing lines, and the clean and direct tone are all distinctive hallmarks of the Bird's impact, even on a jazzman like Johnson, who may have been moving in the direction of such bop methods on his own. Certainly the other soloists on this tune—guitarist Chuck Wayne, pianist Hank Jones, trombonist J. J. Johnson, trumpeter Fats Navarro, and drummer Max Roach—are all unabashed adherents of the bop revolution. As for *Half Step Down Please*, composed by Tadd Dameron, this tune already looks forward to the Miles Davis nonet of 1949, in which Max Roach would also figure prominently, as would J. J. Johnson's sidekick, trombonist Kai Winding. Budd does not solo here, but once again he is present in the ensemble, contributing to the onward force of jazz as it built on the effects of bop and pushed toward the changes wrought by Miles Davis's "the birth of the cool."

During the 1950s, Budd Johnson remained quite active, touring Asia with Benny Goodman in 1957 and recording at times with other Texans, as on an album produced in New York in 1956 and 1957 that includes Lammar Wright and Tyree Glenn. Here Johnson takes an extended solo on *Impressions of New York* and another on *Blues for Me, Myself, and I*, the latter utilizing the full range of Budd's tenor as he digs deeply into this minor blues.[118] The 1956–1957 album offers nothing new, but it is good jazz played in the tried and true styles of the Swing Era. Another recording with Coleman Hawkins, along with Ben Webster and Roy Eldridge, from April 9, 1959, also exhibits a full-blown statement of the blues by Budd on a tune by Webster entitled, after the Texan, *Budd Johnson*.[119]

By this time, Johnson was no longer participating in trailblazing sessions, but he did take part in a historic musical event on July 6, 1961, at the Columbia studios in New York when, for the first time, the bands of Duke Ellington and Count Basie performed side by side in a friendly "battle royal." Budd Johnson solos in the Ellington-Strayhorn classic *Take the "A" Train*, in Frank Wess's *Segue in C*, "one of the outstanding arrangements in the Basie book," and on a piece by Freddie Greene, the Count's longtime guitarist, entitled *Corner Pocket* but renamed here *Until I Met You*.[120] Johnson's solo on *Segue in C* is not exceptional, for even though Stanley Dance calls his four choruses "authoritative," they remain too relaxed and never develop any drive or any sense of form or direction. However, Johnson recorded an earlier solo on this same tune only eight days before, on June 28, 1961, and it is one of his finest outings ever, comparable to his solo work in the late 1930s and on *Sometimes I'm Happy* with Earl Hines in 1965. A live performance with the Basie band at Birdland, this earlier recording of what is given as *Segue in "C"* opens with a classic Basie rhythm section intro (Freddie Greene on guitar, the Count on piano, and Eddie Jones on bass), and Johnson follows with a Prez-like solo that is yet very much Budd's own style, with two sixteenth-note passages that are truly splendid (and quite unlike Lester), flawlessly performed, and at one point with a real Texas "honk." The difference between Budd's live solo and his studio work is quite dramatic and illustrates why the audience regarded the Basie at Birdland performance as "the culmination of all the jazz shows, concerts and events that have ever taken place in New York."[121]

On the July 1961 combined Basie-Ellington recording, Budd's solo on *Take the "A" Train* is obviously inspired by this famous tune, as he trades tasteful fours with the Duke's Jimmy Hamilton. Perhaps it is too much to expect anything new from such a studio album as this, which is essentially given over to replaying memorable tunes on which the soloists in their respective bands recreate their own choruses or those by their legendary predecessors. But what can be said about this historic occasion is concisely summarized by Stanley Dance when he writes, "Gathered this day was the cream of the profession, men with a thoroughly professional and sophisticated attitude, who recognized one another's gifts not only as soloists but as capable musicians with whom they could work harmoniously towards the creation of an orchestral whole."[122]

Johnson would rejoin Basie in 1979 for the album entitled *Get Together*, which marked the only time a Kansas City group (in this case an octet) was composed entirely of musicians who had been members of Basie's small or big bands.[123] Also rejoining the Count is Gus Johnson on drums. Here Budd solos on both baritone and tenor, demonstrating on the former his very considerable power, with an especially strong appearance on *Swinging on the Cusp*. Each of the hornmen—Budd, Lockjaw Davis, Clark Terry, and Sweets Edison—is featured, along with Basie, in a medley of tunes, with Budd taking a masterful solo on *Talk of the Town* that shows him undiminished and even still growing after some fifty years of active playing.

On December 2, 1960, Budd and his brother Keg had recorded the album entitled, appropriately, *Let's Swing*. Of Budd's performance on his own original, *Blues by Budd*, Alun Morgan has written that he "plays the blues with more authority than almost any other tenor saxophonist in jazz."[124] Joe Goldberg, who contributed the liner notes for the album, celebrates another side to this Texas musician when he refers to Budd's wonderfully warm personality, recalling how jazz critic

Martin Williams thought that "one of the most heartening things" he had ever seen was "the look that comes into everyone's face when Budd Johnson walks into a recording date, or, for that matter, any room where he is known."[125] It is clear why the Texan was welcomed by so many bands playing in so many different styles on so many historic occasions. In every capacity—as composer, arranger, soloist, rehearsal director, businessman, and section leader—Budd Johnson was sought out by his fellow musicians because they knew that with his talents available to the group, regardless of the kind of ensemble or the demands of the music, "they could work harmoniously towards the creation of an orchestral whole."

OUT OF BIG D

In 1936, shortly before Count Basie was booked into the Grand Terrace in Chicago by John Hammond, Buster Smith left the band and joined Claude Hopkins in Iowa, after which he returned to Kansas City to play with George E. Lee's sister.[1] Although this was Buster's missed opportunity to make it to the big time with Basie's band, for which he remained "a little sorry" the rest of his life,[2] this did not by any means mark the end of Buster's part in jazz history. In 1937 Smith organized his own band in Kansas City, and "the first in line" to become a member was seventeen-year-old Charlie Parker, who had "idolized Buster since their first meeting in 1932."[3] The extent of Smith's influence on Parker has been the subject of much speculation by the leading writers on Bird's career. As we have seen, Ross Russell finds that Buster's 1929 recording of *Squabblin'* with the Blue Devils "forecasts Charlie Parker."[4] But the very fact that young Yardbird— as he was called in 1932 or 1933 when as a kid he would hang around, with his alto in a paper sack, listening to Smith and the Moten band—spent some two years playing next to his mentor would suggest that Buster's role was indeed significant during the formative years of Parker's career.

If for most listeners the importance of Buster Smith's playing lies in its relationship to Bird's development of a style and technique that changed the course of jazz forever, there is unfortunately a paucity of recorded examples of Buster's alto work on which to base a comparative study. What evidence does exist, however, seems to leave little doubt that "the Professor," as Smith was called, proved a vital precursor of Parker's approach to the alto. (The source of Buster's nickname is suggested by Ross Russell when he notes that "Prof Smith and Herschel Evans . . . had Texas accents and looked like school teachers.")[5] On a more personal level, as well, Smith was close to Bird and served as something of a surrogate father. But in addition to his role as a pre-bop influence, the Prof made a number of recordings in New York with fellow Texans that help fill out the incomplete picture we have of this musician who as arranger, composer, and performer on clarinet and alto reflects many of the major developments in jazz from the late 1920s through the early 1940s.

Buster Smith's 1937 band included several men who would later become prominent members of Jay McShann's orchestra—McShann himself, Orville "Piggy" Minor, Freddie Culliver, and Parker. Buster and Charlie both played alto, with the pair sharing solo time equally. According to Smith, Bird wanted him "to take the first solo. I guess he thought he'd learn something that way. He did play like me quite a bit I guess. But after a while, anything I could make on my horn he could make too—and make something better out of it."[6] Playing with his first organized band, Parker probably learned the kind of "double up" approach that he and Gillespie would later practice during the mid-1940s. As Buster recalled, "We used to do that double time stuff all the time. Only we called it double tongue sometimes in those days. I used to do a lot of that on clarinet."[7] Unfortunately, Buster's band never seems to have recorded, even though it broadcast from Lucille's Band Box on Eighteenth Street in Kaycee. Apparently Buster had ambitions for his band, and in 1938 he went to New York to find work for his group, leaving Charlie and Odel West in charge and intending to send for them. But after waiting three months to gain admittance to the union and finding nothing after seven months, Buster had still not sent for the band, so Parker "got downhearted" and "just caught a train and hoboed up," arriving with his legs "all swollen" from keeping his shoes on for so long.[8] Smith made room at his place for the Bird and during the day let Charlie sleep in his bed, which, according to one report, resulted in the Prof's "losing a wife who objected to Buster's allowing Parker to stay in his less-than-roomy apartment."[9]

With this first stay in New York, Bird was beginning to be listened to by other musicians at such nightspots as Monroe's. But even more important, it was in December 1939 while jamming with guitarist Biddy Fleet at a chili parlor on Seventh Avenue near 140th Street that Charlie stumbled onto what he later claimed was a major discovery when he found in working over *Cherokee* "that by using higher intervals of a chord as a melody line and backing them with appropriately related [chord] changes, he could play this thing he had been 'hearing.' Fleet picked it up behind him and bop was born."[10] Soon after this, however, Parker was called back to Kansas City for his father's funeral and remained there, joining Jay McShann's orchestra for what proved to be a three-year stint, his longest with a big band. As Buster Smith noted, Charlie really wanted "to play in the small groups where he could solo like he wanted to, when he wanted to."[11] Only after Parker's return to

New York City in 1942, and after working there for almost two years with the Earl Hines and Billy Eckstine bands before resigning, was Bird able to devote himself entirely to the bop combos. Subsequently, Parker and Gillespie made the definitive bop recordings of November 26, 1945, with "an astonishing improvisation on *Cherokee*, taken at a reckless tempo," and "a slow blues, *Now's the Time*, . . . perhaps the finest single piece of music produced by the beboppers."[12]

In the meantime, Buster Smith was mostly doing arranging for such big bands as those of Count Basie, Hot Lips Page, and Gene Krupa, turning down Artie Shaw because he wanted three arrangements a week. Buster preferred to take his time, working slowly and carefully on his charts.[13] During this period, the Prof was rarely playing his alto—he had in fact pawned his instrument. However, on June 30, 1939, Pete Johnson and Joe Turner from Kansas City got Buster's sax out of hock for a recording session on which the Prof would once again provide evidence of his superior skills as a soloist. Made in New York City and billed as Pete Johnson's Boogie Woogie Boys, the recording from this date includes on trumpet Buster's former Blue Devils and Moten bandmate, Hot Lips Page. On *Baby, Look at You*, the two Texans play fine obbligatos behind Joe Turner's vocal, and on this tune and on *Cherry Red*, Buster is featured in what Gunther Schuller calls "beautiful and prophetic solos." Schuller goes on to note that "especially characteristic and 'modern' are the sleek downward runs on *Baby* and the bold gestures in bar 5 and 6 of Buster's chorus on *Cherry*."[14] Charles Fox enters a slight demurrer with regard to Buster's "tantalizing performances" on these two tunes: "Hindsight can lead one to read more into short solos like these than they may deserve." However, Fox recounts an anecdote that would seem to support the claim for Buster's influence on Bird: "Jay McShann even recalls hearing a broadcast in Kansas City during 1939 when he failed to realize he was listening to Parker and not to Smith, who had just left for New York."[15] Budd Johnson always contended that "Bird really came from Buster Smith. Because when I was a kid Buster Smith was playing like that then. Way before Bird was ever born. In Dallas, Texas."[16] But Albert McCarthy again suggests that "the stress on [Buster's] 'modern' qualities and his influence on Parker has, possibly, been overdone, for while his recorded solos reveal him as a fine musician they are clearly in the swing tradition."[17]

Certainly the eight-bar solo by Buster on *Cherry Red* has a definite Parker sound, but it is far too brief—one wants more, as is often the case with Herschel Evans, yet even more so with Buster since he recorded far less than one might wish. Page is muted and offers "a searingly 'hot-lipped' growly solo,"[18] and at the end he and

Buster (on clarinet) join for the closing theme. Based in part on this performance, Ross Russell, author of the first biography of Charlie Parker, renders a glowing estimate of Buster's achievement:

> An exalted and highly fluid line is the leading characteristic of Buster Smith's improvisations. He surpasses both Lester Young and Charlie Parker in this respect, for he is smoother. His musical ideas are less spectacular; he is not as daring a musician as they. Smith has a light, silky tone that still manages to retain its blues edge. His time is always perfectly in hand, and he generates an irresistible swing. On the evidence of what little he did record, he deserves a rating with the best alto saxophonists in jazz and is, after Charlie Parker, my favorite on the instrument.[19]

Russell's view is seconded by Samuel Charters and Leonard Kunstadt in their history of the New York jazz scene when they write that Buster "was one of the greatest alto men in jazz, but by staying out of New York at the wrong time he never achieved the fame he deserved."[20]

While still in New York, Buster Smith also recorded eight tunes with Hot Lips Page and His Orchestra on January 23, 1940.[21] Surprisingly, this session has not been discussed either by Ross Russell or Gunther Schuller, both of whom have rendered abundant praise for Smith's brief *Cherry Red* solo but have not mentioned his extended chorus on *I Ain't Got Nobody* from the date with Page.[22] Smith's sound and conception are fully in evidence on this performance, his ideas flowing ceaselessly and unexpectedly as in a Bird solo—from an unusual entrance to many inventive melodic twists and turns that undoubtedly taught Parker so much when he sat beside the Professor back in 1937. In another tune from this 1940 session with Hot Lips, *Walk It to Me*, Buster's approach can be contrasted with that of the fine swing tenorist Sam Davis, whose solos throughout the recording are also quite excellent. But Buster's conception is notably more modern than Davis's Herschel Evans–inspired tenor, as can be heard when the altoist takes an eight-bar chorus following Davis's longer break. From the very first notes of his solo, Buster reveals a newer feeling, a more flowing style that differs dramatically from Davis's on-the-beat rhythms. Also notable in this session is Smith's writing for the ensemble. His arrangement of *A Porter's Love Song to a Chamber Maid* has the saxes biting off their phrases crisply in the Lunceford manner but more subtly. On *I Would Do Anything For You* Buster utilizes the riff from Eddie Durham's *Sent For You Yesterday* and at first achieves a Basie sound (or perhaps it should be called the Basie *Smith* sound) and then more of a Lunceford style, though the writing seems a bit too intricate for Jimmie's more popular approach. In this tune the Prof takes a brief, very

Buster Smith of Altdorf.
Reproduced from
The Legendary Buster Smith
(Atlantic 1323);
photograph by
Bob Tenney.

smooth break on clarinet, though it is not as imaginative as his alto work, which on *I Ain't Got Nobody* firmly supports Budd Johnson's view that "Bird really came from Buster Smith."

Other sessions from Buster's New York period include a July 23, 1941, recording with Bon Bon and His Buddies, on which Buster is joined by Eddie Durham; a February 11, 1942, recording with Snub Mosley and His Band; and a possible session on March 23, 1939, with Don Redman's Orchestra.[23] Yet another recording of two tunes by Eddie Durham and His Band from November 11, 1940, includes both Joe Keyes and Buster Smith, Eddie's former Moten bandmates and fellow Texans, with Durham on electric guitar and Keyes on trumpet contributing some especially fine unison work.[24] In Durham's classic *Moten Swing*, the altoist can be heard in three separate choruses that illustrate the smoothness of Buster's playing, referred to by Ross Russell. Moving beautifully up and down the horn with "a light, silky tone," Buster delivers a marvelous, well-constructed first chorus that, as Russell has observed of his work, "generates an irresistible swing." Following Durham's break on electric guitar, Buster comes back for a second chorus that is not, however, as smooth or as well conceived as the first, though it contains some new ideas that are a bit more "spectacular." The third chorus is the shortest and is closer to the quality and conception of the first. Despite the flaws in Buster's second chorus, which occur mostly in the first part, overall this rare extended offering demonstrates the Texan's adventuresome spirit. Smith's influence on Parker is clearly discernible in certain turns and note choices, and Thomas Owens has observed that "sitting next to Smith night after night apparently had its effect on Parker, for his solo on *Moten Swing* [from November 30, 1940, with the McShann orchestra] is remarkably similar in tone quality and some melodic details to Smith's solo recorded three weeks earlier."[25] In general, this performance fully justifies Russell's rating of Smith "with the best alto saxophonists in jazz."

The other tune from the 1940 session, *I Want a Little Girl*, also recorded earlier with the Kansas City Six, features Durham's electric guitar, which still cannot compare with Charlie Christian's playing for inventiveness and fluidity but is nonetheless satisfying, particularly in tandem with Joe Keyes, who also turns in a fine muted solo chorus. Buster does not solo on this second tune, but his choruses on *Moten Swing* constitute for Russell the most accessible work of this "major saxophonist."[26] Hearing the potential on this recording for even greater things from the altoist makes it all the more disheartening to discover, from the moving account given by Gunther Schuller of his herculean efforts to record Smith, that it was seventeen years between Buster's recording in 1942 with Snub Mosley and his next session, which Schuller organized for the Professor in 1959.

The story Gunther Schuller tells in his insert to the 1959 Atlantic album, *The Legendary Buster Smith*, is a fascinating tale of frustration, impasse, coincidence, and persistence as the composer–jazz historian attempted to locate Smith in Dallas, where he was living "in relative obscurity." Schuller had gone to Big D first with the Metropolitan Opera Orchestra on its spring tour in 1957, when he missed hearing Buster and his band at the annual ball. The following year Schuller finally tracked down the altoist to a dance hall where Buster was playing for a private Shriner's party. Initially Schuller was not allowed in, but later Smith arranged for his admission. The critic describes how he heard Buster's alto "soaring effortlessly above the raucous, rocking Southwestern-style band. . . . In it one could hear the pure, direct sound that Charlie Parker's ear must have absorbed in Kansas City over twenty years ago."

The following June of 1959, Schuller would record Buster and his band at a studio in Fort Worth, but only after more difficulties in making contact with Smith and waiting out his and his band members' arrival for the recording session. Most of the Atlantic album is taken up with choruses played by Buster's sidemen, while the Prof himself solos infrequently. During the time that Schuller and Smith were awaiting the rest of Buster's players to show up, the altoist "became very shy and reluctant" when Schuller suggested that he record "several ballads with just rhythm."[27] Fortunately, Schuller managed to "coax the lovely *September*

Song out of " the Prof, for this is a masterful performance, with great control and tone quality. In an interview with Ira Gitler, Jay McShann recalled how "Buster had it, but you would have to make him play. . . . To me, Buster's one of the greatest clarinet players in the world. We used to feature him, and we'd have to make him play, and also on alto we'd have to make him play."[28] Smith's approach to the ballad *September Song* is quite modern, which might be expected by 1959; yet other early jazzmen did not necessarily keep up, and even Buster admitted that he did not do so well in this department.[29] Nonetheless, it is clear that Smith was still a formidable soloist who had developed or maintained his understanding of the modern jazz idiom.

On *Late, Late*, a Smith original, Buster again exhibits an extremely modern alto sound, nothing really of Parker in it, but rather more of a Los Angeles–West Coast orientation, though with a greater blues feeling. Another Smith original, entitled *Buster's Tune*, contains a brief solo by the altoist that shows a bit of the Parker style, but this similarity is even more apparent in the opening of *Organ Grinder's Swing*, with the little figures Buster repeats but varies by moving up an octave as Parker would often do. Buster's long lines take just the right twists and turns, swinging and revealing the altoist's peculiar rhythmic sense, while the tone is his own rather than that associated with Parker—lighter than the Bird's hard-edged sound. Even so, as Frank Driggs points out, it was Buster's "original sound and lope-along style" that "captured the younger Parker's imagination."[30] *E-Flat Boogie* also offers a brief solo by the altoist, as well as a fine trumpet solo by Charles Gillum, a former member of Boots and His Buddies, the San Antonio band of the 1930s.[31] Finally, *King Alcohol* is a type of ballad that has some nice moments by Buster but nothing to compare with *September Song*, which is surely the high point of this recording. Schuller explains that Buster's band was basically for dancing and that "solid rocking rhythms" were "far more important in Buster's everyday existence than melody or inventive improvisations *per se*. . . . Buster's jazz material, in the 'art' sense of the word, was limited because there is no practical use for it in the Deep South, where Negro musicians are relegated to a strictly servile function of 'entertainin'' the folks for dancin''—and today, dance music means primarily rock and roll."[32]

When Buster Smith left New York in 1942, he was "razzed" for "going back to the sticks," but the jazzman had known the big city and was ready to find time for fishing.[33] In reflecting on Buster's place in jazz history, Jay McShann has been quoted as saying, "You gotta' admit that as an arranger Buster Smith was 20 years ahead of his time and he could always blow—I mean he could really blow."[34] As an influence on Charlie Parker, Buster clearly made his mark on the development of the modern saxophone, and as an arranger it seems that indeed he was "one of a handful of . . . musicians who were responsible for having created the most swinging phase of jazz music."[35] This is much for any man to accomplish, especially a retiring, rather shy, gentlemanly figure who said modestly of himself and his fellow musicians, "We studied our instruments and our arrangements and worked hard at them. The music was the thing."[36]

❧ ❧ ❧

Like Buster Smith, trumpeter Hot Lips Page left the Basie band before it achieved the national recognition that might have assured him of a more secure future and greater exposure as a soloist. But also like Buster, Page did not see his career come to a sudden close, despite the misfortune that followed his decision to go with Louis Armstrong's manager, Joe Glaser. After Glaser signed Page as a bandleader and his band opened in August 1937 at Smalls' Paradise in Harlem, it was less than a year before the group broke up. Although Page tried to keep a smaller band going, he was unsuccessful as a leader, proving too "kindhearted and forever a soft touch . . . victimized by agents, club owners, and, sad to say, his fellow musicians."[37] Nevertheless, Lips made many more recordings than Buster Smith and established himself both as a popular blues singer and a respected soloist on trumpet in the Armstrong tradition, "a master of mutes with a growl style."[38] Most important, Page became in New York "the spirit of the jam session incarnate" and "conquered Harlem and the rest of the jazz scene in the big city."[39]

As we have seen, Page not only missed out on the success of the Count Basie big band, but his place was taken by Carl Tatti Smith in the seminal recordings of Jones-Smith, Inc., in 1936. But with his own big band, with various small groups gathered for record dates, and on the occasion of house parties or of jam sessions at Minton's Uptown House in Harlem, Lips Page demonstrated his many talents as leader, blues and scat singer, trumpet star, and jammer extraordinaire. Regrettably, recordings made by Page and his band from 1938 mostly have him sounding like many of the swing-era trumpeters and his group as fairly indistinguishable from a host of big bands of the day, as on *I'm Gonna Lock My Heart* from June 24, 1938.[40] In this particular tune, however, Page recaptures in his solo some of the old excitement and fire of his work with the 1932 Moten band. More often, as on *At Your Beck and Call*, from April 27, 1938, Page sounds imitative of a number of other swing trumpeters, as if perhaps New York has tamed the "Trumpet King of the West." But then on *If I Were You* from June 24, 1938, Lips takes a fine solo, displaying some of his rapid tonguing and approaching the bop trumpeters of the 1940s in his show of technique. At times, as in the Ellington tune *I Let a Song Go Out of My Heart*, Page employs some half-valve fingering that recalls Armstrong yet is distinctive to the Lips sound, which is more pinched, not so open and singing as

Oran "Hot Lips" Page of Dallas. Reproduced by permission of *Down Beat.*

that of Louis. Page also plays a growl solo that is reminiscent of the Duke's trumpeters, Bubber Miley and Cootie Williams, and even though Dan Morgenstern prefers Page to Williams, this example of Page's growl style is not exemplary, just as his alto player's solo cannot compare with the Johnny Hodges rendition.

In general, Page seems too generous to the band and does not feature himself as the star player as much as one might wish. In a number of selections Lips sings with a mellow voice and fine rhythm, but as Morgenstern concedes, commercial recordings "rarely did Lips justice" and this band was "not a great one," with the critic calling *Skull Duggery* the best it had to offer, and even this second-level swing performance is marred by missed notes. In the same year of 1938, Page was reunited with a great, if not the greatest, band of the period, joining the Basie aggregation for the "Spirituals to Swing" concert at Carnegie Hall in December.[41] Featured on *Blues with Lips,* along with the last recorded tenor solo by Herschel Evans, Page is in an Armstrong mode in the beginning, but on his second chorus he plays more in the Kansas City riff style, with some trumpet shakes à la Louis. However, even here with his old group from the Moten days, Page does not seem to shine as he could, and for the most part the performances by the Basie band on this occasion are not that special.

It was with smaller groups and particularly during jam sessions that Hot Lips Page evinced the kind of trumpet prowess that earned for him Roy Eldridge's acclaim as "the most underrated trumpeter in jazz."[42] Two interesting small group sides from March 21, 1939, find Page a member of Billie Holiday's orchestra. On the take of a tune entitled *Long Gone Blues*, one of the few blues the vocalist ever recorded, the ensemble sound, and even Holiday's entrance, is right out of the 1920s, the heyday of the blues form.[43] Page's obbligato trumpet in the background is barely audible, but it adds to the blues atmosphere, and on his growl solo Lips justifies the high marks given to him by Morgenstern. Lips is also present on the same date for Holiday's touching rendition of *Why Did I Always Depend on You*, and the trumpeter's open solo contains some highly poignant moments.[44] In the estimate of Gunther Schuller, "One of the most remarkable and moving recorded performances in all of jazz is *Piney Brown Blues* by Joe Turner and His Fly Cats, recorded in New York, November 11, 1940." On this "small big band" recording, Page contributes muted trumpet obbligatos to Pete Johnson's "astonishing piano embellishments" behind Turner's "moving and expressive" singing. Schuller goes on to observe that "the two instrumentalists create a constant counterpoint of secondary supportive ideas that pushes the music to the bearable limits of expression."[45]

As we have seen, Page played "a searingly 'hot-lipped' growly solo" on the Pete Johnson–led 1939 recording of *Cherry Red* with Buster Smith on alto.[46] Page's growl trumpet also is quite effective in a series of takes recorded on December 10, 1940, with a trio composed of Leonard Feather on piano, Ernest Hill on bass, and Teddy Bunn on guitar. Especially nice is Page's growl mute work on *My Fightin' Gal*, in which he also sings a classic kind of blues while Bunn lays down a solid beat and blues harmony. (Nat Hentoff tells of how one evening in the late thirties Page "felt a call to sing just about all the blues he knew, and so he did for hours in one of the most moving epic-heroic feats I have ever experienced.")[47] On *Thirsty Mama Blues*, Page sounds like Jimmy Rushing but without that blues shouter's special crying tone. The outstanding side of this series is *Do It, If You Wanna*, a Page original in which he plays some very genuine blues, achieving an unusual sound within a low-down groove. Here Page's muted trumpet duo with Bunn's electric guitar both recalls the Clayton-Durham team and looks forward to the later combination of Cootie Williams and Charlie Christian. Bunn was obviously influenced by Christian, as he repeats certain of Charlie's famous licks, but Teddy does his own thing as well. Throughout this series of recordings both Page and Bunn create many fine moments: Lips with his vocals, his growl-mute and open solos (on mellophone for *Just Another Woman*), and his obbligato behind Bunn's vocal on *Evil*

Man's Blues; and Teddy with his tasteful fills on electric guitar, his pulsing rhythm work along with bassist Hill on *My Fightin' Gal*, and his unassuming solo on *Do It, If You Wanna*.[48]

As noted earlier of the January 23, 1940, Page session with Buster Smith, the six sides produced on this date furnish further evidence of Buster's significant contributions as a soloist and arranger; they also show Hot Lips at his best.[49] In the Page-Smith tune, *I Won't Be Here Long*, the writing for saxes—whose held notes are quite lovely with not a touch of the saccharine—is but one outstanding feature of this classic blueslike performance. Here Lips demonstrates once and for all that Morgenstern is correct in rating Page's wah-wah mute work as superior, for the trumpeter is truly outstanding. Throughout this session Page's playing is not only excellent but quite varied in style, as on the previously mentioned *I Ain't Got Nobody*, where his opening sound is simply beautiful yet not at all like that of Armstrong, while later Lips does evince the influence of Louis's bravura mode. Page's Walleresque vocal on *I Would Do Anything for You* is delightful, and on *Gone with the Gin* Lips takes another fine trumpet solo that again differs from the Armstrong style. With *Walk It to Me* Page's sound is once more quite beautiful against the band's great sax work (thanks, obviously, to the presence of Buster Smith and his scoring for the section). It is apparent, then, that Lips and Buster made for an ideal team, with the fellow Texans producing together a group of sides of considerably higher quality than anything recorded by Page's regular band of 1938.

In 1941 Page was recorded in the pre-bop environment of after-hours Harlem by Jerry Newman on a home tape machine. Called by Dan Morgenstern "a gold mine of private recordings from those carefree days,"[50] the sides from these sessions include Herbie Fields and Jimmy Wright on tenor sax, Rudy Williams on alto, Nick Fenton on bass, Thelonious Monk on piano, Joe Guy on trumpet, and perhaps Kenny Clarke on drums. Morgenstern characterizes the jam session represented by the Newman recordings as a workshop where musicians developed the seeds of bebop, exploring ideas "considered too far out . . . in a working situation." During this formative period, the after-hours setting was a place for musicians to relax and experiment—"to jam meant a welcome and needed chance to stretch out. The jam session was not only a musical but also a social and psychological event, and Lips was a master social director and psychiatric counselor." According to Morgenstern, who was led through Harlem's nightlife by Page, his Texas Virgil, Lips was "electric" and, like Budd Johnson, could light up a room, public or private, "with his mere presence. . . . He was a spreader of joy, a man for all seasons."[51]

Like Budd Johnson, Lips Page was also comfortable in any style, mixing with a number of the major figures in the bop movement before they had "found their legs." Thelonious Monk, for instance, sounds more like Earl Hines than his own unorthodox self, for in his playing of *Sweet Georgia Brown* Monk reveals his Fatha side before he abandoned a showy type of technique for a sparer, more original, modernist approach. In some ways this evidence of Monk's early style is the most historically significant aspect of the Newman recordings. On this particular piece, Lips is *too* relaxed, as Morgenstern accurately observes. With the Eddie Durham composition *Topsy*, a tune that "the 'advanced' swing players were fond of," Joe Guy's trumpet work seems more adventuresome than Page's and even contains a phrase later made famous in 1942 by Dizzy Gillespie in his popular *Salt Peanuts*. Although Lips tends to stick more closely to the theme, with his entrance it is immediately clear that, in comparison with Guy, "the difference in [Page's] sound alone is something." Morgenstern goes on to describe the way Lips works out with the drummer certain "rhythmic patterns, and then the riffs come in behind him as he clinches his inventions with the background."[52] In this way Page generates great swing, yet shows himself to be quite a different trumpeter from Armstrong. Not only does Lips create rising figures that carry his own unique stamp and excitement, but his pace is blistering, so much so that Guy cannot quite keep up with him in the "battle" at the end.

Another take from this jam session with Thelonious Monk features Page as a scat singer on *Old Yazoo*, which illustrates "what a monster he was!" as a "jazz singer."[53] Against the band's solid riffing, Page's scatting is more intense even than that of Cab Calloway and more in the manner of the instrumental improvisations by Rudy Williams and an unidentified tenor. On a piece entitled *Konk*, Page's "soaring ride" strings together "riffs enough for a dozen tunes."[54] A swinging version of *I've Found a New Baby* is quite unlike another 1941 take of the same tune offered on an album entitled *Sweets, Lips, and Lots of Jazz*, where again Monk is on piano. The latter version, also recorded by Jerry Newman, is entitled *Baby Lips*, but it is more in the swing mode than *I've Found a New Baby*, even though it contains a Charlie Christian–inspired guitar solo by Tiny Grimes. On *Baby Lips*, Page trades choruses with an unidentifed tenor who is in the Lester Young mold but repeats himself overmuch (probably Don Byas, or could this be Kermit Scott?). Gary Giddins describes Page's breaks here as "blazing" and three of his last choruses as "glorious . . . with a still exciting rising figure in the third."[55] This exciting performance was equaled in many ways by Page's earlier solo on a November 11, 1940, recording of *Lafayette*, where he rocks and rolls in this Eddie Durham tune with the same "blazing" intensity and swing of the Minton's jam session.[56] Kenny Clarke on drums adds greatly to the *Baby Lips* performance, supporting Page with slashing sticks on his snares and cymbals and his offbeat bombs on his bass drum. Likewise, in the 1940 *Lafayette*, Page was backed marvelously by the "aggressive but controlled playing" of the former Alphonse Trent sideman, A. C. Godley, "the most famous of the early southwestern drummers."[57]

Both of the Page versions of *I've Found a New Baby* show how Lips was "a spellbinding trumpeter who invested every note with its own character"[58] and demonstrated his ability to raise "the swing quotient notably."[59] These qualities are evident as well in some of the tunes recorded by Jerry Newman at a house party, especially on *Tea for Two*, where Page goes into double time at the end. With *Dinah*, Lips makes "use of symmetrical phrasing," which Dan Morgenstern calls "a hallmark of his style . . . as is his genius for building excitement."[60] As Eddie Barefield, Page's former Moten bandmate, once remarked, "Trumpeters such as Roy Eldridge and Hot Lips Page were always ready to jam. . . . They were young athletes, anxious to flex their musical muscles."[61] At the same time, the recordings made by Jerry Newman also illustrate what Morgenstern terms the jam session's "utterly relaxed playing, a kind of groove almost impossible in a commercial . . . setting."[62] It was in this jam session milieu where Lips Page was always at home and where he reigned for many as undisputed champion.

Another Carnegie Hall appearance by Page came in January 1942 in the company of Fats Waller. On this occasion Waller was apparently ill at ease and performed poorly, but Lips, according to one reviewer, "strode resolutely without fear or trepidation on the huge Carnegie Hall Stage, . . . acted as though he were in the Burning Bush Church during a revival," and furnished "the only bright moment" in the concert.[63] In a series of recordings made on September 29, 1944, with a small group that included Don Byas on tenor sax, Earl Bostic on alto, and Clyde Hart on piano, Page delivers a Fats-like novelty vocal on *Fish for Supper*, although this rendition is not up to Waller's vocal on *Hold Tight (Want Some Sea Food Mama)*. However, on *Six, Seven, Eight, or Nine* Lips sings with great conviction this blues-riff of his own making.[64] One admirer called Page "the most original lyricist in the business,"[65] and the words to this song, if not original, are certainly in the grand tradition of blues lyrics, reminding one of Jimmy Rushing's successful 1942 version of *I'm Gonna Move to the Outskirts of Town*.

Dizzy Gillespie once said that "when it came to the blues, nobody could mess with Lips."[66] This is illustrated by Page's fine blues trumpet on *You Need Coachin'*, which also features a solid tenor solo by Byas and some excellent blues on alto by Bostic. In 1941 Earl Bostic had locked horns with Charlie Parker at Monroe's, when Allen Tinney could not "really know who won because it was too tremendous." At Monroe's, Parker listened to "trumpet men like Lips Page, Roy, Dizzy, and Charlie Shavers outblowing each other all night long."[67] From these jam sessions, Tinney recalls, Page influenced such bop trumpeters as Victor Coulson, George Treadwell, and, through Coulson, Fats Navarro.[68] On the 1944 recordings, Page's sound can vary from open and singing on *Six, Seven, Eight, or Nine* to pinched on *You Need Coachin'*, where he plays Armstrong licks in his solo and then leads the ensemble with some stirring trumpet work at the end. Three years later, on October 28, 1947, Page recorded *Walkin' in a Daze*, and once again he delivers a fine blues vocal in the Rushing manner and plays an intense trumpet solo before leading the ensemble with unremitting power.[69] By March 7, 1951, when he performed *Let Me In*, Page could still lead the ensemble with musical muscle, but Dan Morgenstern laments that, even with his prowess intact, "They never did let Lips in."[70]

Even so, Hot Lips Page still enjoyed a number of notable successes in the forties and early fifties before his death on November 9, 1953. In 1941 he became only the second black jazzman "to work as a regular member of a big white band," that of Artie Shaw, who featured him as a trumpet soloist and singer.[71] Following a trip to Europe in 1949, when he took part in the Paris Jazz Festival along with Charlie Parker, Miles Davis, Sidney Bechet, and fellow Texan Kenny Dorham, Lips returned to the States where he was showcased by Eddie Condon on "the earliest of television jazz programs."[72] As a singer, Page made a hit recording, *Baby, It's Cold Outside*, with the up-and-coming new entertainer, Pearl Bailey, who "went on to stardom, while Lips remained in the cold."[73] In spite of Page's failure to gain celebrity status, his place in jazz history seems assured from some 116 recorded sides (the total number of Scott Joplin rag compositions), which document Lips as blues vocalist, trumpet soloist, and jam session "athlete" who won the admiration of his fellow musicians and the devotion of fans like Jerry Newman and has continued to earn the kudos of such critics as Dan Morgenstern and Gary Giddins.

🎵 🎵 🎵

Other than Jack Teagarden, no Texas jazzman revolutionized the role of his instrument in this music more than Charlie Christian, the electric guitarist born in Dallas in 1916. Although Eddie Durham had introduced the amplified guitar circa 1932 and made the first jazz recording with an electric guitar in 1935, it was left for Charlie Christian to exploit the potential of this new instrument for purposes of jazz improvisation. After acknowledging that Christian had predecessors in Lonnie Johnson, Eddie Lang, Django Reinhardt, Floyd Smith, and Eddie Durham, jazz critic Martin Williams declares that Charlie "was, in his brief career, not a major guitarist; he was *the* major guitarist and a major soloist regardless of instrument. Was and still is."[74] As Durham had observed, Christian wanted to sound like the tenor sax players of his day, so his models were not really other guitarists but "most specifically Lester Young."[75] But much of the distinctive sound and phrasing brought to jazz by Christian's guitar playing originated in the

Southwest, which, as Gunther Schuller has indicated, "is guitar country and blues country, the Texas blues tradition particularly being one of the oldest indigenous traditions."[76]

Joe Goldberg notes that the stylistic similarities of Budd Johnson and Lester Young had developed simultaneously and independently, much like the situation in science in which Darwin and Wallace were discovering a theory of evolution at the same moment.[77] This parallel applies as well to Young and Christian: as early as 1938 Charlie was heard in Bismarck, North Dakota, sounding "much like a tenor sax" and playing some of the exact same figures "that Benny [Goodman] recorded later on as *Flying Home, Gone with "What" Wind, Seven Come Eleven*, and all the others."[78] While Christian apparently emulated Lester's tenor sound, he was "more harmonically exact and sophisticated . . . but, like Young, he remained as much a linear melodist."[79] Again, it was the southwestern melodic singing style of the blues and the riff phrasing developed by Blind Lemon Jefferson that formed the basis of Charlie Christian's innovative approach, which Ross Russell, among a number of jazz historians, finds "very close to that of Lester Young. Both have an airy, singing sonority and improvise in long melodic lines, skillfully compounded of short and multinote phrases, indifferent to the old bar divisions and balanced against ample free space."[80] In many ways this is a concise definition of the southwestern tradition of blues-derived jazz.

Charlie Christian reportedly began to play the guitar professionally in Oklahoma City in 1934 at the age of fifteen.[81] As a boy, Charlie guided his father, a blind guitarist and singer, around Oklahoma City and obviously grew up hearing the blues. But in addition to the influence of a blues tradition, Charlie received music appreciation training in the Oklahoma City public schools, including study of harmony and an opportunity to listen to works from the classical repertory.[82] Between 1934 and 1937, Christian performed on bass with the Alphonse Trent band and sextet, working out of Charlie's Dallas hometown. By the age of eighteen, Christian was playing the electric guitar, having been introduced to the instrument by Eddie Durham, according to the latter's account. During the next two years, Charlie's fame as a guitar soloist spread throughout the Midwest and Southwest, and he was heard in Oklahoma City by John Hammond, who in turn passed along the word to Benny Goodman.

When Hammond insisted that Goodman audition the Texan and had him flown to Los Angeles for this purpose, Benny was at first put off by Charlie's attire: "Suddenly, in walks this vision, resplendent in a ten-gallon hat, pointed yellow shoes, a bright green suit over a purple shirt and, for the final elegant touch—a string bowtie."[83] But once bassist Artie Bernstein and vibraharpist Lionel Hampton "conspired to sneak Charlie" into the hotel where the band was playing,

Charlie Christian of Dallas (left) with Don Redman and Count Basie.
Reproduced courtesy of Duncan Schiedt.

bringing him in through the kitchen, Goodman was forced to listen rather than create a scene. As Hammond tells it, he "never saw anyone knocked out as Benny was" when the quartet plus Charlie "played *Rose Room* for forty-eight minutes!"[84] In New York on October 2, 1939, Charlie would record this same tune as a member of Goodman's sextet, with Hampton on vibes and Bernstein on bass, along with Fletcher Henderson on piano and Nick Fatool on drums. Earlier in New York, on September 11, Christian had already recorded for the first time with a group that included Hampton, Coleman Hawkins, and Dizzy Gillespie. Although Charlie was given no solo space on this occasion, it is apparent to John Chilton that "from the first moment . . . the rhythm section of Cozy Cole (drums), Charlie Christian (guitar), Milt Hinton (bass) and Clyde Hart (piano) have achieved a remarkable blend. Each man's contribution is clearly discernible yet the overall impression is one emphatic pulse."[85] This group's recording of *When Lights Are Low* was regarded by French critic André Hodeir as a masterpiece—"the apex of the ascending curve that symbolizes the evolution of swing."[86] It was Hodeir who first praised "the incomparable homogeneity of the accompaniment" and asserted that "such a blending would not have been possible ten years or even five years earlier, when the training of accompanists still had ground to cover."[87]

As for Christian's debut recording with the Benny Goodman Sextet on October 2, 1939, his solo on *Rose Room* is a full chorus that Gunther Schuller calls "a finely formed, logical *composition*" with a "splendid triplet eighth-note run." Referring to the three tunes recorded on this date—the others being *Flying Home* and *Star Dust*—Schuller observes that they contain "all the essential elements of Christian's style: the clean uncluttered lines, often in arching shapes—his favorite phrase contour; his flawless time; his consistently blues-inflected melodic/harmonic language; the structural logic with which he invested form, whether in shorter segments (8-bar structures) or full choruses."[88] Schuller is mystified that Columbia Records did not originally issue *Star Dust*, which appeared only under the CBS label in Japan. Eventually this performance was released in the United States, and it "shows off Christian's full firm expressive tone at its expressive best," as well as his "extraordinary creativity" in superimposing on *Star Dust* minor triads "set in a special blues-ish relaxed swing."[89]

A later recording of *Star Dust* was made by Christian in early March 1940 in Minneapolis, with a member of Goodman's band, tenor saxophonist Jerry Jerome, along with Frankie Hines on piano and unidentified bass and drums. There are similarities in the two renditions, in particular the fact that on both Charlie quotes from the popular song *Pretty Baby*.[90] For the most part, however, the performances are strikingly and instructively different. In the 1939 version, Christian, as Schuller suggests, composes his own piece, never really stating the theme as Goodman does on clarinet. Rhythmically imaginative, Charlie explores his "triadic idea throughout the solo,"[91] and his riffs relate to a basic rhythmic and harmonic pattern. This rendition is clearly moving away from the Goodman and Hampton model, which indicates, in the view of Martin Williams, that "some sort of future crisis was at hand in the music, that—to exaggerate only slightly—a kind of jazz as melodically dull as a set of tone drums might well be in the offing." But for Williams, Charlie Christian's rhythmic imagination and his originality as a melodist provided the basis for a solution to the problem, both of these qualities being shared by Christian with "perhaps the greatest inventor of melodies jazz has seen"—Charlie Parker.[92]

Like Parker and other beboppers, Christian was adept at and inclined toward incorporating quotes from popular songs, as is evident from his working *Pretty Baby* into *Star Dust*. In the March 1940 version, Charlie not only quotes from *Pretty Baby*, but he ends his solo with part of the final phrase of Duke Ellington's *I Let a Song Go Out of My Heart*, with, instead of the expected conclusion of the original, a bluesy southwestern phrase that completely changes the character of the quotation.

Before this, like Blind Lemon Jefferson, Christian creates countless riffs of his own invention, even finding a place in their midst for an allusion to *Moonglow*. The second half of his solo begins with the same rhythmic ideas as the version with the Goodman Sextet but then adds to it a series of Charlie's characteristic single-string melodic lines. The first half of the solo differs in two ways from the earlier recording: Charlie's entrance, following Jerome's introductory solo, is in the electric guitar's lower range and sounds at first like a continuation of the tenor's chorus; and equally different from the 1939 take, the theme of *Star Dust* is stated fully by Christian, as it is by Jerome, with both instrumentalists embellishing the tune, the tenor doing a respectable job even though he is no Lester Young and no match for Charlie as an improviser. Jerome's better outing on this date is his swinging version of *Tea for Two*, while Christian is slow to find his groove, but once he does, he turns in a superb piece of work at the same time that he furnishes a driving accompaniment for both the pianist and tenor.

By general agreement, Christian's finest moment at the December 1939 Carnegie Hall "Spirituals to Swing" concert came when he teamed up with Lester Young and the Kansas City Six on *Paging the Devil*.[93] Interestingly, Christian's solo on this occasion seems more advanced than Young's, more daring and inventive, combining traditional blues phrases with a newer "bop" language. The same holds true for the October 28, 1940, recordings made with a group composed of Goodman, Young, Buck Clayton, Count Basie, Jo Jones, and Artie Bernstein.[94] However, this setting was not conducive to the best work by Christian and Young, with Goodman interrupting just as Charlie digs into his break on *Lester's Dream*, where aptly Lester offers his finest effort. Surprisingly, even on *Charlie's Dream* Christian seems out of place, and on *Ad-Lib Blues* both he and Lester are uninspired, perhaps inhibited by the somewhat straitjacket feeling of a Goodman-led group.

It was nonetheless through Christian's work with the Goodman sextet, septet, octet, and big band that Charlie gained his greatest exposure during his brief lifetime. On the various sides with the Goodman groups, Christian left "a rich recorded heritage, not merely of excellent playing but of exceptional solos."[95] Gunther Schuller has analyzed an example of what he considers to be Christian's best work with the Goodman Sextet, the January 15, 1941, recording of *Breakfast Feud*, which the critic says sounds "utterly logical, effortless, and pleasing" and in which Charlie's solos "became for all forward-looking young guitarists of the time benchmarks to be studied, imitated, and built upon."[96] With Count Basie on piano, Cootie Williams on trumpet, and Jo Jones on drums, this recording has more of a relaxed feeling of Kansas City jazz, and even Goodman begins his solo in a "down and dirty" groove. After Georgie Auld spells Charlie, following his four solos set off by ensemble riffs, the performance returns to the more straitlaced mode of the Goodman Sextet sides with their tame chamber-music endings, except for Cootie Williams, who growls a kind of Dixieland tag. A December 19, 1940, version of *Breakfast Feud* has a totally different character and is not as relaxed as the Basie-inspired session, even though pianist Kenny Kersey takes a nice enough solo. Here Christian is limited to only two choruses and cannot stretch out, with the result that he does not develop the same flowing, supple lines as in the January 1941 version. Schuller describes in detail the later recording: "Not only does Christian emulate the type of twangy slides, scoops, and string crossings" employed by the country blues guitarists "but he also uses less syncopation, staying more on the beat and relying a great deal on straight even eighth-note lines."[97] James Lincoln Collier also points out that "the ordinary swing player might syncopate half his notes," whereas "Charlie was capable of playing almost a whole blues chorus without syncopating a single note." Collier goes on to say that Christian does this in his fourth chorus on *Breakfast Feud*, in which "only four of forty-eight beats are syncopated. This practice became characteristic of bop."[98]

In the third and fourth choruses of the 1941 solo on *Breakfast Feud*, which were "spliced together from three previously unissued takes,"[99] Charlie especially infuses Goodman's original tune with the blues tradition, lifting the performance above the level of polite jazz to the realm of imaginative transformation. Al Avakian and Bob Prince comment on Christian's "rhythmic daring and resourcefulness" in these choruses and suggest that they "provide rich ground for analysis in that they demonstrate, independently one to the other (but here placed in series), the Christian technique in dealing with basically the same blues derivatives."[100] At another recording session on March 13, 1941, when the sextet members were awaiting the arrival of Goodman, Charlie joined Johnny Guarneri on piano and Georgie Auld on tenor to cut loose on a freewheeling *Blues in B* that was happily recorded by the studio engineers. The impromptu *Waitin' for Benny* with Cootie joining in on trumpet was also captured by the engineers, and the jamming here indicates why Christian's participation in the after-hours sessions at Minton's Playhouse led to his vital role in the development of bop: whereas the Goodman recordings had settled into what Schuller calls "a certain mechanical routine quality," the jam sessions at Minton's allowed Christian's playing to move on to "ever greater dimensions of depth and originality."[101] *Waitin' for Benny* from this occasion is also, according to Avakian and Prince, "the only free, jamming, swing-era trumpet" that Cootie Williams ever recorded, and it is thoroughly exciting.[102]

Even though Charlie's tuberculosis was beginning to take its toll, it is obvious from the recordings made by Jerry Newman in 1941 in Harlem that, of all the younger musicians who sat in at Minton's, Christian was, as Schuller argues, "the most advanced, the most original, and musically the most mature—even more than Gillespie and Monk."[103] This is certainly evident on *Swing to Bop* (a retitled version of Eddie Durham's classic *Topsy*), recorded in May 1941 with Thelonious Monk on piano, with Monk's performance not at all identifiable as the work of the true giant of modern jazz that he ultimately would become.[104] Christian, on the other hand, produces a first solo full of drive and imagination that is far ahead of Monk's, which is still in the Hines trumpet style or, as Joe Goldberg suggests, "sounded a good deal like Teddy Wilson," the Texan who passed along the Hines tradition.[105] Charlie's second chorus is again much more inventive both rhythmically and melodically, building a series of riffs into a unified statement and at times sounding like a tenor. From this same collection of Newman tapes, Christian produces a very satisfying second chorus on *Stompin' at the Savoy*, after his first has sounded like too much of his lesser work with Goodman, too restrained and limited. Showing the value of extended solo time for an improviser of Christian's stature, Charlie's second chorus exhibits his considerable talent for variation on a theme, on riffs derived from it, or rhythmic germs from which he develops his inventive ideas. This second solo also illustrates Schuller's notion that Christian's work seems "relentlessly creative, endlessly fertile, and is so in a way that marks a new stylistic departure. Indeed it signals the birth of a new language in jazz, which even Parker did not have as clearly in focus at that time."[106] While Christian takes a very thoughtful solo here, it still does not match his better moments on *Swing to Bop*, which was suitably retitled, for Charlie's swing *is* moving toward bop.[107]

Both Gunther Schuller and Martin Williams single out an early 1941 performance by Christian on acoustic guitar as "a masterpiece of its kind" and "of such exceptional musical and emotional quality as to produce a sense of sustained wonder, both the first time one hears it and the hundredth."[108] Schuller finds in the solo taken by Charlie on *Profoundly Blue*, recorded with Edmond Hall's Celeste Quartet, featuring boogie-woogie pianist Meade Lux Lewis on celeste and Israel Crosby on bass, "three superb blues choruses, fascinating in their 'older' style, showing clearly how far back Christian's roots go in the Southwestern blues tradition, and notable for their pared-down simplicity and sustained, eloquent storytelling mood."[109] Comparing Christian's earlier playing with this and other work from 1941, Schuller also suggests that while Charlie never abandoned the blues, he was "clearly, like Parker in his later years, trying either to break away from the conventions of the blues or to expand them into a wider vision."[110] Al Avakian and Bob Prince summarize perhaps most concisely the impact of Christian's years in New York, recording with Benny Goodman and jamming at Minton's Playhouse before tuberculosis and his own unwillingness to slow down the tempo of his nightlife in the Big Apple cut short his career in 1942: "Charlie Christian's long, clean eighth-note phrases consisting of harmonic extensions and alterations, his rhythmic dexterity and drive, his formalistic sense of balance, and his unpredictable yet recognizable treatment of the blues were heard by and strongly influenced the then inchoate movement later called bebop."[111]

Although Charlie Christian was indubitably *the* major jazz guitarist, it should be noted that another Texan, Oscar Moore, was active contemporaneously with Christian and also recorded with Lionel Hampton only a year after Charlie took part in the *When Lights Are Low* session of September 11, 1939. Born in Austin on December 25, 1912, Moore at age sixteen formed his own unit with his brother Johnny, also a guitarist. In 1937 Oscar joined the original Nat King Cole Trio and stayed with this famed group until 1947, figuring as "the first of the modern combo guitarists, playing single-string amplified solos and chord work in a style that was a highly attractive element of Cole's records during the early 1940s."[112] On May 14, 1940, Moore recorded with Cole and Hampton two tunes, *Central Avenue Breakdown* and *Jack the Bellboy*. In both tunes Oscar takes brief, distinctive solos, while his riffs on *Central Avenue Breakdown* definitely bear the Christian style and sound. On July 17, 1940, Cole, Hampton, and Moore recorded *Jivin' with Jarvis*, which again finds Moore sounding like Christian, even though he does not seem to overflow with ideas the way Charlie did. Moore can be heard on many sides with the Cole Trio and is especially impressive on *What Is This Thing Called Love* from January 17, 1944, as well as on *Sweet Georgia Brown* from May 25, 1945, when the guitarist provides for a fine interplay with the pianist.[113] According to Leonard Feather, Moore's "use of a ninth chord with a flatted fifth at the conclusion of the Trio's recording of *That Ain't Right* [1940] was indeed 'a daring innovation at that point in time.'"[114] More recently, Gene Santoro has found that Moore's "smoothly jagged approach became the standard once bop shook loose the eight-to-the-bar beat dominating swing." This critic contrasts Moore with Christian by pointing out that whereas Charlie "concentrated on the relationship between scales and chords in a proto-bop manner," Oscar "was more interested in delving into melodies and refashioning them in his own image—which often happened to foreshadow bop's expanded harmonic sense."[115]

While Charlie Christian remains the greatest guitarist in jazz, he was not the only Texan on his instrument to contribute to this music's history. From Blind Lemon Jefferson and Eddie Durham to Oscar Moore, and later to Herb Ellis and Larry Coryell,[116] Texans have brought to jazz guitar a distinctive style and sound that may also be heard in the work of such Western Swing guitarists as Leon McAuliffe and Zeke Campbell, who played in the 1930s with Bob Wills and the

Light Crust Doughboys out of Fort Worth. Although guitarists of the Western Swing persuasion remained closer to a traditional country style, they too commonly improvised blues-inflected, single-note lines like those created by jazz musicians. As Gunther Schuller points out, Christian may not have taken his style directly from earlier Texans like McAuliffe and Campbell, yet "a guitar tradition of the kind [Charlie] represented and perfected was already of long standing by the time he burst onto the scene in New York in mid-1939."[117]

WITH BG

Charlie Christian was only the last of a string of Texans who starred in the Benny Goodman groups of the 1930s and 1940s. The earliest to join Goodman was Teddy Wilson, who in 1935 became the first black jazzman to tour as a member of an interracial group, playing piano with the Benny Goodman Trio. Born in Austin on November 24, 1912, Wilson moved with his family when he was six to Tuskegee, Alabama, where his father became the head of the English Department at the Tuskegee Institute and his mother chief librarian.[1] Teddy grew up in Alabama and received musical training on piano and violin and later majored in music theory at Talladega College. Known for his decorative style and outstanding improvisations, Wilson fit perfectly into Benny Goodman's conception of a classically oriented trio, a refined form of jazz that emphasized balance and control yet could produce a driving, exciting swing. Like many of his fellow Texans, Wilson was adaptable to any mood or style and served as a highly inspiring accompanist.

Formed after a June 1935 meeting of Goodman, Wilson, and Gene Krupa, when the three men played for a private party, the trio brought together in the clarinetist and pianist "two of the most technically adroit performers since Louis Armstrong and Earl Hines collaborated in 1928."[2] On the trio's performance of *Body and Soul*, recorded July 13, 1935, Wilson's playing has been called "a kind of miracle of originality in melody and phrasing."[3] For the Carnegie Hall concert of January 16, 1938, by means of which jazz first gained widespread popularity and through the recordings of which was preserved "one of the authentic documents in American musical history,"[4] the original Benny Goodman Trio rendered once again this popular tune, with Teddy's flawless runs and chimed chords ringing tastefully in spite of Gene Krupa's drum thuds and heavy-handed brushes on cymbals and snares. Wilson's role in the trio was crucial to the success of this groundbreaking group, for Teddy made the trio unique through his "vitalizing and strikingly original concept of contrapuntal harmonic movement."[5] In the early days of the trio, Krupa assisted Goodman and Wilson in taking their "collective improvising to a new level of clarity and precision," with Teddy becoming "the first authentically cool and controlled—but deeply involved—solo and ensemble pianist. He proved, as did Lester Young, that understatement can swing. But when called upon, Wilson could also generate terrific heat, as his fast, florid, and flagwaving pieces vividly demonstrate."[6]

On *Rosetta*, a solo recording made by Wilson on October 7, 1935, the pianist's sound is that of a tame Earl Hines or Fats Waller, with the filigree at times much like cocktail music. But even here the technique and swing are solidly in evidence, and as the piece continues Teddy works into a pulsing groove that "distills some of the Hines basics—the rock-steady left hand, with its striding tenths, and the searching, flashing, right-hand octave passages down to his own more evenly balanced and neatly-folded, tucked-in phrasing—all the while propelling the time with his unique, quietly insistent momentum."[7] In Wilson's November 12, 1937, recording of *Don't Blame Me*, he beautifully modulates the walking bass, but very delicately, unlike the more blatant style of boogie or stride piano. From the same date, Wilson's two renditions of *Between the Devil and the Deep Blue Sea* exemplify his distinctive place in the tradition of jazz piano improvisation: the first version is quite like Fats Waller but exhibits a tighter control and longer melodic lines that swing even as they work out fascinating phrases and note relationships; the second version, which is faster, remains perfectly clear and just as swinging but with more varied ideas than Fats generally offered and more intricate thinking, with ringing right-hand chords and once more a tight control over the playing, to all of which is added an intriguing coda. Gunther Schuller notes that by this time there is "increased daring and authority" in Wilson's playing and that technically he could, when he wished, "do almost anything that Hines could do," but his "innate modesty and even temperament precluded his indulging in excessive displays of technical ostentation."[8] In speaking of Wilson as "a Hines disciple," Wilfrid Mellers suggests that Teddy was perhaps "the only pianist to develop [Earl's] harmonic and textural sophistication without losing the rhythmic drive of traditional barrelhouse style," and Mellers cites as an example "his brilliant version of *Between the Devil and the Deep Blue Sea*."[9] Indeed, Wilson's principal importance in jazz history lies in his having absorbed the style of Earl Hines, which he passed along in a modified form to the next generation of pianists, minus the abrupt shifts and the kind of primitive blues that Hines blended with the stride player's right-hand figures. Like Hines, Wilson developed long lines of single notes, but as the best-known jazz pianist of the swing era, it was Teddy more than Earl who revolution-ized jazz piano and influenced musicians in the decade of the 1940s.[10]

At the Carnegie Hall concert of January 16, 1938, the Benny Goodman Quartet, formed by the addition of Lionel Hampton on vibraharp, offered its rendition of *The Man I Love*. And when Gene Krupa lays out and allows Wilson to set his own pace, the pianist responds with an example of what Gunther Schuller calls Teddy's "Mozartean clarity and ease."[11] In combining European and African American musical practices, Wilson achieves "a delicacy and a symmetry otherwise then unheard in jazz." In playing with Teddy, Benny Goodman says that he got "something, in a jazz way, like what I got from playing [Mozart] with the string quartet."[12] Schuller remarks that in an earlier quartet recording of *The Man I Love*, Wilson and Hampton "combine to create an organ-like background to Goodman's theme statement," and there is something of this "dirge- or hymn-like dignity" to the Carnegie Hall version as well.[13] Much of Wilson's best work is generally considered his early 1940s performances, either in solo or with his own trio. *Smoke Gets in Your Eyes*, from April 7, 1941, looks forward to the restrained, sophisticated, but hard-swinging work of John Lewis, who recorded this same tune in the following decade. (While both Wilson and Lewis were classically trained, one important difference between the two pianists is that John, unlike Teddy, draws upon the blues as an "essential impulse . . . even if it is an interpretation of a standard as remote from the blues as *Smoke Gets in Your Eyes*.")[14] Wilson's January 21, 1942, recording of *These Foolish Things* also displays a rhythmic and melodic symmetry that has been called Mozart-like, resulting in a perfomance in which "the unity and totality of Wilson's style" make the bass and drums accompani-ment seem "rather superfluous at times."[15] From this same period, Gunther Schuller considers Teddy's playing of *I Know That You Know* a masterpiece, "a sort of 'perpetual motion' piece," with "Wilson's hands all over the keyboard." Schuller goes on to say that "so often with swing era musicians . . . virtuoso solos tended to be rather mechanical, even contrived. But Wilson rarely loses that spontaneity that is the essence of jazz. . . . The net result is a dazzling counterpoint of ideas: combining, overlapping, contrasting—variety *in* both hands and *between* them."[16]

As we have seen, Wilson joined the Louis Armstrong orchestra in 1933 and worked in Chicago with Budd and Keg Johnson. Teddy also performed in Willie Bryant's band in 1934 with Eddie Durham, in groups that included Benny Goodman and Jack Teagarden, and with several Basie sidemen, including Herschel Evans.[17] It was as the leader or as a member of a number of orchestras backing singer Billie Holiday that Wilson also teamed with Texans Harry James, Herschel Evans, and Kermit Scott. (Texans Hot Lips Page, Tyree Glenn, Dan Minor, and Eddie

Durham also recorded with Holiday but not in the same orchestra with Wilson.) Teddy's work with Billie Holiday produced what many critics consider the singer's finest performances, beginning with the July 2, 1935, recordings of *What a Little Moonlight Can Do* and *Miss Brown to You*. Glenn Coulter, the perceptive Holiday critic, writes that

> the musicians with her were some of the best men jazz has known; simply to list their names gives a jazz fan pleasure—Buck Clayton, Roy Eldridge, Teddy Wilson, Lester Young. . . . There never was such jazz as this for lyrical ardor and informal elegance, natural as breathing and yet as perfectly balanced as the most sophisticated art. Billie's choruses are utterly different in method and intention from their instrumental setting, a perfect counter-balance to the work of Teddy Wilson, for example, whose beautiful transformations of melodies force the listener into a seemingly permanent attitude of wonder and delight.[18]

Coulter singles out the Holiday-Wilson performance of *Easy Living* from June 1, 1937, as an instance of a rare "true simplicity" in the "directness and intimacy" of Billie's delivery. Of Teddy's solo work and his accompaniment of the other musicians (who included Buck Clayton and Lester Young), Coulter writes that these "are enough by themselves to put this on any ten-best list, and Billie never surpassed this vocal with its repose and warmth."[19] For his part, Gunther Schuller points to *It's Like Reaching for the Moon* of June 30, 1936, as "one of Billie's most wistful filled-with-hope performances" and *I've Got My Love to Keep Me Warm* of January 12, 1937, as "one of Billie's greatest performances."[20] In the first of these Wilson contributes a fine solo with echoes of Fats Waller and in the second feeds the chords to Holiday unobtrusively while Teddy subtly keeps the swing pulsing beneath her enchanting voice. Schuller mentions "other superb performances from this period, many of them with Billie in her happiest, most buoyant mood."[21] On all of these—with the exception of the September 13, 1937, *He's Funny That Way*—Wilson is present to lead the various groups sure-handedly and with infectious drive.

Later, in 1945, Teddy Wilson was also on hand for an important recording date with Dizzy Gillespie and Charlie Parker. This session, which took place in New York, was organized by Red Norvo, and naturally the principal interest of the sides—recorded by Comet on June 6, 1945, and later obtained by Ross Russell for his Dial Records—lies with the performances of Dizzy and Bird. However, as Martin Williams observes of the first take of *Hallelujah*, writing in his liner notes for the Dial Master Series reissue, "Wilson's glittering pianistic abilities should not obscure the musical ideas he gets going here."[22] Wilson plays what Williams calls "almost modern comping" behind Red Norvo's vibraharp in the second take of *Hallelujah*, and while Teddy's solo here is largely scalar, it certainly swings. As for Parker, his third take of *Get Happy* is considered by Williams to be "surely one of the most valuable of all Parker alternate takes. And the chorus contains a hint of the brilliant way he could organize a solo with echo phrases that are not repetitious, as he begins the last eight bars of his chorus with an elaboration of a previous phrase. Wilson is fluently effective behind the final chorus." Meanwhile, on the fourth take of *Get Happy*, Dizzy plays a solo containing phrases that "were imitated to death during the next few years by almost a whole generation of young trumpeters." Both Parker and Gillespie are extraordinary on the fifth take of *Congo Blues*, where their "technique is handmaiden to musical ideas," and although Wilson's ideas are different, they are excellent in his older style. The primary value of the Dial reissue is that it preserves the various takes with Parker and Gillespie that were not released on the original Comet recording. However, it is good to have these examples of Wilson's piano, even if they do not represent a revolutionary development but merely support and complement the work of bebop's leading exponents.

Another less frequently mentioned side of Teddy's multitalented career is his work as an orchestrator, especially for his own short-lived band, which he formed in 1939 after leaving Goodman. Leonard Feather regrets that after 1940 Wilson became "inactive as a writer,"[23] and Budd Johnson recalls one particular Wilson chart, written for the Hines band: "I never will forget the time that Teddy Wilson wrote the arrangement of 'Shine' for Earl Hines. And for the trumpets he transcribed Louis's solo in four-part harmony, and it was the rave of New York. That's the thing they came to New York with and tore up the Savoy."[24] While Gunther Schuller finds that Wilson "lost much of the creative focus of his earlier work" by spreading himself thin as a studio musician, touring Europe, teaching at the Juilliard School, and working on Broadway, Teddy had already made a vital contribution to 1930s and early 1940s jazz as a soloist, leader, sideman, orchestrator, and a modest gentleman who broke the race barrier and made possible mixed groups that produced outstanding results. Wilson left Texas at an early age, but since he was recognized as a prodigy—his "artistic personality already expressed itself in a highly individual manner in his teen years"[25]—there may well have been, as a popular adage has it, something in the Austin water to account in part for his "happy, positive, even-tempered spirit" that represented in jazz "a new re-fined classicism."[26] In the same way, Wilson may have felt, through his birthplace, an affinity for performing with other Texans, toward whom he seemed to gravitate throughout his career, joining with his fellow natives in the Armstrong band, in orchestras backing Billie Holiday, and as a sideman in a number of groups that included Eddie Durham and other prominent jazzmen from his home state.

Perhaps because Teddy Wilson was a Texan not really raised in Texas, the pianist rarely played the blues, unlike John Lewis. However, two convincing examples of Wilson's efforts in this idiom are the 1935 *Blues in E Flat* with Red Norvo and His Swing Octet and the 1936 *Blues in C-Sharp Minor* featuring Roy Eldridge on trumpet, Israel Crosby on bass, Buster Bailey on clarinet, and Chu Berry on tenor.[27] Gunther Schuller also recommends the September 1937 recording of *Just a Mood* with Teddy Wilson, Red Norvo, and fellow Texan Harry James. Schuller remarks that James contributes "eloquent, superbly authoritative blues playing," that he is "technically more assured and controlled than either Armstrong and Berigan, but without quite their depth of feeling," and that, at his best, he could "combine a kind of warm romanticism with the earthiness and stark simplicities of the blues."[28] Both Michael Brooks and Gunther Schuller find *Blues in E Flat* a worthy performance, in which Wilson takes what Brooks considers Teddy's "finest solo" on the two dates with the Norvo groups.[29] For his part, Schuller calls *Blues in E Flat* the one classic from the series, featuring "outstanding melodic improvisations" by Norvo, Bunny Berigan, and Wilson. Schuller adds, "It is also a fine example of collective music-making and the high level of mutual inspiration a compatible group of creative musicians could generate."[30] On *Blues in C-Sharp Minor* Wilson is well supported by Crosby's bass, just as he is by Artie Bernstein's on *Blues in E Flat*, and Teddy's opening solo in the former is quite different—in its "dirtier" note choices and its "primitive" sound—from his more typically elegant playing. Both of these recordings demonstrate Teddy's ability to work within the blues tradition when called upon and to do so with a genuine understanding of this basic jazz medium.

❦ ❦ ❦

Born in Albany, Georgia, on March 15, 1916, Harry James moved about the country with his circus family before settling in Beaumont in southeast Texas. Attending high school there, James won a state solo contest on trumpet at age fourteen and soon afterward began to play with a local group led by violinist Joe Gill and with the band of Herman Waldman out of San Antonio. In 1935 James joined the Ben Pollack orchestra, which in 1936 featured Harry on trumpet and Glenn Miller on trombone. In December 1936, James went with the Benny Goodman band and quickly rose "from the ranks to become a stellar partici-pant . . . and one of the most noticed players, after Goodman himself, at the legendary Carnegie Hall Concert, on January 17, 1938."[31]

Typical of James's work with the Goodman band is his stirring performance from a 1937 radio broadcast of Jimmy Mundy's *Jam Session*.[32] Goodman had previously recorded this tune in November 1936, with his first trumpet star, Ziggy

Elman, as the featured soloist. Even though Elman had played almost the very same solo that James reproduces, Ziggy's chorus had lacked Harry's panache, his almost roosterlike crowing that could seemingly make the sun rise and that does in fact bring listeners to their feet with shouts and applause captured on the recording, an electrifying effect that the Goodman band often had on its live audiences.[33] With this radio air check, James creates a spine-tingling piece of excitement, employing some spectacular half-valve glissandos that dip downward and then zoom upward to one of Harry's recognizable sky-rocket bursts, which thrills the listeners and has them cheering as the band rides on. From another broadcast during the 1937–1938 period, James "blows some mad trumpet" on *Ridin' High* that also brings the audience to life,[34] and on *Sunny Disposish*, Harry's flashy chorus again generates excitement as he screams up to one of his favorite high notes with its immediately identifiable sound: a piercing ring that simply sings and cannot be confused with Ziggy Elman's style even when the two trumpeters play the same solos almost note for note. Likewise, on *St. Louis Blues*, James outshines Elman's rather tame solo taken earlier on this tune, as Harry blends some Armstrong acrobatics with a back-to-the-blues ending that is the high point of the entire performance.[35]

For James Lincoln Collier, the finest of James's solos with Goodman and "one of the finest trumpet solos made during the swing era, the equal of the best work of Bunny Berigan, and approaching that of James's own idol, Louis Armstrong," is Harry's chorus in the July 7, 1937, recording by the Benny Goodman Orchestra of the boogie-woogie special, *Roll 'Em*, arranged by Mary Lou Williams.[36] Collier attributes Harry's "best moments in jazz"—on the blues-inspired numbers *Just a Mood*, *Two O'Clock Jump*, and *Roll 'Em*—to his having been "raised in Texas, a blues hotbed during his youth."[37] Because of his blues background, James worked equally well with mixed groups, whether led by Red Norvo or such black jazzmen as Teddy Wilson, Lionel Hampton, or Pete Johnson.[38] On *Boo-Woo*, recorded on February 1, 1939, with Pete Johnson's Boogie Woogie Trio, James demonstrates his understanding of this style as revived in the late 1930s.[39] Muted following Johnson's piano solo, Harry effectively retains the eight-to-the-bar tempo and feeling, and, as critic Charles Fox acknowledges, "James fit[s] in well."[40] This was also true of two earlier sessions held on December 1, 1937, and January 5, 1938, when James made the first recordings under his own name, leading a group that included fellow Texans Eddie Durham and Herschel Evans, along with other members of the Count Basie Orchestra, as well as Harry's fellow Goodman band member, pianist Jess Stacy.

Albert McCarthy was the first critic to consider the 1937–1938 session with the Basie sidemen "probably the best jazz records issued under James's name."[41] But for Chris Sheridan as well, this date "was undoubtedly Harry James' most rewarding session, his monumentally popular big-band recordings notwithstanding."[42] A large part of the credit for the success of these recordings must go to the arrangements by Eddie Durham and the marvelous solo work of Herschel Evans. Like the outstanding recordings made by Jones-Smith, Inc., in 1936 and by the Kansas City Five and Six in March and September of 1938, these sides from the end of 1937 and the beginning of 1938 were arranged by John Hammond. It is clear that Hammond too could appreciate the work of Harry James and the other Texans involved in these sessions that all produced such notable jazz.

Chris Sheridan laments the fact that James chose his fellow Texan over Lester Young for the 1937–1938 recordings, but the selection seems extremely fortunate, for these sides represent some of Herschel Evans's finest work ever. Here Evans plays in a more relaxed manner and at greater length, and as even Sheridan points out, not only was Herschel "otherwise little heard" but with regard to his work on *I Can Dream, Can't I?* few recordings have "advertised Herschel's richness of tone," and it is perhaps beyond anything he ever recorded with Basie. On two James originals, *Life Goes to a Party* and *Texas Chatter*, both of which are wonderfully arranged by Durham, Harry is at his best, delivering a powerhouse solo on the first and on the second an exciting but under-control chorus. Herschel Evans is also tremendous on these two tunes, building up on *Life* a "bruising" break and on *Texas Chatter* "an excellent booting solo" demonstrating a "definitive Texas Tenor." James is also quite effective on *Song of the Wanderer*, though in a different jazz mode from that of Buck Clayton with his obbligato behind Helen Humes's Billie Holiday–inspired vocal. For *It's the Dreamer in Me*, Harry provides what Sheridan calls "an aptly poignant tone" to introduce Humes's treatment of this medium ballad.[43] Indeed, this last performance is vintage James; but owing, it would seem, to his company on this interracial recording, Harry's playing here is more mellow, less showy. Finally, with Basie's theme song, the Durham-Page-Smith "anthem," *One O'Clock Jump*, Stacy, Evans, and James all contribute outstanding solos on this Kaycee classic.

Despite the excellence of these sides with members of the Basie band, it was not such jazz recordings that brought fame to Harry James but rather his time with Benny Goodman in 1937 and 1938, which established the trumpeter's status as a crowd-pleasing swing-era star. Even before James recorded his famous virtuoso solos on *Two O'Clock Jump, Carnival in Venice*, and *Flight of the Bumblebee* with his own band in the early 1940s, Harry awed many trumpet players of his day, including even Dizzy Gillespie, who showed himself, according to James Lincoln Collier, to be on his earliest records "a big-band trumpet player directly in the James mold." Collier concludes his discussion of Harry's work with the Goodman orchestra by declaring, "It is hardly surprising that James was so influential: he was a hot, swinging trumpet player regularly featured with the country's leading swing band and possessed of a flawless technique that was the envy of trumpet players everywhere."[44] Dan Morgenstern has suggested that James was the "most popular of all trumpeters in the forties,"[45] and Jack Chambers reports that Miles Davis told John S. Wilson of the *New York Times*, "Those people who say there's no music but bop are just stupid. It just shows how much they don't know. . . . When I was growing up I played like Roy Eldridge, Harry James, Freddie Webster and anyone else I admired. You've got to start way back before you can play bop. You've got to have a foundation."[46]

In addition to starring in the Goodman band as a trumpet soloist, James "helped Benny make 'swing' a household word in the thirties"[47] by also contributing two of the band's best arrangements during Goodman's finest period. At twenty, James had written *Peckin'* for the Ben Pollack band, and even at this tender age, Harry was already a skilled arranger, exhibiting "an impressive understanding of the [Fletcher] Henderson arranging recipe."[48] Gunther Schuller writes of the Goodman recording that "the last one-and-a-quarter ensemble chorus of *Peckin'* displays best the kind of remarkable talent" the trumpeter-arranger possessed, adding that "for good measure, earlier in the piece, James adds a characteristically swaggering solo and employs in the final brass ensemble what is perhaps the first use of the section trumpet 'shakes' in a white orchestra—all in all a rather impressive debut."[49] One indication of the appeal of James's tune is the fact that on May 20, 1937, over two weeks before the July 6 recording by the Goodman orchestra in Hollywood, Duke Ellington with Johnny Hodges and his orchestra recorded their own version of Harry's *Peckin'*, with words added to the piece and sung in a type of call-and-response exchange led by vocalist Buddy Clark.[50] Part of the tune's attraction for the Duke and his men is explained by the source for James's tune: the trumpet solo by Cootie Williams on a 1931 recording of Ellington's *Rockin' in Rhythm*.[51] The Ellington-Hodges recording of *Peckin'* features the outstanding rhythm section of bassist Hayes Alvis, drummer Sonny Greer, and guitarist Fred Guy. Cootie Williams plays the theme on his muted trumpet, Harry Carney is simply sui generis on baritone as he shifts into a marvelous double-time passage, Barney Bigard's silken New Orleans–style clarinet proves appropriate to any period of jazz, Clark's lyrics are answered by some delightful falsetto voices from the band, and Johnny Hodges dips and soars with a fascinating rhythmic drive. The entire ensemble is like an engine hitting smoothly on every cylinder but with such a relaxed yet visceral swing that no other band could match it, not even Basie's, at least not with the same unhurried rhythmic pulse under soloists whose timing and note choices are unique to the haunting Ellington sound.

While *Peckin'* has been considered to represent a more original piece of arranging by Harry James than his *Life Goes to a Party*, recorded by the Goodman band in New York City on February 12, 1937,[52] the latter is an arrangement that generates greater swing from Benny and his band, with the leader taking an especially driving solo that is supported enthusiastically by the riffing ensemble. James himself, in a muted chorus, is equally energized by this tune, which originated, according to Martin Williams, from the 1929 Ellington-Miley *Doin' the Voom Voom*—"in AABA song form (an obvious Cotton Club specialty)"—by way of a pair of 1931 Horace Henderson–Fletcher Henderson pieces called *Hot and Anxious* (a blues) and *Comin' and Goin'* (partly a blues), which "added the riff later called *In the Mood*." Williams continues,

> These, in turn, became Count Basie's *Swinging the Blues*. Meanwhile, *Doin' the Voom Voom* had obviously inspired the Lunceford–Will Hudson specialties *White Heat* and *Jazznocracy*, and these in turn prompted the Harry James–Benny Goodman *Life Goes to a Party*. In the last piece, the background figure (an up-and-down scalar motive) to one of the trumpet solos in *Voom Voom* had been slightly changed and elevated into a main theme.[53]

In a way this pedigree places James directly in the line of much of the history of big-band jazz, descending from Ellington and Henderson through Basie and Lunceford to Miller and Goodman. With this kind of heritage, it is no wonder that Harry's *Life Goes to a Party* is a winner. But credit must go to the entire band as well, for even Gene Krupa is subdued enough to keep a steady, pulsing beat without overplaying and Benny's brother Harry Goodman, so often maligned as the band's weak link, adds to the forward momentum of this performance. The side not only showcases all the best qualities of the Goodman band and of the leader's swinging clarinet, but it features Harry James as an "irrepressibly spirited" soloist, as a gifted arranger capable of "some strange harmonic alchemy peculiar to jazz," and as a section leader who could stimulate his colleagues to precision ensemble work in "an up-tempo 'killer-diller.'"[54]

On several sides recorded with Teddy Wilson and Billie Holiday in 1938, James had an opportunity once again to play more authentic jazz than he did as a flashy, swing-era soloist in the ranks of the Goodman orchestra or, more especially, Harry's own big band of the 1940s, although later the trumpeter tended to follow with his band of the 1950s "a more committed jazz policy."[55] Gunther Schuller suggests that the "populist direction" of James's early years as a big-band leader may have been owing largely to his discovery of Frank Sinatra, "a major singing and musical talent" who stayed with the James band for about half a year during

Harry James of Beaumont. Reproduced from
Harry James and His Orchestra (Laserlight 15 771);
photograph by Frank Donovan and design by
A. Backhausen, © 1992 Delta Music Inc.

the end of 1939 and the beginning of 1940.[56] Even though the Wilson-led sessions
with Holiday of late 1938 in New York are not among Billie's best, Wilson plays
with his consistently high level of quality, showing perhaps most fully the Hines-
Waller tradition as he refined it for his own uses. Lester Young also makes his
unmistakable presence felt on these sessions, as do both Herschel Evans and Benny
Carter. As he did earlier in December 1937 and January 1938, James in the company
of Evans and these other black jazz masters turns in some very compatible
choruses, even if at times his brash trumpet proves somewhat overbearing. However, on *April in My Heart*, recorded on November 9, 1938, James solos with a mute
and delivers a very restrained and effective response to this Hoagy Carmichael
tune; likewise, on *They Say*, from the same date, Harry plays tastefully and with
feeling on this minor song by Rodgers and Hart. James's "pretty" side is shown
off in his solos on both *April in My Heart* and *Say It with a Kiss*, yet he also digs in

on the latter with some growly moments that suggest his ability to pay homage to the roots of true jazz.[57]

Another dimension of Harry James's talents comes across in these performances with Holiday—his assertiveness as a section leader, for which Albert McCarthy feels he "has never been given sufficient credit."[58] While James's trumpet may lead the Wilson ensemble with too much drive in view of Holiday's and Young's relaxed, behind-the-beat style, the contrast may also contribute to the total effect of these tender renditions of popular songs. Certainly it would seem that playing with Teddy Wilson (who, as we have seen, was noted for holding back) and the rest of this all-black orchestra (which included Walter Page on bass and Jo Jones on drums), James was enabled to "pay a little more attention to the content of his music," as McCarthy found he so often failed to do when he was with Goodman and indulged himself instead in a bit too much theatricality.[59]

In 1939, James organized his own band, which would feature the fine alto saxophonist Willie Smith, who had so effectively led the reed section of the Lunceford orchestra. Noted for "scorching up-tempo numbers" and "sultry" ballads, the James orchestra scored many successes, placing some fifty-seven songs on the popularity charts, including nine No. 1 hits for a total of thirty-two weeks.[60] The band's recording of *I've Heard That Song Before* became in 1942 Columbia Records' all-time biggest seller with the purchase by listeners of 1,250,000 copies. Vocalists that included Frank Sinatra, Dick Haymes, Helen Forrest, and Kitty Kallen assured the popularity of the orchestra during the war years with their recordings of songs that appealed to the troops abroad and the wives and sweethearts at home, among them a hit song entitled *It's Been a Long, Long Time*. Dating from July 24, 1945, this recording includes a string section, which James first added in 1941, and features Kitty Kallen's winsome delivery of the song's sentimental lyrics, a splendid, soaring alto solo by Willie Smith, and, of course, Harry's opening and closing trumpet that made him a superstar of the big-band era.

In 1948 the James orchestra recorded a Basie–Neal Hefti tune, *Bluebeard's Blues*, which demonstrates Harry's ability to play convincingly in the Count's very swinging Kansas City style. Other tunes from this year include the solidly grooving, very satisfying *Roly Poly* and Harry's original *Snooty Fruity*, both of which show off the band and the trumpeter to good advantage. In the latter especially, James takes a particularly flamboyant solo and Willie Smith contributes two fine, driving choruses. A Neal Hefti original, *The Lady Was Moody*, finds the James orchestra leaning about as far as it ever would in the direction of Stan Kenton's progressive jazz, while *King Porter Stomp* takes James back to the Jelly Roll Morton tune that

Harry recorded with his first band in 1939 and that Alan Lomax lists among the best-known recordings of this all-time classic.[61] (Morton's tune had been recorded earlier by Benny Goodman in 1936, with Bunny Berigan as soloist, but another classic from the early period of jazz history recorded by Goodman had featured Harry James on trumpet: King Oliver's *Sugar Foot Stomp*, in which Harry's solo is rated by Albert McCarthy as "one of James's best solos with the band.")[62] Also from 1948 is a rousing version of *Shine*, a full-blown swing rendering of this tune associated with Louis Armstrong and one that differs totally from the version James made on January 16, 1938, at the Carnegie Hall concert with Goodman, when Harry imitated the famous Armstrong solo.[63] While firmly rooted in the Swing Era, Harry James ranged through the jazz repertoire from Morton, Oliver, and Armstrong to Basie and Kenton, paying homage to the many marvelous traditions of this music, even as he himself made his mark as a trumpet virtuoso, section leader, arranger, and one of the longest active big-band leaders, still performing right up to his death in 1983.

❂ ❂ ❂

A third Texan to form part of the Benny Goodman band was Ernesto "Ernie" Caceres, who was born in Rockport on November 22, 1911. In the early 1930s, Ernie, his brother Emilio, and a cousin, Johnny Gomez, provided "some of the hottest music around San Antonio."[64] In 1937, the Emilio Caceres Trio, with Ernie on baritone and clarinet, Emilio on violin, and Johnny on guitar, performed for a national audience on Benny Goodman's "Camel Caravan" radio show. Afterward, the trio recorded in New York, and Gunther Schuller credits this "improbable instrumental combination" with producing "six splendid small group sides" that are "astonishing" for the way "the violin and clarinet blended and, even more surprisingly, how Ernie's gentle, burly baritone functioned so successfully with the violin." Schuller attributes the success of these sides to the fact that the two brothers were "superb musicians, with excellent tone on their respective instruments."[65]

On *What's the Use*, from the trio's New York session of November 5, 1937, Emilio Caceres turns in an absolutely fascinating performance on violin, his solos vintage 1920s hot swing, with Ernie's baritone accompaniment and solos rocking along in the same twenties vein. In contrast, Ernie's rich clarinet chorus is perhaps rather too swing-era in its style and conception for the rest of the recording. On the other hand, Nat Hentoff finds Ernie's clarinet in this performance "assertive and poignant (an uncommon combination)," although he seems to prefer Emilio, who is termed "unmistakably a jazz fiddler in time, phrasing, and harmonic coloration."[66] Ernie is more impressive on clarinet on *I Got Rhythm* from the same recording session and comes across as smooth as Benny Goodman yet more "assertive and poignant." Emilio is again quite impressive on violin, swinging hard and producing this time some quite original swing-era licks on an instrument that found "true jazz expression" most often only "in the context of the small group," as exemplified in this performance by the Caceres Trio.[67] As Gunther Schuller observes, the Caceres brothers blend beautifully, their lines moving together with the perfection of concert chamber music but swinging Gershwin's tune in true jazz style.

Although "resplendent tales" were told of Emilio, he seems to have recorded little,[68] and it was Ernie Caceres who went on to become a member in 1938 of Jack Teagarden's big band, in 1940 of Glenn Miller's orchestra (playing second alto sax and singing), for a month in 1943 and later in 1944 with Goodman, and also in 1944 with the Woody Herman band along with Budd Johnson. Since Caceres played with Goodman during the record-ban years of World War Two, Ernie's solo work is unfortunately not available from his time with Benny's band, and while with Herman, Ernie does not seem to have recorded as a soloist. He appears on a V-Disc recording made on December 7, 1944, with the Hot Lips Page orchestra, which also includes Teagarden and Texas guitarist Herb Ellis.[69] During the war years Ernie also soloed on recordings with the Teagarden and Miller big bands, as well as with the Eddie Condon Sextet.

Ernie created some fine clarinet choruses on the 1939 recordings of *Persian Rug*, *Muddy River Blues*, and *Wolverine* with Teagarden's orchestra. Writing of this group, Albert McCarthy observes that Jack's "best line-up" was that of 1939 and that "as might be expected Teagarden and Caceres make the most impression."[70] On a Miller recording of *Song of the Volga Boatmen*, Ernie solos on alto and demonstrates his proficiency on yet another reed instrument, as well as his admirable capabilities as an improviser.[71] Appearing on many Miller sides recorded from 1940 until Glenn joined the army in 1942, Ernie took choruses on a number of tunes on clarinet but served for the most part as a sideman in the highly successful Miller unit which, as Gunther Schuller points out, "accomplished what no other reed section ever had before: the closest equivalent to a string section without actually resorting to one," and in the process "set the stage for jazz to become among other things the primary American entertainment and dance music."[72]

Ernie Caceres is especially effective on an April 1943 recording made in New York by the Eddie Condon Sextet, playing "with characteristic aplomb" on *I've Got the World on a String*.[73] On a December 14, 1944, recording with the Condon orchestra, which also includes Jack Teagarden, Caceres plays the theme on baritone behind Pee Wee Russell's clarinet solo on *The Sheik of Araby*, as well as engaging in some rousing Dixieland group improvisation following Russell's chorus. On *Somebody Loves Me* from the same 1944 date, Ernie takes a truly robust baritone solo in the fine tradition of bass saxophonists Adrian Rollini and Min Leibrook from the Bix Beiderbecke era.[74] Although Teagarden is the real star of these last two performances, Ernie Caceres most definitely holds his own. From 1950 to 1956, Ernie performed in a studio orchestra for the Garry Moore television show; from 1956 to 1957, he rejoined Bobby Hackett, with whom he had played in the mid-1930s. In his last years, Caceres returned to San Antonio, where he remained active on the local jazz scene, performing with Jim Cullum's Happy Jazz Band and Chuck Reilly's Alamo City Jazz Band. In 1969 Ernie and Emilio made a final recording, entitled simply *Ernie and Emilio Caceres.*[75]

Wilson, James, and Caceres all made important contributions to the Swing Era, the latter two in particular with regard to the popularity of white big bands that resulted in an expanded audience for jazz-oriented music. Wilson's influence on a generation of pianists may not represent an authentic tie with a Texas tradition; yet as a native who often recorded with other musicians from the state, he belongs in this story of Texans in jazz through his various roles as soloist, sideman, leader, and arranger and as the first black member of a mixed group. Along with James and Caceres, Wilson also stands as a versatile figure who contributed to a wide range of ensembles during the 1930s and 1940s. All three of these men carried on their careers into the succeeding decades, but it was their participation in the Swing Era that has placed them among the outstanding names of this important period in jazz history.

OUT OF HOUSTON

Houston in the late 1930s and early 1940s boasted an outstanding band led by Milt Larkin, who was born in this Gulf Coast city on October 10, 1910, and was inspired to take up the trumpet in the 1930s by Bunk Johnson. In 1936, Larkin organized a Houston unit that has been considered "probably the last of the great Texas bands."[1] Frank Driggs has called the Larkin band "legendary" and reports that the Jimmie Lunceford and Cab Calloway orchestras, when they came through Houston, received "rough treatment" at the hands of "the Larkins crew."[2] Active from 1936 until November 1943, when the leader was drafted during World War Two, the Larkin band spent the better part of a year between 1941 and 1942 in Chicago, also playing during this period an engagement at the Apollo Theatre in New York. John Hammond heard the Larkin band in Beaumont in 1939 and was fully impressed; at this time the personnel included three future saxophone stars: Illinois Jacquet, Arnett Cobb, and Eddie Vinson. All three of these reedmen would eventually make names for themselves in New York as members of such bands as those of Lionel Hampton, Count Basie, and Cootie Williams. Jacquet, Cobb, and Vinson were all products of a Houston upbringing, although Illinois was a native of Louisiana, as was his brother Russell, who briefly played trumpet in the Larkin band. Following in the Coleman Hawkins–Herschel Evans tradition, Jacquet and Cobb would help establish the notion of a Texas school of tenor saxophone playing, while Eddie Vinson would form part of the rising bop movement, "playing fantastic alto in the style of Charlie Parker."[3] Vinson would also become a popular blues singer, scoring a hit record in 1945 with his *Kidney Stew Blues*.

Illinois Jacquet was born in Broussard, Louisiana, on October 31, 1922, but before he was one year old, the family moved to Texas, where Jacquet's father, a sometime bass player, worked for the railroad. Although the youngest of three Larkin reedmen, Illinois was the first to make a name for himself. As a featured

Illinois Jacquet of Houston. Reproduced from *Illinois Jacquet Flying Home* (Bluebird 07836, 61123-2) by permission of Frank Driggs and RCA Victor Records.

soloist with the Lionel Hampton orchestra on *Flying Home*, recorded in New York on May 26, 1942, Jacquet played a chorus that "triggered a whole generation of big-toned, extrovert sax solos."[4] Albert McCarthy has placed this recording of *Flying Home* within the history of Hampton and his long association with the tune, which was attributed to Lionel and Benny Goodman, even though *Flying Home* was credited by Mary Osborne to Charlie Christian.[5] As McCarthy writes, "Over the years, this number has become associated with Hampton, who has recorded it many times (the first was under his own name with a section of the Benny Goodman band in February 1940), but this [1942] version with the obligatory tenor saxophone solo played by Illinois Jacquet and high note trumpet from Ernie Royal remains amongst the best, not least because it is exciting without degenerating into musical chaos."[6]

Indicative of the lasting popularity of this recording, which has epitomized the wartime swing band, is the fact that it has served as the film music for three movies. In 1990, *Flying Home* was featured on *Memphis Belle*, a film set in 1943 and depicting the story of a flying fortress crew on its last bomb run over Bremen before being released from active service. In 1992, *Flying Home* was again featured, this time for a dance-floor scene from the early forties, in Penny Marshall's *A League of Their Own*, the tale of women baseball teams during the war and their demise shortly thereafter. Also in 1992, Spike Lee's film biography, *Malcolm X*, returned to *Flying Home* for the opening scene at a Boston dance hall where the young Malcolm, known as "Detroit Red," appears in his "conked" hairdo.[7]

Listening to Illinois Jacquet's extended chorus on the 1942 *Flying Home* after all the hoopla over his flamboyance and exhibitionism, it is hard at first to hear in this highly controlled performance—one that begins with a mellow huffing reminiscent of Coleman Hawkins—the "wild, full-toned solo" credited with establishing "a new approach to tenor saxophone playing," which was labeled "the Texas tenor style" from its use of extremely high notes or harmonics.[8] But after the rather subdued opening, Jacquet slowly builds through repeated phrases and then single notes played with alternate fingerings to the kind of single-minded intensity that characterized his many performances of this tune, identified with Illinois as much as with Lionel Hampton. One reason for the rather subdued beginning has been suggested by drummer George Haynes, a protégé of Jacquet, who was born in Victoria on October 23, 1920. Haynes reports that Jacquet told him that when Hampton called out in the middle of the tune for the tenorist to solo, Illinois was not expecting it and was thinking at the time of *Martha*, another tune that he proceeded to play at the start of his chorus.[9]

Twenty-five years after the 1942 recording, Hampton and Jacquet would join forces again at the Newport Jazz Festival on July 3, 1967, to hammer and honk away on their faithful warhorse. On the recording from this date, one can hear the same riff phrases repeated at greater length, with Illinois both honking in the bottom range of his horn and screaming in the upper register.[10] Jacquet's apprenticeship in the Southwest, where this style of playing was popular—a style he and his fellow Texas tenors helped introduce nationally—would lead, as Gary Giddins has observed, to "generations of rabble-rousing tenors (none as gifted or rounded as [Illinois])."[11] Indeed, Jacquet's playing was not limited to the feeding-frenzy antics of showmanship but encompassed ballads, slow blues, and an impressive up-tempo technique that made him a formidable proponent of the chase chorus, in which he often engaged with the best tenors of the day, beginning in 1941 during Jacquet's first year with the Hampton band when he did battle with an even younger Dexter Gordon on *Po'k Chops*.[12]

Nonetheless, Jacquet's name remained synonymous with the honking tenor, which Giddins says he did not invent but put on the map.[13] Jacquet was also known for his driving one-note reiterations, which can be sampled in Illinois's own composition *Jet Propulsion*, recorded with his brother Russell in New York on December 18, 1947.[14] Although a master like Coleman Hawkins, who shared the stage with Jacquet when both were members of the Jazz at the Philharmonic tour, could admire the Texan's style of playing, even the Hawk would "sometimes put on a rueful smile if the crowd went wild when Jacquet (or some other tenorist on a JATP show) honked on one note for minutes on end."[15] On the other hand, as Dan Morgenstern has observed, "even the honking and overblowing in which [Jacquet] indulged, while roundly condemned for aesthetic reasons, were a genuine contribution to saxophone technique—Dexter Gordon, for one, has made good use of these devices, not to mention their impact on Coltrane and his followers."[16]

After Jacquet left Hampton in 1942, he joined Cab Calloway for two years, but no recordings seem to exist of the tenorist with the Calloway orchestra since this was during the war-years record ban. In 1944 Illinois participated in the first Jazz at the Philharmonic concert in Los Angeles on July 2, 1944, produced by Norman Granz to help fund the defense of a group of Mexican youths accused of a murder during the so-called Zoot Suit riots.[17] This series of jazz concerts offered jam sessions on stage and brought widespread recognition to Jacquet. Leonard Feather notes that, even though Illinois was criticized in the early days by "those who found his squealing high notes offensive . . . he and Granz were aware that [the tenorist's] occasional forays into these explosive areas provided the element of excitement—something too often absent from small combo jazz at that time."[18]

In 1945 Jacquet joined the Basie band and stayed until 1946, recording a number of sides. By then the Count's orchestra may not have been up to its classic groups of the late 1930s; yet Chris Sheridan asserts that the early 1946 recordings represented "Basie's strongest, freshest Columbia session of the immediate post-war period, with a 'modern' feeling that transcends the Bebop influence heard in some solos. *Rambo* in particular looks forward to the approach of the 'New Testament' band of the 1950s, while *The King*, being a development of *Jumpin' at the Woodside* . . . , provides neat contrast or transition between 'old' and 'new.'"[19] Jacquet's solo on *The King* is indeed quite exciting, but the band builds up such ferocious swing behind the tenorist that it is a wonder Illinois is not wilder and more daring, that he does not launch into the kind of stirring performance Eddie "Lockjaw" Davis became noted for in the late 1950s. Jacquet is also featured effectively on *High Tide* and *Mutton-Leg*. Commenting on the former, recorded on July 28, 1946, Alun Morgan and Albert McCarthy call Jacquet's solo "splendid,"[20] and Chris Sheridan sees in the recording of *Mutton-Leg* from July 31, 1946, "the contact with 'swing-bop' that Basie was to maintain for the rest of the decade."[21] Jacquet's solo on *Mutton-Leg* contains all his trademarks: honks, squeals, shakes, and stratospherics, as well as his high-octane intensity that would influence so many tenors to come, especially in Basie's successive bands. When Jacquet left the Count in September 1946, his place was taken by yet another in a long line of Texas tenors, Jesse Powell, "a genial man of gargantuan size," who only remained with Basie for about one month.[22]

During the period from 1945 to 1946, Jacquet also recorded in Los Angeles with his brother Russell and six other musicians, including Charles Mingus on bass. On August 2, 1945, this group produced *Merle's Mood*, an original by Illinois, on which Russell plays a muted trumpet solo and the tenorist contributes a fairly predictable chorus. As a result, the ensemble writing and Mingus's bass here are more interesting than the solos—the former especially nice as John Brown on alto, Illinois, and Arthur Dennis on baritone play a counter line against Russell's chorus. From the same session, *Memories of You* is a Hawkins-inspired romantic reading on which Jacquet does not, however, exhibit the Hawk's ability to make an original jazz piece out of a pop song, as Illinois repeats the melody frequently and limits himself to mere embellishment. In August 1946 the same group recorded *Ghost of a Chance*, and while Jacquet's solo is clearly in the Hawkins tradition, the sound is at times uniquely his, a thinner, lighter legato. Like Hawkins on his famed *Body and Soul* of 1939, here Jacquet moves further away from the melody and ends his chorus with a stirring cadenza. From the August 1946 session, *Bottom's Up*, another Jacquet original, has a Basie-like riff feeling, and appropriately the solo by Illinois is in the Lester Young style with its relaxed swing and identifiably Prez-inspired phraseology. Back in New York in the same month, Jacquet recorded with another group that included Joe Newman on trumpet and Trummy Young on trombone, and on *Jacquet Bound* the tenor continues a kind of Kansas City sound and swing but inserts some of his predictable honks. On *Twelve Minutes to Go* the honks are excessive, as is his one-note routine, but on the other hand Illinois also has some nice call-and-response moments with Newman. Perhaps the most exciting solo by Jacquet from the New York session comes on *Jumpin' at Apollo*, where the tenor really digs in but keeps his exuberance under control. Trummy Young also takes up where he had left off from his Lunceford days, blowing a fine chorus full of his trademark licks, first heard on the 1938 *Margie*.[23]

From the Basie band in September 1946, Jacquet went with Norman Granz's Jazz at the Philharmonic tour, and it was during this period that he committed most of the excesses associated with his career. In response to the tour's Carnegie Hall performances from May 27 to June 3, 1946, which were Jacquet's first with the tour but, as noted earlier, not his first with the Philharmonic, a *Down Beat* writer headlined his review "Granz Bash a Caricature on Jazz—Everything Bad in Jazz

Found Here."[24] What is amazing is how such "grandstanding" could generate so much excitement among fans and could on occasion result in some genuinely fine exchanges when Jacquet traded choruses with the likes of Coleman Hawkins. At the inaugural Jazz at the Philharmonic concert in Los Angeles in 1944, Jacquet can be mistaken for Lester Young on the recording from this historic occasion. With the group's first tune, *Lester Leaps In*, Illinois begins his solo in a relaxed, lightly swinging mode, but thereafter he breaks out his false fingerings, one-note patterns, and squeals, producing a very remarkable low honk as well. J. J. Johnson, who was later with Jacquet in the Basie band in 1946 when he would record at twenty-two a boppish solo on *Rambo*, is also featured on *Lester Leaps In*, already exhibiting the considerable technique that Leonard Feather calls a "primordial form of 'bebop.'"[25] Here Johnson follows Jacquet's lead in repeating phrases to increase the intensity level, in keeping with the Granz prescription for excitement. Illinois particularly wakes up the crowd with his whistling high-note shakes, as the audience can be heard to respond with cheers and applause. In the up-tempo tune entitled simply *Blues*, Jacquet swings hard and is all over his horn, with his high-note shakes and screams even more spectacular than usual.

Another side of Jacquet's talent is represented by his slow blues style, which is evident when he plays with his own band, organized by Illinois and recorded in December 1947. On *Try Me One More Time*, written by Illinois and his brother Russell, the tenorist delivers a lovely rendition of this blues ballad and then Russell sings the traditional lyrics while the band riffs behind, after which Illinois returns for a classic Basie-like ending. Even more satisfying is Jacquet's ballad work on his composition entitled *A Jacquet for Jack the Bellboy*, recorded the following day, on which Illinois demonstrates his very expressive and controlled handling of the tenor. It is on ballads of this sort that Jacquet shows his affinity for the Hawkins–Herschel Evans school, although Illinois lacks the ideas of the one and the special passion of the other.

On the same 1947 date, Jacquet performs *Riffin' at 24th Street*, a composition of his own that exhibits a slight connection with the bop movement of the day. Despite the presence in Jacquet's band of bop trombonist J. J. Johnson, Illinois does not stray far from mainstream swing here, nor did he throughout his career. As Gary Giddins pointedly remarks, Jacquet could have been "squarely in the first generation of bebop," yet "notwithstanding frequent contact with advanced thinkers of all sorts," he remained "the youngest of the great swing saxophonists, a bridling dinosaur."[26] On such a composition as Jacquet and Johnson's *B-Yot*, Illinois sounds a bit dated when he plays next to J. J.'s trombone, Joe Newman's trumpet, and John Lewis's piano, though Jacquet never quite seems out of place in such a bop-inspired setting. Recorded in Hollywood on April 6, 1949, *B-Yot* may not represent Jacquet's ability to adapt to his own group's more modern tendencies, but on *Hot Rod*, recorded back in New York on May 22, 1950, Illinois provides a fine example of his impressive technique and flexibility. A tune written by Cedric Haywood, another Houston native born around 1918 and the pianist-arranger in the Larkin band, *Hot Rod* finds Jacquet in a high-speed chase with baritone saxophonist Maurice Simon and not only holding his own but exploding from the blocks with a burst of energy that must have gotten the attention of many a bebopper. Joe Newman recalled of the earlier 1947 Jacquet band that another sax player with Illinois, Leo Parker, "one of the best modern baritone saxophonists," would "make it pretty hot for Jacquet, without knowing it."[27] One other sideman with Jacquet was pianist Sir Charles Thompson, whose classic *Robbins Nest* was first recorded by the Jacquet band on May 21, 1947. Thompson remembered that "Jacquet had made a lot of noise with Jazz at the Philharmonic, but he made the greatest impression with that little band he had in 1947."[28]

Certainly Jacquet went on successfully to outlive "his somewhat dubious reputation" as an "eccentric" and "freak."[29] Producing dozens of albums, performing with such bop masters as Dizzy Gillespie, J. J. Johnson, and Howard McGhee and recording with fellow tenorists and Texans Arnett Cobb and Buddy Tate, as well as with Hawkins, Young, Gordon, and Eddie "Lockjaw" Davis, Illinois Jacquet would prove himself one of the most enduring and undiminished jazz saxophonists of his or any other generation. Gary Giddins, in a review of the tenorist's big band from the fall of 1983, reported that news of Jacquet's visit to New York for the first time in many years "promised more than could fairly be expected of an opening night performance—i.e., an orchestra that would swing from the gut. Yet Jacquet and company often delivered. The opening salvo—a Jimmy Mundy arrangement of 'The Birth of the Blues'—touched all the bases."[30] Ten years later, at a June 18, 1993, concert of Jazz at the White House, Jacquet loaned President Bill Clinton his tenor with these words, "You ain't heard nothing yet," and Clinton, who had spoken eloquently and knowledgeably of jazz in a fine introduction to the affair, showed his understanding of and appreciation for the music by obliging with a respectable performance on Jacquet's historic horn.[31]

❧ ❧ ❧

When Illinois Jacquet left Lionel Hampton in 1942, his tenor seat was occupied by Arnett Cobb, who was born in Houston on August 10, 1918. Arnett began his professional career at the age of fifteen as the lead tenor with the Milt Larkin band. During his five years with Hampton, Cobb took over the feature role as tenor saxophonist on what became *Flying Home No. 2*, recorded in New York on March 2, 1944.[32] In Arnett's version of this hit tune, the tenorist employs a raspy tone, a gruff kind of tight vibrato that differs noticeably from Jacquet's normally cleaner, more Lester Young–inspired sound. Here Cobb also makes greater use of high and low notes in his solo than even Illinois had, although these would actually become more the trademarks of Jacquet's playing by the summer of 1944 when he performed with Jazz at the Philharmonic in Los Angeles. One commentator observed that to the "wild style" of freak high notes "perfected by Jacquet," Cobb added "a harsh, cutting intonation, a wide vibrato and a sense of swing equalled by few musicians in jazz. Cobb in full flight is one of the most rhythmically exciting sounds in the music, although the excess of vulgarity inherent in much of his work hides this fact."[33]

Essentially, Arnett Cobb's style was well in place by the time of his early recordings with Hampton. In later years, Cobb's remake of *Flyin' Home* on *Party Time*, one of his many Prestige albums from the late 1950s and 1960s, exhibits many of Cobb's favorite devices, a few of which were also Jacquet's: a growling, vocal-like delivery on the tenor; a hard-swinging, unrelenting drive; false-fingering one-note reiterations; generous quotes from everything from *At Sundown* and Gershwin's *Rhapsody in Blue* to *Pop Goes the Weasel*; and of course an opening and closing statement of the crowd-pleasing theme.[34] Even more typical is a 1978 rendition of *Just a Closer Walk with Thee*, where all the basic Cobb ingredients are stirred into this hymn some thirty-four years after Arnett's recording of *Flying Home No. 2*. Fred Bouchard has described the 1978 session at Sandy's in Boston that produced *Just a Closer Walk* and in doing so has summarized Cobb's approach to the tenor as "equally vocal and drawling and thus utterly unique," utilizing "grunts, hoots, and wrenching wails. . . . These elemental components of Cobb's blues style, coupled with extraordinarily deft timing and phrasing throughout, enable[d] him to excite Sandy's crowd."[35]

Following in Jacquet's footsteps, Cobb also recorded at the Apollo in New York City, demonstrating with a six-piece group in 1947 that he was "not just a wild, frenetic big-band blower, with little or nothing to say of any constructive consequence."[36] It was this series of recordings that left "an indelible mark" on the rhythm and blues music scene "in general, then and later."[37] By 1948 Cobb's back problems forced him to retire, and in 1956 a car accident again interrupted his career, but by the late 1950s he had begun to cut his series of Prestige albums with a wide variety of groups. Influenced both by the blues tradition and by his gospel background in the Houston area, Arnett not surprisingly joined forces with pianist Bobby Timmons, one of the leaders of the gospel-rooted hard-bop movement of the mid- to late 1950s. Cobb's tune *Nitty Gritty*, from the album *Movin' Right Along*, is in the same mode as Timmons's famous *Moanin'*, and on Arnett's piece the tenor and piano both produce a "funky," soulful, gospel feeling.[38] David Rosenthal suggests that even though "deep-funk tenor playing should perhaps be traced back to Ben Webster's lusty, swaggering solos, the honkin'-and-screamin' movement is usually lined to Jacquet's outing on 'Flying Home.'" Rosenthal goes on to observe that Cobb and other tenor players "worked in an area on the border between jazz and R & B, creating a new kind of music that ended up being called 'soul jazz.'"[39]

The soul or gospel influence is also evident in the title tune of Cobb's album *Smooth Sailing*, on which Arnett is accompanied by Austin Mitchell on organ. The early jazz interest in this keyboard instrument that Fats Waller referred to as "the God box" goes back to the 1920s and 1930s and to Count Basie in the 1940s; by the 1950s, the electric version of the organ became "a pillar of soul jazz," having "evolved as an important instrument in black music in the context of gospel."[40] Along with this soul/gospel influence, Cobb also remained indebted to Illinois Jacquet, as indicated by Arnett's inclusion of a Jacquet original, *Black Velvet*, on Cobb's album entitled *Sizzlin'*, which features Texas pianist Red Garland's lush chords behind the tenor and Red's own mood-setting chorus.[41] Jacquet had recorded his lovely ballad, in a fine arrangement by Jimmy Mundy, on April 6, 1949, with some excellent piano work by John Lewis.[42] Cobb does not attempt to duplicate the high-intensity performance of his fellow Texan, but he certainly does the ballad justice in his more relaxed, bluesy interpretation.[43] Again, Arnett is ably supported by Garland's comping and the rippling lines of Red's solo style that had already made jazz history with the Miles Davis Quintet.

Arnett Cobb's 1978 recording at Sandy's was itself a historic occasion: for the first time ever two famed "Texas tenors" and a "Texas alto" were together on the same bandstand. For this session, Cobb welcomed Buddy Tate and Eddie Vinson, and on *Broadway* the three show their common musical heritage by echoing one another in the opening to this Woode-McRea pop tune and by sounding in unison as if a single sax. Tate begins the soloing, and his screams, wails, honks, squeals, guttural flutter tonguing, and false fingerings demonstrate his membership in the Herschel Evans line of Texas tenors that also included Jacquet and Cobb. While Vinson on alto may not match the big tenor sound of Tate and Cobb, his roots are no less Texan by way of Buster Smith. For his part, Cobb actually seems intent on showing Vinson that he too can play up to the altoist's range by staying almost entirely in the upper register, but always with Arnett's raspy tenor voice that descends directly from the blues tradition's crying and pleading urgency. In the closing exchange of fours, there are many almost indistinguishable honks and squeals, the song ending with the trio sounding typically "lusty and ragged and full of good spirit."[44] Any doubts about where Cobb's allegiance lay are dispelled in this same session by his performance of the Evans-Durham classic, *Blue and Sentimental*. Backed only by what Cobb called a dream rhythm section of Ray Bryant on piano, Alan Dawson on drums, and George Duvivier on bass, Arnett pays dutiful homage to Herschel Evans's most famous solo, recapturing the sound and feel of *Blue and Sentimental* before going into his own more "vocal" style with its squeezed-out, breathy blues, a departure from Herschel's more elegant, rhapsodic approach. Once again, Cobb sounds closer to the rhythm and blues tradition out of which he emerged and on which he in turn left his own peculiar stamp.

In 1989, the year of Cobb's death, his album entitled *The Wild Man from Texas* was finally released, long after its original recording in June 1971. Along with Arnett, this album features reedman Jimmy Ford, a tenor saxophonist turned altoist who was born in Houston on June 16, 1927. After playing at the Eldorado, Houston's "ballroom of jazz," and doing a tour in the navy, Ford headed for New York in 1947; but after "beginning to form a base of action" there, he returned to Houston, where he played with Milt Larkin at the Silver Moon.[45] By 1948 Ford was back in New York, where he joined the Tadd Dameron band, which included Fats Navarro, Allen Eager, Kenny Clarke, and Curley Russell. In 1950 Ford switched to alto, and in 1951, as a member of the Red Rodney Quintet, he recorded an album from Prestige entitled *Modern Sounds* and one on the Status label entitled *Broadway*. Of the latter, Alan Zeffert writes that this recording offers "a fine example of [Ford's] Parker-Stitt distillations. He and the quintet's leader, trumpeter Red Rodney, indulge in some excellent exchanges on the fast *Red wig*, while the altoist is relaxed and full-toned on Rodney's *Coogan's bluff*."[46] Ford also performed with the Bud Powell Sextet at Birdland, and after a return to Houston, he joined the Maynard Ferguson big band for "thirty nights a year at Birdland" but on the road for the rest of the time, from New York to El Paso and points in between.[47] While with Ferguson, Ford recorded solos on a number of albums from Roulette, including *Maynard Ferguson at Birdland*, which Zeffert calls "a worthy LP that finds that saxophonist in fiery form with the band sounding exuberant and together."[48] In 1961 Ford left the Ferguson band and returned to Houston for good.

On *The Wild Man from Texas* from 1971, Ford is particularly impressive on the Arnett Cobb original *I Stand Alone*, on *Doxy*, and on *Mr. T*, the last two of these exhibiting the altoist's "fiery form" and his "fluent, exciting" execution.[49] As for Cobb, "the wild man" shows "his mastery of his instrument and his penchant for breaking loose into long, soaring solos"[50] as well as his ability to attack the music "with an energy and power that always astonishes the listener as he moves into gospel-tinged shouts and blues-bottomed riffs, or glides into a delicate, breathy ballad as only he can."[51] This ability is illustrated most fully on Cobb's original blues, *Wake Up, M.F.*, with the fine Texas-Mexican pianist-trombonist Joe Gallardo, born on September 22, 1939, in Corpus Christi, laying down some solid chords behind the tenorist.[52] Arnett is also quite into his game in another of his originals, *Mr. T*, where he soars and honks and twists with a Latin tinge, before Gallardo blows a terrific chorus on trombone (as he does on *Medussa* and *Bobby's Blues*), followed by an exciting instance of Jimmy Ford's "Parker-Stitt distillations," which are also evident on *Old Folks*. In this last tune Gallardo shows that his skills at the keyboard are up to his impressive performances on trombone, and on *You Stepped Out of a Dream*, both Ford and Cobb are equally satisfying, with Jimmy opening the number with a beautifully flowing solo and later Cobb doing his own thing, full of witty allusions and bluesy arpeggios. The two saxes on *You Stepped Out of a Dream* also play the theme as one and capture the tune's special timeless quality. Finally, on the Sonny Rollins classic, *Doxy*, the two reedmen take turns in recapping the history of postwar jazz, from Illinois Jacquet's exuberant brand of swing and Charlie Parker's revolutionary bebop to the hard-bop style of Sonny Rollins, doing credit to each of these figures and the movements they helped to found.

❡ ❡ ❡

Eddie "Cleanhead" Vinson, the eldest of the three alumni from the 1939 Larkin band, was born in Houston on December 18, 1917, and like both Jacquet and Cobb, Cleanhead made his name in New York, beginning in 1942 when he joined the Cootie Williams big band.[53] Unlike his tenor-playing fellows, Vinson achieved his fame primarily with the Williams band as a blues singer on hit recordings of *Cherry Red* and *Somebody's Got to Go*. Both of these tunes from August 22, 1944, exhibit Eddie's crying, "broken-toned" blues vocal style, which is also evident when he solos on alto.[54] At the 1944 Cootie Williams session, Vinson also sings on *Is You Is or Is You Ain't*, but here Cleanhead's delivery is smoother and does not employ the crying, falsetto, cracking, primitive, blues-shouter voice of his two hit recordings. Also on *Is You Is*, Vinson engages in a brief exchange on alto with Cootie's trumpet and takes a short opening chorus, though neither gives much of an idea of his playing style. With the Williams band, on an earlier January 6, 1944, recording of *Things Ain't What They Used to Be*, Vinson offers what is basically a swing-era alto solo with a touch of the bebop forties in its piercing, blues-inflected cry. For the August 22 session, Vinson was also present for the first recording of Thelonious Monk's masterpiece, *'Round Midnight*, although it is here only a showcase for Cootie's trumpet, which smoothes out Monk's modern classic and makes it into a romantic ballad. (Williams actually worked with Monk on the composition of this classic.) Present as well at these sessions was Bud Powell, who, on *Blue Garden Blues*, gives hints of the bop revolution to come.[55] The alto solo by Vinson in this last tune definitely provides evidence to support Benny Bailey's view that Eddie could create a sound comparable to that of Charlie Parker, if not at the same technical level or with the same depth of ideas.[56]

After leaving Williams in 1945, Vinson scored another hit by singing with his own sixteen-piece band on the tune entitled *Kidney Stew Blues*, which contains some of the same lyrics as *Somebody's Got to Go*. During this period, Vinson's band included John Coltrane and Red Garland, who toured with Cleanhead down through the South and Southwest. Because Vinson was the altoist in the band and Coltrane was at that time playing alto, Cleanhead convinced John to switch to tenor.[57] According to J. C. Thomas, "No matter what the band was playing, Coltrane, when not sight-reading, watched his boss attentively, picking up whatever saxophone tips he could. Vinson was a superb technician with an agile style; he had a way of bending and sustaining notes that John really liked. Later, [Coltrane] would notice a similar technique with Miles after he joined the Davis band."[58]

By 1949, Vinson's popularity as a blues singer and band leader had begun to decline. But in 1957 Cleanhead would record with an all-star Basie group that included Joe Newman, Frank Foster, Paul Quinichette, Freddie Greene, and two fellow Texans, Gus Johnson and Henry Coker. Like Jacquet and Cobb, Vinson tended to recycle his early hits, and on the 1957 session he performs, once more, *Cherry Red* and *Kidney Stew Blues*.[59] On the former, Vinson does little with the chords in his alto solos, which pale beside those of Buster Smith on the same tune from 1940; nor can Cleanhead's vocal compare with Joe Turner's version from that earlier date. By this time, Vinson's singing had become mannered, his falsetto voice producing high notes that sound hoarse rather than harmonically appealing. Perhaps the best piece from this session is the 1920s classic *Trouble in Mind*, on which Vinson takes a fine alto break, but it is far too brief to gain a sense of his conception on the instrument. Henry Coker's obbligato behind Vinson's effective vocal is another plus for this performance. On *Caldonia*, Vinson pays tribute to Louis Jourdan's alto, his blues vocals, and the jump bands he popularized, but here the only real touch of jazz is found in Coker's trombone solo. Vinson's alto is heard most fully on *Sweet Lovin' Baby*, and Robert Palmer is accurate in observing that Cleanhead's solo "echoes the grainy, choked sound of his voice." Palmer goes on to assert that, "of course, there is a lot of Charlie Parker in Cleanhead's playing, but Parker was himself a product of the Southwestern blues and jump band tradition, and in the beginning he based his style on the work of saxophonist and clarinetist Buster Smith."[60] However, little of the Smith-Parker influence is apparent in these 1957 recordings, although a much later album made in 1980 with Count Basie and Joe Turner does bring to mind the modern alto styles of Buster and Bird.

On the 1980 album entitled *"Kansas City Shout,"* Vinson joins Joe Turner for another rendition of *Cherry Red.* This time Vinson plays the alto while Turner once again does the vocal. If the latter's vocal performance falls short of his earlier version, which is understandable after forty years, Vinson's alto solo is amazingly strong and would seem to confirm the claim of the album's producer, Norman Granz, that Cleanhead was probably "heavily influenced by Bird."[61] In any event, Vinson certainly proves that he was still "a marvelously potent combination of primitive bluesman and sophisticated jazz musician."[62] Especially on *Apollo Daze,* which must look back to the period when Jacquet and Vinson performed at that New York theater, Vinson sounds closer to Buster Smith than anywhere else and at the same time turns in a splendid blues chorus at the end that places him directly in the line of the great southwestern blues singers and alto saxophonists. One other album, entitled *Kidney Stew Is Fine,* recorded with T-Bone Walker on guitar, brings Vinson's career full circle, for it was as a member of the Larkin band that Walker, a Texas blues singer who traveled in the 1920s with Blind Lemon Jefferson, probably first knew Vinson in 1938 and 1939. Here Vinson repeats his vocal on *Things Ain't What They Used to Be* from the Cootie Williams 1944 recording and also performs what is now called *Somebody Sure Has Got to Go.*[63] Even though this is primarily an album featuring Vinson's singing and does not include much in the way of his alto work, it is clear from this recording and *"Kansas City Shout"* that Cleanhead's voice and saxophone "are Janus-like aspects of a single, natural, vernacular individual" and that "almost from the beginning Texas seems to have been a place where blues and jazz were very close."[64]

❧ ❧ ❧

Texas tenor saxophonist John Hardee, who was born in Corsicana on December 20, 1918, played in the Don Albert band out of San Antonio in 1938 and earned his music degree from Bishop College in Marshall in 1941. Despite a difference in background, Hardee too was "cut from the same fabric as fellow tenor saxophonists Arnett Cobb, Illinois Jacquet, Herschel Evans, Buddy Tate and Budd Johnson," being typified along with these men as a "big-toned, robust, soulful player, steeped simultaneously in raw power and gentle lyricism."[65] During the war, Hardee was stationed in Nyack, New York, and would travel into the Big Apple to jam. After being discharged, he and his wife moved to Harlem, where John met Tiny Grimes, through whom the tenorist signed a contract with Blue Note Records.

In August 1946, the same month Illinois Jacquet was recording in New York with Trummy Young, Hardee was included on a date with the ex-Lunceford trombonist as part of the Tiny Grimes Swingtet that cut a two-part version of *Flying Home*, which "generates a lot of excitement in the best Hampton-Jacquet tradition," with Hardee "getting into some Oriental stuff" in his second chorus.[66] An equally exciting performance by this group is on Ellington's *C-Jam Blues*. Earlier in the year, Hardee had recorded with his own Swingtet on February 28 and his own Sextet on May 31, which included fellow Texan Gene Ramey on bass. At the latter session, Hardee employs a Ben Webster–influenced vibrato on *Sweet and Lovely*, where he "gets further away from the melody" in his second sixteen-measure chorus. But the tune from this session that shows off Hardee's more Texas-derived approach is *River Edge Rock*, where the tenorist swings hard with a full-bodied tone, while Ramey and drummer Big Sid Catlett support Hardee to the hilt with a driving, pulsing beat. There are two takes of *River Edge Rock*, and both exhibit Hardee's technique to good effect, especially the alternate, on which he develops some exquisite extended passages—"seven choruses of inspired tenor . . . well worth having."[67] Likewise, on *Hardee's Partee*, a slow blues from the February 28 session, the tenor's playing "has that Texas flavor, though Webster is again in evidence." On this same date, Hardee also plays with gusto in two takes of *Idaho*, a Jesse Stone tune; with its "whole notes and interesting harmonies" this piece was "a favorite of sophisticated jazz players of the period" and "survived into the early bebop repertory."[68]

Like Jacquet and Cobb, John Hardee performed at the Apollo Theater, and during jobs with the Grimes Swingtet, John teamed up with Jimmy Ford for a session at the 845, an important black club in the Bronx.[69] After playing around New York and the East Coast for three more years, which included some "replacement gigs," among them one "in the tenor chair of Count Basie's orchestra,"[70] Hardee returned to Texas, where he took a high school band director's job in Wichita Falls and commuted three nights a week to play at the Harmony Lounge in Dallas, moving there in 1955 to teach at Lincoln High School. In both of these two cities Hardee worked with younger players who would go on to star in their own right: Leo Wright from Wichita Falls and James Clay and Leroy Cooper from Dallas.[71] In 1975, through the good offices of Arnett Cobb, Hardee took part in the Nice Jazz Festival in France, where he was joined by Illinois Jacquet and Eddie "Lockjaw" Davis. John "The Bad Man" said of this occasion that it was "a hell of a night" and that he "hadn't played that well in 25 years."[72] As Michael Cuscuna points out, although Hardee put his horn away for good after this, and although he did not stick "it out in New York" and rack up "an acceptable number of hours in the studio and years on stage," the Texan's recorded legacy is "sufficient testimony to his talent."[73]

In the case of both Illinois Jacquet and Arnett Cobb, these men more than paid their dues on stage and in the studio, leaving their mark as the last in a distinguished line of big-toned Texas tenors, while Eddie "Cleanhead" Vinson contributed to jazz history as a soloist, singer, sideman, bandleader, and an influence on the great tenor star, John Coltrane. Together, these three Texas saxophonists carried on a vital Houston tradition that began with the Thomas family, continued with such bands as those of Johnson's Joymakers and the Milt Larkin organization, and goes on today through an active club scene and through concert appearances by the city's local and visiting artists.

THE RHYTHM SECTION

Probably the most outstanding Dallas jazzman of the second generation was pianist Red Garland, born in Big D on May 13, 1923. In his youth, Red studied the clarinet and even took lessons locally from Buster Smith. However, having taken up the piano in the army, Garland played this instrument in his first professional job at a Fort Worth dance hall. Hot Lips Page discovered Garland when the trumpeter-bandleader was passing through their mutual hometown. Soon after joining Page's orchestra, Red ended up in New York, where his piano style was strongly affected by a close association with Bud Powell and by hearing Art Tatum live at Luckey's.[1] From Powell, the foremost bop pianist (Monk was doing, as we shall see, his own inimitable thing), Garland learned the changes and substitution chords of the new music. Beginning in 1945 Red played in New York with such swing-era greats as Coleman Hawkins, Lester Young, Ben Webster, and Roy Eldridge as well as with bop giants Charlie Parker and Fats Navarro. In 1954 Miles Davis heard Garland working with Hawkins in Boston and invited him to join a group that the trumpet star was planning to put together; it was to include Sonny Rollins, but when he was no longer available, either Red or Philly Joe Jones recommended John Coltrane.[2] The result was the Miles Davis Quintet of 1955, with Coltrane on tenor and with Garland on piano anchoring the group with his block chords—a group that would "set the pattern for most jazz combos in the '50s."[3]

Before the quintet made its historic recordings, Garland was already the pianist on the Miles Davis album entitled *Miles Davis: The Beginning*, which exhibited in quartet form "the first manifestation of the unique Davis theory of small-group jazz."[4] On this recording, made on June 7, 1955, with Garland on piano, Oscar Pettiford on bass, and Philly Joe Jones on drums, Miles for the first time cut an album without another horn, and as a result his trumpet "can be heard with unadorned clarity."[5] This recording also "proves that the group which eventually came into being was not formed without forethought."[6] From *The Beginning*, it is clear that in Garland and Jones Davis had found two members of an ideal rhythm section—with the well-respected Pettiford to be replaced soon by the younger, relatively unknown Paul Chambers. As Dan Morgenstern has suggested, "The fact that Garland had been a professional boxer, and that boxing had become Miles's favorite sport and pastime, would not have had any bearing on the matter if Miles hadn't liked his playing."[7] An example of Miles in his new approach is heard on the Dietz-Schwartz tune *I See Your Face Before Me*, which has Davis performing this ballad in the unique Harmon-mute style that became his most distinctive and popular mode. It was this same mute style just the following month at the Newport Jazz Festival, during the first week of July, that "brought the audience to its feet" when Miles soloed on *'Round Midnight*.[8] With this exposure Davis was said to have made a comeback, but as he himself remarked, "I just played the way I always play,"[9] and Miles's June 1955 recording of *I See Your Face Before Me* with Garland, Jones, and Pettiford perfectly illustrates the trumpeter's point.

Along with Miles's solo on *I See Your Face Before Me*, which Joe Goldberg calls "one of the loveliest tunes [Davis] has ever played and . . . one of his most moving performances,"[10] Garland provides an early example of the delicate block-chord style that would characterize almost all of Red's work with the Davis Quintet. According to Goldberg, credit for this album's material and approach as a prototype of the later group goes in part to the influence of pianist Ahmad Jamal. The trumpeter's biographer, Jack Chambers, also suggests that "melodic under-statement, harmonic inventiveness, and rhythmic lightness were part and parcel of Jamal's style and became central to Davis's style and the style of his finest bands."[11] In fact, according to Chambers, Miles once said, "Red Garland knew I liked Ahmad and at times I used to ask him to play like that. . . . Red was at his best when he did."[12] Another biographer of Davis offers the view that, while Garland was "not really imitative of Jamal," Red's "ability to assimilate much of Jamal's approach" proved helpful in Miles's attempt "to incorporate Jamal's use of space and lyricism" and that, "in addition, Miles enjoyed the exuberance of Garland's playing, which provided a sharp contrast to his own more introspective improvising."[13] Jack Chambers largely attributes the successful relationship be-tween Davis and Garland to the fact that Miles discovered in Red "not only a very capable piano player but that he was malleable, in contrast to Horace Silver and Monk," with whom Davis had previously recorded. As for the difference between the styles of Silver and Garland, Chambers finds that whereas Horace had brought to a 1953 Davis quartet, on a tune entitled *Blue Haze*, "a basic, funky blues, simple and countrified," Red introduced in the playing of *Green Haze* at the July 1955 session a new approach to the blues that was "sophisticated and urbane."[14]

After the Davis Quintet's recording on July 13, 1955, with Sonny Rollins on tenor along with what would become the regular rhythm section of Garland, Paul Chambers, and Philly Joe Jones, a quintet with John Coltrane was formed later in the summer and played its first club date in Baltimore on September 28, 1955. Destined to represent "a high-water mark in post-war jazz,"[15] this Davis Quintet made its first recording on October 27, 1955. Here Garland plays on *Little Melonae* what Jack Chambers calls an "odd, exotic solo in the lower half of the keyboard,"[16] while on *Ah-Leu-Cha*, an up-tempo Charlie Parker tune, Red shows his bop training as he sticks to long, right-hand lines that have nothing to do with his Jamal-requested manner.[17] Behind Coltrane's characteristically hard-bop solo—with its many leaps, turns, slides, glides, and unexpected starts and stops for his daring phrases—Garland comps and fills without intruding or detracting from this giant in the making. The October session was followed quickly by another on November 16, and although Coltrane could sound a bit out of place in the context of the group's Jamal-inspired lightheartedness on Ellington's *Just Squeeze Me*, the results of this second date were mostly well received. Critic Nat Hentoff, for example, found Garland's playing "some of his best choruses on record" but thought that Coltrane's "lack of individuality" lowered the record's rating.[18] Nonetheless, on *Stablemates* by Benny Golson, Trane is beginning to show signs of his very original sound and unique phraseology, and as a whole the quintet is starting to swing as a unit, with Davis driving the group either with his Harmon mute or his glowing open horn.

Even if the November 16 session was only a hint of something new in the offing, the quintet was turning out an enthusiastic audience, and by the spring of 1956 the group was back in New York to record on May 11 a total of fourteen tunes. Jack Chambers singles out *Surrey with the Fringe on Top* as probably "the one title from this session . . . you would most want to take with you to a desert isle,"[19] and Dan Morgenstern characterizes the group's performance of this piece as one of "refreshing gaiety and humor."[20] Although Chambers does not mention Garland's solo, it is in fact one of the most impressive highlights of this recording, along with the muted statement of the theme by Davis—at a slower tempo than might be expected, which transforms "a silly Rodgers and Hammerstein song from *Oklahoma*" into a more thoughtful piece of music; Chambers calls it "the first recorded instance of the arranged dynamism between Davis and Coltrane, as Davis's lacy, romantic exploration of the melody . . . gives way to a four-bar break in which Coltrane comes roaring in to take over in no uncertain terms."[21] Coltrane's solo also serves as a perfect example of how, as Martin Williams observes, the tenor "was reaching for a kind of subdivided bop rhythm, into a sixteenth-note accent pattern" that differed from Armstrong and Parker, who thought in quarter and eighth notes, respectively.[22] Meanwhile, Garland's solo illustrates his Jamal-oriented side with its light touch and block chords, but at times the sound of his piano is also reminiscent of John Lewis's delicate, almost folksy approach, and at other moments the Texan settles into a bluesy groove. Toward the end, Garland's chording recalls the way Erroll Garner would finish off a piece with brightly ringing chords. As Chambers remarks, "The harmonic innovation that [Garland] traces from Garner was also an important element in the fabric of Jamal's style, and Jamal may well have learned it from Garner. . . . But it was Garland, more than either Garner or Jamal, who transmitted the innovation to the younger jazz players, because he had the best forum as a member of the Miles Davis Quintet."[23] In this respect Garland performed a service similar to the one rendered by Teddy Wilson, as a member of the Goodman trio and quartet, in his transmittal of the Hines and Tatum style to a generation of pianists in the 1940s.

Among the fourteen tunes recorded on May 11, 1956, *Salt Peanuts* represents but one of several bop classics—another being *Woody 'n' You*.[24] On the first of these two Gillespie compositions, Garland demonstrates once again how fluent he was in the bop lingo, turning in a performance that sets him apart from Jamal, Lewis, and Garner by virtue of his ability to execute the long, complex lines of that hard-driving idiom. Quite in contrast to this style, Miles and Red create something of a classical treatment of *It Never Entered My Mind*, with "a repeated Chopinesque countermelody on the piano."[25] At the same time, Garland's bluesy handling of *Bye Bye Blackbird* at the June 5 session must have hit many an aspiring hard-bop pianist right where he lived. After Garland's earthy beginning on his *Blackbird* solo, he grows more elegant and then signs off with the dependable Garner-Jamal block chords. Of course, it is Coltrane's solo that deserves the accolades, along with what Chambers considers in Miles's "tightly muted rendition . . . a distillation of everything he ever learned from Billie Holiday."[26] Coltrane plays Parker on tenor but makes the Bird's upward swoops and tag-end flips sound entirely new on the bigger-toned saxophone. As with all of Garland's accompaniments, his work on *Dear Old Stockholm* adds an exquisite touch to this Swedish folk melody. His falling glissandos also fuel a fine chorus by bassist Paul Chambers, and Garland's repeated chords behind Coltrane prompt the hard-bop edge to John's solo, while Red's damped comping behind Miles's muted horn aids in returning the tune to its opening romantic mood.

At another 1956 Columbia session, of September 10, the quintet recorded *All of You*, considered by Jack Chambers to be "one of Davis's finest ballad performances" and a masterly integration of the Jamal style into the style that Davis "had been working toward for some time." Coltrane's solo is especially poignant, and "at his entrance a new force from the rhythm section takes over as [Paul] Chambers walks and Jones hits rim shots to close each bar."[27] Garland swings in the light Jamal style, mixed with block chords and some crisp single-note licks at the treble end of the keyboard. But this fine rendition was "superseded immediately by 'Round Midnight, one of the most striking ballad performances in all of jazz."[28] Accompanied by the subtle comping of Garland and the very moving bass work of Paul Chambers, Davis opens the Monk tune with one of the trumpeter's "cooler tone poems" and then, with mute still in, Miles blasts with Coltrane a stirring introduction to the tenor's lovely ascendant chorus. Garland does not solo, but his fills are particularly tasteful, and perhaps even more so on the Prestige recording of 'Round Midnight of the following October 26. Here Coltrane is especially adventuresome and forceful, as Garland seems to feed the tenor the choicest chords, which help launch him on his magnificent upward sweeps that are something of a foreshadowing of his famous "sheets of sound."[29]

The October 1956 Prestige session also includes a number of pieces that owe much to Garland's presence, both in their having been chosen in the first place and in their successful performance. The history of Tune Up is particularly notable for its Texas connections. In 1947, when Eddie Vinson had started his own band and hired Red Garland and John Coltrane, one of the fast blues they often played was Vinson's Tune Up, which contained "some quirky changes."[30] Once again, Garland renders critical support to Coltrane's solo in this demanding tune. Even though Miles had performed Tune Up on several occasions, beginning with a May 19, 1953, recording, he does not maneuver through the "quirky changes" so effectively as does Coltrane, who seems indebted both to Garland's guidance of the tenorist and to the fact that Red and John had played the tune often together in Vinson's band. Coltrane liked Tune Up so well that he later based his own Countdown on Cleanhead's challenging piece,[31] and Coltrane's version has been called, along with the title tune of his 1959 album, Giant Steps, one of his "two paragons of vertical improvisation," in which he "uses scale patterns and arpeggios to slice swiftly through the densely packed chords with surgical precision."[32] Coltrane is also bolstered by Garland's comping on another up-tempo tune, Sonny Rollins's bop melody Airegin, on which the pianist plays some unusual figures during the ensemble's spirited outchorus.[33] Although the discography in the Miles Davis Chronicle credits Garland with composing Blues by Five, Dan Morgenstern calls it a Davis tune and Jack Chambers both credits it to Davis and calls it a head.[34] In any event, Morgenstern describes "the Davis solo" as "one of [his] very best recorded blues efforts" and praises Coltrane's "blues playing" here as "something to hear."[35] Garland also turns in a marvelous blues chorus of his own, and his feeling for this piece suggests in fact that he may well have been its composer, even if it was only a memorized head rather than a composition committed to paper.

Among the many fine performances from this date is *If I Were a Bell*, on which both a muted Davis and a raucous Coltrane swing wonderfully, as does Paul Chambers, who gives something of a definitive definition of "cooking" as he backs all the soloists with a splendid walking bass.[36] After Garland had recorded this Frank Loesser tune for Prestige with Chambers and Jones as a trio, Davis was so impressed that he immediately added the piece to the quintet's repertoire; as a result, "musicians everywhere were buzzing about" the band.[37] In light of Garland's earlier performance of this tune, it is no wonder that his piano here simply serves up a "full meal deal" that offers everything, from rapid ascending block chords, rocking rhythms, and faultless lines and trills to a John Lewis–like funky blues bit with enough silence to let in the beautiful bass work of Chambers that accompanies Garland every swinging beat of the way. It is also clear from their work together why, as Dan Morgenstern recalls, the trio of Garland, Chambers, and Jones "was affectionately known in jazz circles as simply 'The Rhythm Section'— the first since the glorious 'All American' rhythm quartet of the Count Basie band of the thirties to earn a soubriquet of its own."[38]

Another noteworthy performance from this period is the September 10, 1956, recording of *Sweet Sue*, arranged by Teo Macero and first issued on the delightful and informative album *Leonard Bernstein: What Is Jazz*. Here composer-conductor-pianist Bernstein discusses the elements of jazz music and uses *Sweet Sue* to demonstrate "how modern jazz musicians rework old materials in their own ways."[39] A band assembled especially for *What Is Jazz*, including Texas drummer Gus Johnson, plays Joplin's *Maple Leaf Rag* and other classic pieces, and toward the end of the recording the Miles Davis Quintet performs Teo Maceo's arrangement of *Sweet Sue* and then "improvises on Miles' own series of chords based on the harmony" of this same tune.[40] In performing a modern rendition of this standard song, the quintet begins with Maceo's rather atonal version and then attempts to work within the same mode, which is unusual for the Davis group and especially for Garland, whose solos were normally "attractive and always competent but almost never adventuresome."[41] (Alun Morgan says of Garland that, in many ways, he was "the most orthodox member of the group and his dependability enabled Paul Chambers and Philly Joe Jones to take liberties with time.")[42] Here the pianist is forced to illustrate Bernstein's point about the changing nature of jazz, and although Garland eventually lapses into his predictable patterns, at first he plays what are for him some rather "far-out" progressions. One can sense that he is not that comfortable with this freer approach to jazz, and in fact only a few years later he would dismiss Ornette Coleman's free jazz by saying of it, "Nothing's happening. I wouldn't mind if he were serious. I like to see a struggling cat get a break. But Coleman is faking."[43] Miles, however, disagreed; he liked Ornette "because he doesn't play clichés."[44]

Although Davis was more sympathetic toward Coleman, Miles himself did not stray far from his harmonic and melodic base, and Coltrane began to grow restless, for as John's playing on *Half Nelson* and *Blues by Five* demonstrates, he was moving into some unexplored territory. Meanwhile, Paul Chambers was developing into a more effective soloist who could even dispense with a rhythm section accompaniment, and his powerful lines were beginning to dominate when he played with Garland on Red's choruses, as on *I Could Write a Book*. By November the quintet had been disbanded by Davis, owing almost entirely to the problems his four members were creating as a result of their drug addiction. Despite this unfortunate situation, the Miles Davis Quintet had by then clearly established a reputation with its Columbia and Prestige recordings. As Ralph J. Gleason would comment, this unit "comprised the best musical minds of their generation: John Coltrane, Philly Joe Jones, Paul Chambers, Red Garland. . . . The interplay between these personalities made the group. . . . [In] no group before or since have I ever heard the kind of rhythmic interaction that went on between Garland and Philly Joe."[45] Nonetheless, it was necessary for Coltrane to set out in a new direction, as it was for Davis, who would not only travel to Europe but would work with Gil Evans again, this time on a series of highly successful orchestral albums, having created with the composer the influential "birth of the cool" recordings of 1949–1950. Although Davis re-formed the quintet in December 1956 after his return from Paris, in April of 1957 Coltrane and Jones were fired, with Trane joining forces briefly with Thelonious Monk.

Garland and Chambers continued with Davis during the summer of 1957 and were recorded at New York's Café Bohemia with Sonny Rollins on tenor. By September Jones was back in the quintet, but Garland had been replaced by Tommy Flanagan. In October Cannonball Adderley joined Davis, and then in December Miles rehired Coltrane, at which time Garland returned. In the judgment of Jack Chambers, the Miles Davis Sextet became "perhaps the finest small band in the history of jazz."[46] Yet for Garland, his tenure as a regular member of the sextet would be shortlived, for following its first recording session on April 2 and 3, 1958, Bill Evans took Red's place on piano. Even so, by this date Garland had already made his mark on modern jazz. As Frank Tirro has written,

Postwar jazz took a quantum jump in the late 1950s when Red Garland and Bill Evans, both pianists with the Miles Davis combos, revoiced keyboard chords by omitting the root as the lowest-sounding pitch and replacing it with the seventh or the third of the chord on the bottom. Garland's 1955 and 1956 recordings with Davis show the transition, and Bill Evans's 1959 work on *So What* (*SCCJ*, XI/3) demonstrates the fully developed modern voicings.[47]

Before Bill Evans was substituted for Garland in the sextet—not, it seems, as a result of Red's reportedly having walked out at the April 3 session over his dissatisfaction with the solo space given to Paul Chambers rather than to himself—the Texas pianist would contribute significantly to what jazz saxophonist-composer Benny Golson considered the best track on the sextet's *Milestones* album for Columbia, Thelonious Monk's *Straight, No Chaser*.[48] More notable, perhaps, is the album's title tune, *Miles*, which both Jack Chambers and James Lincoln Collier rate as a masterwork and a breakthrough, with Davis achieving what Coltrane called his "'new stage of jazz development' and his compositions with 'free-flowing lines and chordal direction'" that, according to Nat Hentoff, predicted "'the development of both Coltrane and, to a lesser degree, the more extreme, more melodic, Ornette Coleman.'"[49] Collier, as Jack Chambers points out, recognized that Davis was constructing his pieces "not on chord changes but on modes,"[50] which Chambers says was not discovered by Miles; rather, his contribution lay "in making it work" and thus in his influence on the practice of jazz in the 1960s.[51]

As for Garland's part on the historic *Milestones* album, his solo on the Monk tune *Straight, No Chaser* is certainly one of the finest and most adventuresome of his career and justifies the enthusiasm of Golson, who cited among "the more arcane delights of this music" the way Garland's solo ends with "a beautiful harmonization of Miles' original solo on *Now's the Time*."[52] And in the title tune, Garland is a highly important component of the "brash but sensitive rhythm section" that Golson felt "buoyed" the three horn players' "individualistic explorations" of the *Miles* theme.[53] In addition, this album has Garland's rendition, accompanied only by the other Rhythm Section members, of the tune *Billy Boy*, which critics have unanimously praised as "unabashed fun" and "one of the foremost examples of the use of block chords."[54] Even though Ahmad Jamal had played *Billy Boy* dozens of times, it was Garland who gained the acclaim for his very swinging, expertly executed rendition of the tune, complete with a patented Erroll Garner tremolo. Wilfrid Mellers writes of Garland that "in a sense" he "complements Erroll Garner, for whereas Garner reveals a poetic romanticism beneath the gay gesture, Garland starts with the nostalgic dream but grows increasingly impatient with it. Most of his numbers end with a sudden, rather fierce, barrelhouse-like tremolo, banishing the self-indulgent brooding."[55] Despite his debts to Jamal and Garner, Red Garland was,

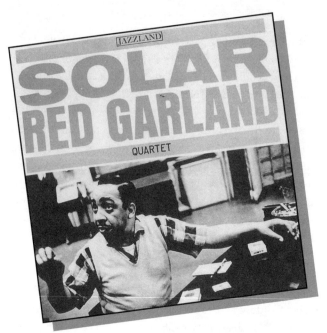

Red Garland of Dallas. Reproduced from *Solar: Red Garland Quartet* (OJC-755) by permission of Fantasy, Inc.; photograph by Steve Shapiro.

according to French critic Henri Renaud, "a marvelous pianist in his own right . . . an original artist with a very personal and creative approach to melody, rhythm, beat and sound." Renaud's comments on Garland aptly summarize the pianist's achievement:

> When he made his first recorded appearance with Miles Davis, he was instrumental in most younger pianists the whole world over going in for both Ahmad Jamal's rhythmic conceptions (the "Charleston" syncopation) and Erroll Garner's harmonic ones. . . . The Garnerian influence is obviously at work in Garland's system of chord inversions: Garner never strikes the tonic with the left hand's little finger. Here indeed lies the essential difference between the pianistic sound that was prevalent during the Parker era and the one that was to supersede it in Coltrane's time.[56]

For most commentators, Red Garland never achieved the same vitality and inventiveness in his playing after he left Davis that he demonstrated during his two and a half years with the trumpet leader. But Red's career did not end in 1958, for he would form a number of trios and quartets and even stage something of a comeback in 1978 after some fifteen years of retirement in Dallas, where he had returned in 1963. On an album like *Solar*, recorded in New York on January 30, 1962, with Les Spann on flute and guitar, Garland offers a representative variety of his wares that includes ballads, the Miles Davis title tune, and two Garland originals (one a minor-key blues), which altogether exemplify his versatility.[57] Even while Red was still with the Davis Quintet, he frequently recorded albums with Coltrane under his own name or under Trane's, among them *The First Trane* (May 31, 1957), *Traneing In* (August 23, 1957),[58] *Soul Junction* (November 15, 1957), *High Pressure* (December 13, 1957), *The Last Trane* (January 10, 1958), *Trane's Reign* (March 26, 1958), *Black Pearls* (May 23, 1958), *Stardust*, and *Standard Coltrane* (the last two from July 11, 1958). None of these albums delineates the more revolutionary side of Coltrane, but many show his development, as on *Black Pearls*, where the tenorist plays some of his "sheets of sound" in the freewheeling *Sweet Sapphire Blues*. This piece also includes what the liner notes, written in April 1964, call "one of Garland's most amazing outings," though it can in no way compare with his best work with the Davis Quintet.[59]

On *Standard Coltrane*, recorded at a difficult period during Trane's time with Miles, the tenorist exhibits with the second chorus of *I'll Get By* what Robert Levin calls "a particularly pointed, woundingly moving example of the artist coping with the torture-chamber of forces of two realities."[60] Garland's solo, preceding Coltrane's second chorus, contains nothing of this sort of excruciating sound, which Levin may exaggerate in an effort to show that Coltrane's playing reflected what Cecil Taylor identified as the "hysteria of the times."[61] By contrast, the pianist rarely if ever attempted what Levin refers to as Coltrane's struggle "to grasp and communicate a churningly vital contemporaneity."[62] Red Garland's solo is, as so often, rather a jaunty, upbeat—if bluesy—treatment of a tune that characterizes the music of this Texan who for almost twenty years not only "got by" but literally had his fingers on the pulse of modern jazz.

FROM BEBOP TO HARD BOP

After recording at Minton's Playhouse with Charlie Christian during after-hours jam sessions in 1941, Thelonious Monk joined with Coleman Hawkins to cut a group of obscure recordings that were released in 1944 and showed that, in Monk, "an original talent was emerging."[1] This date did not include any of Monk's own compositions, even though, as we have seen, his 'Round Midnight was recorded in the same year by Cootie Williams. It was not until 1947 that Monk himself recorded this most famous of all his tunes, along with a number of other pieces that have been considered among his finest. In fact, Monk's performances from the 1947 sessions recorded by Blue Note's Alfred Lion have been labeled the pianist's "most powerful and lasting body of work."[2] On the initial sides issued by Blue Note, Monk was assisted by Texas bassist Gene Ramey, who, with drummer Art Blakey, formed Monk's first recorded trio, which cut three of his tunes that would become standards: *Ruby My Dear, Well You Needn't,* and *Off Minor,* as well as the pop songs *April in Paris* and *Nice Work If You Can Get It.* On the earliest of the 1947 Blue Note recordings, Gene Ramey was also a member of the sextet that recorded Monk's *Humph, Thelonious, Suburban Eyes,* and *Evonce,* along with Blakey, Ike Quebec on alto saxophone, Idrees Sulieman on trumpet, and Billy Smith on tenor.[3]

Thelonious, recorded on October 15, 1947, is a Monk tune that at once places his "piano style historically" and establishes "his heritage in jazz."[4] Called by Martin Williams a "near-parody," this piece contains a clear link with "the style of Harlem stride men like James P. Johnson, Willie 'The Lion' Smith, Fats Waller, and the rest."[5] A ragtime strain emanating from Scott Joplin is also wedded to the blues tradition, for as Williams points out, Monk's playing combines "the regular fulfillment of the expected" in ragtime with "the surprise twist, the sardonically witty phrase, and the unexpected rhythmic movement" that derive from the fact that Monk was "authentically a blues man, as none of the older stride men were."[6] For David Rosenthal, Monk's attachment to stride, boogie-woogie, and gospel is "one of [his] links to hard bop," a style noted for its renewed interest in blues and gospel, "a return to the pulsing rhythms and earthy emotions of jazz's 'roots,'" and a greater emphasis on simplicity of structure.[7] Moreover, hard-bop musicians tended to seek a more personal style that would express a greater emotionalism than is associated with the cerebral, technically virtuosic approach of bebop.

Monk's unique piano style is perhaps more evident on two other of his marvelous originals, *Ruby My Dear* and *Well You Needn't*, recorded on October 24, 1947.[8] Here Monk's spare approach comes to the fore for the first time, a style that owes something to Count Basie but at times can be even more bare-bones. As James Lincoln Collier writes, "Rather than play the four or five notes of a full chord, [Monk] would frequently pick out only two of them to suggest the whole."[9] Monk's playing is also characterized by less manual dexterity—the Hines, Tatum, and Teddy Wilson school—and more hard-bop expressiveness, which is true as well of his compositions in that they call for the unexpected and are often jagged in construction. In describing Monk's style, Wilfrid Mellers reflects some of the special qualities and quirks of a Thelonious performance: "There is a feeling of screwed-up expectancy; the music might, we suspect, break down at any moment, or it might explode into heaven or hell knows what. In fact, it does neither; it simply goes on until it stops. It owes its considerable emotional impact partly to the frustration it generates, partly to the fact that this frustration is accepted with 'a kind of furious calm.'"[10] With all the expectancy and the unexpectedness in Monk's playing and writing, it is perhaps reassuring to hear Gene Ramey's unobtrusive but steady bass maintaining a rock-bottom beat behind the pianist's rhythmically off-center, single-note figures and whole-tone runs. The contrast is effective in setting off Monk's unique rhythmic and melodic sense, and even though Ramey may not have been the ideal hard-bop accompanist (his approach is generally impersonal and unemotional), it seems that he was in fact able to anticipate precisely where Monk was heading and to supply the perfect note that would complement the pianist's melodic lines, his decorative runs, or his ringing note clusters. It is easy to understand why Monk included Ramey on this first recording session to feature the composer-pianist's original compositions.

Well You Needn't finds Ramey especially effective in laying down a well-chosen bass line against Monk's unusual harmonic texture in a tune that has retained an "unflagging freshness."[11] While Thelonious concerns himself with his spare single-note figures, his leaping melodic line, and his embellishing runs, Ramey keeps the pulsing beat clearly in mind, and at times his note choices coincide with Monk's as if by osmosis. Art Blakey on drums remains inconspicuous, merely furnishing an infrequent accent here or there, never intruding into Monk's expressive line of musical thought. In later years Monk could forgo any percussion or bass accompaniment and still achieve an implied beat at the same time that he worked out his unique interpretations, frequently of pop songs. With the early trio recording of *April in Paris*, Monk also demonstrates his special ability to transmute such a popular song into "a composition for piano."[12] Martin Williams's remarks about Monk's subsequent treatment of *Smoke Gets in Your Eyes* apply equally to the earlier recording of *April in Paris*: "His commitment only to the best aspects of the original . . . rid it of its prettiness and its sentimentality and leave it with only its implicit beauty."[13] For Ramey's part, he shows that he knows this tune inside out, as he feeds Monk the key notes he obviously wants to hear for leading him back from his jazz explorations to the original melody, which Thelonious states so concisely but expressively that its "implicit beauty" is at the core of his jazz "composition for piano." The other pop song interpreted by the trio is *Nice Work If You Can Get It*, a George Gershwin classic. Here again, after Blakey's patented press roll, Monk states the theme simply and directly and then launches into his right-hand improvisation, with an occasional chord in the left.[14] Meanwhile, Ramey pumps along with a steady beat that sustains the performance's high energy level and drive as Monk creates his peculiar brand of spellbinding modern jazz.

Despite whatever contributions Monk made to the bebop movement, he has not been labeled, strictly speaking, a bebopper; yet on two tunes by Ike Quebec and Idrees Sulieman, *Suburban Eyes* and *Evonce*, the tendency of the music is clearly in the bop tradition. As far as Mary Lou Williams was concerned, Monk, Charlie Christian, Kenny Clarke, Art Blakey, and Idrees Sulieman were "the first to play bop. . . . Those men played the authentic bop."[15] Art Blakey himself said of Monk that he was "the guy who started it all; he came before both Parker and Gillespie."[16] However, Martin Williams declares that Quebec's *Suburban Eyes* and the Quebec-Sulieman collaboration, *Evonce*, are the exception to the early Monk series, in which otherwise "there is hardly a bop cliché," since Monk "had been working on something else all along."[17] This is evident in Monk's own playing on *Suburban Eyes*, for following the boppish theme, Quebec's Parker-inspired alto flight, and Sulieman's many-note chorus, Monk goes his own way with a much sparer, Basie-like style that illustrates Wilfrid Mellers's view that Monk's music is "separated in space and time, surrounded by silence."[18] Eventually Monk reduces his solo to a few ringing clusters, allowing Ramey's bass to predominate as it runs the chords and fills the emptiness artfully left by Monk. On *Evonce*, Ramey opens with his walking bass, joined by the bop-inclined ensemble, while throughout the following choruses by Quebec, Sulieman, and Billy Smith on tenor, Monk comps with his characteristically percussive clusters and Ramey provides the soloists with a swinging, dependable pulse that booms out the beat and feeds them their needed notes. Working with Monk and Blakey, Gene Ramey supplied a solid if somewhat conservative bass line that in context may have been necessary in keeping time and in reminding the other musicians of the melody and harmony on which they were basing their innovative and at times difficult-to-perform bop-era compositions and improvisations.

In late 1946 and early 1947, Ramey also teamed with Fats Navarro on two classic bebop sessions, the latter of which, on January 16, 1947, produced a version of Miles Davis's *Donna Lee*, based on the chords of *Indiana*.[19] Entitled *Ice Freezes Red*, this Navarro interpretation of *Indiana* has Ramey playing some of his most solid bass behind the bop solos by Fats on trumpet and Leo Parker on baritone, the latter quoting in his chorus from Gillespie's *Bebop*. On *Goin' to Minton's*, Ramey renders excellent support to Navarro behind "another example of his superb control of the horn."[20] At two sessions in 1946, on December 18 and 20, Ramey joined Navarro— along with Eddie "Lockjaw" Davis on tenor, Al Haig on piano, Huey Long on guitar, and Denzil Best on drums—for eight tunes, only two of these not based on the pattern of *I Got Rhythm*, which distinguishes bop from hard bop. That is, the latter, as David Rosenthal explains, is "rarely based on bebop's standard chord changes (for example, 'I Got Rhythm' and 'Indiana')."[21] In these December sessions, Ramey is prominently heard on *Calling Dr. Jazz*, his lines clear and rich, complementing those of the soloists; and on *Fracture* he backs Huey Long's guitar throughout and, as usual, makes excellent note choices. In the latter, Fats is simply fabulous, while Lockjaw plays many of the licks he would later be noted for when he joined Basie; he sounds here at times like Illinois Jacquet, as in his screaming and squealing on *Just a Mystery*. On *Spinal* "the hard-working rhythm section is especially good," and on *Stealin' Trash* Ramey swings in the upper register, his notes precisely timed and well chosen, while on *Maternity* he also walks in the upper register with a firm, resounding beat behind Lockjaw. As might be expected, *Hollerin' and Screamin'* has "some Hampton-styled call-and-response stuff between the horns,"[22] with Ramey really in the groove on this tune that also features a short chase sequence between Fats and Lockjaw.

In 1952, Ramey would again record with Art Blakey, along with pianist Horace Silver, on *Safari*, a showcase for the drummer's talking form of African-inspired percussion playing. Recorded on October 9, 1952, this Silver tune features the pianist at his up-tempo best as he exhibits his "crisp articulation and his melodic imagination, his combination of fierce precision and relaxed swing,"[23] all of which are rather in contrast to Monk's unorthodox nervous style that "lets in the silence."[24] But here too Ramey is quite at home, staying right with Silver and playing with a lighter, fleeter style in keeping with the new "simplified" version of bebop that Blakey and Silver were "accused of playing."[25]

In addition to his work with the bop and hard-bop stars, Ramey could also assist a swing-era great like Lester Young during his last years. On January 12, 1956, Ramey recorded with Young, Teddy Wilson, trumpeter Roy Eldridge, trombonist Vic Dickenson, guitarist Freddie Greene, and drummer Jo Jones. Ramey may have been more comfortable in the company of Lester Young or a "sedate," "calm and measured" Teddy Wilson, but it is clear from the bassist's discography that he could play with any ensemble and could contribute significantly to historical dates with such masters of modern jazz as Charlie Parker, Fats Navarro, and Thelonious Monk, as well as with hard-bop exponents like Art Blakey and Horace Silver.[26] As a highly respected bass player, Ramey was in demand regardless of the style of jazz being performed, and for this reason his timekeeping talents were utilized by the major artists of whatever persuasion.

❂ ❂ ❂

Also joining Charlie Parker, Fats Navarro, Thelonious Monk, Art Blakey, and Horace Silver during their illustrious careers was Kenny Dorham, born on August 30, 1924, in Fairfield, a town in east-central Texas between Waco and Palestine. Dorham began on piano, playing boogie-woogie by the age of seven, and his first wind instrument was the tenor sax. Attending high school in Austin, Kenny took up the trumpet and later continued his musical studies at Wiley College in Marshall, where he majored in chemistry with a minor in physics. Coming on the jazz scene after being discharged from the army in 1942, Dorham had to compete with three major trumpet stars of the bop era: Dizzy Gillespie, Fats Navarro, and Miles Davis. Dorham's career began in California in 1943 with the Russell Jacquet band, and in 1945 he became a member of Dizzy Gillespie's first big band and of Billy Eckstine's organization, composing for the latter "a catchy bop theme entitled *Dead End*," which Charlie Parker regularly featured when Dorham later joined the Bird's quintet in 1948,[27] taking the place of Miles Davis and remaining with Parker until 1950. Dorham was also with Parker at Birdland, along with Art Blakey, on March 4, 1955, for Charlie's last public appearance.

During his time with the Parker quintet, Dorham improved what already was an obvious talent, but one given more to a lyrical gift than to up-tempo pyrotechnics. In an effort to keep up with the fast pace of the bop trumpeters, Dorham at first tended to splatter his attacks and to stumble on double-time runs.[28] His early recordings have been called "dull, flat, and somewhat erratic," but through the years Dorham slowly developed into "a consummate and masterful trumpeter, one of the important voices in modern jazz."[29] Indeed, by the 1950s Dorham had not

Kenny Dorham of Fairfield (left) and Charlie Parker (in pinstripes). Reproduced from the Ross Russell Collection, courtesy of the Harry Ransom Humanities Research Center, University of Texas at Austin.

been "overpowered" by Gillespie and Navarro but had in fact "developed into one of the best trumpeters in modern jazz and perhaps the most personal stylist after Gillespie and Miles Davis."[30]

Before signing up with Parker, Dorham shared the trumpet duties with Fats Navarro on a record date with Sonny Stitt on alto, Bud Powell on piano, and Kenny Clarke on drums. On August 6, 1946, Dorham recorded four tunes: *Boppin' a Riff, Fat Boy, Everything's Cool,* and *Webb City.*[31] On *Boppin' a Riff* (predictably based on *I Got Rhythm*, as are the other tunes, except for *Fat Boy*, the one blues of the session), Dorham's playing here is more satisfying than most commentators have suggested, and even though Navarro is clearly more technically secure, Kenny has much to say in his already lyrical lines. Except for rushing a bit in the second half of his solo, Dorham plays a fine chorus on *Fat Boy*, and he handles the upper register well, though certainly Fats is more relaxed in his own solo.[32] On *Everything's Cool*, Dorham is again lyrical but also executes a sizzling passage that is quite unique. Here Kenny seems more daring than Fats, even though Dan Morgenstern calls Navarro's "one of his best efforts of the date."[33] Playing in unison with Navarro on *Webb City*, Dorham shows that he could keep up with the fleet-fingered Fats, even though Kenny tends to overblow on his solo and perhaps in the end attempts more than he can bring off, while both of Navarro's choruses are "impeccable,"[34] the second even better than the first.

Less than three weeks later, Dorham again joined Navarro and Stitt on August 23 to record three tunes: *Bebop in Pastel*, *Seven Up*, and *Blues in Bebop*. Here the Texan's work has been seen once again as revealing "the less accomplished Kenny Dorham in his formative years."[35] Ira Gitler writes that Bud Powell's composition, *Bouncin' with Bud*, had its debut on August 9, 1949, with Sonny Rollins, Fats Navarro, Tommy Potter, and Roy Haynes, but this tune under the title *Bebop in Pastel* is recorded here by Dorham and the Bebop Boys three years earlier.[36] Admittedly, however, this is Dorham's weakest outing of this session, even though his solo does exhibit his lyrical bent and a knowledge of the bop language, which if he does not yet speak so fluently, he will at a later date. Moreover, Dorham's ensemble work with Stitt is excellent and indicates why Parker would have looked to Dorham to replace Miles Davis. On *Seven Up*, Dorham plays a long, interesting line in the middle of his chorus, to which he manages a stirring if somewhat offbeat ending. Here Dorham demonstrates his ability to play triplets effectively, but more significantly he sings with his trumpet rather than merely running up and down the scales. As for *Blues in Bebop*, this tune contains definite signs of things to come in Dorham's beautifully lyrical style.

In 1947, Dorham performed with an Art Blakey group and composed for it *The Thin Man*, on which Kenny "played convincingly."[37] With Blakey and Horace Silver, Dorham would subsequently become a founding member of the Jazz Messengers, a name that Blakey had used in the late forties but that in 1954 was given to what would prove "one of hard bop's most influential combos."[38]

In 1949, Dorham teamed up with Charlie Parker at The Roost, which billed itself as "the house that Bop built," for this New York nightspot had "adopted a nightly modern jazz policy," providing "proof that bop had arrived."[39] During this period, the arrangements played by the Parker quintet were "identical to the well-known Dial, Guild and Savoy single records" and were "instrumental in building the reputations of Bird, Dizzy, and the whole bebop movement."[40] On *Scrapple from the Apple*, recorded at The Roost on February 12, 1949, Dorham plays perfectly with Bird the up-tempo head but then slows down the pace and intensity with his muted solo, sounding close to Miles Davis in a production of ideas that are more interesting than their performance. On *Barbados*, Dorham sounds better with his open horn, for his ideas come through more clearly and with greater force. Parker is obviously the more adventuresome, quoting in his solo a snatch of *Buttons and Bows*, the 1948 Academy Award–winning song from the Bob Hope film *The Paleface*, which Bird also quotes on *Ooh Bop Sha Bam* from another session with Dorham, as well as on *Scrapple from the Apple* when the two were together in Paris in May 1949 at that city's first international jazz festival.[41]

During his Paris performances with Bird, Dorham would acquit himself admirably with two fine choruses on *Out of Nowhere*, the tune that virtually belonged to Parker. While Bird works in *Happy Birthday* at the end of his solo, Dorham indulges in the bebopper's penchant for incorporating popular tunes by finishing off his second chorus with a quote from Percy Grainger's *Country Gardens*.[42] In Paris Dorham would show as well that he could stay up with Navarro and Gillespie with his up-tempo choruses on *Barbados* and again on *52nd St. Theme*, where he fashions an excellent solo with what sounds like pop-song quotes but could be examples of Kenny's own very melodic conception.

While at The Roost, Dorham developed some "highly inventive bop improvisations,"[43] as on *Groovin' High*. Here he shows off both his melodic talents and his growing control over the execution of his ideas. Dorham also stays right with Bird on this up-tempo and tricky tune, as he does on *Confirmation*, where in trading fours he matches the master bar for bar, then plays the closing theme marvelously, including a perfectly hit high note an octave above the one in the tune's opening statement. On *Salt Peanuts*, Dorham plays the theme as well as any bop trumpeter, holding up his end of the proceedings quite splendidly, with speed and ideas aplenty, while Bird burns as perhaps no one ever has. From two sessions held on February 26 and March 12, 1949, Dorham matches Bird's lovely solo on *Slow Boat to China* with the trumpeter's own mellow, melodic lines, which represent one of Kenny's high points from these Roost recordings. On *Chasin' the Bird*, Dorham engages in some contrapuntal work with Parker and in his solo turns a few humorous phrases that look forward to the late 1950s wit of pocket-trumpeter Don Cherry. Throughout these sessions, Dorham is rarely spectacular but rather quietly supportive, often going his own way, as on *A Night in Tunisia*, which Kenny shows he knows thoroughly and to which at the end of his solo he lends a special touch.

In 1952 Dorham would join Lou Donaldson on alto, Lucky Thompson on tenor, Nelson Boyd on bass, and Max Roach on drums for four sides on which these men helped Thelonious Monk, as arranger-composer, "get away from the usual jazz beat and still swing," with Monk in turn assisting his sidemen to "make their solo power felt."[44] When Dorham recorded with this Monk sextet on May 30, the group performed a Thelonious original entitled *Skippy*, which the composer rarely if ever played again, probably because it is "one of his most intricate and treacherous pieces."[45] An up-tempo tune that displays Monk's considerable and faultless technique, *Skippy* obviously pushes Thompson and Dorham to give their best. Even though the ensemble work definitely stretches the sidemen, Dorham does a superb job to help bring off Monk's difficult but ingenious theme. With Monk's arrangement of *Carolina Moon* in six-eight waltz time, Dorham's ensemble work is again crucial, and he performs ably on this piece in a meter uncommon to earlier jazz. Likewise, on still another piece with a demanding meter, *Hornin' In*, Dorham's ensemble work is equally satisfying. On both tunes, Dorham also solos with distinction, especially on *Carolina Moon*, where his lyricism makes for a beautiful rendering that shows, in addition to a Davis influence, Dorham's own emerging style—a more open, flowing, and melodic sound in which it is evident that he has begun to eschew the thin, piercing tone of a number of the bebop trumpeters. Dorham's playing is clearly becoming more thoughtful and expressive, in the hard-bop vein, instead of depending on the rapid-fire note production of bebop. Like Monk, Dorham is allowing silence to play more a part in the construction of his choruses. In reading Monk's lovely *Let's Cool One*, Dorham once again turns in a highly expressive solo, creating long singing lines as well as shorter swinging phrases, all of which make of his chorus quite a moving performance. Whether or not Martin Williams was specifically thinking of the performances by Gene Ramey and Kenny Dorham when the critic praised the 1947–1952 Monk sessions as "among the most significant and original in modern jazz,"[46] these recordings with the two Texans would certainly seem to qualify.

On October 31, 1953, Ramey and Dorham would record together at Birdland in New York with Art Blakey and Horace Silver, prior to the formation in the following year of the Jazz Messengers by Blakey and Silver, with Dorham, as noted earlier, a founding member.[47] In reaction to the "birth of the cool" movement fostered by the Miles Davis and Gil Evans Nonet recordings of 1949–1950, credited with altering the direction of jazz in the 1950s, Blakey and Silver began a countermovement known variously as funk, hard bop, and postbop, a music that combined blues and gospel with modern jazz and that also changed the character of jazz during this same period. Although Ramey was not present on the earliest Davis-Evans Nonet recordings of January 21 and April 22, 1949, Gene was part of a Stan Getz–Miles Davis sextet whose five air-check sides from a February 1950 performance at Birdland continued the spirit of the Davis-Evans Nonet through a selection of compositions that included *Darn That Dream*, which was subsequently recorded by the nonet on March 9, 1950.[48] Once again, the sides Ramey made with the Davis and Blakey-Silver groups demonstrate the bassist's ability to contribute to two quite different developments in modern jazz. As for Dorham, he can be heard on the 1953 Blakey-Silver session playing in his best bop style on his own tune, *An Oscar for Oscar*, while Ramey proves to be in excellent form as well, pumping away behind Lou Donaldson's alto solo and Silver's already funky piano. Blakey's drum breaks are up to any he recorded throughout the fifties with his various versions of the Jazz Messengers, as is his extended solo on *Get Happy*. Dorham's trumpet work on Silver's *Split Kick* contains a fine example of Kenny's lyrical style at a moderate tempo, and Ramey again accompanies Silver nicely with fine note choices. The final number of the 1953 session, taped around three o'clock in the morning, was appropriately George Shearing's *Lullaby of Birdland*, but unfortunately it can barely be heard behind the announcer, telling the radio audience about upcoming shows with the Modern Jazz Quartet and reminding listeners that the Birdland series was produced by actor Telly Savalas.

While with Blakey's Jazz Messengers from 1954 to 1956, Dorham matured further as a trumpeter and can be heard on recordings of such tunes as *Stop Time* and Silver's *The Preacher*, both of which go back to the roots of jazz, with the latter becoming one of the most influential gospel-based tunes of the hard-bop movement.[49] Working with Horace Silver, who "simplified the shifting patterns of ad-lib passing chords in the accompaniment" but allowed the soloists "plenty of pre-set chord changes," Dorham became a "thoroughly revitalized and highly disciplined performer."[50] This side of Kenny's playing was of course already evident in his work with Monk, but it is while with the Messengers that Dorham "shows conclusively for the first time," especially in the recording of *Yesterdays* from November 23, 1955, that "he is more than just an accomplished and professional soloist. He focuses on the theme and develops it in a melodic improvisation which extends, refashions, and toughens the line into a musical entity obviously related to the original, but goes far beyond it in scope and meaning."[51]

In 1956, Dorham joined the Max Roach Quintet to fill Clifford Brown's seat, which had been tragically vacated with the trumpeter's accidental death at the age of twenty-five. On the Quintet's October 10, 1956, performance of *I Get a Kick Out of You*, Dorham approaches the pyrotechnical level of Gillespie and Navarro, reeling off some impressive runs in the upper register at breakneck speed.[52] On a 1958 album with the Roach Quintet, entitled *Max*, Dorham is featured both as trumpeter and composer.[53] *Crackle Hut*, a tune in the funky style of the period

Kenny Dorham. Reproduced from *Quiet Kenny*
(New Jazz 8225) by permission of Fantasy, Inc.;
photograph by Esmond Edwards. Copyright
©1992 Fantasy, Inc.

cultivated by the Jazz Messengers, finds Dorham playing with a much lighter touch and smoother flow than during his years with Parker. His half-valve effects add to the emotive hard-bop force of his melodic lines, and in his unison work with tenor Hank Mobley the trumpeter performs beautifully and impeccably. For *That Ole Devil Love*, Dorham achieves a very unusual sound with a mute, playing straight ahead in a plain style against Mobley's more florid and soulful approach, after which Dorham changes tactics and becomes more melodic and expressive. On *Audio Blues*, Dorham creates a funky-style blues, working his way around his horn and playing blue notes in unexpected places to create surprises throughout. The only disappointing tune is Dorham's original, entitled *Speculate*, which is too much of a free thing, with too many meaningless notes and scales that go nowhere—a weakness that at times could plague other hard-bop trumpeters of the period— in sum, too abstract, as the title suggests.

As an improviser and composer in the earthy hard-bop mode, Dorham would record in 1959 with his own septet that included Cannonball Adderley on alto sax and fellow Texan Cedar Walton on piano, as well as with his own quartet that featured Tommy Flanagan on piano, Paul Chambers on bass, and Art Taylor on drums. For the septet sessions in New York on January 20 and February 18, 1959, Dorham wrote three originals, all of which relate to the season "when things come into bloom,"[54] as do the pop songs from these two sessions, *Spring Is Here*, *It Might as Well Be Spring*, and *Passion Spring*. On the last of these, Dorham constructs "a marvelously sustained improvisation which is built logically in whole and part."[55] On November 13, Dorham's quartet of Flanagan, Chambers, and Taylor recorded eight tunes, among them a lovely rendering of *My Ideal* and a wonderfully expressive *Alone Together*, marvelous for its masterful execution.[56] On the Dorham original *Blue Friday*, Kenny "sustains a beautiful angular variation which is kept in motion by an amazing and subtle variety of devices of tonal inflection and rhythm."[57] *I Had the Craziest Dream*, recorded by Harry James as one of his "outright lushly sentimental ballads,"[58] was chosen by Dorham because he remembered it "as one of Harry James' best vehicles" and one that "stuck in his mind."[59] Kenny's rendition of *Mack the Knife* bears comparison with Louis Armstrong's versions of this tune, for the hard-bop interpretation measures up well against the New Orleans approach, with Dorham—during his solo and at the end of the piece—even making something of a bow to Satchmo. On *Old Folks* Dorham is not so flawless as elsewhere, but when he played with the Max Roach Quintet, this tune "was one of his most requested numbers."[60]

Based on a "serious examination of the body of Dorham's work," including his quartet and septet recordings of 1959, H. A. Woodfin concludes that Dorham was "one of the modern masters of his instrument and the originator of a style which is both new and impressive."[61] In commenting on the relationship between Dorham's writing for the septet and his own trumpet playing, Zita Carno notes that they both reflect "the same clean-lined construction, the same down-to-earth feeling, and the same wonderful lyricism."[62] The septet recordings are also of particular interest because of the presence on piano of fellow Texan Cedar Walton. Carno points out that Walton is "a thoughtful soloist" who is also "a good accompanist—alert, sure, always there but never overpowering and never getting hung up with the changes."[63] On Dorham's *Blue Spring*, which is very much in the funky Messengers vein, Walton feeds the trumpeter some earthy chords and, following Cannonball Adderley's bluesy solo on alto and Paul Chambers's brief chorus on bass, Walton offers a taste of his Bobby Timmons–inspired soul piano. Here Cedar takes his time and creates an unmistakably funky mood, while on *It Might as Well Be Spring*, he shows that he can play this Broadway ballad just as effectively. On the latter, Walton also backs up Dorham's delicious solo with finesse and feeling, adding immensely to the septet session, which helped establish

Kenny Dorham as "one of the most honestly creative, yet underrated, jazzmen," a musician who had absorbed the lessons of his many years as a practitioner of the bop, hard-bop, and funk-soul schools before emerging "as an individualist in the world of jazz."[64]

In 1960 Dorham continued his growth with an album entitled *Jazz Contemporary*, with Charles Davis on baritone sax and a fine rhythm section made up of Steve Kuhn on piano, Jimmy Garrison or Butch Warren on bass, and Buddy Enlow on drums. In his liner notes for this album, Mark Reilly characterizes the Dorham trumpet style as it had developed to this date, observing that it occupies "a middle area between the virtuosic flights of Gillespie and the brooding intensity of Davis. His tone has a crisp, edgy, natural brassiness and his lines are usually economical and directly to the point." Reilly reveals that Dorham was accustomed to learning the words of songs and that this habit aided in his understanding of the music he played. (Kenny had doubled as a blues singer in Gillespie's big band.) Thus Dorham tended to create highly melodic solo lines as well as tunes like *Tonica*, which Reilly says is "unusual in that it is almost entirely an ensemble piece . . . to keep the focus on the melody."[65] David Rosenthal has noted in this regard that, "along with Miles Davis and Art Farmer," Dorham "helped define an area of melodic invention and tonal nuance that greatly broadened the trumpet's range of expression."[66] Such expressive melodism is especially evident on *This Love of Mine*, as it was even in his earlier work on the 1952 Monk recordings.

Also in 1960 Dorham joined forces with Harold Land, who was born in Houston on December 18, 1928, but after only a few months his family moved to Arizona and then to San Diego. After working with Clifford Brown in the Max Roach Quintet in 1954 and 1955, Land made his most famous recording, *The Fox*, in 1959, with pianist Elmo Hope and trumpeter Dupree Bolton.[67] On July 5 and 8, 1960, Kenny Dorham would record with Land and his fine regular trio for an album entitled *Eastward Ho! Harold Land in New York*, and this date once again finds Dorham in a mellow, lyrical mood, especially on David Raksin's *Slowly*.[68] With Cole Porter's *So in Love* and the rarely jazz-interpreted *On a Little Street in Singapore*, Kenny demonstrates his technical control at an up-tempo pace as he matches Land's driving, hard-bop-inspired solos with smoothly executed runs. On *Singapore* Kenny also contributes some very tasty, thoughtful motifs that have something of a Mile Davis–like whimsicality. But as might be expected of a Texan, Dorham is most impressive on *Okay Blues*, which is quintessential hard bop and sums up superbly what every trumpeter or cornetist of the period was attempting, for instance Nat Adderley. Kenny's use of half-valve and lipping effects and rockingly syncopated rhythmic patterns adds greatly to the power of this performance, lending to his lines an emotively expressive sound production so crucial to hard bop. *Triple Trouble* is a jazz waltz, a form to which hard-bop players were often attracted, beginning, as we have seen, with Monk's *Carolina Moon* and continuing with Nat and Cannonball Adderley's attraction to three-four time. Kenny handles this soul waltz with characteristic lyricism and delicacy. Overall, the Land album shows off Dorham's wide range of stylistic approaches, all within the hard-bop mode of 1950s and early 1960s jazz.

An album on which Dorham would again team up with tenorist Hank Mobley—the two men having first performed together in 1955–1956 with the Jazz Messengers and in Kenny's own sextet and octet from those years—is Dorham's *Whistle Stop*, recorded on January 15, 1961.[69] Michael Shera calls this "probably the best album Dorham has ever made."[70] But in some ways the writing here is more interesting than the improvisations. Dorham composed all seven tunes, with titles that pertain to southwestern motifs—in particular *Windmill*, *Buffalo*, and *Sunrise in Mexico* as well as the album's title tune, which, with its train effects, can be traced to a heritage of East Texas ragtime, blues, and boogie-woogie. In general the tunes are rather typical of the hard-bop period, including as they do the funky *Buffalo*, a modal *Sunset*, and a *Sunrise* that combines hard bop with a "Spanish" tinge, as Jelly Roll Morton recommended, to spice things up nicely. Dorham's best effort is on *Windmill*, where he offers a wide range of techniques in his flowing choruses that slow down and speed up, varying the pace and feeling. *Dorham's Epitaph*, lasting only sixty-nine seconds, is a lovely melody played with Dorham's most passionate yet controlled lyricism. Kenny states the theme but once, and the piece and the album end, with the trumpeter having succinctly summed up the finest qualities of his career.

In 1963, Dorham met Joe Henderson when the tenorman first came to New York, and the two immediately became "a musically inseparable team."[71] On June 3 and September 9, 1963, Dorham and Henderson recorded, respectively, *Blue Bossa* and *Our Thing*. On the former tune Kenny makes very effective use of flutter tonguing, and on the latter (a Henderson tune) the trumpeter and Andrew Hill on piano take outstanding solos, varying the tempi to break up their choruses into complementary fast and slow passages. With regard to *Blue Bossa*, which is a convincing original by Dorham that blends hard bop and bossa nova, it should be noted that Kenny had made a successful trip to Brazil in 1961 to the Rio de Janeiro Jazz Festival.[72] Earlier, in January 1960, Dorham had traveled to Oslo, where he recorded with three local musicians.[73] These were not Kenny's first trips abroad, for, as mentioned earlier, he had attended the Paris Jazz Festival as a member of the Charlie Parker Quintet in May 1948. Like Jack Teagarden, Dorham did his part throughout his career to share with other countries America's highly regarded native music. From his arrival in New York in the mid-forties at the first flowering of the bebop movement through his work in the 1960s, Kenny Dorham may not have won any jazz popularity polls, but he gained the respect of his fellow musicians, effectively took the places of Miles Davis and Clifford Brown in the quintets of Parker and Max Roach, and after his death in 1972 achieved "something like cult status" in the 1980s as "a moving and melodic player" who could also "drive like a row of sabres."[74]

❂ ❂ ❂

Born in Dallas on January 17, 1934, pianist Cedar Walton majored in music at the University of Denver from 1951 to 1954 and performed in the army in Germany with Texas reedman Leo Wright before figuring as a member of a number of important hard-bop combos. After working with Kenny Dorham, Walton played with the J. J. Johnson Sextet, recording in New York on August 1 and 3, 1960, for the album *J. J., Inc.* In Johnson's liner notes, the trombonist glows with the knowledge that the recording was made under conditions that he considered ideal: the material (all written by Johnson) had been "performed nightly in clubs, at jazz concerts and elsewhere" eight months before the recording session.[75] And indeed it is a tight group of performances, with soloing that does not miss a beat. Johnson is smooth as silk and Freddie Hubbard on trumpet, as one of the premier hard-bop trumpeters, is as brassy as ever, while Cedar Walton matches J. J.'s funky feeling on what, for Amiri Baraka, was the last hurrah of hard bop, which by this date "just about destroyed itself as a means toward a moving form of expression."[76] Certainly this album may be overly polished, but this is also one of its positive qualities, for there is no fat in the soloing, no padding, though perhaps a bit too much predictability after so many funky recordings over the previous half a decade or so. And it is for certain that Johnson already had pretty much had his technician's say, along with fellow trombonist Kai Winding, between 1954 and 1956. In many ways, however, Cedar Walton saves the day with his more authentic soul-jazz solos, so much so that one could wish he were turned loose more often and for longer choruses.

Although Walton at one time listed his favorite pianists as Bud Powell, Art Tatum, and Thelonious Monk, it seems from the Johnson album that the influence of Powell and Tatum may have been filtered through the work of Cedar's fellow Texan, Red Garland. On *Fatback*, a "two-beat funk," Walton does his version of the call-and-response routine and merely serves up—behind the trombonist and bassist Arthur Harper—some chording reminiscent of Garland. With

Aquarius, a piece in twelve-eight meter, Walton is simply assigned the task of reiterating the somber theme, until toward the end he again shows off his phrases and chords inspired by Garland. Only on *Shutter-Bug* does Walton lead off with a solo that combines gospel-like repeated phrases with some longer boppish lines, and together these seem to recall to Johnson his own roots, for J. J. comes up with his most imaginative chorus, complete with a quote from *Jericho*, that ageless spiritual. Likewise, Hubbard finally digs in and sounds more committed, as in his own best work with the various groups with which he recorded, from Ornette Coleman and Eric Dolphy to Oliver Nelson and the Jazz Messengers. The trumpeter is equally forceful on *Mohawk*, a tune in six-four time with "an Indian flavor," and Walton also shines on this outing, although he is still indebted to Garland and the gospel tradition for his ideas and pianistic approach. On *Minor Mist* both Johnson and tenorist Clifford Jordan deliver their loveliest solos, with Walton again serving very capably in a supporting role. Appropriately on *In Walked Horace*, Cedar gets in his funky word as a soloist—although only the last to do so and overly short at that, yet undeniably sweet. In general this album demonstrates that Johnson, as the founding father of bop trombone, was a true convert to the hard-bop movement's funk and soul-jazz style. This conversion is heard as much in J. J.'s compositions as in his own playing, and Walton assists ably in the trombonist's preaching of his "new" message.

When Art Blakey organized his 1961 edition of the Jazz Messengers, Cedar Walton took the place of Bobby Timmons on piano. In Michael Cuscuna's view, the leader "outdid himself" in adding "the brilliant complex writing abilities of [Freddie] Hubbard and Walton" to those of tenorist Wayne Shorter.[77] One of Walton's tunes recorded by the Messengers on October 2, 1961, was *Mosaic*, which exhibits the complexity of Cedar's writing, made possible partly by Blakey's addition of trombonist Curtis Fuller to form for the first time a sextet. This tune also illustrates the view of David Rosenthal that "hard bop both needed and got a kind of second wind in the early sixties, and this had something to do with Ornette Coleman's rejection of conventional chord changes, but it had far more to do with developments inside the school: Miles Davis's *Kind of Blue*, Coltrane's evolution, and the influence of Thelonious Monk and Charles Mingus."[78] On the up-tempo *Mosaic*, Walton holds a single chord at a time, against which the horns improvise at length before the pianist moves up a step to the next chord. This device perhaps reflects the impact on Walton of Mingus, who "frequently used what Mal Waldron called 'suspensions' and modes instead of conventional chord changes."[79] (This same type of modal construction seems to be employed by Walton on his title tune for the album *Mode for Joe*, recorded on January 27, 1966, with Joe Henderson on tenor and Kenny Dorham on trumpet.)[80] As for Walton's own solo on *Mosaic*, it proves more swinging than usual and less influenced by predecessors like Horace Silver and Red Garland.

For the most part, Cedar's contributions as a soloist remained minimal, as on the Messengers album entitled *Caravan*, recorded a year later on October 23 and 24, 1962. For the Ellington-Tizol title tune, Walton lays out as a soloist, and on Shorter's hard-bop waltz, *Sweet 'n' Sour*, the pianist sounds much as he did on the Johnson album. Cedar's chorus on *In the Wee Small Hours of the Morning* is brief but fits perfectly into the soulful interpretation created by Curtis Fuller, the featured soloist on this lovely ballad. Shorter's up-tempo tribute to Bud Powell, *This Is for Albert*, finds Walton displaying considerable technique but with his familiar gospel- and Red Garland–inspired style still predominating. Likewise, for another ballad, the beautiful *Skylark*, Walton offers a brief but tasteful chorus with a gospel feeling on this tune featuring trumpeter Freddie Hubbard. Here, as usual, Walton's graceful runs are flawless and played with apparent but obviously deceiving ease. On the final tune, Hubbard's *Thermo*, Walton sounds pretty much like a number of other pianists of the period, and as Rosenthal points out, hard-bop pianists tended not to be innovators and could in fact form a rather "bland pastiche."[81] Certainly there seems little in Walton's playing to distinguish him as a Texas pianist, unless one considers his blues and gospel roots and his attraction for the style of his fellow Texan, Red Garland.

It may be misguided to seek in Cedar Walton an identifiably regional sound, especially when hard bop was essentially a product or an outgrowth of a national movement. One thing that can be said of Walton is that he has played in many different styles and has handled them all with facility and taste, as demonstrated, for example, on *Boss Horn*, an album recorded on November 17, 1966, with trumpeter Blue Mitchell and tenorist Junior Cook.[82] Walton would later record again with Cook when Kenny Dorham served as the trumpeter on Cedar's own 1967 album entitled *Cedar!* Mark Gardner writes in his liner notes to *Cedar!* that "Kenny seems to sound better and better every year and that's saying something considering he was a top-notcher in 1946! His unique tone and fluency have rarely been heard to such good advantage as on this date." As for Walton, he displays on *Cedar!*—in a trio performance with bassist Leroy Vinegar and drummer Billy Higgins—his technical command of the piano on *My Ship*; exhibits his work as a composer on *Head and Shoulders*, which Gardner views as "a more advanced and tricky Walton chart" on which Cedar "is full of surprises";[83] and swings in a funky groove on *Short Stuff*. Dorham is particularly impressive on Ellington's *Come Sunday*, where Kenny's ensemble sound in the upper register is quite unusual, pinched but ringingly penetrating and brassy. Kenny's solo following Cedar's Garlandish runs and block chords is also something special, surprising in its quirky little twists and turns.

As for the Blue Mitchell album, *Boss Horn*, here Walton accompanies the horn players throughout *Millie*, a funky blues, as he maintains the tune's syncopated riff even as he solos in the right hand. On *O Mama Enit* Cedar again accompanies the horns with a constant Latin rhythm, "conveying a carnival atmosphere" before he takes a "coolly textured but strongly pulsing solo."[84] And on the ballad *I Should Care*, Walton's piano supports Blue Mitchell's trumpet with the same kind of ringing chords with which Red Garland backed up Miles Davis and John Coltrane so effectively in the 1950s. Walton's solo on the ballad also recalls Garland, but Cedar's offering has its own rhythmic nuances and note choices that indicate the younger man's background as a university-trained musician. Finally, however, there is little new in this 1966 album, just as Walton's playing is largely indistinguishable from that of other followers of Red Garland. On this same album, another pianist, Chick Corea, also accompanies Mitchell in a style that became famous during Corea's time with Miles Davis beginning in 1968. Walton differs from the more austere Corea, whose approach largely derives from the "delicate articulation" of Bill Evans, who, as we have seen, took Garland's place with the Miles Davis Quintet. Basically, Walton's playing remains true to the blues as it was treated in the funky hard-bop tradition, just as his writing in the blues tradition reflects influences from across the spectrum of fifties and sixties hard bop.

In the liner notes for *Cedar Walton: Piano Solos*, a solo album recorded by Walton in August 1981, Jim Fishel writes that Cedar's playing bridges "the past, present, and future of jazz."[85] This eclecticism may be seen from the wide range of styles reflected in Walton's writing and playing on this album, where at times he sounds funky and blues-inflected and at others almost classical in his Debussy-like quietness. On *Cedar's Blue*, Walton plays traditional blues licks along with lush chords in the Garland style, as well as long bop-like lines that at times show signs of the Bill Evans approach. Walton's very pretty, songlike tune *I'll Let You Know* has a touch of John Lewis in Cedar's light, walking bass under long, delicate lines in the right hand, and from time to time in his elegant chording. The most interesting pieces on the album—all of which are Walton originals except *Over the Rainbow*, a standard he explores through various stylistic approaches or "arrangements"— are *Clockwise*, one of the more quietly swinging numbers, and *Sunday Suite in Four Movements*. The main theme of Walton's suite is a catchy, syncopated phrase that he plays at a moderate, deliberate tempo to emphasize its funky feeling.

With an earlier reading of Walton's *Sunday Suite*, recorded on January 26 and 27, 1977, by Cedar's quartet, featuring Bob Berg on tenor, the four movements were taken at a faster clip and turned into a jazzier version, with much more swing in the first and final sections.[86] The second movement has Walton playing without the accompaniment of bassist Sam Jones and drummer Billy Higgins, but his solo differs from the later 1981 version in being, again, faster, as well as more funky at first before it settles into some virtuoso work mixed with lush chords. Berg is featured in the slow third movement, and his fine solo receives excellent support from Walton's ringing fills. The fourth section is not up to Cedar's more thoughtful solo version, although he and Berg work well together, as they do on other pieces on the 1977 album, particularly *Fantasy in D* and *The Maestro*, the latter marked especially by Walton's fine writing and his unison playing with the saxophonist. A drum solo by Higgins before the final section of *Sunday Suite* is perhaps unnecessary but does make the return to the piece's main theme fresher and more welcome. As a suite, the various movements hang together well and demonstrate "this quiet, unassuming man's impeccable composing and arranging talents."[87] As Gary Giddins has suggested, Cedar Walton, among other hard–bop writers, produced "pieces that could withstand renewed scrutiny."[88]

On February 7–8, 1994, Walton joined forces with tenor saxophonist and fellow Texan Marchel Ivery, who was born in Ennis on September 13, 1938. Although Ivery's *Marchel's Mode*, the tenorist's first album under his own name,[89] may not represent anything new in jazz, it demonstrates the vitality of the hard-bop idiom in the hands of two Texans who have "firm roots," as attested by a Walton tune of this title, in that movement that has inspired a group of stunning performances. Supported by a solid rhythm section of Ed Soph on drums and Lyles West on bass, Ivery and Walton revisit with power and imagination some of the classics of the hard-bop era, from Thelonious Monk's *Nutty* and John Coltrane's *Giant Steps* (both from the late 1950s) to Kenny Dorham's *Escapade* (written for the 1963 Joe Henderson album, *Our Thing*).

In 1958 and 1959 Marchel Ivery was stationed in Europe during military service and performed with Bud Powell at the Cheque Peche; in 1966 Ivery began playing with Red Garland, whom he joined in June of 1983 in New York for Red's last job. With Kenny Dorham's *Escapade* on the 1994 album, Ivery and Walton extend a Texas tradition stretching at least from the 1940s as they pay homage in particular to Dorham and Garland. Ivery's sound is his own, a largely vibratoless, edgy tone that yet has, as Doug Ramsey observes in his liner notes, "blues at the core of the conception, a certain swagger in the execution" characteristic of a "Texas tenor."[90] On the lovely ballad *Don't Blame Me*, Ivery and Walton work beautifully together, with Cedar's Garlandish block chords still in evidence as well as his long, boppish lines. *Wee* shows off Ivery's up-tempo skills on this tune, based, not surprisingly, on the changes of *I Got Rhythm*. Here Walton exhibits his more than considerable technique that is given free and extended rein to grand effect. This is truly a class act. On *Jeannie's Song*, a fine original by Ivery, the tenorist digs in with some imaginative explorations that take him all around his horn technically and in terms of some of his most profound musical thinking. Walton for his part fashions a solo that is quite different in mood yet equally engaging.

As producer Mark Elliott comments in the liner notes to this album made in Dallas, "It is rare for a recording with musicians of this caliber to take place outside of New York or Los Angeles." This is perhaps most evident from the album's last four tracks, beginning with *Firm Roots*, which could have served as the title piece since this and the other final cuts fully confirm the musicians' sources, even though *Marchel's Mode* derives as well from hard bop, in particular the modal approach of Miles Davis and John Coltrane. On *Firm Roots*, Ivery slowly works into this Walton tune, taken at what seems at first an up-tempo beyond Marchel's reach. But by the second half of his solo, the tenorist manages to turn in a quite impressive display of his talents, followed by Cedar, who offers a marvelously varied fare that would have delighted Red Garland to no end. Ivery also does an admirable job with Coltrane's *Giant Steps*, on the original April 1, 1959, recording of which Cedar Walton was the pianist, although he did not solo.[91] It is interesting, then, to hear Cedar's rendition of this tune thirty-five years later, with his still effective block-chord ending. Thelonious Monk's *Nutty* is given a superb reading by both Ivery and Walton, with the former's solo close to Coltrane's nonstop performance on the 1957 quartet recording with Monk.[92] Walton's own solo, which is more reminiscent of Monk's playing on *Nutty* from an August 1958 recording with Johnny Griffin on tenor, is a playful, highly inventive improvisation totally in keeping with the character of Monk's catchy masterpiece.[93] The Ivery album ends poignantly with an appropriate ballad, *Every Time We Say Goodbye*, which leaves the listener longing for more, in the best tradition of Herschel Evans.

❦ ❦ ❦

Taken as a group, Gene Ramey, Kenny Dorham, and Cedar Walton were active participants over the entire period of hard bop, contributing to some of its most significant recordings, with Dorham figuring as one of the movement's most distinguished exponents. As outstanding accompanists, Ramey and Walton imparted knowing support to many of the leading hard-bop soloists, while both Dorham and Walton added substantially to hard bop through their skills as composers as well as interpretive artists. Each in his way helped establish or carry on hard bop's blues and gospel-rooted cause, to which, as we shall see, another trio of Texans also made a fundamental contribution, bringing renewed energy to this vital movement that began in the late 1940s, continued well into the 1970s, and has even survived through Walton and Marchel Ivery into the mid-1990s.

THE MINGUS DYNASTY

In 1953, Charles Mingus organized in Toronto the famous Massey Hall concert, featuring Dizzy Gillespie, Charlie Parker, Bud Powell, Max Roach, and Mingus himself as the premier bassist of the era. Janet Coleman remarks that this project "was a producer's nightmare of personality clashes and frayed nerves. That Mingus persisted in doing it at all is testimony to his sense of obligation to this period of jazz history."[1] In 1955 Mingus would found in New York his Jazz Workshop in order to train musicians to perform his own compositions with their "clearly defined folk music roots and a savage, shouting, blues-derived intensity."[2] Partly because Mingus's own personality was too demanding for some and because he literally clashed with others, the personnel in his Jazz Workshop changed often through the years. But this was also largely due to his "university" system that successfully instilled in his "students" the ability to play *themselves* rather than just *his* music, at which point they "graduated." From the late 1950s and into the early 1960s, Mingus schooled a number of Texans in his "savage, shouting, blues-derived" curriculum.

Although born in Nogales, Arizona, on April 22, 1922, and raised in Los Angeles, Mingus was favorably disposed to working with jazz musicians from Texas. Several reasons may account for his having been a Texophile: his mother was a native of the state; Charles "was raised" with T-Bone Walker,[3] the Linden-born electric guitarist and vocalist who recorded with the Los Angeles band of Les Hite a 1940 hit entitled *T-Bone Blues*; and Mingus gained his first widespread recognition on the Apollo sessions with Russell and Illinois Jacquet in 1945–1946. Describing the Apollo recordings, Brian Priestly writes that on *Merle's Mood* Charles not only "plays a series of double-stops (two strings sounding simultaneously), which was unheard-of except in Jimmy Blanton's work on *Jumpin' Punkins*, but he plays them with a viciously aggressive pizzicato which seems at least fifteen years ahead of its time."[4] Reportedly, Mingus learned to bend a note's pitch on his bass "by the left hand not only stopping the string but stretching it out of true *across* the fingerboard," a practice "probably pioneered in the blues-guitar field by T-Bone Walker."[5] But Charles Mingus was attracted for other reasons to the talents of Texas jazzmen—three in particular: Booker Ervin, John Handy, and Richard Williams.

In 1956 the Mingus Jazz Workshop recorded *Pithecanthropus Erectus*, an album that had an "overwhelming impact" and was termed "astonishingly powerful," winning five years later a Grand Prix in France.[6] But the album that most fully represents the music of Charles Mingus is his best-selling 1959 Columbia album, *Mingus Ah Um*, considered "a *high point* of hard bop" and "perhaps one that is artistically most satisfying."[7] On this recording, the Jazz Workshop members include Texas tenorist Booker Ervin and altoist John Handy. After the success of one outstanding tune on this album, *Better Git It in Your Soul*, which was aired on radio by Symphony Sid, New York's leading disc jockey, a second album, *Blues and Roots*, made up of previously recorded but unissued material, was released by Atlantic Records in April 1960 and also featured Ervin and Handy. With regard to *Better Git It in Your Soul*, Joe Goldberg observes,

> By the time *Mingus Ah Um* was released, "soul" music, which took much of its inspiration from the Negro church, had become an unstimulating backwater devoid of all freshness. . . . Mingus had not only gone to the source, but had grasped its essence, and added elements peculiarly his own. . . . The result, a piece called *Better Git It in Your Soul*, complete with hand clapping and Mingus shouting "Yes, Lord, I know," was stunning proof that nothing is cliché in the hands of a great musician.[8]

In 1959, Texas trumpeter Richard Williams also recorded with Ervin and Handy as part of the Jazz Workshop on the second and final album from Columbia, *Mingus Dynasty*. Following their work with Mingus, all three of these Texas musicians became important members of other bands or recorded under their own names, but the training they received from their association with Mingus was invaluable; in turn, the services these Texans rendered to the Jazz Workshop recordings made in the late 1950s and early 1960s helped Mingus "generate the kind of excitement for which movie and TV jazz scorers are constantly, and unsuccessfully, striving."[9]

Booker Ervin, Jr., was born in Denison on October 31, 1930, and first studied the trombone—since his father had played this instrument, for a time with Buddy Tate. However, while stationed on Okinawa during a stint in the air force from

1950 to 1953, Booker taught himself to play the tenor saxophone, and after his discharge, he studied in Boston at the Berklee School of Music. Following his stay in Boston, he returned to the Southwest and traveled for a year with the band of Ernie Fields, a trombonist and a native of Nacogdoches.[10] After mostly performing rhythm and blues, Booker studied clarinet and flute in Denver, where he reportedly first played jazz, before quitting music and taking a job in the post office, as Charles Mingus had at one point in his own career. Finally, Ervin decided that New York was the only place to be and arrived in May 1958, when he was introduced to Mingus by pianist Horace Parlan, and in November Booker joined the Jazz Workshop. In the allusive words of Alun Morgan, Ervin "seems to have sprung fully grown from the head of Mingus."[11] However, another Mingus saxophonist, Shafi Hadi, suggesting that Ervin arrived in New York with his own style already developed, said at the time: Booker "cuts everybody, me and Sonny and all those cats. I'm a sax player so I know what he's doing on that instrument."[12] Morgan also remarks that Booker was "one of the strongest soloists Mingus . . . employed, and that Ervin played so well with him, argues a basically similar emotional response (if not an identical musical approach)."[13] With the "enrollment" of Ervin and his "scorching tone and polytonal improvisation," the Workshop "added an intensity to Mingus's music hitherto only occasionally matched by Jackie McLean or Jimmy Knepper."[14] Later, when Ervin went off on his own in the mid-1960s, he became one of the most outstanding of the Mingus exes, recording a series of albums for Prestige that would elicit from one writer the claim that "no other tenorman, including the most famous, can out-think and out-swing Booker in the idiom of [1960s] jazz."[15]

Like Ervin, John Handy III came to New York in 1958, arriving in July, and in December he too became an integral part of Mingus's Jazz Workshop. Born in Dallas on February 3, 1933, Handy was self-taught on clarinet by the age of thirteen and, like Red Garland, was an accomplished boxer, becoming an amateur featherweight champion at fourteen. About 1943 Handy had moved with his family to California, but after two years they returned to Dallas until 1948, when they moved back to California. Here, in 1949, Handy began to play the alto saxophone, jamming with musicians in San Francisco and hearing Charlie Parker at the Say When in 1952. Following service in Korea from 1952 to 1953, Handy continued his college studies at San Francisco State, but in 1958 he headed for New York, playing off and on with Mingus, including an appearance as featured tenor soloist at the Seventh Annual Monterey Jazz Festival on September 20, 1964—the first time the Mingus group was invited to participate. As late as April 1974, Handy recorded with Mingus in New York at the third of Mingus's annual concerts there, and Handy was featured among "a number of fairly famous alumni."[16] Although

Handy, like other Mingus sidemen, had his problems with the restrictions placed on him as an improviser by the composer-director's demands, it is clear from his long association that Handy was *his* saxophonist and had been from the first time Mingus heard him in New York at the Five Spot Cafe, yelling to the leader of the band with which the saxman was sitting in, "Hey man, why don't you let this cat play?"[17] Like other Mingus sidemen, Handy was fired and then rehired, receiving his walking papers in 1959 for "practising high notes on the job" but present again on Mingus albums thereafter in 1962 and 1964.[18] In 1965, Handy's own group upstaged his old professor's Workshop band at the Monterey Jazz Festival,[19] but as one critic suggests, Handy and several other Mingus sidemen "never produced work outside his band to match what they had done in it."[20]

Richard "Notes" Williams, a third Texan in the Jazz Workshop, was born in Galveston on May 4, 1931. He began on tenor and then switched to trumpet in his teens. First playing in local bands on the Gulf Coast, Williams later attended Wiley College in Marshall, from which he graduated with a degree in music. After four years in the air force, he went with the Lionel Hampton band, touring Europe in 1956 as the group's principal trumpet. On his return to the States, Williams took a master's degree from the Manhattan School of Music and then began working with a number of units, including the Mingus Workshop from 1959 to 1964. Like Handy, Williams was replaced and then reinstated by Mingus, displeasing him on one occasion "for forgetting his wa-wa mute."[21] Both Williams and Handy could be praised by Mingus for playing "fine solos," but the composer could also complain that their improvisations on the composer's *Far Wells, Mill Valley*, recorded November 1, 1959, were "executed in a diatonic Charlie Parker chordal manner" that did not "utilize the possibilities given by the open fifths."[22] On the other hand, Mingus complimented Booker Ervin's double improvisation on tenor for achieving "the compositional continuity that I'd wanted in the preceding individual solos" by Handy and Williams.[23]

On *Hora Decubitus*, from the 1963 album *Mingus, Mingus, Mingus, Mingus, Mingus*, Richard Williams and Booker Ervin improvise in the hard-bop tradition with so much "fire" that, according to Nat Hentoff, "the overall musical experience reaches deeply into the most basic emotions of both players and listeners." As Hentoff goes on to observe, "The seeming paradox of Mingus is that so forceful a personality can create situations which so irresistibly propel his sidemen to be so fully themselves."[24] In Williams's last years, after having worked with the bands of Duke Ellington (1965, 1971) and Lionel Hampton (1975) and other name bands as well as the Gil Evans orchestra (1973), Williams played in the Illinois Jacquet big band and, along with John Handy, in Mingus Dynasty, a group formed following the death of Mingus in January 1979 to give performances of the composer's compositions.[25] On the Gil Evans album, *Svengali*, recorded May 30, 1973, Williams would be a featured soloist along with two other Texans: Billy Harper, a tenor saxophonist, flutist, and composer born in Houston on January 17, 1943, and Marvin "Hannibal" Peterson, a trumpeter and composer born in Smithville on November 11, 1948.[26] In his solo on *Blues in Orbit*, composed by George Russell, Harper is into what we shall see was a passionate, driving Booker Ervin bag, and on Harper's own tune, *Cry of Hunger*, the Texan builds a gospel-like solo by utilizing repeated phrases in the style of black ministers. In a *Down Beat* article, Chuck Berg suggests that "Harper's playing represents a fusion of the Rollins and Coltrane traditions, tempered with the spirituality derived from his childhood religious experiences."[27]

Hannibal Peterson is the featured soloist on *Svengali* for the tune entitled *Zee Zee*, on which the trumpeter begins with a Miles Davis–influenced sound, reminiscent of the Evans-Davis albums *Porgy and Bess* and *Sketches of Spain*, but then moves into a more Coltrane-inspired approach, with phrasal flurries and scalar runs. Like Harper, Peterson studied at North Texas State University in the 1960s; later he toured with Roland Kirk and jammed in Texas with T-Bone Walker. Peterson, again like Harper, is respected as much for his compositions as for his work as an instrumentalist. With regard to the latter, Gary Giddins has written, "No one plays more trumpet than [Peterson], and his performances throughout [*One with the Wind*] are stunning in their immediacy and drive." Giddins quotes from *The Penguin Guide to Jazz on CD, LP, and Cassette* by way of summarizing Peterson's achievement as a composer between 1977 and 1981: "He seems to encapsulate the whole black music tradition from field songs through gospel and soul to bop and free and onward to the kind of ambitious formal composition one associates with Charles Mingus."[28]

Following his time with Evans, Peterson compiled an extensive discography, recording with such figures as Dewey Redman, Richard Davis, Clifford Jordan, Oliver Lake, Don Pullen, Buster Williams, Billy Hart, and Eddie Henderson. Many of Peterson's recordings were made for European labels and are extremely hard to come by, but in 1994 two albums were released on compact disc: *One with the Wind* and *The Angels of Atlanta*. The latter consists of a five-movement sequence for six-piece combo, vocalist Pat Peterson (a cousin who sang as a Ray Charles Rayette), and the Harlem Boys Choir. Produced on February 15 and 19, 1981, in response to the brutal murders of twenty black children in Atlanta, *The Angels of Atlanta* was written entirely by the trumpeter and has been considered "a document of rare beauty."[29] Peterson is joined on this album by an all-star group: George

Adams on tenor, Kenny Barron on piano, Diedre Murray on cello, Cecil McBee on bass, and former Mingus drummer Dannie Richmond—all heard to grand effect in the final movement, Peterson's arrangement of the traditional *Sometimes I Feel Like a Motherless Child*.

❧ ❧ ❧

What makes Mingus's 1959 album, *Mingus Ah Um*, most representative of the composer-bassist-professor's music is that it "was perhaps the first deliberate attempt to show off [his] many and varied compositional approaches on one record."[30] Many of the pieces performed and recorded by the various Workshop bands, in particular *Fables of Faubus, Better Git It in Your Soul, Wednesday Night Prayer Meeting*, and *Goodbye Pork Pie Hat*, were replayed, rerecorded, and renamed through-out the 1960s and 1970s, especially the last of these and "probably the best-known item" of this "highlight-filled album."[31] Four of the album's nine compositions are Mingus's musical portraits of or tributes to some of his favorite jazz figures: Jelly Roll Morton (*Jelly Roll*), Duke Ellington (*Open Letter to Duke*), Lester Young (*Goodbye Pork Pie Hat*), and Charlie Parker (*Bird Calls*). In all these selections the two Texas saxophonists, Ervin and Handy, have prominent roles to play in realizing the composer's intention of rendering homage to those jazzmen who established the traditions from which Mingus's own music had taken its inspiration.

Although *Jelly Roll* has been called something of a parody of 1920s jazz, "the point" with Mingus, as Gary Giddins has noted, "was always the continuity of tradition and never modernistic putdown."[32] Jimmy Knepper, the fine Mingus trombonist, claimed that each soloist "had to play one old-style chorus, then a more modern-style one. . . . It was meant to be sort of a novelty."[33] After Knepper's introduction and after the ensemble has played the tender theme, John Handy opens the soloing on *Jelly Roll* with a ricky-tick alto break followed by a fine Parker-influenced chorus. (On *My Jelly Roll Soul*, recorded earlier on February 4, 1959, as part of *Blues and Roots*, Handy also plays a fine alto solo.) Ervin comes next with a lovely tenor solo that shows the proper regard with which Morton's work should be revisited in paying such "an affectionate tribute."[34]

Open Letter to Duke is but one of several Mingus homages paid to Ellington, whose music first impressed Charles at the age of eight or nine when he heard a broadcast of *East St. Louis Toodle-oo* and shortly thereafter a live show that had Mingus jumping and screaming.[35] Ervin starts things off with a bang on *Open Letter* and never lets up as he does some of his "high-octane blowing over a shuffle beat" before the ensemble plays Mingus's Ellington-like, rhapsodic theme, with Handy's "languid" alto featured to good effect.[36] Handy also is showcased on *Goodbye Pork Pie Hat*, this time, as would be expected, on tenor. This first recording of the piece, written as soon as Mingus heard of Lester's death, is a moving testament to the tenor giant who Mingus said "towered over most other musicians" with his sensitivity.[37] Handy plays a beautifully "mournful solo . . . that includes some effective flutter tonguing."[38] However, in 1963, when Mingus recorded this tribute as *Theme for Lester Young*, Booker Ervin took the tenor solo and made it an even more thrilling piece of work that shows both Ervin's sensitivity and his "reflective" style at its most "intense."[39]

As for *Bird Calls* on the 1959 album, this homage to Parker demonstrates how highly Mingus admired the saxophonist. The composer said that Parker "was the cause of my realization that jazz improvisation, as well as jazz composition, is the equal of classical music. . . . Bird brought melodic development to a new point in jazz, as far as Bartók or Schoenberg or Hindemith had taken it in the classics. But he also brought to music a primitive, mystic, supra-mind communication that I'd only heard in the late Beethoven quartets and, even more, in Stravinsky."[40] Mingus shows his awareness of these twentieth-century composers in his own writing of *Bird Calls*, which opens with a type of primitive cacophony associated with Stravinsky's *The Rite of Spring* but is quickly followed by Booker Ervin's "fierce" and very intensely swinging hard-bop chorus that surely would have entranced Beethoven and Bartók. Handy's "liquid-toned" alto is equally attuned to the spirit of Mingus's tribute,[41] as both saxophonists do a masterful job of performing the highly demanding and imaginative ensemble passages that fade out with twittering bird sounds from the reeds and the bowed bass of Mingus.

The longest work on *Mingus Ah Um* is *Fables of Faubus*, one of the composer's "political" pieces given over largely to solos by Handy, pianist Horace Parlan, and Ervin, all of whom turn in high-quality performances. The shortest piece on the album is *Self-Portrait in Three Colors*, another work that is very demanding of the saxes, who must read "Mingus's deliriously romantic Ellington-style ballad, complexly voiced with interweaving contrapuntal lines."[42] On *Pussy Cat Dues*, a slow blues, Handy demonstrates his proficiency on clarinet, and on *Boogie Stop Shuffle* Ervin takes one of his keening, swinging solos, after which he, Handy, and Hadi execute the intricate, long-lined written passages with great precision and punch. The second-longest number is *Better Get It in Your Soul*, which was not the first recording of this Mingus hit or the last. Once again the 1963 remake of *Better Get It* is far more exciting, with Richard Williams helping give the gas to this up-tempo burner, while under the title *E's Flat, Ah's Flat Too*, recorded for Atlantic on May 5, 1959, but not released until 1960 on *Blues and Roots*, this same tune also received a more exciting performance, with Ervin and Handy both contributing wailing solos.[43] On the 1963 recording of *Better Get Hit in Yo' Soul*, after it seems the piece is over, Mingus on slapped bass and Jaki Byard on rolling church piano go into a gospel routine that is, if possible, even more swinging than the first part of this spirited performance. Also on this same 1963 album, Williams, Booker Ervin, and Eric Dolphy are all red hot on *Hora Decubitus*. Ervin comes out smoking and is followed by Dolphy, who absolutely explodes, with Mingus right with him on his spark plug of a bass. And not to be outdone, Richard Williams blows one of the most incredible solos of his career, and certainly one of the most dynamite choruses ever recorded by a Mingus trumpeter.

Another such Mingus "masterpiece of planned chaos"[44] is *Wednesday Night Prayer Meeting* on the 1960 album, *Blues and Roots*, with Mingus hollering and Booker Ervin preaching a gospel-inspired sermon while the band claps in amen-assent. Noted for being the "first successful use of a fast 6/4 time-signature," this piece is related to *Slop*, a composition on the 1959 album, *Mingus Dynasty*, which depicts a gathering after the prayer meeting to sing the same gospel songs at the picnic grounds where "the Rev or the Deacon has just sneaked a few nips to a few of the leading voices."[45] This "looser, sloppier approach" to the meeting songs—with shouting and a general drunken stupor suggested in the opening section—finds Ervin in a bluesy solo accompanied by handclapping as he plays some very unusual stuttering phrases at the end of his chorus, as if into his cups; in contrast, Handy's solo is more straight-ahead. Two Ellington tunes on *Mingus Dynasty*—*Things Ain't What They Used To Be* and *Mood Indigo* (the latter is also on the 1963 album but it features the passionate, virtuosic Mingus on bass)—showcase Ervin and Handy with some of their better efforts: Booker as soloist and John as section leader on alto. On *Things Ain't What They Used To Be*, Booker plays a double-time chorus that is both technically and imaginatively fine, while on *Mood Indigo* Handy leads the saxes with authority, especially at the end when the Duke's classic theme returns.

Ervin and Handy can be heard on a number of other Mingus albums from the early to mid-1960s. On the July 13, 1960, recording at the Antibes Jazz Festival, Ervin again performs superbly on *Wednesday Night Prayer Meeting*. On *Folk Forms No. 2*, Booker really has his soul battery charged and his gospel engine revved up by Mingus and Dannie Richmond's jump-start, stop-and-go bass and drums. The same year, on October 20 and November 11, the Workshop recorded *Lock 'Em Up*, where Ervin takes a marvelous extended chorus that suits perfectly the piece's mental hospital motif—the tenorist cued back in toward the end of his solo by Mingus's imitation of a patient's "insane yell."[46] This Ervin solo illustrates what James Lincoln Collier observes about Mingus's choice of personnel: "He has always preferred the direct, passionate players to the more controlled ones, which the second generation of boppers tended to be—the Jimmy Knepper or Booker Irvin [*sic*] to the J. J. Johnson or Paul Desmond."[47] With the November 6, 1961, recording of *Mingus/Oh Yeah*, Ervin shared the spotlight on tenor with Roland

Kirk, or vice versa, since Kirk is really the featured soloist on this album. Ervin does contribute a "searing" chorus on *Devil Woman*, which begins wonderfully with his crying moans and goes on to some rapid bursts executed as beautifully as any saxman ever has.[48] Unfortunately, on *Wham Bam Thank You Ma'am*, Ervin's solo is rather lackluster compared with Kirk's terrific chorus on a type of saxophone known as a strich.

Handy, as noted earlier, took part in the 1964 Monterey Jazz Festival, where after the performance of Mingus's *Meditations on Integration*, a work lasting almost thirty minutes and running "the gamut from tender reflection to mankind-gone-mad chaos," the audience gave the composer and his eleven-piece orchestra a standing ovation.[49] The opening work, a medley of Ellington tunes, features Handy on *Take the "A" Train*, where in playing tenor he turns in a more aggressive solo than he normally attempts on alto. Here too Handy attains a richer sound on this instrument that is closer to the human voice, and at times, with his screams and high-note squeals, he reminds one of Illinois Jacquet.

Even while Booker Ervin and Richard Williams formed part of the Mingus Workshop, the two men also recorded on their own. On May 27, 1960, Williams teamed with Eric Dolphy on a recording under the leadership of reedman and composer Oliver Nelson. Interestingly, the album is entitled *Screamin' the Blues*, after a twelve-bar blues by Nelson that bears the same title as the song recorded by Maggie Jones and Louis Armstrong in December 1924. The Nelson tune is a typical example of the back-to-the-roots tendency of hard bop, and Richard Williams contributes a "striking" solo that "builds with compelling order and heat" and is marked, as so often in his work, by "the hard clarity of his articulation and that soaring sound whose crackling brilliance is effectively set off by contrasting pinched notes."[50] Another representative hard-bop piece is Nelson's gospel-inspired tune entitled appropriately *The Meetin'*, on which Nelson performs as the preacher while Dolphy and Williams respond as members of the congregation, with the trumpeter also "launching into an exceptionally arresting solo."[51] Some ten days later, on June 7, 1960, Williams joined altoist Gigi Gryce to record *The Rat Race Blues*, their second album together, which collects five pieces—all based on the blues, including one, *Strange Feelin'*, which belongs in the gospel camp.[52] Each tune achieves a distinctive style and mood within the blues framework, with *Boxer's Blues* containing a solo by Williams that is similar to those he produced for Mingus but less fiery. Perhaps the trumpeter's finest outing is on *Blues in Bloom*, which features Williams in an intense, virtuosic, bluesy solo that is longer than any taken while with Mingus and that allows Williams to exhibit a searching, thoughtful side to his artistry more than most anywhere else in his recorded work. Likewise, *Monday Through Sunday* provides Williams with an opportunity to stretch out, but the

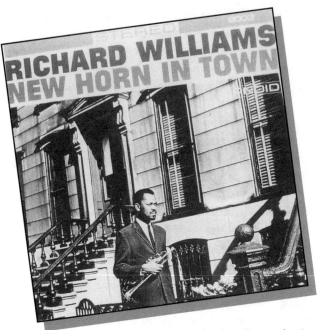

Richard Williams of Galveston. Reproduced from
New Horn in Town (Candid 9003) by permission of
DA Music. Copyright © 1960 Candid Records.

results are not so satisfying as on *Blues in Bloom*, although *Monday Through Sunday* does demonstrate the trumpeter's effective ensemble playing as he opens and closes the tune beautifully in tandem with Gryce's alternately soulful and "screamin'" alto.

On November 19, 1960, Richard Williams recorded the only album under his own name, *Richard Williams: New Horn in Town*. Here the trumpeter is joined by fellow Texan Leo Wright, who also performed with the Mingus Workshop.[53] Williams offers most fully on this album his "sweepingly lyrical, long-lined conception" and a "singing quality" combined with "a technical brilliance that is in the daring tradition of Dizzy Gillespie and Clifford Brown," as well as a "full, warm, assertively *brass* tone."[54] The trumpeter's lyrical, very clearly Clifford Brown–inspired side can be heard on Benny Golson's *I Remember Clifford*, with Wright on flute accompanying Williams's lovely rendering of this classic memorial tune. Wright's own flute chorus following Williams's solo is in itself quite beautiful if not so majestic. *Ferris Wheel* finds Wright and Williams each soloing (with Leo on alto) at a relaxed tempo, while on the trumpeter's original boplike tune, *Raucous Notes*, the two men show off their ability to handle an up-tempo pace with exactitude and swing. Indeed, on *Raucous Notes*, the two hornmen execute the demanding theme as well as Gillespie and Parker did in the performances of their 1940s bop-age masterpieces. With *Over the Rainbow*, Williams creates "the kind of gracefully lyric line that this song requires," and, as Nat Hentoff declares, the trumpeter proves himself to be "one of the most authoritative ballad players in jazz."[55] Here Williams's singing style is simply masterful and his cascading triplets a total delight. *Renita's Bounce*, another Williams original, exhibits one more facet of the trumpeter's musical personality, its sizzling side, found most often on his Mingus recordings. Given Williams's range of expressiveness, his secure technique, and his "ease in all areas of modern jazz argot," it is incomprehensible that this was the trumpeter's first and final album as a leader, for not only is he a consummate soloist on this recording, but here and elsewhere he "leads ensembles with brilliant abandon" yet always with precision and "exultant fervor."[56]

One week later, Williams would join Booker Ervin and a group that included Mingus sidemen Dannie Richmond and Horace Parlan, along with a non-Workshop member, George Tucker on bass, for an album entitled *Booker Ervin: Down in the Dumps*, produced under Ervin's name on November 26, 1960. This recording presents both Ervin and Williams in a particularly relaxed setting, where each stretches out on a slow blues, a ballad, and four originals by Booker. Although laid back, Williams's solos on the funky title tune, on *Well Well*, on the boppish *Mr. Wiggles*, and on *Dee-Da-Do*, with its "roots in the jazz–R & B fifties bands of the Southwest,"[57] all anticipate the trumpeter's fiery chorus on Mingus's *Hora Decubitus*. Many of Williams's phrases will in fact reappear in that Mingus tune, and though more at ease here, Williams's playing is still forceful and compelling. On *Autumn Leaves*, the trumpeter solos first, with some muted choruses that have their mellow moments, followed by Booker with his crying held notes alternating with sixteenth-note runs and a series of accented quarter notes, before a sloweddown and affective closing statement of the ballad theme. Ervin's chorus on the slow blues *Down in the Dumps* has rightly been called by Michael Cuscuna "a rich and mature testament to the fact that the blues is an unendingly resourceful form and feeling for creativity." Cuscuna goes on to offer some unfortunately accurate observations about Ervin's career: "Caught between the onslaught of commercial jazz and angry, iconoclastic experimenters, he became a misunderstood anachronism almost immediately after his impressive New York debut in the Mingus group. Booker would probably have been better suited to this era when a foot in the past and an eye toward the future are not mutually exclusive."[58]

Ervin went on to record on December 3, 1963, his highly regarded album *Booker Ervin: The Freedom Book*, with Jaki Byard, Richard Davis, and Alan Dawson.[59] This same quartet would produce another album on October 2, 1964, entitled *Booker*

Booker Ervin of Denison. Reproduced from *The Blues Book* (PR 7340) by permission of Fantasy, Inc.; photograph by Don Schlitten. Copyright © 1993 Fantasy, Inc.

Ervin: The Space Book, on which the musicians are "extending themselves harmonically, rhythmically, and emotionally," which can be heard especially on *Bass-IX,* a tune not originally issued on the Prestige album but included on a Japanese rerelease of 1991. In 1965 Ira Gitler pointed out that over the past years Ervin had developed not in the manner of the bop and postbop musicians, who played changes, but by building "his own harmonic sequences with high invention in modal or limited chord situations."[60] The English critic Alun Morgan writes that in 1963 and 1964 Ervin produced "a remarkable series of albums" that "shows such maturity and consistency that choice is rendered extremely difficult, but [*The Blues Book*] has four original and varied blues which demonstrate effectively the exciting and distinctive sound of his polytonal approach."[61] Like many more "traditional" jazzmen of the early sixties, Ervin was not, however, able to compete for attention or an audience with the likes of Ornette Coleman and John Coltrane, as Gitler implies in his notes for *The Blues Book,* recorded on June 30, 1964: "His passionate music is of the '60s but it has not lost touch with the tap-roots of jazz. Booker's phrasing (the highly-charged flurries and the excruciating, long-toned cries), harmonic conception (neither pallid nor beyond the pale), and tone (a vox humana) add up to a style that is avant-garde yet evolutionary, and not one that bows to fashion or gropes unprofessionally under the guise of 'freedom.'"[62] It is not to detract from Ervin's achievement to suggest that he did not change with the times, but in many ways Booker, like Handy, had already done his best work with Mingus. While Ervin's later playing may have deepened and advanced to some degree, it was essentially the same as that found on his Mingus albums.[63] What Ervin offered to the Workshop was a passionate, blues-derived sound so dear to Charles Mingus. In the liner notes for Ervin's February 27, 1964, album, *The Song Book*, Dan Morgenstern observes that Mingus liked "his music naked," "full of fire and conviction: nothing about it strikes the ear as forced, contrived or meretricious"; thus it is "no wonder" that the composer-bassist "used Booker whenever he could get him."[64]

Following John Handy's appearance with Mingus at the 1964 Monterey Jazz Festival, the reedman organized his own group in San Francisco. Handy's quintet stunned critic Ralph J. Gleason, who considered his first hearing of the group "one of the great moments of a lifetime of listening to jazz."[65] Handy is especially impressive in his closing chorus of *If Only We Knew*, one of two original Handy tunes on the group's first album, which resulted from the Handy quintet's appearance at the Monterey Jazz Festival in 1965.[66] On this piece, Handy demonstrates convincingly that he has absorbed the innovations of Eric Dolphy and John Coltrane. Previous to this, in 1963, Handy had organized a group called the Freedom Band after taking part in the civil rights march on Washington, D.C. This group was considered "an unusual ten-piece 'protesting' band—unusual because it did *not* play protest music," with the exception perhaps of Handy's *Tears of Ole Miss (Anatomy of a Riot)*, which took shape in 1962 but was not recorded until Handy put out his third Columbia album, *New View!*[67] Unusual too is the makeup of Handy's groups on *New View!* and his 1965 Monterey album, the former with Bobby Hutcherson on vibes and the latter featuring on violin fellow Texan Mike White.[68]

For the most part, these albums present a tamer side to Handy's playing, as indicated by the tune on *New View!* entitled *A Little Quiet*, a light-hearted piece with a bossa-nova beat. On this same album is Handy's tribute to John Coltrane, a softly rendered treatment of Trane's tune *Naima*, with Hutcherson's vibes both here and on *A Little Quiet* giving to the performances a "gorgeously sensuous feeling."[69] *Tears of Ole Miss* recalls more the Mingus years and shows the influence of Eric Dolphy in Handy's opening chorus with its angular flights against a type of ground bass laid down by the rest of the band. Some of the whistle and birdlike sounds that accompany a quote from *Dixie* are reminiscent of Mingus's *A Foggy Day* from his *Pithecanthropus Erectus* album and *Bird Calls* from *Mingus Ah Um*. Handy's work in this *Fables of Faubus* vein seems somewhat derivative, as might be expected from a

Mingus student who learned his lessons well. However, this debt to his professor cannot take away from Handy's own very real and genuine musical commentary on political events of his day.

As a trained and talented musician capable of performing on clarinet, alto, and tenor, John Handy proved his worth on his various Mingus albums and continued to inspire the exuberant praise of critics like Ralph Gleason and Leonard Feather. Along with Booker Ervin, Handy formed a vital part of the premier band that recorded *Mingus Ah Um*, and with both Ervin and Richard Williams, Handy helped make possible the recording of *Far Wells, Mill Valley*, one of Mingus's more ambitious compositions. Together these three Texans brought to the Mingus system many of the components necessary for the success of the composer's major work: a fundamental blues and gospel tradition, the vocal-like sounds produced on their instruments so essential to the Mingus conception, the technical facility to handle difficult notated charts, and, above all, the dispositions and imaginations required for spontaneous improvisation within the constraints of individual and group assignments made by a dictatorial leader-teacher who just happened to be one of the great creative minds in jazz.

PART

4

GOING TO LOS ANGELES

OUT OF DENTON

A number of years before Texas jazzmen like Jack Teagarden, Herschel Evans, and Buddy Tate spent time in California prior to making their reputations in the East, early New Orleans jazz masters such as Jelly Roll Morton, Kid Ory, and King Oliver took the trip the nineteenth-century pioneers and gold prospectors had made and brought their now treasured music to the West Coast. The first printed use of the word "jazz" came on March 6, 1913, in the *San Francisco Bulletin* in "an ambiguous reference to 'ragtime and jazz' in a sports article."[1] A California ragtime brass band, the Black and Tan Orchestra, was originally from Texas and "reached Los Angeles with a carnival" sometime around 1918, calling itself in 1919 the Black and Tan Jazz Orchestra.[2] One of the four musicians credited with the development of jazz on the West Coast during the first decade of the twentieth century was Sonny Clay, who was born on May 15, 1899, in Chapel Hill, Texas.[3] Having met Jelly Roll Morton in Tijuana around 1920, Clay was leading his Eccentric Harmony Six in Los Angeles in 1922. Les Hite, who would figure prominently in West Coast jazz in the late 1930s as a leader of his own orchestra, was a member of Clay's resident band at the Vernon Country Club in Los Angeles in 1928, the same band that was "probably the first black jazz group ever to tour [Australia],"[4] which it did in January 1928 with vocalist Ivie Anderson, who later starred with the Duke Ellington Orchestra.

Lesser- and better-known Texas jazzmen were also active on the West Coast, mostly in the 1930s and early 1940s. Among these was legendary trumpeter Claude "Benno" Kennedy from Dallas, who was with Troy Floyd's San Antonio band and later took a Texas band called the Oleanders to Los Angeles prior to 1932.[5] Other Texans who went west were Tyree Glenn in 1935; Keg Johnson sometime after 1936; Allen Durham in 1939 (recording with Les Hite in 1942 when Dizzy Gillespie recorded *Jersey Bounce* with the Hite band); T-Bone Walker and Russell Jacquet in 1940; Illinois Jacquet in 1941, playing there with Floyd Ray's orchestra; and Arnett Cobb and Eddie Vinson in 1941, performing in Seattle with the Milt Larkin band. But it was following the appearance in 1945 of Charlie Parker and Dizzy Gillespie at Billy Berg's in Los Angeles that there would be "a musical invasion, a D-day landing of bebop on the Pacific seaboard,"[6] after which greater attention was focused on the California jazz scene. Here several Texas musicians eventually played seminal roles—first, in creating a so-called West Coast jazz and, later, in beginning the free jazz movement that remains the most advanced stage in the history of this American music.

The Parker-Gillespie visit to Los Angeles may have had little bearing on the fact that Harry Babasin, a student at North Texas State Teachers College in Denton, decided to head for California and participate in the rise of Pacific jazz. Although eventually Babasin would record there with Parker, it seems unlikely that he had gone west expecting to hook up with the Bird. Whatever Babasin's motive, this bass player and two of his fellow classmates would figure in some of the major events of and developments in jazz on the West Coast. Born in Dallas on March 19, 1921, Babasin was raised in Vernon, and after studying at North Texas State in the early 1940s, he left for New York, where he worked with such big bands as those of Gene Krupa, Boyd Raeburn, and Charlie Barnet. In 1945, Babasin set out for California, where he recorded with Woody Herman and Benny Goodman, including a September 1947 session with Goodman that produced "a quintet version of the bebop anthem" *Cherokee*.[7] More important, Babasin began performing and recording with many of the progressive West Coast players, most notably in 1946 with Dodo Marmarosa, in 1947 with Wardell Gray and Dexter Gordon, in 1952 with Chet Baker, and in 1953 with Laurindo Almeida, Bud Shank, and Shorty Rogers.

Preceding Harry Babasin, another North Texas student and Dallas native, Gene Roland, who was born on September 15, 1921, made his way to California in 1944 to join the Stan Kenton orchestra as a composer-arranger and eventually as fifth and then sixth trumpet, fifth trombone, and valve trombonist. According to *Down Beat* for March 11, 1946, Gene Roland and Kai Winding were "the jazz stars" in Kenton's five-trombone section,[8] but it was primarily as Stan's "first full-time staff arranger" that Roland would make his mark.[9] In 1945, Roland contributed an arrangement that would result in Kenton's first million-selling record, *Tampico*, featuring June Christy as vocalist.[10] By 1946, when he composed *Ain't No Misery in Me*, which was also recorded by Christy, Roland was credited with helping make Kenton's orchestra "one of the most popular bands in America."[11]

A third North Texas student and native of Dallas, multi-instrumentalist and composer Jimmy Giuffre, also ended up in Los Angeles, following in the footsteps of Babasin and Roland, with whom he had shared an eight-room house in Denton, along with a fourth jazz student, guitarist Herb Ellis.[12] Like his three housemates, Jimmy Giuffre was born in 1921, in his case on April 26, and along with his fellows, Jimmy "jammed a lot," playing in local big and small bands. This group of friends, according to Giuffre, "really started the reputation for jazz" at North Texas State, even though the four Texans were never enrolled in the jazz program, which was only established later at the institution when it became "a premier center of jazz education in America."[13] Having begun on clarinet at age nine, Giuffre eventually took a degree in music education in 1942, but the future composer-arranger and clarinet-tenor-baritone star claimed that all his harmonic thinking came from "listening to records: Basie and Benny Goodman."[14] Giuffre was first in California with the air force in 1946, when he entered a master's program at the University of California at Los Angeles; but he gave it up to work with several big bands, composing for Woody Herman in 1947 the classic tune *Four Brothers*, "one of the most conspicuous successes of the modern jazz era."[15] But it was after returning to Los Angeles at the end of the 1940s and studying privately there with Dr. Wesley La Violette that Giuffre would develop from being "a conventional swing-era tenor saxophonist"[16] and doing "pretty standardized . . . dance band writing"[17] to becoming the creator of "a fresh, distinctive sound unlike anything else in jazz."[18] The Texan also would prove to be "arguably the king of cool understatement," and in the company of Shelly Manne, Shorty Rogers, and Howard Rumsey "a bellwether of the new jazz movement on the coast."[19]

Over the years, the big attraction in California for music students at North Texas State Teachers College was not really the bop movement, as introduced by Parker and Gillespie and carried on by certain musicians on the West Coast, but rather the band of Stan Kenton, who up until his death in 1979 continued to seek out graduates of the jazz studies program at what became North Texas State University (now the University of North Texas).[20] First making a name for himself with Kenton beginning in 1944, Gene Roland remained with Stan's orchestra until 1955, "except for brief stints . . . as free-lance arr[anger] . . . w[ith] L[ionel] Hampton, C[harlie] Barnet, C[laude] Thornhill, A[rtie] Shaw, [and] H[arry] James."[21] Roland rejoined Kenton in the 1960s and 1970s, but it was during his stay with Stan's orchestra in the 1940s that he made one of his own favorite arrangements—of the Duke Ellington–Billy Strayhorn tune *Just A-Sittin' and A-Rockin'*, which, like *Tampico* and *Ain't No Misery in Me*, was sung by June Christy. Roland's arrangement of the Ellington-Strayhorn piece captures the feeling of the original but invests it with the Kenton sound by employing the band's predictable blasty trombones and its typical screaming trumpets. The same is true for the five-trumpet section on *Ain't No Misery in Me*, Roland's "modern sophisticated blues."[22]

Such an arrangement as Roland's *Just A-Sittin' and A-Rockin'* was considered "superb" at the time, with its "wild brass kicking throughout,"[23] while Gene's *Tampico* is representative of the more popular approach to big-band arranging, with the full sax section featured in some now rather dated swing-era passages following Christy's singing of this unmemorable theme. *Tampico* has little if any relationship to real jazz and in no way compares with Kenton's successful use of Latin rhythms on *The Peanut Vendor* from the same period; yet Roland's arrangement was obviously a hit, largely, one would suspect, because of June Christy's vocal.[24] In 1947, Roland's arrangement of *Tampico* also formed part of a movie short, *Let's Make Rhythm*, and this was another attraction that California held for jazz musicians—the money to be made playing for film studios. As early as 1940, *Down Beat* reported of the Les Hite band, which had never been farther east than Denver, that "the boys did not want to come East [to New York City] because they did not want to lose movie studio connections (35 dollars for three hours) and they had plenty of it."[25] Roland's arrangements for Kenton also included such tunes as *I Got Rhythm*, *Got a Penny Jenny?*, *Baby Won't You Please Come Home?*, *Are You Livin' Old Man?* (along with *Tampico* and *Just A-Sittin'*, a Roland favorite), *The Mist Is Over the Moon*, *Tortillas and Beans*, *Shoo Fly Pie and Apple Pan Dowdy*, *I Been Down in Texas* (these last two, which also featured June Christy, "perched high on the list of most-played discs"),[26] *Travelin' Man* (sung by Anita O'Day), *Opus in Turquoise*, *Opus in Chartreuse*, and *Four Months, Three Weeks, Two Days, One Hour Blues*.

In 1946 Roland arranged most of the Kenton book, but with the leader's addition of more progressive composer-arrangers like Pete Rugolo and Bob Graettinger, Roland did not contribute to the Kenton band's "new concepts" so much as he represented its earlier "Artistry in Rhythm" period. Essentially, as some of the tunes he arranged suggest, Roland remained close to the southwestern riff and blues tradition, and in later years the Texan would return to the Kenton fold to provide such 1973 compositions as *Country Cousin* and *Blue Gene*. In 1960 Roland did help introduce to the Kenton band a new feature, the mellophonium, a brass instrument "slightly resembling a French horn, keyed in F, to fill the gap between the trumpets and trombones." In order to capitalize on the instrument's "intriguing new ways to shade and dramatize sound," Kenton, Johnny Richards, and Roland wrote forty new scores to usher in what Kenton termed "the New Era in Modern Music."[27] Roland himself can be heard playing the mellophonium on his own *Early Hours (Lady Luck)*, written in 1960 in his "loose, swinging, riff-ish style with which most associate him" and included on a reissue of the Kenton album entitled *Cuban Fire!*[28] A Kenton album from December 1961, entitled *Stan Kenton: Adventures in Blues*, consists entirely of Roland's own compositions.[29] Throughout this album, Gene solos with a true blues feeling that is, for the most part, absent from Kenton's work. Not only does Roland perform on mellophonium but he plays soprano sax as well, attesting to a fellow bandmember's claim that Gene "played everything!"[30]

Adventures in Blues also showcases the work of two graduates of the North Texas State jazz program, trombonist-drummer-composer Dee Barton, to whose writing Kenton also devoted an entire album (*The Jazz Compositions of Dee Barton*), and trumpeter Marv Stamm. Barton's two charts, *Turtle Talk* and *Waltz of the Prophets*, were recorded during the same December 1961 sessions and are included on Kenton's *Adventures in Jazz*, although Roland is not among the personnel. Barton's *Waltz of the Prophets*, a "hypnotic" blues in six-eight time using whole-tone scales, was first performed in 1960 by the North Texas State Lab Band, which won the Best Band title that year at the Annual Notre Dame Collegiate Jazz Festival, with Barton taking an individual award on trombone.[31] Not surprisingly, perhaps, the North Texas State version of Barton's composition is more jazz-oriented than the Kenton version. There is better contrast in dynamics, more drama, more youthful enthusiasm, and the solos by trumpeter Tom Wirtel (also a Kenton member at a later date) and Dee Barton on trombone communicate a jazz feeling that is more bluesy and thoughtful than is Barton's chorus or Marv Stamm's trumpet work on the Kenton recording. While George T. Simon has good words for Barton as "one of Kenton's most creative appointments," the jazz critic remarks that Stamm could be exciting "at fast tempos, but at slower speeds [his] preoccupation with notes at the expense of phrasing and feeling lends an over-cerebral, under-emotional touch unsuited to the new Kenton mood."[32]

On *Adventures in Blues*, it is clear that Roland retained close musical contact with his Texas roots. Although Barton's trombone is aided by Roland's ensemble writing on *The Blue Story*, once on his own Dee does little more than fake his way through the chorus, whereas Gene on soprano immediately settles into a genuine blues groove and then continues it on mellophonium, the latter his most unusual break on the album. Unfortunately, as is too often the case with a Kenton arrangement, Roland resorts to ear-splitting decibels for the full-band ending to his piece. On *Blue Ghost*—Gene's very haunting tune with Kenton featured on piano—Stamm fails to maintain on muted trumpet the unique feeling of this minor blues. However, on *Aphrodisiac* Stamm plays an effective straightforward trumpet introduction, followed by Roland's melancholy mellophonium, expressive of a modern approach to the urban blues Kenton-style. The control of the playing and writing here is in dramatic contrast to the overdependence in Dee

Barton's compositions on screaming trumpets, low tuba and baritone sax, and symphonic proportions that are neither jazz nor concert music. While much of Kenton's music remained in fact far from authentic jazz, his work nonetheless won—thanks in part to Gene Roland—a faithful following during the 1940s and 1950s that often voted Kenton's the best band of the year in the annual *Down Beat* polls. More significantly perhaps, the Kenton organization served as a training ground and meeting place for a number of important West Coast sidemen who would go on to develop in smaller units music that hewed closer—as did much of Roland's writing and playing—to the true roots of jazz. Among the Kentonites to create in the 1950s a softer, more intimate, and more introspective form of jazz were Shelly Manne, Bud Shank, Shorty Rogers, and Jimmy Giuffre.

❂ ❂ ❂

Although Harry Babasin was not associated with Stan Kenton and his orchestra through recordings or radio and television broadcasts,[33] the bassist performed in Los Angeles with several members of the Kenton organization, in particular Brazilian guitarist Laurindo Almeida, alto saxophonist and flutist Bud Shank, and trumpeter-composer-arranger Shorty Rogers. Before recording with these Kenton stars, Babasin worked with Dodo Marmarosa, the Pittsburgh pianist who participated in the first Dial recordings of Charlie Parker produced by Ross Russell on March 28, 1946, as well as in the famous *Relaxin' at Camarillo* session recorded for Dial on February 19, 1947, after Bird had been released from psychiatric treatment at the Camarillo State Hospital. It was with Marmarosa, a fellow sideman from the Boyd Raeburn band, that Babasin recorded five tunes for Dial: *Bopmatism, Dodo's Dance, Trade Winds (You Go to My Head), Dary Departs,* and *Cosmo Street (Lover).* The session for these five cuts—from a total of twenty-nine recorded tracks—took place on December 3, 1947, at a time when Marmarosa was in the running as "the Charlie Parker of the piano."[34] Although Marmarosa won the *Esquire* New Star Award in 1947, Bud Powell would ultimately cross the finish line as the bop pianist par excellence. As for Babasin, he made jazz history on this occasion by playing pizzicato cello, "the first use of that instrument on a jazz record date."[35] However, this use of a cello is not simply a curiosity but a highly effective piece of work by Babasin, who achieves an extremely modern sound as if in the upper register of the bass fiddle.

On the two up-tempo tunes, *Bopmatism* (the title an allusion to Jay McShann's *Swingmatism* of 1942) and *Dodo's Dance*, Babasin plucks the strings firmly and accurately, matching Marmarosa's rapid-fire runs on piano with a light touch that is yet surprisingly resonant. Throughout the series of takes, Babasin's note choices are excellent; at times he doubles the pianist's phrases with precision and swing, and at others creates his own exceptional melodic lines. Marmarosa approved of the five takes on the original ten-inch disc issued in 1950, and *Bopmatism* from these cuts finds Babasin playing an even more ambitious solo than on the alternate take offered on the later twelve-inch disc. On the approved take of *Dodo's Dance*, Babasin seems to push too hard and the results are not so appealing. But on the alternate take of *Dodo's Dance*, Babasin is more effective and lays down a solid line at a faster pace than on *Bopmatism*, even as he executes his accompaniment in the advanced style of the top bass players of the bop period. His light touch and mellow sound are particularly suited to Marmarosa's own approach to the piano, and on *Cosmo Street* the two make a most compatible combination, with Babasin contributing terrific solos on both takes, especially on the one approved by Dodo.

At the slower tempo taken on *Trade Winds* and *Dary Departs*, Babasin achieves an intimacy that is quite amazing. His note choices and tasteful execution go beautifully with Marmarosa's lovely rendering of *Trade Winds*, a ballad based on *You Go to My Head*. On *Dary Departs*, Babasin's opening releases that follow Marmarosa's chords are nicely done, and Harry's walking cello is in wonderful accord with Dodo's Hines-Tatum chorus on this boppish version of a swing-style tune. Babasin's ability to play both up-tempo and slow pieces with finesse and forceful-ness made him an ideal partner for a pianist like Marmarosa, who also exhibits these same qualities. Babasin blends naturally with the pianist's sound production, even as the cellist seems to maintain his own individual tone and musical concep-tion. The smaller instrument in Babasin's hands is no less supportive of the piano than the larger bass would have been, and with the rich sound he was capable of producing, it seems strange that more string players did not utilize the cello on jazz recordings and miked club dates. Only years later, mostly in the 1970s, would other jazz musicians begin to discover the potential for the cello that Babasin reveals in these 1946 Dial recordings.

In 1980, Texan Julius Hemphill's quartet, with Abdul Wadud on cello, would record an album in Milan, Italy, entitled *Flat-Out Jump Suite*. The unsigned liner notes observe that "the cello is a greatly misunderstood instrument in jazz circles, but, thanks largely to the efforts of Wadud, it is becoming more and more of a voice. Frequently, as here [*Mind, First Part*], the instrument is used completely in lieu of a bass. Even the work of Ron Carter on his 'piccolo bass' and Percy Heath on his 'baby bass' is helping to put the sound of the cello in the forefront."[36] Another member of the string family, the viola, also would become "more and more of a voice," as played by Austin jazz musician Will Taylor. Taylor's writing and playing on his album *Reel Life* from 1993 are extraordinary,[37] and the violist (who also plays violin, classical guitar, and piano) has produced a fine rendition of Thelonious Monk's *Well You Needn't*. Taylor is ably assisted on electric guitar by

Clay Moore; on soprano, alto, and tenor saxes by James Elias Haslanger; on bass by Steve Zirkel; and on percussion by Chris Searles.[38] On soprano, Haslanger plays beautifully in both *Dance of the Prairie* and *When Sunset Falls*, and Clay contributes a fine solo on *Cry of Winter*. This album also includes a cello, played by Ed Lawrence, who doubles on viola as well and together with Taylor provides some well-played, driving duets, as on *Blues for Fritz*, which is described by Julie Noble as "a delightful fusion of swing rhythm enmeshed with the melodic language of bop, all grounded in the blues form—a whimsical mirror of a particularly changeable sideswipe of a cat."[39]

In 1947, Harry Babasin became quite active on the Los Angeles scene, which has been vividly described by Ross Russell:

> If you lived in Los Angeles during the war years you saw a city in motion, on its way from a provincial big town to the sprawling metropolis it is today. Transition times are often the best of times, especially for the arts, and this was true of Los Angeles, and the jazz that mushroomed there during the war years. If you loved jazz you spent a lot of time on Central Avenue, the main drag of the Afro-American city. From 1941 to 1946, when servicemen began to drift back from the Pacific theatres, their pockets full of money, many of them to remain in Southern California, Central Avenue came to bear a striking resemblance to another street, remembered from another war, Basin Street, the thoroughfare of legendary Storyville, where jazz began.[40]

On July 6, 1947, at the Elks Auditorium near Central Avenue, a group that included tenor saxophonists Dexter Gordon and Wardell Gray, altoist Sonny Criss, pianist Hampton Hawes, drummer Connie Kay, Barney Kessel on guitar, and Babasin on bass recorded at one of the most famous sessions of the postwar period. Russell writes of this band that its impact "was in every way comparable to that made on the Austin High School Gang of Chicago when the King Oliver Creole Jazz Band played the Lincoln Gardens in 1923."[41] From the session of July 6, the tune entitled *The Hunt* was even celebrated in Jack Kerouac's *On the Road*, the literary work that put California on the Beat Generation map: "He began to learn 'Yes!' to everything, just like Dean at this time, and hasn't stopped since. To the wild sounds of Dexter Gordon and Wardell Gray blowing 'The Hunt,' Dean and I played catch with Marylou over the couch."[42] Babasin can be heard pumping away on *The Hunt*, especially when he backs up Barney Kessel's solo, his bass sound and style clearly recognizable from his work with Marmarosa.[43] Of course, Dexter and Wardell are the real focus of this recording, which offers "a rare glimpse into how the early bop players performed when freed from the time limitations inherent in three-minute-

Harry Babasin of
Dallas (right) with
Charlie Parker and
Chet Baker.
Reproduced with
the permission of
photographer
William Claxton.

long 78s," as the two tenors engage in a dramatic battle that "needed to be spread across several 78 rpm disks" so that "devoted bop fans had to listen to their music piecemeal. Yet this degree of excess may have only added to the music's allure."[44] Behind Hampton Hawes on the Coleman Hawkins tune *Disorder at the Border*, Babasin also makes his effective presence heard and felt on this extraordinary session that produced in *The Hunt* something of a beatnik theme song.

At a Polynesian nightspot called the Trade Winds (thus the title of the Marmarosa version of *You Go to My Head*) in the Los Angeles suburb of Inglewood, Harry Babasin organized a series of "off-night" jam sessions. Although Howard Rumsey's Hermosa Beach gatherings were also important during the early 1950s, as were those at the Haig, Babasin's Monday-night sessions were so popular that "after a few weeks Sundays were included to accommodate the overflow business."[45] The most important Sunday session came on the night of Bloomsday 1952—James Joyce's famous June 16. On this occasion, Babasin "found himself in dazzling company" when Charlie Parker, Chet Baker, and Sonny Criss all "showed up to front a rhythm section consisting of Babasin, Lawrence Marable on drums, and Al Haig and Russ Freeman sharing honors on the out-of-tune piano."[46] This occasion represented the first big break for trumpeter Chet Baker, who had auditioned along with "every trumpet player in L.A." and was chosen by Bird after

Chet played only two tunes that night. Following his hiring of the twenty-two-year-old Baker, Parker, according to photographer William Claxton, phoned Miles Davis and Dizzy Gillespie to tell them, "There's a little white cat out here who's going to give you guys a lot of trouble."[47]

Shortly before the Trade Winds jam session, Parker had been touring the West Coast and apparently was "strung out" and thus susceptible to being "cut" by the unintimidated altoist Sonny Criss. But if Criss burns on the recordings made on Bloomsday night, the Bird is capable of unforgettable flights, as on the opening tune, Tadd Dameron's *The Squirrel*. Although Baker begins in a thoughtful Miles Davis manner that shows why Parker was probably attracted to Chet's approach, Baker demonstrates throughout the session his ability to play bop with the required intensity and stream-of-consciousness invention. From the first, Babasin really works on this Dameron tune, and behind Baker the bassist's note choices are absolutely perfect. After Criss blows and goes on two choruses (the second even more impressive than the first) and Baker takes two, Bird opens his solo by announcing himself with a signature blues phrase and then turns it on with a run of his favorite licks and that marvelous, inimitable sound. Parker's entire chorus is a thing of beauty, and the spontaneous applause of the audience acknowledges the presence of Kerouac's Buddha-like Zen master. In the exchange of fours, Bird is again superb. Criss definitely displays his best stuff as well, but his sound is not so pleasant and he is too nonstop, rarely alternating his tempi or pausing between ideas as Bird does, but rather stringing out one idea without any relief or contrast. Meanwhile, Baker shows how effectively he too could keep pace at this bop tune's scorching speed, in particular with his last four bars.

On *Irresistible You*, Bird and Baker simply sound great together, and Babasin hustles behind Haig's piano and then takes a brief solo before Bird returns with the lovely theme. As would be expected, Bird is out of sight on *Indiana (Donna Lee)*, his flow of ideas unbelievable, and Babasin is right with him, though Harry's playing tends to suffer from the same headlong, unrelieved drive as does Sonny Criss's—both obviously intent on impressing Parker and the audience on hand to hear the star attraction. As for Baker, he provides a sample of his own outpouring of ideas that only a month later would be featured with the Gerry Mulligan Quartet, through which Chet gained international recognition. Baker also joins Bird for the theme statement and matches the kind of flawless performance given by Gillespie and Miles at their best. Closing the session is *Liza*, which opens with a fantastic solo by Parker, his wondrous sound fully audible on every race-speed note. Chet dives in with his highly lyrical style, maintained even at the tune's very demanding clip. Criss once again is simply blistering, and the bassist hangs right in there. Even though a solo taken by Babasin is nothing special, it makes sense and keeps the homefires stoked for the return of the horns, who take up where they left off, first Criss, and then Bird, who plays perhaps more meaningful notes in eight bars than Sonny does in most of his extended choruses. This jam-session production by Harry Babasin helped establish the fact that, despite a feeling held by some that jazz was dead because the big-band era had passed and little was being done in the way of large auditorium performances, the small "nitery-type place" like the Trade Winds was creating the real thing and "the Hollywood area was jumping with jazz of all kinds,"[48] including the work of other Texans: Jack Teagarden at the Royal Room and Jimmy Giuffre with the Lighthouse All-Stars at Hermosa Beach.

When Harry Babasin played bass with a group like the Laurindo Almeida Quartet, he managed the same delicate but firm touch that marked his work with Dodo Marmarosa. Recording in 1953 and 1954 with Almeida on acoustic guitar, Bud Shank on alto or flute, and Roy Harte on drums, Babasin and the Almeida Quartet created one of the early fusions of jazz with Brazilian music like the bossa nova. Although these sides are not considered the progenitors of bossa nova, they "certainly exhibited characteristics of that style some nine years before bossa nova became a national craze."[49] According to Harte, the idea for this quartet was Harry Babasin's, and his bass parts "provided the lead rhythmically." Harte goes on to report that the group's main purpose was "to achieve the light, swinging feel of the baião—combined with jazz blowing."[50] The "chemistry" between Almeida and Babasin had begun to work when the two men first played a club date in 1952 on Sunset Strip. In 1953 they were joined by Shank and Harte for an engagement at the Haig and for a recording session in September at the Pacific Jazz studios. Six tunes were recorded; out of these, three were "standards of the Brazilian repertoire" and one was a Babasin original entitled *Noctambulism*.[51]

Writing of this hybrid album, Robert Gordon declares that "the music is instantly appealing; the infectious samba rhythms fit in quite well with the jazz feeling, and Bud Shank's pure alto tone is a perfect complement to Almeida's unamplified guitar."[52] Ted Gioia calls Shank's playing on this recording "some of the most reflective and unabashedly pretty alto work of his career."[53] On *No No* by Romualdo Peixoto, the lovely blend of guitar and bass opens the tune and presents the ensemble's samba side, after which Shank enters ever so quietly with an airy sound on alto that suddenly turns into a swinging jazz improvisation, though still restrained in keeping with the piece's subdued feeling. Babasin backs up Almeida on the guitarist's extended introduction, the two players seemingly one in a rich string mixture of treble and bass. With Shank's jazz interpretation of the tune, the bassist moves from the samba rhythm to a steady four-beat pulse against which the altoist takes off on his "pretty" flight. At the end Shank returns to more of a samba feeling and then concludes the piece with some lovely fluttering arpeggios.

On *Speak Low*, a tune not included on the original recording but added to a 1955 release, the quartet emphasizes the jazz aspect of its approach. This Kurt Weill tune also opens with bass and guitar stating the theme, with Shank again entering gently and in the Latin mode; afterward, the altoist and the rhythm section engage in something of a group improvisation. Although Almeida is not looked upon as a true jazz instrumentalist, he is able to meld "a new form out of disparate parts."[54] As for Babasin, he demonstrates on this tune his ability to move quite successfully from the classical-sounding touch of his accompaniment work with the guitarist to swinging lines that complement the altoist's whispery but driving improvisations. Babasin's own *Noctambulism* begins with Shank stating the melancholy theme straight, with only a tinge of blues feeling. After Almeida's equally straight treatment, Shank returns for a brief bit of subdued invention. This is probably the least interesting performance on the album, certainly not comparable with Shank's spirited choruses on *Blue Baião*, which is pure swinging jazz from start to finish, with Almeida adding a nice break and the rhythm section cooking all the way—even at the end as the group slows into a *baião* beat. Even so, Babasin's *Noctambulism* does illustrate Ted Gioia's view that on this album Shank plays "some of the most reflective . . . work of his career."

Bud Shank's first recording date as a leader was with the rhythm section of the new Nocturne label, whose creation has been credited either to Babasin or Harte.[55] Nocturne's first record featured Herbie Harper, a Kansas-born trombonist raised in Amarillo, and Bob Gordon, a highly talented baritone saxophonist who died tragically in 1955 at the age of twenty-seven. Babasin and Harte, along with pianist Jimmy Rowles, comprised the Nocturne rhythm section on these first two recordings, with Shank joined by Shorty Rogers on flügelhorn for the label's second album, entitled *Bud Shank Quintet*.[56] All six of the tunes recorded on this 1954 Shank session were written by Rogers, and two of these, *Shank's Pranks* and *Lotus Bud*, were "minor hits at the time."[57] The former tune is typical of Rogers's light-hearted style—he was something of a jazz prankster, as we shall see from his association with Jimmy Giuffre—and the latter is "a beautiful ballad with an engaging alto flute solo by Shank."[58] On *Lotus Bud*, Rowles and Babasin accompany Shank's opening theme statement on flute, which remains largely in the lower register and creates a pensive mood that is richly supported by the note choices in Babasin's lifting and falling bass lines. Rogers's mellow flügelhorn maintains the mood, never rising above the instrument's middle range or increasing the deliberate pace. The quiet, low-toned quality of this performance and the subdued effect sought after in the Almeida recordings were characteristic of the West Coast school and represented an intentional restraint in response to the troubled and, for many listeners, troubling dynamics and intensity of the bop revolution. Not that Shank and Rogers were incapable of bop-inspired fireworks, but perhaps the greatest appeal of the West Coast school lay in its cultivation of a quieter jazz, and Harry Babasin, with his classical training, played an important role in this counterrevolution that arose fittingly on the shores of the Pacific.

❧ ❧ ❧

An even greater and more significant part in the West Coast movement was taken by Jimmy Giuffre, who was a member of the first "official" Lighthouse All-Stars formed in 1951 by Howard Rumsey as the band for the Lighthouse Cafe at Hermosa Beach. The initial recordings issued by the new Contemporary label were under the Lighthouse All-Stars banner and included Giuffre and Shorty Rogers both as composers and outstanding soloists. Giuffre's ballad *Out of Somewhere* (a nod to Charlie Parker's classic recordings of *Out of Nowhere*), his *Big Girl* (a "take-off on a rhythm and blues number, complete with a honking solo by the composer"),[59] and *Four Others* (a title that plays on that of Giuffre's famous Woody Herman arrangement, *Four Brothers*) were all recorded in 1952 and 1953 with the Lighthouse All-Stars.[60] Even earlier, on October 8, 1951, Giuffre had joined Shorty Rogers for a Capitol recording in Los Angeles, although the sides were not released until 1952, when these and sessions by the Gerry Mulligan Quartet with Chet Baker "spread the word that new things were happening on the Coast."[61] Writing of the Capitol sides, Ted Gioia calls these "seminal performances" that are "justifiably considered not only one of the classics of Rogers's career, but also one of the pioneering statements of the 'West Coast sound.'"[62]

While following from the earlier Miles Davis "birth of the cool" recordings of 1949–1950, the 1951 "forerunners of West Coast jazz" by Rogers and Giuffre avoid, in Robert Gordon's view, such pitfalls as overarranging, bland solos, and lifeless rhythm sections that "would come to plague some later examples of the style. Certainly they were far from slavish copies of the Miles Davis recordings."[63] Giuffre's tune *Four Mothers* (yet another play on the title of his Woody Herman classic) is a romping piece of straight-ahead jazz that finds Giuffre swinging as hard as any of the soloists.[64] After the ensemble's statement of the theme, accompanied by exuberant cries of "hey" and "go" (these sounds differing in style from the gospel, church-derived shouts heard on a Mingus album), Rogers rips off a chorus with his characteristic three-note rising and falling scalar phrases. Giuffre follows with an example of what Gioia refers to as the Texan's "powerful no-nonsense tenor work . . . rarely found on [his] leader dates." This is a rocking chorus by Giuffre that may, as Gioia says, "show little of the feel for the bebop idiom" in some of his arrangements,[65] but it is nonetheless a solo totally integrated into the spirit of the overall performance. On *Didi*, a Rogers composition that employs a type of call-and-response figure, Giuffre takes only two short breaks, but they are the most funky of the side and look forward to the tenorist's later development of his basic down-home style. Art Pepper is the Charlie Parker–inspired soloist here, while especially on Rogers's *Popo* Giuffre reveals his own more Lester Young–derived approach. Gioia describes the achievement of this particular "chart" by calling it "a telling indicator of one of the distinctive sounds Rogers was forging. It was nothing short of a new way of playing the blues." Giuffre's solo also shows that he certainly contributed to the creation here of "an effortless swing, an atmosphere in which melody could float above the beat and the blues . . . could take on a new face."[66]

In January 1953, Shorty Rogers and His Giants recorded for RCA Victor and produced an album with the name of this group as its title; Giuffre was included in the group and composed for it two tunes, *The Pesky Serpent* and *Indian Club*. Although Robert Gordon criticizes the latter for its "rather embarrassing tom-tom and minor-key melody line that echoes Hollywood's idea of American Indian music,"[67] the liner notes commend the tune for combining "Indian and swing motifs in an exceptionally clever way."[68] Clearly Giuffre's baritone solo on this number does not measure up to his tenor work on the Capitol recording; yet the arrangement itself is important as something of a harbinger of his later master-piece, *Suspensions*, which makes a more sophisticated use of an American Indian rhythm. *The Pesky Serpent*, which Gordon allows is a "nice enough tune,"[69] harks back to Giuffre's *Four Brothers* in its arranging style. The composer's tenor solo is nothing special here, and in fact his playing is better represented on Rogers's *Morpo*, though nowhere on this album is it up to Giuffre's usual performances with the Giants. One of Jimmy's best outings from this period is on another RCA Victor session from March and April of the same year. Originally entitled *Cool and Crazy* but reissued in July 1956 as *The Big Shorty Rogers Express*, the recording produced on this date has been cited by Rogers as his favorite album.[70] Here Giuffre takes a tremendously exciting solo in the same class with the very best work of Illinois Jacquet, tearing out a page from that jazzman's book of Texas tenor playing. But none of Giuffre's solo performances or his compositions fully prepared listeners for his forthcoming productions, which would grow more and more experimental and would concentrate largely on a new sound developed through the clarinet, an instrument that had been displaced in jazz by the tenor and alto saxophones.

Something of Giuffre's new direction was indicated on a July 20, 1953, session with Shelly Manne for an album entitled *The West Coast Sound*.[71] To the album's eight arrangements, which "set the style for much of what came to be called West Coast jazz," Giuffre contributed *Fugue*, a work that represented "an attempt to stretch the boundaries of jazz writing,"[72] an "atonal piece of counterpoint" that "must have struck most 1953 listeners as an incongruous, if not downright spiteful, contribution from the composer of 'Four Brothers.'"[73] Ted Gioia elaborates on the significance of Giuffre's composition when he states that it "stands out as one of the most strikingly avant-garde pieces any jazz group, on either coast, recorded during the early 1950s. . . . [I]ts atonality and its obvious destruction of the typical roles played by the rhythm instruments . . . made this work especially iconoclastic. Even today, some thirty-five years after it was recorded, it is a disturbing, unnerving piece to listen to."[74] The following month, on August 31, Giuffre joined Shorty Rogers and vibist-leader Teddy Charles for a session that Ira Gitler would proclaim "the most successful wedding of elements from modern serious music and jazz."[75] All the writing for this session was done by Charles, except for two pieces, *Free* and *Evolution*, the first by Rogers and the second by Giuffre.[76] While the Rogers composition predates a seminal work by Ornette Coleman of the same title, there is little in Shorty's piece that looks forward to the free jazz movement. On the other hand, Giuffre's *Evolution* is very much a sign of things to come and in fact contains a number of phrases and tonal combinations that will be heard on his revolutionary *Tangents in Jazz* album of 1955. This composition also seems to represent Giuffre's earliest attempt to write improvisational-like parts for the soloists. Likewise, Giuffre's own tenor playing here may be the earliest instance of his combining written with improvised jazz.

In the tunes by Teddy Charles the Texan proves he is "an almost ideal sideman" who "sounds more comfortable on these sophisticated experimental works than on many of his own compositions from that period."[77] On *Margo*, which Gitler in his liner notes calls "perhaps the first successful slow piece in this new idiom," Giuffre is featured on tenor with some "very sensitive melodic support" that predates the similar work of Charles Mingus's reedmen on his *Pithecanthropus Erectus* album of 1956. For *Bobalob*, Giuffre switches to baritone and plays some licks that will be heard again on the 1955 Rogers album entitled *The Swinging Mr. Rogers*. *Bobalob* was recorded and issued in two takes, with the second "a head arrangement of the ideas that 'happened' in the first."[78] According to Ted Gioia, *Bobalob* "looks ahead to [Miles Davis's] *Kind of Blue* with its pronounced modal emphasis."[79] The group improvisation toward the end of the second take of *Bobalob* is far removed from Dixieland, yet retains the spirit of jazz musicians listening to and responding to one another spontaneously. This development will also prove characteristic of Giuffre's later work with his various groups, just as both his warm, ethereal tenor and his at times gruff baritone are prophetic of the sounds he will come to emphasize on these instruments, along with his low-registered, almost vibratoless clarinet.

The next step along Giuffre's "evolutionary" path is his September 10, 1954, Contemporary recording session with only Shelly Manne on drums and Shorty Rogers on trumpet. This test of the limits of Giuffre's theories of contrapuntal writing and the elimination by the three men of "preconceived chord pattern, melody, or rhythmic structure" on *Abstract No. 1* is, as Ted Gioia properly judges, "perhaps more impressive for what it attempted than for what it actually achieved."[80] Although the tune represents "a completely free improvisation, with no established melody or chord structure,"[81] all three musicians fail to liberate themselves from their own clichés. More interesting is the Rogers tune *Three on a Row*, based on Schoenberg's dodecaphonic serial technique. Here the trio members employ some of the same rhythmic and melodic phrases—drawn in this case from Shorty's twelve-tone row—that will be fully and effectively utilized later on Giuffre's *Tangents in Jazz*. Rogers's composition represents one of the more successful early examples of Third Stream music, to which Giuffre will be attracted not only in his compositions for *Tangents* but in many of his other works that "fuse" classical form with jazz improvisation and feeling. Also at this session the trio recorded Giuffre's *Pas de trois*, in which Manne's drums are used "as a melody instrument, with an equal voice in the structure of the counterpoint,"[82] a technique that looks forward as well to the *Tangents* album with its development of a greater melodic role for the rhythm section.

In March 1955, Giuffre was back with Rogers for a more traditional quintet recording for Atlantic, *The Swinging Mr. Rogers*, the success of which Robert Gordon credits with helping to "ensure the continuation of the Atlantic jazz policy"[83] that would later result in the historic recordings of Ornette Coleman made in 1959 and 1960. One of the principal achievements of the Rogers-Giuffre album was that at the time it convincingly refuted the thesis that "West Coasters couldn't swing."[84] Giuffre was central to this refutation, for he can be heard on all three of his instruments playing with great spirit and drive. Gordon rightly singles out Giuffre's performance on the two standards, *Isn't It Romantic* and *My Heart Stood Still*, for here Jimmy turns in what the critic calls "surging, all-stops-out" solos on baritone that owe "nothing whatsoever to the Mulligan style."[85] Gioia also praises these pieces "as powerful vehicles for improvisations from both Rogers and Giuffre" and as precursors to Rogers's later album from 1957, *Shorty Rogers Plays Richard Rogers.*[86] Giuffre's bluesy, Prez-inspired tenor is notably heard on *That's What I'm Talkin' About*, but the most significant pieces on this album are those in which Giuffre plays clarinet, especially *Martians Go Home*, "the jazz equivalent of a hit."[87] Not only does

Shelly Manne support the Martian theme with his tuned drums and pitched cymbals, but he dazzles the unwelcome visitors from Mars with a coin trick, spinning a fifty-cent piece on his tom-tom and letting it wobble down right in time to the tune's slow-to-medium tempo. More to the point, this piece introduces Giuffre's breathy Chalumeau clarinet, which will become his principal instrument in the creation of a unique sound that attempted to bring out the texture and timbre of each individual note.

With Giuffre's *Tangents in Jazz*, recorded for Capitol in June 1955, Jimmy would produce what remains "the most controversial project of his career."[88] On this album Giuffre's quartet—Jack Sheldon on trumpet, Ralph Peña on bass, Artie Anton on drums, and the leader alternately on tenor, baritone, and clarinet—performs a type of jazz that lacks a steady beat normally provided by piano, bass, or percussion. Here, rather, the pulse is generated by Giuffre's written parts for each instrument, with solos largely replaced by "a wide range of compositional devices: call-and-response figures, two- and three-part counterpoint, unison and harmony lines, canonic devices."[89] This new conception, by questioning "the driving rhythm of modern jazz," challenged what had always been the most sacrosanct aspect of the music: "the propulsive beat . . . viewed by many, both musicians and critics, as the essence of jazz."[90] However, in spite of the absence of "an audible beat—no walking bass, no riding cymbal," Giuffre by the force of his "indomitable folksiness . . . out-thumps the music of most of his heavy-handed neighbors."[91]

Giuffre himself states clearly that "clarity and freedom" prompted him to abandon a pulsating beat: "I've come to feel increasingly inhibited and frustrated by the insistent pounding of the rhythm section."[92] Without it, Giuffre believed the soloist could more "fully concentrate on the solo line." And as a result, the rhythm section members, instead of simply keeping time, have now become soloists as well, as on *Scintilla Two*, where the drummer contributes to the thematic line of this Giuffre tune, represented on the album by four variations. Here Anton's snare drums—played with brushes—take on an integral role, completing or responding to Giuffre's tenor phrases. Similarly, on *Chirpin' Time*, Peña on bass participates in this "blues-type mood in minor" as a melodic instrument on an equal footing with the horns played by Giuffre and Sheldon, as all four instrumentalists function independently yet "trade twos and fours in a kind of question-and-answer routine."[93] On *Chirpin' Time*, Giuffre plays clarinet, as he does on the "ultra-slow and bluesy" *Lazy Tones*, where bass and drums accompany him not with a beat but with punctuations or parallel lines that fill in or move in their own directions. This characteristic applies as well to the trumpet, which creates with the clarinet a lovely, low-keyed duet of independent voices that yet achieve a unified effect. On

Scintilla Two, Sheldon plays parallel lines to those of the tenor or moves counter to the bass, blows held notes under Giuffre's inventions, and breaks out in fiery "sparks" of his own, to which the bass and drums respond energetically. The basic element of constant movement is ever present in these pieces, but it shifts from one instrument to another, with each supplying its own peculiar sound and rhythmic variations toward an overall musical end.

This Is My Beloved, the only "non-Giuffrian, non-jazz tune" on the album, opens with the bass and drums setting the pace of this "stately waltz" and only hinting at the Vernon Duke theme, which later the bass will play in full while tenor and trumpet provide the fills, reversing the normal order of things. Essentially this piece features the bass, although in between Peña's thematic statement and his thematic variations, the horns engage in some affective canonic and contrapuntal "improvisation," which in fact has been written out by Giuffre but sounds spontaneous in the best jazz tradition. With *The Leprechaun*, Giuffre creates his most folksy, countrified song, on which he "pipes" his "plaintive" clarinet. Each instrument takes its turn in "trying a little out-of-tempo improvisation"—that is, a steady beat, even if implicit, is not the concern of the musicians in this "conversation" where all have their "genteel" say, picking up from or anticipating the end of each other's musical phrase.[94] *Scintilla Three* features Sheldon's trumpet with double-time variations on Giuffre's folksy theme, and this spontaneous-sounding performance contrasts dramatically with *Rhetoric*, which makes "free use of classical form, 'The Chorale Figuration with Invention Group,'"[95] a highly experimental "atonal ditty" that still maintains a jazz feeling, if more subdued and structured than the album's other pieces.

Perhaps the most swinging number of all, *Scintilla Four*, is appropriately the album's final tune, which has the percussionist fingering his drums, lending to the opening fanfare a most novel and dark-toned sound in keeping with the piece's very ceremonious character. The finger-played drums also complement Giuffre's baritone and reveal the composer's great sensitivity to tonal color and instrumental timbre. While *Tangents in Jazz* had few if any successors among jazz recordings, and if even Giuffre himself did not really follow up on his revolutionary developments, this album demonstrated that jazz could swing without the soloists having to fight "a pounding beat" and were free to "get a more natural sound out of their horns, try for all sorts of new effects."[96] Had Giuffre continued in this vein he might have merely repeated himself rather than moving on to the next stage in his "evolution," what George Russell called his period of "backwoods impressionism."[97] Don Heckman, however, regrets that Giuffre did not "develop more fully the principle advanced in his *Tangents in Jazz* compositions. His use of meter there was particularly intriguing and might have led to a freer concept of percussion than is generally practiced."[98] In any event, as Ted Gioia has commented, "despite the stereotyped view of these performances as effete attempts to cut off jazz from its vital African roots, one returns to them with a constantly fresh sense of their enormous rhythmic variety." This critic also finds that Giuffre's experiments in various compositional techniques such as counterpoint and atonality are "harbingers of that later [New Age] West Coast style of music."[99]

Giuffre joined Shorty Rogers once again for Atlantic sessions in October, November, and December 1955 that produced two albums—*Martians Come Back!* and *Way Up There*. On the former, Giuffre forecasts his clarinet approach on his own March 1956 Atlantic sessions for his album *The Jimmy Giuffre Clarinet*. Here with Rogers, as in his clarinet work on *Tangents*, Giuffre's playing on this instrument is folksy, even on the tune entitled *Chant of the Cosmos*, a continuation of Shorty's interplanetary metaphor. With both *Martians Come Back!* and *The Jimmy Giuffre Clarinet*, Giuffre solos almost exclusively in the low register, using little vibrato, playing "short, simple phrases, which are sometimes composed of a single repeated note."[100] Above all, the stress is on quietness, as in the title tune *Martians Come Back!*, a placative and highly subdued piece on which Rogers plays his muted trumpet entirely in the lower range. Another piece in this same quiet vein is *Lotus Bud*, which had originally featured Bud Shank on flute when Giuffre's former housemate, Harry Babasin, recorded it on the Nocturne label in 1954. Finally, quietude is taken to its logical extreme on *Chant of the Cosmos* when, as John S. Wilson notes, "one of the great creative moments in jazz may have occurred." Wilson elaborates on this statement and offers a witty prediction: "It happened when Giuffre, huffing away on his clarinet, decided to take a noteless break—nothing but air artfully articulated through the clarinet and phrased with a sensitive beat. This may be the first air break in jazz. Once Giuffre has figured out how to expand the air scale a bit, we may expect a major work in this manner which will presumably be called *Breath, Where Is Thy Swing?*"[101]

In 1956, Giuffre signed with the Atlantic label for the first of what would prove a series of albums reflecting "the 'backwoods impressionistic' period in his creative cycle."[102] Although Ted Gioia considers the first of these albums, *The Jimmy Giuffre Clarinet*, "a clear step back from the experimentation of *Tangents in Jazz*," he can also view it as experimental in a more accessible way and concedes that it "remains Giuffre's finest recording from his most productive decade."[103] If *The Jimmy Giuffre Clarinet* lacks the inventiveness of Giuffre's work on *Tangents in Jazz*, this album— on which Giuffre continues with his composing and performing of tunes having a "blues-tinged . . . and a sort of haunted pastoral quality"[104]—does make up to

Jimmy Giuffre of
Dallas with Jim Hall
and Ralph Peña.
Reproduced from
The Jimmy Giuffre 3
(Atlantic 1254) by
permission of Atlantic
Records; photograph
by William Claxton.

some extent for a less varied rhythmic and melodic fare by offering a number of different instrumental combinations. Along with three outstanding Gershwin songs, *Deep Purple*, *My Funny Valentine*, and *Fascinatin' Rhythm*, the album contains five of Jimmy's wide-ranging original compositions. On seven of the eight tunes, oboe, English horn, flute, alto flute, bass flute, celeste, alto and bass clarinets, and the usual rhythm section join Giuffre on clarinet. However, Jimmy's clarinet playing on this album does not achieve the appeal it has on *Martians Come Back!* nor does it advance his conception of a jazz that abandons a pounding beat, at least beyond the point reached in this regard by the *Tangents* recording. In fact, the first tune, *So Low*, which records Giuffre playing alone in a darkened room, tends to support his own theory by not putting into practice what he had preached. While this work represents "the first recording for solo horn since Coleman Hawkins' *Picasso* in 1948,"[105] it demonstrates how, as Giuffre keeps time by patting his foot on the floor, an "insistent pounding" can become irritating to the listener and can make it impossible "to hear the horn's true sound."[106]

For the most part, this album indicates Giuffre's growing concentration on composition, and a prototypical piece like his *Down Home*, for three trumpets, tenor and baritone saxes, bass, drums, and his own clarinet, predicts his later Third

Stream–school *Suspensions* of 1957, an entirely composed piece for an ensemble larger than the trios and quartets he began working with more and more frequently from this period onward. At the same time, a keyless, atonal work like *The Side Pipers* recalls *Tangents in Jazz* in that drummer Shelly Manne adds to the soft sound desired by Giuffre by using "only his fingers."[107] Yet despite the affective power of the quietness created by his playing on *Martians Come Back!* and by some of the *Tangents* compositions, it is somewhat difficult to agree with Giuffre's ideas when they are applied to the performances on his clarinet album: "It has been said that when jazz gets soft it loses gusto and funkiness. It is my feeling that soft jazz can retain the basic flavor and intensity that it has at a louder volume and at the same time perhaps reveal some new dimensions of feeling that loudness obscures."[108] But if *The Jimmy Giuffre Clarinet* did not illustrate this view as convincingly as Giuffre's previous work, his subsequent album for Atlantic would make the case more effectively and would also produce, after *Four Brothers*, "perhaps Giuffre's most popular composition,"[109] his down-home *The Train and the River*, from the Texan's next album, *The Jimmy Giuffre 3*.[110]

Labeling *The Train and the River* "a 22-carat classic," *The Harmony Illustrated Encyclopedia of Jazz* goes on to say that this piece is "a lesson in spontaneous, blues-laced improvisation and staggering musical empathy."[111] John Litweiler writes that in this composition "the shifting rhythms and textures of [Giuffre's] Appalachian folk variations . . . yield a charm that not only is new to jazz, but also contradicts the assertive expression that is jazz's birthright."[112] Indeed, this entire album displays how much is to be learned from Giuffre's notion that soft jazz can retain the basic flavor and intensity that was traditionally associated with the music's loudness—a tendency exaggerated by the big bands of the 1940s and especially by the various "progressive" units led by Stan Kenton. (It is curious, perhaps, that both Giuffre's school of softness and Kenton's brash, bigger-is-better approach were products of the West Coast and the same sunny, palm-treed climate.[113] The fact that Kenton, though born in Kansas, was raised in Los Angeles suggests that his flashy style was more native to California than the freer, blues-inspired conception favored by Giuffre as a jazzman from North Texas or even by Gene Roland, despite the latter's obstreperous and even shrill arrangements for Kenton.)

Just as Giuffre's other leader dates had been groundbreaking in their use of unusual instrumentation, *The Jimmy Giuffre 3* was once more innovative in dispensing with a drummer and substituting instead a guitar, joined to a bass and Giuffre's clarinet, tenor, or baritone.[114] From the first piece on this recording, Giuffre's *Gotta Dance*, it is clear that the composer has found a new sound even within his "old" folksy approach, having explored again what Fred Bouchard calls Jimmy's "own backwaters" and his "cooler creeks of composition, closely brushing classical and Third Stream."[115] Here, as on the clarinet album, Giuffre combines his own fine bluesy, funky tunes with two standards, and especially in the case of Jerome Kern's *The Song Is You*, the choice is perfect for the folk-songsy mood created throughout the recording and shows how hard yet quietly the trio can swing. In Jim Hall, the leader had found an ideal "running mate," with the guitarist's light touch and his tone that fuses the classical and the down-home. Hall is showcased on *Crazy She Calls Me*, and his "gut-string style" is wonderfully suited to Giuffre's simple but very intimate and emotive sound. Giuffre's *Voodoo*, with the leader on baritone and Ralph Peña on bass featured at a syncopated medium tempo, recaptures in its restrained manner something of the primitive roots of jazz. Unlike the clarinet album, which has moments and even entire tunes that fail to come off, the trio outing contains nothing but winners. Yet it is *The Train and the River* and the longest piece, *Crawdad Suite*, which represent the major developments on this Atlantic recording.

While *Crawdad Suite* does not swing so intensely as *Gotta Dance* or *The Song Is You*, this folksy, bluesy composition is perhaps Giuffre's furthest exploration of the down-home idiom and offers a subtle drive all its own. Peña's relaxed walking bass seems not so much to pulse or push as to carry on a running commentary with the other two voices. When the bassist pauses to listen and then puts in his own knowing "two-bits," the character of the piece changes from a trio conversing as a group to a thoughtful call-and-response discussion of the finer points of pastoral jazz. This composition stands as one of the earliest and most successful Third Stream works, which takes its cue from Debussy's sonata for flute, viola, and harp.[116] In many ways this extended, seven-minute piece is more impressive than *The Train and the River*, but undeniably it is the latter that epitomizes the whole pastoral, down-home approach that Giuffre would continue to exploit in his later 1958 Atlantic albums, *Trav'lin' Light* (which replaced the bass with Bob Brookmeyer's valve trombone) and *Western Suite*.[117] George Russell, Giuffre's fellow Third Stream composer, has written of *Trav'lin' Light* that here the programmatic subject is "hill people" or, as the title of one piece has it, "swamp people," whose "vigorous activities are captured in the camp meeting chants. . . . Brother Giuffre is taken with the holiness tongue and utters in his ecstasy some phrases of remarkable rhythmic virility. Brother Brookmeyer can't contain the spirit any longer on *Pick 'Em Up* and starts preachin' an unaccompanied jump and shout sermon."[118]

As Ted Gioia remarks of this period and Giuffre's "return visits to the jazz heritage," they "never lasted for long," for even the composer's "most conventional works seemed to have a subversive undercurrent."[119] This quality can best be felt on *Crawdad Suite*, in which Giuffre is not content merely with mimetic versions of the pastoral but is obviously seeking more experimental structures that can open up his own playing and that of his sidemen. Like Ornette Coleman, who was beginning to break new ground during these same years, Giuffre "began thinking, as a result of studying composition, of the individual in the music—of each one of the musicians rather than in toto." As Lorin Stephens goes on to say, Giuffre also "began thinking of what you might call 'interesting ideas,' counterpoint, and using the rhythm section in different ways, different forms and different kinds of tones—all these things that weren't conventional in jazz."[120]

During August of 1956, Giuffre continued his studies by attending John Lewis's jazz program at Music Inn in the Berkshire Mountains of Massachusetts, where Lewis, of the Modern Jazz Quartet, would in 1959 also welcome Ornette Coleman. Present with Giuffre at Music Inn in 1956 was another Texan, the early blues and boogie-woogie pianist Sammy Price. Intended as an opportunity to bring together jazz musicians and critics of all persuasions, the Music Inn program was devoted to roundtable discussions followed by a jam session. Earlier, in 1955 in Denver, Lewis and Giuffre had had their first meeting and had discussed a possible record date because Lewis felt that the Texan "was the one jazz musician whose playing was closest to [the Modern Jazz] Quartet's style."[121] As a result, Giuffre was asked during his stay at Music Inn to join the quartet for a recording session at the end of August, to which the Texan contributed his composition *Fun*. For *Serenade* by David Raksin, the composer of *Laura*, Lewis suggested that Giuffre play "straight without variations or interpolations" since the quartet's leader did not offer this tune as "a jazz performance" but "just a piece of music," refusing "to be restricted by any formulas."[122] In so many ways, Lewis's position was indicative of the new directions being pursued by Jimmy Giuffre, Ornette Coleman, and other jazz musicians of this period. As Coleman would comment years later, "I never thought about being called [a jazz saxophone player]—I was just playing the saxophone, you know. It wasn't until I got to California and New York that the word *jazz* started being more constrictingly applied to what I was doing."[123] As for Giuffre, he would be "needled" by Coleman, when the two men met at Music Inn in August 1959, into breaking "out of himself to play free."[124]

As the only musician at Music Inn to respond in a practical sense to Ornette Coleman's "free jazz," Giuffre would organize yet another evolutionary unit, a trio composed of pianist Paul Bley and bassist Steve Swallow. According to Coleman's biographer, John Litweiler, the West Coast musicians were more open to "exploratory works" than the heirs to bebop on the East Coast, who ironically had "internalized one of the nasty features of the social tidepool in which it had spawned: intolerance."[125] Giuffre's "experiments in free harmonic structure"[126] were developed to their most innovative level on his new trio's Verve albums,

Fusion (1961) and *Thesis* (1962).[127] Ted Gioia considers these "difficult works" to have "little of the charm that radiates from Giuffre's most memorable efforts. Especially when he abandons a tonal center in his works, Giuffre seems to lose more of his individuality than he gains by the supposed freedom."[128] Comparing Giuffre's work with his fellow Texan's, the critic concludes that "at their most derivative, [Jimmy's] evocations of Ornette Coleman . . . are nowhere as convincing as the real thing." But Gioia goes on to say that "to be fair, this apparently final stage in Giuffre's development was clearly no haphazard result, but truly the logical end-point of a decade of personal growth."[129] Litweiler finds in Giuffre's venture into "freely moving tempo and meter" one of the boldest steps taken by his generation, while his clarinet playing "arrived at a new expressiveness and angularity of line."[130] Of Giuffre's 1963 album, *Free Fall*, Wilfrid Mellers declares that the clarinetist "takes the ultimate step and dispenses with 'beat' altogether."[131]

A tune on the *Fusion* album, entitled *Venture*, combines the classical and the funky, the syncopated and the pointillistic, while maintaining throughout the piece Giuffre's essential folksy approach. From his *Thesis* album, Giuffre's *Sonic*, as its title suggests, emphasizes sound exclusively, in this case an almost eastern bells-and-sitar effect, so that there is no longer the traditional swing associated with jazz or the blues intonation deriving from the human voice. *Whirr* likewise is basically lacking in any sense of syncopation, blues, or swing, attempting rather through chromatic scales and two-note trills to replicate the sound in the piece's title. Like *Whirr*, *Flight* emphasizes movement but only in terms of sound rather than forward momentum or any particular sense of direction, as in a rag, blues, or pop tune. Two other tunes in this mode with more folksy titles are *Trudgin'* and *Scootin' About*. The former is a free-for-all piece that achieves movement only by means of a repeated figure in Bley's piano whereas the latter tends to speed up or slow down in keeping, once again, with its title. Two other tunes with more colloquial titles are *That's True, That's True* and *Me Too*, both of which are in Giuffre's down-home style, the latter containing syncopated triplets and featuring Swallow's walking bass line and a bluesy, swinging clarinet. The tunes with more colloquial titles tend to contain a greater degree of folksiness, just as those with rather abstract titles are—like *The Gamut*—comparable to any modern classical composition for chamber trio. However, none of the pieces is either completely down-home or strictly abstract, which indicates Giuffre's allegiance to what Gunther Schuller has termed Third Stream, a "fusion" of the two forces of jazz and classical music, a "kind of cross-fertilization" that for Schuller benefits "both musics."[132]

One of the most satisfying examples of Giuffre's "fusion" work is his composition entitled *Suspensions*, an entirely written-out piece performed in 1957 at the Brandeis University Festival of Arts. Here Giuffre created a work for an ensemble that included Teddy Charles on vibes, James Buffington on French horn, Manuel Zegler on bassoon, Robert DiDomenica on flute, and Margaret Ross on harp, along with a contingent of jazz musicians—trumpeter Art Farmer, trombonist Jimmy Knepper, altoist Hal McKusick, and pianist Bill Evans. Giuffre's goal, in his own words, was to write for the individual players in such a way that they could "express themselves as they would in a solo."[133] With a strong folk-blues feeling and at times a solid swing, this work for a number of instruments more common in a classical setting illustrates Schuller's notion of the "mutual fructifying" achieved by Third Stream music "in the hands of gifted people."[134] Certainly Jimmy Giuffre in 1957 was one of those figures who was able to bring his knowledge of and feeling for jazz to the composition of a work that could achieve the wonderful spontaneity of jazz within the formal demands of a wholly notated piece of music. Whether Third Stream compositions will continue to play an important role in the development of jazz or not, the fact remains that Giuffre— along with Harold Shapero in his fascinating piece wittily entitled *On Green Mountain (Chaconne after Monteverdi)*[135]—proved the viability of such a jazz-classical fusion and did so by utilizing those elements closest to Giuffre's own western traditions: the folk song, the blues, and even, on *Suspensions*, a rhythmic pattern borrowed from the American Indian. Like Scott Joplin, Charlie Christian, and, as we shall see, Ornette Coleman, Giuffre made significant use of both "streams"— African and European—and in doing so carried on not only in the ragtime, swing, bop, and free jazz idioms but in a Texas tradition as well.

THE COWTOWN VANGUARD

Of the four major Texas cities—Dallas, Fort Worth, Houston, and San Antonio—it might seem highly unlikely that Cowtown, as Fort Worth has been called since its early days as a center for cattle auctions, slaughterhouses, packing plants, and a railhead for shipping, would give rise to the most avant-garde movement in jazz since bebop. But as a number of leading critics have observed, the free-jazz movement spearheaded by the playing and writing of Ornette Coleman, who was born in Fort Worth on March 19, 1930, marked the beginning of "the present era of jazz."[1] Indeed, Ornette's practice of his theory that a jazz artist must be "free to *create* form" is still the guiding principle "of the best post-Coleman musicians right up to the present."[2] In addition, critics like Martin Williams, Max Harrison, Gunther Schuller, and John Litweiler consider Coleman's "remarkable achievement" one of the three defining moments in all of jazz history, the other two being Louis Armstrong's 1926–1927 Hot Five and Hot Seven recordings—through which he brought to perfection the New Orleans style and forecast the coming of the Swing Era—and the Charlie Parker–Dizzy Gillespie bebop masterpieces of 1945.[3] Martin Williams has flatly declared that Coleman's music "represents the first fundamental reevaluation of basic materials and basic procedures for jazz since the innovations of Charlie Parker,"[4] and Max Harrison has pronounced Coleman "the most far-reaching innovator in jazz's history."[5]

How such a revolutionary musician could emerge from a city known mostly as the place "Where the West Begins" and for its airplane industry and oil-well outfitters may remain as inexplicable as the birth in Texarkana of the King of Ragtime. But just as East Texas, through its meeting grounds for African American musical traditions and the new growth industries of railway and lumberyard, made possible a greater freedom of expression, so too the existence in Fort Worth of a strong war economy produced a rhythm and blues scene that depended on young, undrafted musicians for its very existence and vitality. In turn, this economic and R & B environment enabled a group of Fort Worth jazzmen to develop their talents and eventually to follow the example of Ornette Coleman as he achieved a historic breakthrough into the largely unexplored frontier of free jazz.

Even before the rise of a generation of Cowtown jazzman born around 1930, local and touring bands laid the groundwork for an avant-garde movement that would spread to every part of the country as well as abroad. As we have seen, Euday L. Bowman of Fort Worth performed a significant service to jazz when he composed his *Twelfth Street Rag* in 1914. In 1936, almost twenty years after their first recording session in 1917, the Original Dixieland Jazz Band reunited for a performance at the Texas Centennial Exposition in Dallas, and during the 1930s many big bands passed through Dallas and Fort Worth, performing at the latter's Blackstone Hotel and at its Lake Worth casino. In 1953, Duke Ellington composed a piece commemorating his visit to Texas, whuch he entitled *Dallas Doings*, "a 'stomp' in the terminology of the times" that used riffs in the way Count Basie would in later years.[6] In the 1940s, Dizzy Gillespie and Charlie Parker brought their new bebop to the Recreation Building on East Vickery Street. But it was during the swing era that a number of native musicians from Cowtown took important roles in this period of jazz, notably drummer Ray McKinley and tenor saxophonist Tex Beneke.

Born on June 18, 1910, Ray McKinley began his career with bands in the Fort Worth and Dallas area, after which he played with various groups in Nashville and Pittsburgh and in 1930 at New York's Roseland Ballroon. Later, McKinley worked as a drummer and singer with the Dorsey Brothers during 1934 and 1935 and with Jimmy Dorsey from 1935 to 1939. Following his years with the Dorseys, McKinley and Will Bradley teamed up to form their own band, and at this time Ray scored several hits as a vocalists, including the highly popular boogie-woogie tune *Beat Me Daddy Eight to the Bar*, which "features genial singing by McKinley."[7]

After leaving Bradley to form his own band, Ray created two other boogie–woogie successes, *Rock–a–Bye Boogie* and *Down the Road a Piece*, although later Ray dropped this "bias" and performed "quite respectable jazz," with his tuba player, Joe Parks, "one of the first to play swinging melodic ensemble lines" on that instrument.[8] Although McKinley's own band was short–lived, he did lead a rather progresive band that performed "abstract atonal scores" by Eddie Sauter.[9] During the war, McKinley was a member of the Glenn Miller Army Air Force Band, taking over leadership of the unit along with Jerry Gray after Miller's plane disappeared in December 1944. While with the Miller Army Air Force Band, McKinley was in part responsible for the development of "swinging march arrangments of jazz tunes," one of which, W. C. Handy's *St. Louis Blues*, became the band's "most famous arrangement and recording."[10] As an "imaginative, tasteful" rhythm man, McKinley took "more than capable solos,"[11] and during the late 1930s and early 1940s, he was one of the most popular drummers in Dixeland circles. In general, McKinley "combined elements of showmanship with thoughtful, feeling performances" and is credited with being "a masterful timekeeper."[12]

Born on February 12, 1914, Tex Beneke was another Cowtown native who worked with Glenn Miller. In 1938, he starred in Miller's civilian band as both tenor saxophone soloist and vocalist, enabling Miller to succeed "in crashing the popular market."[13] Beneke was given more solo time by Miller than the orchestra's other tenorist, Al Klink, who "could easily outblow Tex as a swinging jazz musician." As George T. Simpson explains, Miller's preference for the Texan was owing to the fact that Beneke was "not merely a musician but also a commercial personality, and so [Glenn] never missed a chance to feature him."[14] Two of Beneke's biggest vocal successes were *I've Got a Gal in Kalamazoo* and *Chattanooga Choo Choo*, but like a number of other Texan musicians, including Buster Smith, "Tex's big ambition was to go back to Texas, eat some chili and play some blues."[15] Gunther Schuller, while acknowledging that Beneke's style fit Miller's "'smooth–it–out' philosophy to a T," is ruthless in his description of Tex's playing as "a kind of pablum version of [Coleman] Hawkins, to which Beneke in due course added mild dehydrated doses of Chu Berry and Lester Young." However, Schuller does allow that Tex "was a consistent player, reliable within his limitations, and never really embarrassing."[16] Despite the low esteem in which Beneke's playing is held, the Texan nonetheless became "world famous" as the most prominent musician during the heyday of Miller's hugely successful swing–era band.[17]

Neither of these Fort Worthians made, however, the sort of impact on jazz that Ornette Coleman and his generation would in the last years of the 1950s. While McKinley and Beneke paid their respects to the older traditions of the blues and boogie–woogie, Ornette Coleman began his career by hearing quite early the bebop music that a decade or so later his own free jazz would extend or even supersede. Unlike his white precedessors, Coleman was largely unaware of jazz history, as indicated by the fact that when, in 1959, Gunther Schuller introduced Ornette to Jelly Roll Morton's *Black Bottom Stomp*, he thought that the tune was "the best thing he'd ever heard in his life." Schuller adds that he played for Ornette "a lot of Louis Armstrong, Bessie Smith, God knows what, and a lot of this was a revelation to him about his own heritage."[18] However, if Coleman was not schooled in recorded jazz of earlier periods, he nevertheless demonstrates through his performances and his compositions that he experienced and absorbed in Texas—and in his travels to New York City, the Deep South, and the West Coast—the major jazz traditions.[19] For the most part, the music Coleman heard in Fort Worth was either rhythm and blues or in the vintage swing-era style, and Ornette's own favorites were Texas tenormen Illinois Jacquet and Arnett Cobb, as well as Big Jay McNeeley, "whose one-note riffing and antics won him several years of postwar fame."[20] Coleman, who played tenor in his early years and later recorded on this instrument in 1962 and 1986, admitted to being "more like a honker" who played "very freely rhythmically."[21] Another influence was the Louis Jordan jump band. In general, the music played by many of the musicians that Coleman listened to was "the sophisticated kind that marked the intersection of the jazz and blues traditions. Bebop musicians may have played in the Jacquet and Cobb bands, but these and the others . . . were rooted in the Swing Era, both harmonically and rhythmically."[22] Coleman reportedly first heard bebop at the age of fifteen when he visited New York City with an aunt and caught a performance by Dizzy Gillespie's first big band.[23] According to Dewey Redman, one of Coleman's classmates from Fort Worth's I. M. Terrell High School, Ornette soon could "play closest to Bird of anybody I've ever heard."[24]

If Coleman had already mastered the bop idiom by 1947 or thereabouts, it is easy to understand why he would be inspired to indulge "in some improvising in the midst of John Philip Sousa's *Washington Post March*," which resulted in his being booted out of the high school band.[25] This incident would set a pattern for Coleman's early career, for in 1948 he was fired from a job with the Fort Worth band of tenorist Red Connors after the group's employer objected to Ornette's solo on *Star Dust*, during which the saxophonist made "a crucial discovery," comparable to Charlie Parker's "innovatory harmonic extensions while jamming on standard chord changes" of *Cherokee*. Ornette realized that, once he knew all the changes of a tune, he could compact them in his head, which liberated his playing and proved the beginning of his investigation into "how to improvise without following the patterns of chord changes."[26] For this reason as well, it is understandable that when Ornette went on tour in 1949 with the Silas Green Minstrel Show—"a survivor of a much earlier era of American show business" that had launched the careers of such blues singers as Ma Rainey and Bessie Smith—the music he performed, such as Euday L. Bowman's *Twelfth Street Rag*, was "hardly inspiring to a young bebop saxophonist, but just the thing for the show's half-naked shake dancers."[27] Once again, Coleman was fired after trying to teach one of his fellow band members some of his bebop ideas. He was by this time in Natchez, Mississippi, where, after joining the band of blues singer Clarence Samuels, Ornette recorded for the first time, though this evidence of his "conventional R & B phase" was probably never issued.[28]

In writing of Coleman's association with Clarence Samuels, who had been with the Jay McShann band, with which Charlie Parker first recorded, Joachim Berendt remarks that Ornette's "origin in Texas and the world of country blues cannot be overemphasized." Berendt also comments that "jazz had always been superior in intensity to other musical forms of the Western world, but never before had the accent been on intensity in such an ecstatic, orgiastic—sometimes even religious—sense as in free jazz." For Berendt, Coleman and other free-jazz musicians "are closer to the 'concrete,' folk-music-like atonality of the 'field cry' and of the archaic folk blues than to 'abstract,' intellectual European atonality."[29] It was during Coleman's work with the Samuels band that history once again would repeat itself when he traveled with the group to Baton Rouge and his already free-jazz inclinations were visited on another unsuspecting audience. When the listeners at a local dance hall objected to Ornette's blues tenor solo and his long "Jesus-like beard," he was called outside by some men who proceeded to kick him in the stomach and rear until, in Ornette's words, he "blacked out cause blood was everywhere."[30] Fortunately, in suffering a broken collarbone that did not heal properly, Ornette was eventually rejected for service in Korea. In 1950, after landing in New Orleans, he first began to move into his "harmolodics," his method of employing a tune's melody as the basis of harmonic improvisation rather than its chord changes. Following a six-month stay in the Crescent City, Coleman returned to Fort Worth and formed his own group, which included another classmate from high school, Charles Moffett, who at the time played trumpet but would later switch to drums. The band soon secured a job in Amarillo, but when this ended, Ornette returned once more to Fort Worth, where he joined up with the Pee Wee Crayton band for a tour that, after a series of one-nighters, would strand him in Los Angeles.

Coleman's first stay in L.A. resulted in further rejection of his style of playing. James Clay, a tenor and flute man from Dallas, remembered the first time he ever heard Ornette: "He came in a club and started playin . . . and the band got up and left! Just up and split!"[31] The only encouragement came from such musicians as pianist Hampton Hawes and tenor saxophonist Teddy Edwards, who let Coleman sit in with them.[32] Coleman also renewed his friendship with a drummer he had met in New Orleans, Ed Blackwell, who, alternately with drummer Billy Higgins (a native of Los Angeles), would become an important member of Ornette's first major groups. But after enduring mostly scorn from musicians who said he "didn't know the changes and was out of tune," Ornette "telegraphed his mother to send enough money for him to return to Fort Worth."[33] But by 1952, Coleman's former schoolmates with whom he had often practiced in his mother's house—"because their own families objected to their playing in their own homes"[34]—had all left Cowtown. Coleman still found opportunities to jam and even formed another band to play rhythm and blues for local dances. However, once again, as Dallas trumpeter Bobby Bradford reported, Coleman was "doing things that nobody could associate with," and Ornette felt that he was simply marking time, so he determined "to give jazz, and Los Angeles, another chance."[35]

Back in L.A. in 1953, Coleman found that Ed Blackwell was still there, and Bobby Bradford, who had heard Ornette in Fort Worth, had also moved to the West Coast. Three other Texas musicians would eventually make their way to L.A. during the mid- and late 1950s: alto and flute player Prince Lasha, with whom Ornette had played at Terrell High School, moved to California in 1954; James Clay arrived in 1955; and tenor saxophonist Dewey Redman showed up in 1959. In the early 1960s clarinetist John Carter, also from Coleman's Fort Worth high school, would move to Los Angeles and form a group in 1965 with Bobby Bradford. All of these men had been or would be involved in Coleman's development, as would drummer Charles Moffett.

During his second stay in Los Angeles Coleman met Oklahoma City–born trumpeter Don Cherry, who, along with drummers Ed Blackwell and Billy Higgins, began to rehearse Ornette's music, and soon these three found themselves as jazzmen through Coleman's "freely mobile harmonic structures."[36] These rehearsals proved to be "the most important events in Ornette's career up to then" and "the most important events in post-Parker jazz."[37]

Coleman's first break came through his friendship with James Clay, who was born in Dallas on September 8, 1935, and worked there during high school with John Hardee at the Harmony Lounge. Clay's own initial recording date was in 1957 in Los Angeles when he cut an album with Lawrence Marable entitled *Jazz: West*; and that same year, on March 26, he recorded with Red Mitchell on the bass player's first leader date. Of Clay's playing on *Presenting Red Mitchell*, Nat Hentoff writes that "he could well end up laying the foundation for maybe the next step in jazz." However, Hentoff is not only hesitant in his prediction of Clay's future but quite vague as to the direction of this "next step."[38] Certainly Clay did not represent in the long run the kind of innovative thinking and execution achieved by Coleman; yet Clay was important to the furtherance of Ornette's music and contributed not only to the Mitchell recording but to another important album, on which he was featured along with a fellow native of Dallas, tenorist David "Fathead" Newman.

The Mitchell date involved what Robert Gordon terms "definitely a young and forward-looking band," which had Lorraine Geller on piano and Billy Higgins on drums. In Clay, Gordon hears "a proponent of the big-toned tenor style favored in the South West" and on flute finds him "singularly muscular."[39] The opening tune on *Presenting Red Mitchell* is Parker's *Scrapple from the Apple* and has Clay and

Mitchell playing the theme in an unusual tenor-contrabass combination that really works. Clay's solo, however, is eclipsed by that of Geller, who offers a dazzling display of her talents at the keyboard. Clay's flute work on Mitchell's original tune, *Rainy Night*, is much more satisfying, but once again Geller upstages him with a delightfully swinging chorus on piano. Clay's ideas seem half-formed and his playing a bit tentative, although his solo work is more assured on the Sonny Rollins tune, *Paul's Pal*. On *Sandu*, a Clifford Brown original, Clay's solo is especially flawed in comparison with the smooth rendition of this fine piece by Harold Land, who recorded it with Brown in February 1955, a year before the great trumpeter's fatal traffic accident.[40] Clay does, however, attempt more in his solo than does Land, who sticks closer to the melody. And the sound achieved by Clay can be quite appealing, as on *Cheek to Cheek*, which is his best tenor outing on the Mitchell album. Here Clay plays with real authority and swings without a hitch. Throughout his extended solo he is backed propulsively by Red's bass, Geller's tight comping, and Higgins's light cymbal work and his few but well-placed accents on the snare. However, except for Clay's performance on *Cheek to Cheek*, Geller pretty much steals the show, though Mitchell demonstrates how effective he could be as a soloist, in particular on this last tune. Unfortunately, after such an "auspicious debut,"[41] the quartet recorded no more albums because Clay left for Dallas and military service and Geller died tragically of apparent heart failure.

For an album on the Riverside label, Clay was featured with his fellow Texan David "Fathead" Newman, who was born in Dallas on February 24, 1933. Cannonball Adderley, who sponsored this recording session on April 26, 1960, called Clay and Newman "the first to emerge" from the so-called "Texas tenor sound" and its tradition "since Illinois Jacquet and Arnett Cobb made their debut on the national scene in the early 1940s." Adderley observed that neither of the younger tenorists exhibits the "'wildman' characteristics" of their predecessors but that they do have "an 'edge' to the horn sound (but *not* meaning any harshness)" as well as "a moan inside the tone."[42] Orrin Keepnews notes another connection with a Texas tradition when he points out that Newman began his professional career by working in Dallas with Buster Smith, mostly on R & B jobs. Together, Newman and Clay are said to represent "the broad expanses of Texas" in their "wide-open, surging sounds."[43] (In this regard, Arnett Cobb attributed his own "full tone" to "his incessant practice as a teenager in a large field near his Fifth Ward Houston home, where lots of sound was required to fill up the open space," and Booker Ervin's playing is said to have featured "the short, spasmodic, out-of-key runs . . . developed by going out to the woods and trying to frighten the birds.")[44] During this same year of 1960, Newman was with the Ray Charles orchestra when the pianist-singer recorded his smash hit,

Georgia on My Mind. Writing of Newman's tenor work with the band, Leonard Feather remarks that "like Charles himself, Newman has transcended his r & b background to earn a place in jazz as a soloist with a strong beat and funky quality combined with growing elements of individual tone and style."[45] From 1958 Newman can be heard on *Hard Times* playing his own gospel-soul tune, with that crying quality notable in blues-derived jazz, and on *Deed I Do* from 1959 the tenorist solos in a Jacquet-inspired mood.[46] Some of Newman's finest performances come on Ray Charles's *The Genius After Hours*, where with *Joy Ride* Fathead delivers an excellent solo on alto (which Leonard Feather claims is really his principal instrument) and reveals his Buster Smith–Charlie Parker roots. On a beautiful, slowed-down version of Fats Waller's classic, *Ain't Misbehavin'*, Newman offers "a full-toned and unpretentious tenor solo."[47]

In Adderley's comments on Newman's playing on the Riverside album, he singles out in particular the tenorist's tone as the brightest he has heard, attributing this to Fathead's R & B experience. This "same light, bright, buoyant" sound is fully evident in Newman's solo on the first tune, *Wide Open Spaces*, a blues written by Babs Gonzales, primarily known as "one of the first and best of 'bop' singers." As for Clay, his solo on this piece is again flawed, but he is in much better form on the sequence of choruses traded by the two tenors, when Clay blows "fervently" and with a control of his instrument that is lacking in his extended solo. Clay has only a few squawks on *They Can't Take That Away from Me* and crafts a very driving solo that is equaled by Newman's, which shows something of a Coltrane influence. Clay's performance on *Some Kinda Mean* is once again spoiled by squeaks and wrong notes, even though his ideas are solid and in keeping with this minor-key groover. Newman is also at home on this low-down blues, and both tenors create some fine breaks at the bridges. In the ballad *What's New*, Newman plays the melody with, again, more than a touch of the Coltrane style of embellishment, while Clay picks up his flute and shows that he is quite adept at achieving "a rich and sensitive" sound on this instrument, which was a favorite of a number of West Coast musicians, from Bud Shank and Buddy Collette to Texas transplants Prince Lasha and Hubert Laws. The final tune, *Figger-ration*, also by Gonzales, features another set of "rousing tenor 'fours'" following Clay's honking, squawking solo that manages to demonstrate his at times "advanced" conception as contrasted with Newman's smoother, brighter form of straight-ahead blowing. This last piece suggests that, in fact, more than Newman, Clay had the potential for what Nat Hentoff considered a progressive development in jazz. But even though at one time Clay was among "the Southern California jazz elite," his career did not go forward as it might have had he been willing to pursue the line of thinking opened up by Ornette Coleman.[48]

Clay and Newman would reunite for two albums in the 1990s, *Return to the Wide Open Spaces* and *Cookin' at the Continental*. The closing tune on the former album is Gonzales's *Wide Open Spaces*, which was the opener on the 1960 Riverside album, and not much has changed—the blowing is still hard and straight-ahead. Here Newman also plays some beautiful flute on his own tune, *13th Floor*. Of particular interest is *Hard Times*, with solos by both Newman and Clay and some impressive double-time baritone work by Leroy "Hog" Cooper, another Dallas native.[49] But perhaps the standout of this live session from the Caravan of Dreams in Fort Worth is the Texan trumpeter Dennis Dotson.[50] Dotson's clean yet fiery solos, both on Paul Mitchell's *Hard Times* and Gillespie's bop classic, *Night in Tunisia*, offer more than the rather predictable work of trumpeter Roy Hargrove on *Cookin' at the Continental*. Essentially, both Dotson and Hargrove hark back to bop or hard bop and represent retrenchment rather than any real advance.[51] Hargrove, who was born on October 16, 1969 in Waco, is featured on two tracks, Horace Silver's *Sister Sadie* and Bobby Timmons's *Moanin'*, a pair of hard-bop warhorses. Like Kenny Dorham, Richard Williams, and Marvin "Hannibal" Peterson before him, Hargrove has been admired not only for his "bop chops" but for his ballad treatments, which one reviewer characterized as uniting "bravura and lyricism" in a "sweet melancholia."[52] Hargrove has recorded with his own groups as well as with a number of saxmen, including Sonny Rollins. As for Clay, his best outings on the *Cookin' at the Continental* album are his swinging interpretation of Hoagy Carmichael's *Georgia on My Mind* and his interchange with bassist Christian McBride on *Crazeology*, while Clay's playing on *Barbados* and *You're Mine, You!* provide glimpses of a bit more daring than usual. However, Clay ultimately remains a fairly staid and conservative jazzman, even though his work clearly reveals an awareness of not only the great Texas tenor tradition but of certain stylistic developments introduced by Sonny Rollins and John Coltrane.

In 1956, prior to his recordings with Red Mitchell and Fathead Newman, James Clay convinced Ornette Coleman to participate in a bop group known as the Jazz Messiahs, which included Don Cherry and Billy Higgins. At the Haig, the Los Angeles club where the Gerry Mulligan–Chet Baker Quartet had made its reputation in 1952, the Jazz Messiahs performed original tunes by Don Cherry during intermissions. When Coleman attended a Jazz Messiahs rehearsal in the garage of co-leader George Newman, Ornette brought along his own compositions and tried to persuade Clay to join him in a group. But Clay, who found Coleman's music written wrong, even though he could play it, told Coleman that it was not his thing. Nonetheless, when Clay was also working at the Haig, he invited Coleman to sit in, and, as a result, bassist Red Mitchell heard Coleman for the first time. Later, Mitchell would hear Coleman again, and although his reaction was mixed, he was favorably impressed by Ornette's compositions, enough to recommend that Contemporary records listen to his songs. Lester Koenig, the label's producer, asked Coleman and Don Cherry to run through a few of Ornette's pieces, and Koenig was so enthusiastic that he not only offered to buy the composer's tunes but also gave him a recording date as leader.[53]

During three Contemporary sessions on February 10 and 22 and March 24, 1958, Coleman, Cherry, and Higgins, along with Walter Norris on piano and Don Payne on bass, recorded *Something Else! The Music of Ornette Coleman*. Although this first album has generally been considered less successful than Ornette's second recording for Contemporary or his first for Atlantic, owing largely to the fact that the piano was "an inhibiting factor,"[54] *Something Else!* introduced listeners to a music that, as Billy Higgins commented to Nat Hentoff, would "make you think."[55] For the most part, as Don Cherry remarked, this album marked the debut of Ornette's ability to write and play "how he feels. . . . [H]e uses a plastic alto; it has a drier, warmer sound without the ping of the metal. . . . He has real control of pitch, and pitch is so important to him. He now can express on his horn what he hears, and he has a very unusual ear."[56] Above all, this album gave the first hints of the "freedom principle" that would guide the direction of Coleman's music and in turn would begin "the Ornette Coleman era."[57] Coleman himself provides perhaps the most clairvoyant view of what he intended, which sounds in many ways like the theories propounded by such American poets as Walt Whitman, Charles Olson, Robert Creeley, and Robert Duncan: "I think one day music will be a lot freer. Then the pattern for a tune, for instance, will be forgotten and the tune itself will be the pattern, and won't have to be forced into conventional patterns. The creation of music is just as natural as the air we breathe."[58]

The first three tunes are indicative of the revolutionary nature of Coleman's music. With *Invisible*, as the composer notes, "the melodic direction is pretty free," and with *The Blessing* (which was "written in a park at Fort Worth at one or two in the morning"), the melodic line is, as Cherry remarks, "rhythmically free." Likewise, of *Jayne*, named for poet Jayne Cortez and Ornette's wife at the time, the composer observes that "the drummer can help determine direction too, because he can turn phrases around on a different beat, for example, thereby raising the freedom of my playing."[59] Nonetheless, as Martin Williams has pointed out, Coleman's early recordings "do not so much outline his own music as they juxtapose some of his own ideas with those of his predecessors."[60] To Hsio Wen Shih, Coleman "is a highly traditional player" who "loves some of the strong and simple rhythmic ideas of the thirties as much as he does the more complex and subtle conceptions that Parker introduced."[61] Williams finds that Coleman's first album, made up entirely of original tunes written in Fort Worth, still has clinging to it "the rhythms and forms of bebop" and that some of the tunes "use popular song sequences recognizably: *Jayne* echoes *Out of Nowhere* and *Angel Voice* is Ornette's *I Got Rhythm.*" Williams goes on to observe that Ornette's playing is "at its most 'free' and most personal" in the "somewhat tonally ambiguous blues" tune *The Disguise.*[62] If Coleman's debut album was largely a juxtaposition of freedom and traditional form, it had for most listeners a distinctly new sound and rhythmic character, regardless of its debts to the past or its inhibition by a clash of chord changes from the piano and bass against Ornette's freer melodic and harmonic spirit. For those like Bobby Bradford, who first heard Coleman in Fort Worth in 1953, there was most importantly "an urgency and dead seriousness in Ornette's music that said things weren't going to be about Jim Crow or a resigned black man or West Coast cool any longer."[63]

A second album for Contemporary was entitled *Ornette Coleman: "Tomorrow Is the Question!"* and the personnel reflected the producer's idea that, since Coleman's first album did not do well commercially, he would "stir up more marketplace action" by bringing in Red Mitchell on bass and Shelly Manne on drums.[64] The results were not entirely satisfying, in part because Mitchell and Manne did not quite grasp Coleman's "free" approach. An indication of Coleman's own dissatisfaction was his seeking out Modern Jazz Quartet bassist Percy Heath—who had spoken glowingly of Ornette's music—as a replacement for Mitchell on a second studio session of March 9–10, 1959, the first sessions having taken place on January 16 and February 23. Despite a certain conservatism that characterizes this album in comparison with Coleman's work with his later combos, Martin Williams asserts that "it should certainly not be overlooked."[65] And John Litweiler declares that *Lorraine,* a tribute to pianist Lorraine Geller, contains "one of the most vividly dramatic solos Ornette ever recorded."[66]

From the opening title piece—*Tomorrow Is the Question!*—Coleman and Cherry demonstrate their uncanny ability to play Ornette's angular melodies totally in sync with one another, as could Gillespie and Parker on their albums and Richard Williams and Leo Wright on theirs, although in a more "orthodox" bebop manner. Here for the first time Cherry uses his Pakistani pocket trumpet that complements so wonderfully Coleman's plastic alto. Overall, the album displays the wide emotional range of Coleman's compositions, from *Lorraine,* a gripping lament that heralds the coming of Ornette's classic *Lonely Woman,* to the humor of *Giggin',* the philosophical *Mind and Time* that, in Cherry's words, "gives the soloist the freedom to establish new pitches, new forms and rhythms," and the moving *Compassion,* written by Ornette to counter the notion, as he says, that "human emotion and mind" are "just a matter of environment."[67] Both *Lorraine* and the twelve-bar blues *Tears Inside* exhibit Coleman's patented keening cry that is so penetratingly human and that brings to a new level the long tradition of blues singing as developed from slavery's field hollers and African American church songs. Although both Mitchell and Heath were obviously sympathetic to Coleman's music, they were neither right nor ready for his revolutionary approach that encouraged greater freedom and responsiveness from each member of the group. While Don Cherry praises Manne's drum solo on *Lorraine*, Shelly simply belongs to another school of jazz, and Martin Williams is correct when he states that Manne plays "almost carelessly,"[68] despite from time to time an effective roll on snare or cymbal. As for Ornette's playing and writing, they answer any question as to where jazz would be tomorrow.

Coleman's first album for Atlantic, the New York label he moved to with the support of John Lewis and the assent of Contemporary, was aptly entitled *The Shape of Jazz to Come* and opens with *Lonely Woman*, which probably remains Ornette's most "popular" composition. This album also introduces for the first time a completely unified and mutually compatible group that includes, along with Coleman and Cherry, bassist Charlie Haden and drummer Billy Higgins. Recorded in May 1959, *The Shape of Jazz to Come* is the culmination of Ornette's early work and stands as the clearest statement of his musical thinking. Here again is a wide variety of compositional styles, which are characterized by Whitney Balliett when he writes that Coleman "has invented his own language, and it is abstract, aphoristic, poetic, philosophical, comic, and nonsensical."[69] Along with *Lonely Woman* and *Peace*, which "quickly went into the repertoires of other jazz musicians," John Litweiler singles out Ornette's *Focus on Sanity* as perhaps the album's "most remarkable work . . . a composition, with several tempos and themes, that could only be realized through improvisation—and not the role-playing kinds of improvisation that Charles Mingus often called for from his interpreters. Ornette, instead, used his players' own choices to unite in a whole musical statement."[70] A humorous piece, *Congeniality*, has a slower second theme that suggested to composer Andrew Rudin—with whom I first heard the piece in 1961—a countrified utterance of the words "Ah'm goin' tooooooo Foat Wuth." Here Coleman's solo combines the down-home with phrases from Tchaikovsky's Piano Concerto in B-flat Minor at the same time that it contains the keening and soulful sounds found in Ornette's more melancholy tunes. Cherry's solo is equally comical, as he too interpolates unexpected phrases, in his case from *Surrey with the Fringe on Top*. Martin Williams, speaking of Coleman's quotation of *Do I Love You* on *Turnaround* (on the second Contemporary album), is pleased that Ornette rarely resorts to such a bebop practice.[71] Yet both Coleman and Cherry integrate their interpolations into the overall structure and meaning of their solos to achieve a motivic unity that is logical and witty. Williams does concede that *Congeniality* is an excellent introduc-

Ornette Coleman
of Fort Worth.
Reproduced from the
Ross Russell Collec-
tion, courtesy of the
Harry Ransom
Humanities Research
Center, University of
Texas at Austin.

tion to the way Coleman "is extending the whole idea of instrumental composition in jazz."[72]

As for *Lonely Woman*, in this classic tune the two horns play with exemplary sensitivity to one another, and they are supported brilliantly and tastefully by Haden on bass and Higgins on drums, who open the piece, respectively, with subtle and suggestive pluckings of strings and double-time tappings on tom-tom. Haden responds melodically to Coleman and creates another voice rather than restricting himself to a timekeeping role, which even Red Mitchell, Shelly Manne, and Percy Heath tended to do despite their attraction to greater independence. John Litweiler concisely describes the important achievement of this group performance of Coleman's composition: "'Lonely Woman' turns the conventional bop ensemble structure inside out, with its fast tempo set by the drummer, the bass playing accents rather than meter or velocity, and the two horns playing the slow, rubato theme over it all. Pity, sorrow, sympathy, and resignation emerge in succession from the theme, qualities amplified in Ornette's solo."[73] For the tune *Eventually*, Litweiler likewise supplies an excellent description of the way Coleman's three-note motif "makes for compact construction" even as it evolves through "varied thrusts" that stab "up, then down, beginning phrases, or leading to fearful, trapped phrases that alternate with long screams and saxophone squalls."[74] Unlike James Clay's accidental squeaks and squawks, Ornette's screams and squalls are intentional and create the agony that contrasts with "the optimistic composed portions" of the *Eventually* theme.[75] Close analysis of these Coleman pieces not only supports Bobby Bradford's view that there is "an urgency and dead seriousness in Ornette's music" but reveals the artistic unity and emotional design of Coleman's compositions and of their performances by Ornette and his first ideally suited ensemble.

In October 1959, Coleman's group flew to New York to record more sides for Atlantic, and most of these would be issued on *Change of the Century*. The first two tunes on this album, *Ramblin'* and *Free*, have each received close analysis by Don Heckman and John Litweiler (in the latter case with the assistance of David Wild). As their titles suggest, *Ramblin'* in many ways represents a return to the roots of jazz, while *Free* stands as the doorway to the future of this music, which, as we have seen, had many of its beginnings in Texas and would now be carried forward by Ornette Coleman and other Texan and non-Texan exponents of the free-jazz movement. However, in certain respects both of these pieces derive from earlier styles even as they typify the tendencies of the postbebop era. For example, Heckman observes that Coleman's solo on *Ramblin'* "illuminates the connection between the old and new jazz, at the same time underlining the vast differences,"[76] while Hsio Wen Shih points out that *Free* is "almost no more than a boogie-woogie bass line, but who would have expected those quarter notes on the beat, mostly broken chords, to be played to give that effortless soaring quality?" *Ramblin'*, which Wen Shih calls "a good hillbilly flavored jazz tune" and "the only unqualified success on the record, theme, ensembles, solos and all,"[77] was described by Coleman himself as "basically a blues, but it has a modern, more independent melodic line than older blues have, of course."[78]

In his close analysis of Ornette's chorus on *Ramblin'*, Heckman finds that it is "shaped like a blues, with each of the three primary sections separated by a rhythmic vamp." And the piece "makes extensive use of familiar blues fragments," but these are "subjected to Coleman's special pitch production and free rhythmic placement." Yet the critic goes on to say that "unlike some of Coleman's other works, *Ramblin'* does not permit the soloist complete freedom. Each solo is accompanied by a recurring rhythm section pattern of alternating 16- and 12-bar sections." Of Coleman's own solo, Heckman notes that it "both ignores and conforms to" the rhythm section pattern and that while his playing can fall behind this accompaniment and develop a "relatively free phrasing," Ornette's "over-all improvisational conception in this work is dominated by the three-part sectionalization characteristic of the blues."[79] Heckman and a number of other commentators on Coleman's music have remarked that it shares with that of Lester Young a "prolific use of harmonic melodies, and [Young's] flowing, Southwestern-styled rhythms," which often come behind the beat. Heckman also refers to Young's "low-note honks" and a use of "noise elements" as being employed by Coleman "for accent and punctuation."[80] In discussing the parallels between Young and Coleman, jazz composer George Russell calls the latter's "horizontal chromaticism," which had been "unexplored up until Ornette," "the logical end of the way Lester Young started out playing."[81] Even on *Ramblin'*, which Martin Williams terms "a sort of light, blues impression of a Southwestern hoe-down,"[82] Coleman demonstrates that he is not only the "logical end" of a development from the blues through swing and bop but that he is "the most dramatic example of a new music."[83]

John Litweiler, who considers the early period of Coleman's career his greatest, has found Ornette's solo on *Free* from the 1960 *Change of the Century* album "among his very best, for its construction and for its great fire."[84] Applying to Coleman's chorus the phrase "sheets of sound"—first used by Ira Gitler to describe the "superhuman" music of John Coltrane[85]—Litweiler analyzes the opening of Ornette's solo on *Free* as being composed of "rising and falling eighth notes" that "begin and end irregularly" in contrast to the theme of the tune which consists of "arpeggios rising and falling over two whole octaves, in eighth notes," with the alto soloist's phrases coming as "rising sheets of sound and angular tumbles rather than even drops." Litweiler then finds that "a crucial development begins in measure 38" with a "four-note motive," which is "quickly atomized into a three-note motive" that is "embedded in the repetitive passages of measures 52–62." The unity of Coleman's solo results, for Litweiler, in "the rising-falling contours that recur throughout" and in the "further sequencing of a two-note motive in measures 87–96." Litweiler also finds a characteristic development in the jazzman's tendency "within two years" to "begin expending particular energy on the direct statement and variation of small motives." For Litweiler, the conclusion of the solo "not only returns to its initiating contours," but it "transforms the emotional content": "In place of the fiery exultation that had heretofore ruled, measures 123–129 are a single phrase that rises five times and drops precipitously, as much as an entire octave, as though battering against a barrier. And when the alto is suspended, finally, without bass-drums support, the result is the frustration expressed in a four-note trill, before the tumbling angularities of the concluding measures." Litweiler completes his analysis of this solo by contrasting Coleman's playing with that of other soloists of the period, including "some of the best." Whereas "the only element of formal unity in their solos was their adherence to recurring chord changes," Litweiler says, Ornette's *Free* solo of "only a minute and a half in length" is "shattering in its power" and "a particularly remarkable achievement—clearly, 'free form' meant, not 'free from form,' but 'free to create form,' and that remains true of the best post-Coleman musicians right up to the present."[86]

In late 1960 and early 1961, Ornette Coleman produced two other revolutionary albums and participated in a performance of Third Stream compositions by Gunther Schuller as well. On *Jazz Abstractions*, which Litweiler considers "an unfortunately ignored album," Coleman appears as a soloist for Schuller's compositions entitled *Abstraction* and *Variants on a Theme of Thelonious Monk (Criss-Cross)*, recorded in New York on December 19, 1960. Litweiler calls *Abstraction* "among the best demonstrations" of the recurring contrasts in Schuller's Third Stream music between "a seemingly constricted, 'correct' classical ensemble yearning for expressive freedom with jazz's realization of that freedom."[87] In writing of the two-part live performances of *Abstraction* at the Circle in the Square from December 20, 1960, which came before and after intermission, Martin Williams reports that "Coleman's grasp of the piece was so thorough that he was able to find his way in it not only with two different improvisations but in two different ways." Williams compares Ornette's first performance, where "he improvised within the textures," to "an early Mozart concerto," and his second, where he improvised "against and in a parallel foil," to the textures in "a Beethoven concerto."[88] On *Variants on a Theme of Thelonious Monk*, which Williams considers a jazz work and not a classical one (neither term for the critic is "a really accurate description of what one heard that evening, and the second turned out to be nearly nonsense"), Coleman improvised using "Monk's melody as his basis in a way I wish Monk could have heard."[89] Williams points especially to "a kind of overlapping, free polyphony" that occurred when a soloist entered while a preceding soloist was still playing: "Hearing Ornette Coleman and Eric Dolphy improvising simultaneously on a Monk theme was, in itself, more than most jazz concerts have to offer." Williams concludes, on the basis of a single hearing, that *Variants* is "a major work (based on Monk's already major piece!) not only within the jazz idiom, but legitimately extending it."[90]

The day after these live performances, Coleman and Dolphy recorded an album that bears the foundational title of *Free Jazz*, on which two quartets of mirror personnel improvise simultaneously, creating during thirty-eight minutes a collective improvisation that Martin Williams confirms "has the stuff of life in it as no other recorded performance I know of."[91] Earlier, on August 2, 1960, Coleman's quartet (with Ed Blackwell on drums) recorded *Beauty Is a Rare Thing*, on which the four musicians also engaged in a collective improvisation. In the liner notes for *This Is Our Music*, the album containing *Beauty Is a Rare Thing*, Coleman writes that the most important part of our music is the improvisation, which is done as spontaneously as possible, with each man contributing his musical expression to create the form. . . . Group improvisation is not new. In early jazz, that kind of group playing was known as Dixieland. In the swing era, the emphasis changed and improvisation took the form of solos based on riffs. In modern jazz, improvisation is melodic and harmonically progressive. Now we are blending the three together to create and give more freedom to the player and more pleasure to the listener.[92]

But whereas in Dixieland there are generally only three horns improvising (trumpet, clarinet, and trombone), on *Free Jazz* there are eight musicians—two reeds, two trumpets, two basses, and two drummers—performing either as soloists backed by the rest of the ensemble's "comments, encouragements, and counter melodies" or as part of the group response that weaves "turbulent, purposeful, harrowing, and joyous textures."[93] In explaining the intent of this recording, Coleman emphasizes that "the most important thing . . . was for us to play together, all at the same time, without getting in each other's way, and also to have enough room for each player to ad lib alone—and to follow this idea for the duration of the album."[94] In the liner notes to *Free Jazz*, Martin Williams attests that "this is an exceptional record," even as it partakes of the time-honored tradition of collective improvisation established by New Orleans jazz. Here, however, the playing is not determined by a given tune or by chord changes but is polyphony based on musical ideas or directions in one player's improvisation to which other players respond and are propelled forward, with no other guidelines than "a few, brief pre-set sections." The object, Williams explains, is "to encourage the improvisor to be freer, and not obey a pre-conceived chord-pattern according to set ideas of 'proper' harmony and tonality." In Coleman's words, the goal was "to play the music and not the background." Ultimately, as Williams suggests, a listener who is not "bothered about 'newness' or 'difference'" on *Free Jazz* but hears in it only "someone crying, talking, laughing" is having the soundest sort of response to Ornette Coleman's music.[95]

A third recording session from the winter of 1960–1961 took place on January 31 in New York, when the Coleman Quartet, with Scott LaFaro on bass, produced four tunes that would comprise the Atlantic album entitled simply *Ornette!* As with five of the Atlantic albums from 1960 and 1961, with the sole exception of *This Is Our Music*, which contains a Gershwin standard (*Embraceable You*), *Ornette!* consists entirely of Coleman's original compositions. In this album, the titles of the tunes are not as witty or descriptive as usual but are merely enigmatic initials.[96] In the liner notes for *Ornette!*, Gunther Schuller offers the following summary of Coleman's simple proposition: "Release me from the bondage of long out-dated harmonic and formal conventions, and I will take you away from the wall-paper clichés of my contemporaries and let you hear a world of sound which you have never heard before, which is free, and which is beholden only to its *own* innermost logic and discipline."[97]

Despite this revolutionary-sounding pronouncement, Coleman's playing on *Ornette!* may be heard in many respects as a return to the eighteenth-century approach of J. S. Bach's *Partitas for Unaccompanied Violin*. In the famous concluding Chaconne section of Bach's Partita No. 2 in D Minor (BWV 1004), the violin score consists of a series of variations on a few chords stated at the beginning of this movement, which lasts for over thirteen minutes. The chaconne itself has been likened to "those types of jazz in which a fixed bass, reinforced by the rhythm section, becomes the point of departure for virtuosic improvisations by a melody instrument (trumpet, clarinet, saxophone)."[98] Although Bach forgoes any accompanying rhythm section, his composition implies a rhythmic beat, but, more important, it exhibits a seemingly inexhaustible fund of ideas generated by the chords from the opening bars of the chaconne. On Coleman's quartet recording, Ornette is accompanied throughout by LaFaro on bass and Ed Blackwell on drums, who represent the free collective polyphony of Dixieland as they respond to the sax's extended solos, which themselves are variations on riffs or motives derived from the tunes' atonal themes. Coleman's solos on *C. & D.* and *R.P.D.D.* are both amazing examples of "virtuosic improvisations" that, like Bach's chaconne, spin out endless variations on rhythmic and motivic patterns. In terms of duration, *C. & D.* takes up over thirteen minutes, and although Ornette's solo lasts only about half that time, on the two tunes taken together, Coleman's combined improvisations on *C. & D.* and *R.P.D.D.* total about the same length as the violin solo on Bach's final movement of the Partita No. 2.

Gunther Schuller's description of Coleman's solos on his two pieces places them clearly in the same creative realm as that of Bach's chaconne:

Like the theme of *C. & D.*, with its short motive treated sequentially, only to be answered by a tonality-disrupting phrase of rising fourths, his solo on *R.P.D.D.*, in expanded form, follows the same general pattern. Little motives are attacked from every conceivable angle, tried sequentially in numerous ways until they yield a motivic springboard for a new and contrasting idea, which will in turn be developed similarly, only to yield to yet another link in the chain of musical thought, and so on until the entire statement has been made.[99]

Schuller goes on to relate Coleman's "ability to exploit the unusual tonal-timbral characteristics of the alto" to the tradition of jazz sounds produced by Louis Armstrong's "gravel-voiced vocalism or [Joe "Tricky Sam"] Nanton's legendary trombone growls," as well as the "sonority investigations" of Sonny Rollins. He concludes that "the purposely split tones, harmonics, and abrasively guttural low register sounds" in Ornette's playing have not only a beauty of the same sort but "an inevitability about them that removes them from the merely experimental." While there is no denying that Coleman's solo remains largely "a world of sound which you have never heard before," it still belongs to the two grand traditions of European and African music—the theme and variation of a form such as the chaconne and the instrumentalizing of the vocal blues—at the same time that there is in Ornette's "hillbilly" or "hoedown" phrasing, tone quality, and rhythmic patterns something of his southwestern heritage.[100] One view of Coleman's achievement has proclaimed that the new jazz fostered by Ornette "is as organic and inevitable a part of the jazz continuum as it is iconoclastic, and . . . it is among the most important and exciting expressions in the history of music."[101]

In the summer of 1961, Coleman was joined in New York by two musicians from Fort Worth and Dallas, Charles Moffett and Bobby Bradford. A former schoolmate of Ornette's at I. M. Terrell High School and a high school band director for eight years in Texas, Moffett was born in Fort Worth on September 11, 1929, and came to New York in 1961 to try his luck as a professional drummer, becoming a member of Coleman's octet in June of that year. Trumpeter Bobby Bradford, with whom Ornette had worked in Los Angeles, both in Ornette's practicing band and together at a department store, was born in Cleveland, Mississippi, on July 19, 1934. Bradford grew up in Dallas and graduated from Lincoln High School, then attended several Texas colleges (including the University of Texas and Huston-Tillotson College, both in Austin).[102]

Moffett and Bradford would not only form part of Coleman's octet but also of his "working" quartet, which rarely performed publicly during this period, when Ornette began to demand higher pay for his music, tripling the price to bring "it more in line with his music's value."[103] As a result of Coleman's refusal to accept less than he expected, the quartet members found little work during the last months of 1961 and most of 1962 and had to take other jobs to support themselves. Moffett taught as a substitute teacher while Bradford finally returned to Texas before he could record with Coleman. Apparently there were some Atlantic sides with the octet cut in June 1961, but these were never issued.[104]

For Moffett, his first recorded session with Coleman came at a concert at New York's Town Hall on December 21, 1962, which was considered a major event. Ornette's latest bass player, David Izenzon, as well as Moffett made up the Ornette Coleman Trio. In addition to the trio, the concert included a string quartet that performed Coleman's composition entitled *Dedication to Poets and Writers*, a work that achieves what perhaps Scott Joplin, Bix Beiderbecke, and Charlie Parker may have longed to create: a purely classical work of "legitimate" music. A very melodic piece with moving parts for the strings that develop commentaries among the quartet members in the same manner as Coleman's collective group improvisations, *Dedication* is derived from a "five-note cell motive . . . with fast and slow sections, harmonic and contrapuntal turmoil . . . resolving in the end, after agitated dissonance, with an unanticipated consonant, hymnlike chord, a touch of pure Ornette humor."[105] As for Moffett and Izenzon, they seem at times superfluous to Ornette's improvisations, especially on *The Ark*, a twenty-three-minute-plus performance by the trio that itself is more classical than jazz. But for John Litweiler this work represents "drastic changes in Ornette's music," for Izenson and Moffett were "quite unlike any bassists and drummers who had recorded previously" with Coleman. Moffett is described by Litweiler as "a master of several styles" who "often changed the character of his accompaniments." On *The Ark* he, Izenzon, and Coleman remain "seemingly independent of each other at the beginning."[106] With the "non-support" of his fellow Texan, Ornette was once again furthering his principle of musical freedom.

Following this concert, Coleman withdrew from live performances into a silence that endured until January 8, 1965, when the trio reemerged to play for three weeks at New York's Village Vanguard. Afterward, Coleman once more fell silent, only to surface in London for a concert on August 29, this time with the trio and a woodwind quintet, the latter performing Ornette's *Forms and Sounds*, a wholly composed work conforming "to the post-Schoenbergian idiom" and described by the composer as "a combination of diatonic and atonal intervals that creates a form out of a sound and a sound out of a form in which the five instruments blend, not by coming together, but by moving in opposing directions."[107] Just as Coleman's classical piece for woodwind quintet was paradoxical in its unity by opposition, so his piece for the trio, entitled *Silence*, blends periods of silence with sudden bursts of sound for a performance in which these two opposing states complement one another with affective force.

Coleman's self-imposed silence for himself and his trio came dramatically to an end with the August performances of Ornette's "forms and sounds" in London and later in the fall in Stockholm. On *Silence*, Moffett urges Coleman along in his

Ornette Coleman (center) with David Izenzon (left) and Charles Moffett of Fort Worth (right). Reproduced from *The Ornette Coleman Trio at the "Golden Circle," Stockholm* (Blue Note 84224); photograph by Francis Wolff.

energetic passages that alternate with weepy phrases that are directly emotive and deeply moving. For *Ballad*, another simply titled tune on which ironically Ornette achieves a greater level of intensity than perhaps any other jazz musician, Moffett helps to intensify the effect with his tom-toms, until the sax and bass in the upper register end on unbelievably complementary pitches, approved on the recording by a whistling audience. Certainly Charlie Parker could also create such intense musical moments as this, and while of a different sort, Parker's and Coleman's playing is of the same order of magnitude. *Sadness* is another classic performance by Ornette, with his crying alto tone, which is so much a part of jazz's oldest blues tradition, delivering in his theme statement a heavy emotional punch.

As so often in the pieces recorded at the London concert, *Falling Star* finds Moffett echoing on his drums the notes and tonal colors of Coleman's playing, which in this composition is given over to high blasts and clearly articulated, humorous ditties on trumpet, and then to the distinctive swing of Ornette's "sheets of sound" on violin. These last are complemented beautifully by Izenzon on bass, and Moffett responds to them with drum rolls and rising and falling rhythmic patterns that parallel perfectly Coleman's "cascades of very short notes" and the "gloriously tangled textures" produced by the two string players. For Victor Schonfeld, Moffett's "torrential contributions" are in fact "in many ways the focal point of the whole apocalyptic performance."[108] According to Ludvig Rasmusson, Moffett, although standing "somewhat in the shadow of the two greats" (Coleman and Izenzon), was "probably the only [drummer] in today's world who could fit into Ornette Coleman's trio."[109] Discussing Moffett's role on the trio's *Golden Circle* album, recorded in Stockholm, Martin Williams writes that by this time the drummer "had elaborated his basic, down-home style (a style appropriate to Coleman, who is basically a bluesman) so that he became capable of an appropriate variety of textures."[110]

Charles Moffett could also "fit in" with other groups playing the new jazz, as he did on the "first major session" with Archie Shepp as a leader, which the album cover labels a "milestone in the history of jazz music." Recorded on August 10, 1964, during Ornette's "silence," Shepp's *Four for Trane* album features a "really impressive" group that has John Tchicai from Denmark on alto, Roswell Rudd on trombone, Alan Shorter on trumpet, and Reggie Workman on bass, with Moffett "heard to good advantage . . . heavy, precise, driving the beat."[111] On Coltrane's *Cousin Mary*, a "hard blues," Moffett is active throughout, answering with fills that complete the sense of Shepp's phrases, toning down his drum responses behind Shorter and Tchicai in keeping with their less aggressive choruses, and using all his battery of percussion instruments to spur on the hornmen. For Coltrane's classic ballad, *Niema*, Moffett leaves the beat-keeping chores to Workman and only punctuates tastefully when the ensemble enters during Shepp's virtuosic improvisation, which comprises the first half of Rudd's arrangement of Trane's tune. During the second half, which opens with Roswell as featured virtuoso, Moffett does a little beat-keeping behind the trombonist and Shepp, as well as supplying more of the drummer's carefully placed accents.

Rufus, which is closer to Coleman's music in its fast "changes" on repeated motifs, is also ably supported by Moffett, who yet remains independently active, working out his own motivic bits and pieces. Toward the end of *Rufus*, the drummer takes a fairly traditional break that leads into the tune's Mingus-like "insanity" theme. *Syeeda's Song Flute* finds Moffett especially busy behind the horns, as he and Workman maintain the tune's drive while Shepp strains for the ineffable note and Rudd tests for every possibility high and low, fast and double-time, with "his big muscular trombone sound."[112] Accompanying Workman's solo, Moffett seems to know just where the bassist is going and plays the same tones on his drums, after which Moffett himself takes his best solo on the album, full of meaningful rhythmic ideas and percussive tonal colors. On *Mr. Syms*, Moffett's drumming, in its rhythmic and tonal offerings behind Shorter on trumpet and Shepp on tenor, is more appealing than anything these horn soloists manage with repetitive exertions that tend to go nowhere.

As with his later work on the London concert album, where Moffett would blend so effectively with Coleman and Izenzon even as he went his own way, the drummer demonstrates on this Shepp recording that he did not need to resort to dull pounding or senseless banging but could communicate a sense of direction in his tasteful playing both as soloist and accompanist. Although Moffett was fired by Coleman in 1968, apparently after he began to double on trumpet and Ed Blackwell came in on percussion, Charles had already made a significant contribution to Coleman's music, in particular to the trio that represents in some ways Ornette's freest group and that "created a sensation virtually everywhere [the three men] played."[113]

❂ ❂ ❂

William "Prince" Lasha (pronounced la-SHAY), a classmate of Coleman and Moffett, was born in Fort Worth on September 10, 1929. Although Lasha had often practiced with his fellow Fort Worthians and had even co-led a band with Coleman while still in high school, Prince never recorded with Ornette. After living in New York for a time in the early 1950s, Lasha moved in 1954 to California, meeting altoist Sonny Simmons and working with him intermittently.[114] In 1962, Simmons took a trip with Lasha to Fort Worth, where, Sonny remembered, they "met and played with some fabulous musicians . . . and I felt at home because they were really in that thing, that free thing, you know, natural."[115] In 1967, Lasha and Simmons would invite Charles Moffett to serve as the drummer for their second album produced by Contemporary, which, as noted earlier, was the first record label to issue Coleman's music.

Lasha and Simmons made their first recording—*"The Cry!"*—in Los Angeles on November 21, 1962. Just as Coleman's free jazz was being termed at this time "a study in contrast between primitive and ultra modern,"[116] so the Lasha-Simmons album was described as a combination of "the cry of the Negro fieldworker, a victim of slavery and its aftermath, and the cry of the abstract jazzman, caught up in a world of prejudice and atomic tensions . . . both are spontaneous outpourings of protest."[117] Lester Koenig, in his album notes, cites semanticist S. I. Hayakawa's definition of field cries in both vocal and instrumental American music and jazz as "what gives American popular musicians and singers their unique and world-wide appeal."[118] Koenig then connects the work of the Prince Lasha Quintet to the idea that "the cry of new jazz comes from men who know the rules and consciously struggle to free themselves from their tyranny in order to move into less studied, uninhibited expressions of basic human emotions."[119] In all of this, the quintet represents another instance of Ornette Coleman's search for freedom from "the stultifying effects of cadential formulas" and for an effective "unleashing of the jazz soloist."[120] Also like Coleman's music, the quintet's playing on *The Cry!* is a blend of past and present, which in many ways is characteristic of the work of all the Fort Worth jazzmen of Ornette's generation, particularly, as we shall see, the work of John Carter.

The first selection on the quintet's album is *Congo Call*, based on "an impression of African tribal music, gained from listening to recordings."[121] Two string basses, played by Gary Peacock (who also recorded with Jimmy Giuffre) and Mark Proctor, open the piece, with a different ostinato pattern laid down by each bassist. On top of this the alto of Simmons and the flute of Lasha create a primitive but sophisticated sound in which the two instrumentalists complement one another rather than compete. Once the hornmen are on their own as soloists, it is clearly Simmons who is the superior improviser, achieving a cry on his alto that is definitely imitative of Coleman. A similar effect is achieved by Simmons's solo on *Bojangles*, although on this tune, named for the great tap dancer, Sonny does an Ornette imitation after his own manner, which is marked by a lusher sound and more repetition of the same ideas. The drummer on this second piece is Gene Stone, whose playing behind Peacock's fine bass solo is rather dull and probably accounts for the substitution of Moffett on the subsequent Lasha-Simmons Contemporary album.

With *Green and Gold*, Peacock is the only notable soloist on this tune, intended to depict the colors of the African landscape. Here Lasha's playing is technically flawed and lacking in swing and musical ideas. With *Ghost of the Past*, the two bass players engage in some stimulating dual improvisation, which is the most exciting feature of this performance, even though it does not quite manage the intensity of the two bassists on Coleman's *Free Jazz*. *Red's Mood*, a free blues named for Fort Worth tenorist Red Connors, who impressed and influenced Prince Lasha so profoundly, is the latter's best outing on the album as a soloist, achieving as he does more swing and better ideas.[122] Simmons is also better here, with more ideas that make better sense in his "free" improvisation. *Juanita*, named for Prince's mother, is a fine original by Lasha and Simmons (who composed all the tunes on the album), but the composition fails for the most part to inspire a comparable level of improvisation. Nice polyrhythmic work by plucked bass and drums and a duet between bowed bass and Lasha on flute create a primitive mood, which finds Prince in one of his more effective grooves as a soloist.

In general, Lasha tends to solo better on the second side of the album, which begins with *Red's Mood*, continues with *Juanita*, and ends with *A.Y. (Affectionately*

Yours), which contains another example of Simmons's successful adaptation of Ornette's "free" style. The tune preceding *A.Y.*, entitled *Lost Generation*, shows Simmons much indebted to Coleman when Sonny opens with a soliloquy or unaccompanied cadenza that takes up half the five-minute piece. Just as Jimmy Giuffre did not need to pat his foot on *So Low*, so Simmons does not require the rhythm section to achieve his potent solo work that is more flowing than Coleman's style and less sharp-edged in tone but totally dependent on Ornette's free-jazz conception. Simmons ends this number with a cute two-note tag that works—the minor interval a pleasant surprise yet still in keeping with the character of the tune. What is not surprising is that, as Simmons reports, Charlie Parker was his first inspiration, but "when Ornette came along, that did it, because the way he was expressing music, I felt was the way you are supposed to express it—just free, flowing naturally through you."[123]

The following summer, on August 8, 1963, Lasha and Simmons joined forces with drummer Elvin Jones to record a sextet album for Impulse, entitled *Illumination!* Here Prince plays clarinet and flute and Sonny performs on alto sax and English horn, and the sound of much of the music on this album is close to that on the pair's own *Green and Gold* from *"The Cry!"* Lasha does not solo on the Jones album but plays well in the ensemble passages, as on a composition by Simmons entitled *Aborigine Dance in Scotland*, which is referred to as "Afro-Scottish" and has Jones doing the African part on drums while Simmons on alto, Lasha on flute, and Charles Davis on baritone sax create a "bagpipe effect."[124] Lasha's own composition, *Nuttin' Out Jones*, opens the album with a rocking medium tempo and features Simmons on English horn, sounding somewhat like Eric Dolphy on this instrument and certainly in the free-jazz vein. For this second album cut under Elvin Jones's name as leader, the instrumentation is typical of "the new breed, avantgarde but with the substance that could lead to classicism."[125]

More representative of the Lasha-Simmons brand of jazz is their second album for Contemporary, recorded in Los Angeles on September 28 and 29, 1967, and entitled *Firebirds*. In his liner notes for this recording, Nat Hentoff quotes Lasha on the aim of his and Simmons's new quintet, which includes Charles Moffett on drums, Bobby Hutcherson on vibes, and Buster Williams on bass. According to Lasha, the group was trying "to capture the sounds lying in the atmosphere that have been there for centuries. All musical sounds that have been sounded on earth are still hanging in the atmosphere—like a canopy over the earth." Hentoff compares this notion with Jung's theory of the collective unconscious as applied to music. Equally important, in Hentoff's view, is the idea that the new music produced by the Lasha-Simmons Quintet forms part of "a shared common intent" among the new jazz musicians who stress "their conviction that music could be a liberating, a unifying force—a way of transcending present tensions and divisiveness by pointing toward a style and sound of life that would be natural, spontaneous, emotionally direct, and loving."[126] Two of the tunes on this album, *Prelude to Bird* and *The Loved Ones*, pay homage to earlier sounds "still hanging in the atmosphere"—those made by Charlie Parker and John Coltrane. Relating their music on *The Loved Ones* to Coltrane's *A Love Supreme*, Lasha remarks that they are "searching here . . . for a love higher than any man can ever dream of," and Hentoff takes this to mean that a recurring motif in their music is "perfectibility, a reaching out past previous definitions and barriers." The critic considers this recording "one of the most regenerating, and therefore important jazz albums in years. The love of the music is the integrity of Lasha and Simmons. They will only play music that is integral to them."

Once again, the music on this album offers the exotic sound of flute and English horn, complemented by the vibraphone and by Moffett's strong cymbal work. On *Psalms of Solomon*, the group attempts to evoke, in Sonny's words, that king's "fabulous palaces paved with gold and all types of precious stones, emeralds, pearls, sapphires, topaz," and in Prince's, "lovely garments" and "dancing girls." Hutcherson's vibes are quite classical-sounding here, and the woodwinds as well, with only the bass's repeated pattern suggesting a jazz or African rhythm. Lasha's most appealing solo comes on *Prelude to Bird*, where he plays alto and seems better able to express himself on this instrument than on flute or clarinet, which is appropriate for this Parker tribute. Simmons is quite good here as well, more his own man than on *"The Cry!"* When Lasha returns for a second solo, he breaks the mood with some unmelodic warblings that may, nonetheless, represent his own "natural" response to Bird's playing. On *The Loved Ones*, Lasha's alto work is for the most part a distracting force, whereas Simmons contributes a moving solo on English horn. Later on clarinet, Lasha is somewhat better, but both he and Moffett are more distracting than otherwise.

On the album's title composition, *Firebirds*, Lasha and Simmons are both on alto, as they were on *Prelude to Bird*, and here again they work well together in the free-jazz mode, as does Hutcherson on vibes. Simmons and Hutcherson turn in a fine simultaneous improvisation, but in Lasha's solo, once again he tends to break the mood with his beside-the-point runs and inconsequential blurtings. This time, however, Moffett's extended solo is a worthy contribution. While in general Prince Lasha is inconsistent in his solo work, it is clear that he and Simmons formed one of the most uncompromising partnerships in the new-jazz movement.[127] If everything Lasha plays does not completely satisfy, he yet maintains admirably, in Nat Hentoff's view, his philosophical stance "that music does not have to be distorted as a way of bringing out the woes and troubles of the present. That's not what music is for. It's to soothe the mind, release it from today's woes and troubles, and simultaneously let man's deepest feelings come through." As Hentoff observes, in their belief that the roots of jazz go back "to the first musicians on earth" and can be recaptured for the good of the here and now, Lasha and Simmons are "emotional positivists" who assert that "if you tell the truth about a certain event or thing or place, after you say that, it frees you, we become able to express more freedom—with discipline."[128] In all of this, Lasha and Simmons prove themselves to be true disciples of Ornette Coleman.

❡ ❡ ❡

Yet another Fort Worth product to grow up with Coleman is Dewey Redman, who was born in Cowtown on May 17, 1931. Along with Coleman and Prince Lasha, John Carter, and King Curtis,[129] Redman attended I. M. Terrell High School, then received his B.S. degree in 1953 from Prairie View A & M and a master's degree in education from North Texas State University in 1959. After hearing "a whole new world" of sound on "the rambunctious corner of East Rosedale Street and Evans Avenue"[130] in Fort Worth and teaching for three years in the city's public schools from 1956 to 1959, Redman left for Los Angeles in 1959 and then spent seven years in San Francisco, playing with a number of groups, including that of Pharoah Sanders.

In 1967, Redman moved on to New York City, where he performed with Sonny Murray before joining Ornette as a member of his old schoolmate's quartet, along with bassist Jimmy Garrison and drummer Elvin Jones, both of whom had been with John Coltrane up to the time of his death in 1967. On April 29 and May 7, 1968, Redman recorded with the Coleman quartet for two Blue Note albums, *New York Is Now!* and *Love Call*.[131] These sessions from April and May produced two pieces, *The Garden of Souls* and *Broadway Blues*, on which Redman is featured with his simultaneous humming and blowing into his tenor that "startled listeners" when he released "overtones, resulting in harsh, growly multiphonics chords."[132] Here John Litweiler finds that Redman's "phrasing and at times his tone recall the young Ornette" and that "again and again in Redman's playing there are passages with a loping quality that suggests a long, tall Texan,"[133] a description that was also applied often to the style of Buster Smith.

While Litweiler admits that in serving as "the other saxophonist in Ornette Coleman's quartet" Redman faced "the ultimate challenge in modern jazz," the critic does not see him as simply "an Ornette surrogate,"[134] but there is no doubt that beside Coleman the tenorist lacks the leader's intensity and his range of ideas. In a version of *Lonely Woman* recorded in 1976 for a Don Cherry album entitled *Old and New Dreams*, with Redman on tenor, the twelve-minute-plus performance fails to reproduce the unity and drama of the original 1959 recording, and only Charlie

Haden's solo on bass approaches the dramatic sense of Ornette's playing.[135] From this same 1976 album, Redman's solo on *Open or Close*, a Coleman original unrecorded by the composer, is a smoother version of Coleman's style, with a warmer sound than his plastic alto, yet lacking in his emotional appeal. Here, nonetheless, Redman does demonstrate how much he learned from Coleman as he shapes a number of similar phrases and explores in the upper and lower registers of his tenor some of Ornette's same tonal inflections.

On August 11, 1968, Redman would join Coleman, Charlie Haden, and Ornette's son Denardo on drums for a concert at the University of California at Berkeley. The younger Coleman had already appeared on *The Empty Foxhole*, a trio recording with Ornette and Haden that was made on September 9, 1966, when the drummer was only ten years old.[136] Although reactions to Denardo's performance differed when he first recorded—some critics saying it sounded "like a little kid fooling around" and others declaring it to be "quite open and responsive to his father's playing" as he drew "a quite broad range of colors from his drum kit"[137]—there seems no denying that, as John Litweiler remarks, Coleman's choice of his son was appropriate "considering the changes that were occurring in Ornette's own playing," for Denardo's drumming was "loose, erratic," and his "freedom of movement, his imitations of his father's rhythmic patterns, his commentary, are indeed elements of freshness."[138] Certainly by his twelfth year, Denardo had developed into a free drummer who, on the Impulse album *Ornette at 12*, a recording of the 1968 Berkeley concert, "takes responsibility for the music's momentum, which is usually fast."[139] As for Dewey Redman, Ornette writes on the album cover of *Ornette at 12* that "Dewey is the freshest and deepest natural player I played with in quite some years." Ornette also comments that "this record is very important to me if only for the personnel."[140]

With the first tune, *C.O.D.*, Redman once again hums or sings through his tenor as he did on *The Garden of Souls*. On *Bells and Chimes*, Ornette plays violin with an affecting sound production that involves scraping and an electronic-like tone quality; and at times, he plays pure, perfectly in-tune passages that are simply magisterial. Haden on bass follows with a fine solo, and then Redman on tenor imitates the strings' harmonics and their whining and quavering as he slides up the scale by minitones that produce an eerie, stirring effect. Throughout, Denardo lends support to the soloists, who at the end echo one another on their respective instruments. The other two tunes on *Ornette at 12* are notable for Coleman's trumpet playing on *Rainbows* and for Redman's tenor statement on *New York*, where Dewey joins Ornette's alto in delivering the theme that is reminiscent of Henry Mancini's *Moon River* but is less sentimental and more impressive as a melody. On *Rainbows*, Denardo's drumming is quite remarkable when he presses his fingers on the drumhead while playing with his sticks to alter the pitch of his percussive tones, which is not just a gimmick but a completely effective technique within the performance's overall sound. Meanwhile, Redman is into a very free form in his solo, and even though he frequently sequences and repeats phrases, he still manages a variety of unusual licks. With his bowed bass, Haden builds a haunting mood, and Coleman enters with his own uniquely identifiable voice, though now on trumpet. Ornette moves from rapid figures in the upper range of the instrument to more lyrical passages in the lower register and creates a number of nicely syncopated phrases as well.

New York showcases the two-saxophone sound of the quartet when the alto and tenor play the tune's very moving theme, with Ornette's soulful and inimitable crying style either in unison or followed beautifully by Redman's lusher sound in a type of canonic delay. Ornette at times speeds up the tempo with some of his typical wailing phrases that are simply heartrending in timbre and note choice. After Haden's very fine bass solo, Ornette and Dewey reprise the tune's quite touching theme. The combination of a variety of ensemble approaches and of an array of inventive solos on alto, tenor, trumpet, violin, bass, and drums makes this album an amazing performance by only four musicians. Unfortunately, Coleman's *Sun Suite of San Francisco* from the same Berkeley concert remains unissued—a performance by the quartet and a twenty-five-piece orchestra conducted by Ornette and featuring Bobby Bradford as trumpet soloist. Three years later, however, Bradford would finally record with Ornette Coleman.

◐ ◐ ◐

In New York on September 9 and 10, 1971, Bobby Bradford joined Ornette and Dewey Redman to record for Columbia, which released two albums entitled *Broken Shadows* and *Science Fiction*.[141] This year marked Ornette's first appearance at, and the last of the eighteen-season run of, the Newport Jazz Festival. For this occasion, Coleman, who regularly designed his band members' outfits, performed in a watermelon-red suit. Shortly afterward, Coleman was offered a contract by Columbia, and his cousin James Jordan was the producer for two albums from this label. *Broken Shadows* was not released until 1982 as part of Columbia's Contemporary Masters Series, but *Science Fiction* came out in 1972.

The title tune of *Broken Shadows* is vaguely reminiscent of Carl Davis's theme music for the BBC's *The World at War* film series. Here Redman's solo is the most accessible, while the ensemble statement of the theme is far superior to the other solos—to such an extent that perhaps the solos are the broken part of this mournful composition. Bradford's best solo comes on the tune entitled *School Work*, which was also included in Coleman's 1972 symphonic work, *Skies of America*, as the lively section called *The Good Life* and later recorded by Ornette's electric bands as *Theme from a Symphony* and *Dancing in Your Head*. The tune entitled *Happy House* is close to the extended improvisation of the *Free Jazz* album but even more intense and satisfying on a certain controlled level—in that sense perhaps less free. *Good Girl Blues* is a novel work in its use of scoring for a woodwind section that offers no jazz feeling as such. In commenting on this album, John Litweiler finds that both Don Cherry, who had rejoined Ornette for these sessions, and Bobby Bradford incorporate "Ornette-like phrasing" in their playing and that "it is particularly interesting to hear Bradford responding to Ornette's music as he may well have responded a decade earlier as a member of Ornette's quartet."[142]

On *Science Fiction*, Bradford is present for three tunes: the title piece, *Law Years*, and *The Jungle Is a Skyscraper*. Redman also appears on these three numbers, as well as on three others, *What Reason Could I Give*, *Rock the Clock*, and *All My Life*. Comparing Bradford and Cherry, who both "spent years getting next to Ornette's musical vision," Bob Palmer of *Rolling Stone* writes that "Cherry is lithe and lean" and that "Bradford certainly isn't fat, but he's bigger and broader . . . with a deliberate flow of ideas."[143] John Litweiler concurs when he comments that Bradford's solos "have a naturally flowing quality" and that "in general his trumpet work . . . lacks the nervous, tense quality of Cherry's; his sound is warmer, the contours of bop phrasing enter his lines in 'Law Years.'"[144] As might be expected of Coleman here—playing with his original 1958 California quartet of Cherry, Haden, and Higgins, reconstituted for these sessions—he returns to that group's earlier style on *Civilization Day* and *Street Woman*, producing in the latter something of an updated, up-tempo version of *Lonely Woman* and in the former exhibiting his inexhaustible store of rhythmic and motivic ideas that take their own shape and commensurate speed. As Palmer observes, "There's form all right; in fact, this is some of the most formally perfect music you're ever likely to hear."[145]

The title tune of *Science Fiction* showcases a septet in a collective improvisation à la *Free Jazz*, while poet David Henderson recites lines on God, the Bible, man, woman, and child, with the actual screams of a baby incorporated into the recording along with cries from the musicians' anguished instruments. On *Rock the Clock*, Redman first plays musette, a type of recorder or whistle flute, then tenor, sounding on the latter mostly like an R & B sideman.[146] Meanwhile, Ornette trills and screams on trumpet and then switches to violin to accompany both Redman and a growly jam-box sound, with which the tune fades out. Both *What Reason Could I Give* and *All My Life* are ensemble accompaniments to vocals by the Indian singer Asha Puthli. The final tunes bring Bradford and Redman together in a quintet setting that on *Law Years* allows time for some straight-ahead blowing, with Dewey on tenor taking the lead in a swinging, fairly traditional solo, followed by Bobby's mellow, rather laid-back chorus. Only Ornette sounds really free in his improvisation, exploring rhythmic and harmonic possibilities beyond those attempted by his sidemen. On *The Jungle Is a Skyscraper*, Ed Blackwell is heard in an extended solo, and Haden's bass is prominently featured as he accompanies Ornette's chorus. Here Bradford is much more adventuresome, and at the rapid pace of the tune, he approaches Cherry's nervous energy and intensity in keeping with the piece's frenetic character. Bradford's playing here is clearly in the spirit of Coleman's free jazz. The string of solos concludes with Redman's best effort, as he once again sings and yells into his tenor for some of his "multiphonics chords."

As can be heard from Redman's work on *Science Fiction*, Dewey does not stick to any one style, even though he, like Ornette, retains always a touch of the blues feeling from his early days in R & B groups in Texas. Bob Palmer notes that Redman "has kept something of every musical situation he has known, from Southwestern blues bands to the demanding technicalities of bebop, to the cries of freedom music and the calls of African villagers." In speaking of Ornette's group in general, Palmer claims that these musicians have overcome the bitterness of their origins and past experiences and have "managed to hold on to the positive values of roots and self-reliance." And in common with all of Ornette's groups, these ensembles on *Science Fiction* represent a continuation of his musical environment in Texas, which "stressed a spirit of sharing and free exchange of feelings and ideas."[147]

𝕺 𝕺 𝕺

Ornette Coleman would seek to carry on this spirit of "free exchange" throughout the 1970s and 1980s, but in many ways it was something of a one-sided affair since his own ideas were the dominant feature of his recordings of this period. However, what came to be billed as Coleman's Prime Time Band included yet another Fort Worth musician who brought to Coleman's music an additional facet of rhythmic freedom. Born in Cowtown on January 12, 1940, drummer Ronald Shannon Jackson studied music in the third grade with John Carter, his first music teacher;[148] at fifteen, he was already playing professionally with James Clay. After high school, Jackson attended Lincoln University in Jefferson City, Missouri, then tried Texas Southern University and finally Prairie View A & M— both in the Houston area—where he studied history and sociology, after which he transferred to the University of Bridgeport in Connecticut and "was so absorbed in those subjects that he intended not to play music at all."[149] But visiting

New York around 1966, Jackson began to sit in with Charles Mingus, Betty Carter, Kenny Dorham, and Joe Henderson, among others.

Jackson first played with an exponent of free jazz when he joined up with Albert Ayler, "one of the most controversial and virtuosic figures in the avant-garde musical movements of the '60s."[150] Ayler allowed his drummers "to roam freely" in his brand of "bizarre beauty," the "kind of antiswing and calculated carelessness" of this tenorist's "new thing" music,[151] which "remains among the most unique and haunting in the history of black American music."[152] Jackson was present on *Albert Ayler Quintet Live at Slug's Saloon* from 1966, an album that is unfortunately no longer available. After 1967, the drummer was outside the avant-garde movement, having "buried himself in lucrative socials—weddings, bar mitzvahs, local bars."[153] Sometime around 1970, the year in which Ayler's body was found floating in the East River, Jackson essentially went into retirement, although he continued to practice daily. He resurfaced in 1975 and joined Ornette Coleman's Prime Time Band, even moving into the leader's New York loft where, with other sidemen, Jackson studied Ornette's harmolodics. At this time, Jackson would travel with the Coleman band to France, where the group remained from October 1975 to March 1976. Jackson has offered an account of that period:

> Ornette had begun to show me different things: how I was playing *behind* someone and all, and encouraged me to do some writing, and work on my ideas. There was the same freedom to play with Albert, but in this context you'd know everything you could or would play before you got up on the bandstand. Still improvisational, but ordered—no more guessing games. . . . My playing was Ornette's harmolodic concept from a rhythmic point of view. . . . The whole time in Paris was like being in Coleman University. We were totally under his influence.[154]

At the end of 1975, while still in France, Jackson participated in the Coleman quintet's recording of two albums, *Dancing in Your Head* and *Body Meta*. Rafi Zabor and David Breskin call *Dancing* "one of the (ahem) great recordings in the history of jazz" and *Body Meta* "a notch or two lower on the pole but [it] still sets the spirit dancing."[155] On *Dancing*, the band plays two extended variations on Coleman's *Theme from a Symphony*, which became known as the Freedom Hymn of the New Jazz. Here once again Ornette plays with the inventiveness of Bach, with an inexhaustible flow of phrases and rhythms based on the Freedom Hymn, a simple theme that seems rather unpromising at first but proves in Ornette's hands the source of a limitless supply of shifting tonal centers and varied rhythmic accents. In his liner notes for *Dancing in Your Head*, Coleman writes of Prime Time's fusion of rock, classical, folk, and jazz, saying that these "are all yesterday's titles. I feel that the music world is getting closer to being a singular expression, one with endless musical stories of mankind."[156] In Jackson's own playing, the drummer brings a wide variety of styles to his application of Coleman's harmolodic approach that "means the rhythms, harmonies and tempos are all equal in relationship and independent melodies at the same time."[157]

Of his own background as a musician, Jackson has recalled that in the Fort Worth schools he

> had to learn the Sousas, other marches by English composers. By the time I got to junior high, we were playing Wagner. At high school, it was marching during the football season and classical music during the rest of the year. Now for our *own* enjoyment we used to jam during lunch hour. The band director let us have the band room. . . . Dallas was bigger than Fort Worth, but Fort Worth always had the cats who were on the money in terms of the music. It had a lot to do with our music teacher there, Mr. Baxter. He played all the instruments. He loved a perfect band. . . . A lot of people come through this man: he was Ornette Coleman's teacher, he was Dewey Redman's teacher, he was Julius Hemphill's teacher, Charles Moffett's teacher and John Carter's and mine.[158]

Jackson also has commented that in his own musical compositions he has tried to achieve a blend of an East Africa feel with an overlay of the march, a type of spirituality experienced at a football game: "As a young kid I used to sit behind the band at the football games, and they used to spread such joy when there was a touchdown or someone caught a pass. I go there, to that feeling, when I play."[159]

On *Dancing in Your Head*, Jackson's drumming indeed suggests, in conjunction with Coleman and the two guitarists and bass, a complete football band's percussion section, as Jackson whales away with always elemental rhythms. He also picks up the rhythmic patterns in Ornette's playing, as do the other musicians, especially bassist Jamaaladeen Tacuma on Variation Two of *Theme from a Symphony*, where his inventive lines based on the tune's theme match Coleman's, as all three tell their "endless musical stories of mankind." With regard to "the Jackson effect," Zabor and Breskin have defined this as having

> more to do with musical essences than with new stylistic wrinkles or technical nuance; like Coleman before him, he has reconnected himself to traditions that modern jazz has either ignored or put to its own more urban uses. . . . Jackson's

findings have led him back from the cluttered island of modernity to the fruitful and murderous fields of America—its folk continuum, trembling wooden churches and football fields, its festivals in Congo Square and, ultimately, Africa.[160]

Jazz critic Gary Giddins first heard Jackson on the 1976 album *Dancing in Your Head*, which he says is "so cantankerously alive you can't listen to it without moving around,"[161] but it was not until two years later, when Giddins witnessed a recording session by the Cecil Taylor Quintet, that Jackson impressed him "as someone to be reckoned with."[162] This was Jackson's second session with Taylor, whom Martin Williams calls "the first jazz musician to make sustained, serious, and direct use of his knowledge of the most advanced European composers of this century."[163] Jackson's debut album with Cecil Taylor illustrates perfectly this approach to jazz, beginning with the piece entitled *Idut*, with its marchlike opening reminiscent of *The Soldier's March*, which begins Stravinsky's 1918 suite, *The Soldier's Tale*. Here Jackson's hyperactive drumming is in keeping with the rest of the ensemble's frantic pace and complements Taylor's percussive piano, with Jackson's rolls on his different drums almost pianistic.[164] At times this piece also recalls the percussion writing in the experimental music of composer Edgard Varèse, with Jackson's crashing, cascading drums and his thrashing cymbals paralleling the shrieking phrases of Raphé Malik's trumpet and Jimmy Lyons's alto sax. Jackson reverses the normal order of things when he takes a solo over Taylor's chording and scalar runs, with the pianist serving more as the accompanist to the drummer. In the rather lyrical *Serdab*, which opens with a Monk-like theme, Jackson's drums rumble underneath as if some upheaval were lifting up the other instruments. Meanwhile, Taylor's role seems that of a concerto pianist in something of a classical call-and-response, as he offers evidence of what the liner notes refer to as "tiers of sound that Taylor constantly builds with his brief interplay with each instrument."[165] Taylor also plays a classical-sounding, unaccompanied solo that yet retains a jazz feeling through its unsettled tempo, its shifting polyrhythms, and its occasional blue note.

In the thirty-minute *Holiday en Masque*, the timbre of Jackson's cymbals matches that of Taylor's chord clusters, while Jackson's bass drum aids in the creation of what are presumably the composer's planned accents. A duet featuring drummer and pianist again finds the two players quite complementary of one another's styles, with the ensemble passages performed with perfect timing both by the horns and Jackson. At about the seventeenth minute of this piece an incredible "human energy" develops and seems to exemplify the "determinant agent" of Taylor's music, which "has to do with ancestor worship, it has to do with a lot of areas that are magical rather than logical."[166] This entire piece is full of the energetic dynamism of Taylor's work, with its "freedom from predetermined harmonies and rhythms,"[167] but at about the seventeen-minute mark, Jackson's heaving battery of percussion instruments, joined to Taylor's piano, Malik's trumpet, Lyons's alto, and Ramsey Ameen's violin, moves into a superhuman up-tempo section that is beyond what even Coleman's *Free Jazz* attempted. This is contrasted after some one and a half minutes by a slower, pointillistic section, which nevertheless features some of Taylor's inhumanly rapid runs and clusters. The pace picks up again with Taylor leading the way and using every imaginable percussive attack on the piano. Jackson keeps his bass drum, snares, and cymbals going simultaneously, somehow managing to maintain the necessary level of intensity on all three. The effect of this section is to amaze by the sheer physical endurance and to mesmerize as if in a primitive ritual that achieves a spiritual, trancelike state that is nonetheless paradoxically exhilarating.

In all, Jackson made four recordings with Cecil Taylor, and according to Zabor and Breskin, these "reveal Jackson as the most stately free-jazz drummer in the history of the idiom, a regal and thundering presence."[168] After his work with Taylor, Jackson went on to form his own group, the Decoding Society, for whose first recording in 1980, *Eye on You*, the drummer did all the writing and "effectively extended his penchant for polyrhythm into the sphere of composition."[169] Two of Jackson's pieces from *Eye on You* are entitled *Apache Love Song* and *Nightwhistlers*,[170] the first described by the composer as "a symbol for what this country is all about . . . the true spirit of what this country was and still is," and the second as representative of "the way people feel in an environment I used to be a part of— where people worked all week picking cotton and corn, and worked in wheatfields and watermelon patches . . . when they'd get together, starting Saturday afternoon puttin' all the ice on the beer, and then after the sun went down they'd get together and start dancin.'"[171]

While John Litweiler has termed Jackson's Decoding Society "the most extreme music in the harmolodic idiom and a denial of the others in that Jackson seeks to combine the most independent of elements," the drummer's roots have clearly remained in the Southwest, and his memories from his early life have proved a positive force in his music.[172] Although Ornette Coleman may have sought to escape Fort Worth and what Litweiler has considered "a dead end for his talents and his self-aware freedom of spirit,"[173] certainly Ornette's early experiences are also deeply imbedded in his music, which bears the enduring mark of a blues-derived sound and inspiration. Jackson's *Nightwhistlers* is likewise a blues, but as Litweiler has noted, the drummer's influences come from many sources, and "separate cultures coexist" in his music,[174] testifying to Jackson's willingness during his formative years in the Southwest to perform under any conditions, for any kind of audience, with whatever group, in any and every style—from Sousa marches, Wagner, redneck honky-tonks, and *The Yellow Rose of Texas,* to *How Much Is That Doggie in the Window?*. Later, in New York, Jackson would play for bar mitzvahs or weddings, and out of all this wide variety of music the drummer discovered that in the end "the music you play comes from your life" and that "the beat is in your body."[175]

❡ ❡ ❡

On September 29, 1983, Fort Worth welcomed back its most famous native son in the field of jazz as the mayor proclaimed that date Ornette Coleman Day and presented the musician with a key to the city. The occasion was the opening of the Caravan of Dreams, a performance center in Ornette's hometown, and on the evening of this celebration, Ornette's *Skies of America* was performed by the Fort Worth Symphony.[176] Four years later, in 1987, the First International Conference on Jazz Studies, held at the University of Bologna, devoted its entire meeting to the life and music of Ornette Coleman, who at the end of the year was voted by *Down Beat* readers Jazz Musician of the Year. In 1988, Ornette's album *Virgin Beauty* "sold more copies in the first year of its release than any of [his] other recordings."[177] Most symbolic of all, Coleman's free jazz was recognized by the French government, which commissioned him to compose for 1989 and the bicentennial of the French Revolution a piece he entitled *The Country That Gave the Freedom Symbol to America.* In 1990, in Los Angeles, jazz pianist Herbie Hancock pronounced the Texan "a man of great conviction, a pioneer always moving forward down the path he has chosen, a can opener who opens all of us up as musicians. I could not play what I play had it not been for Ornette Coleman."[178] This was equally true of the impact of Coleman on the entire contingent of Fort Worth jazz musicians who worked and studied and even lived with Ornette, their "loving, kind teacher," from whom "the main lines of jazz development" have "continued to descend" since his "innovations of the late 1950s."[179]

AFRICA AND BACK

Among those Texans who followed Ornette Coleman down his chosen path and who could not have played what they did without his example were Bobby Bradford and John Carter. Bradford, who moved to Dallas in 1946 from Mississippi, at age twelve, by way of a year in Los Angeles and another in Detroit, went to Lincoln High School, where he was a classmate of Cedar Walton and James Clay. After graduation, Bobby attended college for a year and a half, then joined the air force and was stationed in Texas for almost four years. When he left the service, Bobby headed for Los Angeles, where he hooked up with Ornette and later joined his group in New York. After leaving Coleman in 1963, Bobby moved back to Dallas and then in 1964 returned to Los Angeles. It was at this time that Ornette suggested to John Carter, his former Fort Worth schoolmate from I. M. Terrell High, that "he would find Bradford a stimulating artist to play music with."[1]

Bradford and Carter had known of each other in Texas, but as Bobby recalled, even though Fort Worth and Dallas are only a short distance apart, "we never crossed trails until we were in California."[2] Carter had to telephone a mutual friend in Texas who had Bobby's brother's phone number, and only in this way did the two make contact—an association that led to their founding of the New Art Jazz Ensemble. Along with Ornette Coleman and other Cowtown jazzmen, Carter and Bradford formed part of what was in the 1940s and 1950s "a loosely intermingling school of musicians that was the progenitor of the new music"; the New Art Jazz Ensemble represented later developments in "a large, active jazz scene that [Ornette Coleman] fathered through his persistence and dedication" and that John Carter and Bobby Bradford advanced through "their commitment to a dynamic musical philosophy."[3]

Following high school in Fort Worth, where Carter was born on September 24, 1929, he earned a B.A. degree in music education from Lincoln University in Jefferson City, Missouri, and a master's in the same field from North Texas State University in Denton in 1956. Inspired by Charlie Parker in the 1940s, Carter joined other Fort Worth musicians in, as he remembered, "an upstairs joint where the management would allow us to session in regular hours. Ornette and Charles Moffett were regular participants and we were all stone boppers at the time. . . . Those sessions . . . allowed us to work hard on our bop repertoire and at the same time develop our personal styles. I later wrote a tune called *Blues Upstairs* to commemorate those days."[4] After playing throughout the Southwest in the late 1940s and early 1950s with jazz and blues groups, Carter became discouraged by the road existence of a professional musician and took up teaching instead, working in the Fort Worth public schools. But in 1961, encouraged by the success of Ornette Coleman, Carter left his hometown and settled in the Los Angeles area, continuing his education at California State University and teaching in the local public schools. When Carter met Bradford, both men were teaching, and the other members of the New Art Jazz Ensemble—Tom Williamson on bass and Bruz Freeman on drums—had regular jobs in addition to their work with the group so that the players could "devote themselves unselfishly to the Ensemble's music with no thought of prostituting it for commercial gain."[5]

The New Art Jazz Ensemble's first album was appropriately entitled *Seeking*, in that both Bradford and Carter seem to be searching for their own voices and ideas beyond the Coleman model. Recorded in Los Angeles on January 16, 1969, *Seeking* opens quite inauspiciously with a piece entitled *In the Vineyard*, which begins with a boppish theme and with Carter on tenor. Although John demonstrates his technical command of this reed instrument, he is short on ideas and his solo is shapeless—in general it pales by comparison with Ornette's work. Bradford just noodles on trumpet and seems totally uninspired; he too is completely under the Coleman influence even though, like Carter, he is lacking in Ornette's vitality and originality. This is not a good piece in the first place, and since it is the longest selection (almost ten and a half minutes), it may have lost the album's listeners from the start. Fortunately, things improve with the second tune, *Karen on Monday*, which opens with an interesting figure plucked at the neck of the bass by Tom Williamson and continued throughout this original by Carter, who wrote all the numbers except for the last, a piece by Bradford entitled *Song for the Unsung*. On *Karen*, Carter plays alto and produces with his vibrato a warmer Ornette sound— which is also somewhat indebted to the Los Angeles school of such altoists as Bud Shank and Art Pepper. Bradford's "fatter" trumpet sound (compared with Don Cherry's) is especially in evidence here, but even while Bobby's solo has more going for it than his playing on *In the Vineyard*, there are still lapses of meaningless noodles and the alto and trumpet do not blend. In his own solo, Carter seems to allude to *Harlem Nocturne*, and it fits in well with the melancholy mood of *Karen*. And even though there is no "new" conception here, *Karen* contains in Carter's dialogue with the bass the album's first appealing exchange between two soloists.

Only with *Sticks and Stones* does Carter's "search" finally turn up a promising development. For this tune, with its bop theme that Bradford and Carter play together with amazing precision in the tradition of Parker and Gillespie and Coleman and Cherry, Carter has switched to clarinet, and ironically—given the "old-fashioned" reputation of this woodwind—his sound and ideas are more up to date with the free-jazz movement. While there are few really striking or meaningful passages in Carter's solo, he seems to have found his modern and personal voice in this instrument that goes back to the beginnings of jazz history—the era of Alphonse Picou of *High Society* fame and Johnny Dodds of the Armstrong Hot Five. Bradford has little to say in his own solo, but he matches Carter's sound magnificently in the ensemble sections. On the next tune, *The Village Dancers*, Bradford is more in the Cherry mold, with a thinner sound and with sudden leaps at the ends of phrases. This is Bobby's best solo of the album, yet it is not really characteristic of his more robust approach to the trumpet.

For the album's title tune, *Seeking*, Carter moves to flute, and even though John Litweiler calls this instrument and the clarinet "less expressive,"[6] here Carter certainly creates a melancholy mood that is warm and pleasingly lyrical. The final piece, Bradford's *Song for the Unsung*, is a nice enough tune, somewhat reminiscent of Jimmy Giuffre's funky blues—at one point Carter on tenor even sounds close to the Giuffre tenor, at another coming on like Stan Getz. The piece's repeated bass figure is also in the Giuffre down-home style. Litweiler somehow finds Bradford's solo a union of "blues phrasing, a wonderful variety of phrase shape, and lyric flow with such elegant poise as to announce a major voice in the new music."[7] However, except for *Sticks and Stones*, with Carter's free-jazz clarinet, the album mostly pays its respects rather than establishing, as the liner notes assert, "a distinguished free-form jazz group" or an "exciting unit that . . . immediately takes its place among the most important such organizations in the entire world of jazz." Perhaps at the time the New Art Jazz Ensemble did have "a significant effect on the rather quiet western jazz scene," but it hardly predicted the important work of the Carter-Bradford alliance that was yet to come.

After recording two other albums with the same personnel, Carter and Bradford made a fourth on November 9, 1971, and April 4, 1972, entitled *Secrets*, for which they expanded the quartet by adding a piano. On the previous pair of albums done for the Flying Dutchman label, the New Art Jazz Ensemble had tried to achieve greater spontaneity and to elaborate in their improvisations "more independent musical statements, ones that were self-activating rather than energised by frequent interjections of the themal substance."[8] The results, however, are not always up to even the best performances of the group's debut album, which would perhaps account for the addition of the piano on *Secrets*, as well as a change of drummer and bass player (although Bruz Freeman does appear on one tune, *Circle*). The pianist, Nate Morgan (except on *Circle*, where Bill Henderson plays the limited keyboard part), stimulates the horns by contributing a fiery undercurrent as well as some fine solos on his own, especially for the first tune, Bradford's *Rosevita's Dance*; here Morgan launches into a version of Cecil Taylor, complete with classical-sounding phrases and a percussive style. The drummer, Ndugu, brings more excitement to his part in the ensemble, and both Bradford and Carter seem more inspired by the new personnel. The interplay between the trumpet and piano is notable, and Carter on alto loosens up to give glimpses of his later work on clarinet, once he had abandoned the saxophones to concentrate on this "less expressive" instrument.

The New Art Jazz Ensemble's fourth album includes two slow pieces, one by Bradford entitled simply *Ballad* and another by Carter labeled *In a Pretty Place*. The former is described by critic Michael James as creating a sense of "benign serenity," which is perhaps the best that can be said for Bradford's piece—a nice enough tune but in no way spectacular. On the other hand, Carter's balladlike number is remarkable for the way the clarinet and trumpet play and breathe together so perfectly, achieving as they do an unusual sound, somewhat reminiscent of Giuffre's *Tangents in Jazz*. There are, indeed, some canonic passages with trumpet, clarinet, and bass that would be right at home on that Giuffre album, especially toward the end of Carter's ten-and-a-half-minute piece. Carter's clarinet playing, however, is quite different from Giuffre's, for while Carter can at times verge on the folksy, he is more often given to rapid runs that are closer to the swing-era clarinetists in the virtuoso school of Barney Bigard, Benny Goodman, Artie Shaw, and Woody Herman. Carter has not yet discovered fully his own voice although he does provide flashes of the Cecil Taylor, Eric Dolphy, Ornette Coleman, Dewey Redman, and classical-electronic style that he will slowly develop, with its "portamentos and blisteringly stark multiphonics."[9]

On *Circle*, another of Carter's originals, the clarinetist gives the clearest indication of the sound he will ultimately create, with its alternation of rapid runs and slow, meditative passages. Carter plays unaccompanied to open the piece and then is joined by Bradford, with each pursuing his own musical ideas and directions at his own chosen tempo, thus fulfilling their desire for greater independence. After the bass and drum quietly replace the horns, the piano enters, followed by Bradford

revelation 18

John Carter/Bobby Bradford

secrets

Bobby Bradford of Dallas (left) and John Carter of Fort Worth (right). Reproduced from *Secrets* (Revelations 18) by permission of J. W. Hardy; photograph by John William Hardy.

and then Carter, with the horns picking up the pace in a free-for-all, chaselike episode. Carter mixes a few swinging figures with scale runs, and Bradford adds some pointillistic patches along with more of his noodling that at times sounds like little more than practice excercises out of Arban. By now the two horns have lost the vitality of the opening sequence and return to the theme, thus completing "the circle" but without a satisfying sense of closure. Michael James's comments on the album's achievements are in general accurate enough: "What Carter and Bradford have succeeded in doing here—and in many respects it is a more momentous feat than breaking new ground—is largely to have resolved the problems of formal integration which had been thrown up by one or two of the longer renditions included in their previous two albums."[10]

Carter and Bradford continued to perform during the 1970s, but mostly with other groups, and they did not record together during the rest of the decade. In this period, Carter devoted himself to the task of developing "the expressive qualities of the clarinet," of reincorporating this instrument "into the mainstream of jazz improvisation."[11] On August 16, 1979, in Düsseldorf, Germany, he recorded *A Suite of Early American Folk Pieces for Solo-Clarinet.*[12] The range of Carter's compositions on this album returns the listener to the history of pre-jazz African American music, at the same time that it is updated by his interpretations of such early dance forms as the cakewalk and the funky butt by means of modern harmonies and techniques. The first tune, entitled *Fast Fannie's Cakewalk,* only hints at this folkish dance that influenced the coming of ragtime; mostly it exhibits multiphonics on clarinet of the sort Dewey Redman created as well as electronic effects after the manner of classical composers Karlheinz Stockhausen and John Cage. Throughout the recording, Carter contrasts his shrill multiphonics with lovely melodic phrases, as on *Star Bright.* On two tunes, *Johnetta's Night* and *Earnestine's Dilemma,*[13] Carter's sound and melodic style recall the clarinet work of Jimmy Giuffre, in particular on the second tune, for which Carter seems quite indebted to his fellow Texan's subdued approach to the instrument. However, Carter departs from Giuffre's practice by interjecting chaotic bursts and blending these with meditative passages that, in keeping with the subject's "dilemma," explore a wider and deeper variety of emotions than does Giuffre on his solo clarinet piece, *So Low.*

Although Carter's music on this album grows increasingly disturbed, it always returns to a touch of folkiness that suggests a type of spiritual center. The album also contains in *Buddy Red, Doing the Funky Butt* a swinging, gut-bucket, free transformation of the early jazz associated with legendary trumpeter Buddy Bolden of New Orleans. A faint flavor of dance-hall jazz is mixed here with multiphonics, flutter-tonguing, honks, squeals, and streaking runs. The final piece, *A Country Blues,* moves between blues phrases—with at times a bit of Dewey Redman's simultaneous humming and blowing—and a leaping from high to low registers and a number of electronic-sounding held notes. Carter not only demonstrates the expressive quality of the clarinet, the instrument he had begun on at age twelve because it "was inexpensive, available and 'could duplicate the human voice,'"[14] but he surveys the history of African American music as it relates both to jazz and to the lives of its creators. In this sense, Carter was preparing the ground for his major production, an epic five-suite work entitled *Roots and Folklore: Episodes in the Development of American Folk Music,* for which his solo clarinet recording served as "an aural sketchbook."[15]

In 1984, two years after Carter had begun the seven-year process of recording the five albums that make up his *Roots and Folklore* series, he founded the collective Clarinet Summit, a group that represents—according to Alvin Batiste, one of its four clarinet players—"the first time in history that clarinet players have formed an ensemble to fully explore the instrument's group timbre."[16] Not until March

29, 1987, however, did the Clarinet Summit produce its first recording, *Southern Bells*, cut in Atlanta, Georgia, with Carter, Batiste, and Jimmy Hamilton all on B-flat clarinets and David Murray on bass clarinet. The opening tune is Duke Ellington's *Don't Get Around Much Anymore*, which is stated without embellishment, and along with Juan Tizol's *Perdido* showcases "the more traditional use of the clarinet with bright, chiming tones and an alluring swing."[17] *Fluffy's Blues*, by Batiste, explores both the traditional blues and the clarinet and bass clarinet as outlets for free-jazz conceptions, with Carter and Murray demonstrating most fully in their modern approach how "the pathetic qualities of the human voice" can "easily be imitated" on their respective instruments.[18] Billy Eckstine's *I Want to Talk About You* comes the closest to the Giuffre sound and phraseology, for here Murray manages to transform his bass clarinet into a tenor, thereby giving to the tune a late swing-era feeling. *Beat Box*, by Batiste, combines a type of bass drone with pointillistic blips and bleeps that suggest "a humorous pairing of New Music and Hip Hop."[19] There is nothing here that sounds dated, and in fact throughout this album the contemporary Clarinet Summit restores the good name of that instrument in a very modern vein, even as the ensemble members conduct the listener on a guided tour of earlier pop-jazz styles.

The album's second side begins with Carter's "folkloric" *Southern Bells*, which "layers two-steps, riffs and cherubic atonal harmonies while evoking the pageantry of a well to do Saturday Night Function."[20] The riffs are vintage 1930s, yet serve meaningfully as interludes between the "atonal harmonies" of a more modern style, with Carter and Murray leading the way and effectively bridging old and new. With *Perdido*, Carter and ex-Ellington clarinetist Jimmy Hamilton engage in a duet that is a worthy tribute to this 1930s standard, with both musicians sticking close to the swing-era sound and idiom of Tizol's tune, even as they improvise freely on its chords. Carter has been called

> a blues player in the Jimmy Hamilton mold, with a few unique twists—meaning a clean, delicate line that occasionally drops into a mumble, or sets off on seemingly unrelated tangents that eventually, inevitably, climb into the strato-sphere, cavort there for a time defying gravity, and finally click into place. You may encounter moments where he approaches the unfettered abandon of Eric Dolphy—pure pleasure—and swings through sheer persistence.[21]

The final piece is a Murray original, *Mbizo*, which is dedicated to a South African bassist, Johnny Dyani. At times Murray can create the sense of a drum and bass rhythm section with his low-note drone, and then again produce a sound that transforms his bass clarinet into a swing-era tenor. Meanwhile, the rest of the ensemble participates in a low-keyed collective improvisation in the spirit of Coleman's *Free Jazz*. Like Carter's solo clarinet album, the *Clarinet Summit* recording traces the roots of New Age jazz back through the 1930s and 1940s swing-band era, the blues and folkloric dance forms of earlier periods, and finally to the elemental rhythms of Africa. This same chronicling of the origins and developments in jazz and black history forms the basis of Carter's epic, *Roots and Folklore*.

Both before and during the period between 1982 and 1989 when Carter was recording his *Roots and Folklore* series, he necessarily devoted much of his energy to his occupation as a public school teacher in Fort Worth and Los Angeles. Like other free-jazz proponents, Carter was uncompromising in his artistic integrity and therefore could not rely on performing his music in order to earn a living. As a result, he depended on his teaching career to support his family, and in this way he came to encourage a number of students who went on to make their own mark in the jazz world. Among these, as we have seen, was Ronald Shannon Jackson. Another of Carter's students was Julius Hemphill, who in 1976 formed the World Saxophone Quartet, an ensemble that explored the potential of the saxophone in much the same way as the Summit concentrated later on the clarinet. Born in Fort Worth on January 24, 1938, Hemphill studied clarinet there with Carter, but by his own admission he "wasn't a serious music student"; yet he did "pick up a lot from him, also from Red Connors."[22] Like Carter and other Fort Worth jazzmen, Hemphill went on to study in Los Angeles at the University of California at Berkeley, at Lincoln University in Missouri, and at North Texas State in Denton. In 1968 Hemphill moved to St. Louis, where he was one of the founders of the Black Artists Group.

Along with Hamiet Bluiett on baritone and flute, Oliver Lake on alto and soprano sax, and David Murray on bass clarinet and tenor, Hemphill performed on alto and soprano for the World Saxophone Quartet's first recording session in December 1978.[23] Joachim Berendt has written that "even without a rhythm section [the World Saxophone Quartet] swung more intensively and vitally than some good jazz groups with bass and drums," and the critic calls the group "jazz's most important and influential saxophone ensemble."[24] Hemphill's compositions for the World Saxophone Quartet and for many other groups would bring him particular praise.[25] Like his teacher, John Carter, Hemphill would influence other jazz musicians, such as Tim Berne and David Sanborn, the latter remarking that Hemphill's music "encompasses so much—pop music, r & b music, blues, jazz, free improvisation, all of that. Structure and non-structure. It's inclusionary."[26] The range of Hemphill's work derives from the wide variety of styles he heard in

Fort Worth, from blues and church music to bop and free jazz: "It was hard not to absorb a little bit of each of it and it was hard not to become a startling amalgam of the entire culture."[27]

In 1973, Hemphill produced a stage version of his film, *The Orientation of Sweet Willie Rollbar*, at Ornette Coleman's Prince Street loft; recorded in 1974 with Anthony Braxton; composed a tribute to Blind Lemon Jefferson; and, most impressively, created a jazz saxophone opera, *Long Tongues*, based in part on Ralph Ellison's novel, *Invisible Man*. Like Hemphill, both Carter and Marvin "Hannibal" Peterson would also compose works that achieve historical perspectives on jazz and African American life. Hemphill's *Long Tongues*, Carter's *Roots and Folklore* series, and Peterson's *African Portraits* all express in epic or operatic form a vision in the tradition of Scott Joplin's *Treemonisha*.[28] Not only is the scope of Joplin's opera reflected in the work of Hemphill, Carter, and Peterson, but *Treemonisha*'s theme of the value of education is illustrated in the lives of a number of Fort Worth and Dallas jazzmen like Hemphill, Carter, Ronald Shannon Jackson, Bobby Bradford, and Cedar Walton, whose professional and artistic success is owing in part to their having pursued and completed college degrees—some of these musicians having studied as well in self-taught Ornette Coleman's University of Free Jazz.[29]

To tell the epic story of what Carter refers to as "American Folk Music," the composer would return in his *Roots and Folklore* series to slavery as it developed in the African nation of Ghana. Carrying forward to the modern day with the experience of Africans in America, Carter would create a five-part work that summarizes the entire history of jazz music as it emerged within the state of Texas and in the leading metropolitan centers of the nation. Through its revisiting of the music's various movements—from ragtime and blues through swing and bop to free jazz—Carter's epic series not only recapitulates the entire story of Texans in jazz but serves to epitomize the work of Carter himself, a figure who "has enriched contemporary clarinet playing with creative new sounds, with exciting whirling sounds (based on circular breathing) and unusual disaltered chords that extend into the region of polyphonic playing." In itself, Carter's *Roots and Folklore* "stands alongside Duke Ellington's *Black, Brown, and Beige* as probably the most successful and creative tone poem depicting over two hundred years of black culture in America."[30]

Like Ornette Coleman, who recorded in Morocco with the Master Musicians of Joujouka in 1973 (part of his album *Dancing in Your Head*, released in 1977); Marvin Peterson, who in the early 1970s lived with the Masai tribe in Kenya and as a result wrote a number of African-related compositions (among them *The Flames of South Africa*); and Ronald Shannon Jackson, who in the early 1980s traveled to Zaire and was inspired to produce his album *When Colors Play*, John Carter took part in a "back to Africa" movement along with his fellow Texans—without, however, visiting that continent himself. It was through Carter's oldest son, who made a trip to Ghana and Nigeria in 1973, that the clarinetist-composer began a search for his and the African American's roots, just as he continued to seek for his own musical voice through the clarinet, the first important woodwind in jazz history. As Norman Weinstein has observed, one aspect of Carter's "historical mission" was to concentrate on the clarinet and to discover antecedents for a style that "placed a premium" on "mirroring speech patterns and timbres: narrating, preaching, sermonizing. Clarinet swoops and glides were part of the New Orleans tradition, harking further back to West Africa where the spirit's excitedly possessed voice careened through wood instruments."[31]

Dauwhe, the first album in Carter's *Roots and Folklore* series, was recorded in Los Angeles on February 25 and 28 and March 8, 1982; and like the other four albums in the series, it depicts one of the stages in what the composer calls a journey that "before its completion, would interrupt and redirect the dynamics of human existence on our planet."[32] Carter is referring to the events and times beginning with slavery in Ghana during the sixteenth century and extending up to the twentieth when "the players in this drama will play vital parts in one of the great social experiments in the history of mankind . . . the melting pot that is to become America."[33] *Dauwhe*, according to Carter, came strictly out of his head: "The idea was to say: here is a setting these people came from and what their lives were about."[34]

Constructed in two parts—a slow, somber section and a faster one with a get-happy feeling—the title section of *Dauwhe* recalls the traditional New Orleans funeral procession. Like the 1926 recording by Jelly Roll Morton and His Red Hot Peppers of *Dead Man Blues*, which "is built around a famous New Orleans funeral piece entitled *Flee as a Bird*," Carter's *Dauwhe* begins "slowly, as is traditional," and then "builds to a fast tempo signifying the return from the graveyard when the musicians take off in jam-style."[35] This first section of the first suite in Carter's *Roots and Folklore* series opens with the playing by percussionist Luis Peralta of a waterphone, which sounds like melancholy electronic music. Then the rest of Carter's octet (including tuba)—a larger ensemble than in any of Carter's previous recording sessions but the same size he would employ for all five albums of the series—plays a purely classical chamber-music passage, after which Bobby Bradford enters on cornet with muted phrases that still do not suggest a jazz approach or style, even though Berendt compares his playing to that of Harry Edison with the Count Basie band.[36] (Except for the final album, *Shadows on a Wall*, which brings the series into the period of modern jazz and on which Bradford plays the trumpet, Bobby returns to the earlier cornet, just as Carter had reverted to the "primitive" clarinet since the late 1970s.) Only with the entrance of Carter and the walking bass of Roberto Miranda does the piece evoke an African and somewhat jazzy texture. Here the musicians "get happy" in a modern, ecstatic manner, which is related to African mythology in that Dauwhe was the Goddess of Happiness. After a line of slowed-down single notes by Carter, Bradford takes up the same kind of line before producing what Berendt in the liner notes calls a sound reminiscent of "the early Ellington trumpet players."

In the second section, entitled *Ode to the Flower Maiden*, Carter opens this pastoral piece by playing alone for a few measures before he is joined by the rest of the ensemble, with Red Callender in the upper register on tuba, which creates an eerie background for Carter's romantic ode. Berendt likens this section to early New Orleans ballads played by clarinetist George Lewis. Although in the beginning Carter's clarinet at times sounds close to that of Jimmy Giuffre, by the end of the section Carter has shifted into his piercing, high-pitched style that is more avant-garde than Giuffre's down-home manner and more convincing and satisfying as free jazz than Giuffre's Third Stream explorations.

The third section, entitled *Enter from the East*, features Luis Peralta on waterphone and percussion in a suggestion of earthy African rhythms and talking drums, until bassist Roberto Miranda and soprano saxophonist Charles Owens introduce a jazzy ritualistic element, after which Owens and Carter engage in what Berendt considers "some of the wildest improvising on clarinet (and on soprano . . .) ever recorded," driven excitingly by Peralta's drumming.[37] Section four, *Soft Dance*, finds Carter in the context of a modern version of a swing-era concerto that shows his great versatility and virtuosity. Bradford makes one of his finest appearances in this section, with his warm cornet sound and his touch of flutter-tonguing, his rapid bursts and his Cherry-like thrusts, all adding up to a satisfying contribution to the proceedings, which end beautifully with Carter's perfect intonation for his multiphonics in the upper register. Carter then continues his high-register playing in the final section, *The Mating Ritual*, which recreates, as the composer proposed, something of the life of the African peoples. Bradford's low-down blues feeling is totally in character and complements Carter's piercing clarinet as they "dance" in ritualistic tandem.

Recorded in November 1985, *Castles of Ghana*, the second album in the series, opens with a section of the same title, an impressionistic piece that captures the exotic nature of West Africa's Gold Coast in the 1700s, with its rhythms tied to activities of a religious-cultural mix, something of a melting pot of African and European influences. The basic octet instrumentation evokes a variety of African sounds, from a repeated drum figure and a primitive rhythm in the bass clarinet to the trombone's Mingus-like wah-wahs. Here too a trumpet (played by Baikida Carroll) and a cornet (played by Bradford) offer a fanfare that alludes to the castles and forts lining the country's shores during the beginnings of the slave trade. The violin, meanwhile, is Ellington-like in its blend of the sophisticated and the folkloric.

Evening Prayer, the second section, presents in its clashing sounds the discord of the era, even if rather subdued and prayerful at first. A mournful voice suggests this "chaotic period" in which "many African chiefs, in collaboration with European traders," formed "a new arena of trade, one involving the illegal gathering and trading of African citizens to be eventually shipped from Africa . . . generally for purposes of uncompensated labor."[38] This second section is quite beautiful with its muted, restrained tones; the vocal by Terry Jenoure, who also plays the violin, is deeply emotive. The third section, entitled *Conversations*, is a duet between clarinet and bass clarinet that is indeed conversational in its folksy, free-jazz swing. This is followed by *The Fallen Prince*, which features trombonist Benny Powell in a lovely lament—complemented by the violin—that pictures the emotional impact of enslavement on a socially prominent figure. Downward glissandos symbolize the prince's fall, even though the dignity of this personage is maintained in the trombone's sensitive and subtly human sound. Certainly Carter's talent for portraiture can be compared here with that of Duke Ellington, even though the Texan denied having been inspired by that great composer of jazz character sketches and suites based on historical and literary themes.[39]

Section five, entitled *Theme of Desperation*, is essentially in the classical style, and it illustrates how close jazz can come to the programmatic approach of concert music. The fact that *Castles of Ghana* was commissioned by the New York Shakespeare Festival for its New Jazz at the Public series suggests this album's link with dramatic works that treat historical and social situations with all their complex issues and repercussions, as do Shakespeare's plays. Instead of the usual repetitive beat of jazz, its reliance on the circular song form, and its dependence on riffs to propel the soloists, this section showcases first the violin, as in a modern classical concerto like that of Alban Berg, and then the voice, in a spiritual–like passage that is complemented by bells that add to the tender, plaintive nature of this touching section. *Capture*, the next section, returns to a traditional rhythm-based procedure for jazz in its depiction of the chasing down of victims, with Carter's clarinet expressive of their painful experience in being hunted as so many animals. The movement utilizes a big-band sound to spin off the customary free-jazz improvisations by Bradford on cornet and by Marty Ehrlich on bass clarinet. After these soloists represent the frightening, desperate chase-down of the victims, Carter's clarinet dramatizes the sense of captivity, of being cut off from one's customs and loved ones. The suite concludes with a *Postlude* in which percussion alone accompanies these spoken words: "The journey facing these captives would prove to be arduous and truly eventful, a journey which, before its completion, would interrupt and redirect the dynamics of human existence on our planet."

Carter's third suite, *Dance of the Love Ghosts*, was recorded in November 1986 and opens with the title section picturing in sound the "teeming thousands" who "passed through the Castles of Ghana" and "the ghosts of those lost loved ones" who "dance in eternal rhythm to the song of a desperate people who would never again view their homeland."[40] In this up-tempo section with its simple but haunting theme, Carter's clarinet proves a perfect vehicle for the shrill, painful feelings of the ghosts, with Bradford's cornet serving as a warm foil to the excruciating sound produced by Carter. After Bradford's fairly straightforward jazz solo, backed by rather traditional piano chords, Carter returns to join the cornetist (now muted) in a free-jazz ghost dance that is followed by more spectral sounds from Don Preston's synthesizer, which leads into a final haunting episode by the ensemble. The second section, entitled *The Silent Drum*, emphasizes once again the percussive and elemental rhythms of Africa for the purpose of remembering and thus overcoming, it would seem, the sadness and suffering caused by the fact that "they have taken our father away and his drums are sitting in a corner idling." The drum patterns underneath the moving dialogue between cornet and trombone and the solos by violin and clarinet contribute to a sense of the ongoing, enduring nature of African culture. This second section appropriately began with the actual Ghanian dialect spoken by Ashanti drummers in their native language and now closes with those same drummers beating out alone their uplifting rhythms.

With the third section, *Journey*, the suite follows the slaves on their voyage across the Atlantic. The liner notes (probably by Carter but left unsigned) allude to evolutionary thought in stating that "only the very strong will survive the travails of this journey. Only the very strong of that group will subsequently survive the life offered by the new land." But the notes go on to say that "Destiny is a passenger in this transfer," as if to suggest that there is more than Darwinian theory involved. The emphasis in the music is on the slaves' survival of inhuman conditions, with the trombone's wails and pedal tones a sound-image of the bowels of a slave ship where those cramped there without light or air yet manage somehow to utter lyrical, manly strains, whether open(ly) or muted(ly). The bass clarinet also echoes the depths of despair surmounted by song and rhythmic play. The violin then swirls into dithyrambic exhilaration, followed by an electrifying free-jazz improvisation, with drum rolls, rim shots, and cymbals supporting and accenting the excitement generated by the entire ensemble participating in a collective improvisation. The bass's reiterated down-up phrase also adds to the effect of a mastering of the journey's travail.

Norman Weinstein observes that "the most chilling moment occurs" in the fourth section of *Dance of the Love Ghosts* when Terry Jenoure recites a text "reflecting her feelings as a slave woman facing the prospect of rape by the slave ship's captain."[41] *The Captain's Dilemma* opens with a beautiful Ellington- and Mingus-like ensemble as Carter's clarinet faintly pipes above it, after which the vocalist enters with the telling combination of a straightforward torch song and the acrobatics of a modern type of scat singing. Jenoure's delivery and control are truly majestic and are followed by Carter's liquid, percolating clarinet, which later breaks into the kind of aerodynamics that duplicate the vocalist's high-pitched leaps. The section concludes with the words "must be free," a phrase that sums up the enduring urge of the African American and that expresses most fully the source of black music and especially of the New Jazz. Section six, *Moon Waltz*, traces "the birth of the blues" to the memory of the African father who "would sing and tell us stories under the moonlight." *Moon Waltz* is not in itself a blues but points to the cause of their birth as an outlet for suffering and suggests the blues at the conclusion of the piece. In the beginning the bass pulsates painfully, and later the piano part is marked by percussive, stabbing pangs, with the violin and clarinet in dual agony. The movement ends as if in the midst of hard labor, a metaphorical image for the life-giving blues that will be born in the fields of Carter's fourth suite.

Recorded in March 1988, *Fields* is subtitled "Seven Vignettes Depicting Life during the Fields Period in Early America." Carter writes in his liner notes that this period "was witness to the labor, grief and pain that harnessed production unseen in the world before" and that it "also cradled the beginnings of national music that would grow to be respected and admired the world over."[42] Throughout *Fields*, Don Preston on keyboards is extremely fine; the bass player, Fred Hopkins, is superb; and Terry Jenoure shows her ability not only as a vocalist but as a violinist who can swing as well as play "legit." The first section, *Ballad to Po' Ben*, begins with a repeated and haunting minor figure through which a voice can be heard but not quite understood. Just before the vocalist enters, Carter treats the listener to a beautifully dramatic passage equal to the best of modern classical music. In its melodic power, Terry Jenoure's song recalls the delta-levy blues as well as Gershwin's *Porgy and Bess*, with the synthesizer contributing a churchy organ sound, after which the muted trombone groans, moans, and growls. This is not the kind of jazz to which one dances or even pats one's foot, but it is rich in its evocations of a race's experiences and requires listening with one's intellect, historical sense, and human emotions in sympathy with those who suffer from man's inhumanity to man. Of course, regardless of whether jazz was intended for the dance or concert hall, there has always been much of the oppressive history of its creators in all of this music, to be heard through the "happy," "upbeat" sounds and rhythms that have won the hearts of listeners worldwide. As Frederick Douglass remarked in 1855 of the singing of slaves, it was "more to *make* themselves happy, than to express their happiness."[43]

Even though the second section may be meant as a critical though subtle commentary on the slave system, *Bootyreba at the Big House* is an all-out swinger and reveals in Bradford's cornet that he has fulfilled here his early potential as a free-jazz exponent. He can be heard especially to full advantage on the 1988 album he and Carter recorded with a quintet that includes Don Preston on piano and synthesizer, Richard Davis on bass, and Andrew Cyrille on drums. Entitled *Comin' On*, this recording perhaps represents the best effort of the Bradford-Carter duo at the same time that it showcases each horn player in his own right at the peak of his career. Of Carter's clarinet mastery, as demonstrated on this album, Art Lange writes that it "is one of modern music's joys. He has expanded the instrument's capabilities into unusual extended ranges while embracing its woody warmth and piercing power . . . his bluesy conviction conveys passion while suggesting the possibility of pain without losing optimism."[44] In a November 11, 1986, performance with the Frank Sullivan Trio in Gainesville, Florida, Bradford had previously recorded *Comin' On*, which serves as the title tune of the 1988 album with Carter. While Bradford turns in a fine version of *All the Things You Are* with the Sullivan Trio, as well as offering a beautiful rendition of *Sho' Nuff Blues*, he seems less inspired on this earlier occasion than with Carter.[45] On the Bradford-Carter album, the two men play the title tune's theme with the precision and feeling of the Coleman-Cherry team, and in their solos both hornmen exhibit great inventiveness and truly original sounds on cornet and clarinet, their respective "old-time" instruments for *Comin' On*.

Juba's Run, the third section of Carter's *Fields*, describes another chase scene, this time a desperate flight of the sort depicted in Blind Lemon Jefferson's *Shanty Blues*, with night and train sounds accompanying Carter's frantic clarinet as the runaway slave or ex-slave attempts to escape the bloodhounds or the Ku Klux Klan's lynch mob. Muffled voices, doglike growls, and other sound effects heighten the drama of this realistic account of those deadly manhunts. Section four, *Seasons*, is a pastoral piece featuring the violin as it evokes a peaceful if painful landscape. Here Carter is definitely in the Ellington tradition of jazz constructed for the purposes of creating a tone poem based on the lives of "black folk." In doing so, Carter, like

Ellington, has universalized the experience of his people, setting their lives against a timeless backdrop of seasonal labor and relaxation, fear and hope, sorrow and irrepressible joy. The section concludes with a text uttered despairingly by Jenoure to the effect that labor in the fields was endless and the workers condemned to a "prison of some ungodly historical circumstance."

Fields, the fifth and title section of the suite, is the longest section, lasting over twenty minutes. If this exemplifies the ability of African Americans to "make themselves happy," it succeeds brilliantly, for the performances throughout are truly magnificent and are even more exciting and inspiring than the long works of Taylor and Coleman. Carter has clearly solved the problem of integrating a great deal of material and yet unifying it and making it vital. Returning to the early period of American life, he combines banjolike sounds on the violin with the voice of his Uncle John, "a musician, poet, preacher, the family historian and a spellbinding storyteller" from a "small, rural community in north central Texas" where as a boy Carter spent several enjoyable summers. Uncle John was near ninety at the time that Carter taped him, and as the composer writes in the liner notes, "It would be our last long talk."[46] A spoken narrative by Uncle John tells of his life as a field hand in north-central Texas while Carter and his group weave modern jazz in and around the words of this great uncle. Along with Carter's grandfather, Uncle John had been a member of marching and dance bands and spoke to Carter of his great-great-grandfather, a virtuoso country fiddler at dances, suppers, wakes, funerals, and the traditional celebrations following graveside obsequies. In sum, this section surveys the entire history of jazz as it developed out of the Carter family tradition in north-central Texas.

Uncle John's voice on *Fields* is backed by the violinist flinging herself into a swinging, free-jazz improvisation propelled by walking bass and slashing drums, while clarinet and bass clarinet add to the section's total effect with melancholy held notes. In general, this piece is a combination of the somber and the determined, with Marty Ehrlich maintaining this affective mix in his Dolphy-like bass clarinet solo. The synthesizer chorus also suggests the spirit of the undaunted drones who toil away and yet endure with dignity. As if there were no relief from the workers' relentless drudgery, the music goes on and on, though there is nothing dull here, for the musicians are impelled by the stimulation of one another instead of being flogged by masters or overseers. The synthesizer's chimelike chords urge the group along, and riffs played by the ensemble encourage soloists as in the call-and-response form so common to jazz by way of African music. Just as the workers plodded on until they or their heirs managed to survive and find a better life, the musicians carry on their improvisations to a triumphant ending, when Uncle John finishes the section singing in the old field-hand style.

The sixth and penultimate section, entitled *Children of the Fields*, incorporates the songs of Carter's own grandchildren. The kids taunt one another while doing their chores to the singing of *Shuckin' Corn*; play a game to the words of *At the Big Tree*, which instructs them to "turn to the one that you love the best"; or watch as clouds pass slowly overhead, their sameness represented by the simple reiteration of a folk-song melody. *On a Country Road*, the seventh and final section of the suite, has Carter's clarinet recorded over a story being told by Uncle John of a horse stuck in a mud hole. The folksy phrase repeated by Carter on clarinet is affecting in its elemental drone rhythm, which is picked up by the bass and then the drum. Afterward, Bradford improvises against this drone and works into a bluesy groove, following which Frederick Phineas plays a country harmonica to end this delightful piece and Carter's fourth suite.

Completing Carter's cycle of suites is the fifth, *Shadows on a Wall*, recorded in April 1989 and called by *Down Beat* reviewer Bill Shoemaker the "fitting conclusion" to the series. Shoemaker also asserts that "anyone claiming a serious interest in American music needs to hear *Roots and Folklore*, and there's no better place to start than at the end" with *Shadows on a Wall*.[47] From the opening section, *Sippie Strut*, with its atonal woodwinds and insistently repetitive figure in the rhythm section, it is clear that we are in the modern age, even as the music pays respects to the blues tradition of the freight train's lonesome whistle and the motif of the "Bird done left me." Whether Sippie of the title refers to Texas blues singer Sippie Wallace remains a supposition, but the words of Carter's verses for this section certainly suggest the possibility. Clearly Carter is aware, in his notes to the album, of the black migration northward, although he emphasizes that his own forebears went "westward from Mississippi and finally settled in Texas." While Carter and his people stayed in the Southwest, he acknowledges that the northern cities proved "great magnets" to attract musicians like Sippie and her brothers George and Hersal. It was especially through the migration north that blacks found employment as entertainers, and Carter recalls in the second section, *Spats*, the creation of the tap dance, "one of the more spectacular developments in dance" brought about by African Americans.[48] Featuring a get-happy solo by trombonist Benny Powell and some extraordinary simultaneous vocal and violin work by Terry Jenoure, this section closes with a slowed-down chorus by Carter.

City Streets, the third section of *Shadows on a Wall*, renders the demanding environment that blacks traded for their life in the fields:

Jobs were difficult to come by and standards of living were generally very low
for most . . . but they came, bringing with them their folk melodies and hymns,
the rhythms, rhymes and dances, ripe for development into the twelve bar blues

and thirty two bar, AABA formats that would become much of the basic foundational materials for American music. Only now did these innate and engrained elements of their music have an opportunity for unhampered development by the Afro-Americans.[49]

This piece is a basic low-down blues, with references in the sung text to New York and Kansas City, where so many Texans took part in the "unhampered development" of "American music." Success in the entertainment field, however, did not necessarily bring respect or better treatment.

The fourth section, *And I Saw Them*, seems to represent the continued struggle to live with the hatred of a racist society, in which the African American existed as a "shadow" or as Ralph Ellison's "invisible man." On the other hand, Carter echoes here the poetry of Langston Hughes as it identified blacks as an integral part of American history, despite the denial of their contributions through prejudice and even jealousy of what they had actually accomplished. The free improvisation of the instruments combines with a text sung by Jenoure to record and reflect on these aspects of the African American experience throughout the nation, from whatever states—Texas, Mississippi, or California—black artists traveled to all parts of the country to make a living through the creation of their imaginative, enlivening music. According to Norman Weinstein, "The gloom introduced by the image of shadows on the wall . . . is a result of trying to escape from the totality of the history of one's people—choosing to remember only a portion, whether African or American."[50] In his epic vision, Carter takes in all periods of the black story, both the African and the American heritage, in order "to recover the full range of history" and to demonstrate "not only the enduring strength of African-American music but the growth and various elaborations (swing, bop) of African roots that continue in it."[51]

Carter next commemorates in particular those who gathered on Fifty-second Street in New York City to develop bebop and to change the entire complexion of jazz. In the fifth section, *52nd Street Stomp*, Bobby Bradford is featured on trumpet and, along with a background of leopardlike screams, recaptures something of the primitive-sophisticated spirit of the bop era, which released its practitioners into a new world of black pride based on self-respect and virtuosic technique and on a return to the roots of an African American consciousness. And last of all, this in turn would lead to the free-jazz movement, perhaps represented by the sixth and final section of this concluding suite, entitled, conceivably with Ornette Coleman in mind, *Hymn to Freedom*.

The text of John Carter's closing theme song, rendered masterfully by vocalist Terry Jenoure, completes the composer-clarinetist's epic *Roots and Folklore* series, as this final section extends an invitation to the "land of the free, home of the brave . . . to men of goodwill" of "all color" to join together, to "Stand Up," to sing, to be strengthened by working side by side. And with Carter's *Hymn to Freedom* "beckoning all . . . to a peaceful life, with hard work . . . unhampered," this study of Texans in jazz history comes full circle, back from Africa to the piney woods and cotton fields of the state where ragtime, blues, and boogie-woogie flourished and on to the streets of Kansas City, New York, Chicago, and Los Angeles where Texas jazzmen congregated with their fellow artists from across the nation to create for America an uplifting music cherished by listeners the world over.

NOTES

INTRODUCTION

1. One possible exception might be Arkansas trombonist Snub Mosley, who performed with the Alphonse Trent orchestra out of Dallas. Gunther Schuller sees him as a musician who exhibited in the 1920s an early form of bebop. See Schuller, *Early Jazz: Its Roots and Musical Development* (New York: Oxford University Press, 1968), p. 302.

2. For the story of the early Texas bands, see Ross Russell, *Jazz Style in Kansas City and the Southwest* (Berkeley: University of California Press, 1971), pp. 53–64; Schuller, *Early Jazz*, pp. 291–293, 299–303; and Gunther Schuller, *The Swing Era: The Development of Jazz, 1930–1945* (New York: Oxford University Press, 1989), pp. 798–805.

3. In *The Swing Era*, Gunther Schuller states that the Southwest, including Texas, developed a regional or territorial style based on the blues that was "so strong and unique" that eventually it asserted itself "as a 'national' style" (p. 805).

4. This study in no way subscribes to the wholesale position taken by a recent history of the state: "Texas never developed a 'jazz' sound as did some other southern states." Robert A. Calvert and Arnoldo De León, *The History of Texas* (Arlington Heights, Ill.: Harlan Davidson, 1990), p. 355.

I. BEGINNINGS IN EAST TEXAS
1. Ragtime

1. Frank Tirro, *Jazz: A History* (New York: W. W. Norton, 1977), pp. 27–29.

2. Gary Giddins, *Riding on a Blue Note: Jazz and American Pop* (New York: Oxford University Press, 1981), pp. 144, 146.

3. Ibid., p. 144.

4. Arnold S. Caplin, liner notes, *Scott Joplin Ragtime*, vol. 3 (Biograph Records, BLP 1010Q, 1972).

5. Along with *The Entertainer* (1902), the film adapted four other of Joplin's compositions: *The Easy Winners* (1901), *The Ragtime Dance* (1906), *Gladiolus Rag* (1907), and *Pineapple Rag* (1908).

6. Tirro, *Jazz*, p. 167.

7. It is possible that Joplin was actually born elsewhere in East Texas. See James Haskins, with Kathleen Benson, *Scott Joplin* (Garden City, N.Y.: Doubleday, 1978), p. 203n.22.

8. Rudi Blesh and Harriet Janis, *They All Played Ragtime* (New York: Knopf, 1950), p. xvi. Other jazz historians have also found a resemblance between ragtime and the European rondo form of the minuet. However, Gunther Schuller observes that this is a "misleading" and "mistaken notion." Schuller only recognizes the music's roots in "the march or the quick step" (*Early Jazz*, pp. 31–32).

9. Theodore Albrecht, "Julius Weiss: Scott Joplin's First Piano Teacher," *College Music Symposium* 19, no. 2 (Fall 1979): 93.

10. Don Gazzaway, "Conversations with Buster Smith," Part 2, *Jazz Review* 3, no. 1 (January 1959): 13.

11. Haskins, *Scott Joplin*, pp. 193–194. Through such pianola rolls created by Joplin and other ragtime pianists, nonreading musicians also learned to train their fingers by placing them where the player piano keys were depressed mechanically by means of a punched paper roll.

12. Blesh and Janis, *They All Played Ragtime*, pp. 52, 76.

13. Haskins, *Scott Joplin*, p. 57.

14. Ibid., pp. 23, 27.

15. Ibid., p. 27.

16. Ibid., p. 41.

17. Ibid., pp. 59–60.

18. Blesh and Janis, *They All Played Ragtime*, p. xxiii. The authors also write that "for at least a dozen years a large proportion of published rags consciously or unconsciously followed the metric patterns or melodic lines of Joplin's prototype, or else had variants or new melodies based on its harmonic progressions."

19. Haskins, *Scott Joplin*, p. 59.

20. Ibid., p. 80n.21.

21. Russell, *Jazz Style in Kansas City*, p. 42.

22. Haskins, *Scott Joplin*, p. 81.

23. Nathaniel Hawthorne, *The House of the Seven Gables* (New York: Oxford University Press, 1992), p. 36.

24. Haskins, *Scott Joplin*, p. 83.

25. Ibid.

26. Ibid., pp. 212n.30 and 85.

27. See Marshall W. Stearns, *The Story of Jazz* (New York: Oxford University Press, 1970), p. 147; H. Wiley Hitchcock, *Music in the United States: A Historical Introduction*, 2d. ed. (Englewood Cliffs, N.J.: Prentice-Hall, 1974), p. 123 (cited in Tirro, *Jazz*, p. 26).

28. Schuller, *Early Jazz*, p. 33.

29. William J. Shafer and Johannes Riedel, *The Art of Ragtime* (Baton Rouge: Louisiana State University Press, 1973), p. 79.

30. Ornette Coleman, liner notes, *The Music of Ornette Coleman* (RCA Victor Records, LSC-2982, 1968).

31. Quoted in Blesh and Janis, *They All Played Ragtime*, pp. 118, 253.

32. Haskins, *Scott Joplin*, p. 90.

33. Blesh and Janis, *They All Played Ragtime*, pp. 50, 31.

34. Haskins, *Scott Joplin*, p. 88.

35. Blesh and Janis, *They All Played Ragtime*, p. 31.

36. John W. "Knocky" Parker, liner notes, *Scott Joplin's Original Ragtime Compositions* (Audiophile Records, 71).

37. Quoted in Haskins, *Scott Joplin*, p. 113.

38. Guy Waterman, "Ragtime," in *The Art of Jazz: Essays on the Nature and Development of Jazz*, ed. Martin T. Williams (New York: Grove Press, 1960), p. 16.

39. Ibid., p. 20.

40. Ibid., pp. 20, 19, 15, 26–27. Joshua Rifkin, the New York pianist who recorded eight Joplin rags for Nonesuch Records in 1970, has observed that "throughout the first decade of the century, [Joplin's] harmonies grow bolder . . . and the keyboard writing fuller and more demanding. The experimentation and searching achieve their fruition in *Scott Joplin's New Rag*, with its fluid harmonies and unmistakable undercurrent of bitterness, and in *Magnetic Rag*, the last piece that Joplin completed. Subtitled *Syncopations classiques*, this valedictory work synthesizes the diverse facets of Joplin's imagination, paying tribute, in its middle sections, to the transplanted Middle-European dance music that influenced early ragtime pianists, the upcoming world of jazz, and the European masters whom Joplin sought to emulate." Liner notes, *Piano Rags by Scott Joplin* (Nonesuch H-71248, 1970).

41. Haskins, *Scott Joplin*, p. 150.

42. Barry Kernfeld, ed., *The New Grove Dictionary of Jazz* (London: Macmillan, 1988), 2:465.

43. James Lincoln Collier, *The Making of Jazz: A Comprehensive History* (New York: Dell Publishing, 1978), p. 52. Collier goes on to say, "These pieces are among the most infectious, joyous pieces of music written by any American, and I have no doubt that they will become part of our heritage, to be sung and danced by school children for generations to come."

44. Schuller, *Early Jazz*, p. 115.

45. Ibid., pp. 375, 146.

46. Ibid., pp. 124–125.

47. This whole area of the sexual or even "bestial" side of ragtime and jazz has been discussed by many commentators. Schafer and Riedel summarize the view that ragtime and jazz were "barbaric and corrupting expressions of a socially debased and genetically inferior people." This "aesthetic Darwinism" found "something fundamentally 'primitive' or 'savage' in black music, an element appealing to the bestial in the listener and provoking him to wickedness, lewdness, or at best indecorousness." Pro-ragtime critics could draw on Darwin, too, finding it "a ligno-musical stimulant. The ordinary music-listener wants to hear something musical that sets the head to nodding and the foot to stamping [as in Joplin's *Stoptime Rag*]; something which he can grasp and comprehend with his present rhythmic sense, somewhat as he does a cane, because of his simian descent" (quoted in *The Art of Ragtime*, pp. 38–40).

48. *Some Day My Prince Will Come* (Columbia Records, CL1656). Jack Chambers writes that "*Pfrancing*, a wonderfully evocative title capturing references to Frances Davis and to a whole semantic field taking in prancing, dancing, and frantic, all of which suit it nicely, quickly became a nightly fixture under the more prosaic title *No Blues*." See *Milestones 2: The Music and Times of Miles*

Davis since 1960 (New York: William Morrow, 1985), p. 32. Wilfrid Mellers describes Fats Waller's technique in part as "prancing," a term that goes back to the cakewalk, the nineteenth-century dance developed by African Americans. See Mellers, *Music in a New Found Land*, rev. ed. (New York: Oxford University Press, 1987), p. 374.

49. Rudi Blesh, *Shining Trumpets: A History of Jazz*, 2d ed. (New York: Knopf, 1958; rpt. Da Capo Press, 1980), p. 269.

50. Addison W. Reed, "Scott Joplin, Pioneer," in *Ragtime: Its History, Composers, and Music*, ed. John Edward Hasse (New York: Macmillan, 1985), p. 132.

51. Haskins, *Scott Joplin*, pp. 122–123.

52. Quoted in Blesh and Janis, *They All Played Ragtime*, p. 181.

53. Quoted in ibid., p. 148.

54. Quoted in Haskins, *Scott Joplin*, p. 122.

55. Alan Lomax, *Mister Jelly Roll: The Fortunes of Jelly Roll Morton, New Orleans Creole and "Inventor of Jazz"* (New York: Grosset and Dunlap, 1950), p. 190. Lomax also quotes Morton's own account of a time in St. Louis around 1912 when he was hired at the Democratic Club and the local pianists brought him "all Scott Joplin's tunes—he was the great St. Louis ragtime composer—and I knew them all by heart and played them right off" (p. 148).

56. Collier, *The Making of Jazz*, p. 49.

57. Blesh and Janis, *They All Played Ragtime*, p. 68.

58. Schafer and Riedel, *The Art of Ragtime*, p. 225.

59. Schuller, *Early Jazz*, pp. 186–187.

60. Max Harrison, liner notes, *New Orleans Rhythm Kings and Jelly Roll Morton* (Milestone M47020, 1974).

61. Ibid.

62. Nat Shapiro and Nat Hentoff, eds., *Hear Me Talkin' to Ya: The Story of Jazz as Told by the Men Who Made It* (1955; reprint, New York: Dover Publications, 1966), pp. 59–60. Jack Weber recalls that "an old circus trumpeter in New Orleans back in 1915 on a dance date, a fellow named Sam Rickey," told him that "they had been playing ragtime down there for thirty years."

63. Ibid., p. 60. An indication of the popularity of Joplin's *Maple Leaf Rag* is found in a private solo recording of this tune by Bunk Johnson, made in New Iberia, Louisiana, on February 2, 1942. Having lost his teeth about 1931, Johnson returned to performing only around 1940, when supporters, led by Frederic Ramsey, Jr., and William Russell, helped fit him with a set of teeth and supplied him with a trumpet. Rudi Blesh writes that "he amazed all who heard him by the vigor, freshness, and creative power of his playing. In the compressed history of jazz this event was as important and revealing as, in European music, it might be to hear Chopin or Beethoven play today" (*Shining Trumpets*, p. 185). This claim is supported by Johnson's solo rendition of Joplin's *Maple Leaf Rag*, which the trumpet player had obviously performed many times when a much younger man. Despite flaws in places, as would be expected in a man over sixty years of age and after some ten years of not playing, the performance exhibits Bunk's sure sense of form and rhythm, his beautiful sound that was so often praised by other players, and his thorough knowledge of Joplin's rag. This remarkable recording is available on *New Orleans Horns (1923–1954)* (Document DLP 501/502, 1986).

64. Schafer and Riedel, *The Art of Ragtime*, p. 146.

65. Joplin made this comment on the scores of his music: "It is never right to play Ragtime fast." See Reed, "Scott Joplin, Pioneer," pp. 130–131. Schafer and Riedel also quote Joplin's piano manual, *The School of Ragtime* (1908), on the adverse effects of "playing too fast" (*The Art of Ragtime*, p. 145).

66. A recording of Joplin's April 1916 Connorized piano roll (no. 10265) is included on *The Smithsonian Collection of Classic Jazz* (Columbia Special Products, Smithsonian Institution, P6 11891, 1987), cassette side A.

67. Schafer and Riedel, *The Art of Ragtime*, p. 145.

68. Jelly Roll Morton, "Discourse on Jazz," in *Classic Jazz Masters*, vol. 8, Library of Congress Recordings (Circle Records CJM9, remastered 1970). Morton was recorded by Alan Lomax, the library's folk music curator, beginning on May 21, 1938.

69. Lomax, *Mister Jelly Roll*, p. 149n.

70. Morton, "Discourse on Jazz."

71. See in particular Tirro, *Jazz*, pp. 109–111.

72. *The Smithsonian Collection of Classic Jazz*, selected and annotated by Martin Williams (Washington, D.C.: Smithsonian Collection of Recordings, 1987), pp. 35, 37.

73. Schuller, *Early Jazz*, pp. 136n, 148.

74. Of his earliest recording Jelly Roll said, "I made my first record . . . in 1918 for some company in California. Reb Spikes, Mutt Carey, Wade Waley, Kid Orey [*sic*], and I recorded *The Wolverines* and *King Porter*, but we never heard from those records." Quoted in Lomax, *Mister Jelly Roll*, p. 300. Lomax lists *The Jelly Roll Blues* of 1915 as Morton's "first published jazz composition?" but indicates that this work was "written in 1905, arranged 1912?" (p. 292).

75. Quoted in ibid., p. 62.

76. Schuller, *Early Jazz*, p. 173.

77. Ibid., pp. 144–145.

78. Waterman, "Ragtime," p. 22.

79. Martin Williams, *The Jazz Tradition* (New York: Oxford University Press, 1983), p. 157.

80. Schuller, *Early Jazz*, p. 144.

81. *The Chronological Jelly-Roll Morton 1930–1939* (Classics Records, 654, 1992).

82. Rudi Blesh, liner notes, William Bolcom, *Heliotrope Bouquet: Piano Rags 1900–1970* (Nonesuch Records, H-71257, 1971).

83. Guy Waterman, "Jelly Roll Morton," in *Jazz Panorama*, ed. Martin Williams (New York: Collier Books, 1967), p. 33.

84. Schafer and Riedel, *The Art of Ragtime*, p. 179.

85. Waterman, "Jelly Roll Morton," p. 32.

86. Ibid., pp. 35, 36–37.

87. Blesh and Janis, *They All Played Ragtime*, p. 271.

88. Camille Paglia, *Sexual Personae: Art and Decadence from Nefertiti to Emily Dickinson* (New York: Vintage Books, 1991), p. 638.

89. From a video of the November 1991 performance of *Five Dances by Martha Graham* at the Opera de Paris Garnier (videocassette, Amaya Distribution).

90. John Edward Hasse, "Euday L. Bowman," in *The New Grove Dictionary of Music*, ed. H. Wiley Hitchcock and Stanley Sadie (London: Macmillan, 1986), 1:281.

91. Blesh and Janis, *They All Played Ragtime*, p. 122.

92. This information comes from a 1992 conversation with an aunt of mine, Irene Shepherd, who, during her girlhood in Fort Worth, heard Bowman practicing as she would pass by the shoeshine parlor. Both this aunt on my mother's side and an uncle on my father's were contestants at a 1926 Charleston contest held in Fort Worth, which was won by Ginger Rogers, who went on to Hollywood fame and fortune. My Uncle Buzz played ragtime at home, and I recall in the late 1940s seeing sheet music for the *Maple Leaf Rag* on his piano. In my grandmother's home in Fort Worth, I listened with delight on her Victrola to George Botsford's *Black and White Rag*, originally published in 1908, "his first and biggest syncopated hit . . . widely recorded for phonograph and pianola" (Blesh and Janis, *They All Played Ragtime*, p. 122).

93. Paul E. Affeldt, liner notes, *The Professors: Brun Campbell, Dink Johnson, Euday L. Bowman*, Piano Series, vol. 2 (Euphonic Records, ESR 1202). This recording was probably made in 1938. Bowman first recorded his rag in 1924 for Gennett Records, but it was not issued. See Hasse, "Euday L. Bowman," in *The New Grove Dictionary of Music*, ed. Hitchcock and Sadie, 1:281. Neither Bowman nor his rag is mentioned in Rick Kennedy, *Jelly Roll, Bix, and Hoagy: Gennett Studios and the Birth of Recorded Jazz* (Bloomington: Indiana University Press, 1994). Paul Affeldt writes in his liner notes that Bowman's piano "was subsequently auctioned off to help with his funeral expenses" since, in having sold outright "royalties and all" for one hundred dollars, the composer died in poverty. Affeldt observes that "Bowman's story is perhaps the classic of all stories of unfair exploitation of musicians, be they ragtime or otherwise."

94. Paul Oliver et al., *The New Grove Gospel, Blues, and Jazz with Spirituals and Ragtime* (New York: W. W. Norton, 1986), p. 49.

95. Hasse, "Euday L. Bowman," in *The New Grove Dictionary of Music*, ed. Hitchcock and Sadie, 1:281. Ross Russell claims that Bowman's rag "commemorated one of the main thoroughfares in Kansas City" (*Jazz Style in Kansas City*, p. 219), while Hasse reports that it "commemorated four streets" (Sixth, Tenth, Eleventh, and Twelfth) in "'Hell's Half Acre,' the former bordello district of Fort Worth" (p. 281).

96. Frank J. Gillis, "Hot Rhythm in Piano Ragtime," in *Ragtime*, ed. Hasse, p. 229.

97. Oliver et al., *The New Grove Gospel, Blues, and Jazz*, p. 29.

98. Schuller, *The Swing Era*, p. 248n.

99. Max Harrison, Charles Fox, and Eric Thacker, *The Essential Jazz Records*, vol. 1, *Ragtime to Swing* (New York: Da Capo Press, 1988), p. 501.

100. Williams, *The Jazz Tradition*, p. 56.

101. John Chilton, liner notes, *Louis Armstrong: The Hot Fives and Hot Sevens*, vol. 2 (Columbia Records, CK 44253, 1988), p. 9.

102. Williams, *The Jazz Tradition*, pp. 56–57.

103. Schuller, *Early Jazz*, p. 283.

104. Brian Rust, liner notes, *Bennie Moten and His Kansas City Orchestra*, vol. 1, *"Moten Stomp"* (Halcyon Records, HDL 108, 1986).

105. Cootie Williams recalled to jazz historian Stanley Dance that it was while playing *Twelfth Street Rag* on trumpet, after having started at seven on trombone and being "transferred to tuba," that his teacher told him, "'That's your instrument' . . . and from there on it was." See Stanley

Dance, *The World of Duke Ellington* (New York: Charles Scribner's Sons, 1970), p. 103.

106. Stanley Dance, liner notes, *Duke Ellington: "Rockin' in Rhythm,"* vol. 3, *1929–1931* (MCA Records, MCA-1360, 1970).

107. *Fats Waller: Ain't Misbehavin'* (Pickwick International Records, England, SMS 20, 1990).

108. Mellers, *Music in a New Found Land*, pp. 374–375.

109. Eric Thacker, reviews of *Lester Young Memorial*, vol. 1 and vol. 2, in Harrison, Fox, and Thacker, *The Essential Jazz Records*, p. 301.

110. Stanley Dance, liner notes, *The Essential Count Basie*, vol. 1 (Columbia Records, CJ 40608, 1987).

111. Albert McCarthy, *Big Band Jazz* (London: Barrie and Jenkins, 1974), p. 206. Another British critic to find Young's performance on Bowman's rag noteworthy is Barry Ulanov, who suggests that Lester's solos could be "as stale and stiff as his competitors'" but that "in Basie's 'Taxi War Dance' and 'Twelfth Street Rag,' in his own 'Lester Leaps In,' . . . the earmarks of a bright style did emerge." See *A History of Jazz in America* (London: Jazz Book Club, 1959), p. 236.

112. Benny Green, "Man with a Hat: An Evaluation of the Work of Lester Young," in *Just Jazz 3*, ed. Sinclair Traill and Gerald Lascelles (London: Landsborough Publications, 1959), pp. 53–54.

113. Schuller, *The Swing Era*, p. 248n. Schuller characterizes a 1940s version of *Twelfth Street Rag* by the Lionel Hampton band as "mindless piano pyrotechnics" (p. 394). The Hampton recording is included on *Lionel Hampton and His Orchestra* (Past Records, 9789). Another recording of Bowman's rag was made by the Fletcher Henderson band in 1931 and featured a solo by Coleman Hawkins on tenor sax. See *Fletcher Henderson: The Crown King of Swing* (Savoy Jazz Records, SV–0254, 1994).

114. *Kansas City Jazz* (Decca Records, DL 8044).

115. Albert McCarthy notes that "an intriguing side of Mary Lou's playing has always been her occasional reversion to ragtime modes" (*Big Band Jazz*, p. 246). Brian Rust, in his *Jazz Records 1897–1942*, vol. 2 (Chigwell, England: Storyville Publications, 1975), credits Williams as the arranger for the band but does not refer to specific tunes. Rex Harris, in his liner notes to *Twelve Clouds of Joy: Andy Kirk* (Decca Records, England, Ace of Hearts, AH 160, 1967), gives Sumner-Bowman for *Twelfth Street Rag*, but it is not clear whether Sumner was an arranger for Kirk.

116. Charles Fox, review of *Andy Kirk: Walking and Swinging*, in Harrison, Fox, and Thacker, *The Essential Jazz Records*, p. 294.

117. Lawson not only served as lead trumpet from around 1935 to 1942 but also composed *Big Jim Blues*, which, as arranged by Mary Lou Williams, was recorded by the Kirk orchestra on November 15, 1939 (*Andy Kirk: "Instrumentally Speaking"* [1936–1942] [Decca Records, DL 9232]). Gunther Schuller calls Lawson's muted solo on *Big Jim Blues* a "highly unusual 18-bar variant of the blues changes" (*The Swing Era*, p. 358).

118. Harris, liner notes, *Twelve Clouds of Joy*.

119. Ralph J. Gleason, jacket copy for *Treat It Gentle*, by Sidney Bechet (New York: Hill and Wang, 1960).

120. Unsigned jacket copy for ibid.

121. George Hoefer, liner notes, *Bechet of New Orleans: A Jazz Pioneer* (RCA Victor Records,

LPV-510, 1965). During the "Spirituals to Swing" concert of 1939 at Carnegie Hall, Texas trombonist Dan Minor was a member of Bechet's New Orleans Feetwarmers, playing traditional tailgate trombone on *Weary Blues* and at greater length on *I Wish I Could Shimmy Like My Sister Kate* on *Spirituals to Swing*, vol. 1 (Fontana Vanguard Records, FJL 401).

122. Hoefer, liner notes, *Bechet of New Orleans*.

123. Eric Thacker, review of *The Blue Bechet*, in Harrison, Fox, and Thacker, *The Essential Jazz Records*, p. 501.

2. Country Blues

1. Schuller, *Early Jazz*, p. 145.

2. Albert Murray, *Stomping the Blues* (1976; reprint, New York: Da Capo Press, 1987), pp. 63–64. Murray mentions the examples of Irving and Jefferson. Thoreau uses both "blues" and "blue devils" in the "Solitude" section of *Walden*, the first in reference to the question of whether he became lonely while staying in his cabin, and the second by way of comparing his own state with that of nature: "I am no more lonely than the loon in the pond that laughs so loud, or than Walden Pond itself. What company has that lonely lake, I pray? And yet it has not the blue devils, but the blue angels in it, in the azure tint of its waters" (*Walden; or, Life in the Woods* [Boston: Ticknor and Fields, 1854], p. 148). The passages containing the terms "blues" and "blue devils" were included in the first version of *Walden*, which possibly dates from as early as the mid-1840s. See James Lyndon Shanley, *The Making of Walden* (Chicago: University of Chicago Press, 1957), pp. 167–168.

3. Schuller, *Early Jazz*, p. 40.

4. Lomax, *Mister Jelly Roll*, p. 89.

5. Ibid., p. 20.

6. William Barlow, *"Looking Up at Down": The Emergence of Blues Culture* (Philadelphia: Temple University Press, 1989), pp. 68, 23. Barlow's study is extremely valuable and is the basis of much of my subsequent discussion of the rural blues tradition in Texas.

7. Schuller, *The Swing Era*, p. 563.

8. Ibid., pp. 156–157.

9. Ibid., p. 186.

10. Paul Oliver, *The Story of the Blues* (Philadelphia: Chilton, 1969), pp. 39–40.

11. Ibid., p. 16.

12. Sidney Finkelstein, *Jazz: A People's Music* (1948; reprint, New York: International Publishers, 1988), p. 97.

13. Gerard Herzhaft, *Encyclopedia of the Blues*, trans. Brigitte Dewd (Fayetteville: University of Arkansas Press, 1992), pp. 341–342.

14. Charles Keil, *Urban Blues* (Chicago: University of Chicago Press, 1966), p. 59.

15. Derrick Stewart-Baxter, review of *Henry Thomas: Ragtime 'Texas,'* *Jazz Journal* 25, no. 5 (May 1975): 44. Stewart-Baxter credits Mack McCormick, who rediscovered Thomas, with "the most remarkable piece of research and documentation I have seen."

16. According to Stephen Calt, liner notes, *Henry Thomas: Texas Worried Blues* (Yazoo Records, 1080/1, 1989), Thomas recorded twenty-four tunes, but there are only twenty-three on this

recording, which is nevertheless billed as Thomas's "complete recorded works."

17. Samuel B. Charters believes that Thomas "was probably the first singer to record using the quills, even though they were at one time widely played throughout the South." See *The Blues Makers* (1967; reprint, New York: Da Capo Press, 1991), p. 191. Charters goes on to say that the quills were "also known as 'pan pipes'"—each of which was "a cross blown cane reed, held against the lips while the player blows across the opening in the top."

18. Stephen Calt makes this suggestion in his liner notes to *Texas Worried Blues*. Much of my discussion thus far is based on Calt's observations.

19. Samuel B. Charters reports that Jefferson recorded *Beggin' Back* in the spring of 1925 but that it was not released until the summer of 1926. See *The Country Blues* (London: Jazz Book Club, 1961), p. 43. *Beggin' Back* is included on *Blind Lemon Jefferson: King of the Country Blues* (Yazoo Records, 1069, 1990).

20. Quoted in Lomax, *Mister Jelly Roll*, p. 89.

21. Calt, liner notes, *Texas Worried Blues*.

22. Barlow, *"Looking Up at Down,"* p. 62.

23. Thomas's own versions of this song are entitled *Don't Ease Me In* and *Don't Leave Me Here*. Of the latter, Stephen Calt writes, "Although the song is not a blues, Thomas gives it a bluesy cast by virtue of his vocal treatment; he adds minor thirds and minor sevenths." Calt, liner notes, *Don't Leave Me Here: The Blues of Texas, Arkansas, and Louisiana 1927–1932* (Yazoo Records, 1004).

24. Barlow, *"Looking Up at Down,"* p. 64.

25. Calt, liner notes, *Texas Worried Blues*.

26. For an enlightening discussion of the banjo and the quills, see Stearns, *The Story of Jazz*, p. 54.

27. Charters, *The Blues Makers*, pp. 193, 195.

28. In his liner notes to *Blind Lemon Jefferson: King of the Country Blues*, Stephen Calt notes that Jefferson's birth date has been given "on poor grounds" as 1897 but that "his true birth year conceivably dates to 1880." William Barlow also takes the earlier date as Jefferson's year of birth (*"Looking Up at Down,"* p. 65).

29. Samuel Charters reports that "there is a story that the first recordings [by Jefferson] were done in a rug department of a Dallas department store" sometime in 1924 (*The Country Blues*, p. 43).

30. Tom Shaw, a "would-be imitator" of Jefferson, quoted in Calt, liner notes, *Blind Lemon Jefferson: King of the Country Blues*.

31. Daphne Duval Harrison, *Black Pearls: Blues Queens of the 1920s* (New Brunswick, N.J.: Rutgers University Press, 1988), p. 150.

32. The date of Jefferson's death "is variously given as from shortly after his last Paramount recording session in September 1929, up until mid-1930." Pete Welding, liner notes, *Blind Lemon Jefferson* (Milestone Records, MCD-47022-2, 1992).

33. Calt, liner notes, *Blind Lemon Jefferson: King of the Country Blues*.

34. Ibid.

35. Welding, liner notes, *Blind Lemon Jefferson*.

36. Calt, liner notes, *Blind Lemon Jefferson: King of the Country Blues*.

37. Barlow, *"Looking Up at Down,"* p. 67.

38. Tirro, *Jazz*, p. 128.

39. Calt, liner notes, *Blind Lemon Jefferson: King of the Country Blues.*

40. Barlow, *"Looking Up at Down,"* p. 67.

41. Ibid.

42. Ibid.

43. Welding, liner notes, *Blind Lemon Jefferson.*

44. Schuller, *Early Jazz*, p. 48.

45. Ibid., pp. 48, 50.

46. Calt, liner notes, *Blind Lemon Jefferson: King of the Country Blues.*

47. Welding, liner notes, *Blind Lemon Jefferson.*

48. Ibid.

49. Calt, liner notes, *Blind Lemon Jefferson: King of the Country Blues.*

50. Schuller, *The Swing Era*, p. 239.

51. Ibid. This version of *Sent for You Yesterday* is included on *The Best of Count Basie* (MCA Records, MCA2-4050, 1980).

52. Murray, *Stomping the Blues*, p. 176.

53. Calt, liner notes, *Blind Lemon Jefferson: King of the Country Blues.*

54. Barlow, *"Looking Up at Down,"* p. 68.

55. Jeff Todd Titon, *Early Downhome Blues: A Musical and Cultural Analysis* (Urbana: University of Illinois Press, 1977), p. 115. Titon explains that a "fatmouth" is a fool. He also notes that *Got the Blues* was "mistakenly identified" as *Long Lonesome Blues* (p. 114).

56. Schuller, *The Swing Era*, p. 17. The 1931 *Beale Street Blues* recording is included on *The Golden Horn of Jack Teagarden* (Decca Records, DL4540).

57. George Hoefer, liner notes, *The King of New Orleans Jazz* (RCA Victor Records, RCA LPM-1649, 1959).

58. Schuller, *Early Jazz*, p. 166.

59. Murray, *Stomping the Blues*, p. 79.

60. After Leadbelly composed his 1924 song *Governor Pat Neff*, "nearly 23 years of his sentence for murder and assault to murder" was commuted, and he "walked out of the penitentiary in Huntsville, Texas, a free man." Kip Lornell, liner notes, *Leadbelly: Midnight Special*, vol. 1, Library of Congress Recordings, recorded by Alan Lomax (Rounder Records, 1044, 1991).

61. See Mary Berry and John Blassingame, "African Slavery and the Roots of Contemporary Black Culture," in *Chant of Saints: A Gathering of Afro-American Literature, Art, and Scholarship*, ed. Michael Harper and Stephen Stepto (Urbana, Ill.: University of Illinois Press, 1979), p. 252, cited in Barlow, *"Looking Up at Down,"* pp. 70, 357n.

62. Calt, liner notes, *Blind Lemon Jefferson: King of the Country Blues.* Jefferson's *See That My Grave Is Kept Clean* is a version of the well-known *Two White Horses Standing in a Line*, "the same folk melody and most of the verses that were sung not only in Texas but in many other areas of the South" (Charters, *The Blues Makers*, pp. 178–179). Barlow refers to this Jefferson piece as a prison work song (*"Looking Up at Down,"* p. 60).

63. Welding, liner notes, *Blind Lemon Jefferson.*

64. See Calt, liner notes, *Blind Lemon Jefferson: King of the Country Blues.*

65. Russell, *Jazz Style in Kansas City*, pp. 35–36.

66. Ibid., pp. 36, 33, 38.

67. Lornell, liner notes, *Leadbelly: Midnight Special.*

68. Barlow, *"Looking Up at Down,"* p. 73. Albert Murray refers to Leadbelly's instrument as his "notorious twelve-string train-whistle guitar" (*Stomping the Blues*, p. 117).

69. Russell, *Jazz Style in Kansas City*, p. 35.

70. Tony Standish, review of Huddie Ledbetter, *Blues Anthology*, vol. 7 (Storyville Records, SLP 124), *Jazz Journal* 15, no. 9 (September 1962): 28.

71. Paul Oliver, liner notes, *The Story of the Blues* (Columbia Records, 30008).

72. On a 78 rpm of *I'm on My Last Go-Around* (Bluebird Records, B-8981-B), Leadbelly imitates a train whistle with his singing while his guitar creates an enginelike beat.

73. Russell, *Jazz Style in Kansas City*, pp. 34–35.

74. Ibid., p. 36. *Matchbox Blues*, *Irene*, and *Ella Speed* are included on *Leadbelly: Midnight Special*; *C. C. Rider* is on *Leadbelly: Gwine Dig a Hole to Put the Devil In*, vol. 2, Library of Congress Recordings (Rounder Records, 1045, 1991).

75. Stearns, *The Story of Jazz*, pp. 157, 158.

3. Classic Blues

1. Schuller, *Early Jazz*, p. 226n.

2. Ibid., p. 209.

3. Sippie Wallace was one of thirteen children born to George W. Thomas, Sr., an itinerant railroad worker and deacon of Shiloh Baptist Church in Houston (Harris, *Blues Who's Who*, p. 507). David Evans, in his liner notes to *Texas Piano*, vol. 1 (Document Records, DOCD-5224, 1994), says that there were twelve Thomas children, which may mean in addition to Sippie.

4. Various dates have been given for Hersal Thomas's birth. Most recently, David Evans claims 1906 as the correct year, apparently based on information obtained from Detroit jazz researcher Mike Montgomery (liner notes, *Texas Piano*).

5. Ernest Borneman, "The Blues: A Study in Ambiguity," in *Just Jazz 3*, ed. Traill and Lascelles, p. 90.

6. George Thomas's 1922 hit, *Muscle Shoal Blues*, was one of two tunes performed by Fats Waller on his first recording, made in 1923. It was also recorded in 1926 by the first major Kansas City jazz band, led by Bennie Moten and featuring at the time Texan Lammar Wright on cornet.

7. Rudi Blesh, *Shining Trumpets*, p. 139. An advertisement for Sippie's recording of *Underworld Blues* offers an example of what Daphne Duval Harrison labels "high-type dialect," but it also suggests something of the singer's style and its effect on her listeners: "Sippie sure totes a mighty mean contralto and it's just suited for 'low-down.' When she lets it loose with her own peppery style of delivery—um-m-m-um—we're telling you you're a-hearin' real 'blues' and we don't mean maybe" (*Black Pearls*, facing p. 125). *Underworld Blues* was written by Sippie Wallace and, according to her account, "came about from watching these women hustling on the street corners." See Eric Townley with Ron Harwood, "The Texas Nightingale: An Interview with

Sippie Wallace," *Storyville*, no. 108 (1983): 228–229.

8. Evans, liner notes, *Texas Piano*, vol. 1. Bernice Edwards recorded sixteen issued sides (twelve in Chicago in 1928), all of which are included on this album. Her vocal delivery ranges from "stage vibrato" and "vaudeville warbling to blues belting," and her accompaniment of herself on piano "displays a fully developed 'Santa Fe' style" with the "typical Texas melodic figure of M3-4-M3-m3-2-1 along with right hand tremoloes and lots of underlying harmonic movement." She did not, however, record with jazz musicians. Her *Southbound Blues* is another instance of the railroad theme, with a pleading to the engineer to "hurry and make up that train" so she can "go home."

9. Harrison, *Black Pearls*, p. 123.

10. Schuller, *Early Jazz*, p. 228.

11. Barlow, *"Looking Up at Down,"* pp. 60, 143.

12. Harrison, *Black Pearls*, p. 123.

13. Ibid., p. 113. Harrison reports that Sippie's first recording "purportedly sold 100,000 copies—quite a feat for a newcomer in a young field" (p. 121).

14. James Cones, *The Spirituals and the Blues: An Interpretation* (New York: Seabury Press, 1972), pp. 111–112; quoted in Harrison, *Black Pearls*, p. 116.

15. Harrison, *Black Pearls*, pp. 114, 117.

16. Blesh, *Shining Trumpets*, p. 139.

17. Ibid., pp. 139–140. *Trouble Everywhere I Roam* and *Baby I Can't Use You No More* are included on *Adam and Eve Had the Blues: Rare Recordings of the Twenties*, vol. 2 (CBS Records, France, 65379). Armstrong played cornet on these two Okeh sides, but they are not included on *The Complete Louis Armstrong and the Singers, 1924/30*, 4 vols. (King Jazz, 1993).

18. Collier, *The Making of Jazz*, p. 111.

19. Ibid.

20. Ibid.

21. Ibid., p. 112.

22. Blesh, *Shining Trumpets*, p. 140.

23. Martin Williams, review of *King Oliver: "Back o' Town"* (Riverside Records, RLP 12-130), *Jazz Review* 2, no. 8 (September 1959): 35. King Oliver, along with pianist Clarence Williams and white guitarist Eddie Lang, also recorded with Alger "Texas" Alexander, whose birthplace has been given as Leon County—either Jewett (in 1900) or Leona (ca. 1890). As a Texas bluesman who did not play the guitar, Alexander was accompanied by such figures as Blind Lemon Jefferson and Lonnie Johnson as well as Oliver. On *Tell Me Woman Blues* and *'Frisco Train Blues*, from November 20, 1928, Oliver on muted trumpet creates with wah-wahs and trills his characteristic responses to Alexander's country blues. On *'Frisco Train Blues*, Oliver also takes a fine full chorus, after which Alexander offers an example of his patented use of a humming moan. Both tunes with Oliver are included on *Texas Alexander*, vol. 2, *1928–1930* (Document Records, France, MBCD 2002, 1993). In his liner notes to this compact disc, blues historian Paul Oliver finds that the King "plays as if he were accompanying a 'classic blues' singer" rather than a rural bluesman like Alexander, who tends to set his own pace in a more free-form style. Robert Santelli has followed Oliver's lead in suggesting that Alexander's vocal approach was "closely linked to the field hollers, work shouts, and prison songs" and his "best songs . . .

reflected East Texas culture." See *The Big Book of Blues: A Biographical Encyclopedia* (New York: Penguin, 1993), pp. 5–6. Alexander was a cousin of Texas singer Lightnin' Hopkins, who was born in Centerville on March 15, 1912, and is considered the last singer in the grand style of Texas blues.

24. These tunes are included on *New Orleans Horns, 1924–1954* (Document Records, DLP 501/502, 1986).

25. Less than a week before this recording session, Sippie and Hersal participated in the Okeh Race Records Artists Night, held on February 27, 1926, at the Chicago Coliseum, along with Armstrong and many others. See "Chicago Jazz History," in *Esquire's 1946 Jazz Book*, ed. Paul Eduard Miller (New York: Smith and Durrell, 1946), p. 25.

26. Liner notes, *Rare Recordings of the Twenties*, vol. 4 (CBS Records, France, 65421).

27. André Hodeir calls *Big Butter and Egg Man* the "most successful of all" the Hot Five recordings and "a masterpiece," saying that "it is impossible to imagine anything more sober and balanced." See *Jazz: Its Evolution and Essence* (New York: Grove Press, 1956), pp. 56–57. Daphne Duval Harrison identifies May Alix as one of several pseudonyms used by singer Alberta Hunter (*Black Pearls*, p. 200).

28. Harrison, *Black Pearls*, p. 125.

29. Ronald P. Harwood, liner notes, *Sippie Wallace with Jim Dapogny's Chicago Jazz Band* (Atlantic Records, SD 19350, 1982); Harwood, "'Mighty Tight Woman': The Thomas Family and Classic Blues," *Storyville*, no. 17 (1968): 22.

30. Townley, "The Texas Nightingale," p. 229.

31. Jefferson's version was recorded on April 1 and 2, 1926. See Welding, liner notes, *Blind Lemon Jefferson*.

32. Hear, for example, Ma Rainey's recording of *See See Rider Blues* with Louis Armstrong from October 1924 on *Ma Rainey* (Milestone Records, MCD-47021-2, 1992) as well as Bessie Smith's *Careless Love Blues* from May 26, 1925, with Armstrong, Charlie Green on trombone, and Fletcher Henderson on piano on *Bessie Smith/Nobody's Blues But Mine* (Columbia Records, G 31093, 1972). Richard Hadlock observes that on *Careless Love Blues* Armstrong is "very much the soloist . . . even to running notes into Bessie's words and attempting ideas not necessarily related to the song material as Bessie understood it." See *Jazz Masters of the Twenties* (1965; reprint, Collier Books, 1974), p. 21.

33. According to "Discographical Notes," *The Complete Louis Armstrong and the Singers, 1924/30*, vol. 4, *1926–1930* (King Jazz, 141 FS, 1993), the pianist is Sippie Wallace. This fact would explain why some observers have mistakenly identified the pianist as Hersal Thomas, for at times Sippie's playing resembles Hersal's.

34. Grainger is given as the composer in the liner notes of both *Rare Recordings of the Twenties*, vol. 1 (CBS Records, France, 64218), and *The Complete Louis Armstrong and the Singers, 1924/30*, vol. 4, *1926–1930*. However, Sippie Wallace reported that she and her brother George wrote *The Flood Blues* (Townley, "The Texas Nightingale," p. 229).

35. Harrison, *Black Pearls*, p. 132. This recording was made on February 7, 1929 (Victrola V38502), and includes Johnny Dodds on clarinet and Natty Dominique on trumpet. An earlier recording entitled *A Mighty Tight Woman* was made on November 20, 1926, with Cicero Thomas on cornet and an unknown pianist. The latter sounds so much like Hersal Thomas, who had

died on July 3 of that year, that Brian Rust suggests that either Sippie accompanied herself or was accompanied by her brother George (*Jazz Records 1897–1942*, 2:1724). The 1926 recording is included on *Sissy Man Blues* (Jass Records, J-C-14, 1991).

36. Blesh, *Shining Trumpets*, p. 141. *Buzz Me* and *Bedroom Blues* were recorded on September 25, 1945, and are on Mercury Z010.

37. Blesh, *Shining Trumpets*, p. 135.

38. Oliver et al., *The New Grove Gospel, Blues, and Jazz*, p. 52.

39. John Chilton, liner notes, *Louis Armstrong: The Hot Fives and Hot Sevens*, vol. 2 (Columbia Records, CK 44253, 1988).

40. Armstrong also plays a similar phrase on *The Mail Train Blues* from the same March 3, 1926, session with Wallace. *I Feel Bad* and *The Mail Train Blues* are included on *The Complete Louis Armstrong and the Singers 1924/30*, vol. 3, *1925–1926* (King Jazz KJ 141 FS). All six of the Armstrong-Jones recordings have been reissued in this series on vol. 1, *1924–1925* (King Jazz KJ 139 FS).

41. William Russell, "Louis Armstrong," in *Jazzmen*, ed. Frederic Ramsey, Jr., and Charles Edward Smith (London: Sidgwick and Jackson, 1958), p. 127.

42. Hadlock, *Jazz Masters of the Twenties*, p. 22. When he speaks of Jones "playing 'second fiddle,'" Hadlock is alluding to his earlier discussion of the Bessie Smith–Louis Armstrong recording of May 1925 of *I Ain't Gonna Play No Second Fiddle*, whose title, the critic suggests, "may have expressed Bessie's feeling about the collaboration" (p. 21).

43. Blesh, *Shining Trumpets*, p. 110.

44. The Hociel Thomas performances, a dozen in all, are included on *The Complete Louis Armstrong and the Singers 1924/30*, vol. 3.

45. Blesh, *Shining Trumpets*, pp. 136–137.

46. Two sides cut by this pair early in June 1925 contain some of their best work together. On *Worried Down with the Blues*, Hersal furnishes a fine introduction; and when both musicians perform together, their lines are perfectly clear, complementary, and yet interesting on their own, especially on *Fish Tail Dance*, which has been called "a splendid tune" (Oliver et al., *The New Grove Gospel, Blues, and Jazz*, p. 52) and which really swings. This recording also exhibits Hociel's best vocal qualities in her breaks and when Hersal backs her up with the melody line. Hociel utilizes some short effective growls, while Hersal embellishes with glissandos, syncopation, and altered chords. Also of interest here are the various lyrics that refer to a number of the period's songs and dances: "heard the band play 'Mussel Shoal Blues'"; "you get sway back and ball the jack"; "do the black bottom and then you got 'em"; "shimmy right onto the floor." This recorded reference to the dance known as the "black bottom" comes two and a half years prior to Ma Rainey's December 1927 recording of the tune *Ma Rainey's Black Bottom*, which served as the basis of Adrian Wilson's 1984 play of the same title. Blind Lemon Jefferson also refers to doing the black bottom in 1927 on *Hot Dogs*, which is said to be "his only recorded work in which singing was secondary to instrumentation" (Calt, liner notes, *Don't Leave Me Here*). *Worried Down with the Blues* and *Fish Tail Dance* are included on *Texas Piano*, vol.1, which also includes three tunes cut by Hersal and Hociel with a dreadful novelty clarinet that pretty much drowns out the piano, although on *I Must Have It* (where Hociel's singing is quite good), Hersal can be heard more clearly with some fine work in the left hand. Like Hersal and Sippie, Hociel was also a talented pianist, as demonstrated by her lively San Francisco performance of *Tebo's Texas Boogie*

(Circle Records 1014) from August 20, 1946. Tebo was Hociel's married name.

47. This recording is apparently the one included on *Sissy Man Blues*. Even though the liner notes for the album give the date of the tune as 1929, no version of Spivey's *Black Snake Blues* is listed for this year in Rust's *Jazz Records 1897–1942*.

48. This view is offered in Tirro, *Jazz*, p. 126. On the other hand, Paul Oliver demonstrates very clear sexual connotations in the lyrics of another Spivey blues, *Handy Man*, recorded September 12, 1928. In discussing Spivey's *Black Snake Blues*, Oliver notes that she was "the first singer on record to use a herpetological symbol" and that this recording "was to make a strong impression on blues symbolism. Combining the qualities of an exceptional tune with striking imagery, her *Black Snake Blues* was copied by innumerable blues singers and reinterpreted by many others" (*Aspects of the Blues Tradition* [New York: Oak Publications, 1970], pp. 209–210). Spivey's *Handy Man* can be compared with *Butcher Shop Blues* by her fellow Houstonian Bernice Edwards as an example of the sexual connotations in the classic blues as composed and performed by women of the period. Edwards's *Butcher Shop Blues* is included on *Texas Piano*, vol. 1.

49. Harrison, *Black Pearls*, p. 150.

50. Ibid., p. 152. Blind Lemon's version is included on *Blind Lemon Jefferson*.

51. Harrison, *Black Pearls*.

52. Ibid., pp. 152–153. *Arkansas Road Blues* was recorded in April 1927 and reissued on *Victoria Spivey Recorded Legacy of the Blues* (Spivey Records, LP 2001, n.d.). *Toothache Blues*, a recording from October 17, 1928, with both Lonnie Johnson and Spivey as vocalists accompanied by Spivey herself on piano, is included on *Sissy Man Blues*.

53. Harrison, *Black Pearls*, p. 151. Spivey's *Black Snake Blues* reportedly sold 150,000 copies in its first month. See Sally Placksin, *American Women in Jazz, 1900 to the Present: Their Words, Lives, and Music* ([New York: Putnam] Wideview Books, 1982), p. 34.

54. Harrison, *Black Pearls*, p. 153.

55. Quoted in Barlow, *"Looking Up at Down,"* p. 153.

56. Quoted in Billy Altman, liner notes, *Better Boot That Thing: Great Women Blues Singers of the 1920's* (RCA Victor, 66065-2, 1992).

57. Ibid.

58. Oliver et al., *The New Grove Gospel, Blues, and Jazz*, p. 58.

59. Hadlock, *Jazz Masters of the Twenties*, p. 42.

60. Stanley Dance, liner notes, *Louis Armstrong*, vol. 5, *Louis in New York* (Columbia Records, CK 46148, 1990), p. 7.

61. Linda Dahl, *Stormy Weather: The Music and Lives of a Century of Jazz Women* (New York: Pantheon Books, 1984), pp. 108, 111.

62. These two tunes are on Vocalion 0336.

63. Harrison, *Black Pearls*, p. 23.

64. Lawrence Cohn, *Nothing but the Blues: The Music and the Musicians* (New York: Abbeville Press, 1993), p. 100.

65. *Lillian Glinn: Complete Recorded Works in Chronological Order 1927–1929* (Document Records, DOCD-5184, 1993).

66. Quoted in Cohn, *Nothing but the Blues*, p. 120.

67. Oliver, *The Story of the Blues*, p. 64. Oliver adds that Glinn toured to New Orleans and Atlanta but appeared most frequently at Ella B. Moore's Park Theatre on Central Tracks in Dallas.

68. Paul Oliver, liner notes, *The Story of the Blues* (Columbia Records, 30008).

69. Oliver, *The Story of the Blues*, p. 40. Texas Alexander first recorded in 1927, and his numerous recordings from 1928 would surely have been known by Glinn.

70. On this same date, Glinn also sang *Packing House Blues*, which employs the food-sex analogy found in Bernice Edwards's *Butcher Shop Blues*.

71. John Wilby, liner notes, *Lillian Glinn*.

72. Oliver et al., *The New Grove Gospel, Blues, and Jazz*, p. 71.

73. Collier, *The Making of Jazz*, p. 113.

74. *Fort Worth Denver Blues* is included on *Better Boot That Thing*. Tucker's 1928 recording session was held at the Memphis Auditorium. At the same time, another singer active in Dallas, Ida May Mack, also recorded there, and her work is included on this same compact disc. Although Mack's performances are not particularly noteworthy, it is pertinent that one of her own original tunes is entitled *Elm Street Blues*. In his liner notes, Billy Altman reports that "both Tucker and Mack either hailed from, or at least were living, in Dallas at the time: the Victor logs note Tucker's address on Central Street, while Mack is listed with a Monger Street address." William Barlow identifies both women as being from East Texas (*"Looking Up at Down,"* p. 180).

75. Placksin, *American Women in Jazz*, p. 9.

4. Boogie-Woogie

1. See especially E. Simms Campbell, "Blues," in *Jazzmen*, ed. Ramsey and Smith, p. 112.

2. Giddins, *Riding on a Blue Note*, p. 105.

3. Max Harrison, "Boogie-Woogie," in *Jazz: New Perspectives on the History of Jazz*, ed. Nat Hentoff and Albert J. McCarthy (1959; reprint, New York: Da Capo Press, 1975), p. 108.

4. William Russell, "Boogie Woogie," in *Jazzmen*, ed. Ramsey and Smith, p. 183.

5. Peter J. Silvester, *A Left Hand Like God: A History of Boogie-Woogie Piano* (New York: Da Capo Press, 1989), p. 42. Silvester also notes that "boogie-woogie style is to all intents and purposes synonymous with the blues in regard to its form and harmony" (p. 39).

6. Ibid., pp. 40–41. Aaron "T-Bone" Walker, a Texas blues singer born in the East Texas town of Linden on May 28, 1910, recalled that the first time he heard a boogie-woogie piano was the first time he went to church: "That was the Holy Ghost Church in Dallas, Texas. That boogie-woogie was a kind of blues, I guess. Then the preacher used to preach in a bluesy tone sometimes. You even got the congregation yelling 'Amen' all the time when his preaching would stir them up—his preaching and his bluesy tone." Quoted in Shapiro and Hentoff, eds., *Hear Me Talkin' to Ya*, p. 250.

7. Silvester, *A Left Hand Like God*, p. 5.

8. Ibid., p. 41.

9. Mellers, *Music in a New Found Land*, p. 273.

10. Oliver, *The Story of the Blues*, p. 40.

11. Silvester, *A Left Hand Like God*, p. 16. A recording of *Hattie Green* was made in Austin in March 1963 by Robert "Fud" Shaw, a Texas barrelhouse pianist born in Stafford on August 9, 1908. Recorded by Mack McCormick, *Texas Barrelhouse Piano* (Arhoolie Records, F1010) has Shaw playing piano and singing in the style he helped develop as a member of the group known as the Texas Santa Fe pianists.

12. Silvester, *A Left Hand Like God*, p. 30.

13. Ibid., p. 25.

14. Ibid., p. 27.

15. Campbell, "Blues," pp. 112–113.

16. Silvester, *A Left Hand Like God*, p. 5.

17. Martin Williams, *Jazz Heritage* (New York: Oxford University Press, 1985), p. 162.

18. Mellers, *Music in a New Found Land*, p. 273.

19. Blesh, *Shining Trumpets*, pp. 295, 302.

20. Silvester, *A Left Hand Like God*, p. 32.

21. Mellers, *Music in a New Found Land*, pp. 278–279.

22. Williams, *Jazz Heritage*, pp. 162–163. Rudi Blesh likewise acknowledges that the origins of boogie-woogie are obscure, but he says that "like the blues, it does not seem to have originated in New Orleans," and suggests that boogie-woogie arose "spontaneously, with strong regional differences, in Texas, Mississippi, Louisiana, Alabama, Arkansas, Tennessee—everywhere, in fact, in the South" (*Shining Trumpets*, pp. 302–303).

23. Williams, *Jazz Heritage*, p. 163.

24. *The Rocks*, under the name Clay Custer, with "George W. Thomas" in parentheses, is included on *Boogie Woogie Stomp!* (Academy Sound and Vision, England, CD AJA 5101, 1993). Liner notes by Pat Hawes credit this 1923 recording with being "the first recording of a piano piece with identifiable boogie elements." In his liner notes to *Texas Piano*, vol. 1, which also includes *The Rocks*, David Evans wonders why Thomas "would use a pseudonym . . . since his real name appears on the record as the composer." Evans adds, "Whoever the player is, the piece is played according to Thomas' published score, which betrays vestiges of formal ragtime with its repeated themes."

25. Silvester, *A Left Hand Like God*, p. 52.

26. Oliver et al., *The New Grove Gospel, Blues, and Jazz*, p. 75.

27. George W. Thomas was born in Little Rock, Arkansas, in 1883. In Houston in 1911 he met songwriter Clarence Williams, with whom he collaborated, and in 1913 the two formed a partnership. According to David Evans, George Thomas reportedly composed "close to a hundred pieces, mostly blues, and is known to have published 27 of them. Several were among the most popular blues of the era, including 'Muscle Shoals Blues,' 'Shorty George Blues,' and 'Houston Blues'" (liner notes, *Texas Piano*, vol. 1).

28. George Avakian, liner notes, *The Bessie Smith Story*, Vol. 2 (Columbia Records, CL 856, 1951).

29. Silvester, *A Left Hand Like God*, p. 48. Silvester notes that the copyright was signed over to Clarence Williams (presumably for a price) because Thomas made a visit to his dying mother. It was Williams who first recorded the song in 1923. William Barlow reports that George Thomas was a piano player for the Theatre Owners Booking Association (also known

as "Tough on Black Asses" among the black entertainers who were contracted by TOBA) in Houston in 1911 when he met Clarence Williams: "At the time, [Thomas's] blues trademark was a boogie-woogie East Texas piece that he eventually entitled 'New Orleans Hop Scop Blues'" (*"Looking Up at Down,"* p. 236).

30. Silvester, *A Left Hand Like God,* p. 48. On the sheet music cover of *The Fives,* reprinted in Silvester's history of boogie-woogie (p. [51]), an express train is pictured with the numeral 5 on the front of the engine (recalling William Carlos Williams's poem "The Great Figure" with its numeral 5 "in gold / on a red / firetruck," based on a Charles Demuth painting). See William Carlos Williams, *Selected Poems* (New York: New Directions, 1985), p. 36.

31. Silvester, *A Left Hand Like God,* p. 38.

32. Ibid., p. 28. Like Robert "Fud" Shaw, Pickens was a member of the Santa Fe group.

33. Oliver et. al, *The New Grove Gospel, Blues, and Jazz,* pp. 29, 74.

34. Silvester, *A Left Hand Like God,* p. 49.

35. Russell, "Boogie Woogie," p. 189.

36. Silvester, *A Left Hand Like God,* p. 81.

37. Russell, "Boogie Woogie," p. 191.

38. Silvester, *A Left Hand Like God,* p. 50.

39. Ibid., p. 47. Thomas's piece is printed as *Mussel Shoal Blues* as well as *Muscle Shoal Blues. Texas Piano,* vol. 1, includes two other Thomas compositions, *Fast Stuff Blues* and *Don't Kill Him in Here,* the latter with "occasional walking bass figures along with right hand tremolo that would be heard in the Texas 'Santa Fe' piano of the 1930's" (David Evans, liner notes). Thomas recorded both *Houston Blues* and *Shorty George Blues* with vocalist Tiny Franklin on December 10, 1923, for the Gennett Company in Richmond, Indiana.

40. Blesh, *Shining Trumpets,* p. 311. *Suitcase Blues* is included on *Cuttin' the Boogie: Piano Blues and Boogie Woogie, 1926–1941* (New World Records, NW259, 1977). In his liner notes to this album, Martin Williams suggests that Hersal's *Suitcase Blues* "probably should not be called true boogie woogie," seemingly on the grounds that one of the two basic chorus ideas "is played over a simple, heavy blues bass of four even accents." However, Ernest Borneman states unequivocally that "boogie *is* the blues as far as melody, harmony and length of theme are concerned. It may differ in time signature (8/8 instead of 4/4), use of chromatics, use of timbre, or in rhythmic accentuation. But thematically it is, and must remain, the blues." See "Boogie Woogie," in *Just Jazz,* ed. Sinclair Traill and Gerald Lascelles (London: Peter Davies, 1957), p. 29.

41. *The Fives* is included on *Boogie Woogie Blues* (Biograph Records, BCD 115, 1991). No month or day is indicated on this recording, and it does not appear in either Brian Rust's *Jazz Records 1897–1942* or Charles Delaunay's *New Hot Discography,* ed. Walter E. Schaap and George Avakian (New York: Criterion, 1948).

42. Cited in Barbara Caplin and Debra C. Rath, liner notes, *Boogie Woogie Blues.*

43. Ibid.

44. Ibid.

45. Borneman, "Boogie Woogie," p. 31.

46. Silvester, *A Left Hand Like God,* p. 291.

47. Harrison, "Boogie-Woogie," pp. 128–129.

48. Silvester, *A Left Hand Like God,* p. 47.

49. Harrison, "Boogie-Woogie," p. 129.

50. Silvester, *A Left Hand Like God*, pp. 274–275. *Hersal's Blues* is included on *The Thomas Family: The Piano Blues*, vol. 4 (Magpie Records, PY 4404). However, I have been unable to find this label from England and have heard Thomas's performance only on a 78 rpm recording (Okeh, no. 8227).

51. Silvester, *A Left Hand Like God*, p. 274.

52. Leonard Feather, *The Book of Jazz* (New York: Meridian Books, 1959), p. 64.

53. Ibid., p. 18. Feather is quoting William L. Grossman and Jack W. Farrell, *The Heart of Jazz* (New York: New York University Press, 1956), p. 254.

54. Williams, *Jazz Heritage*, p. 161.

55. Mellers, *Music in a New Found Land*, pp. 317, 314, 374, 336.

56. Sammy Price, *What Do They Want?: A Jazz Autobiography*, ed. Caroline Richmond (Champaign-Urbana: University of Illinois Press, 1990).

57. Feather, *The Book of Jazz*, p. 64. A recording of *Just Jivin' Around* by Sam Price and His Texas Blusicians with Lester Young, which exhibits good swing but a fairly tame solo from Prez, is included on *52nd Street Swing: New York in the '30s* (Decca Records, GRD-646).

58. Collier, *The Making of Jazz*, p. 230. *Boogie-Woogie* is included on *Lester Young Memorial*, vol. 1 (Epic Records, LG 3107).

59. *Boo Woo* is included on *Boogie Woogie Stomp!*

II. GOING TO KANSAS CITY
5. The Bennie Moten Band, 1921 -1927

1. Schuller, *The Swing Era*, p. 562.

2. Russell, *Jazz Style in Kansas City*, p. 54.

3. Schuller, *The Swing Era*, p. 340n.12. Schuller places Wright in the Moten band as of 1924, but a 1923 Moten recording with Wright on cornet makes clear that he was already a member by that time.

4. Russell, *Jazz Style in Kansas City*, pp. 89, 180. Russell notes that Parker was mostly "an absentee and truant."

5. Ibid., p. 88.

6. Ibid., p. 89.

7. In June 1922, Kid Ory had recorded in Los Angeles his *Ory's Creole Trombone*, which Gunther Schuller calls "a clear, albeit naive example of the kind of ragtime-plus-march-plus minstrel hokum that made up the partly jazz repertoire" (*Early Jazz*, p. 74).

8. Ibid., pp. 83, 85; Tirro, *Jazz*, p. 146.

9. Schuller, *Early Jazz*, p. 284.

10. Blesh, *Shining Trumpets*, p. 184. Years later, in early 1930, Johnson was playing in Electra, Texas, when King Oliver wrote to him there to encourage him to come up to New York: "It's your fault you are still down there working for nothing." But Bunk preferred "to stay in the deep South where he could still 'drive the blues down'" (Frederic Ramsey, Jr., "King Oliver and His Creole Jazz Band," in *Jazzmen*, ed. Ramsey and Smith, p. 84).

11. Bechet, *Treat It Gentle*, pp. 96, 106. Bechet comments that "this blues was different from anything I ever heard." Telling of a man in trouble, the blues sung by his cellmates and played

by Bechet represented "all the wrong that's been done to all my people" (pp. 107–108).

12. Quoted in Lomax, *Mister Jelly Roll*, p. 145. Jelly Roll goes on to say that "the only piano player in Texas I remember was George W. Smith, who gave up the piano when he heard me and moved to California to make his living as a trumpet player."

13. Ibid., p. 146.

14. Shapiro and Hentoff, eds., *Hear Me Talkin' to Ya*, p. 56.

15. Quoted in Frank Driggs, "Kansas City Brass: Ed Lewis' Story as Told to Frank Driggs," part 2, *Jazz Review* 2, no. 9 (October 1959): 26.

16. Russell, *Jazz Style in Kansas City*, p. 93. *Crawdad Blues* and *Elephant Wobble* are included on *Territory Bands 1929–1933* (Historical Records, HLP-9).

17. Russell, *Jazz Style in Kansas City*, p. 93.

18. Ed Steane, liner notes, *Bennie Moten's Kansas City Orchestra 1923–1929* (Historical Records, vol. 9, ASC-5829-9).

19. Schuller, *Early Jazz*, p. 284.

20. Ibid.

21. Collier, *The Making of Jazz*, p. 265.

22. Schuller, *Early Jazz*, p. 283.

23. Russell, *Jazz Style in Kansas City*, p. 96.

24. These recordings are included on *Bennie Moten and His Kansas City Orchestra*, vol. 1 (Halcyon Records, HDL 108, 1986).

25. Schuller, *Early Jazz*, p. 283.

26. Ibid., p. 285.

6. The Blue Devils, 1925-1934

1. Don Gazzaway, "Conversations with Buster Smith," part 1, *Jazz Review* 2, no. 10 (December 1959): 18. This enormous quantity required incredibly backbreaking work, an indication of how badly Buster must have wanted his first instrument.

2. Russell, *Jazz Style in Kansas City*, pp. 80, 74.

3. Quoted in Gazzaway, "Conversations with Buster Smith," part 1, p. 20.

4. Quoted in Frank Driggs, "Budd Johnson: Ageless Jazzman," part 1, *Jazz Review* 3, no. 9 (November 1960): 6.

5. Quoted in Stanley Dance, *The World of Count Basie* (New York: Charles Scribner's Sons, 1980), p. 327.

6. Schuller, *Early Jazz*, p. 302. Trent's first name is usually given as either Alphonso or Alphonse. Schuller uses Alphonse, as does Arnold S. Caplin in the liner notes for the album *Territory Bands 1929–1933*, which reproduces five sides by the Alphonse Trent Orchestra: *Black and Blue Rhapsody*, *After You've Gone*, *St. James Infirmary*, *Clementine*, and *I've Found a New Baby* (Historical Records, HLP 5829-24).

7. Russell, *Jazz Style in Kansas City*, p. 64.

8. Leonard Feather, *The New Edition of the Encyclopedia of Jazz* (New York: Bonanza Books, 1962), p. 388. Albert McCarthy credits Gus Wilson, brother of Texas pianist Teddy Wilson, with the "advanced score" of Trent's *Clementine*, recorded in March 1933. (Gus is not listed among the

personnel of the Trent band.) McCarthy writes that if the group "had never made any other title but *Clementine* this alone would qualify the Trent band's inclusion amongst a list of the greatest big bands" (*Big Band Jazz*, pp. 101–102).

9. Albert McCarthy reproduces a photo from 1932 with Dan Minor pictured among members of the Trent orchestra, which would record *Clementine* and *I've Found a New Baby* in March 1933. See *Big Band Jazz*, p. 100. However, by December 1932, Minor was with the Bennie Moten Orchestra and for this reason probably was not included in the 1933 recording session with Trent.

10. Gazzaway, "Conversations with Buster Smith," part 1, p. 20.

11. Russell, *Jazz Style in Kansas City*, p. 77.

12. Ibid., p. 78.

13. Ibid., pp. 79–80.

14. Barlow, *"Looking Up at Down,"* p. 233.

15. Russell, *Jazz Style in Kansas City*, p. 80.

16. Shapiro and Hentoff, eds., *Hear Me Talkin' to Ya*, p. 296.

17. Ibid., p. 297.

18. Russell, *Jazz Style in Kansas City*, pp. 80–81. Dan Morgenstern reports that Page heard Oliver and Armstrong sometime in the mid-1920s in Chicago. Morgenstern also reports Page's claim that Texas trumpeter Claude "Benno" Kennedy was also an early influence. See "Hot Lips Page," *Jazz Journal* 15, no. 7 (July 1962): 5. Kennedy is discussed in Part IV.

19. Dance, *The World of Count Basie*, p. 61. Eddie Durham also reported that his brother was "as fast on cello as Oscar Pettiford was on bass."

20. George Hoefer, "Held Notes: Eddie Durham," *Down Beat* 29 (July 19, 1962): 57; Schuller, *The Swing Era*, p. 351. Later Allen Durham was also a member of the Dizzy Gillespie big band.

21. Hoefer, "Held Notes," p. 54.

22. J. A. Siegel and J. Obrecht, "Eddie Durham: Charlie Christian's Mentor, Pioneer of the Amplified Guitar," *Guitar Player* 13 (August 1979): 56.

23. Russell, *Jazz Style in Kansas City*, p. 59.

24. Schuller, *The Swing Era*, p. 772.

25. Gazzaway, "Conversations with Buster Smith," part 2, p. 13.

26. Schuller, *The Swing Era*, p. 245.

27. Siegel and Obrecht, "Eddie Durham," pp. 55–56.

28. Quoted in Dance, *The World of Count Basie*, p. 60.

29. It was while with the 101 Ranch Band that Durham began to write music, to express, as he put it, his "own voicing" (quoted in ibid., p. 61). And on another occasion, Durham commented: "I could experiment with harmony because I could get four trombones and four French horns together. I had to learn five- and six-part harmony myself because no one was teaching it" (quoted in Siegel and Obrecht, "Eddie Durham," p. 56).

30. Schuller, *Early Jazz*, p. 378.

31. Quoted in Shapiro and Hentoff, eds., *Hear Me Talkin' to Ya*, p. 299.

32. Quoted in Dance, *The World of Count Basie*, p. 61.

33. Russell, *Jazz Style in Kansas City*, p. 85.

34. Both of these sides are included on *Territory Bands*, vol. 2, *1927–1931* (Historical Records,

HLP 26).

35. Russell, *Jazz Style in Kansas City*, p. 84.

36. Schuller, *Early Jazz*, pp. 298, 297.

37. Shapiro and Hentoff, eds., *Hear Me Talkin' to Ya*, p. 297.

38. Russell, *Jazz Style in Kansas City*, p. 85.

39. Schuller, *Early Jazz*, p. 297.

40. Ibid., pp. 296–298.

41. Russell, *Jazz Style in Kansas City*, p. 80.

42. Schuller, *Early Jazz*, pp. 293, 295.

43. Gazzaway, "Conversations with Buster Smith," part 1, p. 22.

44. Schuller, *Early Jazz*, p. 296.

45. Russell, *Jazz Style in Kansas City*, p. 234.

46. Frank Driggs, "Kansas City and the Southwest," in *Jazz*, ed. Hentoff and McCarthy, p. 192.

47. Almost every jazz musician interviewed in such works as Shapiro and Hentoff's *Hear Me Talkin' to Ya*, Dance's *The World of Count Basie*, and Nathan W. Pearson's *Goin' to Kansas City* (Urbana: University of Illinois Press, 1987) has recalled some figure as equal or superior to the most famous names in jazz. For example, Gene Ramey of Austin remembered the son of a cousin, Parrish Jones, who had taught bop trumpeter Kenny Dorham and "was one of the greatest in the country, but he wouldn't leave Texas. He took up teaching, but he played jazz and Diz[zy Gillespie] and them were afraid of him" (quoted in Dance, *The World of Count Basie*, p. 259). Much later in jazz history, Red Connors of Fort Worth was remembered by Prince Lasha and Ornette Coleman as greater than Lester Young, yet Connors rarely recorded. Buddy Tate remembered saxophonist Red Calhoun, who "played brilliant alto" and performed "the blues better than anybody I ever heard in my life. He never left Dallas, wouldn't go any place else, but he could really have made a name for himself had he come to New York" (quoted in Dance, *The World of Count Basie*, p. 119).

7. Bennie Moten, 1929–1935

1. Schuller, *Early Jazz*, pp. 286–289, 293.

2. *Rhumba Negro, Rit-Dit-Ray, The Jones Law Blues, Small Black, New Vine Street Blues*, and *Band Box Shuffle* are included on *Bennie Moten and His Orchestra 1929–1930*, vol. 1 (RCA Victor Records, LPM 10023).

3. Schuller, *Early Jazz*, p. 304.

4. Ibid.

5. Russell, *Jazz Style in Kansas City*, p. 106.

6. Schuller, *Early Jazz*, p. 304.

7. Quoted in Dance, *The World of Count Basie*, p. 66.

8. Ibid., p. 62.

9. Ibid. For Buster Smith, reading music also meant learning "the value of the notes." See Gazzaway, "Conversations with Buster Smith," part 2, p. 13.

10. An example is *Eddie Durham: Blue 'Bone* (JSP Records, 1030, July 1981).

11. *The Last of the Blue Devils*, directed by Bruce Ricker (New York: Rhapsody Films, 1979).

12. Schuller, *Early Jazz*, p. 305.

13. Russell, *Jazz Style in Kansas City*, p. 101.

14. Schuller, *Early Jazz*, p. 305.

15. Ibid.

16. Russell, *Jazz Style in Kansas City*, p. 102.

17. Martin Williams, liner notes, *Count Basie in Kansas City: Bennie Moten's Great Band of 1930–1932* (RCA Victor Records, LPV-514, 1965). *Oh! Eddie, Moten's Swing, That Too, Do, When I'm Alone*, and *Toby* are on this album.

18. Ibid.

19. John McDonough, "A Century with Count Basie," *Down Beat* 57 (January 1990): 36.

20. Buster Smith reported that he had recruited Keyes before 1929 for the Blue Devils (Pearson, *Goin' to Kansas City*, p. 69). Drummer Jo Jones called Keyes "one of the most wonderful musicians I have known in my life. . . . He was also a guy who taught me how to think" (quoted in Shapiro and Hentoff, eds., *Hear Me Talkin' to Ya*, p. 290).

21. Schuller, *Early Jazz*, p. 313.

22. Schuller, *The Swing Era*, p. 206. Ross Russell calls *Toby* "a Durham riff over the harmonic framework of *Sweet Sue*" (*Jazz Style in Kansas City*, p. 107).

23. Russell, *Jazz Style in Kansas City*, p. 108.

24. Ibid., p. 107.

25. This tune is attributed to Basie and Durham in several sources; see Dance, *The World of Count Basie*, p. 64, and Count Basie, *Good Morning Blues: The Autobiography of Count Basie*, as told to Albert Murray (New York: Random House, 1985), p. 127. The latter contains this account by Basie:

"Eddie Durham and I came up with the number that went into the book as 'Moten Swing.' It started out as our thing on a pop tune called 'You're Driving Me Crazy,' but we were not trying to work that up into anything. . . . I came up with a little something that Eddie liked. . . . We played over what he had put down [Durham notated what Basie tried out on the piano], and then I just went on and tried something, and he picked up on that, and I said, 'You got it.' I cut back out to have another little nip because I knew he knew where it went from there.

"That's how we came up with that one, and we had to name it something, so we just said, 'Hell, call it "Moten Swing,"' because it really was for the band, and it turned out to be the most famous number associated with that band. . . . It was copyrighted in the name of Bennie and [his brother] Buster Moten, but Eddie Durham and I were the ones who wrote it out together."

26. Albert Murray writes that "*Moten Swing*, the Kansas City Anthem, is credited to Bennie and Buster Moten, but was actually composed by Eddie Durham from the chords of *You're Driving Me Crazy*. Durham laid out to do so during a set backstage at the Pearl Theater in Philadelphia in 1931 because a ride-out number was needed for the finale" (*Stomping the Blues*, p. 176, caption).

27. Schuller, *Early Jazz*, p. 316.

28. Ibid.

29. Williams, liner notes, *Count Basie in Kansas City*.

30. Samuel B. Charters and Leonard Kunstadt, *Jazz: A History of the New York Scene* (Garden City, N.Y.: Doubleday and Company, Inc., 1962), pp. 283–284.

8. The Count Basie Orchestra, 1935-1963

1. Russell, *Jazz Style in Kansas City*, p. 135.

2. Ibid., p. 134.

3. Ibid., p. 139.

4. Quoted in Dance, *The World of Count Basie*, p. 274. Ramey discusses how Smith's ability to set riffs at "spook breakfasts" also influenced Charlie Parker.

5. Ibid.

6. Quoted in Shapiro and Hentoff, eds., *Hear Me Talkin' to Ya*, p. 309.

7. Dance, *The World of Count Basie*, p. 6.

8. Eric Thacker, in Harrison, Fox, and Thacker, *The Essential Jazz Records*, pp. 166–167.

9. Schuller, *Early Jazz*, p. 292.

10. Russell, *Jazz Style in Kansas City*, pp. 56–57. *Dreamland* is included on *Territory Bands* (EMI Records, 7082).

11. This performance is included on *One O'Clock Jump: An Album of Classic "Swing" by Count Basie and His Orchestra 1937* (Decca Records, MCA-49394, 1990).

12. Mary Lee Hester, *Going to Kansas City* (Sherman, Tex.: Early Bird Press, 1980), p. 50. Hester's collection of articles on Texas jazz musicians is particularly valuable because it is often based on interviews with the musicians. Originally most of her pieces appeared in *Texas Jazz*, a monthly magazine published in Dallas containing news notes on the Texas jazz scene, record reviews, and Hester's series entitled "Texas Jazz Heritage." Hester's pieces were accompanied by fine line drawings of the jazz musicians, executed by her husband Don and reproduced in *Going to Kansas City*. Hester seemingly edited some of her pieces when she collected them in book form (for example, information in the magazine article on Budd Johnson does not appear in the book version, and this may be true of the other pieces as well). For more on the famous cutting session at the Cherry Blossom, see Russell, *Jazz Style in Kansas City*, pp. 28–30.

13. Schuller, *The Swing Era*, p. 354.

14. Finkelstein, *Jazz*, p. 137.

15. Frank Driggs, liner notes, *The Count at the Chatterbox* (Jazz Archives Records, JA-16, 1974).

16. Ibid.

17. Schuller, *The Swing Era*, p. 237.

18. Dance, *The World of Count Basie*, p. 67.

19. Schuller, *The Swing Era*, p. 237.

20. Both of these air checks of *One O'Clock Jump* are included on *Basic Basie* (Phontastic Records, Sweden, NOST 7640, 1982).

21. Dance, *The World of Count Basie*, p. 67.

22. Joachim E. Berendt, *The Jazz Book: From Ragtime to Fusion and Beyond*, rev. Günther Huesmann; trans. H. and B. Bredigkeit, with Dan Morgenstern and Tim Nevill (New York: Lawrence Hill Books, 1992), p. 242.

23. Schuller, *The Swing Era*, p. 239. *John's Idea, Time Out*, and *Topsy* are included on *One O'Clock Jump: An Album of Classic "Swing"*; *Every Tub* and *Swingin' the Blues* are on *Count Basie and His Orchestra 1937–1943: Jumpin' at the Woodside* (Jazz Roots, CD 56015, 1991). The arrangement of *Every Tub* is credited on the Jazz Roots album to Buck Clayton, but Chris Sheridan lists Eddie Durham as the arranger (*Count Basie: A Bio-Discography* [New York: Greenwood Press, 1986], p. 43).

24. Collier, *The Making of Jazz*, p. 235.

25. Murray, *Stomping the Blues*, p. 159, caption.

26. Schuller, *The Swing Era*, p. 238.

27. *The Best of Count Basie* (MCA Records, MCA2-4050, 1980).

28. *Good Morning Blues* (MCA Records, MCA2-4108, 1977). Durham is credited with the arrangement of *I Keep Remembering* in Sheridan, *Count Basie: A Bio-Discography*, p. 37.

29. Russell, *Jazz Style in Kansas City*, p. 236.

30. Collier, *The Making of Jazz*, p. 235.

31. Schuller, *The Swing Era*, p. 241. The critic even refers to "Evans's nagging, nastily squealy clarinet" on *Jumpin' at the Woodside* as "notable" (p. 242).

32. Ibid., p. 242. André Hodeir is more interested in Dickie Wells's trombone solo on the performance of Herschel's *Texas Shuffle*, for he finds evidence here that Wells is "one of the most perfect constructors of choruses in the history of jazz." Hodeir points to the procedure by which Wells plays "with more intense swing than any but a few trumpeters have attained," sacrificing "in the manner of Lester Young . . . everything else to swing, concentrating all his rhythmic powers on one or two notes repeated at greater or lesser length" (*Jazz*, p. 69).

33. Schuller, *The Swing Era*, pp. 243–244.

34. Russell, *Jazz Style in Kansas City*, p. 133.

35. Schuller, *The Swing Era*, p. 245. *The Blues I Like to Hear* is included on *Good Morning Blues*. The title of Smith's piece is credited to French jazz critic Hugues Panassié, and the story of the recording session is told in Sheridan, *Count Basie: A Bio-Discography*, pp. 59–60. According to Panassié, before the Basie band recorded Buster's riff with a vocal by Rushing, it "had been featured prominently at the Famous Door for at least a month—but as an instrumental yet untitled."

36. Schuller, *The Swing Era*, p. 236n.

37. Murray, *Stomping the Blues*, p. 174.

38. Williams, *The Jazz Tradition*, pp. 128, 129.

39. *Panassie Stomp* is included on *The Best of Count Basie*. Evans's last solo came on *Blues with Lips* at the "Spirituals to Swing" concert of December 23, 1938.

40. Russell, *Jazz Style in Kansas City*, pp. 72–73.

41. Dance, liner notes, *The Essential Count Basie*, vol. 1.

42. *Seventh Avenue Express* is included on *Basie's Basement* (RCA Camden Records, CAL-497, 1959).

43. *The Essential Count Basie*, vol. 1, includes *Taxi War Dance*.

44. Williams, *The Jazz Tradition*, p. 131.

45. Liner notes, *Jumpin' at the Woodside*.

46. Schuller, *The Swing Era*, p. 254.

47. *Bye, Bye, Baby* is included on *The Count* (RCA Camden Records, CAL-395).

48. Joe Goldberg, liner notes, *Buck and Buddy* (Prestige Records, 2017, 1992).

49. *The One for Me, Take the "A" Train*, and *Mean to Me* are included on *The Original Jazz Masters Series*, vols. 1 and 2 (da Music/Black Lion, 3701-2 and 3702-5).

50. *Tate-a-Tate* (Prestige Records, SVLP 2014); Sinclair Traill, "Record Reviews," *Jazz Journal*, vol. 15, no. 9 (1962): 32.

51. *The Texas Twister* (New World Records, NW 352-1).

52. Feather, *The New Edition of the Encyclopedia of Jazz*, p. 272.

53. Richard Cork and Brian Morton, *The Penguin Guide to Jazz on CD, LP, and Cassette* (Harmondsville, England: Penguin, 1992), p. 78.

54. *Blues by Basie* (Columbia Records, CL 901). During this period, Basie cut down the size of his unit but later returned to a full-band format. Another tune with the octet, *I Ain't Got Nobody*, from November 3, 1950, provides an especially fine example of Johnson's drumming. The tune is included on *One O'Clock Jump: Count Basie* (Columbia Records, CL-997).

55. *Basie Rides Again* (Verve Records, MG V-8108). Sheridan refers to this band as the "New Testament" and says that "from 1952 onwards [it] possessed, in its ensemble work, a markedly percussive approach" (*Count Basie: A Bio-Discography*, pp. [325]–326).

56. In an interview, Henry Coker does not indicate which black college he attended, but two were located in Marshall at the time: Bishop College and Wiley College. See Valerie Wilmer, "Texas Trombone: Henry Coker," *Jazz Journal* 15, no. 10 (1962): 11–12. Wilmer comments that Coker's "solo work . . . is at all times interesting, the form being carefully planned and the style lusty and searing" (p. 11).

57. Ibid. *Malibu* was written for the Carter band by Texan Kenny Dorham.

58. *Bop Bounce* is included on *Benny Carter and His Orchestra Live Broadcasts 1939–1948* (Jazz Hour, JH-1005).

59. According to Kernfeld's *New Grove Dictionary of Jazz*, vol. 1, Coker immediately made his presence felt on solos recorded for the 1952 album *Count Basie Big Band*, soloing on *No Name*, *Redhead*, and *Peace Pipe*. Unfortunately, I have been unable to hear this recording (Clef, 89115).

60. These tunes are included on *Count Basie Class of '54* (Black Lion Records, BLCD760924, 1989). Leonard Feather's estimate of Gus Johnson's work Barry McRae's liner notes echo, declaring that "in terms of sheer momentum, the Basie/Green/Lewis and Johnson team were especially impressive and could well be rated amongst the most dynamic of all Basie sections."

61. *"April in Paris"* (Verve Records, 825 575-2).

62. *Basie in London* (Verve Records, MGV-8199).

63. *The Atomic Mr. Basie* (Roulette Records, ROU 1005).

64. *The Count Basie Story* (Roulette Birdland Records, RB-1). Gus Johnson is the drummer for three tunes on this album. In his notes for the album, Leonard Feather comments that Durham's *Swinging the Blues* is "one of the most celebrated early instrumentals," and the entire trombone section beautifully recreates Durham's fine composed break for three trombones. Coker takes four exciting breaks on *Out the Window*, each utilizing a different approach, from laid-back to trills and sparkling high notes. He also solos nicely on *Texas Shuffle*.

65. Unsigned liner notes, *Kansas City Suite* (Forum Records, SF 9032).

66. *Li'l Ol' Groovemaker . . . Basie!* (Verve Records, V/V6-8549). According to Stanley Dance in his liner notes for this album, "wrinkles" may be translated as "chittlin's."

9. Jones-Smith, Inc., and the Kansas City Five and Six

1. Jo Jones has described the atmosphere in this way: "You would hear music twenty-four hours a day in Kansas City. Practically all the little places had piano and a set of drums. I had a little group in one of them with Lester Young and George Hunt on trombone . . . and Ed Durham on guitar. Any drummer who wanted to could sit in because I could play piano" (Shapiro and Hentoff, eds., *Hear Me Talkin' to Ya*, p. 289).

2. Russell, *Jazz Style in Kansas City*, p. 141. The date for this recording session has been listed incorrectly for fifty years, according to Chris Sheridan, who reports that it actually took place in November 1936. See Sheridan's liner notes for *Count Basie—Harry James: Basie Rhythm* (HEP Records, 1032, 1991), which contains all the sides from this famous session.

3. Unsigned liner notes, *The Jazz Makers* (Columbia Records, CL 1036).

4. Schuller, *The Swing Era*, p. 230.

5. Collier, *The Making of Jazz*, p. 230.

6. Harrison, Fox, and Thacker, *The Essential Jazz Records*, p. 301.

7. Ibid. Both *Boogie-Woogie* and *Evenin'*, two of the four tunes from the Jones-Smith session, feature vocals by Jimmy Rushing. On *Evenin'* Smith is only heard riffing behind the blues shouter and does not solo as he does on *Boogie-Woogie*.

8. Schuller, *The Swing Era*, p. 236.

9. Ibid., p. 230.

10. Williams, *The Jazz Tradition*, p. 132.

11. Quoted in Dance, liner notes, *The Essential Count Basie*, vol. 1.

12. Schuller, *The Swing Era*, p. 233.

13. Ibid., pp. 230, 236, 236n.

14. Frank Driggs's comment that, in the 1937 transcriptions of the Basie Chatterbox broadcasts, Clayton and Smith's solos are "hard to separate" suggests the possible influence of Carl Tatti on Buck (liner notes, *The Count at the Chatterbox*).

15. Schuller, *The Swing Era*, pp. 232–233.

16. Ibid., p. 230.

17. John Chilton, *Who's Who of Jazz: Storyville to Swing Street* (1972; reprint, New York: Da Capo Press, 1985), p. 312. James Lincoln Collier suggests that Smith "might have had a successful career with Basie had he not left the band, apparently for emotional reasons" (*The Making of Jazz*, p. 230).

18. Schuller, *The Swing Era*, p. 233.

19. Milt Gabler, liner notes, *Giants of the Tenor Sax: Lester "Prez" Young and Friends* (Commodore Records, CCK 7002, 1988).

20. Earlier Durham had recorded using a homemade amplified guitar when he soloed on *Hittin' the Bottle* with the Jimmie Lunceford Orchestra on September 30, 1935.

21. Gabler bought three sides from Brunswick and added five by the Kansas City Six to make a total of eight sides.

22. Harrison, Fox, and Thacker, *The Essential Jazz Records*, p. 356.

23. Ibid.

24. Ibid.

25. Nat Hentoff, quoted in Gabler, liner notes, *Giants of the Tenor Sax*.

26. Collier, *The Making of Jazz*, p. 233.

27. Harrison, Fox, and Thacker, *The Essential Jazz Records*, p. 357.

28. Quoted in Gabler, liner notes, *Giants of the Tenor Sax*.

29. Harrison, Fox, and Thacker, *The Essential Jazz Records*, p. 356.

10. The Jay McShann Orchestra, 1938–1942

1. Pearson, *Goin' to Kansas City*, p. 205.

2. Dance, *The World of Count Basie*, p. 274; see also Russell, *Jazz Style in Kansas City*, p. 183.

3. Dance, *The World of Count Basie*, p. 269.

4. Russell, *Jazz Style in Kansas City*, p. 189.

5. Dance, *The World of Count Basie*, p. 287.

6. Russell, *Jazz Style in Kansas City*, p. 189; Dance, *The World of Count Basie*, p. 276.

7. Quoted in Dance, *The World of Count Basie*, p. 264.

8. Quoted in Hester, *Going to Kansas City*, p. 174.

9. Dance, *The World of Count Basie*, pp. 262–263.

10. Ross Russell, *Bird Lives!* (New York: Charter house, 1973), p. 110.

11. Quoted in Dance, *The World of Count Basie*, p. 276. See also p. 264 for more on Braud and Greer as well as on Jimmie Lunceford's bass player, Moses Allen.

12. Dan Morgenstern, liner notes, *Charlie Parker with Jay McShann and His Orchestra: Early Bird* (Stash Records, ST-CD-542, 1991).

13. Dance, *The World of Count Basie*, p. 272. See also Pearson, *Goin' to Kansas City*, p. 169.

14. Morgenstern, liner notes, *Early Bird*.

15. Russell, *Jazz Style in Kansas City*, p. 227.

16. Schuller, *The Swing Years*, p. 794. As we shall see in Chapter 13 in the discussion of Buster Smith's solo on *Moten Swing*, recorded on November 11, 1940, there was a precedent in the Texan's work for Parker's stylistic approach.

17. Shapiro and Hentoff, eds., *Hear Me Talkin' to Ya*, p. 355.

18. Ibid., p. 354.

19. Morgenstern, liner notes, *Early Bird*.

20. Robert Bregman, liner notes, *Early Bird*.

21. Ibid.

22. The 1941 version of *Swingmatism* is included on *Blues from Kansas City* (Decca Records, GRD-614, 1992).

23. John S. Wilson, liner notes, *The Drum Suite: A Musical Portrait of Eight Arms from Six Angles* (RCA Victor, LPM-1279, 1956).

24. Bregman, liner notes, *Early Bird*.

25. Ibid.

26. Shapiro and Hentoff, eds., *Hear Me Talkin' to Ya*, p. 354. *Hootie Blues* was also recorded in Dallas on February 13, 1941, and is included on *Blues from Kansas City*.

27. Nat Pierce, liner notes, *Kansas City Piano (1936–1941)* (Decca Records, 79226). These 1941 trio sides have been reissued on *Blues from Kansas City*.

28. Loren Schoenberg, liner notes, *Blues from Kansas City*. *Red River Blues* by Charlie Nelson bears the same title as a "rag ditty" by "Ragtime Texas" Thomas, discussed in Chapter 2.

29. *Say Forward, I'll March* was recorded on December 1, 1943, in New York by the McShann Orchestra and is included on *Blues from Kansas City*. Loren Schoenberg observes in the liner notes that the piece "has one foot in the '30s and the other in the '40s. The melodic figures veer towards bop. . . . Ironically, although it was a big performance number for the band, this forward-looking record for some reason remained unreleased for years."

30. Bill Weilbacher, liner notes, *Going to Kansas City* (MJR Records, 8113, recorded March 6, 1972).

31. *The Best of Basie* (Roulette Records, R52081). Ramey and Johnson would appear together in the Basie band at Birdland on January 1, 1953, when Lester Young returned as a guest soloist. Ramey would also form part of Young's groups in Lester's later years, appearing on such albums as *"Pres"* (Everest, FS 287) and *Lester's Here* (Verve, MG V-8161).

32. Stearns, *The Story of Jazz*, pp. 186–187.

33. Gene Ramey commented that "most jazz musicians from Texas can hardly wait to leave areas where they have practiced their professions over prolonged periods. They are anxious to return to home-base. Texans, of all walks, all races, from every rank of the social strata, are fiercely loyal to their places of origin. It seems more prevalent with Texans than with natives of other states" (quoted in Hester, *Going to Kansas City*, p. 177).

III. GOING TO NEW YORK AND CHICAGO

11. A Trombone Trio

1. Giddins, *Riding on a Blue Note*, p. 74.

2. Quoted in H. J. Waters, Jr., *Jack Teagarden's Music: His Career and Recordings* (Stanhope, N.J.: Walter C. Allen, 1960), p. 15.

3. Artie Shaw, quoted in Shapiro and Hentoff, eds., *Hear Me Talkin' to Ya*, pp. 269–270.

4. Jay D. Smith, "Big T," *Jazz Review* 2, no. 6 (July 1959): 7.

5. Ibid.

6. Hadlock, *Jazz Masters of the Twenties*, p. 191.

7. Ibid., p. 182.

8. Max Harrison, review of *Jack Teagarden*, in Harrison, Fox, and Thacker, *The Essential Jazz Records*, p. 164. In his autobiography, clarinetist Mezz Mezzrow—who, along with many of Chicago's leading white jazz players, left the Windy City for New York in the late 1920s—recalls that "Teagarden sang that lament [*Dirty Dog*] on a record of ours called *Makin' Friends*, and it should have been the theme-song of the Chicagoans" (*Really the Blues* [1946; reprint, New York: Citadel Press, 1990], p. 177). Later Mezzrow remarks, "Even though we played all showtunes . . . things sometimes began to happen when Jack Teagarden . . . would start off the blues in a major key, then change to the minor, same as he does on *Makin' Friends*. Jack could really get in the jazz idiom, and he did a lot to make this job bearable to me" (p. 188). Both *Indiana* and *Dirty Dog* are included on *Jack Teagarden*, vol. 1, *1928–1931* (Jazz Archives, no. 51, France, 157022, 1992).

9. Schuller, *The Swing Era*, p. 600. *That's a Serious Thing* is included on *Jack Teagarden: I Gotta Right to Sing the Blues* (Academy Sound and Vision Ltd., CDAJA 5059, 1989).

10. Williams, *Jazz Heritage*, p. 13. Of this same recording Gunther Schuller comments that along with Teagarden's "effortless sovereign technical mastery" and "richness of tone" there is his "total lack of exhibitionism even in this basically virtuosic setting, and above all, the need to 'sing' on the instrument, no matter what the context" (*The Swing Era*, p. 609).

11. Quoted in Charles Edward Smith, "Jack Teagarden," *The Jazz Makers: Essays on the Greats of Jazz*, ed. Nat Shapiro and Nat Hentoff (1957; reprint, New York: Da Capo Press, 1988), p. 65.

12. Hadlock, *Jazz Masters of the Twenties*, p. 182.

13. Schuller, *The Swing Era*, p. 599.

14. Quoted in Waters, *Jack Teagarden's Music*, p. 3.

15. Charles R. Townsend writes that Wills, who was born in the Panhandle, also in 1905, remembered hearing Bessie Smith as a young man in the 1920s and thinking her "the greatest thing I had ever heard." See *San Antonio Rose: The Life and Music of Bob Wills* (Urbana: University of Illinois Press, 1976), p. 40. Gertrude "Ma" Rainey has often been credited with taking Bessie on tour with her, though no proof of this has been offered. Dan Morgenstern, in notes for the compact disc entitled *Ma Rainey* (Milestone, MCD-47021-2, 1992), reports that "there is some evidence that they did work together briefly near the end of Ma's career, in an early Thirties stock show in Fort Worth."

16. Hadlock, *Jazz Masters of the Twenties*, p. 174.

17. Smith, "Jack Teagarden," p. 34. Peck Kelley, who was born in Houston in 1899, never recorded during the 1920s and in fact was not persuaded to do so until the 1950s, when he "allowed friends to record his solo playing" and later recorded with a group called Shannon & Co. These recordings, produced by Milt Gabler's Commodore Records (Mosaic Records, 1990), are discussed in liner notes by Dan Morgenstern written in June 1990. At times Kelley's piano style sounds like Bix Beiderbecke's *In a Mist* from September 9, 1927 (on *The Bix Beiderbecke Story*, vol. 3, *Whiteman Days* [Columbia Records, CL 846]), with its pounded passages and starts and stops, its key shifts and modulations of the period. But Peck can also suggest the later Earl Hines and Fats Waller in his technique and at times in his rocking rhythms. Often Kelley's playing seems just what it was, a kind of cocktail jazz, with the clinking of glasses and conversation in the background, as on *Lover*, where he improvises on the theme by ripping off scales up and down the keyboard, returning from time to time to remind us of the basis of his excursions; some of this even recalls Bud Powell's explorations of a pop tune or ballad, though in no way boppish in style. On *Honeysuckle Rose 1*, Peck plays more of a contrapuntal, Bach-like version of this classic Waller tune that would have intrigued Fats, who loved the baroque master. Peck can also swing the tune as hard as Waller, but this seems only one of many approaches he likes to try out. This piece demonstrates as well Peck's personal inventiveness, for even as his right hand pursues a Walleresque stride statement of the theme, his left roams in the low bass with a line of its own. Nonetheless, since all of this comes some thirty years after Kelley worked with Teagarden, it had little direct bearing on the development of jazz, so that it is only through the possible influence of Peck on Teagarden that the pianist has a place in the story of Texans and their contribution to the history of jazz.

18. Jay D. Smith and Len Guttridge, *Jack Teagarden: The Story of a Jazz Maverick* (London: Cassell and Company, 1960), p. 42.

19. During a trip to New Orleans while he was with Peck Kelley's Bad Boys in 1921–1922, Teagarden is said to have heard Armstrong "playing on the upper deck of a river boat off Canal Street. They met then and there, in the home city of jazz, and have matched horns in marvelous music, off and on, ever since" (Smith, "Jack Teagarden," pp. 61–62).

20. Williams, *Jazz Heritage*, p. 11.

21. Hadlock, *Jazz Masters of the Twenties*, p. 178. *She's a Great, Great Girl* is on *Jack Teagarden*, vol. 1, *1928–1931*.

22. John Litweiler, *Ornette Coleman: A Harmolodic Life* (New York: William Morrow, 1992), p. 63.

23. Quoted in Hadlock, *Jazz Masters of the Twenties*, p. 185.

24. Ibid., p. 172.

25. Ibid.

26. Ibid., p. 181.

27. Quoted in Shapiro and Hentoff, eds., *Hear Me Talkin' to Ya*, p. 288.

28. Hadlock, *Jazz Masters of the Twenties*, p. 176.

29. Smith and Guttridge, *Jack Teagarden*, p. 25.

30. Hadlock, *Jazz Masters of the Twenties*, p. 174.

31. Smith and Guttridge, *Jack Teagarden*, p. 42.

32. Ibid., p. 45.

33. Ibid., pp. 43, 54.

34. Schuller, *The Swing Era*, p. 600.

35. Ibid.

36. Vic Bellerby, liner notes, *Jack Teagarden: I Gotta Right to Sing the Blues*.

37. According to Stanley Dance, this recording "was unfortunately rejected and the master either lost or destroyed" (liner notes, *Louis Armstrong*, vol. 5, *Louis in New York* [Columbia Records, CK 46148, 1990]).

38. Russell, *Jazz Style in Kansas City*, p. 123.

39. Dance, liner notes, *Louis Armstrong*, vol. 5.

40. Ibid.

41. This day marked a turning point for Armstrong's career, not because of the recording with Teagarden but because he was featured as a virtuoso trumpeter and a vocalist with his nine-piece orchestra on *I Can't Give You Anything But Love*, which was recorded along with *Mahogany Hall Stomp*. Louis's recording of *I Can't Give You Anything But Love* launched him as a popular singer as well as a world-class jazz trumpet star.

42. Schuller, *The Swing Era*, p. 598n.

43. Stanley Dance, liner notes, *The Golden Horn of Jack Teagarden* (Decca Records, DL 4540).

44. Schuller, *The Swing Era*, p. 602.

45. Whitney Balliett, *American Musicians: 56 Portraits in Jazz* (New York: Oxford University Press, 1986), p. 164.

46. Smith, "Jack Teagarden," p. 66.

47. Schuller, *The Swing Era*, p. 605n. All the recordings mentioned in this paragraph are

included on *The Golden Horn of Jack Teagarden.*

48. Smith, "Jack Teagarden," p. 73.

49. George Avakian, liner notes, *The Bessie Smith Story,* vol. 2 (Columbia Records, CL 856, 1951).

50. Schuller, *The Swing Era,* p. 600. *It's So Good* is on *Jack Teagarden.* vol. 1.

51. Schuller, *The Swing Era,* pp. 600–601.

52. Ibid., p. 603.

53. Both of these tunes are included on *Billie Holiday: The Golden Years* (Columbia Records, C3L 21, 1962).

54. Glenn Coulter, "Billie Holiday," in *The Art of Jazz,* ed. Williams, p. 165.

55. Balliett, *American Musicians,* p. 163.

56. The sides from this October 1933 session are included on *Benny Goodman and the Giants of Swing* (Prestige Records, PR 7644).

57. Hadlock, *Jazz Masters of the Twenties,* p. 190.

58. Giddins, *Riding on a Blue Note,* p. 74.

59. Schuller, *The Swing Era,* p. 605n.

60. Jack's sister and two brothers all performed with him at one time or another, and all were born, as he was, in Vernon. Norma, who played the piano in Jack's bands in the mid-1940s, was born on April 28, 1911; Charlie was born on July 19, 1913; and Clois Lee (Cub), who played drums with Jack's big band in 1939 and 1940, was born on December 16, 1915.

61. Russell, *Jazz Style in Kansas City,* p. 127. In 1929 alone, Teagarden made more than 100 recordings (Hadlock, *Jazz Masters of the Twenties,* p. 183).

62. Hadlock, *Jazz Masters of the Twenties,* p. 192.

63. Williams, *Jazz Heritage,* pp. 9, 10.

64. *Satchmo at Symphony Hall* (Decca Records, DXB 195).

65. Hadlock, *Jazz Masters of the Twenties,* p. 188.

66. Giddins, *Riding on a Blue Note,* pp. 75–76, 78.

67. Humphrey Lyttleton, *The Best of Jazz, Basin Street to Harlem: Jazz Masters and Masterpieces, 1917–1930* (London: Robson Books, 1978), p. 200.

68. Quoted in Hadlock, *Jazz Masters of the Twenties,* p. 179.

69. Frank Driggs, "Budd Johnson: Ageless Jazzman," part 1, *Jazz Review* 3, no. 9 (November 1960): 4.

70. Ibid., p. 6.

71. Ibid., p. 7.

72. Schuller, *The Swing Era,* p. 184. This and the other tunes performed by Keg Johnson are on *A Rare Batch of Satch: The Authentic Sound of Louis Armstrong in the '30s* (RCA Victor Records, LPM-2322, 1961).

73. Schuller, *The Swing Era,* p. 183.

74. Quoted in George T. Simon, liner notes, *A Rare Batch of Satch.* Schuller is probably closer to the mark, for *Laughin' Louie* primarily displays Armstrong's high-note acrobatics.

75. James Lincoln Collier, *Louis Armstrong: An American Genius* (New York: Oxford University Press, 1983), p. 258.

76. Johnny Simmen, liner notes, *Benny Carter/1933* (Prestige Records, 7643, 1969).

77. Johnson's solo work with Fletcher Henderson is found on *Swing's the Thing (1931–1934)*, vol. 2 (Decca Records, DL79228).

78. All three recordings are included on *"Chu"* (Epic Records, EE22007).

79. Both tunes are included on *The Most Important Recordings of Cab Calloway* (Official Records, 3041-2, 1989).

80. Johnson is present on the Ray Charles album *Genius Plus Soul Equals Jazz* (Impulse Records, A-2), recorded on December 26, 1960.

81. Sinclair Traill, "Record Reviews," *Jazz Journal* 15, no. 9 (1962): 28.

82. Dance, *The World of Count Basie*, p. 329.

83. McCarthy, *Big Band Jazz*, p. 175. This jazz historian also reports that Keg Johnson was one of a group of musicians who were with the Echols band "at different times over the years."

84. *Benny Carter and His Orchestra Live Broadcasts 1939 / 1948* (Jass Hour, JH-1005).

85. Ross Russell, "Bebop," in *The Art of Jazz*, ed. Williams, p. 205.

86. McCarthy, *Big Band Jazz*, p. 213. *Pickin' the Cabbage* and *Bye Bye Blues* are included on *16 Cab Calloway Classics* (CBS Records, France, CBS 62950).

87. McCarthy, *Big Band Jazz*, p. 214. *King Porter Stomp* is included on *Cruisin' with Cab* (Alamac Records, QSR 2407).

88. In the personnel for the September 19, 1949, recording of *I Beeped When I Shoulda Bopped*, Glenn is listed on trombone even though by this time he was with Duke Ellington's orchestra.

89. Vic Bellerby, "Duke Ellington," in *The Art of Jazz*, ed. Williams, p. 144.

90. Ibid., p. 156. *H'ya Sue* is included on Duke Ellington's ten-inch album, *Mood Ellington* (Columbia Records, CL 6024).

91. Jeff Aldam, "The Ellington Sidemen," in *Duke Ellington: His Life and Music*, ed. Peter Gammon (London: Phoenix House, 1958), p. 199. *Three Cent Stomp* is on *Mood Ellington*.

92. Duke Ellington with Stanley Dance, "The Art Is in the Cooking" (1962), *The Duke Ellington Reader*, ed. Mark Tucker (New York: Oxford University Press, 1993), p. 336.

93. James Lincoln Collier, *Duke Ellington* (New York: Oxford University Press, 1987), pp. 246, 251.

94. Bellerby, "Duke Ellington," p. 146.

95. Ibid. *Mood Indigo* of 1950 is included on *Masterpieces by Ellington* (Columbia Records, JCL 825, 1973).

96. Raymond Horricks, "The Orchestral Suites," in *Duke Ellington*, ed. Gammon, p. 128.

97. Ibid., p. 129. Max Harrison differs with Horricks in finding that Glenn's vibraharp on Dance No. 2 halts "a series of forceful exchanges between clarinet and the rest of the band driven by Sonny Greer in exceptional form" and that Tyree's "banal entry" is "an anti-climax so extreme as to make one laugh out loud" ("Some Reflections on Ellington's Longer Works" [1964; rev. 1991], *The Duke Ellington Reader*, ed. Tucker, p. 393).

98. Jacques B. Hess, liner notes, *Liberian Suite* (CBS Records, France, CBS 62686, 1973).

99. For a moving account of the Teagarden trip to the Far East for the U.S. State Department, see Smith and Guttridge, *Jack Teagarden*, pp. 179–180.

100. See the album entitled *Horace Henderson 1940* (Tax Records, M-8013).

101. Johnson was present for the recording of Ellington's *Second Sacred Concert* (RCA Victor Records, 1968).

102. *Up in Duke's Workshop* (Pablo Records, OJC-633, 1979).

103. There is some confusion in the discographical notes for this album. Stanley Dance's notes correctly identify the soloists for *Blem*, whereas the album dates and personnel do not coincide with tunes as they are listed.

104. Collier, *Louis Armstrong*, p. 313.

105. John F. Szwed, liner notes, *What a Wonderful World* (ABC Records, ABCS-650). On this particular album, Glenn's trombone behind Armstrong on *Cabaret* has just the right mellow tone in support of Louis's vocal, and their playing together is particularly satisfying, each with his own peculiar sound.

106. These tunes are included on *Louis "Satchmo" Armstrong* (Everest Records, FS-258). Dates for the various numbers seem to be as follows: *Short But Sweet*, New York, July 1965; *When the Saints Go Marchin' In*, New York, April 1966; and *Tin Roof Blues* and *Mame*, New York, May 1966. *Bye 'n' Bye* may date from October 29, 1970, when Glenn was with the Armstrong All-Stars at Charity Concert in London. Glenn also was a member of the Armstrong combo when it appeared on the David Frost Show on February 10, 1971, some five months prior to the trumpeter's death on July 6, 1971.

107. *The Circle of Your Arms, So Long Dearie, Tyree's Blues*, and *Pretty Little Missy* are included on *Louis "Satchmo" Armstrong*.

12. By Way of Kaycee

1. Max Harrison, review of *The Missourians*, in Harrison, Fox, and Thacker, *The Essential Jazz Records*, p. 168.

2. Schuller, *Early Jazz*, p. 271.

3. Schuller, *The Swing Era*, p. 328.

4. Schuller, *Early Jazz*, p. 271.

5. These recordings are included on *The Missourians* (RCA Victor Records, France, FPM 17017).

6. Harrison, Fox, and Thacker, *The Essential Jazz Records*, pp. 168–169. *Ozark Mountain Blues* and *Market Street Stomp* are reproduced on *Hot Jazz 1928–1930* (Nimbus Records, England, HRM 6004, 1987).

7. Schuller, *The Swing Era*, p. 328.

8. Harrison, Fox, and Thacker, *The Essential Jazz Records*, p. 168.

9. Schuller, *The Swing Era*, pp. 327–328.

10. Ibid., p. 327.

11. Ibid., pp. 327, 334, 336.

12. All these pieces are included on *The Most Important Recordings of Cab Calloway* (Official Records, 3041-2, 1989).

13. Schuller, *The Swing Era*, p. 349.

14. Ibid., p. 340.

15. Lunceford's recording of *Margie* is included on *Jimmy Lunceford and His Orchestra* (Decca Records, DL 8050, 1953).

16. Alain Gerber, liner notes, *Jimmie Lunceford "Harlem Shout" (1935–1936)*, vol. 2 (Decca

Records, MCA-1305, 1980).

17. Tirro, *Jazz*, p. 227.

18. Feather, *The New Edition of the Encyclopedia of Jazz*, p. 317.

19. Schuller, *The Swing Era*, pp. 203–204, 203n.

20. Ibid., p. 211.

21. Hoefer, "Held Notes," p. 54.

22. Quoted in Dance, *The World of Count Basie*, p. 67.

23. Schuller, *The Swing Era*, p. 211.

24. Quoted in Dance, *The World of Count Basie*, p. 66.

25. Schuller, *The Swing Era*, p. 218.

26. Charles Fox, review of *For Dancers Only*, in Harrison, Fox, and Thacker, *The Essential Jazz Records*, p. 309.

27. All the tunes discussed in these last two paragraphs are included on *Jimmie Lunceford "Harlem Shout,"* vol. 2, and all were recorded in New York.

28. Schuller, *The Swing Era*, p. 356n.

29. Quoted in Alan Govenar, *Meeting the Blues* (Dallas: Taylor Publishing, 1988), p. 35. Stanley Dance quotes Durham as saying that he used the resonator while he was still with Bennie Moten (*The World of Count Basie*, p. 63). Burton W. Peretti, who has made extensive use of a Durham interview housed in the Rutgers Institute of Jazz Studies, reveals that during Eddie's youth his father "instructed him in such folk music practices as tapping his cigar-box fiddle's fingerboard with hatpins and filling its soundbox with snake rattles." See *The Creation of Jazz: Music, Race, and Culture in Urban America* (Urbana: University of Illinois Press, 1992), p. 42.

30. Gerber, liner notes, *Jimmie Lunceford "Harlem Shout,"* vol. 2.

31. Schuller, *The Swing Era*, p. 213.

32. Quoted in Govenar, *Meeting the Blues*, p. 36.

33. Schuller, *The Swing Era*, p. 573.

34. Ibid., pp. 356n, 564–565n, 577.

35. Al Avakian and Bob Prince, "Charlie Christian," in *The Art of Jazz*, ed. Williams, p. 184. This essay is reprinted from Avakian and Prince's liner notes to *Charlie Christian with the Benny Goodman Sextet and Orchestra* (Columbia Records, CL 652).

36. Avakian and Prince, "Charlie Christian," pp. 184–185.

37. Quoted in Dance, *The World of Count Basie*, pp. 66–67.

38. Schuller, *The Swing Era*, pp. 212–213.

39. Fox, review of *For Dancers Only*, in Harrison, Fox, and Thacker, *The Essential Jazz Records*, p. 309.

40. Sheridan, *Count Basie: A Bio-Discography*, p. xxv.

41. Ibid., pp. xxiv–xxv.

42. Schuller, *The Swing Era*, p. 238. While Schuller credits Jimmy Mundy with arranging Durham's composition, Chris Sheridan lists Durham as the arranger for *John's Idea*. See Sheridan, *Count Basie: A Bio-Discography*, p. 40.

43. Harrison, Fox, and Thacker, *The Essential Jazz Records*, p. 309.

44. Ibid., p. 308. The Lunceford performance of *Pigeon Walk* is included on *For Dancers Only*, vol. 3, *1936–1937*; the Basie performance of *Time Out* is included on *One O'Clock Jump* (Decca

Records, MCA-42324, 1990).

45. Schuller, *The Swing Era*, p. 216. This performance is on *For Dancers Only*, vol. 3.

46. Williams, *The Jazz Tradition*, pp. 128–129. Williams's reference to Sampson's *Blue Lou*, arranged for and recorded by the Fletcher Henderson orchestra on March 27, 1936, may relate to some structural similarity between this piece and Durham's *Time Out*, for the tunes are otherwise not at all the same.

47. Leonard Feather, liner notes, *Giants of the Tenor Sax*.

48. Count Basie had studied with Waller, who had himself studied with James P. Johnson, who broke with the Missouri ragtime tradition, which was, as Schuller explains, "essentially more melodic, thematic in conception. With his strong, striding left hand, Johnson focused his attention on the rhythmicization of melodic ideas, often suppressing the latter element to the point of extinction. Many of his 'melodies' are essentially rhythmic figures that happen to have pitches attached to them. But rather than being merely destructive, this approach provided the necessary transition to jazz" (*Early Jazz*, pp. 217–218). Chris Sheridan writes that Basie "rapidly distilled 'stride' to its fundamentals, then rebuilt those essentials as a kind of lattice, through which soloists and rhythm section components alike could weave and interweave" (*Count Basie: A Bio-Discography*, p. xxiv).

49. Murray, *Stomping the Blues*, p. 174.

50. Eddie Durham commented on one occasion that another cause of the big-band business going "wrong" was that "the bands got too wild in their tempo" (Dance, *The World of Count Basie*, p. 65).

51. Schuller, *The Swing Era*, p. 675. While Schuller writes that "Miller became a millionaire on *In the Mood* alone," George T. Simon, in *Glenn Miller and His Orchestra* (New York: Thomas Y. Crowell, 1974), claims that "though 'In the Mood' became one of Glenn's all-time hit records, he was never able to collect anything from the proceeds of its sales. . . . Because he was still bound by his no-royalty contract, . . . all he ever received for 'In the Mood' was the original $175!" (p. 177). Nonetheless, Schuller is probably correct in that the popularity of *In the Mood* made possible many profitable radio broadcasts, public appearances, and endorsements.

52. Quoted in Dance, *The World of Count Basie*, pp. 68–69.

53. Dizzy Gillespie and Al Fraser, *To Be or Not . . . to Bop: Memoirs* (Garden City, N.Y.: Doubleday, 1979), p. 258.

54. John Flower, *Moonlight Serenade: A Bio-Discography of the Glenn Miller Civilian Band* (New Rochelle, N.Y.: Arlington House, 1972), p. 81. See pp. 70, 72, 74–76, and 104 for Durham's contributions to the Miller band. Gunther Schuller speculates that "Eddie Durham did the actual transferring of [Joe] Garland's original arrangement [Garland is credited with the arrangement in the published score], as pruned by Miller, and that Durham is also responsible for the trombone pedals towards the end. He was a trombonist, of course, and had used similar effects for years with the Lunceford band" (*The Swing Era*, p. 675).

55. Placksin, *American Women in Jazz*, pp. 132–151. Clora Bryant, a trumpet player born in Denison, was active during the decade following Durham's work with all-women orchestras. She began her career at Prairie View College and later moved to Los Angeles, where she became "one of the most respected trumpet players on the West Coast" (p. 152).

56. *Swing Today Volume Three* (RCA Victor, LFL1 5067) and *Eddie Durham* (RCA Victor, LPL 5029). Both albums were recorded in New York on July 10, 1973.

57. Stanley Dance, *The World of Earl Hines* (1977; reprint, New York: Da Capo Press, 1983), p. 204.

58. Quoted in Driggs, "Budd Johnson," part 1, p. 6. Gunther Schuller notes that Mosley's "formidable technique clearly forecasts the lightning-fast trombones of the Bop Era" (*Early Jazz*, p. 302).

59. Driggs, "Budd Johnson: Ageless Jazzman," part 2, *Jazz Review* 4, no. 1 (January 1961): 16. Johnson performs on *Blues and Things*, an album with Earl Hines and Jimmy Rushing (Master Jazz Recordings, MJR 8101), dating from July 19, 1967.

60. Dance, *The World of Earl Hines*, pp. 206, 207.

61. Ibid., p. 208.

62. Driggs, "Budd Johnson," part 2, p. 17. *Paseo Street* is on Brunswick 7132.

63. Schuller, *Early Jazz*, p. 298.

64. Quoted in Dance, *The World of Earl Hines*, p. 209.

65. Ibid.

66. Ibid., pp. 209–210.

67. Ibid., p. 212.

68. Driggs, "Budd Johnson," part 2, p. 17. *Mahogany Hall Stomp* and *Some Sweet Day* are included on *A Rare Batch of Satch*.

69. Quoted in Dance, *The World of Earl Hines*, p. 210.

70. Ibid., p. 213.

71. Driggs, "Budd Johnson," part 2, p. 14.

72. Ibid., p. 16. Mary Lee Hester claims that Johnson's nickname came from Hines, who referred to him as "My Buddy"—after the tune of that title—but then shortened it to "My Budd." See "Texas Jazz Heritage," *Texas Jazz* 3, no. 8 (August 1979): 3.

73. Stanley Dance, liner notes, *The Grand Terrace Band: Earl Hines* (RCA Victor Records, LPV-512, 1965). Frank Driggs reports that "by 1942 when the record ban set in, [Johnson had] written the arrangements for half the band's records" ("Budd Johnson," part 2, p. 17).

74. Dance, liner notes, *The Grand Terrace Band*.

75. *Pianology* is included on *Hines Rhythm* (Epic Records, 22021).

76. Schuller, *The Swing Era*, p. 285. Johnson achieves great swing in his solo on *Pianology*, but his "Lester Young" sound seems more in evidence on *Flany Doodle Swing* of the same date. On *Pianology* his swoops and rhythms and tone are more those of a true tenor rather than the altolike sound that Young tended toward in his own tenor playing.

77. Schuller, *The Swing Era*, pp. 288, 286.

78. Hugues Panassié and Madeleine Gautier, *Guide to Jazz*, ed. A. A. Gurwitch; trans. Desmond Flower (Boston: Houghton Mifflin, 1956), p. 146.

79. Schuller, *The Swing Era*, pp. 287, 285.

80. Driggs, "Budd Johnson," part 2, p. 17.

81. Schuller, *The Swing Era*, p. 290.

82. Stanley Dance, liner notes, *Earl Hines Live at the Village Vanguard* (Columbia Records, 44197, 1988), p. 3

83. Ibid. In a review of these performances, Dance also comments that "the piano playing throughout was superb, but we think these recordings will add a great deal to Budd's international reputation. He has seldom been caught before in comparable form" ("Lightly and

Politely," *Jazz Journal* 18, no. 8 [August 1965]: 26).

84. *Blues and Things.*

85. Stanley Dance, liner notes, *"Fatha" Blows Best: Earl Hines and His Quartet* (Decca Records, DL 75048). On this album, recorded on March 8 and 11, 1964, Budd performs two other tunes on soprano, and as Dance points out, "Although [Budd] plays the whole saxophone family (and clarinet), he is best known as one of the most talented tenor improvisers. Since rejoining Hines in 1964, however, he has devoted much time to the soprano, with the result that he is today probably the most fluent of all jazz performers on this instrument, as his brilliant solos testify here."

86. Quoted in Driggs, "Budd Johnson," part 2, p. 16.

87. Feather, *The New Edition of the Encyclopedia of Jazz,* p. 270; Leonard Feather, *Inside Be-Bop* (New York: J. J. Robbins and Sons, 1949), p. 29.

88. Gillespie and Fraser, *To Be, or Not . . . to Bop,* p. 218.

89. McCarthy, *Big Band Jazz,* p. 110.

90. Quoted in Gillespie and Fraser, *To Be, or Not . . . to Bop,* p. 218.

91. Ibid.

92. Ibid., p. 138.

93. Ira Gitler, *Swing to Bop* (New York: Oxford University Press, 1985), p. 81.

94. One tune from the Hawkins sessions, entitled *Serenade to a Sleeping Beauty,* is included on *Swing Street* (Epic Records, SN 6042), but Hawkins is the soloist and the sax section with Scott gives a saccharine imitation of Glenn Miller. The Holiday dates are included on *Billie Holiday/God Bless the Child* (Columbia Records, G30782, 1972).

95. These sides are included on *Billie Holiday, The Golden Years.*

96. Feather, *The New Edition of the Encyclopedia of Jazz,* p. 270.

97. Dan Morgenstern, liner notes, *Coleman Hawkins: Rainbow Mist* (Delmark Records, Denmark, DD-459, 1992).

98. Ibid.

99. John Chilton, *The Song of the Hawk: The Life and Recordings of Coleman Hawkins* (Ann Arbor: University of Michigan Press, 1990), p. 210.

100. Quoted in Gillespie and Fraser, *To Be, or Not . . . to Bop,* p. 215.

101. Chilton, *Song of the Hawk,* p. 211.

102. Gillespie and Fraser, *To Be, or Not . . . to Bop,* p. 186.

103. Morgenstern, liner notes, *Rainbow Mist.*

104. Chilton, *Song of the Hawk,* p. 210.

105. Gitler, *Swing to Bop,* p. 5.

106. Chilton, *Song of the Hawk,* p. 210; Morgenstern, liner notes, *Rainbow Mist.* The 1960 recording of *Yesterdays* is on *Essen Jazz Festival All-Stars* (Fantasy Records, 6015).

107. However, Albert McCarthy calls Johnson's solo on *Cherry* "very good" (*Big Band Jazz,* p. 236).

108. George T. Simon, liner notes, *Woody Herman 1943–1944: "The Turning Point"* (Decca Records, DL 9229).

109. Ibid.

110. Later, in 1959 and 1960, Budd would once again join with white musicians recording another kind of modern jazz—the arrangements of Gil Evans. Following the successful

collaborations between Evans and Miles Davis on the 1949 *The Birth of the Cool* and their later cooperative efforts on the 1957 *Miles Ahead* and the 1958 *Porgy and Bess*, Evans recorded his *Great Jazz Standards* on February 5, 1959 (prior to the 1959–1960 *Sketches of Spain* with Miles Davis) and called on Budd Johnson to play clarinet or tenor in four tunes: Don Redman's *Chant of the Weed*; a blues, spiritual-like rendition of *Ballad of the Sad Young Men*; Clifford Brown's *Joy Spring*; and the Evans original, *Theme*. Budd solos on *Chant of the Weed*, setting the mood with his "rich, full-throated . . . soulful clarinet," and on *Theme* he constructs an "imaginative solo based on thematic material." In selecting Budd Johnson to play the clarinet solo on *Chant of the Weed* and the tenor solo on *Theme*, Gil Evans created "all in all a hell of an album" (Dave Baker, liner notes, *Gil Evans: Pacific Standard Time* [Blue Note Records, BN-LA461-H2]). On another Evans album, recorded December 10 and 11, 1960, as part of the series *The Great Arrangers*, Budd, along with his brother Keg, performs well enough in this progressive idiom, but his tenor solo on *La Nevada* cannot compare with his work in the 1930s and 1940s. Nevertheless, as one of the premier modern arrangers, Evans proves his good taste by his "selection of personnel" (Tom Stewart, liner notes, *The Great Arrangers*, vol. 9 [Impulse Records, 2-4143]). One new wrinkle on this Impulse album occurs in Kurt Weill's *Bilbao*, with Budd on soprano sax. As noted earlier, by 1964 Budd had begun to concentrate on this instrument.

111. Gillespie and Fraser, *To Be, or Not . . . to Bop*, p. 186.

112. Driggs, "Budd Johnson," part 2, pp. 17–18.

113. Mark Gardner, liner notes, *Together: The Legendary Big Band of Billy Eckstine* (Spotlite Records, England, Spotlite 100, 1974).

114. Ibid.

115. Ibid. Gardner's notes were written in 1971.

116. Feather, *The New Edition of the Encyclopedia of Jazz*, p. 270.

117. Dan Morgenstern, liner notes, *Coleman Hawkins: Body and Soul* (RCA Victor Records, 5658-1-RB, 1986). In an anecdote about a concert at Carnegie Hall on September 29, 1947, Johnson described his relationship with Parker: "At that concert, Charlie Parker did something. People try to create some dissension between Charlie Parker and me. They don't know how warm a relationship we had. On the stage, after one of the numbers, Charlie Parker just walked out on the stage with one rose, one long rose—he'd probably spent his last quarter to buy it—and gave it to me. And he kissed me—on the mouth—and then walked off. I get a warm feeling every time I think about Charlie Parker" (quoted in Gillespie and Fraser, *To Be or Not . . . to Bop*, p. 312).

118. *The International Jazz Group*, vol. 2 (Swing Records, SW 8416, 1987).

119. *Compact Jazz* (Verve Records, 833 296-2).

120. Stanley Dance, liner notes, *First Time! The Count Meets the Duke* (Columbia Records, CK 40586), p. 6.

121. Unsigned liner notes, *Basie at Birdland* (Roulette Records, R52065). Johnson was a regular member of the Basie band during 1960 and 1961. Gerald Lascelles reports that in *Segue* Budd "works the crowd into something of a frenzy" and concludes that "pride of place" goes to this side on the album. See his review of *Basie at Birdland*, *Jazz Journal* 15, no. 6 (June 1962): 28.

122. Dance, liner notes, *First Time!* p. 5.

123. Count Basie, *Get Together* (Pablo Records, PACD-2310-924-2, 1986).

124. Albert McCarthy et al., *Jazz on Record: A Critical Guide to the First 50 Years: 1917–1967*

(London: Hanover Books, 1968), p. 154. Johnson's authority is even more apparent in his solo on *Backstage Blues* from *Basie at Birdland*; here Budd blows this blues with complete authority and owes nothing to Lester Young. Fellow Texan Henry Coker also plays an eloquent trombone solo on *Backstage Blues*.

125. Quoted in Joe Goldberg, liner notes, *The Budd Johnson Quintet: Let's Swing* (Prestige Records, OJC-1720). Another album from 1960, *Budd Johnson and the Four Brass Giants* (Riverside Records, 343), recorded on August 22 and September 6, features Johnson on tenor along with trumpeters Nat Adderley, Harry Edison, Ray Nance, and Clark Terry. This album also showcases Johnson's arrangements of standards as well as four originals by the Texan, two of which are tributes to Lester Young. The other two originals are *Driftwood* and *Trinity River Bottom*. The latter, according to Johnson, was "named after a Dallas river which 'has caused a lot of trouble and taken a lot of lives so I always associated it with people having a hard time. I therefore thought there ought to be a blues about it'" (quoted in Chris Albertson, liner notes, *Four Brass Giants*).

13. Out of Big D

1. In an interview, Smith recalled that while with Hopkins he "was playing cool at the time. I really liked being around [Hilton] Jefferson [who was also in the band] but Claude Hopkins and me didn't get along at all. I didn't stay with him for very long. I think I left after about a month with him" (Hester, *Going to Kansas City*, p. 21).

2. Don Gazzaway, "Buster and Bird: Conversations with Buster Smith," part 3, *Jazz Review* 3, no. 2 (February 1960): 13.

3. Ibid., p. 14; Gazzaway, "Conversations with Buster Smith," part 1, p. 18.

4. Russell, *Jazz Style in Kansas City*, p. 84.

5. Ross Russell, *Bird Lives! The High Life and Hard Times of Charlie "Yardbird" Parker* (New York: Charterhouse, 1973), p. 52.

6. Quoted in Gazzaway, "Conversations with Buster Smith," part 3, p. 14.

7. Ibid.

8. Ibid.

9. Tim Schuller, "Music out of Clay," *Texas Jazz* 3, no. 1 (November 1979): [1].

10. Michael Levin and John S. Wilson, "'No Bop Roots in Jazz': Parker," *Down Beat* 16, no. 17 (September 9, 1949): 12.

11. Quoted in Gazzaway, "Conversations with Buster Smith," part 3, p. 13.

12. Russell, *Jazz Style in Kansas City*, p. 201.

13. Gazzaway, "Conversations with Buster Smith," part 2, p. 14.

14. Schuller, *The Swing Era*, p. 797. Both of these sides are included on *Swing Street* (Epic Records, SN 6042, 1962).

15. Harrison, Fox, and Thacker, *The Essential Jazz Records*, p. 549. Fox's review of *Swing Street*, vol. 4, mistakenly gives the date of these recordings by Pete Johnson and His Boogie Woogie Boys as "30 June 1937" rather than 1939.

16. Quoted in Gitler, *Swing to Bop*, p. 60. Mary Lee Hester reports a related statement by Budd Johnson: "Buster Smith was our inspiration. But then he was that to all musicians of our time.

When I was a kid we had this little band. We used to go and hear Buster all the time. He had a great band—a great, great band and always helped us kids, tremendously. That was back in the very early 20's. So you see I've known Buster for an awfully long time" (quoted in *Going to Kansas City*, p. [95]).

17. McCarthy, *Big Band Jazz*, p. 148.

18. Schuller, *The Swing Era*, p. 798.

19. Russell, *Jazz Style in Kansas City*, p. 235.

20. Charters and Kunstadt, *Jazz*, p. 286.

21. Six of these tunes are reproduced on *Hot Lips Page 1938–1940* (Official Records, Denmark, 83 047, 1989).

22. It should be noted as well that no other commentators, not even Dan Morgenstern in his writings on Hot Lips Page, have made reference to Buster's work from this session. Morgenstern does, however, include this recording in his Page discography as among Page's "greatest" sides. See "Hot Lips Page," *Jazz Journal* 15, no. 11 (November 1962): 14. Gazzaway also lists *I Ain't Got Nobody* in "Conversations with Buster Smith," part 3, p. 16. Russell alludes to this session but merely writes that "there are also eight titles, two of them never issued on 33 rpm records, with Lips Page for Decca" (*Jazz Style in Kansas City*, p. 235). Schuller discusses a recording of *I Ain't Got Nobody*, but this version is by Lester Young and Basie's Bad Boys (*The Swing Era*, p. 552).

23. Gazzaway, "Conversations with Buster Smith," part 3, p. 16.

24. *Kansas City Jazz* (Decca Records, 8044).

25. Thomas Owens, *Bebop: The Music and Its Players* (New York: Oxford University Press, 1995), p. 9.

26. Russell, *Jazz Style in Kansas City*, p. 235.

27. Gunther Schuller, "In Search of Buster Smith," insert for *The Legendary Buster Smith* (Atlantic Records, 1323).

28. Quoted in Gitler, *Swing to Bop*, p. 62.

29. Gazzaway, "Conversations with Buster Smith," part 3, p. 15.

30. Frank Driggs, liner notes, *Atlantic Jazz: Kansas City* (Atlantic Records, 78 17011, 1986). This album reproduces two tunes from *The Legendary Buster Smith*: *Buster's Tune* and *E-Flat Boogie*.

31. Gillum is not represented on an album entitled *San Antonio Jazz* (International Association of Jazz Record Collectors, LP No. 3), but the work of other sidemen is included on recordings by two outstanding San Antonio bands from the period 1935–1938: Boots and His Buddies and Don Albert and His Orchestra. Performances by Boots and His Buddies, also available on the compact disc *The Chronological Boots and His Buddies 1935–1937* (Classics Records, France, 7231), are typical of the swing era and show the influence of Don Redman, Moten, and Basie. Some of the band's pieces are quite lively, notably *Rose Room* and *Riffs* from August 14, 1935, which are played in a rougher, more aggressive southwestern style.

Leader Clifford "Boots" Douglas was born in Temple in Central Texas on September 7, 1908, and began on drums at age fifteen, playing his first job at Turner's Park in San Antonio in 1926. Schuller describes Douglas as "a kind of western Chick Webb," one of the swing era's greatest drummer-bandleaders (*The Swing Era*, p. 799). At times Douglas's soloists are extremely fine, with Boots himself quite active on his drum set and Charles Anderson on trumpet and Baker Millian on tenor especially impressive—all three featured well on *The Goo* from September 17, 1937. Schuller comments that Anderson exemplifies the notion that "young territory trumpeters were as influenced and competitively inspired by *each other* as they were by the more famous Eastern soloists" (p. 801n.27). Boots's saxes play beautifully as a section on *Anytime* from August 14, 1935, and on *Jealous* from February 27, 1937. After this early period, however, the Boots band, according to Schuller, deteriorated in quality and never really found its own identity (pp. 800–801).

All the Don Albert sides date from November 18, 1936, the only recordings made by this San Antonio band. According to Albert McCarthy, the group was "the first orchestra to use the word 'swing' in its title," billing itself as "Don Albert and His Music, America's Greatest Swing Band" (*Big Band Jazz*, p. 107). The Albert recordings show the influence in particular of Lunceford and Ellington. *You Don't Love Me* is a fine imitation of the Lunceford style, and *Deep Blue Melody* is an Ellington-like treatment arranged by pianist Lloyd Glenn, who was born in San Antonio on November 21, 1909. Glenn played with the Terrence Holder band in Dallas, joined Don Albert in 1934, and went with Boots Douglas in Shadowland at San Antonio from 1935. For Boots and His Buddies, Glenn arranged the fine *How Long?* which was recorded in two parts in 1935 and 1936 and contains Rushing-like vocals by Celeste Allen. Glenn's piano style has been described as a "lilting, jazz-flavored" one that "contained elements of Texas blues as well as the rhythmic punch of boogie-woogie" (Robert Santelli, *The Big Book of Blues: A Biographical Encyclopedia* [New York: Penguin, 1993], p. 157).

32. Schuller, "In Search of Buster Smith."

33. Gazzaway, "Conversations with Buster Smith," part 3, p. 15; part 1, p. 18.

34. Quoted in Hester, *Going to Kansas City*, p. 15.

35. Ibid.

36. Quoted in Gazzaway, "Conversations with Buster Smith," part 3, p. 16.

37. Dan Morgenstern, liner notes, *Feelin' High and Happy: Hot Lips Page and His Band* (RCA Victor Records, LPV-576). See also Morgenstern, "Hot Lips Page," *Jazz Journal* 15, no. 7 (July 1962): 5–6 and 40; and no. 8 (August 1962): 2–4.

38. Morgenstern, liner notes, *Feelin' High and Happy*. According to an unsigned article in *Jazz Journal International* 30, no. 8 (1981): 16, Page recorded some 116 sides.

39. Dan Morgenstern, liner notes, *Hot Lips Page After Hours in Harlem 1941* (Onyx Records, OR1207).

40. All the 1938 recordings by Page are found on *Feelin' High and Happy*.

41. *Spirituals to Swing*, vol. 1.

42. *Metronome* magazine, 1941, quoted in Morgenstern, liner notes, *Feelin' High and Happy*.

43. This side is included on *Billie Holiday, The Golden Years*.

44. This side is included on *Billie Holiday "The Golden Years,"* vol. 2 (Columbia Records, C3L 40).

45. Schuller, *The Swing Era*, p. 796.

46. Ibid., p. 798.

47. Nat Hentoff, liner notes, *Little Club Jazz: Small Groups in the 30's* (New World Records, NW 250, 1976), p. 1.

48. These sides are all available on *Feelin' High and Happy*.

49. *Hot Lips Page 1938–1940*.

50. Morgenstern, liner notes, *Feelin' High and Happy*.

51. Morgenstern, liner notes, *Hot Lips Page After Hours in Harlem*.

52. Ibid.

53. Ibid.

54. Ibid.

55. Gary Giddins, liner notes, *Sweets, Lips, and Lots of Jazz* (Xanadu Records, 123, 1976).

56. *Hot Lips Page 1938–1940*.

57. Russell, *Jazz Style in Kansas City*, p. 226.

58. Giddins, liner notes, *Sweets, Lips, and Lots of Jazz*.

59. Morgenstern, liner notes, *Hot Lips Page After Hours in Harlem*.

60. Ibid. This album includes both *Tea for Two* and *Dinah*.

61. Quoted in Gitler, *Swing to Bop*, p. 24.

62. Morgenstern, liner notes, *Hot Lips After Hours in Harlem*.

63. Quoted in Charters and Kunstadt, *Jazz*, p. 280.

64. These two tunes plus *You Need Coachin'* and *These Foolish Things* are included on *Jonah Jones/Hot Lips Page* (Columbia Records, XFL 16569).

65. Ernie Anderson, "Lips the Hard-Luck Man," *Melody Maker*, no. 30 (November 20, 1954): 7. Anderson recounts a tale of Page during World War Two: "The draft was breathing down everybody's neck. So Lips walked on stage and sang 'Uncle Sam Ain't No Woman But He Can Certainly Steal Your Man.' Somebody from the War Department was in the audience and they rushed him to a studio and made a V-Disc of it right away." Anderson adds that "Lips made some of his best stuff on V-Discs." Will Friedwall singles out this tune as Page's "most famous record," pointing out that "as a blues-based singer with equal capacity for comedy and tragedy, Page takes a backseat only to Basie's blues giants Jimmy Rushing and Joe Williams" (*Jazz Singing: America's Great Voices from Bessie Smith to Bebop and Beyond* [New York: Charles Scribner's Sons, 1990], p. 350).

66. Quoted in Morgenstern, liner notes, *Feelin' High and Happy*. Gillespie also had this to say: "I know the blues, but Hot Lips Page is a blues man. When he plays trumpet, he plays it like a blues player would play. My music is not that deep—not as deep as his—not as deep as Hot Lips Page or Charlie Parker, because Yard knew the blues. Blues is my music, the music of my people, but I'm not what you call a 'blues' player. I mean in the authentic sense of the blues. I don't want to put myself up as a blues player. I'd love to, I feel it, but I'm not. Because when I hear the blues, I hear Lips play the blues, and it's different from me" (Gillespie and Fraser, *To Be, or Not . . . to Bop*, p. 310).

67. Quoted in Gitler, *Swing to Bop*, p. 75.

68. Ibid., p. 79.

69. *Swing Street* (Epic Records, SN 6042, 1962).

70. Morgenstern, liner notes, *Feelin' High and Happy*.

71. Ibid.

72. Ibid.

73. Ibid.

74. Williams, *Jazz Heritage*, p. 37.

75. Ibid., p. 38.

76. Schuller, *The Swing Era*, p. 563.

77. Goldberg, liner notes, *The Budd Johnson Quintet: Let's Swing*.

78. Mary Osborne, quoted in Avakian and Prince, "Charlie Christian," pp. 181–182. Christian can be heard on *Flying Home* from the 1939 "Spirituals to Swing" concert at Carnegie Hall, with Lionel Hampton on vibraharp (*Spirituals to Swing*, vol. 1. On this same recording, Christian performs with Lester Young, Basie, Walter Page, and Jo Jones (?) in a version of *Jam Session*, where Charlie's solo is a hard-driving example of the southwestern style and sound, combining rifflike phrases with long, inventive lines that are at once lyrical and imaginative, and seem to quote in passing as the beboppers would.

79. Williams, *Jazz Heritage*, p. 38.

80. Russell, *Jazz Style in Kansas City*, p. 230.

81. Avakian and Prince, "Charlie Christian," p. 181.

82. Gunther Schuller discusses at length the combination of blues and classical traditions, as well as other types of music "of diverse ethnic and cultural backgrounds," that served as "a variety of formative influences" on Christian. See *The Swing Era*, pp. 536–566.

83. Bill Simms, "Charlie Christian," in *The Jazz Makers*, ed. Shapiro and Hentoff, p. 322.

84. Quoted in ibid., p. 323.

85. Chilton, *Song of the Hawk*, p. 159. Gunther Schuller also comments on Christian's artistry as an accompanist: "Because of Christian's superiority as a solo-line player, his rhythm playing has been much neglected; occasionally one even reads implications that he was not terribly effective in this area. But if proof of Christian's prowess as rhythm guitarist be needed, we can find it abundantly on such sides as *Hot Mallets* (with Hampton) [from the same September 11, 1939, date], on some of the tracks from the "Spirituals to Swing" Carnegie Hall Concert, both with the Goodman Sextet and the Kansas City Six, but above all with the Edmond Hall Celeste Quartet. Hear the perfect buoyant swing of Christian and bassist Israel Crosby—they sound absolutely like one instrument—on *Jammin' in Four* and *Celestial Express*" (*The Swing Era*, p. 567n). *Hot Mallets* is included on *Lionel Hampton and His Orchestra* (Past Records, CD 9789). Another tune from the September 11 date, *Early Session Hop*, is included on *Body and Soul: A Jazz Autobiography—Coleman Hawkins* (RCA Victor Records, LPV-501, 1964).

86. Hodeir, *Jazz*, p. 217. *When Lights Are Low* is included on *Swing Classics: Lionel Hampton and His Jazz Groups* (RCA Victor Records, LPM-2318, 1961) and in *The Smithsonian Collection of Classic Jazz*, cassette side D. On *Swing Classics*, Christian solos on *Haven't You Named It Yet* from October 12, 1939, hitting some nice licks after Henry "Red" Allen's trumpet break.

87. Hodeir, *Jazz*, p. 215.

88. Schuller, *The Swing Era*, p. 567.

89. Ibid., p. 568. *Star Dust*, from October 2, 1939, is available on *The Benny Goodman Sextet Featuring Charlie Christian: 1939–1941* (Columbia Records, CK 45144, 1989).

90. The March 1940 recording of *Star Dust* is included on *Solo Flight: The Genius of Charlie Christian* (Columbia Records, CG 30779, 1972).

91. Schuller, *The Swing Era*, p. 568.

92. Williams, *The Jazz Tradition*, pp. 142, 143.

93. *Spirituals to Swing*, vol. 2 (Fontana Vanguard Records, FJL 402).

94. *Charlie Christian/Lester Young: Together 1940* (Jazz Archives Records, JA-6).

95. Williams, *Jazz Heritage*, p. 38.

96. Schuller, *The Swing Era*, p. 571. This version is included on *Solo Flight: The Genius of Charlie Christian.*

97. Schuller, *The Swing Era*, p. 573. The December 19, 1940, recording is included on *The Benny Goodman Sextet Featuring Charlie Christian: 1939–1941.*

98. Collier, *The Making of Jazz*, p. 345.

99. Avakian and Prince, "Charlie Christian," p. 185. This essay was originally printed as liner notes for *Charlie Christian with the Benny Goodman Sextet and Orchestra* (Columbia Records, CL 652), which includes the January 15, 1941 *Breakfast Feud.*

100. Avakian and Prince, "Charlie Christian," pp. 185–186.

101. Schuller, *The Swing Era*, p. 576. *Blues in B* and *Waitin' for Benny* are included on both *Solo Flight* and *Charlie Christian with the Benny Goodman Sextet and Orchestra.*

102. Avakian and Prince, "Charlie Christian," p. 183.

103. Schuller, *The Swing Era*, p. 576.

104. *Charlie Christian—Guest Artists: Dizzy Gillespie and Thelonious Monk* (Everest Records, FS-219).

105. Joe Goldberg, *Jazz Masters of the Fifties* (New York: Macmillan, 1965), p. 26. Gunther Schuller also compares Monk at this time to Wilson. See "Reviews: Recordings," *Jazz Review* 1, no. 1 (November 1958): 23.

106. Schuller, *The Swing Era*, p. 577.

107. Dean Tudor and Nancy Tudor write that in *Swing to Bop* "changes and transitional elements abound" and that this tune, based on *Topsy*, "is really a condensed history of jazz as riff after riff from the swing age are laid down until the complex phrases are reached" (*Jazz* [Littleton, Colo.: Libraries Unlimited, 1979], p. 144).

108. Schuller, *The Swing Era*, p. 571; Williams, *Jazz Heritage*, pp. 39–40.

109. Schuller, *The Swing Era*, p. 571. *Profoundly Blue* is included on *"Celestial Express"* (Blue Note Records, B-6505).

110. Schuller, *The Swing Era*, p. 577.

111. Avakian and Prince, "Charlie Christian," p. 186.

112. Feather, *The New Edition of the Encyclopedia of Jazz*, p. 340.

113. *The Best of the Nat King Cole Trio* (Capitol Records, CDP 7 98288 2, 1992).

114. Quoted in Stan Britt, *The Jazz Guitarists* (Poole, England: Blandford Press, 1984), p. 98.

115. Gene Santoro, *Dancing in Your Head: Jazz, Blues, Rock, and Beyond* (New York: Oxford University Press, 1994), p. 202.

116. Herb Ellis is discussed in Chapter 19 in conjunction with Jimmy Giuffre, but it should be noted here that one commentator has asserted that "it's easy to discern that Ellis's conception was shaped by the Charlie Christian of Benny Goodman's versions of 'Memories of You' and 'Rose Room.'" See James Isaacs, liner notes, *The Oscar Peterson Trio at the Stratford Shakespearean Festival* (Verve Records, 314 513 752-2, 1993).

Larry Coryell, who was born in Galveston on April 2, 1943, worked on the West Coast with Chico Hamilton in 1966; beginning in 1969, he led his own jazz-fusion groups, "notably the influential Eleventh House." See Brian Case and Stan Britt, *The Harmony Illustrated Encyclopedia of Jazz*, 3d ed., rev. Chrissie Murray (New York: Harmony Books, 1987), p. 57. Guitarist Pat

Metheny, who would record *Song X* on December 12–14, 1985, with Ornette Coleman (Geffen Records, 924096-2), is quoted as saying that when he heard Coryell in 1968, Larry "revealed a new flexibility and made the opening statement for the next guitar generation." See Leonard Feather, *The Passion for Jazz* (New York: Horizon Press, 1980), p. 106.

117. Schuller, *The Swing Era*, p. 565. Bill C. Malone discusses the work of Leon McAuliffe and the influence of "the Bob Wills style" in *Country Music, U.S.A.* (Austin: University of Texas Press, 1968), pp. 173–181. Malone defines "the Bob Wills variety of western swing" as "characterized by a heavy, insistent beat, the jazz-like improvisations of the steel guitar, and the heavily bowed fiddle. It was a rhythmic, infectious music designed for dancing" (p. 179). Malone also quotes pianist Knocky Parker's remark that "western swing was essentially a mixture of Mexican mariachi music from the south with jazz and country strains coming in from the east" (p. 173).

14. With BG

1. Stanley Dance, *The World of Earl Hines*, p. 184.

2. Dick Katz, liner notes, *Teddy Wilson: Statements and Improvisations, 1934–1942* (Columbia Records, Smithsonian Collection R005, P 13708, 1977).

3. *The Smithsonian Collection of Classic Jazz*, p. 51.

4. Irving Kolodin, liner notes, *Benny Goodman Live at Carnegie Hall* (Columbia Records, J2C 40244).

5. Katz, liner notes, *Teddy Wilson*.

6. Ibid.

7. Ibid.

8. Schuller, *The Swing Era*, p. 509.

9. Mellers, *Music in a New Found Land*, p. 376.

10. Schuller, *The Swing Era*, p. 513. For more on the Hines-Wilson relationship, see Collier, *The Making of Jazz*, pp. 212–213.

11. Schuller, *The Swing Era*, pp. 511–512.

12. Quoted in Katz, liner notes, *Teddy Wilson*.

13. Schuller, *The Swing Era*, p. 508.

14. Horst Lippmann, liner notes, *Improvised Meditations and Excursions: John Lewis* (Atlantic Records, SD-1313).

15. Dick Katz, commentary on *These Foolish Things*, in Martin Williams, Dick Katz, and Francis Davis, *Jazz Piano* (Washington, D.C.: Smithsonian Collection of Recordings, 1989), p. 24.

16. Schuller, *The Swing Era*, p. 511.

17. Gunther Schuller has written of a 1934 recording session with Goodman and Teagarden that "Wilson already reveals his own distinctive voice in a well-formed, typically clean chorus, but it is Teagarden who ultimately dominates the performance—a fact that even Goodman realized by ceding not only a major solo but the closing ensemble to Teagarden. It is one of his solos that seems to contain in it most of the trombone music one was to hear in the bands of others for the next decade or so" (*The Swing Era*, p. 604).

18. Glenn Coulter, "Billie Holiday," in *The Art of Jazz*, ed. Williams, pp. 164–165.

19. Ibid., p. 165. *Easy Living* is included on *The Quintessential Billie Holiday*, vol. 4, 1937 (Columbia Records, CJ 44252, 1988).

20. Schuller, *The Swing Era*, pp. 538, 539. Both of these sides are included on *Billie Holiday: "The Golden Years,"* vol. 2.

21. Schuller, *The Swing Era*, p. 540.

22. Martin Williams, liner notes, *Once There Was Bird* (Parker Records, PLP-408, 1962). Williams's liner notes are reprinted in his *Jazz Heritage*, pp. 184–191.

23. Feather, *The New Edition of the Encyclopedia of Jazz*, p. 466.

24. Quoted in Gitler, *Swing to Bop*, p. 100.

25. Schuller, *The Swing Era*, p. 504.

26. Ibid., p. 507.

27. *Blues in E Flat* is included on *Red Norvo and His All Stars* (Epic Records, EE 22009); *Blues in C-Sharp Minor* is on *The Jazz Makers*.

28. Schuller, *The Swing Era*, p. 522.

29. Michael Brooks, liner notes, *Red Norvo and His All Stars*.

30. Schuller, *The Swing Era*, p. 517.

31. Didier C. Deutsch, liner notes, *The Essence of Harry James* (Columbia Records, 57151, 1994).

32. This performance is included on Benny Goodman's *Jazz Concert No. 2* (Columbia Records, SL-180) and *I Like Jazz* (Columbia Records, JZ 1).

33. Collier, *Benny Goodman and the Swing Era*, p. 233.

34. George Avakian, liner notes, *The King of Swing*, vol. 1, *1937–38 Jazz Concert No. 2* (Columbia Records, CL 817).

35. Both *Sunny Disposish* and *St. Louis Blues* are included on *The King of Swing*, vol. 1.

36. Collier, *Benny Goodman and the Swing Era* (New York: Oxford University Press, 1989), p. 233. At the January 16, 1938, Carnegie Hall concert, James's performance of Armstrong's *Shine* solo is note for note but in the Texan's *own* bravura style. Collier also discusses a series of sixteen sides recorded with Teddy Wilson where, on *Just a Mood*, from the middle of 1937, James "has five choruses which are thoughtfully worked out to build to a climax in the manner suggested by what Louis Armstrong was doing on the Hot Five records a decade earlier." Collier goes on to say, "James's solos on these records show him to be a thoughtful player with an immaculate technique. He virtually never fluffs, a rare thing in an improvising trumpet player. He can stand comparison with most of the today more highly regarded jazz musicians who played on these Wilson sides" (p. 232).

37. Ibid., p. 233.

38. Gunther Schuller refers to James's solo work with Hampton groups as "cocky, irreverent and dashing," observing that Lionel gathered certain sidemen, from the Goodman and Basie bands, on the assumption that "players accustomed to each other would produce better integrated performances." Although Schuller finds the results often "disjointed and impersonal," he judges Harry's playing on *Shoe Shiner's Drag* and *Muskrat Ramble* to be excellent (*The Swing Era*, p. 395).

39. *Boo-Woo* is included on *Boogie Woogie Stomp!*

40. Charles Fox, review of *Café Society Swing and Boogie Woogie*, in Harrison, Fox, and Thacker, *The Essential Jazz Records*, p. 381.

41. McCarthy, *Big Band Jazz*, p. 241.

42. Chris Sheridan, liner notes, *Count Basie / Harry James: Basie Rhythm* (HEP Records, England, CD 1032, 1991).

43. Ibid.

44. Collier, *Benny Goodman and the Swing Era*, p. 234.

45. Dan Morgenstern, liner notes, *Dexter Gordon: Long Tall Dexter* (Savoy Records, SJL 2211, 1976).

46. Quoted in Jack Chambers, *Milestones 1: The Music and Times of Miles Davis to 1960* (New York: William Morrow, 1983), p. 118.

47. Avakian, liner notes, *The King of Swing*, vol. 1.

48. Schuller, *The Swing Era*, p. 24. The Ben Pollack orchestra recorded *Peckin'* on December 18, 1936. George Avakian provides the source for the title *Peckin'* when he writes that the tune "celebrated one of the routines developed by jitterbug dancers, in which the partners each drop to one knee and 'peck' over each other's shoulders in time to the music. Dance is forgotten now, but the music more than stands up" (liner notes, *The King of Swing*, vol. 1).

49. Schuller, *The Swing Era*, p. 24.

50. This recording is included on *Duke Ellington and His Orchestra 1937*, vol. 2 (Classics Records, 687, 1993). For the Goodman recording, see D. Russell Connor and Warren W. Hicks, *BG on the Record: A Bio-Discography of Benny Goodman* (New Rochelle, N.Y.: Arlington House, 1969), p. 191.

51. Avakian, liner notes, *The King of Swing*, vol. 1.

52. *Peckin'* and *Life Goes to a Party* are included on *The Indispensable Benny Goodman*, vols. 3–4, 1936–1937 (RCA Victor Records, France, NL89756[2], 1983). The origin of the second title is accounted for by Ross Firestone: "On November 1 [1937] *Life* magazine, one of the most influential periodicals in the country, devoted its regular 'Life Goes to a Party' feature to a four-page celebration of the Madhattan Room engagement. 'A nightly scene of wild adulation,' the magazine called [the Goodman band's performance at the Hotel Pennsylvania in New York City], 'where intermittent dancing and dining is subordinated to the almost scholarly pleasure of listening to Benny "feel his stuff."' To make the most of this important national publicity, Benny christened a new Harry James jump tune 'Life Goes to a Party,' quickly recorded it [on December 2] and sent the lead sheet off to the *Life* letters to the editor column along with an effusive thank-you note" (*Swing, Swing, Swing: The Life and Times of Benny Goodman* [New York: W. W. Norton, 1993], p. 206).

53. Williams, *The Jazz Tradition*, pp. 124–125n. Out of the three takes of *Life Goes to a Party* recorded by RCA Victor, Goodman preferred the third, but the second replaced this last take after the second was issued illegally in Canada. For a discussion of this matter, see John S. Lewis, "Alternate Takes," *Texas Jazz* 6, no. 12 (December 1982): n.p.

54. Schuller, *The Swing Era*, p. 25.

55. McCarthy, *Big Band Jazz*, p. 241.

56. Schuller, *The Swing Era*, pp. 745, 688. Schuller also notes that "James was the first (except for Ellington) to exploit and capitalize fully on the presence of a band singer by creating special musical frameworks for that singing talent, tailor-made, so to speak, at the same time craftily exploiting the need during the tense wartime years for the comforting reassurance of

sentimental ballads.... "James did not foresee how such a development would affect the future course of jazz. But the results were soon fully audible and visible: as other bands, especially Dorsey (with Sinatra) copied the formula, singers took over the popular music field, jazz as swing was more or less driven out—certainly as a *leading* force. In turn a new form of jazz, namely bop, primarily instrumental and represented by smaller combos, was to take over" (p. 747).

57. These performances are included on *The Quintessential Billie Holiday*, vol. 6, 1938 (Columbia Records, C 45449, 1990).

58. McCarthy, *Big Band Jazz*, p. 228.

59. Ibid., p. 229.

60. Deutsch, liner notes, *The Essence of Harry James*.

61. All of the tunes from 1948 are included on *Harry James and His Orchestra: Stompin' at the Savoy* (Laser Light, 15 771, 1992). The March 6, 1939, recording of *King Porter Stomp* is listed in Lomax, *Mister Jelly Roll*, p. 267.

62. McCarthy, *Big Band Jazz*, p. 228. *Sugar Foot Stomp* is included on *Benny Goodman: The King of Swing*, vol. 2 (Columbia Records, CL 818).

63. The 1938 *Shine* is included on *Benny Goodman Live at Carnegie Hall* (Columbia Records, J2C 40244).

64. Tony Baldwin, liner notes, *Hot Violins* (ABC Records, 836 049–2).

65. Schuller, *The Swing Era*, p. 825n.

66. Nat Hentoff, liner notes, *Little Club Jazz*, p. 4.

67. Baldwin, liner notes, *Hot Violins*. This album includes the ever-popular *I Got Rhythm*. Baldwin informs us that Emilio later became the leader of a Latin American band whereas Ernie stayed in New York. Emilio's place of birth has been given as Corpus Christi and his death date as 1973. In a piece on the Caceres brothers, Mary Lee Hester suggests that by the time Ernesto was five years of age, Emilio already had a band of his own, which would place Emilio's birth close to 1900. See "Texas Jazz Heritage," *Texas Jazz* 4, no. 11 (November 1980): n.p.

68. Hentoff, liner notes, *Little Club Jazz*, p. 4. An article by Debbie Howell entitled "12 Far-Out Bands Bring Jazz Here" in the *Corpus Christi Caller-Times*, June 21, 1964, p. 8-B, reports that Emilio Caceres "played with many big-name bands, including Benny Goodman, Tommy Dorsey, Rudy Vallee, Paul Whiteman, Red Nichols, David Rose, Harry James and the late Jack Teagarden." However, I have yet to find any recordings by these figures with Emilio present. His first recording came in 1932 for Victor—a tune entitled *Jig in G*.

69. See Morgenstern, "Hot Lips Page," *Jazz Journal* 15, no. 8 (August 1962): 5.

70. McCarthy, *Big Band Jazz*, p. 300. The Caceres solos are included on *The Unforgettable Jack Teagarden* (Halcyon Records, England, HAL-4).

71. *Song of the Volga Boatmen* is included on *Glenn Miller: A Legendary Performer* (RCA Records, CPK2-0693, 1974).

72. Schuller, *The Swing Era*, pp. 672, 662.

73. Charles Fox, review of *Lee Wiley Sings Rodgers and Hart and Harold Arlen*, in Harrison, Fox, and Thacker, *The Essential Jazz Records*, p. 447.

74. Both of these tunes are included on *The Golden Horn of Jack Teagarden*.

75. *Ernie and Ernesto Caceres* (Audiophile Records, 101).

15. Out of Houston

1. McCarthy, *Big Band Jazz*, p. 109.

2. Driggs, "Kansas City and the Southwest," p. 224. In 1935 Nat Towles of New Orleans formed a band in Texas that by 1937 included Texans Buddy Tate and Henry Coker. Driggs writes that Towles's band, which Tate rated better than Basie's, and "another fine Texas crew," that of Milt Larkin, "battled every Sunday for years at the old Harlem Square Club in Houston" (p. 223). Most sources give the trumpet-leader's name as Larkins, but his business cards read "Larkin," and this spelling of his name is used in the *Milt Larkin Jazz Society Newsletter*.

3. Benny Bailey, quoted in Gitler, *Swing to Bop*, p. 97.

4. Leonard Feather, liner notes, *Lionel Hampton "Steppin' Out,"* vol. 1, *1942–1945* (Decca Records: DL 79244). This side is also included on *Lionel Hampton (1942–1945) Flying Home* (Decca Records, MCAD-42349, 1990).

5. See Avakian and Prince, "Charlie Christian," p. 182.

6. McCarthy, *Big Band Jazz*, p. 231.

7. In *The Autobiography of Malcolm X* (New York: Grove Press, 1964), Malcolm comments further: "I endured all of that pain, literally burning my flesh with lye, in order to cook my natural hair until it was limp, to have it look like a white man's hair. I had joined that multitude of Negro men and women in America who are brain washed into believing that the black people are so 'inferior'—and white people 'superior'—that they will even violate and mutilate their God-created bodies to try to look 'pretty' by white standards" (p. 55). Earlier, Malcolm discusses his love of jazz, his coming to know many members of the Basie band, including Buddy Tate, and his having had Lionel Hampton sit in his chair when he was a shoeshine boy on first arriving in Boston, where he heard jazz at dances at the Roseland Ballroom (pp. 50–51).

8. Kernfeld, ed., *The New Grove Dictionary of Jazz*, 1:574.

9. This anecdote comes from a conversation with Haynes at a symposium entitled "Texas Jazz: Myth or Reality?" held at the Houston Museum of Fine Arts on August 14, 1993. At the time, Jacquet was living in Houston with George Haynes.

10. *Illinois Jacquet Flying Home* (RCA Records, Bluebird 61123-2, 1992).

11. Gary Giddins, *Rhythm-a-ning: Jazz Tradition and Innovation in the '80s* (New York: Oxford University Press, 1985), p. 179.

12. No recording of *Po'k Chops* has surfaced. See Morgenstern, liner notes, *Long Tall Dexter*. Morgenstern writes that "it is an interesting but little noted fact that the two players [Jacquet and Gordon] who would become the most influential tenor stylists of the later forties sat in the same big band section for several years." Of Jacquet's style, Morgenstern observes that "it combined elements of Lester Young and Coleman Hawkins (the latter via Illinois' idol, Herschel Evans) with a special Texas spice." Gene Ramey is the bassist on five of the tunes on *Long Tall Dexter*, including the title number and *Dexter's Cuttin' Out* (based on *I've Found a New Baby*), which were recorded in New York on October 30, 1945. Of the rhythm section on *Dexter's Cuttin' Out*, Morgenstern comments that it "is solid and shows how quickly jazz players in the New York mainstream adapted themselves to rhythmic innovations."

13. Giddins, *Rhythm-a-ning*, p. 179.

14. *Illinois Jacquet Flying Home*.

15. Chilton, *Song of the Hawk*, p. 243.

16. Morgenstern, liner notes, *Long Tall Dexter*. Morgenstern also points out, in his liner notes to *Coleman Hawkins: Body and Soul*, that on *His Very Own Blues* from January 18, 1956, Hawkins "offers some Illinois Jacquet licks (a legacy from JATP?)."

17. Leonard Feather, liner notes, *Jazz at the Philharmonic: The Historic Recordings* (Verve Records, VE-2-2504, 1976).

18. Ibid.

19. Sheridan, *Count Basie: A Bio-Discography*, p. 260.

20. McCarthy et al., *Jazz on Record*, p. 16.

21. Sheridan, *Count Basie: A Bio-Discography*, p. 264. *The King* and *Rambo* are both included on *Basie's Best* (Columbia Records, Harmony HS 11247); *Mutton-Leg* is on *Count Basie Classics* (Columbia Records, CL-997) and *One O'Clock Jump* (Columbia CL-997).

22. J. C. Thomas, *Chasin' the Trane* (Garden City, N.Y.: Doubleday, 1975), p. 46. Powell, born in Fort Worth on February 27, 1924, had been with a Hot Lips Page band from 1942 to 1943 and with Louis Armstrong from 1944 to 1945. Apparently he was with Basie for the month of September for a trip to California after both Jacquet and Joe Newman left the Count's band on August 16, 1946. Powell led his own band in 1948 before joining the Dizzy Gillespie big band for two years in 1949, recording during that year a solo on *Tally Ho*, which is included on *Dizzy Gillespie and His Orchestra* (Capitol Records, M-11059). See Feather, *The New Edition of the Encyclopedia of Jazz*, p. 386. Sheridan's *Count Basie: A Bio-Discography* does not list Powell in the personnel for any recordings with the Basie band.

23. These tunes from August 1945 and 1946 are included on *Illinois Jacquet: The Fabulous Apollo Sessions* (Vogue Records, France, CLDAP 858).

24. Quoted in Chilton, *Song of the Hawk*, p. 238.

25. Feather, liner notes, *Jazz at the Philharmonic: The Historic Recordings*.

26. Giddins, *Rhythm-a-ning*, p. 181.

27. Quoted in Dance, *The World of Count Basie*, p. 48.

28. Ibid., p. 340.

29. Case and Britt, *The Harmony Illustrated Encyclopedia of Jazz*, p. 99.

30. Giddins, *Rhythm-a-ning*, p. 181.

31. Reportedly, President Clinton, "early in his career as a saxophonist," had memorized Jacquet's "landmark improvisation" on *Flying Home*. See Peter Watrous, "Jazz at the White House (Home of a Serious Fan)," *New York Times*, June 21, 1993, sec. C, p. 13.

32. *Lionel Hampton "Steppin' Out,"* vol. 1. This album also includes solos by Cobb on *In the Bag* (from May 26, 1942), *Chop-Chop* (from the same date as *Flying Home No. 2*), and *Overtime* (from October 16, 1944).

33. G. E. Lambert, "Lionel Hampton—Jazz Giant," part 2, *Jazz Journal* 14, no. 11 (November 1961): 7.

34. *Flyin' Home* is included on *The Best of Arnett Cobb* (Prestige Records, 7711), which is a selection of sides from Cobb's various Prestige albums. Illinois Jacquet also recorded a number of albums for the Prestige label, among them *The Soul Explosion* (7629) and *The Blues: That's Me!* (7731).

35. Frederick L. Bouchard, liner notes, *Live at Sandy's! Arnett Cobb and the Muse All Stars* (Muse

Records, MR 5191, 1979).

36. Case and Britt, *The Harmony Illustrated Encyclopedia of Jazz*, p. 52.

37. Ibid.

38. *Nitty Gritty* is included on *The Best of Arnett Cobb*.

39. David Rosenthal, *Hard Bop: Jazz and Black Music 1955–1965* (New York: Oxford University Press, 1992), pp. 102, 104.

40. Ibid., pp. 109–110. *Smooth Sailin'* is included on *The Best of Arnett Cobb*.

41. *Black Velvet* is included on *The Best of Arnett Cobb*.

42. Jacquet's version of *Black Velvet* is included on *Illinois Jacquet Flying Home*.

43. Alan Zeffert offers this assessment: "Arnett's raw, big-toned excursions have obscured an interesting musician who, when the opportunity occurs as it does on [*Ballads by Cobb* (Prestige/Moodsville 14)], can turn out tender slow blues or ballads. Here, with sympathetic support from Red Garland's piano, he proves to be a stimulating and always interesting saxophonist" (McCarthy et al., *Jazz on Record*, p. 353). Another Prestige album with Cobb and Garland is *Blue and Sentimental* (24122).

44. Bouchard, liner notes, *Live at Sandy's!*

45. Jerry Tumlinson, "Jimmy Ford: Just Jobbing," *Milt Larkin Jazz Society Newsletter* 1, no. 3 (August 1992): [1].

46. Alan Zeffert, in McCarthy et al., *Jazz on Record*, p. 353.

47. Tumlinson, "Jimmy Ford," p. 3.

48. Zeffert, in McCarthy et al., *Jazz on Record*, p. 353. *Maynard Ferguson at Birdland* (Roulette Records, R-52027).

49. Zeffert, in McCarthy et al., *Jazz on Record*, p. 353.

50. Kenneth Randall, liner notes, *The Wild Man from Texas* (Home Cooking Records, HCS-114, 1989).

51. Bob Claypool, quoted in ibid.

52. In the 1950s, Gallardo was a member of the Del Mar College Jazz Club and Ensemble and performed with various local groups, in particular at the Officer's Club of the city's naval base. Gallardo's father reportedly played in the mid-1920s in a New Orleans–style group called the Real Jazz Orchestra, which was originally based in Laredo but whose members migrated to Corpus Christi around 1930. Joe Gallardo is credited with working as a sideman in a number of big bands, including those of Stan Kenton and Woody Herman. At some point in his career Gallardo moved to Germany, where he has enjoyed success as an active jazz musician. For more information on the Gallardo family and on various jazz figures from the Corpus Christi area, see Glen Nicholas M. Evans, "Swingin' and Boppin' South Texas-Style: Toward an Understanding of the Corpus Christi Jazz Scene" (Master of Arts Report, University of Texas at Austin, May 1992). Another Corpus Christi musician, Eddie Galvan, commented in an interview with Evans that Arnett Cobb "plays very few notes, but they were all significant— meant something" (p. 57).

53. Vinson's nickname derived from the fact that he had "lost most of his hair at the tender age of twenty. 'Too much conking,' he told Malcolm X (then called Detroit Red, who henceforth let his own hair grow natural). Disliking both toupees and hats, Mr. Clean upstaged Yul Brynner by a generation and got his head shaved all the way" (Thomas, *Chasin' the Trane*, p. 38).

54. Feather, *The New Edition of the Encyclopedia of Jazz*, p. 450. All of the tunes with Williams are included on *Cootie Williams Sextet and Orchestra: Things Ain't What They Used to Be* (Phoenix Jazz Records LP 1).

55. Ira Gitler notes that the title is really *Royal Garden Blues* (*Jazz Masters of the Forties* [New York: Macmillan, 1966], p. 112). Likewise, *Cherry Red* is listed on the Phoenix album as *Blue Red*. Also in Williams's band during 1943 and 1944 was Pearl Bailey, who took her first professional tour with Cootie and sings nicely and is supported well by the band's swinging versions of *Now I Know* and *Tess's Torch Song* from January 6, 1944.

56. Gitler, *Swing to Bop*, p. 97.

57. Thomas, *Chasin' the Trane*, pp. 38–39.

58. Ibid., pp. 39–40.

59. *Cherry Red* and *Kidney Stew Blues* are included on *Cleanhead's Back in Town* (Bethlehem Records, BCP-6037).

60. Robert Palmer, liner notes, *Cleanhead's Back in Town*.

61. Norman Granz, "Producer's Note," *"Kansas City Shout"* (Pablo Records, D2310859). J. C. Thomas reports that Vinson's saxophone style is "an intriguing blend of blues and bop, the latter directly attributed to the Charlie Parker influence" (*Chasin' the Trane*, p. 38). Thomas adds,

"In 1939, in Shreveport, Louisiana, while touring with the Milt Larkins band, Cleanhead first heard Bird, who was playing there with Jay McShann. At the usual after-hours jam session, Vinson was wiping out everyone in sight until, as he recalls, 'This young kid walked on the stand with his alto in his mouth and started to blow the wildest things I ever heard in my life. He cut me good—he cut me up.' Bird was then nineteen. Vinson continues, 'I put my arm around that boy and told him, man, you're not gonna get out of my sight until you show me how you make your horn go like that.'

"Bird did just that; all night long, and all the next morning."

62. Case and Britt, *The Harmony Illustrated Encyclopedia of Jazz*, p. 182.

63. *Kidney Stew Is Fine* (Delmark Records, DS-631). Jay McShann is on piano.

64. Palmer, liner notes, *Cleanhead's Back in Town*.

65. Michael Cuscuna and Dan Morgenstern, liner notes, *The Complete Blue Note Forties Recordings of Ike Quebec and John Hardee* (Mosaic Records, MR4-107, 1984), p. 6. The Ike Quebec sides are of interest here for the participation of the two Texas trombonists, Tyree Glenn and Keg Johnson, the former recording with Quebec on September 25, 1944, and the latter on July 17, 1945, and September 23, 1946. On *Basically Blue*, from the last of these sessions, Keg takes a solo "with a mute, and full of slurs and trills" that "could almost pass for Dickie Wells" (p. 13). Tyree is "in excellent form" on *Facin' the Face* (p. 11). Glenn had been in the same Corsicana band as Hardee—Dan Carter's Blue Moon Syncopaters—and had played banjo "when Hardee first joined" (p. 6).

66. Ibid., p. 10.

67. Ibid.

68. Ibid., p. 9.

69. Ibid., p. 7 and caption.

70. Ibid., p. 7. Hardee also replaced Ben Webster in the Ellington band in the spring of 1944. The Texan commented of this occasion: "I never had such a background behind me in all my life!" (p. 7).

71. Mary Lee Hester, "Texas Jazz Heritage," *Texas Jazz* 5, no. 12 (December 1981): n.p.

72. Quoted in Cuscuna and Morgenstern, liner notes, *The Complete Blue Note Forties Recordings*, p. 8.

73. Ibid.

16. The Rhythm Section

1. Len Lyons and Don Perlow, *Jazz Portraits: The Lives and Music of the Jazz Masters* (New York: William Morrow, 1989), p. 211.

2. Davis biographer Jack Chambers states that it was Jones who recommended Coltrane (*Milestones 1*, p. 214); however, Lyons and Perlow report that Garland recalled having suggested Coltrane (*Jazz Portraits*, p. 211). According to J. C. Thomas, it was Garland who convinced Coltrane to join the Eddie Vinson band after Red had already signed up (*Chasin' the Trane*, p. 39).

3. Case and Britt, *The Harmony Illustrated Encyclopedia of Jazz*, p. 60.

4. Chambers, *Milestones 1*, pp. 151, 182. Davis recorded with quartets as early as 1951 (on piano with Sonny Rollins) and on May 19, 1953 (with John Lewis, Charles Mingus, and Max Roach).

5. Joe Goldberg, liner notes, *Miles Davis: The Beginning* (Prestige Records, 7221).

6. Ibid.

7. Dan Morgenstern, liner notes, *Miles Davis Chronicle: The Complete Prestige Recordings 1951–1956*. Jack Chambers feels that Garland's rumored boxing career "may also have impressed Davis for entirely extramusical reasons" (*Milestones 1*, p. 200).

8. Chambers, *Milestones 1*, p. 206.

9. Quoted in Goldberg, *Jazz Masters of the Fifties*, p. 73.

10. Goldberg, liner notes, *Miles Davis: The Beginning*.

11. Chambers, *Milestones 1*, p. 201.

12. Quoted in ibid., p. 200.

13. Eric Nisenson, *'Round About Midnight: A Portrait of Miles Davis* (New York: Dial Press, 1982), p. 100.

14. Chambers, *Milestones 1*, p. 201. Both *Blue Haze* and *Green Haze* are included on *Miles Davis Chronicle*.

15. Alun Morgan, quoted in Chambers, *Milestones 1*, p. 216.

16. Chambers, *Milestones 1*, p. 225. For the complicated recording history of this tune, see pp. 223–224.

17. *Little Melonae* and *Ah-Leu-Cha* are included on *The Miles Davis Quintet: 'Round About Midnight* (Columbia Records, CJ 40610).

18. Quoted in Chambers, *Milestones 1*, p. 227. *Just Squeeze Me* and *Stablemates* (discussed next) are included on *Miles Davis Chronicle*.

19. Chambers, *Milestones 1*, p. 235.

20. Morgenstern, liner notes (sessions 16 and 17), *Miles Davis Chronicle*.

21. Chambers, *Milestones 1*, p. 235.

22. Williams, *The Jazz Tradition*, p. 228. See also Thomas, *Chasin' the Trane*, p. 105.

23. Chambers, *Milestones 1*, p. 219.

24. *Surrey with the Fringe on Top* and *Salt Peanuts* originally appeared on *Steamin' with the Miles Davis Quintet* (Prestige Records, 7220).

25. Chambers, *Milestones 1*, p. 235.

26. Ibid., p. 237.

27. Ibid., p. 239.

28. Ibid. *Dear Old Stockholm, Bye Bye Blackbird*, and *'Round Midnight* are all included on *The Miles Davis Quintet: 'Round About Midnight*.

29. Ira Gitler, *Down Beat*, October 16, 1958, cited in Thomas, *Chasin' the Trane*, p. 106.

30. Thomas, *Chasin' the Trane*, p. 40. For an account of Vinson's claim to this tune as well as to *Four*, both credited to Miles Davis when they were first recorded, see Chambers, *Milestones 1*, p. 184. Another Texas jazzman who indirectly affected Coltrane's career was Jesse Powell, the Fort Worth tenorman who, like Garland, toured with Hot Lips Page. Through Powell, Jimmy Heath, a Philadelphia tenorman who was briefly with Texan Kenny Dorham's group during the 1950s, brought Coltrane to an audition with Gillespie in mid-1949 and both were hired by Dizzy (p. 46).

31. Thomas, *Chasin' the Trane*, p. 40; Chambers, *Milestones 1*, p. 311.

32. Lyons and Perlow, *Jazz Portraits*, p. 142.

33. *Tune Up* and *Airegin* originally appeared on *Cookin' with the Miles Davis Quintet* (Prestige Records, 7094).

34. Morgenstern, liner notes, *Miles Davis Chronicle*; Chambers, pp. 328, 245.

35. Morgenstern, liner notes, *Miles Davis Chronicle*.

36. *If I Were a Bell* is included on *Miles Davis Chronicle*.

37. Chambers, *Milestones 1*, p. 245.

38. Morgenstern, *Miles Davis Chronicle*. Ted Gioia also considers this "perhaps the finest working rhythm section in jazz during this period"; of *Art Pepper Meets The Rhythm Section* (Contemporary Records, S7532) with the same trio, Gioia writes that this January 19, 1957, recording by Pepper was "one of the finest albums" of the saxophonist's career. See *West Coast Jazz: Modern Jazz in California 1945–1960* (New York: Oxford University Press, 1992), pp. 296–297. On the Pepper album, Garland plays some of his characteristic block chords on *Imagination*, a Burke–Van Heusen tune in which both Pepper and Garland really shine. Pepper is at his finest on *Straight Life*—his own original, whose title also served for his autobiography—and here all three Rhythm Section members turn in some sterling performances in backing up the altoist, especially Philly Joe Jones.

39. George Avakian, liner notes, *Leonard Bernstein: What Is Jazz* (Columbia Records, CI 919).

40. Ibid.

41. Chambers, *Milestones 1*, p. 211.

42. See Alun Morgan, "Red Garland," in McCarthy et al., *Jazz on Record*, p. 105.

43. Quoted in Eric Nisenson, *'Round About Midnight*, p. 165.

44. Ibid.

45. Ralph J. Gleason, liner notes, *Davis* (Prestige Records, 24001).

46. Chambers, *Milestones 1*, p. 269.

47. Tirro, *Jazz*, p. 362.

48. Ibid., p. 277. Both Chambers and Nisenson do not view Garland's playing or behavior

as the reason for his being replaced; rather, both biographers state that Davis found in Evans a different kind of pianist. According to Nisenson, Miles said he liked Red's way of carrying the rhythm, yet he preferred the way Bill underplayed (*'Round About Midnight*, p. 150).

49. Quoted in Chambers, *Milestones 1*, p. 280. For clarification on the change of the title tune from *Milestones* to *Miles*, see Nisenson, *'Round About Midnight*, p. 148.

50. Collier, *The Making of Jazz*, p. 431.

51. Chambers, *Milestones 1*, p. 280. As Davis's "first completely successful composition based on scales rather than a repeated chord structure" (p. 279), *Milestones* exhibits a feeling that was already present in his playing on the *Miles Ahead* album, recorded with the Gil Evans orchestra in May 1957.

52. Quoted in ibid., p. 278.

53. Ibid., p. 279.

54. Charles Edward Smith, liner notes, *Milestones* (Columbia Records, CK 40837); Lyons and Perlow, *Jazz Portraits*, p. 212; Len Lyons, *The Great Jazz Pianists Speaking of Their Lives* (New York: William Morrow, 1983), p. 145. *Milestones* includes *Miles*, *Billy Boy*, and *Straight, No Chaser*.

55. Mellers, *Music in a New Found Land*, p. 378.

56. Quoted in Chambers, *Milestones 1*, p. 219.

57. *Solar: Red Garland Quartet* (Jazzland Records, JLP 73).

58. In a review of Coltrane's album *Soultrane*, Mimi Clar refers to the title tune of *Traneing In* and remarks that Garland's "misty block chords provide temporary relief to the blasting Coltrane" (*Jazz Review* 2, no. 3 [April 1959]: 24). In her review of four Garland Prestige albums with Paul Chambers on bass and Art Taylor on drums (*Red Garland's Piano*, *Groovy*, *A Garland of Red*, and *Manteca*), Clar confronts the issue of Red's having often been accused of playing "cocktail" piano: "The brand . . . is generally unjustified in Red's case, but probably originates from several stylistic facts. Garland is essentially a very refined pianist. His playing, while modern, is unfunky enough not to tax the aural capacities of the uninitiated who might find Horace Silver or Monk hard to take" (p. 25).

59. Michael Gold, liner notes, *Black Pearls* (Prestige Records, 7316).

60. Robert Levin, liner notes, *Standard Coltrane* (Prestige Records, 7243).

61. Quoted in ibid.

62. Ibid.

17. From Bebop to Hard Bop

1. Williams, *The Jazz Tradition*, p. 156.

2. Michael Cuscuna, liner notes, *The Best of Thelonious Monk* (Blue Note Records, CDP 7 95636 2, 1991).

3. *Ruby My Dear*, *Well You Needn't*, *Off Minor*, *April in Paris*, *Humph*, and *Thelonious* are on *Thelonious Monk: Genius of Modern Music*, vol. 1 (Blue Note Records, BST-81510); *Nice Work*, *Suburban Eyes*, and *Evonce* are on vol. 2 (BST-81511). *Thelonious*, *Ruby My Dear*, *Well You Needn't*, and *April in Paris* are also included on *The Best of Thelonious Monk*.

4. Williams, *The Jazz Tradition*, p. 160.

5. Ibid. Williams considers *Humph* one of Monk's "deliberate parodies" of bop clichés (p. 156).

6. Ibid., pp. 160–161.

7. Rosenthal, *Hard Bop*, pp. 133, 43.

8. Wilfrid Mellers credits *Ruby My Dear* to Coleman Hawkins (*Music in a New Found Land*, p. 337), even though Monk is always given as the composer, as he is on *The Best of Thelonious Monk*.

9. Collier, *The Making of Jazz*, p. 385.

10. Mellers, *Music in a New Found Land*, pp. 337–338.

11. Ira Gitler, liner notes, *Thelonious Monk: Genius of Modern Music*, vol. 2. Martin Williams suggests that the term "harmony" may not accurately apply to Monk's work: "He seems much more interested in sound and in original and arresting combinations of sounds percussively delivered than in harmony per se" (*The Jazz Tradition*, p. 162). This percussive quality is fully evident in Monk's *Off Minor*. It should be noted here that Gunther Schuller does not find these trio recordings of much interest and blames the rhythm section, calling Ramey's a "plunky bass" ("Reviews: Recordings," p. 23).

12. Williams, *The Jazz Tradition*, p. 168.

13. Ibid., p. 163.

14. The piece is included on *Thelonious Monk: Genius of Modern Music*, vol. 2, where the title is given as *Nice Work*.

15. Quoted in Shapiro and Hentoff, eds., *Hear Me Talkin' to Ya*, p. 350.

16. Quoted in Feather, *The New Edition of the Encyclopedia of Jazz*, pp. 337–338.

17. Williams, *The Jazz Tradition*, p. 156. David Rosenthal would probably suggest that this "something else" was hard bop—"an opening out in many directions, an unfolding of much that had been implicit in bebop but held in check by its formulas" (*Hard Bop*, p. 39).

18. Mellers, *Music in a New Found Land*, p. 338.

19. For a brilliant analysis of this side and a history of Davis's tune, see Douglass Parker, "*Donna Lee* and the Ironies of Bebop," in *The Bebop Revolution in Words and Music* (Austin, Tex.: Harry Ransom Humanities Research Center, 1994), pp. 161–201.

20. Dan Morgenstern, liner notes, *Fat Girl: The Savoy Sessions* (Savoy Records, SJL 2216, 1977).

21. Rosenthal, *Hard Bop*, p. 29.

22. Morgenstern, liner notes, *Fat Girl*.

23. Rosenthal, *Hard Bop*, p. 47.

24. Mellers, *Music in a New Found Land*, p. 337.

25. Rosenthal, *Hard Bop*, p. 39.

26. Unsigned liner notes, *The Jazz Giants '56* (Verve Records, UMV 2511, 1982).

27. Gitler, *Jazz Masters of the Forties*, p. 102.

28. Ibid.; Lyons and Perlow, *Jazz Portraits*, p. 173.

29. H. A. Woodfin, "Kenny Dorham," *Jazz Review* 3, no. 7 (August 1960): 7.

30. Gitler, *Jazz Masters of the Forties*, p. 103.

31. These four sides are included on *Fat Girl* and also have Al Hall on bass, Morris Lane on tenor, and Eddie De Verteuil on baritone sax.

32. Morgenstern comments that Dorham seemed "nervous on this date" and that he "came

off much better alongside Fats on the famous Kenny Clarke date for the French Swing label of the day before, which had essentially the same personnel" (liner notes, *Fat Girl*).

33. Ibid.

34. Ibid.

35. Mark Gardner, liner notes, *The Modern Jazz Piano Album* (Savoy Records, SJL 2247).

36. Gitler, *Jazz Masters of the Forties*, p. 117. Max Harrison also notices this fact when he writes that *Bebop in Pastel* is "almost identical in theme and arrangement with . . . *Bouncing with Bud*" (review of *Opus de Bop* [Savoy MG 12114], *Jazz Review* 2, no. 9 [October 1959]: 33).

37. Gitler, *Jazz Masters of the Forties*, p. 102. *The Thin Man* is on *Art Blakey's Jazz Messengers* (Blue Note Records, BLP 5010).

38. Rosenthal, *Hard Bop*, p. 37. John Litweiler suggests that "the source of hard bop was the late-forties Charlie Parker quintets with Max Roach [and Kenny Dorham]" (*Ornette Coleman*, p. 80).

39. Bill Miner, liner notes, *Charlie Parker at the Roost* (Savoy Records, SJL 1108, 1977).

40. Ibid.

41. *Ooh Bop Sha Bam* is included on *Historical Masterpieces* (Charlie Parker Records, PLP-701); *Scrapple from the Apple, Out of Nowhere, Barbados*, and *52nd Street* are on *Bird in Paris* (Yard Records, CP3).

42. Parker's famous *Happy Birthday* quote comes on what is given as the first version of *Out of Nowhere*; Dorham's quote from *Country Gardens* comes on the second version.

43. Miner, liner notes, *Charlie Parker at the Roost*.

44. Gitler, liner notes, *Thelonious Monk: Genius of Modern Music*, vol. 2.

45. Cuscuna, liner notes, *The Best of Thelonious Monk*.

46. Williams, *The Jazz Tradition*, p. 156.

47. The Ramey-Dorham sides are on *Kenny Dorham: New York 1953–1956 and Oslo 1960* (Landscape Records, LS2-918, 1992).

48. Chambers, *Milestones 1*, pp. 124–125.

49. *Horace Silver Quintet* (Blue Note Records, BST-84325). *Stop Time* dates from November 13, 1954, and *The Preacher* from February 6, 1955.

50. Woodfin, "Kenny Dorham," p. 8.

51. Ibid. *Yesterdays* is on *The Jazz Messengers at Cafe Bohemia* (Blue Note Records, BLP 1508).

52. *I Get a Kick Out of You* is included on *Kenny Dorham: New York 1953–1956 and Oslo 1960*. This performance features Sonny Rollins on tenor, Ray Bryant on piano, and George Morrow on bass.

53. *Max* (Argo Records, LP623).

54. Orrin Keepnews, liner notes, *Blue Spring: Kenny Dorham Septet Featuring Cannonball Adderley* (Riverside Records, OJC-134).

55. Woodfin, "Kenny Dorham," p. 9.

56. *Quiet Kenny* (Prestige / New Jazz Records, OJCCD-250-2, 1992). Mark Gardner, in his liner notes to *Cedar!* (Prestige Records, OJCCD-462-2), calls *Quiet Kenny* "a prized item in many a collection" that deserves to be ranked "with the greatest trumpet and rhythm LPs."

57. Woodfin, "Kenny Dorham," p. 9.

58. Schuller, *The Swing Era*, p. 749.

59. Jack Maher, liner notes, *Quiet Kenny*.

60. Ibid.

61. Woodfin, "Kenny Dorham," p. 9.

62. Zita Carno, review of *Blue Spring* by Kenny Dorham, *Jazz Review* 2, no. 7 (August 1959): 26.

63. Ibid. According to Roger Boykin, Walton's first American recording session came on *Kenny Dorham Sings*. See "Cedar Walton Swings Home," *Texas Jazz* 5, no. 6 (June 1981): n.p. *Kenny Dorham Sings* is probably the album entitled *This Is the Moment* (Riverside Records, RLP 12-275), recorded on July 7, 1958, with Walton and G. T. Hogan, a drummer born in Galveston on January 16, 1929, who substituted for Charlie Persip on two tunes. Mark Gardner says that Hogan's work in the early 1960s with Elmo Hope, Walter Bishop, Randy Weston, and Kenny Drew "is especially noteworthy" (*The New Grove Dictionary of Jazz*, ed. Kernfeld, 1:531). *This Is the Moment* includes one vocal by Dorham on *Since I Fell for You*.

64. Don Gold, liner notes, *Max*.

65. *Jazz Contemporary: Kenny Dorham* (Time Records, S/2004).

66. Rosenthal, *Hard Bop*, p. 158. The critic also refers to Dorham's "sharply syncopated phrasing, full of subtle rhythmic displacements, as well as his tart, dark tone and austerely motif-oriented solos."

67. *The Fox* (Contemporary Records, 7619).

68. *Eastward Ho! Harold Land in New York* (Jazzland Records, OJC-493).

69. *Whistle Stop* (Blue Note Records, BLP 4063). Mobley is on *Kenny Dorham, Afro/Cuban* (Blue Note Records, BLP 1535), recorded January 30, 1955. J. J. Johnson is on the same album in an octet recorded on March 29, 1955. For details of the personnel for this recording, see Tom Lord, *The Jazz Discography* (West Vancouver, Canada: Lord Music Reference, 1993), 5:D441.

70. Michael Shera, "Record Reviews," *Jazz Journal* 14, no. 12 (December 1961): 33.

71. Michael Cuscuna, liner notes, *The Best of Joe Henderson* (Blue Note Records, CDP 7 95627-2, 1991).

72. *Hot Stuff from Brazil* (Westwind Records, 2015).

73. *Kenny Dorham: New York 1953–1956 and Oslo 1960*.

74. Case and Britt, *The Harmony Illustrated Encyclopedia of Jazz*, p. 64.

75. J. J. Johnson, liner notes, *J. J., Inc.* (Columbia Records, CL 1606).

76. Quoted in Rosenthal, *Hard Bop*, p. 151.

77. Michael Cuscuna, liner notes, *The Best of Art Blakey and the Jazz Messengers* (Blue Notes Records, CDP 7 93205 2, 1989). Some of Walton's compositions recorded by the Messengers include *Mosaic*, *Plexis*, *Shaky Jake*, *Ugetsu*, and *One Flight Down*.

78. Rosenthal, *Hard Bop*, p. 131.

79. Ibid., p. 139.

80. The title tune from the album *Mode for Joe* is included on *The Best of Joe Henderson*.

81. Rosenthal, *Hard Bop*, p. 278.

82. *Boss Horn* (Blue Note Records, BLP 4257/84257).

83. Gardner, liner notes, *Cedar!*

84. Nat Hentoff, liner notes, *Boss Horn*.

85. Jim Fishel, liner notes, *Cedar Walton: Piano Solos* (Clean Cuts Records, CC 704).

86. *Eastern Rebellion 2* (Timeless Records, SJP 106).

87. Fishel, liner notes, *Cedar Walton: Piano Solos*.

88. Giddins, *Rhythm-a-ning*, p. 134.

89. Ivery is on *Texas Tenors* (Jazz Mark Records, 104), along with James Clay, also of Dallas. Clay is discussed in Chapter 20.

90. Doug Ramsey, liner notes, *Marchel's Mode* (Leaning House Jazz, BB001). In an interview with Red Garland, Ramsey remarks of Ivery that he is "a full-blooded, modern mainstream tenor man with abundant ideas and that peculiarly spacious Texas sound." See his *Jazz Matters: Reflections on the Music and Some of Its Makers* (Fayetteville: University of Arkansas Press, 1989), p. 97. Ramsey's book also contains an interview with Gene Ramey.

91. A later take of this tune, made on May 4, 1959, with Tommy Flanagan on piano, was the one issued in 1960 on the Coltrane album *Giant Steps* (Atlantic 1311), while the earlier take with Walton was not issued until 1974 on *John Coltrane: Alternate Takes*. Both takes of *Giant Steps* have been reissued on Atlantic 1311-2. Although the later take contains, as Ira Gitler points out in the liner notes, Coltrane's "intensely crowded choruses," the original take also offers a fascinating outing by the tenorist.

92. *Thelonious Monk with John Coltrane* (Jazzland, OJCCD-038-2).

93. *Misterioso: Thelonious Monk Quartet* (Riverside Records, 12-279).

18. The Mingus Dynasty

1. Janet Coleman and Al Young, *Mingus/Mingus: Two Memoirs* (Berkeley: Creative Arts, 1989), p. 15.

2. Feather, *The New Edition of the Encyclopedia of Jazz*, p. 335.

3. Nat Hentoff, liner notes, *Mingus/Oh Yeah* (Atlantic Records, 1377). Hentoff may mean only that Mingus grew up listening to T-Bone Walker. Certainly the impact of Walker's music on Mingus has been documented. See Brian Priestley, *Mingus: A Critical Biography* (New York: Quartet Books, 1982). pp. 1, 16, 25.

4. Priestley, *Mingus*, p. 63.

5. Ibid.

6. Martin Williams, *Jazz Masters in Transition, 1957–1969* (London: Macmillan, 1970), pp. 150, 7.

7. Rosenthal, *Hard Bop*, pp. 139, 141. Mingus himself apparently considered the 1957 *Tijuana Moods* (RCA Victor Records, LPM-2533) to be his finest album, according to the jazzman's statement on the album sleeve.

8. Goldberg, *Jazz Masters of the Fifties*, p. 142.

9. Ibid.

10. Born in Nacogdoches on August 26, 1905, Ernie Fields first formed his band about 1930 and made Tulsa his home base for many years. The Fields unit performed in Dallas and Wichita, Kansas, and recorded in New York in August and September 1939. In 1942 the personnel included Paul Quinichette on tenor, and from 1944 to 1945 the band was in Baltimore, Washington, Dallas, and Los Angeles. Again in 1946 the Fields band recorded in New York, and Booker Ervin made his first recording with the band some ten years later, by which time

Fields had gone into rhythm and blues. Albert McCarthy comments that as one of the "earlier territory bands, Fields's was the last to give in, and as the final survivor of a once flourishing tradition it deserves its honourable niche in big band jazz history" (*Big Band Jazz*, p. 112).

11. Alun Morgan, review of four albums by Booker Ervin, in McCarthy et al., *Jazz on Record*, p. 93.

12. Quoted in Diane Dorr-Dorynek, liner notes, *Mingus Ah Um* (Columbia Records, CK 40648). This album was recorded on May 5 and 12, 1959.

13. Morgan, in McCarthy et al., *Jazz on Record*, p. 93.

14. Priestley, *Mingus*, p. 97.

15. Michael Morgan, liner notes (January 1967), *Setting the Pace* (Prestige Records, PRCD-24123-2, 1993).

16. Priestley, *Mingus*, p. 201.

17. Ibid., p. 97. Mingus refers to Handy as "my" saxophonist on the live Monterey Festival recording, *Mingus at Monterey* (Mingus Records, JWS 001 and 002).

18. Ibid., p. 108.

19. Ibid., p. 167.

20. Rosenthal, *Hard Bop*, p. 139.

21. Priestley, *Mingus*, p. 108.

22. Quoted in Diane Dorr-Dorynek, liner notes, *Mingus Dynasty* (Columbia Records, CL 1440).

23. Ibid.

24. Nat Hentoff, liner notes, *Mingus, Mingus, Mingus, Mingus, Mingus* (Impulse! Records, Mono A-54).

25. Williams, who died in 1985, is present on the Mingus Dynasty album, *Reincarnation* (Soul Notes Records, SN 1042, 1982). Another Texan to play with Ellington late in the Duke's life was drummer Quinten "Rocky" White, who was born in San Marcos on November 3, 1952, and performed with the Ellington orchestra at Westminster Abbey in London, on October 24, 1973; the recording from this performance is *Third Sacred Concert* (RCA Victor Records, APLI-0785).

26. *Svengali* (Atlantic Records, 90048-1). Harper also worked as a sideman with James Clay of Dallas as well as with such bands as those of Art Blakey and Max Roach. Harper's best work is perhaps on his first album as a leader, *Capra Black* (1973).

27. Quoted in Leonard Feather and Ira Gitler, *The Encyclopedia of Jazz in the Seventies* (New York: Horizon Press, 1976), p. 167.

28. Gary Giddins, liner notes, *One with the Wind* (Muse Records, MCD 5523, 1994). On this album, recorded September 3, 1993, Peterson's rich, lush sound and penetratingly passionate intensity are akin to but different in kind from the style of Richard Williams. As a balladeer, Peterson exhibits his hard-bop emotionalism on very moving six-minute explorations of Billie Holiday's *God Bless the Child* and Erroll Garner's *Misty*. Perhaps the most impressive performance by the trumpeter is his "soaring gospel feeling" on *Change Is Going to Come*, where, as Giddins observes, "the individual quality of [Peterson's] timbre and projection is every bit as unmistakable as the prodigiousness of his invention." As early as 1975, Giddins had selected Peterson as "one of the 10 most promising new arrivals on the New York jazz scene," and with his

performances on *One with the Wind*, the critic declares that the trumpeter has grown into a warmer, more evocative player, which is evident throughout this entire album, but in particular on *Glow* with Peterson's solo "etched in sorrowful, almost tearful tones" and with his poignant half-valve fade-out at the end.

29. Thomas Fitterling, liner notes, *The Angels of Atlanta* (Enja Records, CD 3085-2, 1994).

30. Priestley, *Mingus*, p. 102.

31. Ibid., p. 104. *Goodbye Pork Pie Hat*, for instance, was renamed *Theme for Lester Young*.

32. Giddins, *Riding on a Blue Note*, p. 171. Joe Goldberg notes that *Jelly Roll* is "a delightful, affectionate burlesque done with real understanding, which stems from Mingus' purchase of a book of Morton tunes" (*Jazz Masters of the Fifties*, p. 142). See also Priestley, *Mingus*, p. 88. An earlier homage to Jelly Roll, entitled *Jelly Roll Jellies*, was performed by the Mingus Workshop on January 16, 1959, at the Nonagon art gallery in New York City. Apparently no tape of this tune exists (see Michael Cuscuna's liner notes for *Jazz Portraits* [Blue Note Records, CDP7243]), but the recording from this performance at the Nonagon represents the first with Mingus for both Handy and Ervin. Whitney Balliett, in reporting on this session, wrote that *Jelly Roll Jellies* was an "attempt to capture the essence of Jelly Roll Morton—a direct forebear of Mingus"— but that "instead of being a celebration, the number turned into a clumsy takeoff" ("Jazz Concerts: Mingus among the Unicorns," *New Yorker*, 34 [January 24, 1959]: 104).

Of the four tunes recorded at the Nonagon, Balliett singles out *Alice's Wonderland* as "a near-perfect piece. Handy was particularly striking . . . he played with flawless control, and although the work of Charlie Parker forms a broad dais for his style, he used, unlike most of his colleagues on the saxophone, a highly selective number of notes, a warm tone, and a couple of devices— a frequently prolonged trill astonishingly like that of the old New Orleans clarinetist George Baguet, and ivory-like sorties into the upper register reminiscent of Benny Carter's smooth ascents" ("Jazz Concerts," p. 104). Handy's Bird-inspired alto is also featured prominently on *I Can't Get Started*. According to Brian Priestley, *No Private Income Blues* is perhaps "the most impressive" piece on the album, "a themeless up-tempo twelve-bar blues whose heated exchanges and counterpoint between the saxes [Handy and Ervin] looks forward directly to the celebrated *Folk Forms*" (*Mingus*, p. 99). Bob Burns remarks that at first he did not care for *Jazz Portraits* but that the more he listened to the album, the more he grew to like it: "The reason, I feel, is the complete sincerity of Mingus and his players" ("Record Reviews," *Jazz Journal* 15, no. 11 [November 1962]: 30).

33. Quoted in Priestley, *Mingus*, p. 88.

34. Rosenthal, *Hard Bop*, p. 141.

35. Priestley, *Mingus*, pp. 6–7.

36. Rosenthal, *Hard Bop*, p. 140.

37. Quoted in Hentoff, liner notes, *Mingus, Mingus, Mingus, Mingus, Mingus*.

38. Rosenthal, *Hard Bop*, p. 140.

39. Hentoff, liner notes, *Mingus, Mingus, Mingus, Mingus, Mingus*.

40. Quoted in Dorr-Dorynek, liner notes, *Mingus Dynasty*.

41. Rosenthal, *Hard Bop*, p. 140.

42. Ibid.

43. *Blues and Roots* (Atlantic Records, 1305).

44. Priestley, *Mingus*, p. 101.

45. Quoted in Dorr-Dorynek, liner notes, *Mingus Dynasty*.

46. Priestley, *Mingus*, p. 120. *Lock 'Em Up* is included on *Mingus: The Candid Recordings* (Barnaby Records, KZ 31034).

47. Collier, *The Making of Jazz*, p. 448.

48. Hentoff, liner notes, *Mingus/Oh Yeah*.

49. Don DeMichael, "Monterey Moments," *Down Beat*, 31, no. 29 (November 5, 1964): 18, reproduced in liner notes, *Mingus at Monterey*.

50. Nat Hentoff, liner notes, *Screamin' the Blues* (Prestige/New Jazz Records, OJCCD-080-2).

51. Ibid.

52. *The Rat Race Blues* (Prestige/New Jazz Records, OJCCD-081-2). The first Gryce-Williams album, *Sayin' Something* (Prestige/New Jazz Records, 8230), recorded on November 3, 1960, was also devoted entirely to the blues. In a review of this earlier album, Michael Shera calls Williams "the most important new trumpeter to emerge since Clifford Brown" and adds that he "blows some incredibly long phrases, without any deterioration in tone or volume—a tribute to his excellent breath control" (*Jazz Journal* 15, no. 3 [March 1962]: 33).

53. Leo Wright appeared in a Mingus concert at the Newport Jazz Festival in 1959 but apparently never recorded with the Workshop. Wright, born in Wichita Falls on December 14, 1933, studied music at Huston-Tillotson College in Austin and joined Dizzy Gillespie in 1959, appearing on the album *Dizzy Gillespie Quintet* (Verve Records, MV 2605), recorded in New York at the Museum of Modern Art on February 9, 1961. Under his own name, Wright recorded *Blues Shout* (Atlantic Records, 1358), which also has Richard Williams on trumpet. Leo's father Mel Wright played professionally in Texas with Booker Ervin's father and was associated with Boots and His Buddies out of San Antonio. In 1977 another Texan, guitarist Larry Coryell, recorded with Mingus for the album *Three or Four Shades of Blue* (Atlantic Records, 1700-2).

54. Nat Hentoff, liner notes, *Richard Williams: New Horn in Town* (Candid Records, CD 9003).

55. Ibid.

56. John S. Wilson, review of *Sayin' Something* by Gigi Gryce and Richard Williams, *High Fidelity*, 10, no. 10 (October 1960): 111. In his liner notes to *Richard Williams*, Hentoff refers to Wilson of the *New York Times* as Williams's "most enthusiastic supporter among the critics."

57. Michael Cuscuna, liner notes, *Booker Ervin: Down in the Dumps* (Savoy Records, SJL 1119).

58. Ibid.

59. *Booker Ervin: The Freedom Book* (Prestige Records, 7295).

60. Ira Gitler, liner notes, *Booker Ervin: The Space Book* (Wings Records, VICJ-23784).

61. Alun Morgan, review of four albums by Booker Ervin, in McCarthy et al., *Jazz on Record*, p. 94.

62. Ira Gitler, liner notes, *Booker Ervin: The Blues Book* (Prestige Records, 7340). Ervin is joined on this album by the infrequently recorded trumpeter Carmell Jones, of whom Alun Morgan writes that he "has rarely played so well" (McCarthy et al., *Jazz on Record*, p. 94).

63. Ervin's playing on *Setting the Pace*, the title tune of his October 27, 1965, recording, is perhaps an example of his "advancement," for here he certainly turns up the heat. Or—to borrow David Himmelstein's description of Dexter Gordon, who splits the soloing on this album—Booker "erupts like a volcano, flowing molten from great depths." Himmelstein's

metaphor for Ervin is "a dragon breathing flames," but the more earthy comparison suggests the source for Booker's eruption: his core of gospel-based blues. See Himmelstein, liner notes (September 1966), *Setting the Pace* (Prestige Records, PRCD-24123-2).

64. Dan Morgenstern, liner notes, *Booker Ervin: The Song Book* (Prestige Records, 7318).

65. Ralph J. Gleason, liner notes, *John Handy Recorded Live at the Monterey Jazz Festival* (Columbia Records, CS 9262).

66. Leonard Feather calls the other tune on the album, *Spanish Lady*, "the highlight of [Handy's] performance . . . a fascinating display of new rhythms and use of the violin in an avant-garde setting" (*The Encyclopedia of Jazz in the Sixties* [New York: Horizon Press, 1966], p. 151).

67. *New View! The New John Handy Quintet* (Columbia Records, CL 2697). This recording was preceded by *The Second John Handy Album* (Columbia Records, CL 2567).

68. Mike White was born in Houston on May 24, 1933, and attended McClymonds High School in Oakland with Handy.

69. Gordon Donaldson, liner notes, *New View!*

IV. GOING TO LOS ANGELES
19. Out of Denton

1. Gioia, *West Coast Jazz*, p. 61. Frank Tirro clarifies this reference somewhat by explaining that the "team" mentioned in the *San Francisco Bulletin* article is a baseball team, whose members "have trained on ragtime and 'jazz'" (*Jazz*, p. 51).

2. McCarthy, *Big Band Jazz*, p. 169; Gioia, *West Coast Jazz*, p. 8n.

3. McCarthy, *Big Band Jazz*, p. 168. It is unclear which Chapel Hill is meant. One community with this name is located near Brenham, between Houston and Austin; at one time spelled Chapel Hill, it is now Chappell Hill. Another Chapel Hill exists in Upshur County near Tyler in the northeastern part of the state. Gunther Schuller identifies Clay as being from Arizona, probably because the 1972 edition of John Chilton's *Who's Who of Jazz* gave Clay's birthplace as Phoenix, but Chilton's 1985 edition accords with McCarthy and gives Clay's place of birth as Chapel Hill. (McCarthy does say that Clay moved with his family to Phoenix in 1908.)

Following Chilton, Schuller refers to Clay as "a multi-instrumentalist" who was "one of the earliest black jazz musicians to settle in Los Angeles (around 1916)." Schuller adds to Chilton and McCarthy in describing Clay's best efforts with his Stompin' Six in the mid-twenties as exhibiting "a style that is a pleasant but at times uneasy amalgam of ragtime, jazz (as filtered through the Original Dixieland Jazz Band and King Oliver's Creole Band), and primitive early instrumental blues" (*The Swing Era*, p. 779). Tirro lists two recordings with Clay from 1925: *Bogaloosa Blues* and *Jambled Blues* (both on Vocalion 15078). See *Jazz: A History*, pp. 187 and 213. Two pieces by Sonny Clay's Plantation Orchestra in Los Angeles from August 1926 are on *Territory Bands*, vol. 2, 1927–31: *California Stomp* and *Chicago Breakdown*, the former featuring a fine piano solo by Clay.

4. McCarthy, *Big Band Jazz*, p. 173.

5. Frank Driggs, "My Story by Buddy Tate as told to Frank Driggs," *Jazz Review* 1, no. 2 (December 1958): 18. Tate recalls that Kennedy was "very far advanced over everyone else then," but apparently he never recorded. See Russell, *Jazz Style in Kansas City*, p. 242.

6. Gioia, *West Coast Jazz*, p. 16.

7. Collier, *Benny Goodman and the Swing Era*, p. 327. Collier comments that "it is impossible to put percentages to anything as elusive as the amount of bebop in a given performance, but this version of 'Cherokee' is certainly brushed with bop. It sounds today rather mild; but at the time it sounded disquietingly modern to Goodman's older fans" (p. 328).

8. Quoted in William F. Lee, *Stan Kenton: Artistry in Rhythm* (Los Angeles: Creative Press of Los Angeles, 1980), p. 85.

9. Carol Easton, *Straight Ahead: The Story of Stan Kenton* (New York: William Morrow, 1973), p. 99. Easton reveals that it was Roland who expanded the Kenton trumpet section to five by sitting in and writing himself an extra part: "It sounded terrific—so much so that Stan began paying Roland for playing as well as for arranging." After Roland left the band in 1945 and returned a few months later, he "began sitting in again—this time playing a *fifth* trombone" (p. 99). Still later Roland came up with the idea of adding a sixth trumpet (p. 100).

10. Lee, *Stan Kenton*, p. 74.

11. Robert Gordon, *Jazz West Coast: The Los Angeles Jazz Scene of the 1950s* (London: Quartet Books, 1986), p. 57.

12. Herb Ellis, born in Farmersville on August 4, 1921, has been considered one of the swingingest of jazz guitarists, but since he did not follow his fellow Texans to California, his work will be noted only in passing. The guitarist's career began in 1944 with Glen Gray's Casa Loma Orchestra, and from 1945 to 1948 he was with Jimmy Dorsey. Later he formed part of the popular Soft Winds instrumental-vocal trio and in 1953 took Barney Kessel's place in the Oscar Peterson Trio, with which he recorded extensively during the six years he remained with Peterson. Ellis acknowledges that his own inspiration came from Charlie Christian, but only after his roommates insisted that he was missing out on the "message" in Christian's playing: "It really hit me, like a spiritual awakening. How much depth he had. And how scummy I sounded. His playing sounded deep and mine sounded shallow. . . . Now I went from all notes to no notes. Each note had to drip with emotion, and be sent from heaven. I went from one extreme ridiculously the other way. So that's how I got some direction" (quoted in Gene Lees, *Oscar Peterson: The Will to Swing* [Rocklin, Calif.: Prima, 1990], p. 106). Ellis does not solo on the Dizzy Gillespie–Stan Getz album *Diz and Getz* (Verve Records, V6-8141), but he can be heard on *The Oscar Peterson Trio at the Stratford Shakespearean Festival*, where his solos on Peterson's *Noreen's Nocturne* and on *Gypsy in My Soul* are a mixture of smeary Les Paul–like chords, repeated notes using alternate fingerings, and scalar runs that swing but amount to very little. Ellis can also be heard with Texans Buddy Tate and Gus Johnson on *Herb's Here* from *50 Years of Jazz Guitar* (Columbia Records, 33566). In commenting on the guitarist's work on the album entitled *Herb Ellis Meets Jimmy Giuffre* (Verve Records, MG V-8331), Don Heckman remarks that while "the album is tasty, quiet, and refined . . . it could never convince [me] that Herb Ellis is anything more than a competent journeyman" (review of *Jimmy Giuffre: "The Easy Way"* [Verve MG V-8337], *Jazz Review* 3, no. 2 [July 1960]: 27).

13. Gioia, *West Coast Jazz*, p. 228. Morris Eugene (Gene) Hall, born in Whitewright in northeast Texas on December 6, 1913, played with a number of prominent bands in the 1930s and 1940s, including those of Isham Jones and Ray McKinley, before he joined the staff at North Texas State, where "he set up a musical education program leading to a major in dance

band work. He was the first educator to put jazz on a formal credit basis of this kind." See Feather, *The New Edition of the Encyclopedia of Jazz*, p. 240.

14. Lorin Stephens, "The Passionate Conviction: An Interview with Jimmy Giuffre," *Jazz Review* 3, no. 2 (February 1960): 8.

15. Schuller, *The Swing Era*, p. 744. This tune is included on *Woody Herman: The Thundering Herds 1945–1947* (Columbia Records, CJ44108). Giuffre utilized in his composition the voicing for three tenors and a baritone that he had developed from an earlier use of four tenors made in 1946 by Gene Roland, with whom Giuffre had formed a band in the air force. Thomas Owens refers to Giuffre's *Four Brothers* as "perhaps the finest example of big-band bebop in the 1940s," calling his theme "an attractive, arpeggio-filled melody," with the bridge moving the four Herman saxophonists—Serge Chaloff, Herbie Stewart, Stan Getz, and Zoot Sims—"rapidly through chords and key areas" (*Bebop*, p. 21).

16. Gioia, *West Coast Jazz*, p. 230.

17. Stephens, "The Passionate Conviction," p. 8.

18. Gioia, *West Coast Jazz*, p. 243.

19. Ibid., pp. 200, 201.

20. Val Kolar, a bass player with Kenton in 1962, remembers vividly the call he received from the bandleader who had always been Kolar's "idol": "In the '50s I was a Kenton nut. I bought all his records. . . . I saw him in Texas when I was at North Texas State University. . . . I really wanted to play in the Kenton band, so it was a proud moment and fulfilled an ambition" (quoted in Lee, *Stan Kenton*, p. 294).

21. Feather, *The New Edition of the Encyclopedia of Jazz*, p. 400. Feather believes that Roland was "potentially a valuable writer, though very many of his arr[angement]s are based on thin riffs that seem to have been mass-produced." After joining Woody Herman's band in 1956, Roland had created sixty-five arrangements for Herman by February 1958.

22. Unsigned liner notes, *Stan Kenton and His Orchestra: Artistry in Rhythm* (Capitol Records, T167). This album includes *Just A-Sittin' and A-Rockin'* and *Ain't No Misery in Me*.

23. [Don C. Haynes,] "Diggin' the Discs with Don," *Down Beat* 13, no. 1 (January 1, 1946): 8.

24. *Tampico* is included on *Stan Kenton Retrospective* (Capitol Records, CDP 7 97350 2), as is *The Peanut Vendor* (originally on *Kenton in Hi-Fi* [Capitol Records, W724]).

25. Quoted in McCarthy, *Big Band Jazz*, p. 178.

26. Lee, *Stan Kenton*, p. 86.

27. Ibid., p. 275.

28. *Cuban Fire!* (Capitol Records, CDP 7 96260 2, 1991). *Early Hours (Lady Luck)* was recorded in Los Angeles on September 21, 1960. Another Roland tune, *Carnival*, was cut on September 20. See Ted Daryll's liner notes.

29. *Stan Kenton: Adventures in Blues* (Capitol Records, ST1985).

30. Dwight Carver, quoted in Lee, *Stan Kenton*, p. 281. Carver was a mellophonium player who was with Kenton in 1961 and 1962.

31. Hugh Lampman, liner notes, *North Texas State College* (90th Floor Records, Dallas, 1961).

32. George T. Simon, *New York Herald Tribune*, September 23, 1961, quoted in Lee, *Stan Kenton*, pp. 288–289. None of these three ex-North Texas students is a native Texan.

33. Lee, *Stan Kenton*, p. 569.

34. Unsigned liner notes, *Dodo Marmarosa* (Spotlite Records, 108). While the liner notes give the year as 1946, elsewhere on the album cover the year is given as 1947, which conforms with the date on the original Dial 10-inch recording (no. 208).

35. Ibid. Although Babasin was the first jazzman to record on cello, Oscar Pettiford became the most noted jazz cellist: "From about 1950, [Pettiford] transferred his solo style to amplified cello, which he played in a bouncy, dexterous style, reminiscent of Charlie Christian" (Kernfeld, ed., *The New Grove Dictionary of Jazz*, 2:306). In 1955, Fred Katz recorded on cello—both bowed and pizzicato—with the Chico Hamilton Quintet. Ted Gioia calls Katz "perhaps the first significant jazz player to play [the cello] without doubling on the contrabass" (*West Coast Jazz*, p. 188), whereas Robert Gordon writes of Katz that his "cello, which undoubtedly attracted the greatest initial attention to the [Hamilton] group, is at times an intrinsic component of the quintet and at others a slightly embarrassing fifth wheel" (*Jazz West Coast*, p. 138).

36. Unsigned liner notes, *Julius Hemphill Quartet: Flat-Out Jump Suite* (Black Saint Records, BSR 0040). Hemphill's career is discussed later in relation to the work of his teacher, Texas reedman John Carter.

37. *Reel Life* (Amazing Records, AMZ1033.2, 1993). Taylor was born on November 30, 1968, in DeKalb, Illinois, but moved with his family to San Angelo at the age of two and later to Austin, where he has lived ever since.

38. Haslanger was born in Austin on July 9, 1969; Zirkel, in McAllen on February 11, 1957; and Searles, in Austin on July 14, 1971.

39. Julie Noble, liner notes, *Reel Life*. Both Taylor and Haslanger can be heard on Taylor's first album, *RadioEdge* (Dolby B HX Pro, 1991), which includes an earlier version of *Blues for Fritz*, and on Taylor's third album, *Simple Gifts* (Impro Vision, WT1034, 1994), which also has Zirkel on trumpet and Searles on percussion. On *Simple Gifts* Taylor demonstrates his ability to handle many different styles, as does Haslanger, who is especially fine on tenor on *Sweet Stefanie*. Haslanger's playing can be sampled as well on three tracks from *Loose Ends* (1994), a compact disc produced by the University of Texas at Austin's Jazz Orchestra, directed by Rick Lawn. Steve Zirkel was the original trumpeter with another Austin band, Beto y los Fairlanes.

40. Ross Russell, liner notes, *Dexter Gordon and Wardell Gray: The Hunt* (Savoy Records, 2222, 1977).

41. Ibid. Russell gives Babasin's name as Babison, which may indicate its proper pronunciation. All other sources consulted give Babasin as the correct spelling, except the album *Way Out Wardell* (Crown Records, CLP 5004), which also gives his name as Harry Babison.

42. Jack Kerouac, *On the Road* (New York: Signet, New American Library, 1958), p. 105. Kerouac also mentions Hot Lips Page and the Bennie Moten band when he gives a brief survey of jazz (p. 197).

43. Another session, held on June 12, had already produced *The Chase*, an equally famous side, "a thirty-two bar AABA tune based—at least in the A sections—on the old Basie specialty 'Doggin' Around' (a tune that featured contrasting solos by Basie's great tenor men, Herschel Evans and Lester Young)" (Gordon, *Jazz West Coast*, p. 32). Babasin, however, was not present at this earlier date.

44. Gioia, *West Coast Jazz*, p. 36.

45. Jordi Pujol, liner notes, *Bird and Chet: Inglewood Jam* (Fresh Sound Records, FSR-CD 17).

46. Gioia, *West Coast Jazz*, p. 127.

47. Quoted in Pujol, liner notes, *Bird and Chet*.

48. Ibid.

49. Gordon, *Jazz West Coast*, p. 98.

50. Quoted in ibid., p. 97.

51. Ibid., p. 98. These sides are included on *Laurindo Almeida Quartet Featuring Bud Shank* (Pacific Jazz Records, PJ-1204, 1955).

52. Gordon, *Jazz West Coast*, p. 98.

53. Gioia, *West Coast Jazz*, p. 211.

54. Will MacFarland, liner notes, *Laurindo Almeida Quartet Featuring Bud Shank*.

55. Kernfeld, ed., *The New Grove Dictionary of Jazz*, attributes the label's founding to Babasin (1:49), whereas Robert Gordon credits Harte with forming "his own label" (*Jazz West Coast*, p. 98).

56. This album was later released with additional material as Pacific Jazz 1205.

57. Gordon, *Jazz West Coast*, p. 100.

58. Ibid.

59. Ibid., p. 62.

60. An excellent sampler of Giuffre's varied approaches to the tenor sax is included on *Sunday Jazz: A La Lighthouse*, vol. 1 (Contemporary Records, C3501, 1953). On *Four Others* he takes a relaxed but driving Prez-inspired solo, and on another Giuffre original, *Creme de Menthe*, Jimmy digs in on his pop-tune-like melody with some of his characteristic folksy choruses. On Shorty Rogers's *Viva Zapata!* Giuffre comes up with a Latin-flavored solo that adds considerably to this Lighthouse performance that Ted Gioia calls "surprisingly successful, with none of the awkwardness one finds in many other early recordings of jazz players attempting Latin music" (*West Coast Jazz*, p. 202). Giuffre also turns in some fine solos on *Bernie's Tune*, on *Solitaire* (where he plays this ballad with subtlety and feeling), and on *Morgan Davis*. The Texan also composed and arranged a Shelly Manne feature, *La Soncailli*.

61. Gordon, *Jazz West Coast*, p. 63. Giuffre can be heard playing clarinet with the Chet Baker Quintet on *There Will Never Be Another You* from 1955. This side is included on *Jazz West Coast: An Anthology of California Music* (Pacific Jazz Records, JWC-500, 1957). Giuffre is also with Baker on the album entitled *Witch Doctor* (Contemporary Records, OJCCD-609-2), recorded on September 13, 1953, with the Lighthouse All-Stars at Hermosa Beach. Giuffre's tenor solo on *I'll Remember April* is more interesting than his chorus on *Loaded*, but neither improvisation compares with his work with Shorty Rogers.

62. Gioia, *West Coast Jazz*, p. 252.

63. Gordon, *Jazz West Coast*, p. 60.

64. The recordings from this session are included on *The Birth of the Cool*, vol. 2 (Capitol Records, CDP 7 98935 2).

65. Gioia, *West Coast Jazz*, pp. 257, 231.

66. Ibid., pp. 252–253.

67. Gordon, *Jazz West Coast*, p. 63.

68. Unsigned liner notes, *Shorty Rogers and His Giants* (RCA Victor Records, LPM-1195).

69. Gordon, *Jazz West Coast*, p. 63.

70. Gioia, *West Coast Jazz*, p. 255. *The Big Shorty Rogers Express* ((RCA Victor Records, LPM-1350).

71. *The West Coast Sound* (Contemporary Records, 3507).

72. Gordon, *Jazz West Coast*, p. 89.

73. Gioia, *West Coast Jazz*, p. 231.

74. Ibid., p. 268.

75. Ira Gitler, liner notes, *Collaboration: West* (Prestige Records, OJCCD-122-2 [P-7028]).

76. These two tunes from the August 1953 session are also included on *Evolution* (Prestige Records, OJCCD-1731-2 [P-7078]) as well as on *Collaboration: West*. Neither Robert Gordon nor Ted Gioia makes mention of these sides.

77. Gioia, *West Coast Jazz*, p. 232.

78. Gitler, liner notes, *Collaboration: West*.

79. Gioia, *West Coast Jazz*, p. 232.

80. Ibid., p. 234.

81. Lester Koenig, liner notes, *Shelly Manne's "The Three" and "The Two"* (Contemporary Records, OJCCD-172-2).

82. Ibid.

83. Gordon, *Jazz West Coast*, p. 128.

84. Ibid., p. 126.

85. Ibid. p. 127. On January 25, 1955, Giuffre recorded on baritone with the Stan Kenton orchestra, and two of the tunes from that session, *Malagueña* and *Dark Eyes*, are included on Kenton's *Sketches on Standards* (Capitol Records, T426). Earlier, in 1953, on Kenton arranger Pete Rugolo's extremely fine first album under his own name, *Adventures in Rhythm* (Columbia Records, CL604), both Giuffre and Bob Gordon took rousing solos on Jelly Roll Morton's classic *King Porter Stomp*.

86. Gioia, *West Coast Jazz*, p. 259. Giuffre is not present on *Shorty Rogers Plays Richard Rogers* (RCA Victor Records, LPM-1428).

87. Gordon, *Jazz West Coast*, p. 128.

88. Gioia, *West Coast Jazz*, p. 234.

89. Ibid., p. 235.

90. Ibid.

91. Will Farland, liner notes, *Tangents in Jazz* (Capitol Records, T634).

92. Giuffre, comments following liner notes, *Tangents in Jazz*.

93. McFarland, liner notes, *Tangents in Jazz*.

94. Ibid.

95. Ibid.

96. Giuffre, comments following liner notes, *Tangents in Jazz*.

97. George Russell, review of *Jimmy Giuffre 3: Trav'lin' Light*, *Jazz Review* 1, no. 1 (November 1958): 35.

98. Heckman, review of *Jimmy Giuffre: "The Easy Way,"* p. 27. Another Verve album by Giuffre is entitled *Ad Lib* (MGV-8361) and features the Texan on tenor and clarinet along with a

traditional rhythm section of Red Mitchell on bass, Lawrence Marable on drums, and Jimmy Rowles on piano. This is what Martin Williams in his liner notes calls a straight blowing session, with Giuffre showing on tenor more technique than usual. He is particularly freewheeling in his tune entitled *Problems*. His clarinet is generally folksy and relaxed, as on *I Hear Red* and *Stella by Starlight*.

99. Gioia, *West Coast Jazz*, pp. 236, 237.

100. W. G. Fargo, liner notes, *The Jimmy Giuffre Clarinet* (Atlantic Records, 1238).

101. John S. Wilson, liner notes, *Martians Come Back!* (Atlantic Records, 1232).

102. Russell, review of *Jimmy Giuffre 3: Trav'lin' Light*, p. 35.

103. Gioia, *West Coast Jazz*, p. 237.

104. Fargo, liner notes, *The Jimmy Giuffre Clarinet*.

105. Fred Bouchard, "Jimmy Giuffre: Four Brothers + 3 Decades," *Down Beat* (December 1981): 28.

106. Giuffre, comments following liner notes, *Tangents in Jazz*. In Giuffre's liner notes to his 1963 album, *Free Fall* (Columbia Records, CL 1994), Jimmy recalls that when he was thirteen, he performed his "first unaccompanied clarinet solos for night campfire meetings at Camp Crockett (a YMCA boys' camp) near Granbury, Texas. Performing unaccompanied, therefore, is very natural to me. A player has the opportunity to stop or go—in any direction, speed or fashion—at will."

107. Fargo, liner notes, *The Jimmy Giuffre Clarinet*.

108. Giuffre, comments following liner notes, *Tangents in Jazz*.

109. Gioia, *West Coast Jazz*, p. 239.

110. *The Jimmy Giuffre 3* (Atlantic 1254).

111. Case and Britt, *The Harmony Illustrated Encyclopedia of Jazz*, p. 79.

112. John Litweiler, *The Freedom Principle: Jazz after 1958* (New York: William Morrow, 1984), p. 18.

113. Gordon, *Jazz West Coast*, p. 57.

114. The drummerless Nat King Cole trio with Oscar Moore had earlier made "musical history," but it had done so without a wind instrument as well. See Michael Cuscuna, liner notes, *The Best of the Nat King Cole Trio*. Of course, the drummerless Emilio Caceres Trio of the mid-1930s predates both of these groups.

115. Bouchard, "Jimmy Giuffre," p. 28.

116. Gioia, *West Coast Jazz*, p. 239.

117. *Trav'lin' Light* (Atlantic Records, 1282); *Western Suite* (Atlantic Records, 1330).

118. Russell, review of *Jimmy Giuffre 3: Trav'lin' Light*, p. 35. *Trav'lin' Light* is not as stimulating as the earlier Giuffre trio recording for Atlantic, *The Jimmy Giuffre 3*, for Brookmeyer does not come up to his capabilities as a soloist, and Giuffre seems to be going through the same rhythmic motions. One interesting fact about the title tune is mentioned by Nat Hentoff in his liner notes: "Jimmy has been intrigued with [*Trav'lin' Light*] since he first heard the Paul Whiteman recording of it with Billie Holiday while he was still in Texas in the early forties."

119. Gioia, *West Coast Jazz*, p. 239.

120. Stephens, "The Passionate Conviction," p. 9.

121. John S. Wilson, liner notes, *The Modern Jazz Quartet at Music Inn, Guest Artist: Jimmy Giuffre* (Atlantic Records, 90049-1, 1982).

122. Ibid.

123. Quoted in Litweiler, *Ornette Coleman*, p. 30.

124. Gunther Schuller, quoted in ibid., p. 69.

125. Litweiler, *Ornette Coleman*, p. 64.

126. Ibid.

127. *Fusion* (Verve Records, V-8402); *Thesis* (Verve V-8397).

128. Gioia, *West Coast Jazz*, p. 242.

129. Ibid.

130. Litweiler, *Ornette Coleman*, pp. 111–112.

131. Mellers, *Music in a New Found Land*, p. 362. Mellers allows that even if Giuffre's music "hasn't the passionate authenticity of the 'advanced' music of Coleman and Coltrane," it "at least seems relevant" (p. 363).

132. Gunther Schuller, *Musings: The Musical Worlds of Gunther Schuller, A Collection of His Writings* (New York: Oxford University Press, 1986), pp. 114, 117. Another type of "fusion" music is represented by the jazz/rock/soul/pop work of an entirely native Houston group known originally as the Swingsters when they organized in the early 1950s while still in high school. Composed of Stix Hooper (born August 15, 1938) on drums, Hubert Laws (born November 10, 1939) on reeds, Wilton Felder (born August 31, 1940) on tenor, and Joe Sample (born February 1, 1939) on piano, the group derived its "natural feeling" from "learning the blues and getting all those old gospel influences, the old Baptist churches that had tambourines, piano and choirs." Joe Sample, quoted in Lee Underwood, "The Crusaders: Knights without Jazz," *Down Beat* 43, no. 12 (June 17, 1976): 13, cited in Len Lyons and Don Perlow, *The 101 Best Jazz Albums* (New York: William Morrow, 1980), p. 341. After attending Texas Southern University, the group dropped out and moved to Los Angeles in 1968 where they became the Jazz Crusaders and later simply the Crusaders, with Wayne Henderson (born September 24, 1939) added on trombone. Lyons judges the 1974 album *Scratch* (Blue Thumb, BTS-6010) to be the group's best effort: "Joe Sample's gospel-influenced piano is gripping and authentic. Wilton Felder, with his big, rough 'Texas-tenor' sound derivative of Lockjaw Davis, Harold Land, and the southwestern R & B style, reaches beyond his immediate grasp with exciting results. . . . Wayne Henderson . . . achieves intense moments on 'Hard Times' and 'Eleanor Rigby' . . . . *Scratch* is looser than the other Crusader LP's, leaving the most room for spontaneity within the naturally confining R & B context" (p. 342). Although he did not record with the group, Hubert Laws, who became a much sought-after flutist with the Metropolitan Opera Orchestra and the New York Philharmonic, went on to make numerous recordings performing what he called his Afro-Classic music—everything from Bach and Mozart to James Taylor—as on the album *The Best of Hubert Laws* (Columbia Records, 5C 36365). His album entitled *The Laws of Jazz* (Atlantic Records, SD 8813), recorded on April 2 and 22, 1964, has Chick Corea on piano and includes such representative Laws pieces as his own original funky blues, *Black-Eyed Peas and Rice*, as well as *All Soul*. Hubert's younger brother, Ronnie Laws (born in Houston on October 3, 1950), would record with him in 1974 on tenor and soprano saxophone on *In the Beginning* (CTI Records, 6065).

133. Quoted in Gunther Schuller, liner notes, *Modern Jazz Concert* (Columbia Records, WL 127).

134. Schuller, *Musings*, p. 117.

135. This piece is one of the six compositions commissioned by Brandeis University for its 1957 Festival of the Arts and included on *Modern Jazz Concert*. The others are by Charles Mingus, Charles Russell, Milton Babbitt, and Gunther Schuller. The Mingus piece, *Revelations (First Movement)*, is a marvelous mix of gospel and classical.

20. The Cowtown Vanguard

1. Litweiler, *Ornette Coleman*, p. 54. Litweiler notes that Ornette's sister Truvenza gives her brother's birthdate as March 9, 1931 (p. 21).

2. Ibid., p. 204.

3. Ibid. and p. 68.

4. Williams, *The Jazz Tradition*, p. 235.

5. Quoted in Litweiler, *Ornette Coleman*, p. 16.

6. Stanley Dance, liner notes, *Duke Ellington: Daybreak Express* (RCA Victor Records, LPV-506, 1964).

7. Charles Fox, review of *Swing Street Vol. 4*, in Harrison, Fox, and Thacker, *The Essential Jazz Records*, p. 549.

8. Schuller, *The Swing Era*, p. 765.

9. Ibid., p. 764n.

10. Simon, *Glenn Miller and His Orchestra*, pp. 337–338.

11. Schuller, *The Swing Era*, p. 764.

12. Ronald Spagnardi, *The Great Jazz Drummers*, ed. William F. Miller (Cedar Grove, NJ: Modern Drummer Publications, Inc., 1992), p. 25.

13. Tirro, *Jazz*, p. 549.

14. Simon, *Glenn Miller*, p. 124. Klink himself is quoted as saying, "All the guys in the band, and even Tex, would say, 'Klink, you ought to play more solos.' The arrangers would write things for me, but Glenn would cut them out" (pp. 127–128).

15. Ibid., pp. 126–127. Simon is quoting drummer Maurice Purtill.

16. Schuller, *The Swing Era*, p. 673.

17. Ibid., p. 666.

18. Quoted in Litweiler, *Ornette Coleman*, p. 69.

19. Litweiler quotes Schuller on the effect of Coleman's own peculiar training: "Over a period of years, when I think he was playing in blues bands in Texas, he had for some reason begun to associate certain pitches with certain characters. In other words, certain notes were always upbeats and they could only be upbeats. Certain other notes were always downbeats. I have always said that because he did not learn these things in the traditional way, he became the extraordinarily original improviser that he is, it's his genius. To this day he has people translate, I don't know what the word is, transcribe, transmogrify the things he writes down into some kind of normal notation, and nobody really knows whether those people do it accurately or not" (ibid., p. 94).

20. Ibid., p. 31.

21. Quoted in ibid. On the album *Ornette on Tenor* (Atlantic Records, 1394), Coleman's explanation for making a recording on this instrument is quoted in A. B. Spellman's liner notes:

"The tenor is a rhythm instrument, and the best statements Negroes have made, of what their soul is, have been on tenor saxophone. . . . The tenor's got that thing, that honk, you can get to people with it." See also A. B. Spellman, *Four Lives in the Bebop Business* (New York: Pantheon, 1966).

22. Litweiler, *Ornette Coleman*, p. 30.

23. Ibid., p. 28.

24. Quoted in ibid.

25. Ibid., p. 27.

26. Ibid., p. 33. Litweiler reports that tenor saxophonist Red Connors, who was also an influence on Coleman and other Fort Worth musicians, "impressed upon Ornette the importance of reading music fluently" (p. 32).

27. Ibid., pp. 35–36.

28. Ibid., pp. 36–37.

29. Berendt, *The Jazz Book*, pp. 112, 24, 26.

30. Quoted in Litweiler, *Ornette Coleman*, p. 37.

31. Quoted in Tim Schuller, "Music out of Clay," p. [1].

32. Litweiler, *Ornette Coleman*, p. 42.

33. Ibid., p. 43. Among the musicians in Los Angeles to reject Coleman was, according to British critic Sinclair Traill, a band that recorded under the name of Texas trombonist Ernie Fields: "This is the sort of group which paid Ornette Coleman not to play. I wouldn't buy the record [by the Fields band] just because of that" ("Record Reviews," review of *Ernie Fields: Saxy!*, *Jazz Journal* 14, no. 1 [January 1961]: 31). At the time of this review, Traill was unusual among British critics in appreciating Coleman's music.

34. Litweiler, *Ornette Coleman*, p. 28.

35. Quoted in ibid., p. 44.

36. Ibid., p. 54. Martin Banks, a trumpeter born in Austin on June 21, 1936, may have been the person to introduce Ornette to Don Cherry. Banks was in L.A. beginning in 1955 and could have joined up with Coleman; but in a telephone interview of November 6, 1994, Banks told me that, as he recalls, he was looking for a different kind of music at the time. Banks did appear on the 1960 album entitled *The Resurgence of Dexter Gordon* (Jazzland Records, JLP-29). Subsequently, he performed with most of the major big bands, including those of Count Basie (serving as a relief trumpeter), Duke Ellington (performing in 1968 alongside Harold "Money" Johnson), Dizzy Gillespie, the Dorham-Henderson big band, and for some four years with the Sun Ra Arkestra. Banks also appeared in mid-September of 1967 with Booker Ervin on an album entitled *Booker and Brass* (Pacific Jazz Records, ST 20127), which has Banks, Ray Copeland, Freddie Hubbard, and Richard Williams on trumpet. From about 1962 to 1970 Banks played off and on at the Apollo Theatre in New York.

In recent years Martin Banks has worked steadily in Austin, recording in 1989 with Countenance, a local group led by pianist Rich Harney and including reedman Alex Coke (born in Dallas on November 13, 1953, and now with the Willem Breuker Kollektief orchestra in Holland) and bassist Evan Arredondo (born in Alice on September 18, 1951), with vocals by Beth Ullman. Ullman is especially fine in her scat singing of *Blue Skies* on a trio recording (see *You've Been Haunting My Dreams* [1989] and *Aren't We the Lucky Ones* [Soul Prayer Records, 1994]). Banks and Coke are also together on *Jamad*, recorded in Austin on April 2 and 3, 1990, along with pianist James Polk. Born in Yoakum on September 10, 1940, Polk was a writer-arranger for the Ray Charles Orchestra from 1978 to 1988 and received Grammy Award nominations in 1979 and 1983. Banks also can be heard on *The Heaven Line* (CreOp Muse 002, 1994), a recording from January 25, 1992, cut by Austin's Creative Opportunity Orchestra, led by the superb vocalist Tina Marsh. Here Banks solos on *Circle* and sounds slightly reminiscent of Don Cherry.

37. Litweiler, *Ornette Coleman*, p. 54.

38. Nat Hentoff, liner notes, *Presenting Red Mitchell* (Contemporary Records, C7538).

39. Gordon, *Jazz West Coast*, p. 153.

40. Land's performance of *Sandu* is on *Study in Brown* (Emarcy Records, MG 36037).

41. Gordon, *Jazz West Coast*, p. 154.

42. Quoted in Orrin Keepnews, liner notes, *The Sound of the Wide Open Spaces!!!! James Clay and David "Fathead" Newman* (Riverside Records, 1178).

43. Ibid.

44. Kenneth Randall, liner notes, *The Wild Man from Texas: Arnett Cobb* (Home Cooking Records, HCS-114); Bob Burns, "Record Reviews," *Jazz Journal* 15, no. 11 (November 1962): 30.

45. Feather, *The New Edition of the Encyclopedia of Jazz*, p. 350.

46. *Hard Times* is included on *The Jazz Years* (Atlantic Records, SD2-316); *Deed I Do* is on *The Genius of Ray Charles* (Atlantic Records, 1312).

47. Leonard Feather, liner notes, *The Genius After Hours* (Atlantic Records, 1369).

48. Gioia, *West Coast Jazz*, p. 358. Seven years before his death in January 1995, Clay would record with Coleman's original quintet, minus Ornette, when Clay joined Don Cherry, Charlie Haden, and Billy Higgins for making Cherry's *Art Deco* (A & M Records, SP 5258, 1989). Cut in New Jersey on August 27, 28, and 30, 1988, this recording features Clay on two standard ballads, *Body and Soul* and *I've Grown Accustomed to Your Face*. According to Doug Ramsey in his liner notes to the album, Clay's solo on *Body and Soul* fashions a melody "at the beginning of the bridge of the second chorus" that is "a jewel, a tiny self-contained masterpiece." More important, Ramsey is correct when he observes that Clay's performance on *Compute*, a tune by Ornette, demonstrates that "All that woodshedding with Cherry and Coleman so long ago apparently planted the seeds of free jazz, and here they are germinating." On *Compute*, Clay shows that he was capable of echoing Coleman's style when Clay employs squeals, cries, and low-note double-time passages—all convincingly executed in the free-jazz mode. Clay himself remarks in the liner notes that "Texas tenor players are known for playing in a raunchy, straight-forward manner, with lots of emotion and few frills. I'm a typical example of that style of player." He admits that he had rarely played without a comping piano to supply the chords, so to record with Cherry's group was "like a Baptism in fire." Clay's christening, however, did not lead to any fundamental change from his faith in mainstream jazz.

49. Cooper, born on August 31, 1928, was with the Ernie Fields band between 1948 and 1951 on both alto and baritone, then with the Ray Charles orchestra for twenty years. At the present writing, Cooper performs regularly at Disney World in Orlando, Florida.

50. Dotson, born in the East Texas town of Jacksonville on June 18, 1946, recorded with Woody Herman in 1975 and has performed with Texas reedmen Arnett Cobb, Edgar Winter, and Tony Campise. Winter, a native of Beaumont, is a rock-and-roll tenorman whose work can

be sampled on *Texas Sax Greats* (Home Cooking Records, COL-CD-5261, 1992). Campise, born in Houston on January 22, 1943, played lead alto and flute with Stan Kenton in 1974 and appears on *Kenton Plays Chicago* and *Fire, Fury, and Fun*; he has been active on the Austin jazz scene for a number of years. Campise's album, *Ballads Blues Bebop and Beyond* (Heart Music, 006, 1994), includes Dotson on two tunes, Miles Davis's *Teo* and Charles Mingus's *Haitian Fight Song*; in both, the trumpeter does justice to these classic pieces.

51. This is true as well of the work of blind drummer Sebastian Whittaker, who was born in Houston on September 12, 1966. Dotson performs on Whittaker's *First Outing* (Justice Records, 0201-2, 1990), where the trumpeter is featured on the drummer's touching, extended composition *Waltz for Tiny* as well as on bassist David Craig's *Hangin' with Lee*, a tribute, most likely, to trumpeter Lee Morgan. Whittaker's group in fact looks back to the Blue Note era of Morgan, a member of Art Blakey's Jazz Messengers, and the Houston drummer's own tasteful and musical performances are very solidly and convincingly rooted in Blakey's hard-bop tradition. Whittaker's *Homage to Tony*, in reference it would seem to drummer Tony Williams, is a virtuoso display devoted to Sebastian's own classy percussion artistry.

52. Bret Primack, review of Roy Hargrove's *Public Eye* (Novus Records, 67:34), *Jazz Times* 21, no. 5 (August 1991): 58. This was Hargrove's second album; his first, *Diamond in the Rough* (Novus Records, 3082), was also praised for the trumpeter's sweet ballad treatments.

53. Litweiler, *Ornette Coleman*, pp. 52–56.

54. Ibid., p. 57.

55. Nat Hentoff, liner notes, *Something Else! The Music of Ornette Coleman* (Contemporary Records, S7551).

56. Quoted in ibid. Charlie Parker had recorded for the only time in his career on a plastic alto at the 1953 Massey Hall concert in Toronto, but only with a few high and low notes on this instrument (for example in *All the Things You Are* and *Perdido*) does Parker's sound make one think of Coleman's.

57. Litweiler, *Ornette Coleman*, p. 16.

58. Quoted in Hentoff, liner notes, *Something Else!*

59. Quoted in ibid.

60. Williams, *The Jazz Tradition*, p. 236.

61. Hsio Wen Shih, "Ornette Coleman," in *Jazz Panorama*, ed. Williams, p. 290.

62. Williams, *The Jazz Tradition*, pp. 236, 237.

63. Quoted in Litweiler, *Ornette Coleman*, p. 57.

64. Ibid., p. 64.

65. Martin Williams, "Ornette Coleman," in *Jazz Panorama*, ed. Williams, p. 287.

66. Litweiler, *Ornette Coleman*, p. 65.

67. Quoted in Nat Hentoff, liner notes, *Ornette Coleman: "Tomorrow Is the Question!"* (Contemporary Records, S7569).

68. Williams, *Jazz Panorama*, p. 287.

69. Balliett, *American Musicians*, p. 402.

70. Litweiler, *Ornette Coleman*, p. 67.

71. Williams, *Jazz Panorama*, p. 288.

72. Martin Williams, liner notes, *The Shape of Jazz to Come* (Atlantic Records, 1317).

73. Litweiler, *Ornette Coleman*, pp. 67–68.

74. Ibid., p. 68.

75. Ibid.

76. Don Heckman, "Inside Ornette Coleman," part 1, *Down Beat*, September 9, 1965, p. 14.

77. Wen Shih, "Ornette Coleman," pp. 289–290.

78. Ornette Coleman, as told to Gary Kramer, liner notes, *Change of the Century* (Atlantic Records, SD-1327).

79. Heckman, "Inside Ornette Coleman," p. 15.

80. Ibid.

81. George Russell and Martin Williams, "Ornette Coleman and Tonality," *Jazz Review* 3, no. 5 (June 1960): 8.

82. Williams, *The Jazz Tradition*, p. 244. T. E. Martin has described *Ramblin'* as having "an outmoving prairie theme over an excellently defined rhythm in which bassist Charlie Haden's repetitive figures fill the expressive gaps. These gaps seem to create the sense of western emptiness across which men (the horns) move with their mixture of bravado and loneliness" (quoted in Litweiler, *Ornette Coleman*, p. 74).

83. Russell and Williams, "Ornette Coleman and Tonality," p. 10. Williams, in this same conversation with Russell, asks, "Did you hear about the time when somebody asked [Coleman] to play like Buster Smith, then play like Bird, then play like Ornette, and he did—each one?" In his liner notes to *The Art of the Improvisers* (Atlantic Records, SD 1572), Martin Williams observes that on *The Legend of Bebop* Coleman utilizes "that minor seventh bebop line" and uses "some straightforwardly boppish phrases too."

84. Litweiler, *Ornette Coleman*, pp. 203–204.

85. See Ira Gitler, "Trane on the Track," *Down Beat* 25, no. 21 (October 16, 1958): 17, quoted in Thomas, *Chasin' the Trane*, p. 106.

86. Litweiler, *Ornette Coleman*, p. 204.

87. Ibid., p. 95. *Jazz Abstractions* (Atlantic Records, 1365).

88. Williams, *Jazz Panorama*, p. 303.

89. Ibid., pp. 302, 304.

90. Ibid., p. 305.

91. Williams, *The Jazz Tradition*, p. 245.

92. Ornette Coleman, liner notes, *This Is Our Music* (Atlantic Records, 1353).

93. Williams, *The Jazz Tradition*, p. 244.

94. Quoted in Martin Williams, liner notes, *Free Jazz* (Atlantic Records, 1364).

95. Ibid.

96. The five Atlantic albums are *The Shape of Jazz to Come, Change of the Century, Free Jazz, This Is Our Music,* and *Ornette!* In addition to these, a sixth Atlantic album, *Ornette on Tenor* (Atlantic Records, 1394), was cut in March 1961, and seventh and eighth albums, *The Art of the Improvisers* and *Twins* (Atlantic Records, SD 1588), were released in 1970 and 1971, respectively, but contain sides recorded in 1959, 1960, and 1961. *Check Up* on *Twins* was originally recorded on the *Ornette!* date and had only initials for a title. Martin Williams, in the liner notes for *Twins*, observes that the melody of this piece has a "decidedly Southwestern, almost Mexican, quality (echoing Ornette's Texas up-bringing of course)."

97. Gunther Schuller, liner notes, *Ornette!* (Atlantic Records, 1378).

98. Sergiu Luca, liner notes, *Johann Sebastian Bach: The Sonatas and Partitas for Unaccompanied Violin* (Nonesuch Records, HC-73030), pp. 7–8.

99. Schuller, liner notes, *Ornette!*

100. Ibid.

101. Pauline Rivelli and Robert Levin, ed., *Giants of Black Music* (1970; reprint, New York: Da Capo Press, 1979), p. [1].

102. As a student at the University of Texas in 1964, I once caught Bradford performing with a pick-up group in the Student Union as I happened to be passing by and could not believe my ears, never having heard such a live trumpet player of Bobby's caliber. It was an unforgettable, chance encounter with this outstanding jazzman, and regrettably was to be the only time I have ever heard in live performance any of the marvelous figures associated with the free-jazz movement.

103. Litweiler, *Ornette Coleman*, p. 103.

104. Ibid., p. 215.

105. Ibid., p. 105.

106. Ibid.

107. Ornette Coleman, liner notes, *The Music of Ornette Coleman* (RCA Victor Records, LSC-2982). The original performance of *Forms and Sounds* appears, along with the rest of the London concert, on *An Evening with Ornette Coleman* (Arista-Freedom Records, AL1900).

108. Victor Schonfeld, liner notes, *An Evening with Ornette Coleman.*

109. Ludvig Rasmusson, liner notes, *The Ornette Coleman Trio at the "Golden Circle," Stockholm,* vol. 1 (Blue Note Records, 84224).

110. Williams, *Jazz Masters in Transition,* pp. 203–204.

111. LeRoi Jones, liner notes, *Four for Trane* (Impulse Records, A-71).

112. Ibid.

113. Litweiler, *Ornette Coleman,* p. 119.

114. According to John Litweiler, Moffett, Lasha, and Sonny Simmons had performed together at the Village Vanguard with Eric Dolphy in the spring of 1963 during "a major breakthrough in Dolphy's evolving art. They [Lasha and Simmons] did not, however, record with Ornette" (ibid., p. 109).

115. Quoted in Lester Koenig, liner notes, *"The Cry!": Prince Lasha Quintet Featuring Sonny Simmons* (Contemporary Records, S7610).

116. Harvey Pekar, "Tomorrow Is the Question," *Jazz Journal* 15, no. 11 (November 1962): 10.

117. Koenig, liner notes, *"The Cry!"*

118. Quoted in ibid. Hayakawa is referring to a Willis James article in *Phylon* entitled "The Romance of the Folk Cry in America."

119. Koenig, liner notes, *"The Cry!"*

120. Don Heckman, "Ornette Coleman and the Quiet Revolution," *Saturday Review,* January 12, 1963, quoted in Lester Koenig, liner notes, *"The Cry!"*

121. Koenig, liner notes, *"The Cry!"*

122. Lasha claimed that Connors was "the greatest inspiration in the South-West"; Ornette Coleman said that he was better than Lester Young; and Dewey Redman called Connors "the

John Coltrane of that time." Coleman also reported that Connors made some records and was taped, but he did not know any details about these recordings. See Litweiler, *Ornette Coleman*, p. 27.

123. Quoted in Koenig, liner notes, *"The Cry!"*

124. Stephen James, liner notes, *Illumination!* (Impulse Records, A-49).

125. Ibid.

126. Nat Hentoff, liner notes, *Firebirds* (Contemporary Records, 7617).

127. Around 1981, Prince Lasha recorded an album under his own name entitled *Inside Story* (Enja Records, 3044), which includes Herbie Hancock on piano and Cecil McBee on bass. Ira Bernstein, in a review in the "texwax" section of *Texas Jazz* 5, no. 8 (August 1981), n.p., refers to Lasha's "unique alto style."

128. Hentoff, liner notes, *Firebirds*.

129. King Curtis, the youngest of this group, was born in Fort Worth on February 7, 1934, and died in New York City in 1971 of a stab wound. Known mostly as a major R & B figure, Curtis made a number of albums as a jazz tenorist in the tradition of Gene Ammons's "uncomplicated, warm-hearted, free-wheeling approach." Curtis's sound has been characterized as "a big, hoarse, utterly masculine tone with which he communicates a primal, savagely intense kind of musical feeling cloaked in the melodic and harmonic metaphor of mainstream jazz." Although Curtis remained close to his R & B roots and did not form part of the free-jazz movement, on September 9, 1960, he recorded on an album with Oliver Nelson, a trained musician capable of combining jazz, pop, and classical music in a style approaching that of John Coltrane. On *Soul Battle*, Curtis shows that he could handle the modal orientation of the tune *Anacruses* "with an almost off-hand manner" and with "carefree confidence." Following the "exalted beauty" of a Nelson solo played "against a continually shifting harmonic background" on *In Passing*, Curtis "launches what is perhaps the most exciting solo on the album. It is pervaded with a singing quality, an ultra-melodiousness seldom heard in modern jazz improvisation." See Tom Wilson, liner notes, *Soul Battle* (Prestige Records, OJC-325).

130. Christopher Evans, interview, *Fort Worth Star-Telegram*, February 13, 1994, sec. A & E. In this interview conducted in late 1993, Evans refers to the section of Rosedale Street and Evans Avenue as a vortex of a five- or six-block area "on the city's short southeast side" where dozens of "uniquely trained young musicians . . . were either born or weaned musically." Evans quotes Redman as saying, "Fort Worth, that's my theme. I'm just a country boy from Fort Worth, Texas, who came to New York and made it." These last comments by Redman come from the complete text of the interview before it was edited and printed. I am grateful to T. Sumter Bruton III for supplying me with a copy of Evans's original text.

131. *New York Is Now!* (Blue Note Records, BST 84267).

132. Litweiler, *Ornette Coleman*, p. 130.

133. Ibid., p. 128.

134. Ibid., pp. 129, 171.

135. *Old and New Dreams* (ECM Records, 829379-2).

136. *The Empty Foxhole* (Blue Note Records, 84246).

137. Quoted in Litweiler, *Ornette Coleman*, p. 121.

138. Ibid.

139. Ibid., p. 130.

140. Ornette Coleman, liner notes, *Ornette at 12* (Impulse Records, 9178).

141. *Broken Shadows* (Columbia Records, FC38029); *Science Fiction* (Columbia Records, KC31061).

142. Litweiler, *Ornette Coleman*, p. 141. For an interview with Bradford conducted during his period with Coleman during the early 1960s, see LeRoi Jones, "Introducing Bobby Bradford," in *Black Music* (New York: William Morrow, 1967), pp. 99–103.

143. Bob Palmer, liner notes, *Science Fiction*.

144. Litweiler, *Ornette Coleman*, p. 141.

145. Palmer, liner notes, *Science Fiction*.

146. Ibid. Redman can also be heard on musette on his own tune, *Orbit of La-B*, from the 1976 album *Old and New Dreams*.

147. Palmer, liner notes, *Science Fiction*.

148. Rafi Zabor and David Breskin, "Ronald Shannon Jackson: The Future of Jazz Drumming," *Musician, Player, and Listener*, no. 33 (June 1981): 61.

149. Quoted in Giddins, *Rhythm-a-ning*, p. 97.

150. Ibid., pp. 97–98.

151. Williams, *Jazz Masters in Transition*, pp. 194–195.

152. Michael Cuscuna, quoted in Feather and Gitler, *The Encyclopedia of Jazz in the Seventies*, p. 57.

153. Giddins, *Rhythm-a-ning*, p. 98.

154. Quoted in Zabor and Breskin, "Ronald Shannon Jackson," p. 65.

155. Ibid.

156. Ornette Coleman, liner notes, *Dancing in Your Head* (A & M/Horizon Records, SP-722).

157. Ibid.

158. Quoted in Zabor and Breskin, "Ronald Shannon Jackson," p. 61.

159. Ibid., pp. 68–70.

160. Ibid., p. 66.

161. Giddins, *Riding on a Blue Note*, p. 181.

162. Giddins, *Rhythm-a-ning*, p. 95.

163. Williams, *Jazz Masters in Transition*, p. 222.

164. In describing Jackson's music, John Litweiler observes that "hyperstimulation charac-terizes harmolodic music in any case, but Jackson's . . . extremes of adrenaline bring about extraordinary juxtapositions of textures" (*The Freedom Principle*, p. 292).

165. Spenser Richards and Ramsey Ameen, "The World of Cecil Taylor," liner notes, *Cecil Taylor* (New World Records, NW 201-2).

166. Giddins, *Riding on a Blue Note*, p. 282.

167. Ibid., p. 281.

168. Zabor and Breskin, "Ronald Shannon Jackson," p. 66.

169. Ibid.

170. *Eye on You* (About Time Records, 1980).

171. Quoted in Zabor and Breskin, "Ronald Shannon Jackson," p. 70.

172. Litweiler, *The Freedom Principle*, p. 291.

173. Litweiler, *Ornette Coleman*, p. 34.

174. Litweiler, *The Freedom Principle*, p. 292.

175. Quoted in Zabor and Breskin, "Ronald Shannon Jackson," p. 62. An album recorded in 1987 by Jackson and his Decoding Society is entitled *Texas* (Caravan of Dreams Productions, CDPT 85012). Although three tunes, *Panhandling, Shotgun Wedding,* and *Sheep in Wolf's Clothing,* offer something of a southwestern feeling, especially in the saxophone solos on the first two and the guitar riffs on the third, this production is disappointing, not only because it seems to have little to do with the album's title but because too much of it is given over to mood music associated with film soundtracks.

176. *Skies of America* (Columbia Records, KC 31562). An album by Coleman's Prime Time Band, with Denardo and Sabir Kamal on drums, recorded in celebration of this event, is entitled *Opening the Caravan of Dreams* (Caravan of Dreams Productions, CDP 85001, 1985). It includes among its fascinating, high-energy offerings *Harmolodic Bebop* and *Sex Spy,* with the former containing Ornette's version of wailing, swinging, R & B harmolodics and the latter one of his classic Texas honks.

177. Litweiler, *Ornette Coleman*, p. 195. *Virgin Beauty* (CBS Records, OR 44301, 1988) is most memorable for the haunting theme of its title tune.

178. Quoted in Litweiler, *Ornette Coleman*, p. 195.

179. Ibid., pp. 180, 173.

21. Africa and Back

1. Litweiler, *Ornette Coleman*, p. 125.

2. Quoted in Rivelli and Levin, *Giants of Black Music*, p. [41].

3. Michael James, liner notes, *Seeking/The New Art Jazz Ensemble* (Revelation Records, REV-9).

4. Quoted in ibid.

5. Ibid.

6. Litweiler, *The Freedom Principle*, p. 149.

7. Ibid., p. 150.

8. Michael James, liner notes, *Secrets* (Revelation Records, Revelation 18).

9. Norman C. Weinstein, *A Night in Tunisia: Imaginings of Africa in Jazz* (Metuchen, N.J.: Scarecrow Press, 1992), p. 90.

10. James, liner notes, *Secrets*.

11. Don Palmer, liner notes, *The Clarinet Summit* (Black Saint Records, BSR 0107, 1987).

12. *A Suite of Early American Folk Pieces for Solo-Clarinet* (Moers Music, 02086).

13. The album gives the name as "Earnestine," which Carter may have intended (rather than the more usual Ernestine), but since the text on the compact disc commits a number of typographical errors, this is possibly another.

14. Palmer, liner notes, *The Clarinet Summit*.

15. Weinstein, *A Night in Tunisia*, p. 87.

16. Palmer, liner notes, *The Clarinet Summit*.

17. Ibid.

18. Ibid.

19. Ibid.

20. Ibid.

21. Art Lange, liner notes, *The Dark Tree*, vol. 2 (Hat Art, 6083, July 1990). This album contains two tracks with Carter performing with fellow Texan Horace Tapscott, who was born in Houston on April 6, 1934; in 1945 Tapscott moved to Los Angeles, where he worked with such local groups as the Gerald Wilson orchestra and with such figures as Eric Dolphy and Don Cherry before touring with Lionel Hampton from 1959 to 1961. Returning to Los Angeles, Tapscott formed his own group and became a leading educator and promoter of what Stanley Crouch calls "a new Black music . . . because, as an African writer once said, 'time is flow.' Tapscott and his men know that all of the time, if it's carrying the feeling of the people, it is new, is free" (quoted in Feather and Gitler, *The Encyclopedia of Jazz in the Seventies*, p. 321).

22. Quoted in Bill Smith, liner notes, *Buster Bee* (Sackville Records, 3018).

23. *Steppin' with the World Saxophone Quartet* (Black Saint Records, BSR 0027).

24. Berendt, *The Jazz Book*, p. 261. Mark C. Gridley writes that the World Saxophone Quartet's "style is fundamentally original, though they have drawn extensively on rhythmic, melodic, and timbral traditions of blues-flavored black-American popular music, and the jazz approaches of Ornette Coleman and Albert Ayler. . . . Although the quartet occasionally plays passages of free jazz, by deftly interweaving composed parts with improvised solos and ensembles, the musicians achieve a greater balance of contrasts than Coleman" (*New Grove Encyclopedia of Jazz*, ed. Kernfeld, pp. 640–641).

25. See Litweiler, *The Freedom Principle*, p. 294.

26. Quoted in Howard Mandel, "The Three Outsketeers," *Down Beat* 60, no. 1 (October 1993): 31.

27. Quoted in unsigned liner notes, *Julius Hemphill Quartet: Flat-Out Jump Suite*.

28. In his *African Portraits*, written for a performance by the American Composers Orchestra at Carnegie Hall on November 11, 1990, Marvin "Hannibal" Peterson created a work that surveys the story of African Americans and their music. On November 17, 1994, the San Antonio Symphony Orchestra gave the Texas premier of this composition for full orchestra, chorus, solo vocalists, a four-man South African drum choir, and Peterson's jazz quartet (with James Polk on piano). Among the vocal soloists were T. D. Bell, born in 1922, who performed a blues, accompanying himself on guitar, and Bernice Williams, a graduate of San Antonio's Incarnate Word College and Trinity University, who sang a gospel piece entitled "Victor Nelson's Cotton Field: Elgin, Texas, 1940." As we shall see, Carter's *Roots and Folklore* series from the 1980s includes, as does Peterson's *African Portraits*, the depiction of a slave ship making the Atlantic crossing with its human cargo, as well as the violent disruption of African lives and their subsequent inhuman treatment at the hands of slave owners and plantation overseers. Peterson's work was scheduled to be recorded in 1995 by the Chicago Symphony Orchestra. In addition to his *African Portraits*, Peterson has written more than 150 compositions that include operas and masses.

29. Ronald Shannon Jackson's Decoding Society album, *Barbequed Dog* (Antilles Records, 422-848 817-2), recorded in New York in 1983, includes two tunes that in some ways approach, as we shall see, the work of Carter and Bradford: *When Cherry Trees Bloom in Winter, You Can Smell Last Summer* and *Harlem Opera*. On the former, trumpeter Henry Scott is quite impressive, as is

Jackson, while on *Harlem Opera* the drummer's writing for his ensemble (including voices) and his own playing, along with that of Zane Massey on alto, show Jackson attempting one of his fullest, most ambitious statements.

30. Berendt, *The Jazz Book*, pp. 227–228.

31. Weinstein, *A Night in Tunisia*, p. 83.

32. Quoted in ibid., p. 88.

33. John Carter, liner notes, *Dance of the Love Ghosts* (Gramavision Records, R2 79424).

34. Quoted in Weinstein, *A Night in Tunisia*, p. 87.

35. George Hoefer, liner notes, *The King of New Orleans Jazz* (RCA Victor Records, LPM-1649).

36. Joachim Berendt, liner notes, *Dauwhe* (Black Saint Records, BSR 0057, 1982).

37. Ibid.

38. John Carter, liner notes, *Castles of Ghana* (Gramavision, R2 79423). Throughout his liner notes, Carter's descriptions recall Letter IX of Michel-Guillaume-Jean de Crèvecoeur's *Letters from an American Farmer* (1782). Crèvecoeur had described much the same situation as Carter depicts both verbally and aurally: "Here the horrors of slavery, the hardship of incessant toils, are unseen, and no one thinks with compassion of those showers of sweat and of tears which from the bodies of Africans daily drop and moisten the ground they till. . . . Wars, murders, and devastations are committed in some harmless, peaceable African neighborhood where dwelt innocent people who even knew not but that all men were black. The daughter torn from her weeping mother, the child from the wretched parents, the wife from the loving husband, whole families swept away and brought through storms and tempests to this rich metropolis! There, arranged like horses at a fair, they are branded like cattle and then driven to toil, to starve, and to languish for a few years on the different plantations of these citizens."

39. For Carter's denial, see Weinstein, *A Night in Tunisia*, p. 82.

40. Unsigned liner notes, *Dance of the Love Ghosts* (Gramavision, R2 79424-2).

41. Weinstein, *A Night in Tunisia*, p. 90.

42. John Carter, liner notes, *Fields* (Gramavision, R2 79425).

43. Frederick Douglass, *My Bondage and My Freedom* (1855), in *Readings in Black American Music*, ed. Eileen Southern (New York: W. W. Norton, 1983), p. 84.

44. Art Lange, liner notes, *Comin' On* (Hat Art, 6016).

45. *Bobby Bradford with the Frank Sullivan Trio, One Night Stand* (Soul Note, 121168-2).

46. Carter, liner notes, *Fields*.

47. Bill Shoemaker, review of *Shadows on a Wall*, *Down Beat* (March 1990): 29.

48. John Carter, liner notes, *Shadows on a Wall* (Gramavision Records, R2 79422, 1989).

49. Ibid.

50. Weinstein, *A Night in Tunisia*, p. 92.

51. Ibid.

SELECTED BIBLIOGRAPHY

Albrecht, Theodore. "Julius Weiss: Scott Joplin's First Piano Teacher." *College Music Symposium* 19, no. 2 (Fall 1979).

Aldam, Jeff. "The Ellington Sidemen." In *Duke Ellington: His Life and Music*, ed. Peter Gammon. London: Phoenix House, 1958.

Anderson, Ernie. "Lips the Hard-Luck Man." *Melody Maker*, no. 30 (November 20, 1954).

Avakian, Al, and Bob Prince. "Charlie Christian." In *The Art of Jazz*, ed. Martin T. Williams. New York: Grove Press, 1960.

Balliett, Whitney. *American Musicians: 56 Portraits in Jazz*. New York: Oxford University Press, 1986.

————. Review of Charles Mingus Jazz Workshop. *New Yorker*, January 24, 1959.

Barlow, William. *"Looking Up at Down": The Emergence of Blues Culture*. Philadelphia: Temple University Press, 1989.

Basie, Count. *Good Morning Blues: The Autobiography of Count Basie*, as told to Albert Murray. New York: Random House, 1985.

Bechet, Sidney. *Treat It Gentle*. New York: Hill and Wang, 1960.

Bellerby, Vic. "Duke Ellington." In *The Art of Jazz*, ed. Martin T. Williams. New York: Grove Press, 1960.

Berendt, Joachim E. *The Jazz Book: From Ragtime to Fusion and Beyond*, rev. Günther Huesmann; trans. H. and B. Bredigkeit, with Dan Morgenstern and Tim Nevill. New York: Lawrence Hill Books, 1992.

Blesh, Rudi. *Shining Trumpets: A History of Jazz*. 2d ed. 1958. Reprint, New York: Da Capo Press, 1980.

Blesh, Rudi, and Harriet Janis. *They All Played Ragtime*. New York: Knopf, 1950.

Borneman, Ernest. "The Blues: A Study in Ambiguity." In *Just Jazz 3*, ed. Sinclair Traill and Gerald Lascelles. London: Landsborough Publications, 1959.

————. "Boogie Woogie." In *Just Jazz*, ed. Sinclair Traill and Gerald Lascelles. London: Peter Davies, 1957.

Bouchard, Fred. "Jimmy Giuffre: Four Brothers + 3 Decades." *Down Beat* 48, no. 12 (December 1981).

Britt, Stan. *The Jazz Guitarists*. Poole, England: Blandford Press, 1984.

Burns, Bob. "Record Reviews." *Jazz Journal* 15, no. 11 (November 1962).

Campbell, E. Simms. "Blues." In *Jazzmen*, ed. Frederic Ramsey, Jr., and Charles Edward Smith. London: Sidgwick and Jackson, 1958.

Carno, Zita. Review of Kenny Dorham's *Blue Spring*. *Jazz Review* 2, no. 7 (August 1959).

Case, Brian, and Stan Britt. *The Harmony Illustrated Encyclopedia of Jazz*. 3d ed. Revised by Chrissie Murray. New York: Harmony Books, 1987.

Chambers, Jack. *Milestones 1: The Music and Times of Miles Davis to 1960*. New York: William Morrow, 1983.

———. *Milestones 2: The Music and Times of Miles Davis since 1960*. New York: William Morrow, 1985.

Charters, Samuel B. *The Blues Makers*. 1967. Reprint, New York: Da Capo Press, 1991.

———. *The Country Blues*. London: Jazz Book Club, 1961.

Charters, Samuel B., and Leonard Kunstadt. *Jazz: A History of the New York Scene*. Garden City, N.Y.: Doubleday and Company, 1962.

"Chicago Jazz History." In *Esquire's 1946 Jazz Book*, ed. Paul Eduard Miller. New York: Smith and Durrell, 1946.

Chilton, John. *The Song of the Hawk: The Life and Recordings of Coleman Hawkins*. Ann Arbor: University of Michigan Press, 1990.

———. *Who's Who of Jazz: Storyville to Swing Street*. 1972. Reprint, New York: Da Capo Press, 1985.

Clar, Mimi. Review of four albums by Red Garland and *Soultrane* by John Coltrane. *Jazz Review* 2, no. 3 (April 1959).

Collier, James Lincoln. *Benny Goodman and the Swing Era*. New York: Oxford University Press, 1989.

———. *Duke Ellington*. New York: Oxford University Press, 1987.

———. *Louis Armstrong: An American Genius*. New York: Oxford University Press, 1983.

———. *The Making of Jazz: A Comprehensive History*. New York: Dell Publishing, 1978.

Coleman, Janet, and Al Young, *Mingus/Mingus: Two Memoirs*. Berkeley: Creative Arts, 1989.

Cork, Richard, and Brian Morton. *The Penguin Guide to Jazz on CD, LP, and Cassette*. Harmondsville, England: Penguin, 1992.

Coulter, Glenn. "Billie Holiday." In *The Art of Jazz*, ed. Martin T. Williams. New York: Grove Press, 1960.

Dahl, Linda. *Stormy Weather: The Music and Lives of a Century of Jazz Women*. New York: Pantheon Books, 1984.

Dance, Stanley. "Lightly and Politely." *Jazz Journal* 18, no. 8 (August 1965).

———. *The World of Count Basie*. New York: Charles Scribner's Sons, 1980.

———. *The World of Earl Hines*. 1977. Reprint, New York: Da Capo Press, 1983.

Driggs, Frank. "Budd Johnson: Ageless Jazzman." Part 1. *Jazz Review* 3, no. 9 (November 1960).

———. "Budd Johnson: Ageless Jazzman." Part 2. *Jazz Review* 4, no. 1 (January 1961).

———. "Kansas City Brass: Ed Lewis' Story as Told to Frank Driggs." Part 2. *Jazz Review* 2, no. 9 (October 1959).

———. "Kansas City and the Southwest." In *Jazz: New Perspectives on the History of Jazz*, ed. Nat

Hentoff and Albert J. McCarthy. 1959. Reprint, New York: Da Capo Press, 1975.

———. "My Story by Buddy Tate as told to Frank Driggs." *Jazz Review* 1, no. 2 (December 1958).

Easton, Carol. *Straight Ahead: The Story of Stan Kenton.* New York: William Morrow, 1973.

Evans, Christopher. Interview with Dewey Redman. *Fort Worth Star-Telegram,* February 13, 1994.

Evans, Glen Nicholas M. "Swingin' and Boppin' South Texas–Style." Master of Arts report, University of Texas at Austin, May 1992.

Feather, Leonard. *The Book of Jazz.* New York: Meridian Books, 1959.

———. *The Encyclopedia of Jazz in the Sixties.* New York: Horizon Press, 1966.

———. *Inside Be-Bop.* New York: J. J. Robbins and Sons, 1949.

———. *The New Edition of the Encyclopedia of Jazz.* New York: Bonanza Books, 1962.

———. *The Passion for Jazz.* New York: Horizon Press, 1980.

Feather, Leonard, and Ira Gitler. *The Encyclopedia of Jazz in the Seventies.* New York: Horizon Press, 1976.

Finkelstein, Sidney. *Jazz: A People's Music.* 1948. Reprint, New York: International Publishers, 1988.

Firestone, Ross. *Swing, Swing, Swing: The Life and Times of Benny Goodman.* New York: W. W. Norton, 1993.

Flower, John. *Moonlight Serenade: A Bio-Discography of the Glenn Miller Civilian Band.* New Rochelle, N.Y.: Arlington House, 1972.

Friedwall, Will. *Jazz Singing: America's Great Voices from Bessie Smith to Bebop and Beyond.* New York: Charles Scribner's Sons, 1990.

Gammon, Peter, ed. *Duke Ellington: His Life and Music.* London: Phoenix House, 1958.

Gazzaway, Don. "Conversations with Buster Smith." Part 1. *Jazz Review* 2, no. 10 (December 1959).

———. "Conversations with Buster Smith." Part 2. *Jazz Review* 3, no. 1 (January 1959).

———. "Buster and Bird: Conversations with Buster Smith." Part 3. *Jazz Review* 3, no. 2 (February 1960).

Giddins, Gary. *Rhythm-a-ning: Jazz Tradition and Innovation in the '80s.* New York: Oxford University Press, 1985.

———. *Riding on a Blue Note: Jazz and American Pop.* New York: Oxford University Press, 1981.

Gillespie, Dizzy, and Al Fraser, *To Be, or Not . . . to Bop: Memoirs.* Garden City, N.Y.: Doubleday, 1979.

Gillis, Frank J. "Hot Rhythm in Piano Ragtime." In *Ragtime: Its History, Composers, and Music,* ed. John Edward Hasse. New York: Macmillan, 1985.

Gioia, Ted. *West Coast Jazz: Modern Jazz in California 1945–1960.* New York: Oxford University Press, 1992.

Gitler, Ira. *Jazz Masters of the Forties.* New York: Macmillan, 1966.

———. *Swing to Bop.* New York: Oxford University Press, 1985.

Goldberg, Joe. *Jazz Masters of the Fifties.* New York: Macmillan, 1965.

Gordon, Robert. *Jazz West Coast: The Los Angeles Jazz Scene of the 1950s.* London: Quartet Books, 1986.

SELECTED BIBLIOGRAPHY ✐ 445

Govenar, Alan. *Meeting the Blues*. Dallas: Taylor Publishing, 1988.

Green, Benny. "Man with a Hat: An Evaluation of the Work of Lester Young." In *Just Jazz 3*, ed. Sinclair Traill and Gerald Lascelles. London: Landsborough Publications, 1959.

Hadlock, Richard. *Jazz Masters of the Twenties*. 1965. Reprint, New York: Collier Books, 1974.

Harris, Sheldon. *Blues Who's Who: A Biographical Dictionary of Blues Singers*. New Rochelle, N.Y.: Arlington House, 1979.

Harrison, Daphne Duval. *Black Pearls: Blues Queens of the 1920s*. New Brunswick, N.J.: Rutgers University Press, 1988.

Harrison, Max. "Boogie-Woogie." In *Jazz: New Perspectives on the History of Jazz*, ed. Nat Hentoff and Albert J. McCarthy. 1959. Reprint, New York: Da Capo Press, 1975.

———. Review of *Opus de Bop. Jazz Review* 2, no. 9 (October 1959).

Harrison, Max, Charles Fox, and Eric Thacker. *The Essential Jazz Records*. Vol. 1, *Ragtime to Swing*. New York: Da Capo Press, 1988.

Harwood, Ronald P. "'Mighty Tight Woman': The Thomas Family and Classic Blues." *Storyville*, no. 17 (1968).

Haskins, James, with Kathleen Benson. *Scott Joplin*. Garden City, N.Y.: Doubleday, 1978.

Hasse, John Edward, ed. *Ragtime: Its History, Composers, and Music*. New York: Macmillan, 1985.

Heckman, Don. "Inside Ornette Coleman." Part 1. *Down Beat*, September 9, 1965.

———. "Ornette Coleman and the Quiet Revolution." *Saturday Review*, January 12, 1963.

———. Review of *Jimmy Giuffre: "The Easy Way." Jazz Review* 3, no. 2 (July 1960).

Hentoff, Nat, and Albert J. McCarthy, eds. *Jazz: New Perspectives on the History of Jazz*. 1959. Reprint, New York: Da Capo Press, 1975.

Herzhaft, Gerard. *Encyclopedia of the Blues*, trans. Brigitte Dewd. Fayetteville: University of Arkansas Press, 1992.

Hester, Mary Lee. *Going to Kansas City*. Sherman, Tex.: Early Bird Press, 1980.

———. "Texas Jazz Heritage." *Texas Jazz* 5, no. 12 (December 1981).

Hitchcock, H. Wiley, and Stanley Sadie, eds. *The New Grove Dictionary of Music*. Vol. 1. London: Macmillan, 1986.

Hodeir, André. *Jazz: Its Evolution and Essence*. New York: Grove Press, 1956.

Hoefer, George. "Held Notes: Eddie Durham." *Down Beat* 29 (July 19, 1962).

Horricks, Raymond. "The Orchestral Suites." In *Duke Ellington: His Life and Music*, ed. Peter Gammon. London: Phoenix House, 1958.

Jones, LeRoi. "Introducing Bobby Bradford." In *Black Music*. New York: William Morrow, 1967.

Kennedy, Rick. *Jelly Roll, Bix, and Hoagy: Gennett Studios and the Birth of Recorded Jazz*. Bloomington: Indiana University Press, 1994.

Kernfeld, Barry, ed. *The New Grove Dictionary of Jazz*. 2 vols. London: Macmillan, 1988.

Lascelles, Gerald. Review of *Basie at Birdland. Jazz Journal* 15, no. 6 (June 1962).

Lee, William F. *Stan Kenton: Artistry in Rhythm*. Los Angeles: Creative Press of Los Angeles, 1980.

Lees, Gene. *Oscar Peterson: The Will to Swing*. Rocklin, Calif.: Prima, 1990.

Lewis, John S. "Alternate Takes." *Texas Jazz* 6, no. 12 (December 1982).

Litweiler, John. *The Freedom Principle: Jazz after 1958*. New York: William Morrow, 1984.

———. *Ornette Coleman: A Harmolodic Life*. New York: William Morrow, 1992.

Lomax, Alan. *Mister Jelly Roll: The Fortunes of Jelly Roll Morton, New Orleans Creole and "Inventor of Jazz."* New York: Grosset and Dunlap, 1950.

Lord, Tom. *The Jazz Discography.* Vol 5. West Vancouver, Canada: Lord Music Reference, 1993.

Lyons, Len. *The Great Jazz Pianists Speaking of Their Lives.* New York: William Morrow, 1983.

———. *The One Hundred Best Jazz Albums.* New York: William Morrow, 1980.

Lyons, Len, and Don Perlow. *Jazz Portraits: The Lives and Music of the Jazz Masters.* New York: William Morrow, 1989.

Lyttleton, Humphrey. *The Best of Jazz, Basin Street to Harlem: Jazz Masters and Masterpieces, 1917–1930.* London: Robson Books, 1978.

McCarthy, Albert. *Big Band Jazz.* London: Barrie and Jenkins, 1974.

McCarthy, Albert, et al. *Jazz on Record: A Critical Guide to the First 50 Years: 1917–1967.* London: Hanover Books, 1968.

McDonough, John. "A Century with Count Basie." *Down Beat* (January 1990).

Malone, Bill C. *Country Music, U.S.A.* Austin: University of Texas Press, 1968.

Mellers, Wilfrid. *Music in a New Found Land.* Rev. ed. New York: Oxford University Press, 1987.

Mezzrow, Mezz. *Really the Blues.* 1946. Reprint, New York: Citadel Press, 1990.

Morgenstern, Dan. "Hot Lips Page." *Jazz Journal* 15, no. 7 (July 1962); no. 8 (August 1962); no. 11 (November 1962).

———. "Miles Davis." In *Miles Davis Chronicle: The Complete Prestige Recordings 1951–1956.* Berkeley, Calif.: Fantasy Records, 1987.

Murray, Albert. *Stomping the Blues.* 1976. Reprint, New York: Da Capo Press, 1987.

Nisenson, Eric. *'Round About Midnight: A Portrait of Miles Davis.* New York: Dial Press, 1982.

Oliver, Paul. *Aspects of the Blues Tradition.* New York: Oak Publications, 1970.

———. *The Story of the Blues.* Philadelphia: Chilton, 1969.

Oliver, Paul, et al. *The New Grove Gospel, Blues, and Jazz with Spirituals and Ragtime.* New York: W. W. Norton, 1986.

Owens, Thomas. *Bebop: The Music and Its Players.* New York: Oxford University Press, 1995.

Panassié, Hugues, and Madeleine Gautier. *Guide to Jazz.* Edited by A. A. Gurwitch. Translated by Desmond Flower. Boston: Houghton Mifflin, 1956.

Parker, Douglass. "*Donna Lee* and the Ironies of Bebop." In *The Bebop Revolution in Words and Music,* ed. Dave Oliphant. Austin, Tex.: Harry Ransom Humanities Research Center, 1994.

Pearson, Nathan W. *Goin' to Kansas City.* Urbana: University of Illinois Press, 1987.

Pekar, Harvey. "Tomorrow Is the Question." *Jazz Journal* 15, no. 11 (November 1962).

Peretti, Burton W. *The Creation of Jazz: Music, Race, and Culture in Urban America.* Urbana: University of Illinois Press, 1992.

Placksin, Sally. *American Women in Jazz, 1900 to the Present: Their Words, Lives, and Music.* [New York: Putnam] Wideview Books, 1982.

Price, Sammy. *What Do They Want?: A Jazz Autobiography.* Edited by Caroline Richmond, with a discography compiled by Bob Weir. Champaign-Urbana: University of Illinois Press, 1990.

Priestley, Brian. *Mingus: A Critical Biography.* New York: Quartet Books, 1982.

Primack, Bret. Review of *Public Eye* by Roy Hargrove. *Jazz Times* 21, no. 5 (August 1991).

Ramsey, Doug. *Jazz Matters: Reflections on the Music and Some of Its Makers.* Fayetteville: University of Arkansas Press, 1989.

Ramsey, Frederic, Jr., and Charles Edward Smith, eds. *Jazzmen*. London: Sidgwick and Jackson, 1958.

Reed, Addison W. "Scott Joplin, Pioneer." In *Ragtime: Its History, Composers, and Music*, ed. John Edward Hasse. New York: Macmillan, 1985.

Rivelli, Pauline, and Robert Levin, eds. *Giants of Black Music*. 1970. Reprint, New York: Da Capo Press, 1979.

Rosenthal, David. *Hard Bop: Jazz and Black Music, 1955–1965*. New York: Oxford University Press, 1992.

Russell, George. Review of *Jimmy Giuffre 3: Trav'lin' Light*. *Jazz Review* 1, no. 1 (November 1958).

Russell, George, and Martin Williams. "Ornette Coleman and Tonality." *Jazz Review* 3, no. 5 (June 1960).

Russell, Ross. "Bebop." In *The Art of Jazz*, ed. Martin T. Williams. New York: Grove Press, 1960.

———. *Bird Lives! The High Life and Hard Times of Charlie "Yardbird" Parker*. New York: Charterhouse, 1973.

———. *Jazz Style in Kansas City and the Southwest*. Berkeley: University of California Press, 1971.

Russell, William. "Boogie Woogie." In *Jazzmen*, ed. Frederic Ramsey, Jr., and Charles Edward Smith. London: Sidgwick and Jackson, 1958.

———. "Louis Armstrong." In *Jazzmen*, ed. Frederic Ramsey, Jr., and Charles Edward Smith. London: Sidgwick and Jackson, 1958.

Rust, Brian. *Jazz Records 1897–1942*. 2 vols. Chigwell, England: Storyville Publications, 1975.

Santelli, Robert. *The Big Book of Blues: A Biographical Encyclopedia*. New York: Penguin, 1993.

Santoro, Gene. *Dancing in Your Head: Jazz, Blues, Rock, and Beyond*. New York: Oxford University Press, 1994.

Schafer, William J., and Johannes Riedel. *The Art of Ragtime*. Baton Rouge: Louisiana State University Press, 1973.

Schuller, Gunther. *Early Jazz: Its Roots and Musical Development*. New York: Oxford University Press, 1968.

———. *Musings: The Musical Worlds of Gunther Schuller, A Collection of His Writings*. New York: Oxford University Press, 1986.

———. "Reviews: Recordings." *Jazz Review* 1, no. 1 (November 1958).

———. *The Swing Era: The Development of Jazz, 1930–1945*. New York: Oxford University Press, 1989.

Schuller, Tim. "Music out of Clay." *Texas Jazz* 3, no. 1 (November 1979).

Shapiro, Nat, and Nat Hentoff, eds. *Hear Me Talkin' to Ya: The Story of Jazz as Told by the Men Who Made It*. 1955. Reprint, New York: Dover Publications, 1966.

———. *The Jazz Makers: Essays on the Greats of Jazz*. 1957. Reprint, New York: Da Capo Press, 1988.

Shera, Michael. "Record Reviews." *Jazz Journal* 14, no. 12 (December 1961); 15, no. 3 (March 1962).

Sheridan, Chris, comp. *Count Basie: A Bio-Discography*. New York: Greenwood Press, 1986.

Shoemaker, Bill. Review of John Carter's *Shadows on a Wall*. *Down Beat* (March 1990).

Siegel, J. A., and J. Obrecht. "Eddie Durham: Charlie Christian's Mentor, Pioneer of the

Amplified Guitar." *Guitar Player* 13 (August 1979).

Silvester, Peter J. *A Left Hand Like God: A History of Boogie-Woogie Piano*. New York: Da Capo Press, 1989.

Simms, Bill. "Charlie Christian." In *The Jazz Makers: Essays on the Greats of Jazz*, ed. Nat Shapiro and Nat Hentoff. 1957. Reprint, New York: Da Capo Press, 1988.

Simon, George T. *Glenn Miller and His Orchestra*. New York: Thomas Y. Crowell, 1974.

Smith, Charles Edward. "Jack Teagarden." In *The Jazz Makers: Essays on the Greats of Jazz*, ed. Nat Shapiro and Nat Hentoff. 1957. Reprint, New York: Da Capo Press, 1988.

Smith, Jay D. "Big T." *Jazz Review* 2, no. 6 (July 1959).

Smith, Jay D., and Len Guttridge. *Jack Teagarden: The Story of a Jazz Maverick*. London: Cassell and Company, 1960.

The Smithsonian Collection of Classic Jazz. Selected and annotated by Martin Williams. Washington, D.C.: Smithsonian Collection of Recordings, 1987.

Southern, Eileen, ed. *Readings in Black American Music*. New York: W. W. Norton, 1983.

Spellman, A. B. *Four Lives in the Bebop Business*. New York: Pantheon, 1966. Reprinted as *Black Music: Four Lives*. New York: Schocken Books, 1970.

Standish, Tony. Review of *Blues Anthology* by Leadbelly. *Jazz Journal* 15, no. 9 (September 1962).

Stearns, Marshall W. *The Story of Jazz*. New York: Oxford University Press, 1970.

Stephens, Lorin. "The Passionate Conviction: An Interview with Jimmy Giuffre." *Jazz Review* 3, no. 2 (February 1960).

Stewart-Baxter, Derrick. Review of *Henry Thomas: Ragtime 'Texas.'* *Jazz Journal* 25, no. 5 (May 1975).

Thomas, J. C. *Chasin' the Trane*. Garden City, N.Y.: Doubleday, 1975.

Tirro, Frank. *Jazz: A History*. New York: W. W. Norton, 1977.

Titon, Jeff Todd. *Early Downhome Blues: A Musical and Cultural Analysis*. Urbana: University of Illinois Press, 1977.

Townley, Eric, with Ron Harwood. "The Texas Nightingale: An Interview with Sippie Wallace." *Storyville*, no. 108 (1983).

Townsend, Charles R. *San Antonio Rose: The Life and Music of Bob Wills*. Urbana: University of Illinois Press, 1976.

Traill, Sinclair. "Record Reviews." *Jazz Journal* 14, no. 1 (January 1961); 15, no. 9 (September 1962).

Traill, Sinclair, and Gerald Lascelles, eds. *Just Jazz*. London: Peter Davies, 1957.

———. *Just Jazz 3*. London: Landsborough Publications, 1959.

Tucker, Mark, ed. *The Duke Ellington Reader*. New York: Oxford University Press, 1993.

Tudor, Dean, and Nancy Tudor. *Jazz*. Littleton, Colo.: Libraries Unlimited, 1979.

Tumlinson, Jerry. "Jimmy Ford: Just Jobbing." *Milt Larkin Jazz Society Newsletter* 1, no. 3 (August 1992).

Ulanov, Barry. *A History of Jazz in America*. London: Jazz Book Club, 1959.

Waterman, Guy. "Jelly Roll Morton." In *Jazz Panorama*, ed. Martin Williams. New York: Collier Books, 1967.

———. "Ragtime." In *The Art of Jazz*, ed. Martin T. Williams. New York: Grove Press, 1960.

Waters, H. J., Jr. *Jack Teagarden's Music: His Career and Recordings*. Stanhope, N.J.: Walter C. Allen, 1960.

Wen Shih, Hsio. "Ornette Coleman." In *Jazz Panorama*, ed. Martin Williams. New York: Collier Books, 1967.

Williams, Martin. *Jazz Heritage*. New York: Oxford University Press, 1985.

———. *Jazz Masters in Transition, 1957–1969*. London: Macmillan, 1970.

———. *The Jazz Tradition*. New York: Oxford University Press, 1983.

Williams, Martin, Dick Katz, and Francis Davis. *Jazz Piano*. Washington, D.C.: Smithsonian Collection of Recordings, 1989.

Williams, Martin, ed. *The Art of Jazz: Essays on the Nature and Development of Jazz*. New York: Grove Press, 1960.

———, ed. *Jazz Panorama*. New York: Collier Books, 1967.

Wilmer, Valerie. "Texas Trombone: Henry Coker." *Jazz Journal* 15, no. 10 (1962).

Wilson, John S. Review of *Sayin' Something* by Gigi Gryce and Richard Williams. *High Fidelity* 10, no. 10 (October 1960).

Weinstein, Norman C. *A Night in Tunisia: Imaginings of Africa in Jazz*. Metuchen, N.J.: Scarecrow Press, 1992.

Woodfin, H. A. "Kenny Dorham." *Jazz Review* 3, no. 7 (August 1960).

Zabor, Rafi, and David Breskin. "Ronald Shannon Jackson: The Future of Jazz Drumming." *Musician, Player, and Listener*, no. 33 (June 1981).

INDEX

Edison, Harry "Sweets," 32–33, 48, 108, 110, 112, 119, 180, 351

Edwards, Esmond, 254

Edwards, Moanin' Bernice, 55, 372, 375

Edwards, Teddy, 310

E-Flat Boogie, 188

Ehrlich, Marty, 353, 357

Eighteenth Street Blues, 89

Eighteenth Street Strut, 89

Eldridge, Roy, 145, 176, 179, 191, 194, 207, 209, 212, 234, 248

Elephant Wobble, 88

Ella Speed, 52

Ellington, Duke, vii, viii, 2, 17, 24, 26, 29–35, 43, 62, 81, 97, 100, 106, 114, 126, 146, 149, 151–155, 159, 179–180, 189, 198, 212–213, 232, 236, 260, 268, 270–273, 281, 283, 307, 348, 350, 352–353, 355

Elliott, Mark, 263

Ellis, Herb (b. 1921), 3, 202, 217, 283, 425

Ellison, Ralph, 350, 359

Elman, Ziggy, 209

Elm Street Blues, 375

Embraceable You, 322

Emerson, Ralph Waldo, 169

Enlow, Buddy, 256

Enois, Leonard, 130

Enter from the East, 352

Entertainer, The, 10, 12

Ernst, Alfred, 19

Ervin, Booker, Jr. (1930–1970), 2–3, 101, 266–268, 270–273, 275–278, 312, 422–424

Escapade, 262

E's Flat, Ah's Flat Too, 271

Euphonic Sounds, 19

Evans, Bill, 240–241, 261, 305

Evans, Christopher, 438

Evans, Gil, 149, 240, 252, 253, 268, 269

Evans, Herschel (1909–1939), 2–3, 48, 94, 105–114, 116, 126, 130, 150, 161, 166, 173–174, 182, 184–185, 190, 206, 210–211, 214, 219, 224, 227–228, 231, 263, 281

Evenin', 387

Evening Prayer, 353

Eventually, 318–319

Every Dog Has Its Day, 57

Everything's Cool, 249

Every Time We Say Goodbye, 263

Every Tub, 110, 115

Evil Man's Blues, 191

Evolution, 295

Evonce, 244, 246, 416

Exactly Like You, 174

Fables of Faubus, 270–271, 277

Facin' the Face, 413

Fallen Prince, The, 353

Falling in Love Again, 176

Falling Star, 326

Fantasy in D, 262

Farewell Blues, 142

Farmer, Art, 256, 305

Far Wells, Mill Valley, 268, 278

Fascinatin' Rhythm, 300

Fast Fannie's Cakewalk, 347

Fast Stuff Blues, 378

Fatback, 258

Fat Boy, 249

Father Steps In, 172, 178

Fatool, Nick, 197

Feather, Leonard, 82, 166, 174, 178, 191, 202, 208, 222, 224, 278, 313

Felder, Wilton (b. 1940), 3, 431

Fenton, Nick, 175, 192

Ferguson, Maynard, 228

Ferris Wheel, 274

Fickle Fay Creep, 25

Fields, 355–357

Fields, Ernie (b. 1905), 267, 420–421, 433

Fields, Herbie, 192

52nd Street Stomp, 359

52nd St. Theme, 251, 418

Figger-ration, 313

Finegan, Bill, 157
Finkelstein, Sidney, 37, 108
Firm Roots, 263
First Outing, 435
Fishel, Jim, 261
Fish for Supper, 194
Fishing Blues, 41–42
Fish Tail Dance, 374
Fives, The, 77–78, 378
Flames of South Africa, The, 350
Flanagan, Tommy, 240, 255
Flany Doodle Swing, 397
Flee as a Bird, 351
Fleet, Biddy, 183
Flight, 304
Flight of the Bumblebee, 211
Flood Blues, The, 61
Flower, John, 168
Floyd, Troy (1898–196?), 92, 99, 105, 107, 113, 281
Fluffy's Blues, 348
Flying Home, 196, 198, 220–221, 227, 232, 411
Flying Home No. 2, 226
Flyin' Home, 226, 411
Focus on Sanity, 317
Foggy Day, A, 277
Folk Forms No. 2, 272
Ford, Jimmy (b. 1927), 3, 228–229, 232
Forms and Sounds, 325, 437
For No Reason at All in C, 100
Forrest, Helen, 215
Fort Worth Denver Blues, 72, 376
Foster, Frank, 230
Foster, Stephen, 18
Four, 415
Four Brothers, 283, 293–295, 301, 426
400 Hop, 156
Four Months, Three Weeks, Two Days, One Hour Blues, 284
Four Mothers, 293
Four Others, 293, 428
Fox, Charles, 162, 165, 184, 210

Fracture, 247
Free, 295, 319–320
Free Jazz, 321–322, 329, 335, 340, 349
Freeman, Bruz, 343, 345
Freeman, Bud, 143
Freeman, Russ, 289
'Frisco Train Blues, 372
Front and Centre, 169
Fugue, 295
Fuller, Curtis, 259–260
Fuller, John R., 16
Fuller, Walter Gilbert, 168
Fun, 303
Funny Feathers, 69

G.T. Stomp, 172
Gabler, Milt, 120
Gallardo, Joe (b. 1939), 3, 229, 412
Gambler's Dream, 65–66
Gamut, The, 304
Garden of Souls, The, 332–333
Gardner, Mark, 178, 260
Garland, Red (1923–1984), 2–3, 20, 227, 230, 234–243, 258–263, 267, 415–416, 420
Garner, Erroll, 237, 241–242
Garrison, Jimmy, 256, 332
Gaspard, Octave, 70
Geller, Lorraine, 311–312, 316
Georgia on My Mind, 313–314
Gerber, Alain, 162
Gershwin, George, 118–119, 165, 217, 226, 246, 300, 322, 355
Get Happy, 208, 253
Get Together, 180
Getz, Stan, 253, 344
Ghost of a Chance, 223
Ghost of the Past, 329
Giant Steps, 262–263
Giddins, Gary, 10, 145–147, 193, 195, 221, 224–225, 262, 269–270, 339
Giggin', 316

Hackett, Bobby, 218
Haden, Charlie, 317–318, 332–336
Hadi, Shafi, 267, 271
Hadlock, Richard, 65, 69, 136
Haig, Al, 247, 289
Haitian Fight Song, 435
Half Nelson, 240
Half Step Down Please, 179
Hall, Edmond, 201
Hall, Jim, 300, 302
Hall, Morris Eugene, 425
Hallelujah, 207, 208
Hamilton, Jimmy, 180, 348
Hamlisch, Marvin, 10
Hammerstein, Oscar, 236
Hammond, John, 106, 117, 120, 182, 196–
     197, 211
Hampton, Lionel, 105, 152, 171, 196–197,
     202, 206, 210, 219–222, 225, 226, 232,
     247, 268, 283
Hancock, Herbie, 341
Handy, John, III (b. 1933), 3, 49, 266–268,
     270–273, 277–278, 422
Handy, W. C., 16, 39, 48, 142, 307
Handy Man, 375
Hangin' with Lee, 435
Hangman's Blues, 50
Happy Birthday, 251
Happy House, 335
Hardee, John (b. 1918), 3, 231–232, 311,
     413
Hardee's Partee, 232
Hardin, Lil, 66
Hardluck Blues, 79
Hard Times, 313–314
Hardy, John William, 346
Hargrove, Roy (b. 1969), 3, 314, 435
Harlem Nocturne, 344
Harlem Opera, 441, 442
Harlem Rag, 18
Harlem Shout, 160–161, 164
Harmony Club Waltz, 16

Harper, Arthur, 258
Harper, Billy (b. 1943), 3, 268
Harper, Herbie, 292
Harris, Rex, 33
Harris, Wynonie, 51
Harrison, Daphne Duval, 55, 59
Harrison, Jimmy, 140–141, 148
Harrison, Louis, ix
Harrison, Max, 80, 136, 155, 306
Hart, Billy, 269
Hart, Clyde, 177, 194, 197
Hart, Lorenz, 214
Harte, Roy, 291–292
Harwood, Ronald P., 60
Haskins, James, 17
Haslanger, James Elias (b. 1969), 288, 427
Hattie Green, 75, 376
Haven't You Named It Yet, 404
Have You Ever Been Down?, 61
Hawes, Hampton, 288–289, 310
Hawkins, Coleman, 43, 107–108, 111, 113,
     126, 136, 140, 146–147, 149, 170, 174–179,
     197, 219, 221, 223–225, 234, 244, 289,
     300, 308, 367
Hawthorne, Nathaniel, 16
Hayakawa, S. I., 328
Hayden, Belle, 19
Hayden, Scott, 18–19
Haydn, Joseph, 19
Haymes, Dick, 215
Haynes, George (b. 1920), 221, 410
Haynes, Roy, 250
Haywood, Cedric (b. c. 1918), 175, 225
Head and Shoulders, 260
Hear Me Talkin' to You, 20
Heath, Percy, 287, 316–318
Heaven Line, The, 434
Heckman, Don, 298, 319–320
Hefti, Neal, 177, 215
Hello Dolly, 154
Hemphill, Julius (b. 1938), 3, 287, 338, 349–
     350

Henderson, Bill, 345

Henderson, David, 335

Henderson, Eddie, 269

Henderson, Fletcher, 57, 62–63, 65, 76, 99, 101–102, 107, 135, 148, 155, 167, 170–171, 197, 212–213

Henderson, Horace, 153, 213

Henderson, Joe, 260, 267, 337

Henderson, Wayne (b. 1939), 3, 4, 431

Hennessey, Thomas, vii

Hentoff, Nat, 122, 191, 217, 236, 241, 268, 275, 311, 313, 315, 330–332

Herb's Here, 425

Herman, Woody, 2, 172, 174, 177–178, 217, 282–283, 293, 345

Hersal's Blues, 80, 378

He's Funny That Way, 207

Hey Doc!, 150

Heywood, Eddie, Sr., 55

Hi De Ho Man, 151

Higginbotham, J. C., 69, 141

Higgins, Billy, 260, 262, 310–312, 314–315, 317–318, 335

Higginson, Fred, 125

High Life, 114

High Society, 344

High Tide, 222

Hill, Andrew, 267

Hill, Bertha, 65

Hill, Ernest, 191–192

Hindemith, Paul, 19, 271

Hines, Earl "Fatha," 2, 20, 30, 58, 66, 153, 171–174, 178, 180, 184, 192–193, 201, 204–206, 214, 245, 287

Hines, Frankie, 198

Hinton, Milt, 197

His Very Own Blues, 411

Hite, Les, 265, 281, 282, 284

Hittin' the Bottle, 158–159, 162–164, 387

Hodeir, André, 197

Hodges, Johnny, 106, 190, 212–213

Hoefer, George, 136

Hogan, Granville Theodore, Jr. (b. 1929), 3, 419

Hold 'Em Hootie, 130

Holder, Terrence T., 92–93, 98–99, 105, 113, 170

Hold Tight (Want Some Sea Food Mama), 194

Holiday, Billie, 97, 142–146, 176, 191, 206–207, 211, 213–215, 237

Holiday en Masque, 339

Holland, Peanuts, 92

Hollerin' and Screamin', 247

Hollingsworth, Dell, ix

Homage to Tony, 435

Honey, Won't You Allow Me One More Chance, 41

Honeydripper, The, 151

Honeysuckle Rose, 127, 172, 390

Honky Tonk Train Blues, 17, 78

Hooker, John Lee, 51

Hooper, Nesbert "Stix" (b. 1938), 3, 431

Hootie Blues, 129

Hootie's Ignorant Oil, 130

Hope, Elmo, 256

Hopkins, Claude, 182

Hopkins, Fred, 355

Hopkins, Sam "Lightnin'" (b. 1912), 51, 373

Hora Decubitus, 268, 272, 275

Hornin' In, 252

Horricks, Raymond, 152

Horst, Louis, 28

Hot and Anxious, 213

Hot Mallets, 404

Hot Rod, 225

Hotter Than That, 30, 39

Houston Blues, 78, 378

How Do You Do It That Way?, 70

How Long?, 402

How Much Is That Doggie in the Window?, 341

Hubbard, Freddie, 258–260

Hudson, Will, 213

Hughes, Langston, 359

Humes, Helen, 211

Humph, 244, 416, 417

Warren, Butch, 256
Washington, Booker T., 10, 147
Washington, Jack, 100, 102, 105, 157
Washington, Mag, 12
Washington Post March, 309
Wash Woman Blues, 66
Waterman, Guy, 19, 27
Waters, Ethel, 155
Waters, Howard, 139
Way Down Yonder in New Orleans, 122
Wayne, Chuck, 179
Weary Blues, 22
Weather Bird, 20
Webb, Chick, 167
Webb City, 249
Webster, Ben, 102–104, 108, 148, 170, 175,
　179, 227, 232, 234
Webster, Freddie, 212
Wednesday Night Prayer Meeting, 270, 272
Wee, 262
Weilbacher, Bill, 130
Weill, Kurt, 292
Weinstein, Norman, 351, 355, 359
Weiss, Julius, 12
Welding, Pete, 45–46, 51
Well, Well, 275
Wells, Dickie, 43, 102, 108–109, 112, 152, 385
Well You Needn't, 244–245, 287, 416
Wen Shih, Hsio, 315, 319
Wess, Frank, 179
West, Lyles, 262
West, Odel, 183
West End Blues, 20, 30
Wham, 168
Wham Bam Thank You Ma'am, 273
What a Little Moonlight Can Do, 207
What Is This Thing Called Love, 202
What Reason Could I Give, 335
What's New, 313
What's the Use, 216
Wheat, John, ix
When Cherry Trees Bloom in Winter, 441

When Colors Play, 350
When I'm Alone, 102
When Lights Are Low, 197, 202, 404
When Sunset Falls, 288
When the Saints Go Marchin' In, 153, 394
Whetsol, Arthur, 152
Whirr, 304
Whistle Stop, 267
Whistling Woman Blues, 72
White, John, 115
White, Michael (b. 1933), 4, 277, 424
White, Morris, 158
White, Quinten "Rocky" (b. 1952), 3, 421
White, Voddie, 91
White Heat, 213
Whiteman, Paul, 142, 144, 146, 159
Whiteman, Wilburforce, 159
Whitman, Walt, 315
Whittaker, Sebastian (b. 1966), 3, 435
Why Did I Always Depend on You, 191
Wide Open Spaces, 313–314
Wilcox, Ed, 159
Wild, David, 319
Wild Party, 148
Wilkins, Ernie, 129
Williams, Buster, 269, 330
Williams, Clarence, 48, 56, 58, 62, 88
Williams, Cootie, 31, 153, 190, 191, 199–200,
　212, 219, 229–231, 244, 366
Williams, J. Mayo, 43
Williams, Joe, 39, 121
Williams, Martin, 26, 30, 57, 76, 81, 101–
　102, 104, 113, 118, 137, 146, 166, 181, 195,
　198, 201, 207, 213, 236, 244, 246, 252,
　306, 315–317, 320–322, 327, 339, 378
Williams, Mary Lou, 33, 35, 94, 139, 210,
　246
Williams, Richard "Notes" (1931–1985), 3,
　266, 268, 271–274, 278, 314, 316, 421, 423
Williams, Rudy, 192, 193
Williams, Spencer, 65
Williams, William Carlos, 378